Lecture Notes in Computer Science 13296

More information about this series at https://link.springer.com/bookseries/558

Alexander S. Kulikov ·
Sofya Raskhodnikova (Eds.)

Computer Science – Theory and Applications

17th International Computer Science Symposium in Russia, CSR 2022
Virtual Event, June 29 – July 1, 2022
Proceedings

Editors
Alexander S. Kulikov
Steklov Institute of Mathematics
St. Petersburg, Russia

Sofya Raskhodnikova
Boston University
Boston, MA, USA

ISSN 0302-9743 ISSN 1611-3349 (electronic)
Lecture Notes in Computer Science
ISBN 978-3-031-09573-3 ISBN 978-3-031-09574-0 (eBook)
https://doi.org/10.1007/978-3-031-09574-0

This Springer imprint is published by the registered company Springer Nature Switzerland AG
The registered company address is: Gewerbestrasse 11, 6330 Cham, Switzerland

Preface

This volume contains the papers presented at CSR 2022, the 17th International Computer Science Symposium in Russia, held online during June 29 – July 1, 2022. CSR covers a wide range of areas in theoretical computer science and its applications. Initially, CSR 2022 was planned as a satellite event for the International Congress of Mathematicians (ICM) in St. Petersburg, Russia. However, as the Program Committee (PC) was starting its deliberations after completing submission reviews, Russia attacked Ukraine. As a result, ICM and CSR 2022 were moved online. Many PC members expressed dismay at the attack and three PC members resigned. Others chose to continue their work, but many wanted to emphasize that they did not support or condone the actions of the Russian government against Ukrainian people.

We received 51 submissions, and out of these the Program Committee selected 21 papers for presentation at the symposium and for publication in the proceedings. Each submission was reviewed by at least three Program Committee members. Submissions by Program Committee members were reviewed by at least four other members of the Program Committee.

The opening lecture at CSR 2022 was given by Umesh Vazirani (University of California at Berkeley), the closing lecture was given by Mark Braverman (Princeton University). Three invited plenary lectures were given by Irit Dinur (Weizmann Institute of Science), Jelani Nelson (University of California at Berkeley), and Mary Wootters (Stanford University).

Many people and organizations contributed to the smooth running and the success of CSR 2022. In particular, our thanks go to

- all authors who submitted their work to CSR;
- the members of the Program Committee who graciously devoted their time and energy to the evaluation process;
- the expert reviewers who helped us evaluate the papers;
- the invited speakers; and
- the members of the local Organizing Committee who made the conference possible.

May 2022

Alexander S. Kulikov
Organizing Committee Chair
Sofya Raskhodnikova
Program Committee Chair

Organization

Program Committee

Alexander Belov	University of Latvia, Latvia
Sergio Cabello	University of Ljubljana, Slovenia
Michael Elkin	Ben-Gurion University of the Negev, Israel (Resigned on March 1, 2022)
Edith Elkind	University of Oxford, UK
Nathanaël Fijalkow	CNRS, LaBRI, University of Bordeaux, France
Fedor Fomin	University of Bergen, Norway
Moses Ganardi	Max Planck Institute for Software Systems, Germany (Resigned on March 3, 2022)
Alexander Golovnev	Georgetown University, USA
Prahladh Harsha	Tata Institute of Fundamental Research, India
Oded Lachish	Birkbeck, University of London, UK
Daniel Lokshtanov	University of California, Santa Barbara, USA
Dániel Marx	Max Planck Institute for Informatics, Germany (Resigned on March 1, 2022)
Pierre Ohlmann	University of Warsaw, Poland
Alexander Okhotin	Saint Petersburg State University, Russia
Madhusudan Parthasarathy	University of Illinois at Urbana-Champaign, USA
Vladimir Podolskii	Steklov Mathematical Institute, Russia
Svetlana Puzynina	Saint Petersburg State University, Russia
Ramyaa Ramyaa	New Mexico Institute of Mining and Technology
Sofya Raskhodnikova	Boston University, USA
Barna Saha	University of California, Berkeley, USA
Jeffrey Shallit	University of Waterloo, Canada
Alexander Shen	LIRMM, CNRS and Université de Montpellier, France, on leave from IITP RAS, Russia

Additional Reviewers

Some chose to remain anonymous.
Anand, Ashwani
Babu, Jasine
Barenboim, Leonid
Bergsträßer, Pascal
Bienvenu, Laurent
Cenzer, Douglas
Chakraborty, Dibyayan
Chen, Lijie
Chew, Leroy
Chou, Chi-Ning
Das, Bireswar
Dorfman, Dani
Efremenko, Klim

Eiben, Eduard
Erlebach, Thomas
Gawrychowski, Pawel
Giannopoulos, Panos
Goldberg, Paul
Gurvich, Vladimir
Haviv, Ishay
Hirahara, Shuichi
Itsykson, Dmitry
Kalimullin, Iskander
Kavitha, Telikepalli
Knop, Alexander
Kozachinskiy, Alexander
Kumar, Mrinal
Köppl, Dominik
Li, Jason
M. Sridharan, Ramanujan
Makarov, Vladislav
Meeks, Kitty
Michielini, Vincent
Milovanov, Alexey
Mozes, Shay
Nanashima, Mikito
Neiman, Ofer
Neuen, Daniel
Ochem, Pascal
Parreaux, Julie
Paul, Erik
Pentus, Mati
Perifel, Sylvain
Peters, Spencer
Pruhs, Kirk
Pérez-Lantero, Pablo
Raskin, Michael
Renault, Marc
Romashchenko, Andrei
Rosenfeld, Matthieu
Schlöter, Miriam
Seelbach Benkner, Louisa
Selivanov, Victor
Sering, Leon
Serre, Olivier
Slivovsky, Friedrich
Solomon, Shay
Spoerhase, Joachim
Srinivasan, Srikanth
Suksompong, Warut
Trehan, Chhaya
Vereshchagin, Nikolay
Vinyals, Marc
Wlodarczyk, Michal

Invited Talks

Optimization-Friendly Generic Mechanisms Without Money

Mark Braverman

Princeton University, Princeton, NJ 08540, USA
https://mbraverm.princeton.edu

Our goal is to develop a generic framework for converting modern gradient-descent based optimization algorithms into mechanisms where inputs come from self-interested agents.

We focus on aggregating preferences from n players in a context without money. Special cases of this setting include voting, allocation of items by lottery, and matching. Our key technical contribution is a new meta-algorithm we call **APEX** (Adaptive Pricing Equalizing Externalities). The framework is sufficiently general to be combined with any optimization algorithm that is based on local search. In the talk we outline the algorithm, and open problem/research directions that it raises, with a particular focus towards mechanism design + machine learning.

We discuss a special case of applying the framework to the problem of one-sided allocation with lotteries. In this case, we obtain a strengthening of the 1979 result by Hylland and Zeckhauser on allocation via a competitive equilibrium from equal incomes (CEEI). The [HZ79] result posits that there is a (fractional) allocation and a set of item prices such that the allocation is a competitive equilibrium given prices. We further show that there is always a reweighing of the players' utility values such that running the standard unit-demand VCG with reweighed utilities leads to a HZ-equilibrium prices. Interestingly, not all HZ competitive equilibria come from VCG prices.

Reference

[HZ79] Hylland, A., Zeckhauser, R.: The efficient allocation of individuals to positions. J. Polit. Econ. **87**(2), 293–314 (1979)

Expanders in Higher Dimensions

Irit Dinur

Weizmann Institute of Science

Expander graphs have been studied in many areas of mathematics and in computer science with versatile applications, including coding theory, networking, computational complexity and geometry.

High-dimensional expanders are a generalization that has been studied in recent years and their promise is beginning to bear fruit. In the talk, I will survey some powerful local to global properties of high-dimensional expanders, and describe several interesting applications, ranging from convergence of random walks to construction of locally testable codes that prove the c^3 conjecture (namely, codes with **c**onstant rate, **c**onstant distance, and **c**onstant locality).

Private Frequency Estimation via Projective Geometry

Jelani Nelson

UC Berkeley, Berkeley, CA 94705, USA
https://people.eecs.berkeley.edu/~minilek

We propose a new algorithm ProjectiveGeometryResponse (PGR) for locally differentially private (LDP) frequency estimation. For a universe size of k and with n users, our ε-LDP algorithm has communication cost $\lceil \log_2 k \rceil$ bits in the private coin setting and $\varepsilon \log_2 e + O(1)$ in the public coin setting, and has computation cost $O(n + k \exp(\varepsilon) \log k)$ for the server to approximately reconstruct the frequency histogram, while achieving optimal privacy/utility tradeoff, including optimality of the leading constant factor. Our empirical evaluation shows a speedup of over 50x over PI-RAPPOR [FT21], while using approximately 75x less memory for practically relevant parameter settings. In addition, the running time of our algorithm is within an order of magnitude of HadamardResponse [ASZ19] and RecursiveHadamardResponse [CKO20] which have significantly worse reconstruction error. Our new algorithm is based on using Projective Planes over a finite field to define a small collection of sets that are close to being pairwise independent and a dynamic programming algorithm for approximate histogram reconstruction on the server side. We also give an extension of PGR, which we call HybridProjectiveGeometryResponse, that allows trading off computation time with utility smoothly.

Joint work with Vitaly Feldman (Apple), Huy Le Nguyen (Northeastern), and Kunal Talwar (Apple). This work is to appear in ICML 2022.

References

[ASZ19] Acharya, J., Sun, Z., Zhang, H.: Hadamard response: estimating distributions privately, efficiently, and with little communication. In: Proceedings of the 22nd International Conference on Artificial Intelligence and Statistics (AISTATS), pp. 1120–129 (2019)

[CKO20] Chen, W.-N., Kairouz, p., Özgür, A.: Breaking the communication-privacy-accuracy trilemma. In: Proceedings of the 32nd Annual Conference on Advances in Neural Information Processing Systems (NeurIPS) (2020)

[FT21] Feldman, V., Talwar, K.: Lossless compression of efficient private local randomizers. In: Proceedings of the 38th International Conference on Machine Learning (ICML), pp. 3208–3219 (2021)

Contents

Parameterized Algorithms for Finding Highly Connected Solution

Ankit Abhinav[1], Susobhan Bandopadhyay[1(✉)], Aritra Banik[1], and Saket Saurabh[2]

[1] National Institute of Science, Education and Research, An OCC of Homi Bhabha National Institute, Bhubaneswar 752050, Odisha, India
{ankit.abhinav,susobhan.bandopadhyay,aritra}@niser.ac.in
[2] The Institute of Mathematical Sciences, HBNI, Chennai, India
saket@imsc.res.in

Abstract. To introduce our question and the parameterization, consider the classical VERTEX COVER problem. In this problem, the input is a graph G on n vertices and a positive integer ℓ, and the goal is to find a vertex subset S of size at most ℓ such that $G - S$ is an independent set. Further, we want that $G[S]$ is highly connected. That is, $G[S]$ should be $n - k$ edge-connected. Clearly, the problem is NP-complete, as substituting $k = n-1$, we obtain the CONNECTED VERTEX COVER problem. A simple observation also shows that the problem admits an algorithm with running time $n^{\mathcal{O}(k)}$. Since the problem is polynomial-time solvable for every fixed integer k, a natural parameter is the integer k. In all the problems we consider, the parameter is k, and the goal is to find a solution S of size at most ℓ, such that $G[S]$ is $n - k$ edge-connected and $G - S$ satisfies a property. We show that this version of well-known problems such as VERTEX COVER, FEEDBACK VERTEX SET, ODD CYCLE TRANSVERSAL and MULTIWAY CUT admit an algorithm with running time $f(k) \cdot n^{\mathcal{O}(1)}$, that is, they are FPT with the parameter k. One of our main subroutines to obtain these algorithms is an FPT algorithm for $n - k$ edge connected STEINER SUBGRAPH, which could be of an independent interest. Finally, we also show that such an algorithm is not possible for MULTICUT.

Keywords: subset problems · parameterized algorithms · connectivity

1 Introduction

Vertex deletion (subset) problems form an important sub-area of graph optimization problems. An input to a prototype vertex deletion problem consists of a graph G and an integer ℓ and the objective is to find a vertex subset S of size at most ℓ such that $G - S$ satisfies a property, such as being an edgeless graph (VERTEX COVER), an acyclic graph (FVS), a bipartite graph(OCT), a chordal graph(CVD), a planar graph (PVD), and a (topological) minor-free graph. In literature, several variants of these classical vertex deletion problems are considered. The most notable ones

A. S. Kulikov and S. Raskhodnikova (Eds.): CSR 2022, LNCS 13296, pp. 1–16, 2022.
https://doi.org/10.1007/978-3-031-09574-0_1

include those where we demand that $G[S]$ is connected, λ-edge-connected (that is, for every pair of vertices in S there are at least λ edge-disjoint paths in $G[S]$) and an edgeless graph (S is an independent set). A classical result by Lewis and Yannakakis [7] shows that most of the vertex deletion problems are NP-complete and so are its variants [10,11]. These problems have been studied extensively from the perspective of the Approximation Algorithms and the Parameterized Complexity to overcome these intractability results.

The objective of this article is to initiate a systematic study of finding a "highly connected" solution for vertex subset problems in the realm of Parameterized Complexity, with respect to a "parameterization involving connectivity."

We first take a detour and give the basic definitions from Parameterized Complexity. The goal of parameterized complexity is to find ways of solving NP-hard problems more efficiently than brute force: here the aim is to restrict the combinatorial explosion to a parameter that is hopefully much smaller than the input size. Formally, a *parameterization* of a problem is assigning an integer k to each input instance, and we say that a parameterized problem is *fixed-parameter tractable (*FPT*)* if there is an algorithm that solves the problem in time $f(k) \cdot |I|^{\mathcal{O}(1)}$, where $|I|$ is the size of the input and f is an arbitrary computable function depending on the parameter k only. For more background, the reader is referred to the monographs [1,3,5,8].

Problem and Parameterization. To introduce our question and the parameterization, we fix a concrete vertex subset problem, namely, the classical VERTEX COVER problem. In this vertex subset problem, the graph $G - S$ is an edgeless graph. In other words, the set S of size at most ℓ must include at least one end-point of every edge of G. When we demand that $G[S]$ is connected or more general λ-edge-connected then the problem is called CONNECTED VERTEX COVER (CVC) or more generally λEDGE-CONNECTED VC (λ-ECVC), respectively. While, the study of CVC is quite old in Parameterized Complexity [6], only recently Einarson et al. [4] studied λ-ECVC and designed lossy kernel as well as an algorithm with running time $2^{\mathcal{O}(\lambda\ell)}n^{\mathcal{O}(1)}$. In some sense, the algorithm for λ-ECVC is the starting point of our work and one of our main motivations. A question that triggered this work was the following:

What happens when we seek S such that $G[S]$ is highly connected. In particular, $(n-1)$-edge-connected, or $(n$-$k)$-edge-connected, where $n = |V(G)|$?

Let us call this version of VERTEX COVER as HC-VC. Observe that when we are seeking $(n$-$k)$-edge-connected subgraph, then the size of S is at least $n - k + 1$, as every vertex in $G[S]$ must have at least $n - k$ neighbors. So, if we apply the algorithm of Einarson et al. [4], then we get an algorithm with running time $2^{\mathcal{O}((n-k)^2)}n^{\mathcal{O}(1)}$. On the other hand, since S contains all but at most $k-1$ vertices of $V(G)$, there is an algorithm running in time $n^{\mathcal{O}(k)}$, that tries all vertex subsets of size at least $n-k+1$ as a potential solution. Given an algorithm with running time $n^{\mathcal{O}(k)}$, a natural question that arises is the following.

Is HC-VC FPT parameterized by k?

The above algorithm for HC-VC, that runs in $n^{\mathcal{O}(k)}$ time, does not use any property of vertex cover! It seemlessly works for HC-FVS, HC-OCT, HC-CVD and HC-PVD. In fact, this algorithm also works for domination (Dominating Set) as well as cut (Multiway Cut, Multicut) problems. In Dominating Set (DS), we seek S such that every vertex in $G-S$ has a neighbor in S. In Multiway Cut, apart from G and an integer ℓ, we are given a vertex subset $T \subseteq V(G)$, called terminals, and the objective is to find an ℓ-sized vertex subset S, such that in $G-S$ there is no path from s to t, for any pair of vertices $s,t \in T$. In Multicut, apart from G and an integer ℓ, we are given t pairs of terminals (s_i, t_i), and the objective is to find a ℓ-sized vertex subset S, such that in $G-S$ there is no path from s_i to t_i, $i \in \{1, \ldots, t\}$. Thus, naturally we ask whether HC-FVS, HC-OCT, HC-CVD, HC-PVD, HC-DS, HC-Multiway Cut and HC-Multicut are FPT.

Our Results and Methods. We show that HC-VC, HC-FVS, HC-OCT, HC-PVD, HC-DS, and HC-Multiway Cut are FPT. To design some of our FPT algorithms we consider a generic vertex deletion problem, whose specific instantiation leads to HC-VC, HC-FVS, and HC-PVD. Let $\mathcal{F}$ be a family of graphs. In the $\mathcal{F}$-Deletion problem, we need to ensure that $G-S$ does not contain any graph in $L \in \mathcal{F}$ as a minor (a graph L is a minor of $G-S$, if it can be obtained from $G-S$ by vertex deletions, edge deletions and edge contractions). If $\mathcal{F}$ is an edge, or a triangle, or a K_5 and $K_{3,3}$, then it corresponds to HC-VC, HC-FVS, and HC-PVD, respectively. The main idea of the algorithms for $\mathcal{F}$-Deletion problems is as follows. Let H be the subset of vertices in G such that the degree of every vertex in H is at least $n-k$. We find a constant size subset of vertices of H, say Z, that does not belong to S, but whose all but $\mathcal{O}(1)$ number of common neighbors do belong to S. Since the size of common neighbors of Z is at least $n-|Z|k$, we have that all but $\mathcal{O}(k)$ vertices get fixed. For the remaining $\mathcal{O}(k)$ vertices, we can guess which one of them belongs to S in $2^{\mathcal{O}(k)}$ time, leading to the desired FPT algorithm.

For HC-DS and HC-Multiway Cut we need additional ideas. We first show that a graph G with n vertices and given integer k and $n > 2k$, is (n-k)-edge-connected if and only if for every vertex $v \in V(G)$, $\mathsf{deg}(v) \geq n-k$. This helps us in characterizing the solution S as a subset where every vertex has degree at least $n-k$. Furthermore, we need an algorithm for HC-Steiner Subgraph, as a subroutine. Here, given a graph G, positive integers ℓ, k and a subset of terminals T, the objective is to find a vertex subset S of size at most ℓ such that $G[S]$ is (n-k)-edge-connected and $T \subseteq S$. We show that HC-Steiner Subgraph admits an algorithm with running time $2^{\mathcal{O}(k \log k)}n^{\mathcal{O}(1)}$. Using this as a subroutine we show that HC-DS and HC-MULTIWAY CUT admit $2^{\mathcal{O}(k \log k)} n^{\mathcal{O}(1)}$ time algorithms. We also prove that HC-MULTICUT problem is W[1]-hard.

2 Preliminaries

We first set up notations and give a characterization of (n-k)-edge-connected subgraph.

Notations. Let G be a graph. We use $V(G)$ and $E(G)$ to denote the set of vertices and edges of G, respectively. Throughout the paper we use n and m to denote $|V(G)|$ and $|E(G)|$, respectively. For a set S, by $G - S$, we mean $G[V(G) \setminus S]$. For a set of vertices $A \subseteq V(G)$, denote $\overline{A} = V(G) \setminus A$. For a vertex v, we use $N(v)$ to denote the set of its neighbors, and use $\mathsf{deg}(v)$ to denote $|N(v)|$. We use $\delta(G)$ to denote the smallest degree of a vertex in G. For a vertex v and a subset $V' \subset V(G)$, define $N_{V'}(v) = N(v) \cap V'$. Given a graph G and an integer k, define $V_L = \{u \in V \mid \mathsf{deg}(u) < n - k\}$ and $V_H = \{u \in V \mid \mathsf{deg}(u) \geq n - k\}$. Most of the symbols and notations of graph theory used are standard and taken form [2].

A reduction rule that replaces an instance (I, k) of a parameterized language L by a reduced instance (I', k') is said to be *safe*, if $(I, k) \in L$ if and only if $(I', k') \in L$.

2.1 Properties of (n-k)-Edge-Connected Subgraph

The next result characterizes (n-k)-edge-connected graphs in terms of degrees of vertices.

Theorem 1. *A graph G with n vertices and given integer k and $n > 2k$, is (n-k)-edge-connected if and only if for every vertex $v \in V(G), \mathsf{deg}(v) \geq n - k$.*

Proof. First, assume that the graph G is (n-k)-edge-connected. For the sake of contradiction, assume that there exists a vertex $v \in V(G)$ such that, $\mathsf{deg}(v) < n - k$. So, by deleting less than $n - k$ many edges, v can be disconnected from the other vertices in G, which contradicts that G is (n-k)-edge-connected.

Next, we prove the reverse direction. Towards this we will show that any partition of the vertex set into two parts contains at least $n - k$ crossing edges. Let A and B any two disjoint subset of $V(G)$ such that $A \uplus B = V(G)$ and $A \cap B = \emptyset$. We show that there are at least $(n - k)$ edges between the vertices in A and the vertices in B. Let $|A| = p$ and $|B| = q$. Without loss of generality assume that $p \geq q$. We divide the proof into two cases. In the first case assume that $p \leq n - k$. Any vertex $x \in A$ can have at most $p - 1$ many neighbors inside A and can have at least $((n - k) - (p - 1))$ neighbors in B. So, the total number of edges from A to B is at least

$$\begin{aligned} p(n - k - p + 1) &= n - k + (p - 1)(n - k) - p(p - 1) \\ &\geq n - k + (p - 1)p - p(p - 1) \qquad (\text{as}\, n - k \geq p) \\ &= n - k. \end{aligned}$$

Thus the claim holds in this case.

In the second case we have that $p \geq n-k+1$, and $n \geq 2k$. Thus $n-k \geq k \geq n-p+1$ (as $p \geq n-k+1$). Therefore, we have $n-k \geq q+1$ ($q = n-p$). Any vertex $y \in B$ has at most $q-1$ neighbors inside B, and at least $(n-k-q+1)$ neighbors in A. Therefore, the total number of crossing edges between A and B is at least

$$\begin{aligned} q(n-k-q+1) &= n-k+(q-1)(n-k)-q(q-1) \\ &\geq n-k+(q-1)(q+1)-q(q-1) \qquad (\text{as}\, n-k \geq q+1) \\ &= n-k+q-1 \geq n-k. \end{aligned}$$

This concludes the proof. □

Let G be a graph on n vertices and S be a vertex subset such that $G[S]$ is (n-k)-edge-connected, then any vertex $v \in V(G)$ with $\mathsf{deg}(v) < n-k$ can not be part of S (follows from Theorem 1). Recall that $V_L = \{v | \mathsf{deg}(v) < n-k\}$ and $V_H = \{v | \mathsf{deg}(v) \geq n-k\}$. Since, $|S| \geq n-k+1$, we have that $|V_L| < k$. Next, we obtain a result that bounds from below the size of the common intersection of any two vertices belonging to V_H.

Observation 1. *For any two vertices u and v in G such that $\mathsf{deg}(u), \mathsf{deg}(v) \geq n-k$, $|N(u) \cap N(v)| \geq n-2k$.*

Proof. We know that $|N(v)| \geq n-k$, and thus, $|\overline{N(v)}| = |V(G) \setminus N(v)| \leq k$. In the worst case all of $\overline{N(v)}$ can be a subset of $N(u)$. So, the other neighbors of u must be a subset of $N(v)$. Hence, $|N(u) \cap N(v)| \geq n-2k$. □

Remark 1. Observation 1, can be generalized for a set X. That is, we can show that for a vertex subset $X \subseteq V(G)$, such that for all $u \in X$, $\mathsf{deg}(u) \geq n-k$, $|\bigcap_{u \in X} N(u)| \geq n-|X|k$.

3 Vertex Subset Problems

In this section, we give two simple algorithms for HC-VC and HC-FVS, that illustrate the idea of "common neighbors branching". Then we provide an algorithm for HC-$\mathcal{F}$-Deletion.

3.1 Vertex Cover and Feedback Vertex Set

The HC-VC is formally stated below.

HC-VC **Parameter:** k
Input: An undirected graph G with n vertices and two integers k and ℓ.
Question: Does there exist a vertex cover S for G of size at most ℓ such that $G[S]$ is $(n-k)$-edge connected?

From Theorem 1 we know, if there exists a solution S, $V_L \cap S = \emptyset$. Notice that if $|V_L| \geq k$ or $\ell \leq n-k$, then we have a No instance. So we proceed assuming that $|V_L| < k$ for both the problems HC-VC and HC-FVS. Thus we have $|V(H)| > n-k$.

Theorem 2. HC-VC *can be solved in* $\mathcal{O}(2^k mn)$ *time.*

Proof. We divide the proof into two cases. In case 1, let $|V_H| = n-k+1$. If V_H is a vertex cover and $G[V_H]$ is (n-k)-edge-connected, then we return Yes. We remark that $G[S]$ being (n-k)-edge-connected can be verified in $\mathcal{O}(m)$ time, using Theorem 1. Otherwise we return a No. In case 2, We assume $|V_H| > n-k+1$. If there exists a solution S, then there exists a vertex $v \in V_H \setminus S$. Since $v \notin S$, $N(v) \subseteq S$. As $|N(v)| \geq n-k$, $|V_H \setminus N(v)| \leq k$. If there exists a subset $X \subseteq V_H \setminus N(v)$ such that $G[X \cup N(v)]$ is (n-k)-edge-connected and is a vertex cover of cardinality at most ℓ, return Yes. If for all $v \in V_H$, there does not exist $X \subseteq V_H \setminus N(v)$ such that $G[X \cup N(v)]$ is (n-k)-edge-connected and is a vertex cover of cardinality at most ℓ, return a No. Observe that there are at most $n2^k$ many choices for v and X. Given a set S in $\mathcal{O}(m)$ time, we can find out whether S is a vertex cover. This completes the proof. □

Next, we give an FPT algorithm for HC-FVS which is similar to the algorithm for HC-VC. The problem is defined as follows.

> HC-FVS **Parameter:** k
> **Input:** An undirected graph G with n vertices and two integers k and ℓ.
> **Question:** Does there exist a feedback vertex set S for G of size at most ℓ such that $G[S]$ is $(n-k)$-edge connected?

Theorem 3. HC-FVS *can be solved in* $\mathcal{O}(4^k n^{\mathcal{O}(1)})$ *time.*

Proof. We divide the proof into three cases. In case 1, let $|V_H| = n-k+1$. If V_H is a feedback vertex set and $G[V_H]$ is (n-k)-edge-connected, then we return Yes. Otherwise, we return a No. From now onwards we assume $|V_H| > n-k+1$. In case 2, we deal with the case when there exist two vertices $u, v \in (V_H \setminus S)$ such that, $uv \in E(G)$. In this case, from Observation 1, it follows that the vertices of $N(u) \cap N(v)$ along with the edge uv forms cycles (in fact, triangles). As u, v are not part of the solution, all the common neighbors of u and v should be part of the solution. This implies that $|V_H \setminus ((N(u) \cap N(v))| \leq n - (n-2k) \leq 2k$. If there exists a subset $X \subseteq V_H \setminus (N(u) \cap N(v))$ such that $G[X \cup (N(u) \cap N(v))]$ is (n-k)-edge-connected and is a feedback vertex set of cardinality ℓ, return Yes. This case can be carried out in time $\mathcal{O}(4^k n^{\mathcal{O}(1)})$.

Finally, if $|V_H| > n-k+1$ and the case 2 does not occur, we know that for all the vertices $v \in (V_H \setminus S)$, $N(v) \cap V_H \subseteq S$. Observe, $|N(v) \cap V_H| \geq n-k$. Therefore $|V_H \setminus N(v)| \leq k$. If there exist a subset $X \subseteq V_H \setminus N(v)$ such that $G[X \cup (N(v) \cap V_H)]$ is (n-k)-edge-connected and is a feedback vertex set of cardinality ℓ, return Yes. This case can be carried out in time $\mathcal{O}(2^k n^{\mathcal{O}(1)})$. Finally, if we do not find the solution in either of the cases, we return that the given instance is a No instance. This completes the proof. □

In the proof of Theorem 3, whenever we considered a cycle, it was a triangle, an odd cycle, and thus a proof identical to Theorem 3 implies that HC-OCT is FPT. In particular, we get the following result.

Theorem 4. HC-OCT *can be solved in* $\mathcal{O}(4^k n^{\mathcal{O}(1)})$ *time.*

3.2 $\mathcal{F}$-Deletion

In this section, we design an FPT algorithm for HC-$\mathcal{F}$-Deletion, defined below.

> HC-$\mathcal{F}$-Deletion **Parameter:** k
> **Input:** An undirected graph G with n vertices, two integers k, ℓ and a finite family $\mathcal{F}$ of graphs.
> **Question:** Does there exist a set $S \subseteq V(G)$ of size at most ℓ such that $G[S]$ is (n-k)-edge-connected and $G \setminus S$ does not contain any graph from $\mathcal{F}$ as a minor.

We assume that the maximum cardinality of the vertex set of a graph in $\mathcal{F}$ is bounded by a constant, $c_{\mathcal{F}}$.

Theorem 5. HC-$\mathcal{F}$-Deletion *can be solved in time* $\mathcal{O}(2^{\mathcal{O}(kc_{\mathcal{F}})} n^{\mathcal{O}(c_{\mathcal{F}})})$.

Proof. From Theorem 1 we know, if there exists a solution S, $V_L \cap S = \emptyset$. Notice that if $|V_L| > k$ or $|V_H| < \ell$ exists, then we have a No instance. So we assume that $|V_L| \leq k$ and $|V_H| \geq \ell$. In case 1, let $|V_H| = \ell$. If V_H is a solution and $G[V_H]$ is (n-k)-edge-connected, then we return Yes. Next we divide the proof into two cases: (a) $|V_H \setminus S| < c_{\mathcal{F}}$ or (b) $|V_H \setminus S| \geq c_{\mathcal{F}}$. The first case is easy to handle. In time $\mathcal{O}(n^{\mathcal{O}(c_{\mathcal{F}})})$ we can try all possible subsets $A \subseteq V_H$ of cardinality at most $c_{\mathcal{F}}$ to find out whether $V_H \setminus A$ is a solution to our problem using an algorithm for graph minor testing [9].

Now we handle the case when $|V_H \setminus S| \geq c_{\mathcal{F}}$. Towards this, we guess a subset X of size $c_{\mathcal{F}}$ of V_H as a potential subset of vertices belonging to $V_H \setminus S$. Clearly, there are at most $\mathcal{O}(n^{\mathcal{O}(c_{\mathcal{F}})})$ choices for X. Now we fix such an X and give an algorithm that checks if there exists a solution S to our problem such that $X \cap S = \emptyset$.

Let W be the set of vertices which are neighbors of every vertex of X, i.e. $W = \{u \mid X \subseteq N(u)\}$. As $X \subseteq V_H$, every vertex $v \in X$ has at most k many non-neighbors. Since $|X| = c_{\mathcal{F}}$, there can be at most $k \cdot c_{\mathcal{F}}$ many non-neighbors of X. Therefore, $|W| \geq n - k \cdot c_{\mathcal{F}}$. Next, we show that at most $c_{\mathcal{F}} - 1$ vertices of W can be outside S.

For the sake of contradiction assume that there exists a solution S such that $|W \setminus S| \geq c_{\mathcal{F}}$. Denote, $A = W \setminus S$. Observe that the graph induced by $A \cup X$ contains $\mathcal{K}_{c_{\mathcal{F}},c_{\mathcal{F}}}$ as a subgraph (and hence a minor). Further $\mathcal{K}_{c_{\mathcal{F}},c_{\mathcal{F}}}$ has $\mathcal{K}_{c_{\mathcal{F}}}$ as a minor (take a $c_{\mathcal{F}}$ sized matching in $\mathcal{K}_{c_{\mathcal{F}},c_{\mathcal{F}}}$ and contract it), and any graph of at most $c_{\mathcal{F}}$ vertices is a minor of $\mathcal{K}_{c_{\mathcal{F}}}$, which contradicts the fact that S is a solution.

Thus we know for any solution S, $|S \cap W| \geq |W| - (c_{\mathcal{F}} - 1) \geq n - kc_{\mathcal{F}} - (c_{\mathcal{F}} - 1)$. Therefore, we can try all possible subsets $B \subseteq W$ of cardinality at most $c_{\mathcal{F}} - 1$ and try to find a solution S such that $B = W \setminus S$. By doing so, we fix at least $n - kc_{\mathcal{F}} - (c_{\mathcal{F}} - 1)$ many vertices of S. From the remaining $kc_{\mathcal{F}} + c_{\mathcal{F}}$ many vertices we need to select $\ell - (n - kc_{\mathcal{F}} - (c_{\mathcal{F}} - 1))$ many vertices. Observe, as $\ell \leq n$, therefore $\ell - (n - kc_{\mathcal{F}} - c_{\mathcal{F}}) \leq kc_{\mathcal{F}}$. Thus in time $2^{\mathcal{O}(kc_{\mathcal{F}} + c_{\mathcal{F}})}$, we can try all possible subsets of $C \subset V(G) \setminus B$ to check whether $B \cup C$ is a solution to the HC-$\mathcal{F}$-Deletion. To test whether $G - (B \cup C)$ does not contain a graph in $\mathcal{F}$ as a minor, we can use the $\mathcal{O}(f(c_{\mathcal{F}})k^3)$ time algorithm of Robertson and Seymour [9]. Alternatively, we could test this as follows. A *model* of a graph H in a graph $G^\star$ is a function μ assigning to the vertices of H vertex disjoint connected subgraphs of $G^\star$, such that if $uv \in E(H)$ then some edge of $G^\star$ joins a vertex of $\mu(u)$ to a vertex of $\mu(v)$. It is well known that there exists a model of a graph H in a graph $G^\star$ if and only if H is a minor of $G^\star$. Using this definition we can test if some graph $H \in \mathcal{F}$ is a minor of $G - (B \cup C)$, in time $2^{\mathcal{O}(kc_{\mathcal{F}})}$. Thus, the algorithm takes $\mathcal{O}(2^{\mathcal{O}(kc_{\mathcal{F}})} n^{\mathcal{O}(c_{\mathcal{F}})})$ in this case. All the cases together imply the theorem. □

4 Steiner Subgraph

In this section, we present an FPT algorithm for HC-Steiner Subgraph. An algorithm for this problem is used as a subroutine for an algorithm for HC-Multicut and HC-DS. The problem itself is defined as follows.

> HC-Steiner Subgraph **Parameter:** k
> **Input:** An undirected graph G with n vertices, a set $T \subseteq V(G)$ of terminals and two integers k and ℓ.
> **Question:** Does there exists a subset $S \subseteq V(G)$ of size *exactly* ℓ such that $T \subseteq S$ and $G[S]$ is $(n-k)$-edge connected.

In what follows, we prepare ourselves to give an FPT algorithm for HC-Steiner Subgraph. Recall $V_L = \{u \mid \mathsf{deg}(u) < n-k\}$ and $V_H = \{u \mid \mathsf{deg}(u) \geq n-k\}$. From Theorem 1 we know, if there exist a solution S, $V_L \cap S = \emptyset$. This leads to the following simple reduction rule.

Reduction Rule 1. *Let (G, T, k, ℓ) be an instance of* HC-Steiner Subgraph *and $v \in V_L$. If $k \leq 1$ or $v \in T$ then return* No. *Otherwise set $(G' = G \setminus \{v\}, T, k-1, \ell)$ as the reduced instance.*

Lemma 1. *Reduction Rule 1 is safe.*

Proof. If $k \leq 1$, then we know that the only potential solution is G itself but since it contains a low degree vertex by Theorem 1 we know that (G, T, k, ℓ) is a No instance. Furthermore, if $v \in T$, then clearly (G, T, k, ℓ) is a No instance.

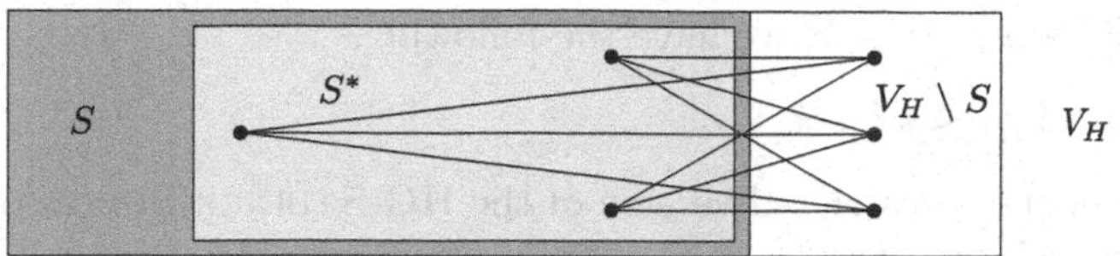

Fig. 1. Illustration of Lemma 2

Suppose $(G' = G, T, k, \ell)$ is a Yes instance of HC-Steiner Subgraph, then there exists a subset $S \subseteq V(G)$ of size exactly ℓ such that $T \subseteq S$, $v \notin S$, and $G[S]$ is $(n-k)$-edge connected. Clearly, $G[S] = G'[S]$ and hence, $G'[S]$ is $(n-k)$-edge connected. However, $n-k = (|V(G')|+1)-k = |V(G')|-(k-1)$. Hence $G'[S]$ is $(n-1)-(k-1)$ edge connected.

For the reverse direction suppose there exists a subset $S \subseteq V(G')$ of size exactly ℓ such that $T \subseteq S$, and $G'[S]$ is $(n-1)-(k-1)$-edge connected. Then, since $G' = G[V(G) \setminus \{v\}]$, we have that $G'[S] = G[S]$ is $(n-1)-(k-1)$-edge connected, which implies that $G[S]$ is $(n-k)$-edge connected. This concludes the proof. □

From now onwards, we assume that Reduction Rule 1 is exhaustively applied. This implies that $V_L = \emptyset$ (that is, $\delta(G) \geq n-k$). Further, notice that if $|V_H| = |V(G)| < \ell$, then we have a No instance. So we assume that $|V(G)| \geq \ell$. Finally, we also assume that $|V(G)| > 2k$, otherwise we could find the desired solution in time $4^k n^{\mathcal{O}(1)}$.

Any solution S excludes exactly $n-\ell$ many vertices from $V(G) = V_H$. We partition V_H into two sets, $V_H^1 = \{v \mid n-k \leq \mathsf{deg}(v) < (n-k)+(|V_H|-\ell)\}$ and $V_H^2 = \{w \mid \mathsf{deg}(w) \geq (n-k)+(|V_H|-\ell)\}$. Our next lemma shows that all but $\mathcal{O}(k^2)$ vertices of V_H must belong to V_H^2.

Lemma 2. *Let* (G, T, k, ℓ) *be a* Yes *instance of* HC-Steiner Subgraph, *then* $|V_H^2| \geq n-k^2-k$.

Proof. Let S be a solution to (G, T, k, ℓ). Since, (G, T, k, ℓ) is a Yes instance of HC-Steiner Subgraph, we have that $\ell = |S| \geq n-k$ as $G[S]$ is $(n-k)$ edge connected. Let $V_{H \setminus S} = V_H \setminus S$ and let $S^\star \subseteq S$ be the set of vertices that are neighbors to every vertex in $V_{H\setminus S}$. That is, $S^\star = \{v \in S \mid V_{H\setminus S} \subset N(v)\}$. Observe that the degree of any vertex $v \in S^\star$ is at least $(n-k)+(|V_H|-\ell)$ (v has at least $n-k$ neighbors in S). Therefore, $S^\star \subseteq V_H^2$. Refer to Fig. 1 for an illustration. Observe, $|V_H| = n$ (as, Reduction Rule 1 is exhaustively applied) and $\ell > n-k$. Hence, $|V_H|-\ell \leq k$. Note that the degree of each vertex in $V_{H\setminus S}$ is at least $n-k$. Hence, the total number of non-neighbors of $V_{H\setminus S}$ in S is at most $k \cdot (|V_H|-\ell) < k^2$. Thus, $|V_H^2| \geq |S^\star| \geq \ell - k^2 \geq n-k-k^2$. This completes the proof. □

Since $|V_H^2| \geq n - k^2 - k$, we have the following.

Corollary 1. $|V_H^1| \leq k^2 + k$.

Next, we define a restricted version of the HC-Steiner Subgraph problem with which we will work.

Annotated HC-Steiner Subgraph	**Parameter:** k
Input: An undirected graph G with n vertices, $\delta(G) \geq n - k$, two sets $T \subseteq V(G)$ (of terminals), and $X \subseteq V(G)$, and two integers k and ℓ. **Question:** Does there exist a subset $S \subseteq V(G)$ of G of size *exactly* ℓ such that $T \subseteq S$, $X = S \cap V_H^1$ and $G[S]$ is $(n-k)$-edge connected.	

Next, we establish a relation between Annotated HC-Steiner Subgraph and HC-Steiner Subgraph. Towards doing so, we prove the following lemma.

Lemma 3. *If* Annotated HC-Steiner Subgraph *is solvable in time* $f(k)n^{\mathcal{O}(1)}$, *then* HC-Steiner Subgraph *can be solved in time* $2^{\mathcal{O}(k \log k)}$ $f(k)n^{\mathcal{O}(1)}$.

Proof. Given a set $X = S \cap V_H^1$, assume Annotated HC-Steiner Subgraph is solvable in time $f(k)n^{\mathcal{O}(1)}$. Observe that $X \subseteq V_H^1$ and $|V_H^1 \setminus X| \leq k$. By Corollary 1, $|V_H^1| \leq k^2 + k$, and thus, there can be at most $\sum_{i=0}^{k} \binom{k^2+k}{i} = 2^{\mathcal{O}(k \log k)}$ many choices for X (guess the complement which is of size at most k). Thus the claim holds. □

Now we show that Annotated HC-Steiner Subgraph can be solved in time $f(k)n^{\mathcal{O}(1)}$. A subset $Y \subseteq X$ is called a *realizable subset*, if there exists a vertex $v \in V_H^2$ such that $N(v) \cap X = Y$. Let $\{X_1, \ldots, X_\psi\}$, be the set of all realizable subsets of X. Next we define $H_i(X)$ as the set of vertices in V_H^2 whose neighborhood is exactly equal to X_i in X. Namely, $H_i(X) = \{v \mid v \in V_H^2 \text{ and } N(v) \cap X = X_i\}$. Next we show a lemma which essentially shows that every vertex in $H_i(X)$ are identical from the perspective of solution S.

Lemma 4 (Exchange Lemma). *Let S be a solution and $\{X_1, X_2, \cdots, X_\psi\}$ be the set of all realizable subsets of X. Furthermore, let $u \in S \cap (H_i(X) \setminus T)$ and $v \in H_i(X) \setminus S$, then $S \cup \{v\} \setminus \{u\}$ is also a solution. See Fig. 2 for an illustration.*

Proof. Let $S_v = S \cup \{v\} \setminus \{u\}$. Observe that $T \subseteq S_v$. We need to show that $G[S_v]$ is $(n-k)$-edge connected. Here we can safely assume that $|S_v| > n - 2k$, otherwise $n \leq 3k$ and we have a trivial kernel. Thus using Theorem 1 it suffices to show that all vertices in S_v have degree at least $n-k$ in $G[S_v]$. Recall that for any vertex $w \in S_v \cap V_H^2$, $\mathsf{deg}(w) \geq n - k + |V_H| - \ell$ and there are at most $|V_H| - \ell$ vertices from $V(G) \setminus S$. Thus for any vertex $w \in V_H^2 \cap S_v$, $|N_{S_v}(w)| \geq n-k$. Next we argue about the degree of a vertex in V_H^1. Recall that both $u, v \in H_i(X)$, and hence $|N_{S_v}(x)| = |N_S(x)|$ for each vertex $x \in S_v \cap V_H^1$. This implies that for every vertex z in $V_H^1 \cap S_v$, $|N_{S_v}(z)| \geq n-k$. Thus if S is $(n-k)$-edge connected, then so is S_v. This concludes the proof. □

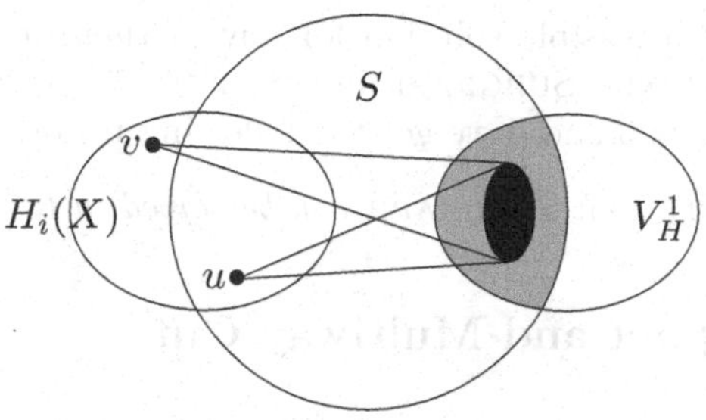

Fig. 2. Illustration of Lemma 4

From Lemma 4 it follows that, if we know $|H_i(X) \setminus S| = b_i$ (that is, there are b_i vertices in $H_i(X)$ that are not part of S), then any b_i vertices can be removed from $H_i(X)$. This observation essentially leads us to the following lemma.

Lemma 5. ANNOTATED HC-STEINER SUBGRAPH *can be solved in time* $2^{\mathcal{O}(k \log k)} \cdot n^{\mathcal{O}(1)}$.

Proof. Let S be a hypothetical solution and let $X = V_H^1 \cap S$. If $|(V_H^1 \setminus X) \cap T| \geq 1$, then return a No. So we assume that $(V_H^1 \setminus X) \cap T = \emptyset$. Denote $\tilde{X} = S \setminus X$. Our objective is to find the set $\tilde{X}$. We partition the vertices of V_H^2 on the basis of neighborhoods into X. Let $\{X_1, \cdots, X_\psi\}$, be the set of all realizable subsets of X. Next we define $H_i(X)$ as the set of vertices in V_H^2 whose neighborhood is exactly equal to X_i in X. Namely, $H_i(X) = \{v \mid v \in V_H^2 \text{ and } N(v) \cap X = X_i\}$. We will show that ψ is upper bounded by $\mathcal{O}(k^3)$. Every vertex in X has degree at least $n - k$ and hence each vertex has at most k non-neighbors. Since, $|X| \leq |V_H^1| \leq \mathcal{O}(k^2)$ (Corollary 1), we have that the number of vertices in V_H^2 that is a non-neighbor to a vertex in X is bounded from above by $\mathcal{O}(k^3)$. In other words, all but $\mathcal{O}(k^3)$ vertices of V_H^2, say v, have the property that $X \subseteq N(v)$. This immediately implies that the number of realizable subsets of X is bounded from above by $\mathcal{O}(k^3)$. Let $b = n - \ell - (|V_H^1| - |X|)$.

Claim: Given X and the vector $\langle b_1, b_2, \cdots, b_\psi \rangle$, in polynomial time we can test whether there exists a solution S for ANNOTATED HC-STEINER SUBGRAPH.

Proof. From Lemma 4 we know that given $\langle b_1, b_2, \cdots, b_\psi \rangle$ we can discard b_i many vertices, that are not terminals, from $H_i(X)$ arbitrarily. If for some i we have that $|H_i(X) \setminus T| < b_i$, return a No. Otherwise, let W_i be a subset of $H_i(X)$ containing arbitrary b_i vertices. Let $S^\star = V_H^2 \setminus (\cup_i W)$. If $G[S^\star \cup X]$ forms an $(n\text{-}k)$-edge-connected graph we return Yes, else, we return a No. □

Observe that $b \leq k$, thus to enumerate $\langle b_1, b_2, \cdots, b_\psi \rangle$, we first guess which of these b_i's are non-zero. This is bounded from above by $\binom{\mathcal{O}(k^3)}{k} = 2^{\mathcal{O}(k \log k)}$. Now indices that are non-zero, we guess the partition of b into these. This is bounded from above by $2^{\mathcal{O}(b)} = 2^{\mathcal{O}(k)}$. This implies that the total number of legal vectors is bounded from above by $2^{\mathcal{O}(k \log k)}$. By enumerating all such vectors and checking whether there exists a feasible solution for any of them it is possible to solve Annotated HC-Steiner Subgraph in time $2^{\mathcal{O}(k \log k)} \cdot n^{\mathcal{O}(1)}$. □

Combining Lemmas 3 and 5 we get the following result.

Theorem 6. HC-Steiner Subgraph *can be solved in time* $2^{\mathcal{O}(k \log k)} \cdot n^{\mathcal{O}(1)}$.

5 Dominating Set and Multiway Cut

In this section we give algorithms for (n-k)-edge-connected version of the classical Dominating Set and Multiway Cut problems.

5.1 Dominating Set

Next, using the algorithm for HC-Steiner Subgraph, we show that HC-DS is FPT.

> HC-DS **Parameter:** k
> **Input:** An undirected graph G with n vertices and two integers k and ℓ.
> **Question:** Does there exists a dominating set S of size exactly ℓ such that $G[S]$ is $(n-k)$-edge connected?

From Theorem 1 we know, if there exist a solution S, $V_L \cap S = \emptyset$. Notice that if $|V_L| > k$ or $|V_H| < \ell$, then we have a No instance. So we assume that $|V_L| \leq k$, $|V_H| \geq \ell$, and $\ell > n - k$. Let $V_{\geq k+1}$ be the set of vertices in $V(G)$ whose degree is at least $k+1$ and $V_{\leq k} = V(G) \setminus V_{k+1}$. We first show that dominating vertices in V_{k+1} is an artifact of the solution size, and we need not worry about them.

Observation 2. *Any set of vertices* $A \subseteq V_H$ *of cardinality at least* $n-k$ *dominates all the vertices in* $V_{\geq k+1}$.

The proof follows from the fact that every vertex in $V_{\geq k+1}$ has at least $k+1$ neighbors.

We assume that $n > 3k$, otherwise we can find a solution by trying all possible subsets of $V(G)$. Observe that any (n-k)-edge-connected subset $S \subseteq V_H$ of cardinality ℓ is a HC-DS for G if and only if S dominates every vertex in $V_{\leq k}$ (follows from Observation 2). In other words, for any solution S, there exists a subset of vertices $S_L \subseteq S \cap N(V_{\leq k})$ of size at most $|V_{\leq k}|$, which dominates every vertex in $V_{\leq k}$. Observe that the cardinality of $V_{\leq k} \subseteq V_L$ is bounded by k. Therefore, $|N(V_{\leq k})| \leq k^2$. For every subset $A \subseteq N(V_{\leq k})$ of size at most k, we can check whether A dominates all the vertices in $V_{\leq k}$. Finally, applying the algorithm for HC-Steiner Subgraph, Theorem 6, on an instance (G, A, k, ℓ), we can check whether there exists a solution of size ℓ. Therefore, we have the following theorem.

Theorem 7. HC-DS *can be solved in time* $2^{\mathcal{O}(k \log k)} \cdot n^{\mathcal{O}(1)}$.

5.2 Multiway Cut

We first state the problem formally.

> HC-MULTIWAY CUT **Parameter:** k
> **Input:** An undirected graph G with n vertices, a set T of terminals $\{t_1, t_2, \ldots, t_q\}$ and two integers k and ℓ.
> **Question:** Does there exists a set $S \subseteq V(G)$ of size at most ℓ such that there does not exist a path between any pair of vertices t_i and t_j in $G \setminus S$ and $G[S]$ is $(n\text{-}k)$-edge-connected?

We first give a reduction rule which takes care of some trivial No instances. Let $t_i, t_j \in T$. We call a path P, from t_i to t_j, *invalid*, if all the vertices on P belongs to V_L.

Reduction Rule 2. *Let (G, T, k, ℓ) be an instance of* HC-MULTIWAY CUT. *If $|V_L| > k$ or $|V_H| < \ell$ then return a* No. *Furthermore, if there exists two terminals $t_i, t_j \in T$ such that there exists an invalid path from t_i to t_j, then return a* No.

Safeness of Reduction Rule 2 is obvious and thus omitted. For a vertex v, a low degree reachable set for v, called $\mathsf{LDR}(v)$, is defined as follows.

$$\mathsf{LDR}(v) = \{u \mid u \in V_H \text{ and} \, \exists \, \text{a path} \, \lambda \, \text{from} v \text{to} \, u \text{such that } \, V(\lambda) \setminus u \subseteq V_L\}$$

In simple words, $\mathsf{LDR}(v)$ contains all high degree vertices which have a path starting at v and whose all the internal vertices are of low degree. In this language, *for a vertex $v \in V_H$*, $\mathsf{LDR}(v) = \{v\}$. Next, we define "low degree' vertices reachable from a vertex via a low degree path". More formally,

$$\mathsf{LR}(v) = \{w \mid \exists \, \text{path} \, \lambda \, \text{from} \, v \, \text{to} \, w \, \text{such that } \, V(\lambda) \subseteq V_L\}.$$

> From now onwards, we assume that Reduction Rule 2 is exhaustively applied. This implies that $|V_L| \leq k$, $|V_H| \geq \ell$, and there is no invalid path in G. The last assumption implies that for any pair of terminals $t_i, t_j \in (T \cap V_L)$, $\mathsf{LR}(t_i) \cap \mathsf{LR}(t_j) = \emptyset$. Let $\mathcal{T} = \{\mathsf{LDR}(t_i) \mid t_i \in T\}$.

Lemma 6. *Let (G, T, k, ℓ) be an instance of* HC-MULTIWAY CUT. *Further, let us assume that there exists a solution S such that there exists a pair of terminals t_i, t_j, and a pair of vertices $x, y \notin S$, $x \neq y$, $x \in \mathsf{LDR}(t_i)$ and $y \in \mathsf{LDR}(t_j)$, then* HC-MULTIWAY CUT *can be solved in time $\mathcal{O}(4^k \cdot n^{\mathcal{O}(1)})$.*

Proof. We first show that if x, y of the kind described in the statement of the lemma exists, then all the common neighbors of x and y must be in S. Suppose not, then there exists a vertex $z \in (N(x) \cap N(y)) \setminus S$. Since $x \in \mathsf{LDR}(t_i)$, there exists a path λ_i from t_i to x such that all the internal vertices on this path belong to V_L. We can similarly get a path λ_j from t_j to y. Let $\overline{\lambda_j}$ be the path λ_j, when traversed from y to t_j. We remark that t_i could be same as x and t_j could be the same as y. Let $P = \lambda_i z \overline{\lambda_j}$ be the walk from t_i to t_j. We claim that all the vertices of P are outside S. We have four cases: (a) $t_i \neq x$ and $t_j \neq y$; (b) $t_i = x$ and $t_j \neq y$; (c) $t_i \neq x$ and $t_j = y$; and (d) (a) $t_i = x$ and $t_j = y$. We only prove the case (a), as all other cases are identical. Indeed, if $t_i \neq x$, then we know that $t_i \in V_L$, and hence by construction every vertex of λ_i is outside S. Similarly, we can show that every vertex of λ_j is outside S. This implies, that the walk P does not contain any vertex of S. Hence, from this walk we can construct a path P' from t_i to t_j whose intersection with S is empty, contradicting the fact that S is a solution.

Thus, to design the desired algorithm in this case, for each pair of vertices x and y of the kind described in the lemma, and for each subset $Z \cup (N(x) \cap N(y))$, $Z \subseteq (V_H \setminus ((N(x) \cap N(y)) \cup \{x, y\}))$, check if $Z \cup (N(x) \cap N(y))$, is a solution to the problem. Since, $|N(x) \cap N(y)| \geq n - 2k$ (Observation 1), the number of choices we need to go through is upper bounded by $n^2 4^k$. This completes the proof. □

Theorem 8. HC-MULTIWAY CUT *can be solved in time* $2^{\mathcal{O}(k \log k)} \cdot n^{\mathcal{O}(1)}$.

Proof. Let (G, T, k, ℓ) be an instance of HC-MULTIWAY CUT and let $\mathcal{T} = \{\mathsf{LDR}(t_i) \mid t_i \in T\}$. If for any terminals t_i and t_j, we have that $\mathsf{LDR}(t_i) \cap \mathsf{LDR}(t_j) \neq \emptyset$, then $\mathsf{LDR}(t_i) \cap \mathsf{LDR}(t_j) \subseteq S$. First of all, observe that if $\mathsf{LDR}(t_i) \cap \mathsf{LDR}(t_j) \neq \emptyset$, then either $t_i \in V_L$ or $t_j \in V_L$. In either case, if $(\mathsf{LDR}(t_i) \cap \mathsf{LDR}(t_j)) \setminus S \neq \emptyset$, then we will get a path from t_i to t_j without a vertex from S. In other words, for any two terminals t_i and t_j, if $\mathsf{LDR}(t_i) \cap \mathsf{LDR}(t_j) \neq \emptyset$, then $\mathsf{LDR}(t_i) \cap \mathsf{LDR}(t_j) \subseteq S$. Let for all $t_i \in T$, $\mathsf{LDR}'(t_i) = \mathsf{LDR}(t_i) \setminus \bigcup_{i \neq j} \mathsf{LDR}(t_j)$. Observe that, $\mathsf{LDR}'(t_i) \cap \mathsf{LDR}'(t_j) = \emptyset$ for all $t_i, t_j \in T$. Let $\mathcal{T}' = \{\mathsf{LDR}'(t_i) \mid t_i \in T\}$.

We first check, using Lemma 6, whether there exists a solution S such that there exists a pair of terminals t_i, t_j, and a pair of vertices $x, y \notin S$, $x \neq y$, $x \in \mathsf{LDR}'(t_i)$ and $y \in \mathsf{LDR}'(t_j)$. We can find a solution of this kind, if exists, in time $\mathcal{O}(4^k \cdot n^{\mathcal{O}(1)})$. From now onwards we assume that such a solution does not exist. That is, there do not exist, t_i and t_j, $t_i \neq t_j$, such that $A = (\mathsf{LDR}'(t_i) \setminus \mathsf{LDR}'(t_j)) \neq \emptyset$, $B = (\mathsf{LDR}'(t_j) \setminus \mathsf{LDR}'(t_i)) \neq \emptyset$, and $(A \setminus S) \neq \emptyset$ and $(B \setminus S) \neq \emptyset$.

Let $W = \cup_{t \in T} \mathsf{LDR}(t)$ and $W' = \cup_{t \in T} \mathsf{LDR}'(t)$. Then the discussion in the above paragraph implies that, there exists a terminal $t \in T$ such that $(W \setminus \mathsf{LDR}'(t)) \subseteq S$. We guess this terminal, say t. Finally, applying the algorithm for HC-STEINER SUBGRAPH, Theorem 6, on an instance $(G, (W \setminus \mathsf{LDR}'(t)), k, \ell)$, we can check in time $2^{\mathcal{O}(k \log k)} n^{\mathcal{O}(1)}$, whether there exists a solution of size ℓ. Let S the solution returned by the algorithm. Let us now prove that there is no path between two terminals t_i and t_j in $G - S$. In fact one of these must be t. Let $t_j = t$. Suppose such a path P, exists then it must have a vertex from $\mathsf{LDR}'(t_i)$, and a vertex from $\mathsf{LDR}'(t)$. However, that will imply that P contains a vertex from two such sets, and by the construction of $(W \setminus \mathsf{LDR}'(t))$ that can only happen if $\mathsf{LDR}'(t_i) \cap \mathsf{LDR}'(t) \neq \emptyset$, a contradiction. This implies that S is indeed a solution, concluding the proof. □

6 Vertex Multicut

In this section, we give a hardness reduction for (n-k)-edge-connected version of the classical VERTEX MULTICUT problem. Let us first define the problem formally.

HC-MULTICUT **Parameter:** k
Input: An undirected graph G with n vertices, a set T of pairs of terminals $\{(s_i, t_i)|i \in [q]\}$ and two integers k and ℓ.
Question: Does there exist a set $S \subseteq V(G)$ of size at most ℓ such that there does not exist a path between any pair of vertices s_i and t_i in $G - S$ and $G[S]$ is (n-k)-edge-connected?

Here we give a reduction from the INDEPENDENT SET problem to HC-MULTICUT.

Theorem 9. *The* HC-MULTICUT *is* W[1]-hard.

Proof. Let $\mathcal{I} = (G, k - 1)$ be an INDEPENDENT SET problem instance, where $|V(G)| = n$. We assume that the parameter is $k - 1$ for INDEPENDENT SET, for simplicity. The question is whether there exists a subset of vertices of cardinality (at least) $k - 1$ such that any two vertices in that subset are non-adjacent in the graph G. Given an instance of the INDEPENDENT SET problem, we first construct an instance of HC-MULTICUT problem, as follows. Consider a clique G' of size n where $V(G') = V(G)$. Let $T = \{(u, v) : (u, v) \in E(G)\}$ i.e. for each edge $(u, v) \in E(G)$ we include the terminal pair (u, v) in T. Now we prove the following claim.

Claim. G has an independent set of cardinality $k - 1$ if and only if G' has a (n-k)-edge-connected multicut of size at most $n - k + 1$.

Proof. Let S be an independent set of cardinality $k - 1$ in the graph G. As G' is a clique, graph induced on $\overline{S}$ in G', $G'[\overline{S}]$ is also a clique with $|\overline{S}| = n - k + 1$. Therefore, the degree of each vertex in $G'[\overline{S}]$ is $(n-k)$. Thus, by Theorem 1, $G'[\overline{S}]$ is (n-k)-edge-connected. Next we show that $\overline{S}$ is a multicut for (G', T). Observe that for any terminal pair $(u, v) \in T$, $(u, v) \in E(G)$. Thus $|\{u, v\} \cap S| \leq 1$. Hence at most one of the terminals from each pair of terminals can be outside $\overline{S}$. Thus $\overline{S}$ is a multicut for (G', T).

Now we prove the other direction. Assume that W is a (n-k)-edge-connected multicut of size at most $n-k+1$ for G'. We prove that $\overline{W}$ is a independent set G. Observe that for all $(u, v) \in E(G)$, $(u, v) \in T$. As G' is a clique, $(u, v) \in E(G')$. Thus at most one of u or v can be in $\overline{W}$ otherwise there is a path between u and v in $G'[\overline{W}]$. Hence, for all $(u, v) \in E(G)$, $|\{u, v\} \cap \overline{W}| \leq 1$. Further, since $|W| \leq n - k + 1$, we have that $|\overline{W}| \geq k - 1$. Thus proving the claim. □

This concludes the proof. □

7 Conclusion

In this paper, we designed FPT algorithms for the highly connected versions of several natural graph problems, with the parameter being the distance from being "$n-1$ connected". Developing polynomial kernels or showing the nonexistence of polynomial kernels remains an interesting direction to pursue.

Acknowledgment. We thank anonymous referees of an earlier version of the paper for several suggestions. Especially for finding a fatal flaw and giving suggestions for improving the running time of the algorithm.

References

1. Cygan, M., et al. (eds.): Parameterized Algorithms. Springer, Cham (2015). https://doi.org/10.1007/978-3-319-21275-3
2. Diestel, R.: Graph Theory. Graduate Texts in Mathematics, vol. 173, p. 7 (2012)
3. Downey, R.G., Fellows, M.R.: Fundamentals of Parameterized Complexity. Texts in Computer Science, Springer, London (2013). https://doi.org/10.1007/978-1-4471-5559-1
4. Einarson, C., Gutin, G.Z., Jansen, B.M.P., Majumdar, D., Wahlström, M.: p-edge/vertex-connected vertex cover: parameterized and approximation algorithms. CoRR, abs/2009.08158 (2020)
5. Fomin, F.V., Lokshtanov, D., Saurabh, S., Zehavi, M.: Kernelization: Theory of Parameterized Preprocessing. Cambridge University Press, Cambridge (2019)
6. Guo, J., Niedermeier, R., Wernicke, S.: Parameterized complexity of vertex cover variants. Theory Comput. Syst. **41**(3), 501–520 (2007)
7. Lewis, J.M., Yannakakis, M.: The node-deletion problem for hereditary properties is np-complete. J. Comput. Syst. Sci. **20**(2), 219–230 (1980)
8. Niedermeier, R.: Invitation to Fixed-Parameter Algorithms. Oxford University Press, Oxford (2006)
9. Robertson, N., Seymour, P.D.: Graph minors. XIII. the disjoint paths problem. J. Comb. Theory Ser. B **63**(1), 65–110 (1995)
10. Yannakakis, M.: The effect of a connectivity requirement on the complexity of maximum subgraph problems. J. ACM **26**(4), 618–630 (1979)
11. Yannakakis, M.: Node-deletion problems on bipartite graphs. SIAM J. Comput. **10**(2), 310–327 (1981)

Coloring a Dominating Set Without Conflicts: q-Subset Square Coloring

V. P. Abidha(✉), Pradeesha Ashok, Avi Tomar, and Dolly Yadav

International Institute of Information Technology Bangalore, Bangalore, India
{abidha.vp,pradeesha,Avi.Tomar,dolly.yadav}@iiitb.ac.in

Abstract. The *Square Coloring* of a graph G refers to coloring of vertices of a graph such that any two distinct vertices which are at distance at most two receive different colors. In this paper, we initiate the study of a related coloring problem called the *subset square coloring* of graphs. Broadly, the subset square coloring of a graph studies the square coloring of a dominating set of a graph using q colors. Here the aim is to optimize the number of colors used. This also generalizes the well-studied Efficient Dominating Set problem. We show that the q-Subset Square Coloring problem is NP-hard for all values of q even on bipartite graphs. We further study the parameterized complexity of this problem when parameterized by a number of structural parameters. We further show bounds on the number of colors needed to subset square color some graph classes.

Keywords: Graph coloring · Square coloring · Subset square coloring · Parameterized algorithm · Dominating set

1 Introduction

Graph coloring is an important problem in the area of graph theory. For a graph $G(V, E)$, the vertex coloring of G refers to a function f from the vertex set V to a set of colors. There are different types of graph coloring problems based on the constraints imposed on this function. A very popular graph coloring question is the Proper Coloring where any two adjacent vertices are to be assigned different colors. Also, several other variants of graph coloring exist, like harmonious coloring, sigma coloring, metric coloring and acyclic coloring. In addition to the theoretical interest, graph coloring problems are motivated by applications in various fields like register allocation in compilers, job scheduling, transportation networks, etc. See [6] for a detailed reading of graph coloring.

A number of graph coloring problems are motivated by a problem in Communication called the *Channel Allocation* problem. Here there exist transmitters $v_1, v_2, \ldots, v_n$ and a transmitter may interfere with another transmitter due to a number of reasons. Now the goal is to assign frequencies to the transmitters such that clear reception of signals is guaranteed. This can be represented as a graph where every vertex corresponds to a transmitter and the interference between transmitters is captured by the distance between the corresponding vertices in

A. S. Kulikov and S. Raskhodnikova (Eds.): CSR 2022, LNCS 13296, pp. 17–34, 2022.
https://doi.org/10.1007/978-3-031-09574-0_2

the graph. Here the frequency assigned to a transmitter corresponds to the color assigned to the corresponding vertex. In the 90s,.Griggs and Yeh [15], introduced a concept of assigning colors (equivalently, non-negative integers) to vertices such that the assignment of colors to any two vertices depends on whether they are at distance at most two. This is called the $L(h,k)$-coloring of graphs. A coloring c of graph G is an $L(h.k)$-coloring if for any two vertices $u, v \in V(G)$, $|c(u) - c(v)| \geq h$ if u and v are at distance 1 and $|c(u) - c(v)| \geq k$ if u and v are at distance 2. Thus, $L(1,0)$- coloring is the proper coloring itself. Other versions of this problem based on different values of h and k are well-studied [5]. Note that $L(1,1)$-coloring involves coloring of vertices with non-negative integers such that the colors on adjacent vertices differ by at least 1 and the colors on vertices at distance 2 also differ by at least 1. This graph coloring is also referred to as *Square coloring* [4,21] since it is equivalent to the proper coloring of the square of a graph.

We initiate the study of a variant of Square coloring called subset square coloring. This is defined as follows:

Definition 1. *Let $G = (V, E)$ be an undirected graph. A coloring function $c : V(G) \to \{c_0, c_1 \cdots c_q\}$ is called a q-*subset square coloring *of G if it satisfies the following constraints:*

- *For every vertex v and every color $c_i, 1 \leq i \leq q$, we have $|c^{-1}(c_i) \cap N(v)| \leq 1$.*
- *A vertex v can have at most $deg(v)$ vertices with color c_0 in $N[v]$, where $deg(v)$ refers to degree of v.*

Here, intuitively, assigning the color c_0 to a vertex v corresponds to v being uncolored. In this paper we refer to a vertex being uncolored and a vertex colored c_0, interchangably. Thus the definition implies that every vertex has at least one colored vertex in its closed neighborhood and no color is repeated in the closed neighborhood. Note that the set of colored vertices form a dominating set of the graph G (A vertex is said to be dominated, if coloured vertices in its closed neighbourhood is from the set $\{c_1 \cdots c_q\}$). Therefore the subset square coloring is equivalent to square coloring a dominating set of the graph using q colors.

For a given graph G, let $\chi_{ssc}(G)$ represent the minimum value of q such that there exists a q-subset square coloring of G. We also study the following algorithmic question. Given a graph G, the q-Subset Square Coloring problem is defined as follows,

Input: Graph G and $q \in \mathbb{N}$.
Question: Can G be q-subset square colored?

The concept of subset square coloring is previously studied in the context of a classic problem in Computational Geometry called the Art Gallery Problem. Given a polygon P, along with two sets, M and G, of points in P, the Art Gallery problem is to find $G' \subseteq G$ such that every point in M is seen by at least one point in G'. Motivated by applications in Robotics, Erickson and LaValle [9], introduced the *Chromatic Art Gallery Problem*. Here, the aim is to find a subset $G' \subseteq G$ such that G' can be colored using q colors and every point $m \in M$ is seen by at least one point in G' and moreover, every point in G' that sees m gets a distinct color. It is easy to see that for the case where M and G are the same finite sets, the Chromatic Art Gallery Problem can be reduced to subset square coloring of a visibility graph. We believe there exists many other application areas related to Channel Allocation where the subset square coloring of graphs becomes useful.

Another motivation for studying the q-SUBSET SQUARE COLORING problem is that many graphs tend to use much smaller number of colors for subset square coloring when compared to number of colors needed for square coloring. For example, complete graphs, star graphs, wheel graphs etc. need $O(n)$ colors for square coloring whereas subset square coloring can be done using one color. This will be useful in many applications where the number of colors corresponds to a resource that needs to be optimized.

We now explore some problems that are related to the q-SUBSET SQUARE COLORING problem.

Related Problems: The problem of Harmonious coloring, was first introduced in 1983 by Hopcroft and Krishnamoorthy [16] which is defined as follows: The harmonious chromatic number of a graph G, denoted by $h(G)$, is the least number of colors which can be assigned to the vertices of G such that each vertex has exactly one color, adjacent vertices have different colors, and any two edges have different color pairs. Later, Yue Li Wang et al. [22] developed the concept of $d-$ Local Harmonious Chromatic problem which generalized the Harmonious Chromatic problem. The $d-$Local Harmonious (or just d-Harmonious) chromatic problem imposes a restriction that the different color-pair requirement is only asked to be satisfied for every edge within distance d for any vertex. Thus the 1-Harmonious chromatic problem is same as the Square coloring problem.

The problem of Efficent Dominating Set [1] for a given graph is also of interest while we study the subset square coloring problem. An efficent dominating set is one which is simultaneously an independent and a perfect dominating set. A perfect dominating set P is one in which each vertex $v \in V(G)$ has exactly one neighbor in $N(v)$ that belongs to P, whereas an independent dominating set I satisfies the condition that set of vertices in I form an independent set. Specifically, efficent dominating set is a special case of a subset square coloring with $q = 1$.

2 A Discussion of Results

In this section, we give a summary of our results.

We have already mentioned that the EFFICIENT DOMINATING SET problem is a special case of q-SUBSET SQUARE COLORING. The EFFICIENT DOMINATING SET problem is already known to be NP-hard [1]. Thus the q-SUBSET SQUARE COLORING problem is NP-hard for $q = 1$. We prove that the q-SUBSET SQUARE COLORING problem with $q = 2$ is NP-hard even on planar bipartite graphs and the q-SUBSET SQUARE COLORING problem is NP-hard even on bipartite graphs, for all values of q. Moreover, it is known that for an arbitrary graph G, it is NP-hard to check if G admits an efficient dominating set.

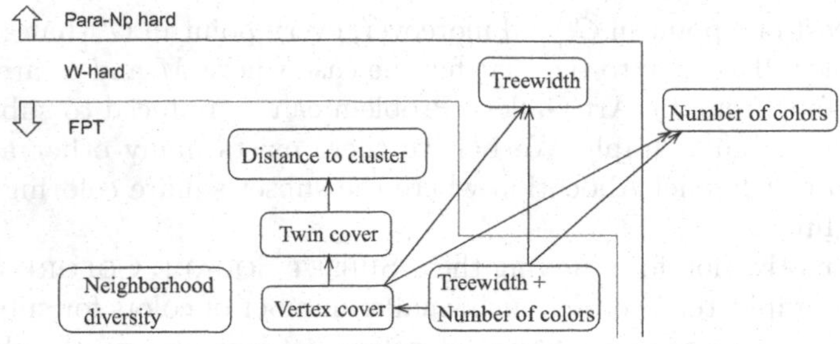

Fig. 1. Summary of parameterized results.

We consider the parameterized complexity of the q-SUBSET SQUARE COLORING problem. For any problem, an interesting parameter to be studied is the size of the solution. For the q-SUBSET SQUARE COLORING problem, this parameter will be q, the number of colors used. However, this turns out to be much harder than a W-hard problem in that it is unlikely to admit an algorithm of running time of the form $f(q)n^{g(q)}$.

Lemma 1. *The q-SUBSET SQUARE COLORING problem parameterized by q is para-NP-hard.*

The lemma follows from the fact that the q-SUBSET SQUARE COLORING problem is NP-hard even for $q = 1$. Moreover, the next result shows that the problem remains W-hard even on graphs of diameter 2.

Theorem 1. *The q-SUBSET SQUARE COLORING problem parameterized by q is $W[2]-$hard on graphs of diameter 2.*

Proof. For a graph G, $\chi_{ssc}(G)$ is bounded by the size of the minimum dominating set of G. When the diameter of a graph is two, all vertices in any dominating set are at distance at most two. Therefore we can not repeat the colors of vertices in a dominating set. This implies that $\chi_{ssc}(G)$ is equal to the size of the minimum dominating set. The minimum dominating set problem is known to be $W[2]-$hard on graphs of diameter 2 [17]. Thus the result follows. □

With respect to Theorem 1, we note that the q-SUBSET SQUARE COLORING problem is polynomial time solvable on planar graphs with diameter 2 [18]. Next, we consider several structural parameters. A well studied structural parameter for graph problems is the treewidth of the graph. Several hard problems are shown to be FPT when parameterized by treewidth. However, the q-SUBSET SQUARE COLORING problem can be shown to be W-hard when parameterized by treewidth. Next we consider treewidth and number of colors as a combined parameter and show that this is FPT. This result is proved using a standard technique in the fixed parameter tractable algorithm design called dynamic programming over treewidth.

Next we consider structural parameters which are possibly larger than treewidth. One such well-studied parameter is the size of the vertex cover of the graph. We give an FPT algorithm for the q-SUBSET SQUARE COLORING problem parameterized by the size of the vertex cover. The size of vertex cover is usually a large parameter, especially for dense graphs. Therefore, we study a parameter whose value is small on dense graphs called the neighborhood diversity. It is also a parameter whose value can be computed in polynomial time. We give an FPT algorithm for the q-SUBSET SQUARE COLORING problem parameterized by neighborhood diversity. We further consider a parameter that is provably smaller than the size of vertex cover, called the *distance to cluster graph* and show that the q-SUBSET SQUARE COLORING problem parameterized by distance to cluster graph is also FPT. We further consider a parameter called *twin cover* whose value typically lies between those of distance to cluster graph and size of vertex cover. Since the q-SUBSET SQUARE COLORING problem parameterized by distance to cluster graph is FPT, the q-SUBSET SQUARE COLORING problem parameterized by twin cover is also FPT. However, we give an algorithm with a better running time.

For these problems, as our goal is to only show whether or not the problem is FPT, we do not try to optimize the running times. See Fig. 1 for a summary of the results in parameterized complexity of the q-SUBSET SQUARE COLORING problem.

Table 1. Summary of bounds for χ_{ssc} for different graph classes.

Graph classes	χ_{ssc}: Upper bound	χ_{ssc}: Lower bound
Path P_n	1	1
Cycle C_{3n}	1	1
Cycle C_{3n+1} or C_{3n+2}	2	2
Complete graph K_n	1	1
Complete bipartite graph $G_{n,m}$	2	2
Bipartite permutation graph $G_{n,m}$	4	2
Planar graphs with diameter 2	3	2
Grid graph $G_{n\times m}$	2	2
Cograph G_n	2	2
Threshold graph G_n	1	1
Caterpillar graph $G(n, r_1, r_2, \cdots r_t)$	3	3
Tree $T(V, E)$	$O(\Delta)$	$O(\Delta - 1)$
Tree $T(V, E)$	$O(n)$	$\Omega(\sqrt{n})$
Split graph $T(V, E)$	$O(n)$	$\Omega(\sqrt{n})$

Next we study bounds on $\chi_{ssc}(G)$ when G belongs to certain graph classes. It is easy to see that various graph classes (that include many sparse and dense graph classes) like complete graphs, cluster graphs, star graphs, wheel graphs, paths, cycles, grid graphs etc. are q-subset square colorable where q is a constant. However, when we consider trees, we show that there exist trees with n vertices, that requires $O(\sqrt{n})$ colors to be subset square colored. As trees form a sub-class of bipartite graphs, this result extends for the class of bipartite graphs also. However, we show that a well-defined sub-class of bipartite graphs, called the Bipartite permutation graphs are 4-subset square colorable. We further show that the class of threshold graphs are 1-subset square colorable. Note that threshold graphs lie in the intersection of split graphs and cographs. We observe that, while cographs, like threshold graphs, are subset square colorable using a constant number of colors, there exist split graphs which require $O(\sqrt{n})$ colors to be subset square colored. See Table 1 for a summary of results.

3 NP−Hardness

In this section, we show that the q-Subset Square Coloring problem is NP-hard, for all values of q. Note that the result is known for $q = 1$. Now, we consider $q = 2$.

Theorem 2. *The q-*Subset Square Coloring *problem, where $q = 2$ is NP-hard, even on planar bipartite graphs.*

Proof. We give a reduction from the planar Exact cover by 3-sets(X3C) problem.

Planar X3C (Exact cover by 3-sets)

Input: A finite set X with $|X| = 3n$ and a collection S of 3−element subsets of X with $|S| = m$.

Question: Does S contain an exact cover for X, i.e., a sub collection $S' \subseteq S$ such that every element of X occurs in exactly one member of S'?

In Planar X3C problem, we have the added constraint that a bipartite graph M such that $V(M)$ corresponds to $X \cup S$ and $E(M)$ is $\{(x, s)|x \in X, s \in S, x \in s\}$ is planar.

Let (U, S) be an instance of the planar X3C problem, where $U = \{u_1, u_2, .., u_{3n}\}$ and $S = \{S_1, S_2, ..., S_m\}$. We construct a planar bipartite graph G as follows: For every element u_i, we add a vertex x_i in G and connect it with an *element gadget* D_i in G. For $1 \leq i \leq 3n$, D_i is a tree rooted at a vertex d_i, as shown in Fig. 3(a). Each of the two child nodes of d_i are connected to three leaves. For every set S_j, $1 \leq j \leq m$, we add a *set gadget* T_j with a vertex t_j attached to two leaves v_j and v'_j. We also add a *palette gadget* P which has two vertices p_1 and p_2 adjacent to each other and each of them attached to three vertices of degree one. See Fig. 3(b).

Further, for $1 \leq i \leq 3n, 1 \leq j \leq m$, we add an edge between x_i and t_j in G, if $u_i \in S_j$ in (U, S). We also add the edge between v_j and $p_1 \in P$, for all $1 \leq j \leq m$.

We claim that (U, S) has an exact-3-cover if and only if $G(V, E)$ has a subset square coloring using two colors (proof is given in the full version).

Now, the result follows from the NP-hardness of the planar X3C problem [12] (Fig. 2). □

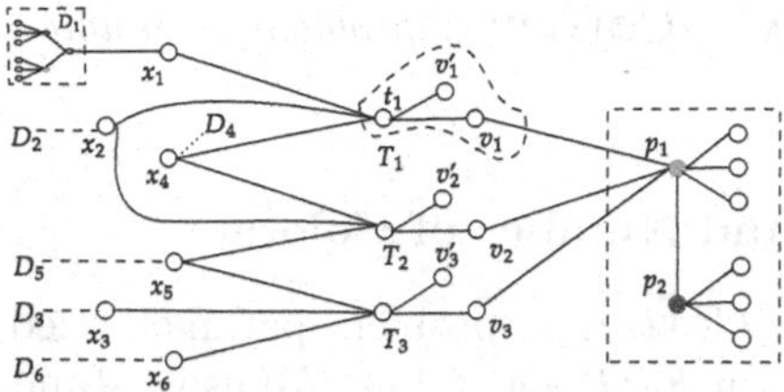

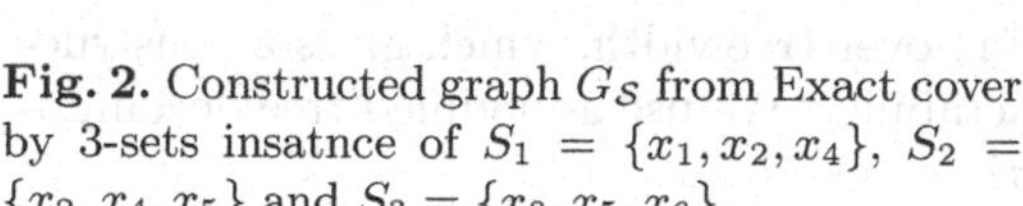

Fig. 2. Constructed graph G_S from Exact cover by 3-sets insatnce of $S_1 = \{x_1, x_2, x_4\}$, $S_2 = \{x_2, x_4, x_5\}$ and $S_3 = \{x_3, x_5, x_6\}$.

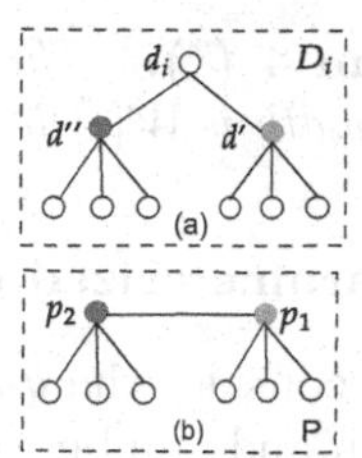

Fig. 3. (a) Element gadget, (b) Palette gadget

Theorem 3 (*).[1] *The* q-SUBSET SQUARE COLORING *problem, where* $q > 2$ *is NP-hard, even on bipartite graphs.*

4 Parameterized Complexity

In this section, we study the parameterized complexity of the q-SUBSET SQUARE COLORING problem.

A parameterized problem is a language $L \subseteq \Sigma^* \times \mathbb{N}$, where Σ is a fixed, finite alphabet. For an instance $(x, k) \in \Sigma^* \times \mathbb{N}$, k is called the parameter. The complexity class FPT contains all fixed parameter tractable problems that have an algorithm, a computable function $f : \mathbb{N} \to \mathbb{N}$, and a constant c such that, given $(x, k) \in \Sigma^* \times \mathbb{N}$, the algorithm correctly decides whether $(x, k) \in L$ in time bounded by $f(k) \cdot |(x, k)|^c$. Theory of intractability of parameterized problems orders the problems into a hierarchy called the W-hierarchy based on its complexity. It is organized as FPT $\subseteq W[1] \subseteq W[2] \cdots$. Under standard complexity theoretical assumptions, a problem which is $W[i]$-hard does not admit FPT algorithms, where $i > 0$. For detailed reading of parameterized complexity refer [8].

4.1 Parameterized by Treewidth

We first consider the treewidth of the graph as a parameter. We begin by defining treewidth.

Tree Decomposition: [8] A tree decomposition of a graph G is a tree T in which each vertex $i \in T$ has an assigned set of vertices $X_i \subseteq V$, called the bag, such that $\bigcup_{i \in T} X_i = V$, with some properties:($a$) if $u \in X_i$ and $u \in X_k$, then $u \in X_j$ for all j on the path from i to k in T.(b)For any edge $e(u, v) \in E(G)$, there exists an $i \in T$ such that $u, v \in X_i$.

The width of a tree decomposition T is the size of the largest bag of T minus one, and the treewidth of a graph G, denoted by $\tau(G)$, is the minimum width over all possible tree decompositions of G.

[1] Proofs of results that are marked with a star are given in the full version.

Theorem 4 (*). *The q-*SUBSET SQUARE COLORING *problem parameterized by tree-width is W[1]-hard.*

4.2 Parameterized by Treewidth and Number of Colors

We now consider the q-SUBSET SQUARE COLORING problem parameterized by treewidth and number of colors and give an FPT algorithm. We use a standard technique called dynamic programming over treewidth, which gives a constructive proof for the fixed parameter tractability. We use a modified tree decomposition called the nice tree decomposition.

Nice Tree Decomposition: [8] A tree decomposition with a distinguished root is called a *nice tree decomposition* if:

- All leaf nodes and the root node have empty bags, i.e., $X_l = X_r = \phi$, where r is the root node and l is a leaf node.
- Every other node in the tree decomposition falls in one of the three categories:

Introduce Node: An introduce vertex node t has exactly one child t' such that $X_t = X_{t'} \cup \{v\}$ for some $v \notin X_{t'}$.

Forget Node: A forget node t has exactly one child t' such that $X_t = X_{t'} \setminus \{w\}$ for some $w \in X_{t'}$.

Join Node: A join node t has exactly two children t_1 and t_2, such that $X_t = X_{t_1} = X_{t_2}$.

Introduce Edge Node: An introduce edge node is labeled with an edge $uv \in E(G)$ such that $u, v \in X_t$ and has exactly one child node t' such that $X_t = X_{t'}$.

Note that we assume every edge is introduced exactly once and we say that edge uv is *introduced* at t. If a join node contains both u and v, and the edge uv exists in $E(G)$, we can note that edge uv will be introduced in the subtree above the join node. Nice tree decomposition enables us to add edges and vertices one by one and perform operations accordingly. This variant of tree decomposition still has $O(\tau \cdot n)$ nodes, where τ is the treewidth of the graph G.

The following result is known.

Proposition 1. *Given a graph G, in time $2^{O(\tau)}n$, we can compute a nice tree decomposition $(T, \mathcal{X})$ of G with $|V(T)| \in |V(G)|^{O(1)}$ and of width at most 5τ, where τ is the treewidth of G [3].*

With each node t of the tree decomposition we associate a subgraph G_t of G defined as: $G_t = (V_t, E_t = \{e : e \text{ is introduced in the subtree rooted at t}\})$. Here, V_t is the union of all bags present in the subtree rooted at t.

Theorem 5. *The q-*SUBSET SQUARE COLORING *is FPT when parameterized by the treewidth τ of the input graph and the number of colors q.*

Proof. We give an algorithm based on dynamic programming over nice tree decomposition $(T, \mathcal{X})$ of G, computed in time $2^{O(\tau)}n$, using Proposition 1, of width at most 5τ, where τ is the treewidth of G. We define subproblems on $t \in V(T)$

for the graph G_t. We consider a *partitioning* of bag X_t by a mapping $f : X_t \to \{B, W, R\}$. For simplicity, we refer to the vertices in each partition respectively as black, white and grey. Each vertex is also assigned another color by a function $c : X_t \to \{c_0, c_1, ..., c_q\}$ and a q-length tuple, by a function $\Gamma : X_t \to \{0, 1, \hat{1}\}^q$. Roughly speaking, these functions will determine how the "partial" square coloring looks like, when restricted to G_t and vertices of X_t. $c(v)$ denotes the color assigned to v and $c(v) = c_0$ denotes that v is not colored. $\Gamma(v)[i]$ indicates whether v has (either in the current graph, or in the "future") a vertex in its closed neighborhood that has color c_i. $\Gamma(v)[i] = 1$ denotes that vertex v has a vertex in its closed neighborhood of color c_i in G_t, $\Gamma(v)[i] = \hat{1}$ denotes that vertex v has a vertex in its closed neighborhood of color c_i, that is not present in G_t, but will appear in the "future", and $\Gamma(v)[i] = 0$ denotes the absence of color c_i in the closed neighborhood of v. We slightly abuse the notation and use $\Gamma(v)[c_i]$ and $\Gamma(v)[i]$ interchangeably. In the following we give a detailed insight into the functions f, c and Γ.

Black, represented by B. Every black vertex v is given a color $c(v) \neq c_0$ in a subset square coloring.
Grey, represented by R. A grey vertex v is not colored, not dominated, i.e. $c(v) = c_0$ and for each $i \in [q]$, it has $\Gamma(v)[i] \in \{0, \hat{1}\}$.
White, represented by W. A vertex v that is neither black nor grey is a white vertex. Note that for a white vertex v, $c(v) = c_0$ and there is $i \in [q]$, such that $\Gamma(v)[i] = 1$.

A tuple (t, c, Γ, f) is *valid* if the following conditions hold for every vertex $v \in X_t$:
1. $f(v) = B \implies c(v) \neq c_0$ and $\Gamma(v)[c(v)] = 1$,
2. $f(v) = R \implies c(v) = c_0$ and $\Gamma(v)[i] \in \{0, \hat{1}\}$, $\forall i \in \{1...q\}$, and
3. $f(v) = W \implies c(v) = c_0$ and $\Gamma(v)[i] = 1$ for some $i \in \{1...q\}$.

For a node $t \in V(T)$, for each valid tuple (t, c, Γ, f), we have a table entry denoted by $D[t, c, \Gamma, f]$. We have $D[t, c, \Gamma, f] = true$ if and only if there is $\mathsf{col} : V_t \to \{c_0, c_1, \ldots, c_q\}$ (where c_0 denotes no color assignment), such that:
1. $\mathsf{col}|_{X_t} = c$,
2. for each $v \in X_t$ and $i \in \{1, 2, \ldots q\}$ with $\Gamma(v)[i] = 1$, there is exactly one vertex $u \in N_{G_t}[v]$, such that $\mathsf{col}(\mathsf{u}) = \mathsf{c_i}$,
3. for each $v \in X_t$ and $i \in [q]$ with $\Gamma(v)[i] \in \{0, \hat{1}\}$, there is no vertex $u \in N_{G_t}[v]$, such that $\mathsf{col}(\mathsf{u}) = \mathsf{c_i}$, and
4. for each $v \in V_t \setminus X_t$, there is at least one vertex $u \in N_{G_t}[v]$, such that $\mathsf{col}(\mathsf{u}) \neq \mathsf{c_0}$, and for all such vertices u, every other $u' \in N_{G_t}[v]$ have $\mathsf{col}(u') \neq \mathsf{col}(u)$.

In the above, such a coloring col is called a (t, c, Γ, f)-*good* coloring. (At any point of time wherever we query an invalid tuple, then its value is $false$ by default.) Note that $D[r, \emptyset, \emptyset, \emptyset] = true$, where r is the root of the tree decomposition, if and only if G admits a subset square coloring using (at most) q colors.

We define $f_{v \to \gamma}$ where $\gamma \in \{B, W, R\}$, as the function where $f_{v \to \gamma}(x) = f(x)$, if $x \neq v$, and $f_{v \to \gamma}(x) = \gamma$, otherwise. Similarly, we define the functions $c_{v \to c_i}$ and $\Gamma_{v[i] \to \alpha}$ where $\alpha \in \{0, \hat{1}, 1\}$. We now proceed to define the recursive formulas for the values of D.

Leaf Node. For a leaf node t, we have $X_t = \emptyset$. Hence, the only entry is $D[t, \emptyset, \emptyset, \emptyset]$. Moreover, by definition, we have $D[t, \emptyset, \emptyset, \emptyset] = true$.

Introduce Vertex Node. Let t be the introduce vertex node with a child t' such that $X_t = X_{t'} \cup \{v\}$ for some $v \notin X_{t'}$. Since the vertex v is isolated in G_t, the following recurrence follows.

$$D[t, c, \Gamma, f] = \begin{cases} D[t', c_{|X'}, \Gamma_{|X'}, f_{|X'}] \text{ if } & f(v) = B \text{ and } \Gamma(v)[c_i] \in \{0, \hat{1}\} \;, \forall\; c_i \neq c(v) \\ D[t', c_{|X'}, \Gamma_{|X'}, f_{|X'}] \text{ if } & f(v) = R \\ \text{False} & \text{otherwise} \end{cases}$$

Introduce Edge Node. Let t be an introduce edge node labeled with an edge u^*v^* and let t' be the child of it. Thus $G_{t'}$ does not have the edge u^*v^* but G_t has. Consider distinct $u, v \in \{u^*, v^*\}$.

1. If $f(u) = B$, $f(v) = W$ and $\Gamma(v)[c(u)] = 1$. We set $D[t, c, \Gamma, f] = D[t', c, \Gamma_{v[c(u)]\to\hat{1}}, f_{v\to R}] \vee D[t', c, \Gamma_{v[c(u)]\to\hat{1}}, f_{v\to W}]$ (if any of the entries are invalid, then it is $false$).
2. If $f(u) = f(v) = B$ and $\Gamma(v[c(u)]) = \Gamma(u[c(v)]) = 1$, set $D[t, c, \Gamma, f] = D[t', c, \Gamma_{v[c(u)]\to\hat{1}, u[c(v)]\to\hat{1}}, f]$.
3. If $\{f(u), f(v)\} \cap \{B\} = \emptyset$, then $D[t, c, \Gamma, f] = D[t', c, \Gamma, f]$.
4. If none of the above conditions hold then $D[t, c, \Gamma, f] = false$.

Lemma 2 (*). *Recurrence for introduce edge node is correct.*

Forget Node. Let t be a forget node with child t' such that $X_t = X_{t'} \setminus \{v\}$ for some $v \in X_{t'}$. Since the vertex v does not appear again in any bag of a node above t, v must be either black or white (otherwise, we set the entry to $false$).

$$D[t, c, \Gamma, f] = \bigvee_{\substack{1 \leq i \leq q \\ \alpha \in \{0,1\}^q}} (D[t', c_{v\to c_0}, \Gamma_{v\to\alpha}, f_{v\to W}] \vee D[t', c_{v\to c_i}, \Gamma_{v\to\alpha}, f_{v\to B}])$$

Join Node. Let us denote the join node by t. Let t_1 and t_2 be the children of t. We know that $X_t = X_{t_1} = X_{t_2}$ and X_t induces an independent set in the graphs G_t, G_{t_1} and G_{t_2}. We say that the pair of tuples $[t_1, f_1, c_1, \Gamma_1]$ and $[t_2, f_2, c_2, \Gamma_2]$ are $[t, f, c, \Gamma]$-consistent if for every $v \in X_t$ the following conditions hold.

- If $f(v) = B$ then $(f_1(v), f_2(v)) = (B, B)$ and $c_1(v) = c_2(v) = c(v)$.
- If $f(v) = W$ then $(f_1(v), f_2(v)) \in \{(W, R), (R, W), (W, W)\}$.
- If $f(v) = R$ then $(f_1(v), f_2(v)) = (R, R)$.
- If $\Gamma(v)[i] = 0$ then $(\Gamma_1(v)[i], \Gamma_2(v)[i]) \in \{(0, 0)\}$ for $1 \leq i \leq q$.
- If $\Gamma(v)[i] = 1$ then $(\Gamma_1(v)[i], \Gamma_2(v)[i]) \in \{(1, \hat{1}), (\hat{1}, 1)\}$ for $1 \leq i \leq q$.
- If $\Gamma(v)[i] = \hat{1}$ then $(\Gamma_1(v)[i], \Gamma_2(v)[i]) \in \{(\hat{1}, \hat{1})\}$ for $1 \leq i \leq q$.

It is easy to see that a vertex v belongs to Black partition in X_t if it is Black in X_{t_1} and X_{t_2} and the color $c(v)$ that is assigned to v is same in these bags. Similarly, we can understand for a vertex in Grey partition. If vertex v

belongs to White partition, it implies that it is dominated in exactly one of the bags X_{t_1} and X_{t_2} or both. However if v is dominated in both the bags, then the color that dominates it is different which is taken care by $\Gamma(v)[i]$. The value of $\Gamma(v)[i]$ is set to 1 for different values of the q-length tuple. Therefore, for a vertex to belong to White partition requires one of the three combinations: $\{(W,R),(R,W),(W,W)\}$. Now consider the values that $\Gamma(v)[i]$ can take in X_t. If color i is not present in $N[v]$ in any of the child nodes t_1 and t_2, then it will naturally not be present in $N[v]$ in G_t, implying $\Gamma(v)[i] = 0$. However, $\Gamma(v)[i] = 1$ indicates the presence of a vertex with color i in $N[v]$ in G_t. We further note that color i appears in exactly one of the child nodes X_{t_1} or X_{t_2} but not both because presence of color i in both child nodes implies the presence of two vertices with color i in $N[v]$ in G_t. This follows from the observation that X_t induces an independent set in G_t, by the property of nice tree decomposition. The next possibility of $\Gamma(v)[i]$ is $\hat{1}$. For this to be true, the color i should not be present in G_t seen so far but will appear in the tree decomposition eventually.

We set $D[t,c,\Gamma,f] = \bigvee_{(f_1,f_2)} (D[t_1,c_1,\Gamma_1,f_1] \wedge D[t_2,c_2,\Gamma_2,f_2])$, where $[t_1,f_1,c_1,\Gamma_1]$ and $[t_2,f_2,c_2,\Gamma_2]$ is $[t,f,c,\Gamma]$-consistent.

We have described the recursive formulas for the values of $D[\cdot]$. Note that we can compute each entry in time bounded by $2^{O(q\tau)} \cdot q^{O(\tau)} n^{O(1)}$. Moreover, the number of (valid) entries for a node $t \in V(T)$ is bounded by $2^{O(q\tau)} \cdot q^{O(\tau)} n^{O(1)}$, and $V(T) \in n^{O(1)}$. Thus we can obtain that the overall running time of the algorithm is bounded by $2^{O(q\tau)} n^{O(1)}$.

4.3 Parameterized by the Size of Vertex Cover

In this section, we prove that the q-Subset Square Coloring parameterized by the size of vertex cover is FPT. Let X be a vertex cover of G, $|X| = k$. First we prove the following result.

Lemma 3 (*). *The number of colors required to subset square color the vertices of graph G is at most the size of vertex cover of G.*

Since both the treewidth and number of colors required to subset square coloring is bounded by $|X|$, the result follows from Theorem 5.

Theorem 6. *The q-Subset Square Coloring parameterized by the size of vertex cover is FPT.*

4.4 Parameterized by Neighborhood Diversity Number

We start by defining the neighborhood diversity number of a graph.

Definition 2. *[13] Given a graph $G = (V,E)$, two vertices $u,v \in V$ have the same type if and only if $N(v)\setminus\{u\} = N(u)\setminus\{v\}$. The graph G has a neighborhood diversity t, if there exists a partition of V into at most t sets, $V_1, V_2, \ldots, V_t$ such that all the vertices in V_i have the same type for $i = 1,2,\ldots,t$. The family $\nu = \{V_1, V_2, \ldots, V_t\}$ is called the type partition of G.*

On creating such a type partition of $V(G)$, we observe that the vertices within a partition either induces a clique or is an independent set. Further, for $1 \leq i, j \leq t$, each vertex in a partition V_i is either adjacent to every vertex in another partition V_j or there are no edges between vertices of V_i and V_j.

Lemma 4 (*). *The number of colors required to subset square color a graph G is at most its neighborhood diversity, that is,* $\chi_{ssc}(G) \leq t$.

Now we show that q-Subset Square Coloring parameterized by t is FPT by giving a polynomial kernel.

Theorem 7. *The q-Subset Square Coloring problem parameterized by neighborhood diversity admits a polynomial kernel of size $O(t^2)$.*

Proof. Let G be a connected graph, along with a type partition of size t, $t > 1$. Let $G'(V', E')$ be the graph obtained from $G(V, E)$ by deleting all but $q+1$ vertices from each type partition. We will show that G' can be q-subset square colored if and only if G can be q-subset square colored. Note that G' is also a connected graph.

Let χ be a q-subset square coloring of G'. We claim χ is a q-subset square coloring of G as well. Let $V_i' = \{v_1, v_2, \cdots, v_{q+1}\}$ be a vertex set in the type partition of $V(G')$. If v_i and v_j, $1 \leq i, j \leq q+1, i \neq j$, are colored, then $\chi(v_i) \neq \chi(v_j)$. Otherwise, there exists at least one common neighbor for all vertices in V_i', since G' is connected and this is a contradiction. Since there are at most q colors, there exists at least one uncolored vertex, say v_i in V_i'. Now, every vertex in $V_i \setminus V_i'$ is dominated in G by the same vertices that dominate v_i in G'.

In the reverse direction, assume that G admits a q-subset square coloring, χ. Then we color the vertices $v_1, v_2, \cdots, v_{q+1}$ in V_i' arbitrarily using the colors, if any, used by χ on V_i. Now it is easy to see that this is a valid q-subset square coloring for G' as well.

Now $|V(G')| \leq (q+1)t$. If $q \geq t$, the problem is trivially a YES instance, by Lemma 4. Therefore $|V(G')| = O(t^2)$. Now the result follows.

4.5 Parameterized by Distance to Cluster Graph

Definition 3. *A cluster graph is a disjoint union of complete graphs.*

It is easy to see that cluster graphs can be 1-subset square colored. In this section, let $X \subseteq V(G)$ such that $G[V \setminus X]$ is a cluster graph and $|X| = k$. Now we observe the connection between $\chi_{ssc}(G)$ and k.

Lemma 5 (*). $\chi_{ssc}(G) \leq |X| + 1$.

Theorem 8. *The q-Subset Square Coloring is FPT when parameterized by distance to cluster graph.*

Proof. If $q \geq |X| + 1$, then by Lemma 5 it is trivially true that a subset square coloring exists. Therefore, we assume that $q \leq k$.

If two or more vertices in a clique in $G[V \setminus X]$ have the same neighborhood in X, delete all but one of those vertices. This does not affect the solution as the closed neighborhood of the vertices are the same. Therefore every clique in $G[V \setminus X]$ has at most 2^k vertices.

Now we bound the number of cliques in $G[V \setminus X]$. Let $\{\mathcal{X}_1, \mathcal{X}_2, \ldots, \mathcal{X}_{2^k}\}$ be the family of subsets of X. For two cliques C_a and C_b in $G[V \setminus X]$, we say C_a and C_b have the same *type* if for all $1 \leq i \leq 2^k$, either both C_a and C_b each have a vertex whose neighborhood in X is $\mathcal{X}_i$ or neither of them has such a vertex. Note that there can be at most 2^{2^k} distinct types of cliques. Now we use the following reduction exhaustively to get a reduced graph G'. If there exists more than $q2^k + 1$ cliques of the same type, delete all but $q2^k + 1$ of them. Thus there are at most $k + 2^{2^k} \cdot (q2^k + 1)$ vertices in G'.

We claim that G has a q-subset square coloring if and only if G' has a q-subset square coloring. Assume G' admits a q-subset square coloring. Let C_i be a clique in $G \setminus G'$. Therefore G' has $(q2^k + 1)$ cliques of the same type as C_i, let them be $C'_1, C'_2, \ldots, C'_{q2^k+1}$. Similarly, for $v \in V(C_i)$, there exists $v_j \in V(C'_j)$ for all $1 \leq j \leq q2^k + 1$ such that $N(v) \cap X = N(v_j) \cap X$. We show that there exists at least one C_j such that one of the conditions is true.

- C_j contains a vertex v_j such that $N(v_j) \cap X = \emptyset$ and v_j is colored.
- none of the vertices in C_j is colored.

If the first condition is true, then we can dominate all vertices in C_i by coloring the corresponding vertex v using the same color as v_j. Now, assume that the first condition is not true. Consider the vertices $v_j \in V(C'_j)$ for all $1 \leq j \leq q2^k + 1$. Since all of them have common neighbors in X, we can color at most q such vertices. Since there are at most 2^k vertices in a cliques, there can be at most $q2^k$ cliques with colored vertices. All the uncolored vertices in a clique is dominated by vertices in X. The same set of vertices can dominate the vertices in C_j in G. The other direction is easy to see.

Since the size of the reduced instance is bounded by a function of k, it follows that the q-Subset Square Coloring is FPT when parameterized by distance to cluster graph.

4.6 Parameterized by the Size of Twin Cover

Definition 4. *[11] For a graph $G(V, E)$ a subset X of vertices is a* twin cover *if for every edge $e = uv \in E(G)$ either (a) $u \in X$ or $v \in X$, or (b) u and v are true twins.*

Two vertices u and v are true twins if every other vertex is either adjacent to both u and v or neither of them and u and v has an edge between them. It follows from the definition that if X is a twin cover, then $G[V \setminus X]$ is a disjoint union of cliques and for every vertex $v \in X$ and every clique in $G[V \setminus X]$, v is either adjacent to every vertex in the clique or v is not adjacent to any vertex in the clique. Thus for every graph G, distance to cluster graph of $G \leq$ size of twin cover $\leq$ size of vertex cover. Thus it follows from Theorem 8 that the q-SUBSET SQUARE COLORING problem parameterized by twin cover is FPT. Here, we give an algorithm with better running time.

Theorem 9. *The q-SUBSET SQUARE COLORING problem parameterized by the size of twin cover is FPT.*

Proof. Let $X \subset V$ be a twin cover of the graph $G(V, E)$ and $|X| = k$. It can be seen that $\chi_{ssc}(G) \leq |X|$. If $q \geq k$, then return $TRUE$. Now, we assume that $q < k$.

Consider all possible $(q+1)^k$ colorings of X using $\{c_0, c_1, \ldots c_q\}$. Now similar to the proof of Theorem 6, we can try to extend each of these colorings to get a valid subset square coloring. Since all the vertices in the clique in $G[V \setminus X]$ are true twins, we can delete all but one vertex from every clique to get an equivalent reduced instance. Now the reduced instance is very similar to that in the proof of Theorem 6, and the same algorithm applies.

Therefore the running time of the q-SUBSET SQUARE COLORING problem parameterized by the size of twin cover is $\mathcal{O}(k^{2^k})$. □

5 Bounds on the Number of Colors for the q-SUBSET SQUARE COLORING

In this section, we discuss bounds on the minimum number of colors needed for subset square coloring some graph classes.

5.1 Trees

We show that $\chi_{ssc}(G)$ can be bounded by maximum degree, when G is a tree. As a corollary, we also show there exists a lower bound on $\chi_{ssc}(G)$ as a function of n.

Lemma 6 (*). *Let Δ be the maximum degree of a tree. Then Δ colors are sufficient to subset square color the tree. Moreover, $\Delta - 1$ colors are sometimes necessary.*

Corollary 1. *There exist trees that require $\Omega(\sqrt{n})$ colors to be subset square colored.*

Now, we know that Trees are a subclass of Bipartite graphs. Therefore the lower bound applies to the class of Bipartite graphs too. In the next result, we show a sub-class of Bipartite graphs can be subset square colored using constant number of colors.

5.2 Bipartite Permutation Graphs

In this section we discuss bounds on χ_{ssc} for bipartite permutation graphs.

A graph is a bipartite permutation graph if it is both bipartite and permutation graph. Let $G(A \uplus B, E)$ be a connected bipartite permutation graph, then it admits the strong ordering, adjacency and enclosure properties, as defined below [20].

(**1**) An ordering of the vertices A in a bipartite graph $G(A \uplus B, E)$ has the *adjacency property* if for each vertex $v \in B$, the vertices in $N(v)$ are consecutive in the ordering of A.
(**2**) An ordering of the vertices A in a bipartite graph $G(A \uplus B, E)$ has the *enclosure property* if for every pair of vertices $v, u \in B$ such that $N(v)$ is a subset of $N(u)$, vertices in $N(u) - N(v)$ occur consecutively in the ordering of A.
(**3**)*A strong ordering* of the vertices of a bipartite graph $G(A \uplus B, E)$ consists of an ordering of A and an ordering of B such that for all (a, b'), (a', b) in E, where a, a' are in A and b, b' are in B, $a < a'$ and $b < b'$ imply (a, b) and (a', b') are in E.

Lemma 7. *If G is a connected bipartite permutation graph then $\chi_{ssc}(G) \leq 4$.*

Let $A = \{a_1, a_2, \cdots a_n\}$ and $B = \{b_1, b_2, \cdots b_m\}$ have the strong ordering property. For $a_j \in A$, let $s(a_j) = \min\{i | b_i \in N(a_j)\}$ and $l(a_j) = \max\{i | b_i \in N(a_j)\}$ be the smallest and largest vertex adjacent to a_j respectively. (Symmetrically defined for B).

Now we color a set of vertices from A, such that all vertices in B are dominated. In the first step, we color the first vertex from A, a_1, using color one.

In the kth step we consider the smallest j such that $b_j \in B$ is not dominated. Then we color $a_i \in A$ such that i is the largest integer such that $N(a_i)$ contains b_j, using color one, if k is odd, or otherwise, using color two. Repeat this till every vertex in B is dominated. Now, if $a_i, a_j, a_k \in A$ are colored in consecutive steps, then $N(a_i)$ and $N(a_k)$ are disjoint. For contradiction, assume that $N(a_i) \cap N(a_k) \neq \emptyset$. Let $j' = l(a_i)$. Then the vertex $b_{j'+1}$ is dominated by both a_j and a_k. This contradicts that a_j was colored by the algorithm to dominate $b_{j'+1}$. Thus no vertex in B has repeating colors in its neighborhood.

Similarly we can dominate all vertices in A by coloring vertices in B using colors three and four. This proves the result. □

Further, we show that the class of Caterpillar graphs which is a subclass of Bipartite Permutation graphs are 3-subset square colorable.

Definition 5. *[19] A* Caterpillar graph *is a tree such that every vertex is at distance at most one from a central path.*

Lemma 8. *$\chi_{ssc}(G) \leq 3$ when G is a caterpillar graph.*

Proof. Let P be the central path of G with vertices $v_1, v_2, \ldots v_{n'}$. Now coloring vertices in P such that v_i, for $1 \leq i \leq n'$, is given color ($i \mod 3 + 1$) is a valid 3-subset square coloring. The result follows.

5.3 Threshold Graph

Definition 6. *[14] A graph is a threshold graph if it can constructed from the empty graph by repeatedly adding either an isolated vertex or a dominating vertex.*

Lemma 9. *If G is a threshold graph then $\chi_{ssc}(G) = 1$.*

Proof. If isolated vertices are present, color them using the same color. By coloring the last introduced dominating vertex v, we satisfy subset square coloring G as each vertex in G has only one colored vertex v in its closed neighborhood.

We know that the family of threshold graphs lie in the intersection of split graphs and cographs. We consider these graph classes in subsequent sections.

5.4 Split Graph

Definition 7. *[2] A graph G is a split graph if $V(G)$ can be partitioned into two sets A and B such that A induces a clique and B induces an independent set.*

Theorem 10. *There exist split graphs with n vertices that require $\Omega(\sqrt{n})$ colors to be subset square colored.*

Proof. We will construct a split graph $G = (A \uplus B, E)$ as follows. Here A induces a clique and B induces an independent set. Let $A = \{v_1, v_2, \cdots v_n\}$ and $B = \{v_{i,j} | 1 \leq i, j \leq n\}$. Further we add edges from $v_{i,j} \in B$ to $v_i \in A$ and $v_j \in A$, for all $1 \leq i, j \leq n$. Note that G has $n^2 + n$ vertices.

All vertices $v_{i,i} \in B$ are of degree 1. To dominate $v_{i,i} \in B$, either we need to color v_i or $v_{i,i}$, for all $1 \leq i \leq n$. If v_i is colored for all i, $1 \leq i \leq n$, then we need n colors since all these vertices are adjacent to each other. Otherwise, assume there exists an i such that v_i is not colored and $v_{i,i}$ is colored. Now the $n-1$ vertices $v_{i,j} \in B$, where $i \neq j$ are dominated either by themselves or by their other neighbor $v_j \in A$. Note that here every vertex is dominated by a distinct vertex. Thus $O(n)$ vertices are colored from at least one of the sets, $\{v_{i,j} | i \neq j\}$ and $\{v_j | j \neq i\}$. Since any two vertices from one of these sets are at distance at most 2, $O(n)$ colors are to be used.

5.5 Cographs

We start by showing the connection between $\chi_{ssc}(G)$ and the modular width of the graph. We first define the modular width of a graph. The modular width of graph G is computed by virtue of four operations, namely creation of isolated vertex, disjoint union, complete join and substitution. More precisely, the modular width of G equals the maximum number of operands used by any occurrence of substitution operation. These four operations that are involved in modular decomposition of graph G are described in [10]. For the sake of completeness, we mention the four operations here.

Definition 8. *[10] Algebraic operations involved to compute modular width of graph G.*

- *Create an isolated vertex;*
- *The disjoint union of two graphs, i.e., the disjoint union of two graph G_1 and G_2, denoted by $G_1 \otimes G_2$, is the graph with vertex set $V(G_1) \cup V(G_2)$ and edge set $E(G_1) \cup E(G_2)$;*

- *The complete join of two graphs, i.e., the complete join of two graphs G_1 and G_2, denoted by $G_1 \oplus G_2$, is the graph with vertex set $V(G_1) \cup V(G_2)$ and edge set $E(G_1) \cup E(G_2) \cup \{\{v, u\} : v \in V(G_1)$ and $u \in V(G_2)\}$.*
- *The substitution operation with respect to some graph G with vertices $v_1, \ldots, v_n$, i.e., for graphs $G_1, \ldots, G_n$ the substitution of the vertices of G by the graphs $G_1, \ldots, G_n$, denoted by $G(G_1, \ldots, G_n)$, is the graph with vertex set $\bigcup_{1 \le i \le n} V(G_i)$ and edge set $\bigcup_{1 \le i \le n} E(G_i) \cup \{\{u, v\} : u \in V(G_i)$ and $v \in V(G_j)$, $v_i, v_j \in E(G)$ and $i \neq j\}$. Hence, $G(G_1, \ldots, G_n)$ is obtained from G by substituting every vertex $v_i \in V(G)$ with the graph G_i and adding all edges between the vertices of a graph G_i and the vertices of a graph G_j whenever $\{v_i, v_j\} \in E(G)$.*

Definition 9. *[10] Let A be an algebraic expression that uses only the four operation as mentioned in Definition 8. We define the width of A as the maximum number of operands used by any occurrence of the substitution operation in A. Modular width of graph G, denoted as $w(G)$, is the least integer m such that G can be obtained from such an algebraic expression of width at most m.*

Cographs are the graphs that can be constructed from operations–creation of an isolated vertex, disjoint union of two graphs and complete join of two graphs. By definition, the modular width of cographs is two [7].

Now we state our result.

Lemma 10. *The maximum number of colors required to subset square color a graph G equals the modular width of G, that is, $\chi_{ssc}(G) \le w(G)$.*

Proof. Now we discuss the maximum number of colors required to subset square color G while we perform those operations. On introducing an isolated vertex, we color it by using one color. To dominate the vertices created as a result of disjoint union of two graphs, we can use maximum number of colors that were used in subset square coloring each subgraphs in the disjoint union operation. Now we consider the complete join operation on the subgraph G_c. Let $G_c = G_{c1} \otimes G_{c2}$. If a vertex v in $V(G_{ci})$, $i = \{1, 2\}$ has degree $G_i(V) - 1$, then $\chi_{ssc}(G_c) = 1$. Otherwise we can color an arbitrary vertex from G_{c1} and G_{c2} using two distinct colors. Therefore the value of χ_{ssc} is ≤ 2. Finally, we examine the substitution operation. We color an arbitrary vertex v in each G_i using distinct colors. Besides the presence of coloured neighbour(s) in G_i, a vertex may possibly be adjacent to another coloured vertex in G_j. Therefore the value of χ_{ssc} can be at most w.

Corollary 2. *If G is a cograph, then $\chi_{ssc}(G) \le 2$.*

References

1. Bange, D.W.: Efficient dominating sets in graphs. Appl. Discrete Math. **189**, 189–199 (1988)
2. Bertossi, A.A.: Dominating sets for split and bipartite graphs. Inf. Process. Lett. **19**(1), 37–40 (1984)

3. Bodlaender, H.L., Drange, P.G., Dregi, M.S., Fomin, F.V., Lokshtanov, D., Pilipczuk, M.: A c∧kn 5-approximation algorithm for treewidth. SIAM J. Comput. **45**(2), 317–378 (2016)
4. Yuehua, B., Zhu, X.: An optimal square coloring of planar graphs. J. Comb. Optim. **24**(4), 580–592 (2012)
5. Calamoneri, T.: The l (h, k)-labelling problem: a survey and annotated bibliography. Comput. J. **49**(5), 585–608 (2006)
6. Chartrand, G., Zhang, P.: Chromatic Graph Theory. Chapman and Hall/CRC, London (2008)
7. Coudert, D., Ducoffe, G., Popa, A.: Fully polynomial FPT algorithms for some classes of bounded clique-width graphs. ACM Trans. Algorithms (TALG) **15**(3), 1–57 (2019)
8. Cygan, M., et al.: Parameterized Algorithms, vol. 5. Springer, Cham (2015). https://doi.org/10.1007/978-3-319-21275-3
9. Erickson, L., LaValle, S.M.: A chromatic art gallery problem. Technical report (2010)
10. Gajarský, J., Lampis, M., Ordyniak, S.: Parameterized algorithms for modular-width. In: Gutin, G., Szeider, S. (eds.) IPEC 2013. LNCS, vol. 8246, pp. 163–176. Springer, Cham (2013). https://doi.org/10.1007/978-3-319-03898-8_15
11. Ganian, R.: Improving vertex cover as a graph parameter. Discrete Math. Theor. Comput. Sci. **17** (2015)
12. Garey, M.R., Johnson, D.S.: Computers and Intractability: A Guide to the Theory of NP-Completeness (Series of Books in the Mathematical Sciences), 1st edn. W. H. Freeman, New York (1979)
13. Gargano, L., Rescigno, A.A.: Complexity of conflict-free colorings of graphs. Theoret. Comput. Sci. **566**, 39–49 (2015)
14. Golumbic, M.C.: Algorithmic graph theory and perfect graphs (2004)
15. Griggs, J., Yeh, R.: Labelling graphs with a condition at distance 2. SIAM J. Discrete Math. **5**, 586–595 (1992)
16. Hopcroft, J., Krishnamoorthy, M.: On the harmonious coloring of graphs. SIAM J. Algebraic Discrete Methods **4**, 306–311 (1983)
17. Lokshtanov, D., Misra, N., Philip, G., Ramanujan, M.S., Saurabh, S.: Hardness of r-dominating set on graphs of diameter (r+1). In: Gutin, G., Szeider, S. (eds.) IPEC 2013. LNCS, vol. 8246, pp. 255–267. Springer, Cham (2013). https://doi.org/10.1007/978-3-319-03898-8_22
18. MacGillivray, G., Seyffarth, K.: Domination numbers of planar graphs. J. Graph Theory **22**(3), 213–229 (1996)
19. Ortiz, C., Villanueva, M.: Maximal independent sets in caterpillar graphs. Discret. Appl. Math. **160**(3), 259–266 (2012)
20. Spinrad, J., Brandstädt, A., Stewart, L.: Bipartite permutation graphs. Discret. Appl. Math. **18**(3), 279–292 (1987)
21. van den Heuvel, J., McGuinness, S.: Coloring the square of a planar graph. J. Graph Theory **42**(2), 110–124 (2003)
22. Wang, Y.L., Lin, T.W., Wang, L.: The local harmonious chromatic problem. In: Proceedings of the 27th Workshop on Combinatorial Mathematices and Computation Theory, Taichung, Taiwan (2010)

Quotient Structures and Groups Computable in Polynomial Time

Pavel Alaev(✉)

Sobolev Institute of Mathematics SB RAS, Novosibirsk, Russia
alaev@math.nsc.ru

Abstract. We prove that every quotient structure of the form $\mathcal{A}/E$, where $\mathcal{A}$ is a structure computable in polynomial time (P-computable), and E is a P-computable congruence in $\mathcal{A}$, is isomorphic to a P-computable structure. We also prove that for every P-computable group $\mathcal{A} = (A, \cdot)$, there is a P-computable group $\mathcal{B} \cong \mathcal{A}$, in which the inversion operation x^{-1} is also P-computable.

Keywords: polynomial computability · computable structures · primitive recursive structures · groups

1 Introduction

If Σ is a finite alphabet then we denote the set of all words in this alphabet by Σ^*. If $x \in \Sigma^*$ then $|x|$ is the length of x. Let $f : A \to \Sigma^*$, where $A \subseteq (\Sigma^*)^n$. We say that f is *computable in polynomial time* (shortly, P-*computable*) if there exists a Turing machine T that, given an input set of words $\bar{x} = \langle x_1, \ldots, x_n \rangle$, computes the word $f(x_1, \ldots, x_n)$ in no more than $P(|\bar{x}|)$ steps, where $|\bar{x}| = \max_{i \leqslant n} |x_i|$ and $P(n) \in \mathbb{N}[n]$ is a polynomial with natural coefficients. Such functions can be considered as a theoretical attempt to define the concept of a quickly computable function. It is known that this definition does not depend on the choice of a particular Turing machine.

We can transfer the notion of P-computability to many other natural objects. If $A \subseteq (\Sigma^*)^n$ then we say that the set A is P-*computable* if $\chi_A : (\Sigma^*)^n \to \{0, 1\}$ is P-computable.

The main object considered in the paper is defined as follows. Let $\mathcal{A} = (A, L^A)$ be a structure of a finite signature L. We say that $\mathcal{A}$ is a P-*computable structure* if there exists a finite alphabet Σ such that $A \subseteq \Sigma^*$, and A itself and all functions and predicates in L^A are P-computable. A structure $\mathcal{A}$ is called a P-*computable presentation* of an abstract structure $\mathcal{B}$ if $\mathcal{A}$ is P-computable and $\mathcal{A} \cong \mathcal{B}$.

The author is grateful to S. S. Goncharov, N. A. Bazhenov, V. L. Selivanov, S. S. Ospichev, and A. V. Seliverstov for fruitful discussions that allowed to improve the quality of the article.

A. S. Kulikov and S. Raskhodnikova (Eds.): CSR 2022, LNCS 13296, pp. 35–45, 2022.
https://doi.org/10.1007/978-3-031-09574-0_3

This definition can be found, for example, in [1]. It is proved there that every computable structure of a finite signature without functions has a P-computable presentation. In [2], it is proved that every torsion Abelian group or a structure with injection is isomorphic to a P-computable structure. In addition, it is noted there that the questions about abstract isomorphisms and, for example, computable isomorphisms are essentially different. In [3], it is proved that every locally finite structure of a finite signature also has a P-computable presentation. In [4,5], it is proved that every finitely generated substructure of a P-computable structure also has a P-computable presentation. In addition, a criterion of P-computability of a finitely generated structure is proved there. In [6], it is proved that the field of complex algebraic numbers and the ordered field of real algebraic numbers have P-computable presentations. In general, the question of the existence of a P-computable presentation for a given structure is quite difficult. Some overview of this theme can be found in [7]. In [12], it is proved that the index set of the class of computable structures having a P-computable presentation is a Σ_1^1-complete set, i.e., has a very high complexity.

Let $\mathcal{A}$ and $\mathcal{B}$ be two isomorphic P-computable structures. We say that $f : \mathcal{A} \to \mathcal{B}$ is a P-*computable isomorphism* if f is an isomorphism and simultaneously a P-computable function. We say that $\mathcal{A}$ and $\mathcal{B}$ are P-*computably isomorphic*, $\mathcal{A} \cong_{\mathrm{p}} \mathcal{B}$, if there is an isomorphism $f : \mathcal{A} \to \mathcal{B}$ such that f and f^{-1} are P-computable. These two definitions are essentially different. The last means that $\mathcal{A}$ and $\mathcal{B}$ are practically identical from the point of view of polynomial computability. In [3], it is proved that for every infinite P-computable structure $\mathcal{A}$, there are infinitely many its P-computable presentations not P-computably isomorphic to each other.

Besides P-computable structures, we can also consider P-*computable quotient structures*, i.e., structures of the form $\mathcal{A}/E$, where $\mathcal{A}$ is a P-computable structure and E is a P-computable congruence in $\mathcal{A}$. The universe of such a structure has the form $A/E = \{[x]_E \mid x \in A\}$, where $A \subseteq \Sigma^*$ is a P-computable set, $E \subseteq A^2$ is a P-computable equivalence relation, and $[x]_E = \{y \in A \mid xEy\}$ is an equivalence class. Sets of this form can be called P-*computable quotient sets.* Identifying a set $A \subseteq \Sigma^*$ with the quotient set A/id_A, we can consider P-computable structures as a partial case of P-computable quotient structures.

In general, P-computable quotient structures are very natural objects. For example, every free group of a finite rank has a natural P-computable presentation. If a group is defined by finitely many generators and relations, and its word problem is decidable in polynomial time, then we obtain a natural P-computable quotient structure.

Let A/E, B/F be two quotient sets. We say that a function $f : A/E \to B/F$ is P-*computable* if there is a P-computable function $f_0 : A \to B$ such that $f([x]_E) = [f_0(x)]_F$ for $x \in A$. This definition allows us to define the notion of a P-computable isomorphism $f : \mathcal{A}/E \to \mathcal{B}/F$ between quotient structures literally as above, as well as the relation $\mathcal{A}/E \cong_{\mathrm{p}} \mathcal{B}/F$.

In [8], it is shown that P-computable quotient structures naturally arise when working with algebraic numbers, and two questions are posed.

1. Is it true that every P-computable quotient structure $\mathcal{A}/E$ is isomorphic to a P-computable structure?
2. Is it true that every P-computable quotient structure $\mathcal{A}/E$ is P-computably isomorphic to a P-computable structure?

In the same article (see also [9]), it was proved that Question 2 almost equivalent to the problem P = NP: if P = NP, then the answer is yes, and if P $\neq$ NP and, moreover, $\Sigma_2^P \neq \Pi_2^P$, then the answer is no.

In this paper, we give the positive answer to Question 1. This means that for every structure consisting of classes of words, we can find a presentation in which each class is replaced by one canonical word (an invariant for this class), and the relations and operations remains P-computable.

To do this, we in particular prove that every P-computable structure $\mathcal{A}$ has a P-computable presentation $\mathcal{B}$ with universe $B \subseteq \mathrm{Tal}(\omega) = \{0\} \cup \{1^x \mid x \geqslant 1\}$, where $1^x = 11\ldots1$ is the word of length x.

Removing all time limits from the definition, we can define a *computable function* $f : A \to \Sigma^*$, $A \subseteq (\Sigma^*)^n$, as a function computable on a Turing machine. Using an appropriate natural numbering $\gamma : \omega \to \Sigma^*$, we can also define the notion of a primitive recursive function $f : A \to \Sigma^*$. Note that for the class of computable or primitive recursive structures, Questions 1 and 2 are trivial.

As an application of the obtained theorems and the technique used, we prove that for every P-computable group $\mathcal{A} = (A, \cdot)$, there is a P-computable group $\mathcal{B} \cong \mathcal{A}$, in which the inversion operation x^{-1} is also P-computable, i.e., $\mathcal{A}$ can be essentially improved.

2 The Universe of P-computable Structures and Quotient Structures

As the basic computing device, we use multi-tape Turing machines described in [11]. If $x \in \omega$ then we define $\mathrm{tal}(x) \in \{0,1\}^*$ as follows: $\mathrm{tal}(0) = 0$ and $\mathrm{tal}(x) = 1^x$ for $x \geqslant 1$. Let $\mathrm{Tal}(\omega) = \{\mathrm{tal}(x) \mid x \in \omega\}$.

Theorem 1. *Let $\mathcal{A} = (A, L^A)$ be a P-computable structure of a finite signature L. Then there exist a P-computable structure $\mathcal{B} = (B, L^B) \cong \mathcal{A}$ with universe $B \subseteq Tal(\omega)$ and a P-computable isomorphism $g : \mathcal{B} \to \mathcal{A}$.*

Proof. Let $A \subseteq \Sigma^*$, where Σ is a finite alphabet. We may assume that all words in A have length at least 2. Consider only the case where L contains one k-place function f, and all other symbols are predicates or constants. The case of several functions looks exactly the same. Increasing $d \geqslant 1$, we may assume that $f^A(a_1, \ldots, a_k)$ is computed in time $\max_{i \leqslant k}\{|a_i|\}^d$, and the same estimate holds for $|f^A(a_1, \ldots, a_k)|$.

In the construction, we define the following series of finite objects by induction on $t \in \omega$: a number $n_t = 2^{c^t}$, a finite set $B_t \subseteq \{1^1, 1^2, \ldots, 1^{n_t}\}$, finite $A_t \subseteq A$, and a bijection $g_t : B_t \to A_t$. They all grow monotonically, i.e., $B_t \subseteq B_{t+1}$,

$A_t \subseteq A_{t+1}$, and $g_t \subseteq g_{t+1}$ for $t \in \omega$. The constant c is specified below. All these objects are encoded in one word

$$W_t = g_t(1^1) * g_t(1^2) * \ldots * g_t(1^{n_t}),$$

where we assume that $g_t(1^x) = 0$ for $1^x \notin B_t$, and $0, * \notin \Sigma$. The word W_t will be an initial subword in W_{t+1}. Here the estimation $|a| \leqslant n_t$ holds for $a \in A_t$. Then $|W_t| \leqslant n_t(n_t+1) = P(n_t)$, where $P(n) \in \mathbb{N}[n]$ is a polynomial with natural coefficients.

We fix a natural order $\leqslant$ on Σ^*, comparing words first by length, and then lexicographically. Then $\Sigma^* = \{u_0 < u_1 < \ldots\}$. In the construction, we will satisfy the following conditions for every $t \in \omega$:

1) there is an algorithm that, given 1^t and W_t, finds W_{t+1} in polynomial time;
2) if $a_1, \ldots, a_k \in A_t$ then $f^A(a_1, \ldots, a_k) \in A_{t+1}$;
3) if $u_t \in A$ then $u_t \in A_{t+1}$.

Let $A_0 = \{a_1, a_2\}$, $B_0 = \{1, 11\}$, and $g_0 : B_0 \to A_0$. We assume that A includes at least two words a_1, a_2 of length 2, since $n_0 = 2$. We can achieve this with a finite permutation in A. Then $W_0 = a_1 * a_2$.

At the end of the construction, we define $g = \bigcup_{t\in\omega} g_t$ and $B = \bigcup_{t\in\omega} B_t$. By 3), $\bigcup_{t\in\omega} A_t = A$. Prove that the set B is P-computable. Let $x > n_0$. Starting from W_0, we successively compute words $W_1, W_2, \ldots$, waiting for a step t for which $n_t < x \leqslant n_{t+1}$. We estimate the working time. If $i \leqslant t$ then $|W_i| \leqslant P(n_i) \leqslant P(n_t) \leqslant P(x)$, where $x = |1^x|$. If the algorithm that finds W_{i+1} from W_i requires $Q(|W_i|)$ steps, where $Q(n) \in \mathbb{N}[n]$, then the total time for computing $W_1, W_2, \ldots, W_{t+1}$ can be estimated as $x \cdot Q(P(x))$, since $t < n_t < x$. Adding some time for auxiliary operations, we obtain a polynomial estimation for the time of computing W_{t+1}.

Now we can find $g_t(1^x)$ in the word W_{t+1}. If $g_t(1^x) = 0$ then $1^x \notin B$, otherwise $1^x \in B$. If $1^x \in B$ then we also know $g(1^x)$. Therefore the function g is also P-computable.

We define an interpretation of L on B so that g is an isomorphism. Clearly, all predicates are P-computable in $\mathcal{B} = (B, L^B)$, since if $P \in L$ and $1^{x_1}, \ldots, 1^{x_k} \in B$, then $P^B(1^{x_1}, \ldots, 1^{x_k}) \Leftrightarrow P^A(g(1^{x_1}), \ldots, g(1^{x_k}))$.

We prove that f^B is P-computable. Consider $1^{x_1}, \ldots, 1^{x_k} \in B$ and assume that $x_i \leqslant x_1$ for $i \leqslant k$. Let $x_1 > n_0$. Just as above, we find W_{t+1} such that $n_t < x_1 \leqslant n_{t+1}$. Then $1^{x_i} \in \mathrm{dom}(g_{t+1})$ for all $i \leqslant k$. We find in W_{t+1} the words $a_i = g_{t+1}(1^{x_i})$, $i \leqslant k$, and compute the word $a = f^A(a_1, \ldots, a_k)$ in $\mathcal{A}$, which is in A_{t+2} by 2). Then we find W_{t+2}. There is $y \leqslant n_{t+2} = n_t^{c^2}$ such that $g_{t+2}(1^y) = a$. Passing through the word W_{t+2} and comparing all its components with a, we find $1^y = f^B(1^{x_1}, \ldots, 1^{x_k})$.

Now we describe an algorithm for the transition from $1^t, W_t$ to W_{t+1}, and define the constant c. Passing through W_t, we write out a list $a_1 * a_2 * \ldots * a_{r_t}$ of all elements of A_t. To obtain A_{t+1}, pass through all tuples $\langle b_1, b_2, \ldots, b_k \rangle$ in A_t^k, for each compute $f^A(b_1, \ldots, b_k)$, and compare it with the previously obtained elements. If it is new then add it to A_{t+1}. Next, passing through all words

$u_0, u_1, \ldots, u_t$, we find u_t and add it to A_{t+1}, if $u_t \in A$ and it was not added before. As a result, we obtain a list $a_1 * \ldots * a_{r_t} * a_{r_t+1} * \ldots * a_{r_{t+1}}$ of all elements of A_{t+1} in polynomial time. Since $|a| \leqslant n_t$ for $a \in A_t$, and $|u_t| \leqslant t \leqslant n_t$, we see that $|a| \leqslant n_t^d$ for $a \in A_{t+1}$. If $c \geqslant d$ then $|a| \leqslant n_{t+1}$.

Clearly $r_{t+1} - r_t \leqslant r_t^k + 1$. Suppose $c \geqslant k+2$. Then $n_{t+1} \geqslant n_t^{k+2} \geqslant 3n_t^k \geqslant n_t^k + n_t + 1 \geqslant r_t^k + n_t + 1$, hence, $n_{t+1} - n_t \geqslant r_t^k + 1$. We add all elements $a_{r_t+1}, \ldots, a_{r_{t+1}}$ to the word W_{t+1}, and complete it by a set of 0 so that it consists of n_{t+1} components. We see that all required estimations holds if $c = \max\{d, k+2\}$. □

In the theorem, the universe of the constructed structure $\mathcal{B}$ is a subset of $\mathrm{Tal}(\omega)$. Can it always be chosen equal to $\mathrm{Tal}(\omega)$? In [10], an example of an infinite computable graph is constructed which does not have a primitive recursive isomorphic presentation with universe ω. Since this graph is a structure without functions, it has a P-computable presentation $\mathcal{A} = (A, P)$, where P is a two-place predicate [1]. However, it cannot have a P-computable presentation with universe $\mathrm{Tal}(\omega)$, since such a presentation easily produces a primitive recursive presentation with universe ω. We give a description of P-computable structures whose universe can be chosen equal to $\mathrm{Tal}(\omega)$.

Theorem 2. *Let $\mathcal{A}$ be a structure of a finite signature L. Then the following are equivalent:*

a) *$\mathcal{A}$ is isomorphic to a P-computable structure $\mathcal{B}$ with universe $Tal(\omega)$;*

b) *$\mathcal{A}$ is isomorphic to a P-computable structure $\mathcal{B}' = (B', L^{B'})$ for which there exists a P-computable injection $h : Tal(\omega) \to B'$.*

Proof. The implication (a$\Rightarrow$b) is clear. Let $\mathcal{B}' = \mathcal{B}$ and $h(x) = x$ for $x \in \mathrm{Tal}(\omega)$. We prove (b$\Rightarrow$a). We assume that the structure $\mathcal{A} = (A, L^A)$ is P-computable itself and $h : \mathrm{Tal}(\omega) \to A$ is a P-computable injection. The proof is very close to the proof of Theorem 1. Let $A \subseteq \Sigma^*$ and L includes only one k-place function f. The case of several functions differs only in a more bulky notation. We assume that $f^A(a_1, \ldots, a_k)$ is computed in time $\max_{i \leqslant k}\{|a_i|\}^d$, and $h(1^x)$ is computed in time x^d for $x \geqslant 2$. Then $|h(1^x)| \leqslant x^d$.

We again construct monotonically growing finite objects $n_t = 2^{c^t}$, B_t, $A_t \subseteq A$, and a bijection $g_t : B_t \to A_t$ by induction on t. The difference is that $B_t = \{1^1, 1^2, \ldots, 1^{n_t}\}$ now. This means that all components $g_t(1^x)$ in the word

$$W_t = g_t(1^1) * g_t(1^2) * \ldots * g_t(1^{n_t})$$

are elements of A_t. Here the estimate $|a| \leqslant n_t^d$ holds for $a \in A_t$, and hence $|W_t| \leqslant n_t(n_t^d + 1) = P(n_t)$. We satisfy the following conditions for every $t \in \omega$:

1) there exists an algorithm that, given 1^t and W_t, finds W_{t+1} in polynomial time;
2) if $a_1, \ldots, a_k \in A_t$ then $f^A(a_1, \ldots, a_k) \in A_{t+1}$;
3) if $u_t \in A$ then $u_t \in A_{t+1}$.

Let $A_0 = \{a_1, a_2\}$, $B_0 = \{1, 11\}$, and $g_0 : B_0 \to A_0$.

At the end of the construction, we define $g = \bigcup_{t\in\omega} g_t$ and $B = \bigcup_{t\in\omega} B_t$, and obtain a bijection $g : B \to A$. In this case, we construct the universe $B = \{1^x \mid x \geqslant 1\}$, but it can easily be transformed to $\mathrm{Tal}(\omega)$. Literally as in Theorem 1, we can show that g is P-computable. Define an interpretation L^B on B so that g becomes an isomorphism. Arguing as in Theorem 1, we see that $\mathcal{B}$ is a P-computable structure.

It remains to describe an algorithm that, given 1^t and W_t, finds W_{t+1}, and to define the constant c. We again pass through all tuples $\langle b_1, \ldots, b_k\rangle$ in A_t^k, computes $f^A(b_1, \ldots, b_k)$, and form a list $a_1 * \ldots * a_{r_{t+1}}$ of all elements that should get into A_{t+1}. If $c \geqslant d$ then $|a_i| \leqslant n_{t+1}$ for all $i \leqslant r_{t+1}$. If $c \geqslant k+2$ then $n_{t+1} - n_t \geqslant n_t^k + 1$, i.e., $n_{t+1} \geqslant r_{t+1}$.

Find $m = n_{t+1} - r_{t+1}$. We need to add m new elements to A_{t+1}, to get a bijection $g_{t+1} : B_{t+1} \to A_{t+1}$, where $|B_{t+1}| = n_{t+1}$. To do this, we compute the list of all elements $h(1^2) * h(1^3) * \ldots * h(1^{n_{t+1}})$, and choose there m elements that are not yet in A_{t+1}. Since $h(1^x)$ is computed in time x^d, the whole list requires $O(n_{t+1}^d \cdot n_{t+1})$ steps. Since $n_{t+1} = n_t^d$ and $n_t \leqslant |W_t|$, this time is polynomial.

Next, $|h(1^x)| \leqslant n_{t+1}^d$ for $x \leqslant n_{t+1}$, i.e., the required estimation of $|a|$ holds for $a \in A_{t+1}$. □

As in Theorem 1, when we prove (b ⇒ a) here, we get a P-computable isomorphism $g : \mathcal{B} \to \mathcal{B}'$.

Theorem 3. *Let $\mathcal{A} = (A, L^A)$ be a P-computable structure of a finite signature L, and let $E \subseteq A^2$ be a P-computable congruence in $\mathcal{A}$. Then there is a P-computable structure $\mathcal{B}$, isomorphic to $\mathcal{A}/E$, and a P-computable isomorphism $f : \mathcal{B} \to \mathcal{A}/E$.*

Proof. By Theorem 1, there exists a P-computable structure $\mathcal{B}_0 = (B_0, L^{B_0})$ with universe $B_0 \subseteq \mathrm{Tal}(\omega)$, and a P-computable isomorphism $g : \mathcal{B}_0 \to \mathcal{A}$. Define $F = \{\langle a, b\rangle \in B_0^2 \mid \langle g(a), g(b)\rangle \in E\}$. Then F is a P-computable congruence in $\mathcal{B}_0$. To simplify the notation, we assume that $B_0 \subseteq \{1^x \mid x \geqslant 1\}$, i.e., $\mathrm{tal}(0) \notin B_0$. Let $B = \{1^y \in B_0 \mid \forall z < y\ \langle 1^y, 1^z\rangle \notin F\}$. It is a P-computable set which contains exactly one element from every equivalence class in B_0/F. If $1^x \in B_0$ then define $\pi(1^x) = 1^y$, where $1^y \in B$ and $\langle 1^x, 1^y\rangle \in F$. To find $\pi(1^x)$, we need to pass through all $y = 1, 2, \ldots, x$, and check the specified condition for each. The function $\pi : B_0 \to B$ is P-computable.

We define an interpretation L^B in B so that the function $\mathrm{id}_B : B \to B_0$ generates an isomorphism from $\mathcal{B}$ to $\mathcal{B}_0/F$. If P is a predicate in L, then $P^B(1^{x_1}, \ldots, 1^{x_n}) \Leftrightarrow P^{B_0}(1^{x_1}, \ldots, 1^{x_n})$. If h is a function in L, then

$$h^B(1^{x_1}, \ldots, 1^{x_n}) = \pi(h^{B_0}(1^{x_1}, \ldots, 1^{x_n})).$$

We obtain a P-computable structure $\mathcal{B}$ for which $g|_B$ generates a P-computable isomorphism $f : \mathcal{B} \to \mathcal{A}/E$, $f(1^x) = [g(1^x)]_E$. □

As mentioned above, if $\Sigma_2^P \neq \Pi_2^P$ then f^{-1} in the theorem is not P-computable in general.

Is it true that if the structure $\mathcal{A}$ in this theorem has universe $\mathrm{Tal}(\omega)$, then we can find $\mathcal{B}$ with universe $\mathrm{Tal}(\omega)$? The answer is no. Let $\mathcal{A}_0 = (A_0, P_0)$, where $A_0 \subseteq \mathrm{Tal}(\omega)$, be the P-computable graph mentioned above which has no P-computable presentation with universe $\mathrm{Tal}(\omega)$. We can easily present it as a quotient structure. Let $A = \mathrm{Tal}(\omega)$. Choose $a \in A_0$. Define $xEy \Leftrightarrow x = y$ for $x, y \in A_0$, and xEa for $x \in A \setminus A_0$. Then E is an equivalence relation on A. Construct $\mathcal{A} = (A, P)$ as follows. If $x, y \in A_0$ then $P(x, y) \Leftrightarrow P_0(x, y)$. If $x, y \in A \setminus A_0$ then $P(x, y) \Leftrightarrow P_0(a, a)$. If $x \in A_0, y \in A \setminus A_0$ then $P(x, y) \Leftrightarrow P_0(x, a)$. Clearly, $\mathcal{A}/E \cong \mathcal{A}_0$.

3 Groups with Quick Inversion Operation

If $x \in \omega$ then $\mathrm{bin}(x) \in \{0,1\}^*$ denotes the standard binary representation of x, where $\mathrm{bin}(0) = 0$. If $x \in \mathbb{Z} \setminus \omega$ then $\mathrm{bin}(x) = 0\,\mathrm{bin}(-x)$. By $\log x$ we denote $\log_2 x$ for $x \geqslant 1$.

Theorem 4. *Let $\mathcal{A} = (A, \cdot)$ be a P-computable group. Then there exists a P-computable group $\mathcal{A}_1 \cong \mathcal{A}$, in which the operation $x \mapsto x^{-1}$ is also P-computable, and a P-computable isomorphism $f : \mathcal{A}_1 \to \mathcal{A}$.*

Proof. Let Σ be a finite alphabet and $A \subseteq \Sigma^*$. We may assume that A is infinite, all words in A have length at least 2, and $x \cdot y$ is computed in $\mathcal{A}$ in time $\max\{|x|, |y|\}^d$, where $d \geqslant 2$ is a constant. Let $L = \{a_i, b_i \mid i \in \omega\}$ be a countable alphabet. We fix a natural order $\leqslant$ on Σ^*, comparing words first by length, and then lexicographically. Then $\Sigma^* = \{u_0 < u_1 < u_2 < \ldots\}$.

The set A can also be represented as a sequence of words $\{e_0 < e_1 < e_2 < \ldots\}$. We construct $h : L \to A$ as follows: $h(a_i) = e_i$ and $h(b_i) = e_i^{-1}$ for $i \in \omega$. Encoding symbol a_i as $a\,\mathrm{bin}(i)$ and b_i as $b\,\mathrm{bin}(i)$, we can consider L as a set of words in the alphabet $\{0, 1, a, b\}$. Then h is a computable function. Let $S = L^*$. The defined function can be naturally extended to $h : S \to A$ so that $h(s_1 s_2 \ldots s_n) = h(s_1)h(s_2)\ldots h(s_n)$ and $h(\varnothing)$ is the unit 1^A of $\mathcal{A}$.

We define two natural operations on S as follows: the multiplication $u \cdot v = uv$ and u^{-1} such that if $u = s_1 s_2 \ldots s_n$ then $u^{-1} = \bar{s}_n \ldots \bar{s}_2 \bar{s}_1$, where $\bar{a}_i = b_i$ and $\bar{b}_i = a_i$. Then h is a homomorphism, since clearly $h(u \cdot v) = h(u) \cdot h(v)$ and $h(u) \cdot h(u^{-1}) = 1$.

Now we define $L_0 = \{a_0, b_0\}$ and

$$L_t = \{a_0, b_0\} \cup \{a_i, b_i \mid i < t \text{ and } h(a_i), h(b_i) \in \{u_0, u_1, \ldots, u_t\}\}.$$

Then $L_t \subseteq L_{t+1}$ for $t \in \omega$, and $\bigcup_{t \in \omega} L_t = L$. Next, let

$$S_t = \{u \in L_t^* \mid |u| < 2^t\}.$$

We again see that $S_t \subseteq S_{t+1}$ and $\bigcup_{t \in \omega} S_t = S$.

In the construction, we define a series of finite objects by induction on $t \in \omega$: the number $n_t = 2^{c^t}$, a finite set $B_t \subseteq \{1^1, 1^2, \ldots, 1^{n_t}\}$, and a bijection $g_t : B_t \to S_t$. All of them grow monotonically: $n_t < n_{t+1}$, $B_t \subset B_{t+1}$, and $g_t \subset g_{t+1}$ for

$t \in \omega$. The constant $c \geqslant 2$ is defined below. All these objects are encoded by one word

$$W_t = g_t(1^1) * g_t(1^2) * \ldots * g_t(1^{n_t}).$$

If $1^x \notin B_t$ then we assume that $g_t(1^x) = 0$. We consider a word $s_1 s_2 \ldots s_n \in L^*$ as the sequence of the codes for $s_1, s_2, \ldots, s_n$, and thus code it as a word in the alphabet $\{0, 1, a, b\}$. The word W_t is an initial subword of W_{t+1}. In the construction, we satisfy the following conditions for every $t \in \omega$:

1) there is an algorithm that, given the words 1^t and W_t, finds W_{t+1} in polynomial time;
2) if $1^x \in B_t$ then $|g_t(1^x)| \leqslant n_t$.

By definition $L_0 = \{a_0, b_0\}$ and $S_0 = \{\varnothing\}$. Let $B_0 = \{1\}$ and $g_0 : B_0 \to S_0$. Then $W_0 = *0$. It follows from 2) that $|W_t| \leqslant n_t(n_t + 1) = P(n_t)$, where $P(n) \in \mathbb{N}[n]$.

At the end of the construction, we define $B = \bigcup_{t \in \omega} B_t$ and $g = \bigcup_{t \in \omega} g_t$, obtaining a bijection $g : B \to S$. Show that B is P-computable. Suppose $x > n_0$. Starting from W_0, we successively compute the words $W_1, W_2, \ldots$ until we find W_{t+1} such that $n_t < x \leqslant n_{t+1}$. Prove that the time of the search depends polynomially on $x = |1^x|$. If $i \leqslant t$ then $|W_i| \leqslant |W_t| \leqslant P(n_t) \leqslant P(x)$. Hence, the total time of computing all words $\{W_i \mid i \leqslant t + 1\}$ can be estimated as $O(x \cdot Q(P(x)))$, if W_{i+1} is computed from W_i in $Q(|W_i|)$ steps, $Q(n) \in \mathbb{N}[n]$, since $t < n_t \leqslant x$. We have a polynomial estimate.

Moving along the word W_{t+1}, we find $g_{t+1}(1^x)$. If $g_{t+1}(1^x) = 0$ then $1^x \notin B$, otherwise $1^x \in B$. If $1^x \in B$ then we have $g(1^x) = g_{t+1}(1^x)$. Therefore, function g is also P-computable.

The set S is a structure with the operations $\cdot$ and $^{-1}$. We transfer these operations to B so that g becomes an isomorphism between $\mathcal{B} = (B, \cdot, ^{-1})$ and $(S, \cdot, ^{-1})$. Prove that $\mathcal{B}$ is a P-computable structure. Suppose that $1^x, 1^y \in B$ and $y \leqslant x$. Arguing as above, we find W_{t+1} for which $1^x \in \mathrm{dom}(g_{t+1})$ in polynomial time. Then $1^y \in \mathrm{dom}(g_{t+1})$. Find in W_{t+1} words $u = g_{t+1}(1^x)$ and $v = g_{t+1}(1^y)$. Then $u, v \in L^*_{t+1}$ and $|u|, |v| < 2^{t+1}$. Hence $|uv| < 2^{t+2}$ and $uv \in S_{t+2}$. Computing W_{t+2}, we can find z such that $g_{t+2}(1^z) = uv$, and obtain that $1^x \cdot 1^y = 1^z$. Computation of $(1^x)^{-1}$ looks even simpler.

We now describe an algorithm of computing W_{t+1} from $1^t, W_t$. First, we need to find L_{t+1}. Since $|u_t| \leqslant t$, we can compute the list $u_0 * u_1 * \ldots * u_t$ and check the condition $u_i \in A$ for each $i \leqslant t$ in polynomial in t time. Let $e_0 < e_1 < \ldots < e_m$ be all the elements of the list from A. Then $h(a_i) = e_i$. If $0 < i \leqslant m$ and $b_i \in L_{t+1}$, then $h(b_i) = e_i^{-1} \in \{e_j \mid j \leqslant m\}$. Passing through the list $e_0 * e_1 * \ldots * e_m$, we check the condition $e_i \cdot e_j = 1$ for each $j \leqslant m$. As a result, we find L_{t+1} in time that polynomially depends on t.

Further steps look quite straightforward: we find a list of all words in S_{t+1}, exclude the elements of S_t that are already in W_t, and then map some initial interval of the set $\{1^x \mid n_t < x \leqslant n_{t+1}\}$ to $S_{t+1} \setminus S_t$, obtaining g_{t+1} and W_{t+1}. Some calculations are needed here, since the number $n_{t+1} - n_t$ must be greater or equal to $|S_{t+1} \setminus S_t|$. If $t = 0$ then $|S_1 \setminus S_0| = 2$ and $n_1 - n_0 = 2^c - 1$. The condition $c \geqslant 2$ is sufficient. Let $t \geqslant 1$. Clearly $|L_{t+1}| \leqslant 2t+2$. Let $2t+2=e$. The number of words in L_{t+1}^* of length at most n can be estimated as

$$e^0 + e^1 + \ldots + e^n = \frac{e^{n+1}-1}{e-1} \leqslant e^{n+1}.$$

Therefore $|S_{t+1}| \leqslant (2t+2)^{2^{t+1}} = 2^{2^{t+1}\cdot\log(2t+2)}$. Next,

$$n_{t+1} - n_t = 2^{c^{t+1}} - 2^{c^t} = 2^{c^t}(2^{c^t(c-1)} - 1).$$

If the estimate $2^{t+1}\cdot\log(2t+2) \leqslant c^t$ holds, i.e., $2(1+\log(t+1)) \leqslant (\frac{c}{2})^t$, then we have that $|S_{t+1}| \leqslant n_{t+1} - n_t$. For sufficiently large t, the condition $c \geqslant 3$ suffices. If $c \geqslant 8$ then the estimate holds for all $t \geqslant 1$.

If $i \geqslant 1$ then $|\mathrm{bin}(i)| = [\log i]+1 \leqslant i$. If $t \geqslant 1$ and $u \in S_t$, then $u = s_1 s_2 \ldots s_n$, $n < 2^t$, and $s_r \in \{a\,\mathrm{bin}(i), b\,\mathrm{bin}(i)\}$, where $i < t$, for $r \leqslant n$. Clearly, $|u| \leqslant (t+1)2^t$ in this case. The same estimate works for $t = 0$. To satisfy 2), we need to check that $(t+1)2^t \leqslant 2^{c^t}$, i.e., $t\log(t+1) \leqslant c^t$. This holds if $c \geqslant 2$.

We now establish the most difficult estimate in this theorem: show that $h \circ g : B \to A$ is also a P-computable function. For this, we prove the following lemma.

Lemma 1. *There is an algorithm that, given 1^t and $u \in S_t$, finds $h(u)$ in time polynomial in n_t.*

Proof. First, we estimate the length of $|h(u)|$. If $s \in L_t$ then $s \in \{a_0, b_0\}$ or $|h(s)| \leqslant t$. Since every function is polynomial on a finite set, it is sufficient to consider the case when $t \geqslant |h(a_0)|, |h(b_0)|, |1^A|$. Then $|h(s)| \leqslant t$ for $s \in L_t$. We prove by induction on $k \leqslant t$ the following assertion: if $u \in S_t$ and $|u| \leqslant 2^k$, then $|h(u)| \leqslant t^{d^k}$. For $k = 0$, this has been proved.

We suppose that $u \in S_t$ and $u = s_1 s_2 \ldots s_n$, where $2^k < n \leqslant 2^{k+1}$ and $s_i \in L_t$ for $i \leqslant n$. Then there is a decomposition $n = n_1 + n_2$, where $n_1, n_2 \leqslant 2^k$. If n is even and $n = 2n_1$, then $n_1 \leqslant 2^k$. If n is odd and $n = 2n_1 + 1$, then $n_1 + \frac{1}{2} \leqslant 2^k$, and if $n_2 = n_1 + 1$ then $n_1, n_2 \leqslant 2^k$. Let $u' = s_1 s_2 \ldots s_{n_1}$ and $u'' = s_{n_1+1} \ldots s_n$. Then $u = u'u''$ and $h(u) = h(u')h(u'')$. By the induction hypothesis, $|h(u')|, |h(u'')| \leqslant t^{d^k}$, hence $|h(u)| \leqslant t^{d^{k+1}}$.

We now describe the computation of $h(u)$. Denote by $t(k)$ an upper bound for the computing time of $h(u)$ for $|u| \leqslant 2^k$. Suppose that $k = 0$ and $u = \varnothing$ or $u \in \{a_i, b_i\} \subseteq L_t$. Above, we constructed an algorithm that, given t, finds a list of all characters in L_t, and then finds $h(s)$ for each $s \in L_t$. Its working time is estimated by a polynomial $R(t) \in \mathbb{N}[t]$. We have that $t(0) = R(t)$.

We suppose now that $|u| = n$ and $2^k < n \leqslant 2^{k+1}$. The algorithm of computing $h(u)$ is specified above: we find a decomposition $n = n_1 + n_2$, where $n_1, n_2 \leqslant 2^k$, present $u = u'u''$, where $|u'| = n_1$ and $|u''| = n_2$, compute $h(u'), h(u'')$ in time $t(k)$, and then obtain $h(u) = h(u') \cdot h(u'')$.

This procedure uses recursion, which requires some effort and an additional time on a Turing machine with finite number of tapes. We will not describe this mechanism in detail, and only note that the costs for the induction step can be estimated as $O(|h(u)|)$, since $|u|, |h(u')|, |h(u'')| \leqslant |h(u)|$. For example, a more detailed algorithm for computing terms in semigroups is given in [5]. As a result, we obtain the formula

$$t(k+1) \leqslant 2t(k) + c_1 \cdot t^{d^{k+1}},$$

where a constant $c_1 \geqslant 1$ does not depend on t and k. Therefore

$$t(k) \leqslant 2^k t(0) + c_1(2^{k-1}t^{d^1} + 2^{k-2}t^{d^2} + \ldots + 2^1 t^{d^{k-1}} + 2^0 t^{d^k}).$$

It can be coarsened to

$$t(k) \leqslant c_1 2^k (t(0) + kt^{d^k}).$$

Since $k = t$ in the worst case, the computing time for $h(u)$ is estimated by the expression $c_1 2^t (R(t) + t \cdot t^{d^k})$. Replacing $R(t)$ by $c_2 t^p$, where c_2, p are fixed, we obtain an estimate of the form $O(t^p 2^t t^{d^t})$, or $O(2^{p \log t + t + \log t \cdot d^t})$. If $c \geqslant d+1$ then this expression can be replaced by $O(2^{c^t})$ for $t \geqslant t_0$. The lemma is proved. □

The P-computability of $h \circ g$ follows from this lemma as above. If $1^x \in B$ then we find W_{t+1} such that $n_t < x \leqslant n_{t+1}$, get $u = g_{t+1}(1^x)$, and find $h(u)$ in time polynomial in n_{t+1}, where $n_{t+1} = n_t^c \leqslant x^c$.

Let $f_0 = h \circ g$. Since g is an isomorphism, and h is an epimorphism preserving the operation x^{-1}, $f_0 : (B, \cdot, ^{-1}) \to (A, \cdot, ^{-1})$ is also an epimorphism. If $E = \{\langle x, y\rangle \in B^2 \mid f_0(x) = f_0(y)\}$ then E is a P-computable congruence in $\mathcal{B}$, and f_0 generates a P-computable isomorphism $f_1 : \mathcal{B}/E \to \mathcal{A}$. By Theorem 3, there are a P-computable structure $\mathcal{A}_1$ and a P-computable isomorphism $f_2 : \mathcal{A}_1 \to \mathcal{B}/E$. Let $f = f_1 \circ f_2$. The theorem is proved. □

We note that Theorem 4 can be easily transferred to the case of primitive recursive (p.r.) structures.

Corollary 1. *Let $\mathcal{A} = (A, \cdot)$ be a p.r. group. Then there exist a p.r. group $\mathcal{A}_1 \cong \mathcal{A}$ in which the operation $x \mapsto x^{-1}$ is also p.r., and a p.r. isomorphism $f : \mathcal{A}_1 \to \mathcal{A}$.*

Proof. The proof of this fact is essentially the same as the proof of Theorem 4. We only need to throw out all polynomial estimates from the text. The function h remains computable. The sets L_t and S_t are defined literally as above. We define the same number n_t and finite objects B_t and $g_t : B_t \to S_t$, but the sequence of words $\{W_t\}_{t\in\omega}$ is now p.r. The word W_t can be replaced by some natural code of g_t.

Condition 1) says now that W_{t+1} is constructed from W_t with a p.r. function. Condition 2) and the estimate for $|W_t|$ should be removed from the text. The set B, the function g, and the structure $\mathcal{B}$ are p.r. If $c = 8$ then the estimation $|S_{t+1} \setminus S_t| \leqslant n_{t+1} - n_t$ holds.

Lemma 1 now states that the function $t, u \mapsto h(u)$ is primitive recursive. Hence, $h \circ g$ is also primitive recursive, and the relation E is a p.r. congruence in $\mathcal{B}$. Choosing the least element in every equivalence class, we obtain a p.r. structure $\mathcal{A}_1$.

We note that the number n_t can be removed from the proof, and we can define $\mathrm{dom}(g_t)$ as an initial segment in ω. In this case, the universe of $\mathcal{B}$ would be equal to ω. However, the factorization by E does not allow to obtain $\mathcal{A}_1$ with universe ω. □

Probably, the idea of the proof is more clear in this case, when polynomial estimations are eliminated. Initially, we construct our group as all group words with generators $\{a_0, b_0\}$. For them, the procedure of finding inverse elements is clear, as far as checking the equality of words. We wait for the moment when $b_1 = a_1^{-1}$ is computed, and then start to enumerate all words with generators $\{a_0, b_0, a_1, b_1\}$. When $b_2 = a_2^{-1}$ is computed, we add $\{a_2, b_2\}$ to the generators, and so on. As the result, we obtain a p.r. quotient structure isomorphic to $\mathcal{A}$.

For computable structures, Theorem 4 is trivial, since the computability of multiplication implies the computability of inversion.

Acknowledgement. The study was carried out within the framework of the state contract of the Sobolev Institute of Mathematics (project no FWNF-2022-0011), and partially supported by RFBR according to the research project no. 20-01-00300.

References

1. Cenzer, D., Remmel, J.: Polynomial time versus recursive models. Ann. Pure Appl. Logic **54**(1), 17–58 (1991)
2. Cenzer, D., Remmel, J.: Polynomial-time abelian groups. Ann. Pure Appl. Logic **56**(1–3), 313–363 (1992)
3. Alaev, P.E.: Structures computable in polynomial time. I. Algebra Logic **55**(6), 421–435 (2016)
4. Alaev, P.E.: Polynomially computable structures with finitely many generators. Algebra Logic **59**(3), 266–272 (2020)
5. Alaev, P.E.: Finitely generated structures computable in polynomial time. Siberian Math. J. (submitted)
6. Alaev, P.E., Selivanov, V.L.: Fields of algebraic numbers computable in polynomial time. I. Algebra Logic **58**(6), 447–469 (2019)
7. Cenzer, D., Remmel, J. B.: Complexity theoretic model theory and algebra. In: Handbook of Recursive Mathematics, vol. 1, pp. 381–513. Elsevier (1998)
8. Alaev, P.E., Selivanov, V.L.: Fields of algebraic numbers computable in polynomial time. II. Algebra Logic **60**(6) (2021)
9. Alaev, P.E., Selivanov, V.L.: Searching for applicable versions of computable structures. In: De Mol, L., Weiermann, A., Manea, F., Fernández-Duque, D. (eds.) CiE 2021. LNCS, vol. 12813, pp. 1–11. Springer, Cham (2021). https://doi.org/10.1007/978-3-030-80049-9_1
10. Kalimullin, I., Melnikov, A., Ng, K.M.: Algebraic structures computable without delay. Theoret. Comput. Sci. **674**, 73–98 (2017)
11. Aho, A.V., Hopcroft, J.E., Ullman, J.D.: The Design and Analysis of Computer Algorithms. Addison-Wesley, Reading (1974)
12. Bazhenov, N., Harrison-Trainor, M., Kalimullin, I., Melnikov, A., Ng, K.M.: Automatic and polynomial-time algebraic structures. J. Symb. Logic **84**(4), 1630–1669 (2019)

Parameterized Complexity of List Coloring and Max Coloring

Bardiya Aryanfard[1(✉)] and Fahad Panolan[2]

[1] Sharif University of Technology, Tehran, Iran
bardiya.aryanfard@gmail.com
[2] Department of Computer Science and Engineering, IIT Hyderabad, Sangareddy, India
fahad@cse.iith.ac.in

Abstract. In the List Coloring problem, the input is a graph G and list of colors $L\colon V(G) \to \mathbb{N}$ for each vertex $v \in V(G)$. The objective is to test the existence of a coloring $\lambda\colon V(G) \to \mathbb{N}$ such that for each $v \in V(G)$, $\lambda(v) \in L(v)$ and for each edge $(u,v) \in E(G)$, $\lambda(u) \neq \lambda(v)$. Fiala et al. (TCS 2011) proved that List Coloring is W[1]-hard when parameterized by the vertex cover number of the input graph. Recently, Gutin et al. (STACS 2020, SIDMA 2021) designed an $O^*(2^k)$ time randomized algorithm for List Coloring where k is the size of the given clique modulator of the input graph. Since List Coloring is W[1]-hard parameterized by the vertex cover number, List Coloring is W[1]-hard parameterized by the size of a cluster modulator. In this work we study the problem parameteized by the size of ℓ-cluster modulator. That is, along with the input we are also given a vertex subset D such that $G-D$ is cluster graph with ℓ connected components. We prove that assuming Exponential Time Hypothesis (ETH), List Coloring can not be solved in time $f(|D|+\ell)n^{o(\frac{|D|+\ell}{\log|D|+\ell})}$ for any computable function f.

In the Max Coloring problem, we are given a graph G and a weight function $w\colon V(G) \to \mathbb{N}$. For a *proper coloring* λ, the cost of λ is defined as follows. For each color i, $w(i)$ is the maximum weight of a vertex colored i. Then, the cost of λ is $\sum_{i\in C} w(i)$, where $C = \{\lambda(v) \mid v \in V(G)\}$. In the Max Coloring problem, our objective is to find a proper coloring with minimum cost. Araújo et al. (TCS 2018) proved that Max Coloring is W[1]-hard even on forests when parameterized by the size of the largest connected component in the input forest. Here, we prove that Max Coloring is FPT with respect to parameters (i) the size of a vertex cover, (ii) the size of a clique modulator, and (iii) the size of a 2-cluster modulator.

Keywords: Graph Coloring · Fixed Parameter Tractability · Randomized algorithms · Reduction · Exponential Time Hypothesis

1 Introduction

Graph coloring is a fundamental topic in algorithms and graph theory. A *proper coloring* of a graph G is a function $\lambda\colon V(G) \to \mathbb{N}$ such that for any edge

A. S. Kulikov and S. Raskhodnikova (Eds.): CSR 2022, LNCS 13296, pp. 46–63, 2022.
https://doi.org/10.1007/978-3-031-09574-0_4

$(u, v) \in E(G)$, $\lambda(u) \neq \lambda(v)$. In the COLORING problem, the input is a graph G and an integer q, and the objective is to test whether there is a proper coloring $\lambda\colon V(G) \to [q]$ of G[1]. The q-COLORING problem is a special case of COLORING where q is fixed and not part of the input. The chromatic number of a graph G is the minimum q for which G is a yes-instance of q-COLORING. It is well known that 2-COLORING is polynomial time solvable and q-COLORING is NP-hard for any $q \geq 3$. In fact, the 3-COLORING problem remains NP-hard even on 4-regular planar graphs [5]. The best known algorithm for computing the chromatic number of a given n-vertex graph is $O^*(2^n)$ and it is a long standing open problem to improve this running time to $O^*((2-\epsilon)^n)$ or to prove that such running time is not possible under some complexity theory assumptions like Strong Exponential Time Hypothesis (SETH)[2].

In this work we consider two generalizations of COLORING, namely LIST COLORING and MAX COLORING in the realm of parameterized complexity and fill in some gaps about these problems in the parameterized complexity setting. In the LIST COLORING problem, for each vertex v in the input graph, we are also given a list $L(v)$ of colors. The objective is to find a proper coloring λ such that for each vertex v, $\lambda(v) \in L(v)$. In the MAX COLORING problem, along with the input graph we are also given a weight function $w\colon V(G) \to \mathbb{N}$. For a proper coloring λ, the cost of λ is defined as follows. For each color i, $w(i)$ is the maximum weight of a vertex colored i (if no such vertex exists, then it is zero). That is, $w(i) = \max_{v \in \lambda^{-1}(i)} w(v)$[3]. Then, the cost of λ is $\sum_{i \in C} w(i)$, where $C = \{\lambda(v) \mid v \in V(G)\}$. In the MAX COLORING problem, our objective is to find a proper coloring with minimum cost. This problem is also called as WEIGHTED COLORING in the literature.

Fiala et al. [10] proved that LIST COLORING is W[1]-hard parameterized by the vertex cover number of the input graph. Recently, Gutin et al. [12] designed an $O^*(2^k)$ time randomized algorithm for LIST COLORING parameterized by the clique modulator number of the input graph. All the randomized algorithms mentioned in this work are Monte Carlo algorithms with one sided error. That is, if the output of the algorithm is No, then it may be wrong with probability at most 1/3. A clique modulator of a graph G is a vertex subset D such that $G - D$ is clique. A cluster modulator is a vertex subset D such that $G - D$ is a cluster graph (i.e., each connected component is a clique). Since LIST COLORING is W[1]-hard parameterized by the vertex cover number, LIST COLORING is W[1]-hard parameterized by the size of a cluster modulator. This motivates us to study LIST COLORING parameterized by the size of the cluster modulator D and the number of clusters (connected components) in $G - D$. Formally, this problem is defined as follows.

[1] Throughout the paper, we use $[q]$ to denote the set $\{1, 2, \ldots, q\}$.

[2] O^* notation hides polynomial factor in the input size.

[3] For a function $f\colon X \to Y$ and $y \in Y$, $f^{-1}(y)$ denotes the set $\{x \mid f(x) = y\}$.

LIST COLORING ℓ-CLUSTER MODULATOR **Parameter:** $|D| + \ell$
Input: A graph G, a set of colors C, for all $v \in V(G)$ a list $L(v) \subseteq C$, and a vertex subset D such that $G - D$ is an ℓ-cluster graph
Question: Is there a proper list coloring of G?

We prove the following result.

Theorem 11. LIST COLORING ℓ-CLUSTER MODULATOR *can not be solved in* $f(|D|+\ell)n^{o(\frac{|D|+\ell}{\log |D|+\ell})}$ *for any computable function* f *unless the Exponential Time Hypothesis (ETH) fails, where* $n = |V(G)|$.

COLORING is a special case of MAX COLORING where each vertex has weight 1. MAX COLORING is NP-hard even on split graphs, interval graphs, triangle-free planar graphs with bounded degree, and bipartite graphs [6,9,17]. Araújo et al. [3] proved that MAX COLORING can not be solved in time $n^{o(\log n)}$ even on trees unless ETH fails. Escoffier et al. [9] designed a polynomial time approximation scheme for MAX COLORING on bounded treewidth graphs. Araújo et al. [2] studied MAX COLORING in the parameterized complexity setting and proved that it is W[1]-hard even on forests when parameterized by the size of the largest connected component in the input forest. Escoffier [8] studied the problem on different graph classes when parameterized by the cost of the coloring. In particular Escoffier [8] proved that the problem is FPT on chordal graphs, but para-NP-hard on bipartite graphs. That is, given a weighted bipartite graph, it is NP-hard to test whether there is a proper coloring of cost at most 7. Escoffier [8] and Araújo et al. [2] also studied MAX COLORING with dual parameter. In this work we study the following parameterized problems around MAX COLORING.

MAX COLORING VERTEX COVER **Parameter:** k
Input: A graph G where every vertex v has a non-negative weight $w(v)$, a vertex cover X of size k, a non-negative integer $\mathcal{W}$
Question: Is there a proper max coloring of cost at most $\mathcal{W}$?

MAX COLORING CLIQUE MODULATOR **Parameter:** k
Input: A graph G where every vertex v has a non-negative weight $w(v)$, a clique modulator D of size k, a non-negative integer $\mathcal{W}$
Question: Is there a proper max coloring of cost at most $\mathcal{W}$?

MAX COLORING 2-CLUSTER MODULATOR **Parameter:** k
Input: A graph G where every vertex v has a non-negative weight $w(v)$, a subset $D \subset V(G)$ of size k such that $G - D = C_1 \uplus C_2$ where C_1 and C_2 are two disjoint cliques, a non-negative integer $\mathcal{W}$
Question: Is there a proper max coloring of cost at most $\mathcal{W}$?

We prove the following results.

Theorem 12. MAX COLORING VERTEX COVER *admits a kernel with* $2^k + k$ *vertices.*

Theorem 13. MAX COLORING CLIQUE MODULATOR *admits a kernel of size* $(2^k \cdot k) + k$.

Theorem 14. *There is a randomized algorithm for* MAX COLORING 2-CLUSTER MODULATOR *running in time* $k^{O(k)}\mathcal{W}n^{O(1)}$.

Our Methods. To prove Theorem 11 we give an FPT reduction from the COLORED SUBGRAPH ISOMORPHISM problem. This result is explained in Sect. 3. We use algebraic technique to prove Theorem 14. Towards that we define the following problem which could be of independent interest.

PERFECT COLORFUL MATCHING **Parameter:** k
Input: A bipartite weighted graph G, a non-negative integer $\mathcal{W}$, a coloring λ for edges, where $L = \{\lambda(e) \mid e \in E(G)\}$ and $\|L\| = k$.
Question: Is there a perfect matching of weight at most $\mathcal{W}$ where every color in L appears at least once?

We give a polynomial time Turing reduction from MAX COLORING 2-CLUSTER MODULATOR to PERFECT COLORFUL MATCHING and prove the following theorem.

Theorem 15. *There is a randomized algorithm for* PERFECT COLORFUL MATCHING *running in time* $2^{O(k)}\mathcal{W}n^{O(1)}$.

To prove Theorem 15 we notice that each term in the permanent of the bipartite adjacency matrix corresponds to a matching. Thus, by suitably labeling each edge with variables we can succinctly represent all the perfect matchings. Moreover, the permanent of a matrix is the same as the determinant of the matrix in the case of field of characteristic two. Thus, we construct a matrix with variables where the monomials of the determinant polynomial represent perfect matchings. Then, from this polynomial using known randomized techniques we check the existence of the required matching.

Bannach et al. [4] have independently proved a more general case of PERFECT COLORFUL MATCHING to be FPT using a reduction to the CONJOINING BIPARTITE MATCHING problem which Gutin et al. (JCSS, 2017) [11] proved its fixed parameter tractability using algebraic methods similar to ours.

2 Preliminaries

2.1 Parameterized Complexity

An instance of a parameterized problem Q is a pair (I, k) where I is called the input and $k \in \mathbb{N}$ is the parameter. A problem Q is called fixed-parameter tractable (FPT) if there exists an algorithm $\mathcal{A}$ to solve this problem in time

$f(k)n^{\mathcal{O}(1)}$ for some function f, where n is equal to the size of input, denoted by $|I|$. In this case, $\mathcal{A}$ is also called an FPT algorithm. Some times in the literature of parameterized complexity, we write the complexity of such an algorithm as $\mathcal{O}^*(f(k))$. Since it is widely believed that FPT $\neq$ W[1], in order to show that a problem is not FPT, we prove that it is W[1]-hard.

Kernelization. A kernelization algorithm $\mathcal{A}$ for a parameterized problem Q, is a polynomial time algorithm that given an instance (I, k) of problem Q, outputs an instance (I', k') of problem Q such that (I, k) and (I', k') are equivalent (i.e., (I, k) is a yes-instance if and only if (I', k') is a yes-instance) and $|I'| + k' \leq g(k)$ for some computable function g. If g is a polynomial function, then we say that Q admits a polynomial kernel.

Exponential Time Hypothesis (ETH). In the framework of parameterized complexity and exact exponential time algorithms, Exponential Time Hypothesis (ETH) of Impagliazzo and Paturi, is a conjecture that states 3-SAT has no subexponential (in number of variables) algorithm. [13] That is, ETH implies that 3-SAT can not be solved in $2^{o(n)}$ time. Recall that ETH will imply that FPT $\neq$ W[1] and therefore ETH can also help us to prove that some problems are not FPT. Moreover, ETH allows us to prove more finer algorithmic lower bounds.

2.2 Graph Theory

In this paper, all of the graphs are undirected and all of the weighted vertices and edges have non-negative weights.

Proper List Coloring. For an undirected graph G where for every vertex $v \in V(G)$ we have a list $L(v)$ of possible colors for this vertex, a coloring λ is called a proper list coloring if for every vertex $v \in V(G)$, $\lambda(v) \in L(v)$ and for every edge $(v, u) \in E(G)$, $\lambda(v) \neq \lambda(u)$.

Max Coloring. In this problem, every vertex v has a weight $w(v)$ and weight of a color c in a certain coloring λ is $w(c) = max_{v:\lambda(v)=c} w(v)$. The total cost of a coloring (to be minimized) is $\sum_{c \in L} w(c)$ where $L = \{c | \exists v \in V(G) : \lambda(v) = c\}$.

Vertex Cover. For an undirected graph G, a subset $X \subset V(G)$ is a vertex cover of G if $G - X$ is an independent set.

Clique Modulator, ℓ-Cluster Modulator. For an undirected graph G, a subset $D \subset V(G)$ is called a clique modulator if $G - D = C$ where C is a clique. Also, a set $D \subset V(G)$ is an ℓ-cluster modulator if $G - D = C_1 \uplus ... \uplus C_\ell$ where $C_1, ..., C_\ell$ are disjoint clusters.

3 List Coloring ℓ-Cluster Modulator

In this section we prove that List Coloring ℓ-Cluster Modulator can not be solved in time $f(|D|+\ell)n^{o(\frac{|D|+\ell}{\log|D|+\ell})}$ unless ETH fails by giving a parameterized reduction from the Colored Subgraph Isomorphism problem which is formally defined as follows.

Colored Subgraph Isomorphism	**Parameter:** k
Input: A graph H, a positive integer m and a partition $V_1 \uplus V_2 \uplus \ldots \uplus V_m$ of $V(H)$, a graph G_s with m vertices and k edges. (The graph G_s is called the small graph) **Question:** Is there a subgraph S of H such that $|V_i \cap S| = 1$ for all $i \in \{1,\ldots,m\}$ and S is isomorphic to G_s? That is, for any edge $(i,j) \in E(G_s)$, there is an edge in S between $S \cap V_i$ and $S \cap V_j$.	

Colored Subgraph Isomorphism can not be solved in time $f(G_s)n^{o(\frac{k}{\log k})}$ unless ETH fails (Corollary 6.3 from [14]). Let $(H, G_s, m, k, (V_1, ..., V_m))$ be an instance of Colored Subgraph Isomorphism. Here, we denote $E_{i,j}$ to represent the set of edges between V_i and V_j where $i < j$. Moreover, here for each edge between $v \in V_i$ and $u \in V_j$ we denote the edge by (v, u) (i.e., the order is from a vertex in V_i to a vertex in V_j, where $i < j$). That is, for $i < j$, $E_{i,j} = \{(v, u)|(v, u) \in E(H), v \in V_i, u \in V_j\}$.

Now we explain how to construct the output instance $(G, L\colon V(G) \mapsto 2^C, D \subseteq V(G))$ as follows. The color set C is defined as below:

$$C = \{1_{(v,u)} \mid (v, u) \in E(H)\} \cup \{2_v \mid v \in V(H)\}.$$

Now, we construct the graph G and the modulator D in the following way: (See Fig. 1 for an illustration.)

1. We introduce a set D of vertices of size $k+m$, which is a $(2k)$-cluster modulator of the graph G. For every pair (i, j) where $(i, j) \in E(G_s)$, D contains vertex $z_{i,j}$ with $L(z_{i,j}) = \{1_{(v,u)}|(v, u) \in E_{i,j}\}$. Also, for every $1 \leq i \leq m$, D contains x_i where $L(x_i) = \{2_v|v \in V_i\}$. This completes the construction of the vertex subset D. Notice that $|D| = k + m$.
2. For every pair (i, j) where $(i, j) \in E(G_s)$ we introduce two cliques K^i_j and K^j_i. Here, the vertex set of K^i_j is partitioned into two blocks $W^i_j \uplus R^i_j$, where R^i_j contains $|V_i| - 1$ vertices and W^i_j is defined as follows.

$$W^i_j = \{w^v_u \mid v \in V_i, u \in V_j, (v, u) \in E_{i,j}\}$$

Next, we explain the list of colors for each vertex in K^i_j. For the vertex w^v_u in W^i_j, we set $L(w^v_u) = \{1_{(v,u)}, 2_v\}$. For each vertex $y \in R^i_j$, we set $L(y) = \{2_v|v \in V_i\}$. The clique K^j_i is defined similarly. That is, the vertex set of K^j_i is partitioned into two blocks $W^j_i \uplus R^j_i$, where R^j_i contains $|V_j| - 1$ vertices and W^j_i is defined as follows.

$$W^j_i = \{w^u_v \mid u \in V_j, v \in V_i, (v, u) \in E_{i,j}\}$$

Next, we explain the list of colors for each vertex in K_i^j. For the vertex w_v^u in W_i^j, we set $L(w_v^u) = \{1_{(v,u)}, 2_u\}$. For each vertex $y \in R_i^j$, we set $L(y) = \{2_u \mid u \in V_j\}$.
Next, we explain the adjacencies among K_j^i, K_i^j and D. We have already mentioned that K_j^i and K_i^j are cliques in G. We make all of the vertices in $W_j^i \cup W_i^j$ adjacent to $z_{i,j}$, all of the vertices in R_j^i adjacent to x_i, and all of the vertices in R_i^j adjacent to x_j.

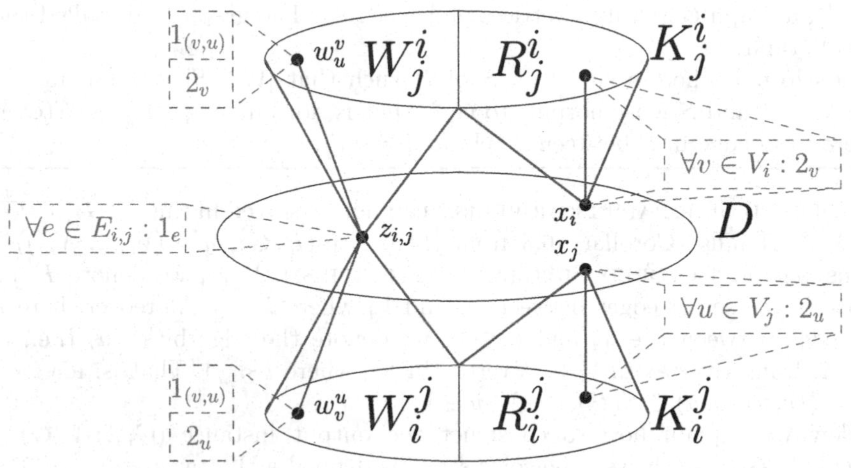

Fig. 1. An illustration of the adjacencies among K_j^i, K_i^j and D in the graph G.

This completes the construction of the output instance (G, L, D) where $|D| = k + m$. Here $G - D$ is a $(2k)$-cluster graph. Moreover, the instance (G, L, D) can be computed in polynomial time.

The intuitive idea of the reduction is the following. Let S be a subgraph in H with exactly one vertex from each one of $V_1, \ldots, V_m$ and isomorphic to G_s. We know that S must have exactly one edge (say $e_{i,j}$) from $E_{i,j}$ for each $(i,j) \in E(G_s)$ and for every i, all of the edges $e_{i,j}$ must have the same endpoint v_i in V_i. For every $1 \le i < j \le m$, the corresponding proper list coloring of G will have $1_{e_{i,j}}$ as the color of vertex $z_{i,j}$ and 2_{v_i} as the color of x_i for every $1 \le i \le m$. That is the selection of colors for $z_{i,j}$ for $1 \le i < j \le m$ where $(i,j) \in E(G_s)$ and x_i for $1 \le i \le m$, is corresponding to the edges and vertices in the solution of Colored Subgraph Isomorphism. As we will see in the correctness proof, such a coloring can be extended to a proper list coloring of G.

Lemma 1. *Graph G has a proper list coloring if and only if H has a subgraph S of size m with exactly one vertex from each of $V_1, \ldots, V_m$ and isomorphic to G_s.*

Proof. First, we prove that if a subgraph S (isomorphic to G_s and with exactly one vertex in each V_i) exists for the instance $(H, G_s, m, k, (V_1, \ldots, V_m))$, then a proper list coloring c exists for G. For each $i \in \{1, \ldots, m\}$, let v_i be the vertex of S which is in V_i. That is, $S = \{v_1, \ldots, v_m\}$ where $\{v_i\} = V_i \cap S$ for all $i \in \{1, \ldots, m\}$. Now we introduce a proper list coloring of G, $c\colon V(G) \mapsto C$ as follows.

- For every $1 \le i \le m$, $c(x_i) = 2_{v_i}$.
- For every $(i,j) \in E(G_s)$, $c(z_{i,j}) = 1_{(v_i,v_j)}$, $c(w_{v_j}^{v_i}) = 2_{v_i}$, and $c(w_{v_i}^{v_j}) = 2_{v_j}$.
- For every $(i,j) \in E(G_s)$ and $(v,u) \in E_{i,j} \setminus \{(v_i,v_j)\}$, $c(w_u^v) = c(w_v^u) = 1_{(v,u)}$.
- For every $(i,j) \in E(G_s)$, each vertex in R_j^i is colored with an arbitrary and unique color from $\{2_v | v \in V_i \setminus \{2_{v_i}\}\}$. That is, c restricted to R_j^i, is a bijection from R_j^i to $\{2_v \mid v \in V_i \setminus \{2_{v_i}\}\}$. Similarly, each vertex in R_i^j is colored with an arbitrary and unique color from $\{2_u \mid u \in V_j \setminus \{2_{v_j}\}\}$.

This completes the definition of the coloring function c. Moreover, it is easy to see that for any $y \in V(G)$, $c(y) \in L(y)$. Next, we prove that c is indeed a proper coloring of G. From the definition of c, notice that for each $(i,j) \in E(G_s)$, the vertices in K_j^i get distinct colors and the vertices in K_i^j get distinct colors. Moreover, no vertex $W_j^i \cup W_i^j$ is colored with $1_{(v_i,v_j)} = c(z_{i,j})$. Also, no vertex in R_j^i is colored with $2_{v_i} = c(x_i)$ and no vertex in R_i^j is colored with $2_{v_j} = c(x_j)$. This completes the proof of the forward direction of the proof.

For the reverse direction, we show that if G has a proper list coloring c, then there exists a subgraph S in H such that S has exactly one vertex in each V_i and is isomorphic to G_s. We define a function $h\colon C \mapsto E(H) \cup V(H)$ as follows.

$$h(s) = \begin{cases} e \text{ if } s = 1_e \text{ for some } e \in E(H) \\ v \text{ if } s = 2_v \text{ for some } v \in V(H) \end{cases}$$

Now, let $S = \{h(c(x_i)) \mid i \in \{1, \ldots, m\}\}$. Next, we prove that S has a subgraph isomorphic to G_s and one vertex in each V_i in G. Notice that for each $i \in \{1, \ldots, m\}$, $c(x_i) \in \{2_v \mid v \in V_i\}$. Therefore, $|S \cap V_i| = 1$. Let v_i be $h(c(x_i))$ for all $i \in \{1, \ldots, m\}$. Next, we prove that for each $(i,j) \in E(G_s)$, $h(c(z_{i,j})) = (v_i, v_j)$ and this will prove that S has a subgraph that is isomorphic to G_s. It can be trivially shown that $h(c(z_{i,j})) \in E_{i,j}$ and $v_i = h(c(x_i)) \in V_i$. To complete the proof, it is enough to show that for every $(i,j) \in E(G_s)$, v_i and v_j are the endpoints of the edge $h(c(z_{i,j}))$. Fix $i, j \in \{1, \ldots, m\}$ such that $i < j$ and $(i,j) \in E(G_s)$. Let $h(c(z_{i,j})) = (u,v)$ such that $v \in V_i$ and $u \in V_j$. Since $c(z_{i,j}) = 1_{(u,v)}$, the only possible color for w_u^v by the coloring c, is 2_v. Also, we know that $|R_j^i| = |V_i| - 1$, hence by the construction of the color lists of the vertices in R_j^i there exists only one vertex $v' \in V_i$ such that $2_{v'}$ is not used to color any vertex in R_j^i by the coloring c. This implies that $v = v'$. Moreover, v is the only vertex in V_i such that 2_v is not used in R_j^i and hence we conclude that $c(x_i) = 2_v$ (since x_i is connected to all of the vertices in R_j^i and $L(x_i) = \{2_{v'} \mid v' \in V_i\}$). This implies that $v = v_i$. By similar arguments, we can show that $h(c(x_j)) = u$ and hence $v_j = u$. This completes the proof of the lemma.

The following theorem follows from the above reduction and Lemma 1. Note that in the graph G constructed as above, $|D| = k+m$ and the number of clusters is $2k$ and also, it is not hard to see that we can assume that G_s is connected (otherwise, it can be solved for each component separately). Therefore, we can assume that $|D| + \ell = \Theta(k)$.

Theorem 11. List Coloring ℓ-Cluster Modulator *can not be solved in* $f(|D|+\ell)n^{o(\frac{|D|+\ell}{\log |D|+\ell})}$ *for any computable function* f *unless the Exponential Time Hypothesis (ETH) fails, where* $n = |V(G)|$.

4 Max Coloring Vertex Cover

In this section we introduce a kernelization for the Max Coloring Vertex Cover problem. Let $I = G - X$ and $\{I_1, ..., I_{2^k}\}$ be the partitioning of I into its equivalence classes with respect to $N(v)$ (where $N(v)$ is the set of vertices of X that are connected to v) and m_i ($i \in [2^k]$) be a vertex in I_i with maximum weight ($\forall i \in [2^k], v \in I_i : w(m_i) \geq w(v)$). Let $M = \{m_1, ..., m_{2^k}\}$ and $R = I \backslash M$. For every color c in a coloring λ, define $\lambda^{-1}(c)$ as the set of all of vertices v such that $\lambda(v) = c$.

Lemma 2. *Instance* (G, X, k) *has a proper coloring with cost at most* $\mathcal{W}$ *if and only if instance* $(G - R, X, k)$ *has a proper coloring with cost at most* $\mathcal{W}$.

Proof. The forward direction is trivial. Since $G - R$ is a subgraph of G, any proper coloring of G is also a proper coloring of $G - R$. Moreover, since the weight of each vertex in $G - R$ is same as the weight in G, the cost of the coloring in $G - R$ will be at most the cost of the coloring in G.

Now, we prove the reverse direction. Let λ_2 be a proper coloring of $G - R$ with weight at most $\mathcal{W}$. We prove the coloring below is a proper coloring of G with cost at most $\mathcal{W}$.

$$\lambda_1(v) = \begin{cases} \lambda_2(m_i) & \text{If there exists } i \text{ such that } v \in I_i \\ \lambda_2(v) & \textit{otherwise} \end{cases}$$

In the coloring above it is not hard to see that for every color c, $\lambda_2^{-1}(c) \subset \lambda_1^{-1}(c)$ and for every vertex $v \in \lambda_1^{-1}(c) \setminus \lambda_2^{-1}(c)$ such that $v \in I_i$, m_i is also in $\lambda_1^{-1}(c)$. Thus, cost of c in λ_1 is equal to cost of c in λ_2. Therefore, total cost of λ_1 is equal to total cost of λ_2. Hence, λ_1 is a proper max coloring of cost at most $\mathcal{W}$.

Lemma 2 implies the following.

Theorem 12. Max Coloring Vertex Cover *admits a kernel with* $2^k + k$ *vertices.*

5 Max Coloring Clique Modulator

In this section we introduce a kernelization algorithm for Max Coloring Clique Modulator. Let $(G, D, \mathcal{W})$ be the input instance and $C = V(G - D)$. For every $v \in C$ we define $N_D(v)$ to be the set of vertices in D that are adjacent to v. Using $N_D(v)$, C will be partitioned into equivalence classes $C_1, \ldots, C_{2^k}$, such that two distinct vertices $v, u \in C$ are in the same equivalence class C_i if and only if $N_D(v) = N_D(u)$. Now, for every equivalence class C_i, define M_i to be the set of t vertices in C_i with the largest weights, where $t = \min\{|C_i|, k\}$. Formally, M_i is a subset of C_i such that $|M_i| = \min\{|C_i|, k\}$ and for any two vertices $v \in M_i$ and $u \in C_i \setminus M_i$, $w(v) \geq w(u)$. We call a vertex $v \in C$ *unaccompanied* in a proper coloring λ if there does not exist another vertex that has the same color as v. That is, v is the only vertex colored with the color $\lambda(v)$.

Lemma 3. *If there exists a proper coloring λ that is a solution for an instance $(G, D, k, \mathcal{W})$ of* Max Coloring Clique Modulator, *then there exists a solution λ' such that for every $i \in [2^k]$, all of the vertices in $C_i \setminus M_i$ are unaccompanied.*

Proof. Let $v \in C_i \setminus M_i$ be a vertex that is not unaccompanied in λ. That is, there exists j such that v has the same color as D_j ($\lambda(v) = \lambda(D_j)$), where D_j is a nonempty subset of D. Since $C_i \setminus M_i \neq \emptyset$, M_i has strictly more than k vertices. We know that some vertices in D have the same color as v, and M_i is a clique. This implies that at most $k-1$ vertices of M_i are not unaccompanied, and so there exists $u \in M_i$ that is unaccompanied. Let λ' be the coloring made by switching the color of vertices u and v from coloring λ (i.e., $\lambda'(v) = \lambda(u)$, $\lambda'(u) = \lambda(v)$ and λ and λ' are the same for the rest of the vertices). Note that since v and u are from the same equivalence class C_i, λ' is still a proper coloring. We claim λ' has a total cost not greater than λ. Let Δ be the total cost of λ' minus total cost of λ, also let a be the largest weight among the other vertices with color $\lambda(v)$. For every color c, define $w(c)$ to be the maximum weight among vertices with color c. Since $w(v) \leq w(u)$ (due to construction) we can have three cases:

i) $a \leq w(v) \leq w(u)$: In this case maximum weight of none of the colors will change, so $\Delta = 0$.
ii) $w(v) \leq a \leq w(u)$: In this case $w(\lambda(u)) = w(u)$ and $w(\lambda(v)) = a$ but after the change, we will have that $w(\lambda'(v)) = w(v)$ and $w(\lambda'(u)) = w(u)$ therefore $\Delta = w(u) + w(v) - (w(u) + a) \leq 0$.
iii) $w(v) \leq w(u) \leq a$: In this case $w(\lambda(u)) = w(u)$ and $w(\lambda(v)) = a$ but after the change, we will have that $w(\lambda'(u)) = a$ and $w(\lambda'(v)) = w(v)$ therefore $\Delta = w(v) + a - (w(u) + a) \leq 0$.

Hence, Δ is always less than or equal to zero. Therefore, λ' is a coloring with total cost at most equal to the total cost of λ and with less vertices in $C_i \setminus M_i$ that are not unaccompanied than λ. Thus, we can decrease the number of such vertices (vertices in $C_i \setminus M_i$ for some i that are not unaccompanied) as long as they exist. Therefore, there is a proper coloring with no such vertices and cost at most the cost of λ. This completes the proof of the lemma.

Since for an unaccompanied vertex u the maximum weight of its color class is $w(u)$, by the lemma above, we can say that instance $(G, D, k, \mathcal{W})$ is a yes-instance if and only if $(G - R, D, k, \mathcal{W} - S)$ is a yes-instance; where $R = \bigcup_{i \in [2^k]}(C_i - M_i)$ and $S = \sum_{v \in R} w(v)$. Hence, we have the following theorem.

Theorem 13. MAX COLORING CLIQUE MODULATOR *admits a kernel of size* $(2^k \cdot k) + k$.

6 MAX COLORING 2-CLUSTER MODULATOR

In this section we give a Turing reduction running in time $k^{O(k)}n^{O(1)}$ from MAX COLORING 2-CLUSTER MODULATOR to PERFECT COLORFUL MATCHING. In Sect. 7 we prove that PERFECT COLORFUL MATCHING is fixed parameter tractable. The Turing reduction is formulated in the following lemma.

Lemma 4. *There is an algorithm running in time* $k^{O(k)}n^{O(1)}$ *that given an instance* $(G, D, \mathcal{W})$ *outputs a collection* $\mathcal{I}$ *of* $k^{O(k)}$ *instances of* PERFECT COLORFUL MATCHING *with the following properties.*

- *The parameter associated with each instance in* $\mathcal{I}$ *is at most* $|D| + 1$.
- $(G, D, \mathcal{W})$ *is a yes-instance of* MAX COLORING 2-CLUSTER MODULATOR *if and only if there is a yes-instance of* PERFECT COLORFUL MATCHING *in* $\mathcal{I}$.

Let $(G, D, \mathcal{W})$ be the given input instance of MAX COLORING 2-CLUSTER MODULATOR. Let C_1 and C_2 be the two connected components of $G - D$. Recall that both C_1 and C_2 are cliques. Let $\mathcal{D} = \{D_1, ..., D_t\}$ be a partitioning of D such that there is no edge in G between two vertices of D_i for any $i \in \{1, ..., t\}$, and let A_0, A_1, A_2, A_{12} be a partitioning of $\mathcal{D}$. For each such choice of $\mathcal{D}$ and A_0, A_1, A_2, A_{12} we construct an instance of PERFECT COLORFUL MATCHING. Towards that let us fix $\mathcal{D} = \{D_1, ..., D_t\}$ and A_0, A_1, A_2, A_{12} with the above mentioned properties.

For every $i \in \{1, ..., t\}$, let m_i be a vertex of D_i with maximum weight. For this choice, we would like to encode an instance I of PERFECT COLORFUL MATCHING, such that for each proper coloring λ of G with the following properties, there is a perfect matching in the instance I with a weight equal to the cost of λ.

- For every $v, u \in V(D)$, $\lambda(v) = \lambda(u)$ if and only if there exists i such that $v, u \in D_i$. In other words $D_1, ..., D_t$ are color classes of D and let $\lambda(D_i)$ be the color of the vertices in D_i.
- For every $D_i \in A_0$, $|\lambda^{-1}(\lambda(D_i)) \cap C_1| = |\lambda^{-1}(\lambda(D_i)) \cap C_2| = 0$.
- For every $D_i \in A_1$, $|\lambda^{-1}(\lambda(D_i)) \cap C_1| = 1$ and $|\lambda^{-1}(\lambda(D_i)) \cap C_2| = 0$.
- For every $D_i \in A_2$, $|\lambda^{-1}(\lambda(D_i)) \cap C_1| = 0$ and $|\lambda^{-1}(\lambda(D_i)) \cap C_2| = 1$.
- For every $D_i \in A_{12}$, $|\lambda^{-1}(\lambda(D_i)) \cap C_1| = |\lambda^{-1}(\lambda(D_i)) \cap C_2| = 1$.

We say that a proper coloring is *compatible* with $(\mathcal{D}, A_0, A_1, A_2, A_{12})$, if it satisfies the above mentioned properties. Now, we construct a weighted edge colored bipartite graph H with bipartition $V(H) = H_1 \uplus H_2$ as follows. Notice that H will have parallel edges.

- Vertex set H_1 initially contains $V(C_1) \cup \{d_i \mid D_i \in A_2\}$ and vertex set of H_2 initially contains $V(C_2) \cup \{d_i \mid D_i \in A_1\}$. That is, for each vertex in C_1, we have a vertex in H_1 and for each set D_i in A_2, we have a vertex in H_1.
- For every $i \in \{1, \ldots, t\}$ and $v \in C_2$ with $D_i \in A_2$, if $D_i \cup \{v\}$ is an independent set in G, then we add an edge between d_i and v with weight $\max\{w(v), w(m_i)\}$ and color the edge with $t + 1$.
- For every $i \in \{1, \ldots, t\}$ and $v \in C_1$ with $D_i \in A_1$, if $D_i \cup \{v\}$ is an independent set in G, then we add an edge between d_i and v with weight $\max\{w(v), w(m_i)\}$ and color the edge with $t + 1$.
- For every $i \in \{1, \ldots, t\}$, $v \in C_1$, and $u \in C_2$ with $D_i \in A_{12}$, if $D_i \cup \{v, u\}$ is an independent set in G, then we add an edge between v and u with weight $\max\{w(v), w(u), w(m_i)\}$ and color the edge with i.
- For every $v \in C_1$ and $u \in C_2$, we add an edge between v and u with weight $\max\{w(v), w(u)\}$ and color the edge with $t + 1$.
- Pad the partition with smaller number of vertices among H_1 and H_2 with new dummy vertices $R = \{r_1, ..., r_p\}$ where $p = ||H_1| - |H_2|| = ||C_1 \cup A_2| - |C_2 \cup A_1||$. We add an edge between every vertex in R and every vertex v of the other partition which is in $C_1 \cup C_2$. This edge has weight $w(v)$ and color $t + 1$. Note that, now we have that $|H_1| = |H_2|$.

Intuitively, in the graph H, choosing an edge between vertices $v \in C_1$ and $u \in C_2$ to be in the matching of graph H, represents the idea of using the same color for both v and u in the coloring of graph G and if the color of this edge is i where $i \leq t$, vertices of D_i (which by construction, is in A_{12}) will also have the same color. Also, choosing an edge between a vertex d_i and v for the matching in graph H, represents using the same color for vertices in D_i and v in the coloring. Furthermore, picking an edge between a vertex $v \in C_1 \cup C_2$ and a dummy vertex $r \in R$, corresponds to v using the color of no other vertices (that is, there will be a color class that only contains v).

In this setting, it can be seen that if the matching contains edges of all colors, then we will have exactly one color class for every vertex in $C_1 \cup C_2 \cup A_1 \cup A_2$ and at least one color for every vertex in A_{12} (for these vertices we can choose an arbitrary color class from these options). Besides, we know that all of the colors used in A_0, are only used for one of the sets $D_i \in A_0$, thus we can color them independent of the color of all of the other vertices in G. As implied above, every edge in the matching of H corresponds to a potential color class in H and furthermore, it can be seen that weight of the potential color class is equal to the weight of its corresponding edge in H. See Fig. 2 for an illustration.

This brings us to the following lemma:

Lemma 5. *There exists an optimal proper coloring of G of cost at most $\mathcal{W}$ that is compatible with $(\mathcal{D}, A_0, A_1, A_2, A_{12})$ if and only if there exists a perfect colorful matching of H with weight at most $\mathcal{W} - \sum_{i:D_i \in A_0} w(m_i)$.*

Proof. Suppose λ is a proper coloring of G that is compatible with $(\mathcal{D}, A_0, A_1, A_2, A_{12})$ and cost of λ is $\mathcal{W}$. Now we construct a perfect colorful matching M of H with weight $\mathcal{W} - \sum_{i:D_i \in A_0} w(m_i)$. For every $D_i \in A_1$, we

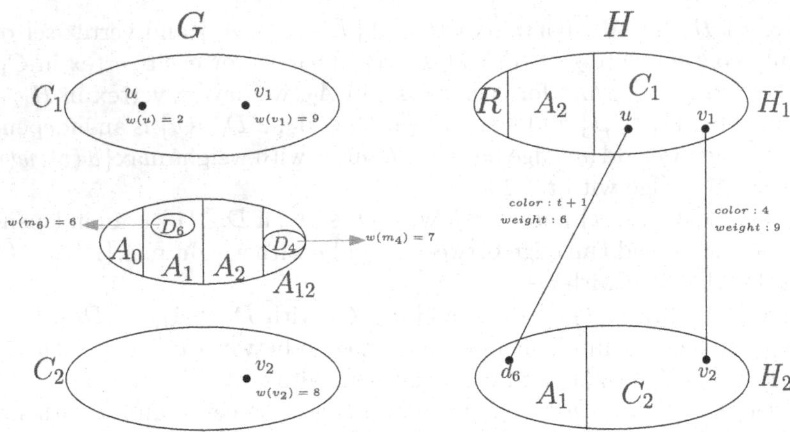

Fig. 2. An example of construction of graph H from G

know that $\lambda^{-1}(\lambda(D_i)) = D_i \cup \{v\}$ for some $v \in C_1$. So we add the unique edge between v and d_i (in H) to M. Note that weight of this edge is equal to the weight of $\lambda(D_i)$ and the color of the edge is $t+1$. Similarly, for every $D_i \in A_2$, we know that $\lambda^{-1}(\lambda(D_j)) = D_j \cup \{u\}$ for some $u \in C_2$. So we add the unique edge between u and d_j (in H) to M. Also here, the weight of this edge is equal to the weight of $\lambda(D_j)$ and the color of the edge is $t+1$. For every $D_i \in A_{12}$, we know that $\lambda^{-1}(\lambda(D_i)) = D_i \cup \{u, v\}$ for some $u' \in C_1$ and $v' \in C_2$, and therefore we know that there exists an edge e' between v' and u' with color i and weight of e' is equal to the weight of $\lambda(D_i)$. We add this edge e' to M. Note that now, every vertex in $C_1 \cup C_2$ which is sharing its color (in the coloring of λ) with a vertex in D, has appeared in exactly one edge in M.

Also, since every pair of vertices v and u ($v \in C_1$ and $u \in C_2$) that are not sharing the colors with vertices of D can clearly use the same color, we can assume that in an optimal coloring λ of G, there do not exist two vertices v and u ($v \in C_1$ and $u \in C_2$) such that neither of them share their colors with other vertices (because we can construct another coloring λ' which uses exact same coloring as λ but color classes of v and u are merged, and then the cost of λ' will be $\min\{w(v), w(u)\}$ less than λ). Therefore, only the clique with more vertices left has vertices that do not share their color with any other vertices. Let us assume that this clique is C_1 (the other case is similar and hence omitted). For every two vertices $v \in C_1$ and $u \in C_2$ such that $\lambda^{-1}(\lambda(v)) = \lambda^{-1}(\lambda(u)) = \{v, u\}$ we add the unique edge e with color $t+1$ in between them to the matching M. We know that the weight of e is equal to the weight of $\lambda(v) = \lambda(u)$.

Finally, for all of the remaining vertices (which we know that they are vertices that do not share their color with any other vertex and are in C_1) we choose a unique vertex of R for each one of them (by construction of R we know that they are exactly the same size) and add the edge between each two of them to

M. Note that for each one of these edges, their weight is equal to the weight of corresponding color in the coloring λ of G.

We can see that by the construction above, M is a perfect matching and since for every $D_i \in A_{12}$ we added an edge of color i and also an edge of color $t+1$ is added to M. Here, we may assume that $\max\{|C_1|, |C_2|\} > t$, and otherwise the instance has size bounded by $O(k)$. Because of this assumption, we have also added an edge to M with color $t+1$. Therefore, M is a colorful perfect matching.

Also, it can be easily seen that for every vertex in $C_1 \cup C_2$ maximum weight of its color in G is appeared exactly once in M (on its corresponding edge in M) and there is no other edge weights appearing on edges of M. Therefore, weight of M is equal to sum of the weights of color classes $\{c \mid \exists v \in C_1 \cup C_2 : \lambda(v) = c\}$ which we know that is equal to the sum of weights of the color classes $\{c \mid \exists v \in V(G) : \lambda(v) = c\} \setminus \{c | \exists D_i \in A_0 : \lambda(D_i) = c\}$. This weight is equal to $\mathcal{W} - \sum_{i:D_1 \in A_0} w(m_i)$. Therefore, $w(M) = \mathcal{W} - \sum_{i:D_1 \in A_0} w(m_i)$.

Now, we prove the reverse direction. Let M be a perfect colorful matching of H with weight $\mathcal{W}'$. Now, we introduce a coloring λ which is compatible with $(\mathcal{D}, A_0, A_1, A_2, A_{12})$ and has weight $\mathcal{W}' + \sum_{i:D_i \in A_0} w(m_i)$.

First, we arrange edges of M in an arbitrary order $e_1, e_2, ..., e_\ell$. Now, for every vertex $x \in \{d_i \mid D_i \in A_1 \cup A_2\} \cup C_1 \cup C_2$ we know that it appears in exactly one edge of M (say e_r). If $x \in C_1 \cup C_2$, we set $\lambda(v) = r$. If $x = d_i$ for some i, then for each $v \in D_i$, we set $\lambda(v) = r$. Also, for every $D_i \in A_{12}$ we know that at least one of the edges in M has color i. Let j be the least value such that e_j has color i. Then, set $\lambda(u) = j$ for all $u \in D_i$. Finally, for every $D_i \in A_0$, set $\lambda(D_i)$ a unique distinct color other than the previously used colors.

By construction of H it can be easily seen that the described coloring λ is a proper coloring of G. Also, it can be seen that there is a one-to-one mapping between edges of M and colors used for the vertices in $V(G) - (\bigcup_{D_i \in A_0} D_i)$ such that the weight of every edge is equal to maximum weight of vertices in its corresponding color class in G. Since colors used for vertices in $(\bigcup_{D_i \in A_0} D_i)$ and $V(G) - (\bigcup_{D_i \in A_0} D_i)$ are disjoint, it can be seen that the cost of λ is equal to $\mathcal{W}' + \sum_{i:D_i \in A_0} w(m_i)$.

It is not hard to see that number of different tuples $(\mathcal{D}, A_0, A_1, A_2, A_{12})$ is upper bounded by $k^{O(k)}$. Note that the reduction above will result an instance of Perfect Colorful Matching with parameter at most $k+1$. Thus, the above construction of H and Lemma 5 implies Lemma 4.

Lemma 4 and Theorem 15 implies the following theorem.

Theorem 14. *There is a randomized algorithm for* Max Coloring 2-Cluster Modulator *running in time* $k^{O(k)}\mathcal{W}n^{O(1)}$.

7 Perfect Colorful Matching

In this section we discuss an FPT algorithm for Perfect Colorful Matching. In order to do this, first we construct a matrix A with multivariate polynomial elements. After that we use an algebraic sieving method to find the answer from this matrix.

7.1 Matrix Construction

First, we introduce variables $X = \{x_c | c \in L\}$, $Y = \{y_e | e \in E(G)\}$ and z. Note that it can be assumed that colors are $1, 2, 3, ..., k$ (i.e., $L = [k]$ and $X = \{x_1, ..., x_k\}$). Let V_1 and V_2 be the two partitions of G (i.e., $G = (V_1, V_2, E)$). Now, construct matrix A with each dimension representing one of the partitions of G such that for every edge $e = (v, u) \in E(G)$ $(v \in V_1,\ u \in V_2)$, $A_{v,u} = y_e x_{\lambda(e)} z^{w(e)}$ where $w(e)$ is weight of edge e (In case of multiple edges $A_{v,u}$ is sum of monomials corresponding to all of these edges) and otherwise (if $(v, u) \notin E(G)$) $A_{v,u} = 0$. Note that every monomial of permanent of A, denoted by *per*(A), corresponds to a perfect matching in G (and vice versa). For every perfect matching M in G, monomial $\Pi_{e \in M} y_e x_{\lambda(e)} z^{w(e)}$ is a monomial of *per*(A) which is equal to $(\Pi_{e \in M} y_e)(\Pi_{e \in M}) x_{\lambda(e)}) z^{\sum_{e \in M} w(e)}$ and because of unique appearances of variables in Y, none of them will be canceled even if we consider this matrix is over a field of characteristic two. We will consider this matrix over a field of characteristic two and the reason for it is the following. In a field of characteristic two, the permanent of a matrix is equal to its determinant and hence this can be computed in polynomial time.

Next, we present the following lemma:

Lemma 6. *$(G, \lambda, L, k, \mathcal{W})$ is a yes-instance if and only if permanent of A has a monomial divisible by $\Pi_{c \in L} x_c$ and not divisible by $z^{\mathcal{W}+1}$.*

Proof. First, we prove that if there exists a colorful perfect matching M with total weight of at most $\mathcal{W}$ then there exists a monomial of A divisible by $\Pi_{c \in L} x_c$ and not divisible by $z^{\mathcal{W}+1}$. The monomial corresponding to M in *per*(A) is equal to $(\Pi_{e \in M} y_e)(\Pi_{e \in M}) x_{\lambda(e)}) z^{\sum_{e \in M} w(e)}$. Since M is a perfect colorful matching, $L = \{\lambda(e) | e \in M\}$. Therefore $\Pi_{e \in M} x_{\lambda(e)}$ is divisible by $\Pi_{c \in L} x_c$. Also, M has weight at most $\mathcal{W}$ so $\sum_{e \in M} w(e) < \mathcal{W} + 1$, and hence the corresponding monomial is not divisible by $z^{\mathcal{W}+1}$.

Now, we prove the reverse direction. If there exists a monomial P in *per*(A) with the stated properties, then its corresponding perfect matching M can be uniquely recovered using appearances of variables in Y. Since P is divisible by $\Pi_{c \in L} x_c$, for every $c \in L$, M has at least one edge from color c, thus M is a perfect colorful matching. Also, since weight of M is equal to the greatest power of z appeared in P and P is not divisible by $z^{\mathcal{W}+1}$, M has a total weight of at most $\mathcal{W}$.

7.2 Evaluation

Now, we discuss an FPT algorithm to find out if *per*(A) has a monomial divisible by $\Pi_{c \in L} x_c$ and not divisible by $z^{\mathcal{W}+1}$. First we state some of the known results which we use for this computation.

Lemma 7 (DeMillo-Lipton-Schwartz-Zippel [7,15,18]**).** *If $B(x_1, ..., x_n)$ is a multivariate not identically zero polynomial of degree d over a field $\mathcal{F}$, then for $a_1, ..., a_n$ that are picked uniformly at random from $\mathcal{F}$,* $\Pr[B(a_1, ..., a_n) = 0] \leq \frac{d}{|\mathcal{F}|}$.

In order to use this lemma, we need to find a finite field of large order and for purposes used later, we find this field such that its characteristic is 2. We do that by finding an irreducible polynomial $f \in \mathbb{F}_2[x]$ of degree at least $6n + 3\mathcal{W}$ and extending $\mathbb{F}_2$ (the Galois field of size 2) by defining $\mathcal{F}$ as $\frac{\mathbb{F}[x]}{f}$. We can find such a polynomial f using the following lemma:

Lemma 8 **([1]).** *For a prime p and an integer r, there exists an algorithm to find an irreducible polynomial $f \in \mathbb{F}_p$ such that $r \leq deg(f) \leq cr \log p$ for a constant c such that its running time is $(cr(\log p^2))^2$.*

For a polynomial $B(x_1, ..., x_n)$ and a subset $I \subset [n]$, define $B_{-I}(x_1, \ldots, x_n) = B(y_1, ..., y_n)$ where $y_i = x_i$ if $i \in I$ and $y_i = 0$ otherwise. We also use the following result.

Lemma 9 **([16]).** *For a polynomial $B(x_1, ..., x_n)$ over a field of characteristic 2 and $J \subset [n]$, if we define $Q(x_1, ..., x_n) = \sum_{I \subset J} B_{-I}(x_1, ..., x_n)$ then for any monomial M, $coef_Q M = coef_B M$ if M is divisible by $\Pi_{j \in J} x_j$ and $coef_Q M = 0$ otherwise.*

Because of Lemma 8, we assume that A is a matrix over a field $\mathcal{F}[X]$ of characteristic two such that the number of elements in $\mathcal{F}$ is at least three time the degree of the polynomial $perm(A)$. By the construction of matrix A, we know that for every v and u, there exists polynomials $P_0^{v,u}(x_1, ..., x_k)$, $P_1^{v,u}(x_1, ..., x_k)$, $P_2^{v,u}(x_1, ..., x_k)$, ... such that $A_{v,u} = y_{v,u} \sum_{i=0}^{\mathcal{W}} P_i^{v,u}(x_1, ..., x_k) z^i$. For a set $I \subset [k]$, define A_{-I} to be a matrix such that $(A_{-I})_{v,u} = y_{v,u} \sum_{i=0}^{\mathcal{W}} (P_i^{v,u})_{-I}(x_1, ..., x_k) z^i$.

Lemma 10 **([12]).** *Given an evaluation of the variables in set X, the value of $P_i^{v,u}(x_1, ..., x_k)$ and therefore A_{-I} can be computed for all $I \subset [k]$ and all $(v, u) \in E(G)$ in time and space $\mathcal{O}^*(2^k)$.*

Note that since $\mathcal{F}$ is a field of characteristic 2, in this field for every matrix M, $det(M) = per(M)$. Therefore, instead of looking for a monomial with stated properties in $per(A)$, we can look for it in $det(A)$. Let us continue the algorithm using the stated lemmas. Next, we pick X and Y uniformly at random from a sufficiently large field $\mathcal{F}$ stated as above. Now, it can be seen that in A and A_{-I} (for every $I \subset [k]$), every element is a polynomial of z with degree at most $\mathcal{W}$. We know that there exists a polynomial algorithm to compute determinant of a matrix, therefore there exists a circuit with polynomial number of nodes and operations multiplication and addition to calculate determinant of a matrix over a field of characteristic 2. Also, we know that in the computations of the determinant used for this problem, monomials with power of z greater than $\mathcal{W}$ are not important, therefore we can define our definition of addition and multiplication by just looking at monomials of power at most $\mathcal{W}$ of z so that every operation is done in $\mathcal{O}(\mathcal{W})$. Now, using this circuit, for every matrix A_{-I}, $det(A_{-I})$ and therefore $det(A)_{-I}$ can be calculated with in $O^*(2^k)$ time. Thus, by Lemma 9 (if we set $J = [k]$ in that theorem), it can be seen that with high probability $det(A)$ has a monomial divisible by $\Pi_{c\in[k]}x_c$ and not divisible by $x^{\mathcal{W}+1}$ if and only if $\sum_{I\subset[k]} det(A_{-I}) = \sum_{I\subset[k]} det(A)_{-I}$ calculated uniformly picked X and Y as above has a non-zero coefficient for $z^{\mathcal{W}'}$ where $\mathcal{W}'$ is at most $\mathcal{W}$. Now from the single variate polynomial we compute the coefficients of $z^{\mathcal{W}'}$ for all $\mathcal{W}' \leq \mathcal{W}$. This completes the proof of following theorem.

Theorem 15. *There is a randomized algorithm for* PERFECT COLORFUL MATCHING *running in time* $2^{O(k)}\mathcal{W}n^{O(1)}$.

8 Conclusion

We proved several results about parameterized complexity of different variations of list coloring and max coloring. First, we used a reduction from COLORED SUBGRAPH ISOMORPHISM to prove that not only LIST COLORING ℓ-CLUSTER MODULATOR is W[1]-hard, but also it cannot be solved in time $f(|D|+\ell)n^{o(\frac{|D|+\ell}{\log|D|+\ell})}$ unless ETH fails. This answers a natural problem raised after Gutin et al. [12] proved fixed parameterized tractability of this problem where $\ell = 1$. However, parameterized complexity of this problem with $\ell = c$ for some constant $c > 1$ is still unknown. Then we gave a kernel with $2^k + k$ vertices for MAX COLORING VERTEX COVER and a kernel of size $2^k.k+k$ for MAX COLORING CLIQUE MODULATOR. One obvious open problem is to give polynomial kernels for this problems. Finally, we presented an FPT algorithm for MAX COLORING 2-CLUSTER MODULATOR using a reduction to PERFECT COLORFUL MATCHING. It could be interesting to derandomize the algorithm for PERFECT COLORFUL MATCHING.

References

1. Adleman, L.M., Jr., H.W.L.: Finding irreducible polynomials over finite fields. In: Hartmanis, J. (ed.) Proceedings of the 18th Annual ACM Symposium on Theory of Computing, Berkeley, California, USA, 28–30 May 1986, pp. 350–355. ACM (1986). https://doi.org/10.1145/12130.12166
2. Araújo, J., Baste, J., Sau, I.: Ruling out FPT algorithms for weighted coloring on forests. Theor. Comput. Sci. **729**, 11–19 (2018). https://doi.org/10.1016/j.tcs.2018.03.013
3. Araújo, J., Nisse, N., Pérennes, S.: Weighted coloring in trees. SIAM J. Discret. Math. **28**(4), 2029–2041 (2014). https://doi.org/10.1137/140954167
4. Bannach, M., et al.: Solving packing problems with few small items using rainbow matchings. arXiv abs/2007.02660 (2020)
5. Dailey, D.P.: Uniqueness of colorability and colorability of planar 4-regular graphs are np-complete. Discret. Math. **30**(3), 289–293 (1980). https://doi.org/10.1016/0012-365X(80)90236-8. https://www.sciencedirect.com/science/article/pii/0012365X80902368
6. Demange, M., Werra, D., Monnot, J., Paschos, V.T.: Weighted node coloring: when stable sets are expensive. In: Goos, G., Hartmanis, J., van Leeuwen, J., Kučera, L. (eds.) WG 2002. LNCS, vol. 2573, pp. 114–125. Springer, Heidelberg (2002). https://doi.org/10.1007/3-540-36379-3_11

7. DeMillo, R.A., Lipton, R.J.: A probabilistic remark on algebraic program testing. Inf. Process. Lett. **7**(4), 193–195 (1978). https://doi.org/10.1016/0020-0190(78)90067-4
8. Escoffier, B.: Saving colors and max coloring: some fixed-parameter tractability results. Theor. Comput. Sci. **758**, 30–41 (2019). https://doi.org/10.1016/j.tcs.2018.08.002
9. Escoffier, B., Monnot, J., Paschos, V.T.: Weighted coloring: further complexity and approximability results. Inf. Process. Lett. **97**(3), 98–103 (2006). https://doi.org/10.1016/j.ipl.2005.09.013
10. Fiala, J., Golovach, P.A., Kratochvíl, J.: Parameterized complexity of coloring problems: treewidth versus vertex cover. Theor. Comput. Sci. **412**(23), 2513–2523 (2011). https://doi.org/10.1016/j.tcs.2010.10.043
11. Gutin, G., Wahlström, M., Yeo, A.: Rural postman parameterized by the number of components of required edges. J. Comput. Syst. Sci. **83**(1), 121–131 (2017). https://doi.org/10.1016/j.jcss.2016.06.001. https://www.sciencedirect.com/science/article/pii/S0022000016300411
12. Gutin, G.Z., Majumdar, D., Ordyniak, S., Wahlström, M.: Parameterized precoloring extension and list coloring problems. SIAM J. Discret. Math. **35**(1), 575–596 (2021). https://doi.org/10.1137/20M1323369
13. Impagliazzo, R., Paturi, R.: Complexity of k-SAT. In: Proceedings of Fourteenth Annual IEEE Conference on Computational Complexity (Formerly: Structure in Complexity Theory Conference) (Cat. No. 99CB36317), pp. 237–240 (1999). https://doi.org/10.1109/CCC.1999.766282
14. Marx, D.: Can you beat treewidth? Theory Comput. **6**(1), 85–112 (2010). https://doi.org/10.4086/toc.2010.v006a005
15. Schwartz, J.T.: Fast probabilistic algorithms for verification of polynomial identities. J. ACM **27**(4), 701–717 (1980). https://doi.org/10.1145/322217.322225
16. Wahlström, M.: Abusing the tutte matrix: an algebraic instance compression for the k-set-cycle problem. In: Portier, N., Wilke, T. (eds.) 30th International Symposium on Theoretical Aspects of Computer Science, STACS 2013, Kiel, Germany, 27 February–2 March 2013. LIPIcs, vol. 20, pp. 341–352. Schloss Dagstuhl - Leibniz-Zentrum für Informatik (2013). https://doi.org/10.4230/LIPIcs.STACS.2013.341
17. de Werra, D., Demange, M., Escoffier, B., Monnot, J., Paschos, V.T.: Weighted coloring on planar, bipartite and split graphs: complexity and approximation. Discret. Appl. Math. **157**(4), 819–832 (2009). https://doi.org/10.1016/j.dam.2008.06.013
18. Zippel, R.: Probabilistic algorithms for sparse polynomials. In: Ng, E.W. (ed.) Symbolic and Algebraic Computation. LNCS, vol. 72, pp. 216–226. Springer, Heidelberg (1979). https://doi.org/10.1007/3-540-09519-5_73

Eternal Vertex Cover on Bipartite Graphs

Jasine Babu[1], Neeldhara Misra[2(✉)], and Saraswati Girish Nanoti[2]

[1] Indian Institute of Technology, Palakkad, Palakkad, India
jasine@iitpkd.ac.in
[2] Indian Institute of Technology, Gandhinagar, Gandhinagar, India
{neeldhara.m,nanoti_saraswati}@iitgn.ac.in
http://www.iitpkd.ac.in/
http://www.iitgn.ac.in

Dedicated to the memory of Professor Rolf Niedermeier.

Abstract. The Eternal Vertex Cover problem is a dynamic variant of the vertex cover problem. We have a two player game in which guards are placed on some vertices of a graph. In every move, one player (the attacker) attacks an edge. In response to the attack, the second player (the defender) moves some of the guards along the edges of the graph in such a manner that at least one guard moves along the attacked edge. If such a movement is not possible, then the attacker wins. If the defender can defend the graph against an infinite sequence of attacks, then the defender wins.

The minimum number of guards with which the defender has a winning strategy is called the eternal vertex cover number of the graph G. On general graphs, the computational problem of determining the minimum eternal vertex cover number is NP-hard and admits a 2-approximation algorithm and an exponential kernel. The complexity of the problem on bipartite graphs is open, as is the question of whether the problem admits a polynomial kernel.

We settle both these questions by showing that Eternal Vertex Cover is NP-hard and does not admit a polynomial compression even on bipartite graphs of diameter six. We also show that the problem admits a polynomial time algorithm on the class of cobipartite graphs.

1 Introduction

The Eternal Vertex Cover problem is a dynamic variant of the vertex cover problem introduced by Klostermeyer and Mynhardt (2009). The setting is the following. We have a two player game—between players whom we will refer to as the *attacker* and *defender*—on a simple, undirected graph G. In the beginning, the defender can choose to place guards on some of the vertices of

The second author acknowledges support from the SERB-MATRICS grant MTR/2017/001033 and IIT Gandhinagar. The third author acknowledges support from CSIR.

A. S. Kulikov and S. Raskhodnikova (Eds.): CSR 2022, LNCS 13296, pp. 64–76, 2022.
https://doi.org/10.1007/978-3-031-09574-0_5

G. The attacker's move involve choosing an edge to "attack". The defender is able to "defend" this attack if she can move the guards along the edges of the graph in such a way that at least one guard moves along the attacked edge. If such a movement is not possible, then the attacker wins. If the defender can defend the graph against an infinite sequence of attacks, then the defender wins (see Fig. 1). The minimum number of guards with which the defender has a winning strategy is called the *eternal vertex cover number* of the graph G and is denoted by $\mathsf{evc}(G)$.

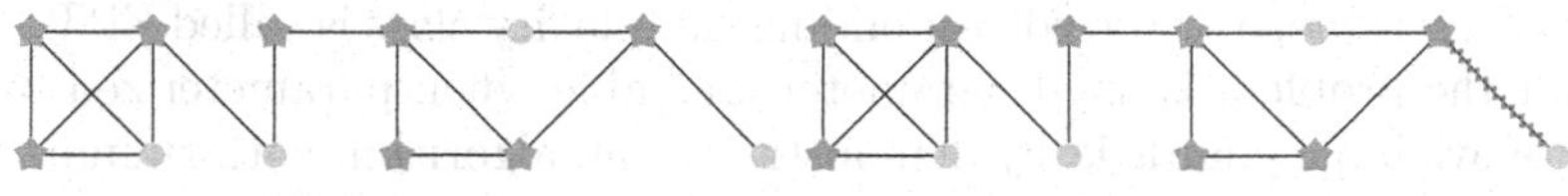

(a) The intial positions of the guards are denoted by the star-shaped vertices.

(b) The attacker's move targets the edge to the far-right, highighted by a wavy red line.

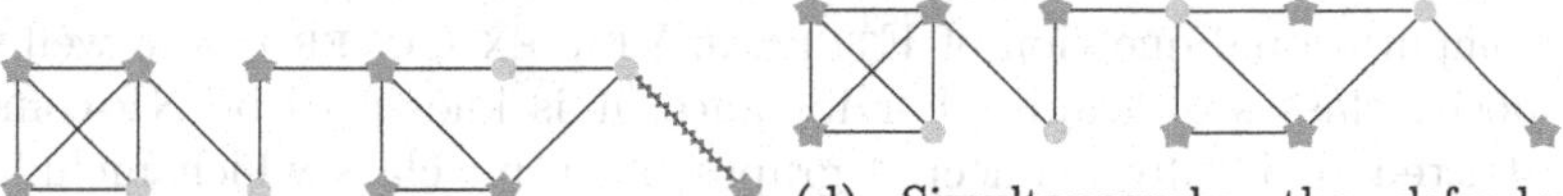

(c) The defender responds to defend the attack by moving a guard along the attacked edge.

(d) Simultaneously, the defender moves another guard to ensure that no edges are left vulnerable. This is the resultant position of the guards.

Fig. 1. An attack that is defended by moving two guards.

If S_ℓ is the subset of vertices that have guards on them after the defender has played her ℓ-th move, and S_ℓ is not a vertex cover of G, then the attacker can target any of the uncovered edges to win the game. Therefore, when the defender has a winning strategy, it implies that she can always "reconfigure" one vertex cover into another in response to any attack, where the reconfiguration is constrained by the rules of how the guards can move and the requirement that at least one of these guards needs to move along the attacked edge. Therefore, it is clear that $\mathsf{evc}(G) \geqslant \mathsf{mvc}(G)$, where $\mathsf{mvc}(G)$ denotes the minimum size of a vertex cover of G. It also turns out that twice as many vertices as the $\mathsf{mvc}(G)$ also suffice the defend against any sequence of attacks. This might be achieved, for example, by placing guards on both endpoints of any maximum matching to begin with and after any attack, reconfiguring the guards to obtain another maximum matching. Using this strategy, a 2–approximation algorithm for ETERNAL VERTEX COVER was obtained by Fomin et al. (2010). This also implies $\mathsf{mvc}(G) \leqslant \mathsf{evc}(G) \leqslant 2\mathsf{mvc}(G)$.

Klostermeyer and Mynhardt (2009) gave a characterization of the graphs for which the upper bound is achieved. A characterization for graphs for which lower bound is achieved remains open, but several special cases have been addressed in the literature (see, for instance Babu et al. 2021a). Also, Klostermeyer and Mynhardt (2011) study graphs with equal eternal vertex cover and eternal domination numbers, which is a closely related dynamic variant of the dominating set problem.

The natural computational question associated with this parameter is the following: given a graph G and a positive integer k, determine if $evc(G) \leqslant k$. The problem is only known to be in PSPACE in general. Fomin et al. (2010) show that this problem is NP-hard by a reduction from vertex cover, and admits a 2-approximation algorithm based on both endpoints of a maximum matching. They also study the problem from a parameterized perspective. In parameterized complexity, one asks if for an instance of size n and a parameter k, a problem can be solved in time $f(k)n^{\mathcal{O}(1)}$ where f is an arbitrary computable function independent of n. Problems that can be solved in that time are said to be fixed parameter tractable, and the corresponding complexity class is called FPT. They show that the problem is fixed parameter tractable when parameterized by the number of available guards k, by demonstrating an algorithm with running time $\mathcal{O}\left(2^{O(k^2)} + nm\right)$ for ETERNAL VERTEX COVER, where n is the number of vertices and m the number of edges of the input graph. This work leaves open the question of whether ETERNAL VERTEX COVER admits a polynomial kernel[1].

The computational question of ETERNAL VERTEX COVER is also well studied on special classes of graphs. For instance, it is known to be NP-complete when restricted to locally connected graphs, a graph class which includes all biconnected internally triangulated planar graphs (Babu et al. 2021a). It can also be solved in linear time on the class of cactus graphs (Babu et al. 2021b), quadratic time on chordal graphs (Babu and Prabhakaran 2021; Babu et al. 2021b) and in polynomial time on "generalized" trees (Araki et al. 2015). However, the complexity of the problem on biparitite graphs remains open, and is an intriguing question especially considering that the vertex cover problem is tractable on biparitite graphs.

1.1 Our Contributions

We resolve the question of the complexity of ETERNAL VERTEX COVER on bipartite graphs by showing NP-hardness even on bipartite graphs of constant diameter. It turns out that the same result can also be used to argue the likely non-existence of a polynomial compression, which resolves the question of whether ETERNAL VERTEX COVER has a polynomial kernel in the negative. Finally, we also observe that the hardness results carry over to the related problem of ETERNAL CONNECTED VERTEX COVER (Fujito and Nakamura 2020), where we would like the vertex covers at every step to induce connected subgraphs.

Summarizing, our main result is the following:

Theorem 1 (EVC on Bipartite Graphs). *Both the* ETERNAL VERTEX COVER *and* ETERNAL CONNECTED VERTEX COVER *problems are* NP*-hard and do not admit a polynomial compression parameterized by the number of guards (unless* NP $\subseteq$ coNP */poly), even on bipartite graphs of diameter six.*

We also show that ETERNAL VERTEX COVER is tractable on the class of cobipartite graphs.

[1] We refer the reader to Sect. 2 for the definition of the notion of a polynomial kernel.

Theorem 2 (EVC on Co-Bipartite Graphs). *There is a quadratic-time algorithm for* Eternal Vertex Cover *on the class of cobipartite graphs.*

Organization. We establish notation and provide relevant definitions in Sect. 2. The proof of Theorem 1 follows from the construction described in Lemma 1, and is the main focus of Sect. 3, while the proof of Theorem 2 can be found in Sect. 4. In Sect. 5, we suggest some directions for further work.

2 Preliminaries and Notations

All graphs in this paper are finite, undirected and without multiple edges and loops. For terminology not defined in this paper we refer to Diestel (2017).

Let $G = (V, E)$ be a graph. We will typically use n and m to denote $|V|$ and $|E|$, respectively. The set of neighbours of a vertex v in G is denoted by $N_G(v)$, or briefly by $N(v)$[2]. More generally, for $U \subseteq V$, the neighbours in $V \setminus U$ of vertices in U are called neighbours of U; their set is denoted by $N(U)$. A subset $S \subseteq V$ is said to be *independent* if for all $u, v \in S$, $(u, v) \notin E$.

A path is a non-empty graph $P = (V, E)$ of the form $V = \{x_0, x_1, \ldots, x_k\}$ and $E = \{x_0x_1, x_1x_2, \ldots, x_{k-1}x_k\}$, where the x_i's are all distinct. The number of edges of a path is its length, and the path of length k is denoted by P^k. The distance $d_G(x, y)$ in G of two vertices x, y is the length of a shortest $x - y$ path in G; if no such path exists, we set $d(x, y) := \infty$. The greatest distance between any two vertices in G is the diameter of G, denoted by $\text{diam}(G)$.

A *vertex cover* of a graph $G = (V, E)$ is a subset S of the vertex set such that every edge has at least one of its endpoints in S. Note that $V \setminus S$ is an independent set. We use $\text{mvc}(G)$ to denote the size of a minimum vertex cover of G. A *dominating set* of a graph G is a subset X of the vertex set such that every vertex of G either belongs to X or has a neighbor in X.

Consider a graph $G = (V, E)$ on n vertices and m edges. Guards are placed on the vertices of the graph in order to protect it from an infinite sequence (which is not known to the guards in advance) of attacks on the edges of the graph. In each round, one edge $uv \in E$ is attacked, and each guard either stays on the vertex it is occupying or moves to a neighboring vertex.

Moreover, the guards are bound to move in such a way that at least one guard moves from u to v or from v to u. The minimum number of guards which can protect all the edges of G is called the eternal vertex cover number of G and is denoted by $\text{evc}(G)$.

A *bipartite* graph is a graph whose vertex set can be partitioned into at most two independent sets. A *co-bipartite graph* is a graph which is the complement of a bipartite graph. In other words, a co-bipartite graph is a graph whose vertex set can be partitioned into at most two cliques.

---

[2] Here, as elsewhere, we drop the index referring to the underlying graph if the reference is clear.

Parameterized Complexity. A parameterized problem L is a subset of $\Sigma^* \times \mathbb{N}$ for some finite alphabet Σ. An instance of a parameterized problem consists of (x, k), where k is called the parameter. A central notion in parameterized complexity is fixed parameter tractability (FPT), which means for a given instance (x, k) solvability in time $f(k) \cdot p(|x|)$, where f is an arbitrary function of k and p is a polynomial in the input size. The notions of kernelization and compression are defined as follows.

Definition 1. *A kernelization algorithm, or in short, a kernel for a parameterized problem $Q \subseteq \Sigma^* \times \mathbb{N}$ is an algorithm that, given $(x, k) \in \Sigma^* \times \mathbb{N}$, outputs in time polynomial in $|x| + k$ a pair $(x', k') \in \Sigma^* \times \mathbb{N}$ such that (a) $(x, k) \in Q$ if and only if $(x', k') \in Q$ and (b) $|x'| + k' \leqslant g(k)$, where g is an arbitrary computable function. The function g is referred to as the size of the kernel. If g is a polynomial function then we say that Q admits a polynomial kernel.*

Definition 2. *A polynomial compression of a parameterized language $Q \subseteq \Sigma^* \times \mathbb{N}$ into a language $R \subseteq \Sigma^*$ is an algorithm that takes as input an instance $(x, k) \in \Sigma^* \times \mathbb{N}$, works in time polynomial in $|x| + k$, and returns a string y such that:*

1. $|y| \leqslant p(k)$ *for some polynomial* $p(\cdot)$, *and*
2. $y \in R$ *if and only if* $(x, k) \in Q$.

Our focus in this paper is the Eternal Vertex Cover problem, in which we are interested in computing $\text{evc}(G)$ for a graph G, and its parameterized complexity with respect to the number of guards:

> Eternal Vertex Cover
> **Input:** A graph $G = (V, E)$ and a positive integer $k \in \mathbb{Z}^+$.
> **Parameter:** k
> **Question:** Does G have an eternal vertex cover of size at most k?

Eternal Vertex Cover is known to admit an exponential kernel of size $4^k(k+1) + 2k$ (Fomin et al. 2010). We use the following standard framework to show that it is unlikely to admit a polynomial compression.

Definition 3. *Let P and Q be parameterized problems. We say that P is polynomial parameter reducible to Q, written $P \leqslant_{ppt} Q$, if there exists a polynomial time computable function $f : \Sigma^* \times \mathbb{N} \to \Sigma^* \times \mathbb{N}$ and a polynomial p, such that for all $(x, k) \in \Sigma^* \times \mathbb{N}$ (a) $(x, k) \in P$ if and only $(x', k') = f(x, k) \in Q$ and (b) $k' \leqslant p(k)$. The function f is called polynomial parameter transformation.*

Proposition 1. *Let P and Q be parameterized problems such that there is a polynomial parameter transformation from P to Q. If Q has a polynomial compression, then P also has a polynomial compression.*

In the Red Blue Dominating Set problem, we are given a bipartite graph $G = (B \cup R, E)$ and an integer k and asked whether there exists a vertex set

$S \subseteq R$ of size at most k such that every vertex in B has at least one neighbor in S. In the literature, the sets B and R are called "blue vertices" and "red vertices", respectively. It is known (see Dom et al. 2014, Theorem 4.1) that RBDS parameterized by $(|B|, k)$ does not have a polynomial kernel, and more generally, a polynomial compression (see Fomin et al. 2019, Corollary 19.6):

Proposition 2 (Corollary 19.6 Fomin et al. (2019)). *The* RED BLUE DOMINATING SET *problem, parameterized by* $|B| + k$, *does not admit a polynomial compression unless* coNP $\subseteq$ NP/*poly.*

Note that based on Propositions 1 and 2, to show that a polynomial compression for ETERNAL VERTEX COVER parameterized by the number of guards implies coNP $\subseteq$ NP/poly, it suffices to show a polynomial parameter transformation from RED BLUE DOMINATING SET to ETERNAL VERTEX COVER.

For more background on parameterized complexity and algorithms, the reader is referred to the books Cygan et al. (2015); Fomin et al. (2019); Niedermeier (2006); Flum and Grohe (2006); Downey and Fellows (2013).

3 Hardness on Bipartite Graphs

In this section we demonstrate the intractability of ETERNAL VERTEX COVER on the class of bipartite graphs of diameter six. Our key tool is a reduction from RED BLUE DOMINATING SET which also happens to be a polynomial parameter transformation.

Lemma 1. *There is a polynomial parameter transformation from* RED BLUE DOMINATING SET *parameterized by* $|B|+k$ *to* ETERNAL VERTEX COVER *parameterized by solution size.*

Proof. Let $\langle G = (V, E), b + k\rangle$ be an instance of RED BLUE DOMINATING SET. We have $V = R \cup B$. We denote the vertices in R by $\{v_1, \ldots, v_r\}$, the vertices in B by $\{u_1, \ldots, u_b\}$ and use m to denote $|E|$. We assume that G is connected, since RED BLUE DOMINATING SET does not have a polynomial sized kernel even for connected graphs.

We assume that every blue vertex has at least one red neighbour and by returning a trivial NO-instance of ETERNAL VERTEX COVER if some blue vertex has no red neighbour. The correctness of this follows from the fact that if some blue vertex does not have a red neighbour then it cannot be dominated by any subset of R.

Further, we assume that $k < b$ by returning a trivial YES-instance of ETERNAL VERTEX COVER if $k \geqslant b$. Also we assume $b > 1$, since when $b = 1$, the instance is easily resolved and we may return an appropriate instance of ETERNAL VERTEX COVER (a trivial YES instance if $k \geqslant 1$ and a trivial NO instance otherwise).

The Construction. We will develop an instance of ETERNAL VERTEX COVER which we denote by $\langle H, \ell \rangle$ based on $\langle G, k \rangle$ as follows (see also Fig. 2). First, we introduce r *red* vertices, denoted by $A := \{v_i \mid 1 \leqslant i \leqslant r\}$ and b *blue* vertices, denoted by $B := \{u_i \mid 1 \leqslant i \leqslant b\}$. Next, for all $i \in [b]$, we add b^2+3 *dependent* vertices of type i, denoted by $C_i := \{w_j^i \mid 1 \leqslant j \leqslant b^2+3\}$. Now, we add b^2+3 *dependent* vertices of type $\star$, denoted by $D := \{w_j^i \mid 1 \leqslant j \leqslant b^2+3\}$. Finally, we add two special vertices denoted by $\star$ and $\dagger$, which we will refer to as the *universal* and *backup* vertices respectively. To summarize, the vertex set consists of the following $r + (b^3 + b^2 + 4b + 5)$ vertices:

$$V(H) := A \cup B \cup C_1 \cup \cdots \cup C_b \cup D \cup \{\star, \dagger\}.$$

We now describe the edges in H:

- There are m *structural* edges given by (v_p, u_q) for every pair (p, q) such that $(v_p, u_q) \in E(G)$. In other words, for every edge (v_p, u_q) in the graph G, the original vertex v_p is adjacent to the partner vertex u_q.
- The dependent vertices of type i are adjacent to the ith blue vertex, i.e., for every $i \in [b]$, we have a *sliding* edge (u_i, w) for each $w \in C_i$.
- The dependent vertices of type $\star$ are adjacent to the universal vertex, i.e., we have a *sliding* edge $(\star, w)$ for each $w \in D$.
- The universal vertex $\star$ is adjacent to every red vertex via a *supplier* edge. For every $i \in [r]$, we have the edge $(v_i, \star)$.
- Finally, we have the edge $(\star, \dagger)$, indicating that the backup vertex $\dagger$ is adjacent to the universal vertex. We call this edge a *bridge*.

To summarize, we have the following edges in H:

$$\begin{aligned}
E(H) = &\{(v_p, u_q) \mid 1 \leqslant p \leqslant r; 1 \leqslant q \leqslant b; \text{ and } (v_p, u_q) \in E(H)\} \longleftarrow \text{ the structural edges} \\
&\cup \{(u_1, w) \mid w \in C_1)\} \longleftarrow \text{ the type 1 sliding edges} \\
&\cup \vdots \\
&\cup \{(u_i, w) \mid w \in C_i)\} \longleftarrow \text{ the type } i \text{ sliding edges} \\
&\cup \vdots \\
&\cup \{(u_b, w) \mid w \in C_b)\} \longleftarrow \text{ the type } b \text{ sliding edges} \\
&\cup \{(\star, w) \mid w \in D)\} \longleftarrow \text{ the type } \star \text{ sliding edges} \\
&\cup \{(v_i, \star) \mid 1 \leqslant i \leqslant r\} \longleftarrow \text{ the supplier edges} \\
&\cup \{(\star, \dagger)\} \longleftarrow \text{ the bridge edge.}
\end{aligned} \tag{1}$$

We now let $\ell := b + k + 2$, and this completes the description of the reduced instance $\langle H, \ell \rangle$.

Claim. The vertex cover number of H is $b + 1$.

Proof. This follows from the fact that there is a matching of size $b+1$ in H, consisting of edges joining each blue vertex and $\star$ to one of their adjacent dependent vertices. (showing the lower bound), and that $B \cup \{\star\}$ is a vertex cover in H (which implies the upper bound).

Proposition 3. *Any vertex cover of* H *that has at most* ℓ *vertices must contain* $B \cup \{\star\}$.

Proof. Consider a vertex cover $S \subseteq V(H)$ that does not contain some blue vertex $u_i \in B$. Then S must contain all the dependent vertices in C_i, but since $|C_i| = b^2 + 3$, this contradicts our assumption that $|S| \leqslant \ell$. Consider a vertex cover $S \subseteq V(H)$ that does not contain the universal vertex $\star$. Then S must contain all the dependent vertices in D, but since $|D| = b^2 + 3$, this contradicts our assumption that $|S| \leqslant \ell$.

Proposition 4. *If* G *has a red blue dominating set of size* k*, then the connected vertex cover number of* H *is at most* $b+k+1$.

Proof. Let S be a Red Blue Dominating Set of size k in G. Consider the set $T = B \cup \{\star\} \cup S$. First we show that $H[T]$ is connected. It is sufficient to show that each vertex has a path joining it to the universal vertex. Clearly the universal vertex is a neighbour of all the red vertices and hence it is connected to them. Any blue vertex has a neighbour in the dominating set and this red neighbour is adjacent to the universal vertex. So all the blue vertices are connected to the universal vertex.

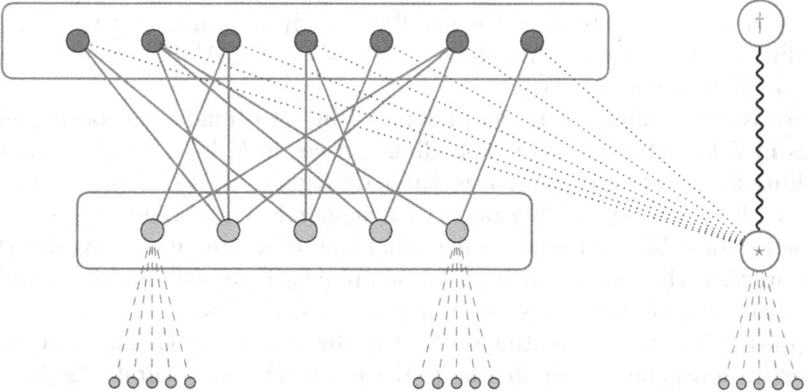

Fig. 2. A schematic depicting the construction of (H, ℓ) starting with an instance (G, k) of Red Blue Dominating Set. The red vertices from G instance are shown in the red rectangle on the top while the blue vertices are in the blue rectangle positioned at the bottom. The solid green lines correspond to edges in $E(G)$. The small orange vertices are the dependent vertices (some of them are omitted for clarity), while the global and backup vertices are shown by nodes labeled $\star$ and † respectively. The wavy line shows the bridge, the dotted lines shows the supplier edges while the dashed lines show the sliding edges.

Next we show that T is a vertex cover of H. Any structural edge has both its endpoints in T. Since $B \cup \{\star\} \subset T$, any sliding edge has one endpoint in T. All the supplier edges and the bridge edge have one endpoint in T which is the universal vertex $\star$. Thus $\mathrm{cvc}(H) \leqslant b + k + 1$.

The Forward Direction. Suppose $\langle G = (V, E), k \rangle$ is a YES-instance of RED BLUE DOMINATING SET. We argue that $\langle H, \ell \rangle$ is a YES-instance of ETERNAL VERTEX COVER. From Klostermeyer and Mynhardt (2009), we have $\mathrm{evc}(H) \leqslant \mathrm{cvc}(H)+1$. Further, Proposition 4 implies that $\mathrm{evc}(H) \leqslant b + k + 2$ i.e. $\mathrm{evc}(H) \leqslant \ell$. Thus $\langle H, \ell \rangle$ is a YES-instance of ETERNAL VERTEX COVER.

The Backward Direction. Suppose $\langle H, \ell \rangle$ is a YES-instance of ETERNAL VERTEX COVER. We argue that $\langle G = (V, E), k \rangle$ is a YES-instance of RED BLUE DOMINATING SET.

We know that any sequence of edge attacks in H can be defended by deploying at most $\ell = b + k + 2$ guards. Let $\mathcal{S}$ denote the initial placement of guards.

We now consider two cases:

Case 1. $\mathcal{S}$ contains the backup vertex. We already know that $\mathcal{S}$ contains all the blue vertices and the universal vertex by Proposition 3. This accounts for the positions of $(b+1)$ guards. Additionally, because of the case we are in, we have one guard on the backup vertex. So the remaining k guards occupy either red or dependent vertices. We will define a corresponding dominating set of size at most k in G.

Specifically, let $A' := \{j \mid 1 \leqslant j \leqslant r \text{ and } v_i \in \mathcal{S}\}$ and $B' := \{j \mid 1 \leqslant j \leqslant b \text{ and } C_j \cap \mathcal{S} \neq \emptyset\}$. For each $j \in B'$, let ℓ_j be such that v_{ℓ_j} is an arbitrarily chosen neighbor of u_j in G. Note that it is possible that $j_1 \neq j_2$ in B' but $\ell_{j_1} = \ell_{j_2}$. We now define $C' := \{\ell_j \mid j \in B'\}$. We claim that $S := \{v_i \mid i \in A' \cup C'\}$ is a dominating set for the blue vertices in G.

Intuitively speaking, our choice of dominating set is made by choosing all red vertices in G for whom the corresponding vertices in H have a guard on them, and additionally, for all blue vertices who have a guard on a dependent neighbor vertex in H, we choose an arbitrary red neighbor in G—while this choice may coincide for some blue vertices, we note that the total number of chosen vertices is no more than the number of guards who are positioned on dependent and red vertices, i.e., k. In other words, we have that $|A' \cup C'| \leqslant k$.

Suppose S is not a dominating set for the blue vertices in G. Then, let $u_t \in B$ be a vertex that is not dominated by S. Let us attack a structural edge (u_t, v_q). Note that v_q is not occupied by a guard, and the guard on u_t is forced to move to v_q to defend this attack. However, observe that our assumption that u_t is not dominated in G implies that no neighbor of u_t has a guard in $\mathcal{S}$. Therefore, there is no guard that can move to u_t now. But, by Proposition 3, the new configuration must contain a guard on u_t, because it is a vertex cover of H of size at most l. This is a contradiction. Therefore, S is indeed a dominating set in G of size at most k.

Case 2. $\mathcal{S}$ does not contain the backup vertex. In this case, we attack the bridge. Let $\mathcal{S}'$ denote the placement of the guards obtained by defending this attack. Note that $\mathcal{S}'$ must contain the backup vertex. Now we argue as we did in the previous case. This concludes the proof in the reverse direction.

Observe that the instance that we construct in the proof of Lemma 1 is both bipartite and has diameter at most six.

Recall that any vertex cover of H that has at most ℓ vertices must contain $\mathsf{B} \cup \{\star\}$. It is easy to verify that all the vertex covers used by the defense in the forward direction induced connected subgraphs, since every vertex cover contains all the blue vertices, a dominating set for the blue vertices, and a universal vertex that is adjacent to all the vertices in the dominating set; and any other vertex is adjacent to one of the blue vertices (or the universal vertex). Therefore, the reduction above also serves to demonstrate the hardness of ETERNAL CONNECTED VERTEX COVER on bipartite graphs—note that the argument for the reverse direction is exactly the same since every connected vertex cover is also a vertex cover.

Overall, Lemma 1 along with Proposition 2 and the remarks above lead to our main result.

Theorem 1 (EVC on Bipartite Graphs). *Both the* ETERNAL VERTEX COVER *and* ETERNAL CONNECTED VERTEX COVER *problems are* NP*-hard and do not admit a polynomial compression parameterized by the number of guards (unless* NP $\subseteq$ coNP */poly), even on bipartite graphs of diameter six.*

4 A Polynomial-Time Algorithm for Co-bipartite Graphs

In this section, we focus on a proof of Theorem 2.

Theorem 2 (EVC on Co-Bipartite Graphs). *There is a quadratic-time algorithm for* ETERNAL VERTEX COVER *on the class of cobipartite graphs.*

The proof of this theorem is derived essentially by combining some existing results. To the best of our knowledge, this result has not been stated explicitly elsewhere and is not subsumed by known polynomial-time algorithms for special classes of graphs like chordal graphs, cactus graphs, and generalized trees[3].

Let $\mathsf{G} = (\mathsf{V} = \mathsf{A} \uplus \mathsf{B}, \mathsf{E})$ be a cobipartite graph with bipartition A, B. Recall that $\mathsf{G}[\mathsf{A}]$ and $\mathsf{G}[\mathsf{B}]$ are cliques. Consider that A has p vertices $\{a_1, a_2, \ldots, a_p\}$ and B has q vertices $\{b_1, b_2, \ldots, b_q\}$. Without loss of generality we assume that $\mathsf{p} \leqslant \mathsf{q}$ and that no vertex in A is universal. (If there is some such universal vertex in A, simply shift that vertex to B). We also assume throughout that G

[3] The notion of generalized trees in the context of eternal vertex cover was considered by Araki et al. (2015). Such graphs are characterized by the following property: every block is an elementary bipartite graph or a clique having at most two cut-vertices in it. Note that a cobipartite graph with four vertices in both parts with two disjoint edges across the parts is not a generalized tree.

is connected and $p \geqslant 1$: if $p = 0$ then G is a clique and $evc(G) = mvc(G) = |V(G)| - 1$.

Since the cliques require $p - 1$ and $q - 1$ vertices respectively for a vertex cover, we have $mvc(G) \geqslant p + q - 2$. Since $p = |A| \geqslant 1$, there exists a (non-universal) vertex a_i on the A side and therefore it has at least one non-neighbor (say b_j) and thus we have a vertex cover of size $p+q-2$ given by $V(G) \setminus \{a_i, b_j\}$. Therefore, $mvc(G) = p + q - 2$. We make a note of this fact in the following claim.

Claim. For any co-bipartite graph G with bipartitions A and B with all the notations as described above, if there are no universal vertices in A and $|A| \geqslant 1$, $mvc(G) = p + q - 2$.

It is easy to see that for any graph G, if the number of guards is one less than the number of vertices, the defender always has a winning strategy. Therefore, in our case, $evc(G) \leqslant p + q - 1$.

Thus, for all co-bipartite graphs (other than cliques) we have:

$$mvc(G) = p + q - 2 \text{ and } p + q - 2 \leqslant evc(G) \leqslant p + q - 1.$$

Now, one easy way to obtain a polynomial time algorithm for co-bipartite graphs is to use the PSPACE algorithm given by Fomin et al. (2010), as follows. When G is a co-bipartite graph on n vertices which is not a clique, the based on the above, we have that $mvc(G)$ is $n - 2$ and $evc(G)$ is either $n - 2$ or $n - 1$. For $k \in \{n - 2, n - 1\}$, the value of $\binom{n}{k}$ is at most n^2. This is the number of vertices in the multigraph obtained by Fomin et al. (2010). The number of edges of the multigraph is at most the square of number of vertices, multiplied by the number of edges of G. The construction of this graph can therefore be done in polynomial time, using the procedure given by Fomin et al. (2010). It is also possible to identify whether $evc(G) = k$ where $k \in \{n - 2, n - 1\}$ in polynomial time using the algorithm given by Fomin et al. (2010).

This running time can be improved to $O(n^2)$ as follows. Since G is not a clique, at least one vertex of A is not a universal vertex. From results in Babu et al. (2020), it follows that for $evc(G) = mvc(G) = n - 2$, for each vertex v there must be a vertex cover of G of size $n - 2$ that contains v and all cut vertices of G. Note that a cobipartite graph with bipartition (A, B) can have at most one cut vertex in A and at most one B. Further, a vertex $u \in A$ is a cut vertex if and only if $N(B) \cap A = \{u\}$. Likewise, a vertex $u \in B$ is a cut vertex if and only if $N(A) \cap B = \{u\}$. Therefore, we can enumerate the set of cut vertices in linear time, and check if the necessary condition holds in $O(n^2)$ time.

We will also argue that this necessary condition is also sufficient to guarantee $evc(G) = n - 2$, thus completing the description of an $O(n^2)$ algorithm to determine $evc(G)$ when G is a cobipartite graph. Suppose that the necessary condition for $evc(G) = mvc(G) = n - 2$ holds. Then every minimum vertex cover of G must contain exactly $|A| - 1$ vertices of A and exactly $|B| - 1$ vertices from B. Therefore, if v is a universal vertex in B, then v must be present in every minimum vertex cover of G. Further, $|A| > 1$ and no vertex of A is a pendant vertex. It also follows from the necessary condition that A must have at least two non-cut, non-universal vertices. Similarly, B must also contain at least two non-universal, non-cut vertices.

Under the necessary condition, we can now show that $evc(G) = n - 2$. Each configuration will have the following invariant: all cut vertices occupied by guards, exactly one of the non-cut, non-universal vertex of A and exactly one of the non-cut non-universal vertex of B are unoccupied and all other vertices occupied. If an attack on an edge inside A or B happens, the unguarded endpoint of that edge must be a non-cut, non-universal vertex of G. A rearrangement of guards to achieve a symmetric configuration can be done easily. Consider an attack on an edge $u - v$ with $u \in A$ and $v \in B$, when v is not occupied. Then v is not a cut vertex of G and there is another $v' \in B$ which has a neighbor u' in A and v' has a guard. We can move the guards from u to v, v' to u' and a sequence of other movements inside cliques B and A to maintain our invariant. This concludes our proof.

Remark 1. We note that the problem of determining the EVC of cobipartite graphs can also be reduced the problem to a "reachability game" played on a graph of size poly(n), leading to an $O(n^4)$ algorithm Grädel et al. (2002).

5 Concluding Remarks

We established the hardness of ETERNAL VERTEX COVER on bipartite graphs of constant diameter. We also showed that, under standard complexity-theoretic assumptions, the problem does not admit a polynomial compression on these graph classes when parameterized by the number of guards. Because of the relationship between $mvc(G)$ and $evc(G)$, this also implies hardness when parameterized by the vertex cover number. In the light of these developments, it will be interesting to pursue improved FPT and approximation algorithms for these classes of graphs. It is also unclear if ETERNAL VERTEX COVER is in NP even on these classes of graphs.

Remark 2. The full version of this paper can be found on ArXiV (Babu et al. 2022). The Appendix has a different algorithm with a comparable running time in the context of Theorem 2.

Acknowledgments. The authors thank Pratik Tale for pointing out a correction in a previous version of this paper, and to the anonymous reviewers of CSR for their very detailed comments that have helped improve the presentation of the paper. In particular, we note that the suggestion in Remark 1 was pointed out by one of the reviewers.

References

Araki, H., Fujito, T., Inoue, S.: On the eternal vertex cover numbers of generalized trees. IEICE Trans. Fundam. Electron. Commun. Comput. Sci. **98–A**(6), 1153–1160 (2015)

Babu, J., Chandran, L.S., Francis, M.C., Prabhakaran, V., Rajendraprasad, D., Warrier, N.J.: On graphs whose eternal vertex cover number and vertex cover number coincide. Discret. Appl. Math. (2021a, in press)

Babu, J., Misra, N., Nanoti, S.: Eternal vertex cover on bipartite and co-bipartite graphs. CoRR, abs/2201.03820 (2022)

Babu, J., Prabhakaran, V.: A new lower bound for the eternal vertex cover number of graphs. J. Comb. Optim. 27–39 (2021)

Babu, J., Prabhakaran, V., Sharma, A.: A linear time algorithm for computing the eternal vertex cover number of cactus graphs. arXiv, Discrete Mathematics (2020)

Babu, J., Prabhakaran, V., Sharma, A.: A substructure based lower bound for eternal vertex cover number. Theoret. Comput. Sci. **890**, 87–104 (2021)

Cygan, M., et al.: Parameterized Algorithms. Springer, Cham (2015). https://doi.org/10.1007/978-3-319-21275-3

Diestel, R.: Graph Theory. Springer, Cham (2017)

Dom, M., Lokshtanov, D., Saurabh, S.: Kernelization lower bounds through colors and IDs. ACM Trans. Algorithms **11**(2), 13:1–13:20 (2014)

Downey, R.G., Fellows, M.R.: Fundamentals of Parameterized Complexity. Springer, London (2013). https://doi.org/10.1007/978-1-4471-5559-1

Flum, J., Grohe, M.: Parameterized Complexity Theory. Springer, Heidelberg (2006). https://doi.org/10.1007/3-540-29953-X

Fomin, F.V., Gaspers, S., Golovach, P.A., Kratsch, D., Saurabh, S.: Parameterized algorithm for eternal vertex cover. Inf. Process. Lett. **110**(16), 702–706 (2010)

Fomin, F.V., Lokshtanov, D., Saurabh, S., Zehavi, M.: Kernelization: Theory of Parameterized Preprocessing. Cambridge University Press, Cambridge (2019)

Fujito, T., Nakamura, T.: Eternal connected vertex cover problem. In: Chen, J., Feng, Q., Xu, J. (eds.) TAMC 2020. LNCS, vol. 12337, pp. 181–192. Springer, Cham (2020). https://doi.org/10.1007/978-3-030-59267-7_16

Grädel, E., Thomas, W., Wilke, T. (eds.): Automata, Logics, and Infinite Games: A Guide to Current Research. LNCS, vol. 2500. Springer, Heidelberg (2002). https://doi.org/10.1007/3-540-36387-4

Klostermeyer, W., Mynhardt, C.M.: Graphs with equal eternal vertex cover and eternal domination numbers. Discret. Math. **311**(14), 1371–1379 (2011)

Klostermeyer, W.F., Mynhardt, C.M.: Edge protection in graphs. Australas. J. Comb. **45**, 235–250 (2009)

Niedermeier, R.: Invitation to Fixed-Parameter Algorithms. Oxford University Press, Oxford (2006)

Non-crossing Shortest Paths in Undirected Unweighted Planar Graphs in Linear Time

Lorenzo Balzotti[1(✉)] and Paolo G. Franciosa[2]

[1] Dipartimento di Scienze di Base e Applicate per l'Ingegneria, Sapienza Università di Roma, Via Antonio Scarpa, 16, 00161 Rome, Italy
lorenzo.balzotti@sbai.uniroma1.it

[2] Dipartimento di Scienze Statistiche, Sapienza Università di Roma, p.le Aldo Moro 5, 00185 Rome, Italy
paolo.franciosa@uniroma1.it

Abstract. Given a set of terminal pairs on the external face of an undirected unweighted planar graph, we give a linear-time algorithm for computing the union of non-crossing shortest paths joining each terminal pair, if such paths exist. This allows us to compute distances between each terminal pair, within the same time bound.

We also give a novel concept of *incremental shortest path* subgraph of a planar graph, i.e., a partition of the planar embedding in subregions that preserve distances, that can be of interest itself.

Keywords: planar graphs · non-crossing paths · shortest paths · undirected unweighted graphs · multiple pairs · external face

1 Introduction

The problem of computing shortest paths in planar graphs arises in application fields such as intelligent transportation system (ITS) and geographic information system (GIS) [22,36], route planning [6,16,30], logistic [27], traffic simulations [3] and robotics [23]. In particular, non-crossing paths in a planar graph are studied to optimize VLSI layout [7], where two *non-crossing* paths may share edges and vertices, but they do not cross each other in the plane.

We are given a planar graph $G = (V, E)$, where V is a set of n vertices and E is a set of edges, with $|E| = O(n)$. The graph has a fixed embedding, and we are also given a set of k terminal pairs $(s_1, t_1), (s_2, t_2), \ldots, (s_k, t_k)$ lying on the external face of G. The non-crossing shortest paths problem (NCSP problem) consists in computing the union of k non-crossing shortest paths in G, each joining a terminal pair (s_i, t_i), provided that such non-crossing paths exist (they exist if and only if the terminal pairs are *well-formed*, see Subsect. 2.2).

A. S. Kulikov and S. Raskhodnikova (Eds.): CSR 2022, LNCS 13296, pp. 77–95, 2022.
https://doi.org/10.1007/978-3-031-09574-0_6

State of the Art. Takahashi *et al.* [33] solved the NCSP problem in a non-negative edge-weighted planar graph in $O(n \log k)$ time (actually, in their paper the time complexity is $O(n \log n)$, that can easily reduced to $O(n \log k)$ by applying the planar single source shortest path algorithm by Henzinger *et al.* [20]). Their result is improved by Steiger in $O(n \log\log k)$ time [32], exploiting the algorithm by Italiano *et al.* [21]. These two algorithms maintain the same time complexity also in the unweighted case.

Our Results. In this paper, we solve the NCSP problem on unweighted planar graphs in $O(n)$ time. We improve, in the unweighted case, the results in [32,33]. By applying the technique in [4] we can compute distances between all terminal pairs in linear time.

Our algorithm relies on two main results:

- an algorithm due to Eisenstat and Klein [11], that gives in $O(n)$ time an implicit representation of a sequence of shortest-path trees in an undirected unweighted planar graph G, where each tree is rooted in a vertex of the external face of G. Note that, if we want to compute shortest paths from the implicit representation of shortest path trees given in [11], then we spend $\Theta(kn)$ time; this happens when all k shortest paths share a subpath of $\Theta(n)$ edges.
- the novel concept of *incremental shortest paths (ISP) subgraph* of a graph G, introduced in Sect. 3, that is a subgraph incrementally built by adding a sequence of shortest paths in G starting from the infinite face of G. We show that an ISP subgraph of G partitions the embedding of G into *distance preserving* regions, i.e., for any two vertices a, b in G lying in the same region R it is always possible to find a shortest path in G joining a and b that is contained in R.

Related Work. Our article fits into a wider context of computing many distances in planar graphs. In the positive weighted case, the all pairs shortest paths (APSP) problem is solved by Frederickson in $O(n^2)$ time [14], while the single source shortest paths (SSSP) problem is solved in linear time by Henzinger *et al.* [20]. The best known algorithm for computing many distances in planar graphs is due to Gawrychowski *et al.* [15] and it allows us to compute the distance between any two vertices in $O(\log n)$ time after a preprocessing requiring $O(n^{3/2})$ time. In the planar unweighted case, SSSP trees rooted at vertices in the external face can be computed in linear time as in [11]. More results on many distances problem can be found in [8–10,13,28,29].

If we are interested in distances from any vertex in the external face to any other vertex, then we can use Klein's algorithm [24] that, with a preprocessing of $O(n \log n)$ time, answers to each distance query in $O(\log n)$ time.

Kowalik and Kurowski [25] deal with the problem of deciding whether any two query vertices of an unweighted planar graph are closer than a fixed constant k. After a preprocessing of $O(n)$ time, their algorithm answers in $O(1)$ time, and, if so, a shortest path between them is returned.

Non-crossing shortest paths are also used to compute max-flow in undirected planar graphs [18,19,31]. In particular, they are used to compute the vitality of edges and vertices with respect to the max-flow [1,2,5].

Balzotti and Franciosa [4] show that, given the union of a set of non-crossing shortest paths in a planar graph, the lengths of each shortest path can be computed in linear time. This improves the result of [33], that can only be applied when the union of the shortest paths is a forest.

Wagner and Weihe [35] present an $O(n)$ time algorithm for finding edge-disjoint (not necessarily shortest) paths in a undirected planar graph such that each path connects two specified vertices on the infinite face of the graph.

Improved Results. We specialize the problem of finding k non-crossing shortest paths in [33] to the unweighted case, decreasing the time complexity from $O(n \log k)$ to $O(n)$ (for every k). Therefore, in the case of unweighted graphs we improve the results in [12,26,34].

Erickson and Nayyeri [12] generalized the work in [33] to the case in which the k terminal pairs lie on h face boundaries. They prove that k non-crossing paths, if they exists, can be found in $2^{O(h^2)} n \log k$ time. Applying our results, if the graph is unweighted, then the time complexity decreases to $2^{O(h^2)} n$.

The same authors of [33] used their algorithm to compute k non-crossing rectilinear paths with minimum total length in a plane with r obstacles [34]. They found such paths in $O(n \log n)$ time, where $n = r + k$, which reduces to $O(n)$ time if the graph is unweighted by using our results.

Kusakari *et al.* [26] showed that a set of non-crossing forests in a planar graph can be found in $O(n \log n)$ time, where two forest F_1 and F_2 are *non-crossing* if for any pair of paths $p_1 \subseteq F_1$ and $p_2 \subseteq F_2$, p_1 and p_2 are non-crossing. With our results, if the graph is unweighted, then the time complexity becomes linear.

Our Approach. We represent the structure of terminal pairs by a partial order called *genealogy tree.* We introduce a new class of graphs, ISP subgraphs, that partition a planar graph into regions that preserve distances. Our algorithm is split in two parts.

In the first part we use Eisenstat and Klein's algorithm that gives a sequence of shortest path trees rooted in the vertices of the external face. We choose some specific shortest paths from each tree to obtain a sequence of ISP subgraphs $X_1, \ldots X_k$. By using the distance preserving property of regions generated by ISP subgraphs', we prove that X_i contains a shortest s_i-t_i path, for all $i \in \{1, \ldots, k\}$.

In the second part of our algorithm, we extract from each X_i a shortest s_i-t_i path and we obtain a set of non-crossing shortest paths that is our goal. In this part we strongly use the partial order given by the genealogy tree.

Structure of the Paper. After giving some definitions in Sect. 2, in Sect. 3 we explain the main theoretical novelty. In Sect. 4 first we resume Eisenstat and Klein's algorithm in Subsect. 4.1, then in Subsects. 4.2 and 4.3 we show the two parts of our algorithm, and we prove the whole computational complexity. Conclusions are given in Sect. 5.

2 Definitions

Let G be a plane graph, i.e., a planar graph with a fixed planar embedding. We denote by f_G^∞ (or simply f^∞) its unique infinite face, it will be also referred to as the *external* face of G. Given a face f of G we denote by ∂f its boundary cycle. Topological and combinatorial definitions of planar graph, embedding and face can be found in [17].

We recall standard union and intersection operators on graphs, for convenience we define the empty graph as a graph without edges.

Definition 1. *Given two undirected (or directed) graphs $G = (V(G), E(G))$ and $H = (V(H), E(H))$, we define the following operations and relations:*

- $G \cup H = (V(G) \cup V(H), E(G) \cup E(H))$,
- $G \cap H = (V(G) \cap V(H), E(G) \cap E(H))$,
- $G \subseteq H \iff V(G) \subseteq V(H)$ *and* $E(G) \subseteq E(H)$,
- $G \setminus H = (V(G), E(G) \setminus E(H))$.

Given an undirected (resp., directed) graph $G = (V(G), E(G))$, given an edge (resp., dart) e and a vertex v we write, for short, $e \in G$ in place of $e \in E(G)$ and $v \in G$ in place of $v \in V(G)$.

We denote by uv the edge whose endpoints are u and v and we denote by $\overrightarrow{uv}$ the dart from u to v. For every dart $\overrightarrow{uv}$ we define $\text{rev}[\overrightarrow{uv}] = \overrightarrow{vu}$ and $\text{head}[\overrightarrow{uv}] = v$. For every vertex $v \in V(G)$ we define the *degree of* v as $deg(v) = |\{e \in E(G) \mid v \text{ is an endpoint of } e\}|$.

For each $\ell \in \mathbb{N}$ we denote by $[\ell]$ the set $\{1, \ldots, \ell\}$.

Given a (possibly not simple) cycle C, we define the *region bounded by* C, denoted by R_C, as the maximal subgraph of G whose external face has C as boundary.

2.1 Paths and Non-crossing Paths

Given a directed path p we denote by $\overline{p}$ its undirected version, in which each dart $\overrightarrow{ab}$ is replaced by edge ab; moreover, we denote by $\text{rev}[p]$ its reverse version, in which each dart $\overrightarrow{ab}$ is replaced by dart $\overrightarrow{ba}$.

We say that a path p is an *a-b path* if its extremal vertices are a and b; clearly, if p is a directed path, then p starts in a and it ends in b. Moreover, given $i \in [k]$, we denote by *i-path* an s_i-t_i path, where s_i, t_i is one of the terminal pairs on the external face.

Given an a-b path p and a b-c path q, we define $p \circ q$ as the (possibly not simple) a-c path obtained by the union of p and q.

Let p be a simple path and let $a, b \in V(p)$. We denote by $p[a, b]$ the subpath of p with extremal vertices a and b.

We denote by $w(p)$ the length of a path p of a general positive weighted graph G. If G is unweighted, then we denote the length of p as $|p|$, that is the number of edges.

We say that two paths in a plane graph G are *non-crossing* if the (undirected) curves they describe in the graph embedding do not cross each other, non-crossing paths may share vertices and/or edges or darts. This property obviously depends on the embedding of the graph; a combinatorial definition of non-crossing paths can be based on the *Heffter-Edmonds-Ringel rotation principle* [17]. Crossing and non-crossing paths are given in Fig. 1.

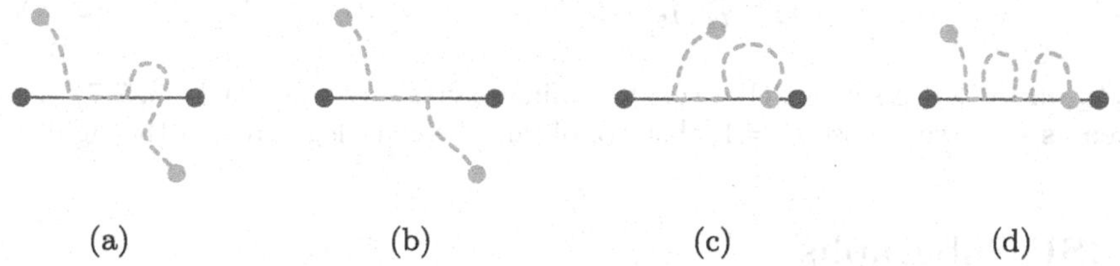

Fig. 1. paths in (a) and (b) are crossing, while paths in (c) and (d) are non-crossing.

2.2 Genealogy Tree

W.l.o.g., we assume that terminal pairs are distinct, i.e., there is no pair $i, j \in [k]$ such that $\{s_i, t_i\} = \{s_j, t_j\}$. Let γ_i be the path in f_G^∞ that goes clockwise from s_i to t_i, for $i \in [k]$. We also assume that pairs $\{(s_i, t_i)\}_{i\in[k]}$ are *well-formed*, i.e., for all $j, \ell \in [k]$ either $\gamma_j \subset \gamma_\ell$ or $\gamma_j \supset \gamma_\ell$ or γ_j and γ_ℓ have no common edges; otherwise it can be easily seen that it is not possible to find a set of k non-crossing paths joining terminal pairs. This property can be easily verified in linear time, since it corresponds to checking that a string of parentheses is balanced, and it can be done by a sequential scan of the string.

We define here a partial ordering as in [4,33] that represents the inclusion relation between γ_i's. This relation intuitively corresponds to an *adjacency* relation between non-crossing shortest paths joining each pair. Choose an arbitrary i^* such that there are neither s_j nor t_j, with $j \neq i^*$, walking on f^∞ from s_{i^*} to t_{i^*} (either clockwise or counterclockwise), and let e^* be an arbitrary edge on that walk. For each $j \in [k]$, we can assume that $e^* \notin \gamma_j$, indeed if it is not true, then it suffices to switch s_j with t_j. We say that $i \prec j$ if $\gamma_i \subset \gamma_j$. We define the *genealogy tree* T_G of a set of well-formed terminal pairs as the transitive reduction of poset $([k], \prec)$. W.l.o.g., we assume that $i^* = 1$, hence the root of T_G is 1.

If $i \prec j$, then we say that i is a *descendant* of j and j is an *ancestor* of i. Moreover, we say that j is the *parent of* i, and we write $p(i) = j$, if $i \prec j$ and there is no r such that $i \prec r$ and $r \prec j$. Figure 2 shows a set of well-formed terminal pairs, and the corresponding genealogy tree for $i^* = 1$.

From now on, in all figures we draw f_G^∞ by a solid light grey line. W.l.o.g., we assume that the external face is a simple cycle, hence, G is a biconnected graph. Indeed, if not, it suffices to solve the NCSP problem in each biconnected component.

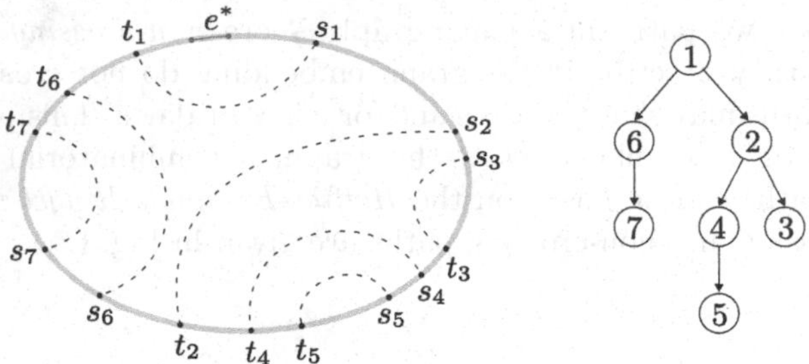

Fig. 2. on the left a set of well-formed terminal pairs. Any value in $\{1,3,5,7\}$ can be chosen as i^*. If we choose $i^* = 1$, then we obtain the genealogy tree on the right.

3 ISP Subgraphs

In this section we introduce the concept of *incremental shortest paths (ISP) subgraph* of a graph G, that is a subgraph incrementally built by adding a sequence of shortest paths in G starting from f_G^∞ (see Definition 2). The interest towards ISP subgraphs is due to the fact that for any two vertices a, b in G lying in a same face f of the ISP subgraph there is always a shortest path in G joining a and b contained in f (boundary included). All the results of this section hold for positive weighted graphs, where the length of a path is the sum of edge weights instead of the number of edges.

This is the main novel result of this paper, that allows us to prove that, in order to build the union of shortest paths joining terminal pairs, we can start from the union of some of the shortest paths computed by the algorithm in [11].

Definition 2. *A graph X is an* incremental shortest paths (ISP) subgraph *of a positive weighted graph G if $X = X_r$, where $X_0, X_1, \ldots, X_r$ is a sequence of subgraphs of G built in the following way: $X_0 = f_G^\infty$ and $X_i = X_{i-1} \cup p_i$, where p_i is a shortest x_i-y_i path in G with $x_i, y_i \in X_{i-1}$.*

Remark 1. All degree one vertices of an ISP subgraph of G are in f_G^∞.

We define now operator $\downarrow$, that given a path π and a cycle C, in case π crosses C, replaces some subpaths of π by some portions of C, as depicted in Fig. 3(b). We observe that $\pi \downarrow \partial f$ could be not a simple path even if π is.

Definition 3. *Let C be a cycle in a positive weighted graph G. Let a, b be two vertices in R_C and let π be a simple a-b path. In case $\pi \subseteq R_C$ we define $\pi \downarrow C = \pi$. Otherwise, let $(v_1, v_2, \ldots, v_{2r})$ be the ordered subset of vertices of π that satisfies the following: $\pi[a, v_1] \subseteq R_C$, $\pi[v_{2r}, b] \subseteq R_C$, $\pi[v_{2i-1}, v_{2i}]$ and R_C have no common edges and $\pi[v_{2i}, v_{2i-1}] \subseteq R_C$, for all $i \in [r]$. For every $i \in [r]$,* *let* μ_i *be the* v_{2i-1}-v_{2i} *path on* C *such that the region bounded by* $\mu_i \circ \pi[v_{2i-1}, v_{2i}]$ *does not contain* R_C*. We define* $\pi \downarrow C = \pi[a, v_1] \circ \mu_1 \circ \pi[v_2, v_3] \circ \mu_2 \ldots \circ \pi[v_{2r-2}, v_{2r-1}] \circ \mu_r \circ \pi[v_{2r}, b]$.

Definition 2 and Definition 3 are depicted in Fig. 3.

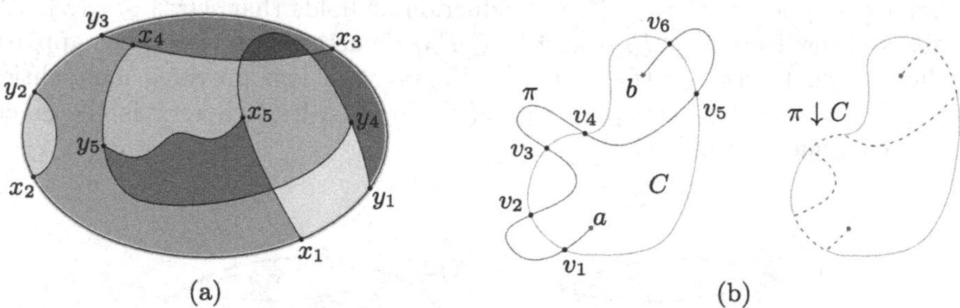

Fig. 3. (a) an ISP subgraph X of G; extremal vertices x_i, y_i of p_i are drawn, for $i \in [5]$. Different faces of X have different colors. An example of Definition 3 is given in (b).

In the following theorem we show that, given any face f of an ISP subgraph X of G, every path π in G whose extremal vertices are in $R_{\partial f}$ is not shorter than $\pi \downarrow \partial f$.

Theorem 1. *Let* X *be an ISP subgraph of a positive weighted graph* G*. Let* f *be any face of* X*, and let* a, b *be two distinct vertices in* $R_{\partial f}$*. For any* a-b *path* π *we have* $w(\pi \downarrow \partial f) \leq w(\pi)$.

Proof. Let $\{X_i\}_{i\in[r]}$ be the sequence of ISP subgraphs such that $X = X_r$, and let p_i be the path that builds X_i from X_{i-1}. We assume that p_i has no vertices in X_{i-1} other than its endpoints x_i and y_i, otherwise we can split p_i on intersections with X_{i-1} and repeatedly apply the same proof to each portion of p_i. We prove the thesis by induction on j for every choice of a face f of X_j, $a, b \in R_{\partial f}$ and a-b path π.

In the base case, where $j = 1$, there are exactly two faces A and B in X_1 other than f_G^∞. Let $a, b \in V(R_{\partial A})$ (the same argument holds for B) and let π be any a-b path. In case $\pi \subseteq R_{\partial A}$ we have $\pi \downarrow \partial A = \pi$, hence the thesis trivially holds. In case $\pi \nsubseteq R_{\partial A}$, then $\pi \downarrow \partial A$ is not longer than π because some subpaths of π have been replaced by subpaths of p_1 with the same extremal vertices and p_1 is a shortest path.

We assume that the thesis holds for all $i < j$ and we prove it for j. Let f be a face of X_j and let f' be the unique face of X_{j-1} such that $f \subset f'$ (Fig. 4(a) and Fig. 4(b) show faces f and f', respectively). Let $a, b \in V(R_{\partial f})$ and let π be an a-b path. Three cases may occur:

case $\pi \subseteq R_{\partial f}$**:** the thesis trivial holds, since $\pi \downarrow \partial f = \pi$;

case $\pi \subseteq R_{\partial f'}$ **and** $\pi \not\subseteq R_{\partial f}$**:** since $\pi \subseteq R_{\partial f'}$ and $\pi \not\subseteq R_{\partial f}$, then π crosses p_j an even number of times, thus $\pi \downarrow \partial f$ is not longer than π, since some subpaths of π have been replaced by subpaths of p_j with the same extremal vertices and p_j is a shortest path (see Fig. 4(c) where π is the red and dashed path);

case $\pi \not\subseteq R_{\partial f'}$**:** since $f \subseteq f'$, it is easy to see that $\pi \downarrow \partial f = (\pi \downarrow \partial f') \downarrow \partial f$. Let us consider $\pi' = \pi \downarrow \partial f'$. By induction, it holds that $w(\pi') \leq w(\pi)$. We observe now that $\pi' \subseteq R_{\partial f'}$ and $\pi' \not\subseteq R_{\partial f}$, hence the previous case applies, showing that $w(\pi' \downarrow \partial f) \leq w(\pi')$. Finally, the two previous inequalities imply $w(\pi \downarrow \partial f) \leq w(\pi \downarrow \partial f') \leq w(\pi)$ (see Fig. 4(c) where π is the green and continue path). □

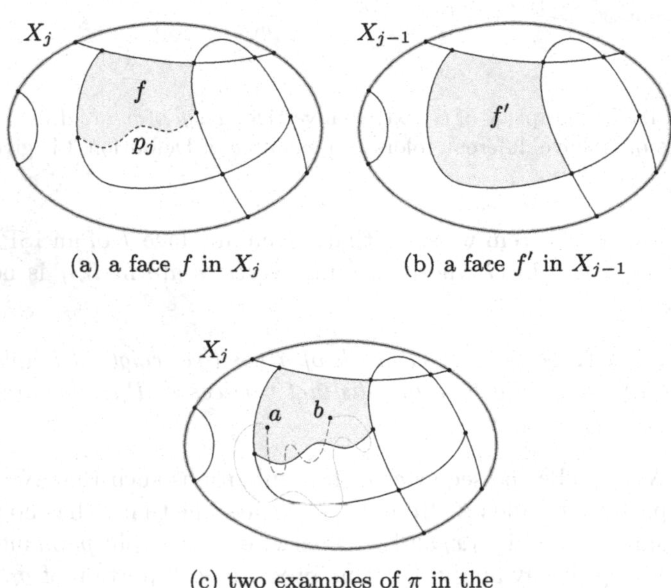

(a) a face f in X_j

(b) a face f' in X_{j-1}

(c) two examples of π in the second case (dashed red) and third case (continuous green)

Fig. 4. in (a) and (b) faces f and f' build on the ISP graph in Fig. 3(a). In (c) we depict the second and third case of the proof of Theorem 1.

We can state now the main property of ISP subgraphs.

Corollary 1. *Let X be an ISP subgraph of G and let f be any face of X. For every $a, b \in R_{\partial f}$ there exists a shortest a-b path of G contained in $R_{\partial f}$.*

4 Our Algorithm

We summarize in Subsect. 4.1 the result of Eisenstat and Klein's paper [11], that deals with the multiple-source shortest paths problem. For the sake of clarity, we split our algorithm in two parts:

- in Subsect. 4.2 we introduce algorithm **NCSPsupergraph**, that builds a sequence $\{X_i\}_{i\in[k]}$ of subgraphs of G such that X_k contains a shortest path for each terminal pair, and it possibly contains some extra edges. We anticipate that $X_i \cup f_G^\infty$ is an ISP subgraph of G, for all $i \in [k]$.
- in Subsect. 4.3 we present algorithm **NCSPunion** that, by using the sequence of graphs $\{X_i\}_{i\in[k]}$ found by algorithm **NCSPsupergraph**, builds a directed graph that is exactly the union of the shortest directed paths joining each terminal pair contained in the output of algorithm **NCSPsupergraph**.

4.1 Eisenstat and Klein's Result

The algorithm in [11] takes as input an undirected unweighted planar graph G, where $v_1, v_2, \ldots, v_r$ is the sequence of vertices in the external face of G in clockwise order, and returns an implicit representation of a sequence of shortest path trees $\mathcal{T}_i$, for $i \in [r]$, where each $\mathcal{T}_i$ is rooted in v_i.

The sequence of trees $\mathcal{T}_i$, for $i \in [r]$, is represented by explicitly listing the darts in $\mathcal{T}_1$, and listing the darts that are added to transform $\mathcal{T}_i$ into $\mathcal{T}_{i+1}$, for $1 < i \leq r$ (for each added dart from x to y, the unique dart that goes to y in $\mathcal{T}_i$ is deleted; with the only two exceptions of the added dart leading to v_i, and the deleted dart leading to v_{i+1}). Hence, the output of their algorithm is $\mathcal{T}_1$ and a sequence of sets of darts. A key result in [11] shows that if a dart d appears in $\mathcal{T}_{i+1} \setminus \mathcal{T}_i$, then d cannot appear in any $\mathcal{T}_{j+1} \setminus \mathcal{T}_j$, for $j > i$. Thus the implicit representation of the sequence of shortest path trees has size $O(n)$. This representation can be computed in $O(n)$ time.

4.2 Algorithm NCSPsupergraph

Algorithm **NCSPsupergraph** builds a sequence $\{X_i\}_{i\in[k]}$ of subgraphs of G by using the sequence of shortest path trees given by Eisenstat and Klein's algorithm. We point out that we are not interested in the shortest path trees rooted at every vertex of f_G^∞, but we only need the shortest path trees rooted in s_i's. So, we define T_i as the shortest path tree rooted in s_i, for $i \in [k]$, i.e., $T_i = \mathcal{T}_{s_i}$. We denote by $T_i[v]$ the path in T_i from s_i to v.

The algorithm starts by computing the first subgraph X_1, that is just the undirected 1-path in T_1, i.e., $\overline{T_1[t_1]}$ (we recall that all T_i's trees given by algorithm in [11] are rooted directed tree, thus $\overline{T_1[t_1]}$ is the undirected version of T_1). Then the sequence of subgraphs X_i, for $i = 2, \ldots, k$ is computed by adding some undirected paths extracted from the shortest path trees T_i's defined by Eisenstat and Klein's algorithm.

We define the set $H_i \subseteq X_i$ of vertices h such that at least one dart d is added while passing from T_{i-1} to T_i such that head$[d] = h$. Hence, H_i is the set of vertices of X_i whose parent in T_i differs from the parent in T_{i-1}. At iteration i, we add path $\overline{T_i[h]}$ to X_i, for each h in H_i.

Algorithm `NCSPsupergraph`**:**

Input: an undirected unweighted planar embedded graph G and k well-formed terminal pairs of vertices (s_i, t_i), for $i \in [k]$, on the external face of G
Output: an undirected graph X_k that contains a set of non-crossing paths $P = \{\pi_1, \ldots, \pi_k\}$, where π_i is a shortest s_i-t_i path, for $i \in [k]$

1 Compute a shortest path tree T_1 rooted in s_1;
2 $X_1 = \overline{T_1[t_1]}$;
3 **for** $i = 2, \ldots, k$ **do**
4     $X_i = X_{i-1}$;
5   Compute T_i from T_{i-1} by the algorithm of Eisenstat and Klein [11];
6   Compute the set H_i of vertices of X_i whose parent in T_i differs from the parent in T_{i-1};
7   For all $h \in H_i$, $X_i = X_i \cup \overline{T_i[h]}$;
8   Let η_i be the undirected path on T_i that starts in t_i and walks backwards until a vertex in X_i is reached;
9     $X_i = X_i \cup \eta_i$;

Lemma 1. *Algorithm* `NCSPsupergraph` *has* $O(n)$ *time complexity.*

Proof. Eisenstat and Klein's algorithm requires $O(n)$ time, implying that the H_i's and the T_i's can be found in $O(n)$ time. Algorithm `NCSPsupergraph` visits each edge of G at most $O(1)$ times (in Line 7, $\overline{T_i[h]}$ can be found by starting in h and by walking backwards on T_i until a vertex of X_i is found). The thesis follows. □

Figure 5 shows how algorithm `NCSPsupergraph` builds X_4 starting from X_3. Starting from X_3 in Fig. 5(a), Fig. 5(b) shows the darts whose head is in H_4. Consider the unique dart d whose head is the vertex x: we observe that $\overline{d}$ is already in X_3, this happens because rev$[d] \in T_3[t_3]$. Indeed, it is possible that at iteration i some portions of some undirected paths that we add in Line 7 are already in X_{i-1}. Figure 5(c) highlights $\bigcup_{h \in H_4} T_4[h]$ and η_4, while in Fig. 5(d) X_4 is drawn.

Subgraphs $\{X_i\}_{i \in [k]}$ built by algorithm `NCSPsupergraph`, together with f_G^∞, satisfy all the hypothesis of Theorem 1. Indeed, paths added in Line 7 and Line 9 are shortest paths in G joining vertices in X_{i-1}, thus fulfilling Definition 2. So, we exploit Theorem 1 to prove that X_i contains an i-path, for $i \in [k]$, and, in particular, X_k contains a set of non-crossing paths $P = \{\pi_1, \ldots, \pi_k\}$, where π_i is a shortest i-path, for $i \in [k]$. The main idea is to show that X_i contains an

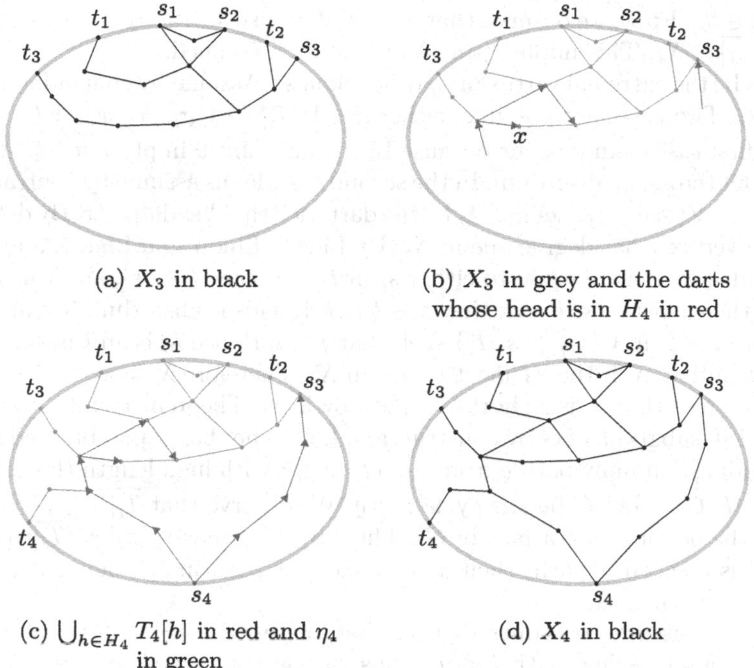

(a) X_3 in black

(b) X_3 in grey and the darts whose head is in H_4 in red

(c) $\bigcup_{h \in H_4} T_4[h]$ in red and η_4 in green

(d) X_4 in black

Fig. 5. algorithm `NCSPsupergraph`: graph X_4 is built starting from X_3.

undirected path that has the same length as the shortest i-path found by the algorithm by Eisenstat and Klein. This is proved in Theorem 2.

Given a subgraph X of G, we say that an i-path p is the *leftmost i-path in X* if for every i-path $q \subseteq X$ it holds $R_{p \circ \gamma_i} \subseteq R_{q \circ \gamma_i}$.

We say that an undirected path p *always turns left* if p chooses the leftmost edge, w.r.t. the fixed embedding, in each vertex going from a to b, where a and b are the extremal vertices of p. Note that not the leftmost a-b path is not necessarily the path that starts in a and always turns left until b is reached.

Theorem 2. *Let π_i be the undirected leftmost i-path in X_i, for $i \in [k]$. The following statements hold:*

2.(1) π_i is the s_i-t_i path in X_i that always turns left, for $i \in [k]$,
2.(2) π_i is a shortest i-path, for $i \in [k]$,
2.(3) for all $i, j \in [k]$, π_i and π_j are non-crossing.

Proof. We prove all the statements separately.

2.(1) For convenience, for every $i \in [k]$, let λ_i be the undirected path on X_i that starts in s_i and always turns left until it reaches either t_i or a vertex x of degree one in X_i; we observe that λ_i is well defined and, by Remark 1, $x \in f^{\infty}_G$. We have to prove that $\lambda_i = \pi_i$.

Let $i \in [k]$. First, we observe that $s_i \in X_i$ because $s_{i-1} \in H_i$, thus, by Line 7, $\overline{T_i[s_{i-1}]} \subseteq X_i$. This implies $s_i \in X_i$ as we have claimed.
Let x be the extremal vertex of λ_i other than s_i. Assume by contradiction that $x \neq t_i$. Two cases are possible: either $x \in V(f_G^\infty) \setminus V(\gamma_i)$ or $x \in V(\gamma_i) \setminus \{t_i\}$. The first case cannot occur because Line 7 and Line 9 imply $\overline{T_i[t_i]} \subseteq X_i$, thus λ_i would cross η_i, absurdum. In the second case, let us assume by contradiction that $x \in V(\gamma_i) \setminus \{t_i\}$. Let $d \in \lambda_i$ be the dart such that head$[d] = x$. By definition of λ_i, vertex x has degree one in X_i. By Line 2, Line 7 and Line 9, all vertices with degree one are equal to either s_ℓ or t_ℓ, for some $\ell \in [k]$, and this implies that there exists $j < i$ such that $x \in \{s_j, t_j\}$. This is absurdum because there is not s_j or t_j in $V(\gamma_i) \setminus \{s_i, t_i\}$ such that $j < i$. Hence λ_i is an i-path, and, by its definition, λ_i is the leftmost i-path in X_i. Therefore $\lambda_i = \pi_i$.

2.(2) We prove that π_i is a shortest i-path by using Theorem 1, indeed, $X_i \cup f_G^\infty$ is an ISP subgraph of G by construction. Let G' be the graph obtained from G by adding a dummy path q from s_i to t_i in f_G^∞ with high length (for example, $|q| = |E(G)|$). Let C be the cycle $\pi_i \circ q$. We observe that $\overline{T_i[t_i]} \downarrow C = \pi_i$ and C is the boundary of a face of G'. Thus, by Theorem 1, $|\pi_i| \leq |\overline{T_i[t_i]}|$. Since $\overline{T_i[t_i]}$ is a shortest path, then π_i is a shortest path in G', hence it also is a shortest path in G.

2.(3) Let us assume by contradiction that there exist $i, j \in [k]$ such that π_i and π_j are crossing, with $i < j$. Thus π_j has not turned always left in X_j, absurdum. □

4.3 Algorithm NCSPunion

The graph X_k given by the algorithm **NCSPsupergraph** contains a shortest path for each terminal pair, but X_k may also contain edges that do not belong to any shortest path. To overcome this problem we apply algorithm **NCSPunion**, that builds a directed graph $Y_k = \bigcup_{i \in [k]} \rho_i$, where ρ_i is a directed shortest i-path, for $i \in [k]$. Moreover, we prove that Y_k can be built in linear time. This implies that, by using the results in [4], we can compute the length of all shortest i-paths, for $i \in [k]$, in $O(n)$ time (see Theorem 4).

We use the sequence of subgraphs $\{X_i\}_{i \in [k]}$. By Theorem 2, we know that X_i contains a shortest undirected i-path π_i and we can list its edges in $O(|\pi_i|)$ time. But if an edge e is shared by many π_i's, then e is visited many times. Thus obtaining $\bigcup_{i \in [k]} \pi_i$ by this easy procedure requires $O(kn)$ time. To overcome this problem, we should visit every edge in $\bigcup_{i \in [k]} \pi_i$ only a constant number of times.

Now we introduce two useful lemmata the will be used later. The first lemma shows that two uncomparable directed paths π_i and π_j (i.e., such that $i \not\prec j$ and $j \not\prec i$) in the genealogy tree T_G cannot share a dart, although it is possible that $\overrightarrow{ab} \in \pi_i$ and $\overrightarrow{ba} \in \pi_j$. The second lemma deals with the intersection of non-crossing paths joining comparable pairs.

Lemma 2. *Let π_i be a shortest directed i-path and let π_j be a shortest directed j-path, for some $i, j \in [k]$. If j is not an ancestor neither a descendant of i in T_G, then π_i and π_j have no common darts.*

Proof. Let us assume by contradiction that π_i and π_j have at least one common dart, and let d be the dart in $\pi_i \cap \pi_j$ that appears first in π_i. Let R be the region bounded by $\overline{\pi_j[s_j, \text{tail}(d)]}$, $\overline{\pi_i[s_i, \text{tail}(d)]}$ and the clockwise undirected $s_i - s_j$ path in f^∞ (Fig. 6(a) shows π_i, π_j and R). Being π_j a simple path, then π_j crosses π_i in at least one vertex in $\pi_i[s_i, \text{tail}(d)]$. Let x be the first vertex in $\pi_i[s_i, \text{tail}(d)]$ after head(d) in π_j. Now by looking to the cycle $\pi_i[x, \text{head}(d)] \circ \pi_j[\text{head}(d), x]$, it follows that π_i and π_j can be both shortest paths, absurdum (Fig. 6(b) shows this cycle). □

Lemma 3. *Let $\{\pi_i\}_{i \in [k]}$ be a set of non-crossing directed paths. Let $i, j \in [k]$, if i is a descendant of j, then $\pi_i \cap \pi_j \subseteq \pi_\ell$, for all $\ell \in [k]$ such that $i \prec \ell \prec j$.*

Proof. Let us assume π_i and π_j have at least one common vertex and choose $\ell \in [k]$ such that $i \prec \ell \prec j$. Let v be a vertex in $\pi_i \cap \pi_j$ and let Q be the region bounded by $\overline{\pi_j[s_j, v]}$, $\overline{\pi_i[s_i, v]}$ and the clockwise undirected $s_j - s_i$ path in f^∞ (region Q and vertex v are shown in Fig. 6(c)). It is clear that if $v \notin \pi_\ell$, then $\{\pi_i, \pi_j, \pi_\ell\}$ is not a set of non-crossing paths, absurdum. □

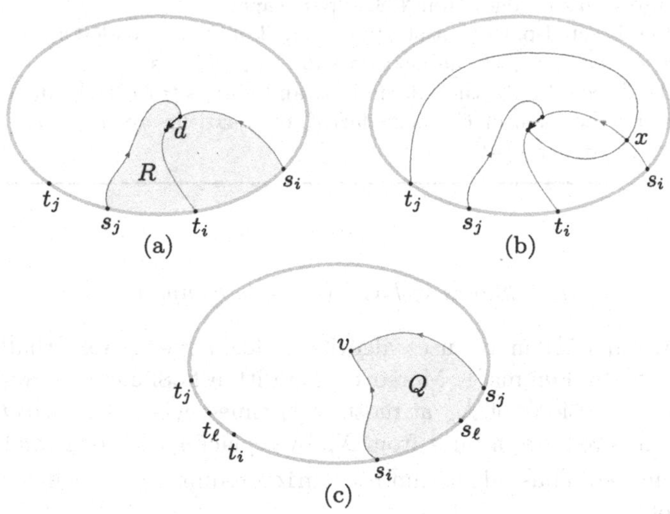

Fig. 6. in (a) and (b) paths π_j and π_i, dart d, region R and vertex x used in the proof of Lemma 2. In (c) region Q and vertex v used in the proof of Lemma 3.

Now we show how to use these two lemmata for our goals. Let ρ_i be a shortest directed i-path and let ρ_j be a shortest directed j-path, for some $i, j \in [k]$, $i \neq j$. By Lemma 2, if i and j are not comparable in T_G, then ρ_i and ρ_j have no common darts. Moreover, by Lemma 3, if i is an ancestor of j in T_G, then $\rho_i \cap \rho_j \subseteq \rho_{p(j)}$. By using these two facts, in order to list darts in ρ_i, then it suffices to find darts in $\rho_i \setminus \rho_{p(i)}$, for all $i \in [k] \setminus \{1\}$ (we remind that 1 is the root of T_G). To this goal we use algorithm NCSPunion, that builds a sequence of directed graphs $\{Y_i\}_{i\in[k]}$ such that Y_k is equal to $\bigcup_{i\in[k]} \rho_i$, where ρ_i is a shortest directed i-path, for $i \in [k]$.

We prove the correctness of algorithm NCSPunion in Theorem 3. At iteration i we compute $\rho_i \setminus \rho_{p(i)}$, showing that $\rho_i \setminus \rho_{p(i)} = \sigma_i \cup \mathrm{rev}[\tau_i]$, where σ_i and τ_i are computed in Line 5 and Line 6, respectively. We observe that if ρ_i and $\rho_{p(i)}$ have no common darts, then $\sigma_i = \mathrm{rev}[\tau_i] = \rho_i$.

To better understand Line 2 of algorithm NCSPunion, we recall that X_1 is an undirected 1-path, hence Y_1 is the directed version of this path.

Algorithm NCSPunion:

Input: an undirected unweighted planar embedded graph G and k well-formed terminal pairs of vertices (s_i, t_i), for $i \in [k]$, on the external face of G

Output: a directed graph Y_k formed by the union of directed non-crossing shortest paths from s_i to t_i, for $i \in [k]$

1 Compute X_1 as in algorithm NCSPsupergraph;
2 Y_1 is the directed version of X_1 oriented from s_1 to t_1;
3 **for** $i = 2, \ldots, k$ **do**
4   Compute X_i as in algorithm NCSPsupergraph;
5   σ_i is the directed path that starts in s_i and always turns left in X_i until either σ_i reaches t_i or the next dart d_i of σ_i satisfies $d_i \in Y_{i-1}$;
6   τ_i is the directed path that starts in t_i and always turns right in X_i until either τ_i reaches s_i or the next dart d'_i of τ_i satisfies $\mathrm{rev}[d'_i] \in Y_{i-1}$;
7     $Y_i = Y_{i-1} \cup \sigma_i \cup \mathrm{rev}[\tau_i]$;

Lemma 4. *Algorithm NCSPunion has $O(n)$ time complexity.*

Proof. Algorithm NCSPunion uses algorithm NCSPsupergraph, that has $O(n)$ time complexity by Lemma 1. Moreover, algorithm NCSPunion visits each dart of the "directed version" of X_k at most $O(1)$ times, where the *directed version of* X_k is the directed graph built from X_k by replacing each edge ab by the pair of darts $\overrightarrow{ab}$ and $\overrightarrow{ba}$. Thus, algorithm NCSPunion requires $O(n)$ time, since X_k is a subgraph of G. □

Theorem 3. *Graph Y_k computed by algorithm NCSPunion is the union of k shortest directed non-crossing i-paths, for $i \in [k]$.*

Proof. Let $\{\pi_i\}_{i\in[k]}$ be the set of paths defined in Theorem 2. For all $i \in [k]$, we denote by $\overrightarrow{\pi_i}$ the directed version of π_i, oriented from s_i to t_i.

First we define $\rho_1 = \overrightarrow{\pi_1}$ and for all $i \in [k] \setminus \{1\}$ we define

$$\rho_i = \begin{cases} \overrightarrow{\pi_i}[s_i, u_i] \circ \rho_{p(i)}[u_i, v_i] \circ \overrightarrow{\pi_i}[v_i, t_i], & \text{if } \overrightarrow{\pi_i} \text{ and } \rho_{p(i)} \text{ share no darts,} \\ \overrightarrow{\pi_i}, & \text{otherwise,} \end{cases} \tag{1}$$

where we assume that if $V(\overrightarrow{\pi_i} \cap \rho_{p(i)}) \neq \emptyset$, then u_i and v_i are the vertices in $V(\overrightarrow{\pi_i} \cap \rho_{p(i)})$ that appear first and last in $\overrightarrow{\pi_i}$, respectively; the definition of ρ_i as in (1) is shown in Fig. 7. Now we split the proof into three parts: first we prove that $\{\rho_i\}_{i\in[k]}$ is a set of shortest paths (we need it to apply Lemma 2); second we prove that $\{\rho_i\}_{i\in[k]}$ is a set of non-crossing paths (we need it to apply Lemma 3); third we prove that $Y = \bigcup_{i\in[k]} \rho_i$ (we prove it by Lemma 2 and Lemma 3).

$\{\rho_i\}_{i\in[k]}$ is a set of shortest paths: we proceed by induction on i. The base case is trivial because π_1 is a shortest path by definition. Let us assume that ρ_j is a shortest j-path, for $j < i$, we have to prove that ρ_i is a shortest i-path. If $\overrightarrow{\pi_i}$ and $\rho_{p(i)}$ have no common darts, then $\rho_i = \overrightarrow{\pi_i}$ by (1), thus the thesis holds because $\{\pi_i\}_{i\in[k]}$ a set of shortest paths. Hence let us assume that $\overrightarrow{\pi_i}$ and $\rho_{p(i)}$ have at least one common dart, then it suffices, by definition of ρ_i, that $|\pi_i[u_i, v_i]| = |\rho_{p(i)}[u_i, v_i]|$. It is true by induction.

$\{\rho_i\}_{i\in[k]}$ is a set of non-crossing paths: we proceed by induction on i. The base case is trivial because there is only one path. Let us assume that $\{\rho_j\}_{j\in[i-1]}$ is a set of non-crossing paths, we have to prove that ρ_i does not cross ρ_j, for any $j < i$.

If ρ_i and ρ_j are crossing and j is not an ancestor of i, then, by construction of ρ_i, either $\rho_{p(i)}$ and ρ_j are crossing or π_i and π_j are crossing; that is absurdum in both cases by induction and Theorem 2. Moreover, by definition, ρ_i does not cross $\rho_{p(i)}$, and by induction, if ℓ is an ancestor of i such that $\ell \neq p(i)$, then ρ_i does not cross ρ_ℓ, indeed, if not, then ρ_ℓ would cross $\rho_{p(i)}$, absurdum. Hence $\{\rho_i\}_{i\in[k]}$ is a set of non-crossing paths.

Y is the union of ρ_i's: now we prove that $Y = \bigcup_{i\in[k]} \rho_i$. In particular we show that $\rho_1 = \overrightarrow{\pi_1}$ and for all $i \in [k] \setminus \{1\}$

$$\rho_i = \begin{cases} \sigma_i \circ \rho_{p(i)}[u_i, v_i] \circ \mathrm{rev}[\tau_i], & \text{if } \overrightarrow{\pi_i} \text{ and } \rho_{p(i)} \text{ share no darts,} \\ \overrightarrow{\pi_i}, & \text{otherwise.} \end{cases} \quad (2)$$

Again, we proceed by induction on i. The base case is trivial, thus we assume that (1) is equivalent to (2) for all $i < \ell$. We have to prove that (1) is equivalent to (2) for $i = \ell$.

If $\overrightarrow{\pi_\ell}$ does not intersect any dart of $\rho_{p(\ell)}$, then (1) is equivalent to (2). Thus we assume that $\overrightarrow{\pi_\ell}$ and $\rho_{p(\ell)}$ have at least one common dart. By (1) and (2) and by definition of σ_i and τ_i in Line 5 and Line 6, respectively, it suffices to prove that $d_i \in \rho_{p(i)}$ and $\mathrm{rev}[d'_i] \in \rho_{p(i)}$.

Now, by induction we know that $d_i \in \rho_\ell$ for some $\ell < i$, we have to show that $d_i \in \rho_{p(i)}$. By Lemma 2 and being $\{\rho_j\}_{j\in[k]}$ a set of shortest paths, it holds that ℓ is an ancestor or a descendant of i. Being the s_j's visited clockwise by starting from s_1, then ℓ is an ancestor of i. Finally, by Lemma 3 and being $\{\rho_j\}_{j\in[k]}$ a set of non-crossing path, it holds that $\rho_i \cap \rho_\ell \subseteq \rho_{p(i)}$. Being $p(i) < i$, then $d_i \in \rho_{p(i)}$ as we claimed. By a similar argument, it holds that $\mathrm{rev}[d'_i] \in \rho_{p(i)}$. □

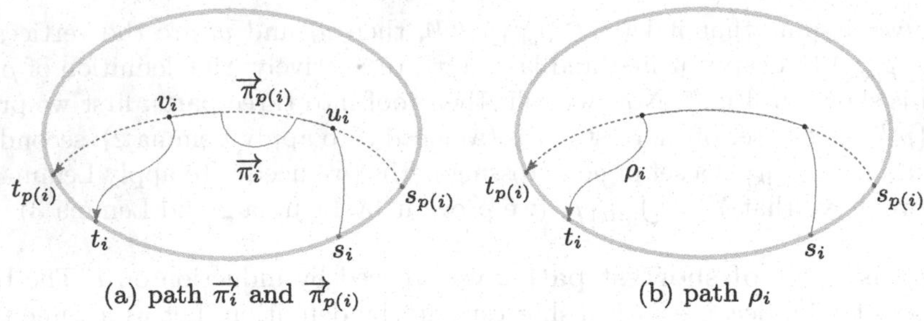

(a) path $\overrightarrow{\pi}_i$ and $\overrightarrow{\pi}_{p(i)}$ (b) path ρ_i

Fig. 7. Proof of Theorem 3, explanation of (1).

It is proved in [4] that, starting from the union of a set of shortest (not necessarily non-crossing) paths between well-formed terminal pairs, distances between terminal pairs can be computed in linear time. Thus we can give the following main theorem.

Theorem 4. *Given an undirected unweighted plane graph G and a set of well-formed terminal pairs $\{(s_i, t_i)\}$ on the external face f^∞ of G we can compute $U = \bigcup_{i \in [k]} p_i$ and the lengths of all p_i, for $i \in [k]$, where p_i is a shortest i-path and $\{p_i\}_{i \in [k]}$ is a set of non-crossing paths, in $O(n)$ time.*

Proof. By Theorem 3, the required graph U is the undirected version $\overline{Y_k}$ of the graph computed by algorithm `NCSPunion`, that has $O(n)$ time complexity by Lemma 4. Moreover, we compute the length of p_i, for all $i \in [k]$, in $O(n)$ time by using the results in [4]. □

Remark 2. For graphs with small integer weights, we can obtain all the previous results in $O(n + L)$ time, where L is the sum of all edge weights, by splitting an edge of weight r in r unweighted edges.

5 Conclusions

In this paper we have shown a linear time algorithm to compute the union of non-crossing shortest paths whose extremal vertices are in the external face of an undirected unweighted planar graph.

The algorithm relies on the algorithm by Eisenstat and Klein for computing SSSP trees rooted on the vertices of the external face and on the novel concept of ISP subgraph of a planar graph, that can be of interest itself. The same approach cannot be extended to weighted graphs, because the algorithm of Eisenstat and Klein works only in the unweighted case.

As stated in [12] our results may be applied in the case of terminal pairs lying on h face boundaries.

We wish to investigate the non-crossing shortest paths problem when each terminal pair contains only one vertex on the external face.

References

1. Ausiello, G., Balzotti, L., Franciosa, P.G., Lari, I., Ribichini, A.: A Linear Time Algorithm for Computing Max-Flow Vitality in Undirected Unweighted Planar Graphs, CoRR, abs/2204.10568 (2022)
2. Ausiello, G., Franciosa, P.G., Lari, I., Ribichini, A.: Max flow vitality in general and ST-planar graphs. Networks **74**, 70–78 (2019)
3. Baker, Z.K., Gokhale, M.B.: On the acceleration of shortest path calculations in transportation networks. In: IEEE Symposium on Field-Programmable Custom Computing Machines, FCCM 2007, pp. 23–34 (2007)
4. Balzotti, L., Franciosa, P.G.: Computing Lengths of Non-Crossing Shortest Paths in Planar Graphs, CoRR, abs/2011.04047 (2020)
5. Balzotti, L., Franciosa, P.G.: Max Flow Vitality of Edges and Vertices in Undirected Planar Graphs, CoRR, abs/2201.13099 (2022)
6. Bauer, R., Delling, D., Sanders, P., Schieferdecker, D., Schultes, D., Wagner, D.: Combining hierarchical and goal-directed speed-up techniques for Dijkstra's algorithm. ACM J. Exp. Algorithmics **15** (2010)
7. Bhatt, S.N., Leighton, F.T.: A framework for solving VLSI graph layout problems. J. Comput. Syst. Sci. **28**, 300–343 (1984)
8. Cabello, S.: Many distances in planar graphs. Algorithmica **62**, 361–381 (2012)
9. Chen, D.Z., Xu, J.: Shortest path queries in planar graphs. In: Proceedings of the Thirty-Second Annual ACM Symposium on Theory of Computing, pp. 469–478. ACM (2000)
10. Djidjev, H.N.: Efficient algorithms for shortest path queries in planar digraphs. In: d'Amore, F., Franciosa, P.G., Marchetti-Spaccamela, A. (eds.) WG 1996. LNCS, vol. 1197, pp. 151–165. Springer, Heidelberg (1997). https://doi.org/10.1007/3-540-62559-3_14
11. Eisenstat, D., Klein, P.N.: Linear-time algorithms for max flow and multiple-source shortest paths in unit-weight planar graphs. In: Symposium on Theory of Computing Conference, pp. 735–744. ACM (2013)
12. Erickson, J., Nayyeri, A.: Shortest non-crossing walks in the plane. In: Proceedings of the Twenty-Second Annual ACM-SIAM Symposium on Discrete Algorithms, pp. 297–208. SIAM (2011)
13. Fakcharoenphol, J., Rao, S.: Planar graphs, negative weight edges, shortest paths, and near linear time. J. Comput. Syst. Sci. **72**, 868–889 (2006)
14. Frederickson, G.N.: Fast algorithms for shortest paths in planar graphs, with applications. SIAM J. Comput. **16**, 1004–1022 (1987)
15. Gawrychowski, P., Mozes, S., Weimann, O., Wulff-Nilsen, C.: Better tradeoffs for exact distance oracles in planar graphs. In: Proceedings of the Twenty-Ninth Annual ACM-SIAM Symposium on Discrete Algorithms, pp. 515–529. SIAM (2018)
16. Goldberg, A.V.: Point-to-point shortest path algorithms with preprocessing. In: van Leeuwen, J., Italiano, G.F., van der Hoek, W., Meinel, C., Sack, H., Plášil, F. (eds.) SOFSEM 2007. LNCS, vol. 4362, pp. 88–102. Springer, Heidelberg (2007). https://doi.org/10.1007/978-3-540-69507-3_6

17. Gross, J.L., Tucker, T.W.: Topological Graph Theory. Courier Corporation (2001)
18. Hassin, R.: Maximum flow in (s, t) planar networks. Inf. Process. Lett. **13**, 107 (1981)
19. Hassin, R., Johnson, D.B.: An O(n $\log^2$n) algorithm for maximum flow in undirected planar networks. SIAM J. Comput. **14**, 612–624 (1985)
20. Henzinger, M.R., Klein, P.N., Rao, S., Subramanian, S.: Faster shortest-path algorithms for planar graphs. J. Comput. Syst. Sci. **55**, 3–23 (1997)
21. Italiano, G.F., Nussbaum, Y., Sankowski, P., Wulff-Nilsen, C.: Improved algorithms for min cut and max flow in undirected planar graphs. In: Proceedings of the 43rd ACM Symposium on Theory of Computing, pp. 313–322. ACM (2011)
22. Jing, N., Huang, Y., Rundensteiner, E.A.: Hierarchical optimization of optimal path finding for transportation applications. In: CIKM 1996, Proceedings of the Fifth International Conference on Information and Knowledge Management, pp. 261–268. ACM (1996)
23. Kim, D., Maxemchuk, N.F.: Simple robotic routing in ad hoc networks. In: 13th IEEE International Conference on Network Protocols (ICNP 2005), pp. 159–168. IEEE Computer Society (2005)
24. Klein, P.N.: Multiple-source shortest paths in planar graphs. In: Proceedings of the Sixteenth Annual ACM-SIAM Symposium on Discrete Algorithms, pp. 146–155. SIAM (2005)
25. Kowalik, L., Kurowski, M.: Short path queries in planar graphs in constant time. In: Proceedings of the 35th Annual ACM Symposium on Theory of Computing, pp. 143–148. ACM (2003)
26. Kusakari, Y., Masubuchi, D., Nishizeki, T.: Finding a noncrossing steiner forest in plane graphs under a 2-face condition. J. Comb. Optim. **5**, 249–266 (2001)
27. Masucci, A.P., Stanilov, K., Batty, M.: Exploring the evolution of London's street network in the information space: a dual approach. Phys. Rev. E **89**, 012805 (2014)
28. Mozes, S., Sommer, C.: Exact distance oracles for planar graphs. In: Proceedings of the Twenty-Third Annual ACM-SIAM Symposium on Discrete Algorithms, pp. 209–222. SIAM (2012)
29. Nussbaum, Y.: Improved distance queries in planar graphs. In: Dehne, F., Iacono, J., Sack, J.-R. (eds.) WADS 2011. LNCS, vol. 6844, pp. 642–653. Springer, Heidelberg (2011). https://doi.org/10.1007/978-3-642-22300-6_54
30. Raney, B., Nagel, K.: Iterative route planning for large-scale modular transportation simulations. Future Gener. Comput. Syst. **20**, 1101–1118 (2004)
31. Reif, J.H.: Minimum s-t cut of a planar undirected network in $O(n \log^2(n))$ time. SIAM J. Comput. **12**, 71–81 (1983)
32. Steiger, A.J.: Single-face non-crossing shortest paths in planar graphs. M.S. thesis, University of Illinois at Urbana-Champaign (2017). http://hdl.handle.net/2142/98345
33. Takahashi, J., Suzuki, H., Nishizeki, T.: Shortest Noncrossing Paths in Plane Graphs. Algorithmica **16**, 339–357 (1996)

34. Takahashi, J., Suzuki, H., Nishizeki, T.: Shortest non-crossing rectilinear paths in plane regions. Int. J. Comput. Geom. Appl. **7**, 419–436 (1997)
35. Wagner, D., Weihe, K.: A linear-time algorithm for edge-disjoint paths in planar graphs. Combinatorica **15**, 135–150 (1995)
36. Ziliaskopoulos, A., Kotzinos, D., Mahmassani, H.S.: Design and implementation of parallel time-dependent least time path algorithms for intelligent transportation systems applications. Transp. Res. Part C: Emerg. Technol. **5**, 95–107 (1997)

Lossy Kernelization of Same-Size Clustering

Sayan Bandyapadhyay[1], Fedor V. Fomin[1], Petr A. Golovach[1], Nidhi Purohit[1(✉)], and Kirill Siminov[2]

[1] Department of Informatics, University of Bergen, Bergen, Norway
{Fedor.Fomin,Petr.Golovach,Nidhi.Purohit}@uib.no
[2] Algorithms and Complexity Group, TU Wien, Vienna, Austria

Abstract. In this work, we study the k-median clustering problem with an additional equal-size constraint on the clusters, from the perspective of parameterized preprocessing. Our main result is the first lossy (2-approximate) polynomial kernel for this problem, parameterized by the cost of clustering. We complement this result by establishing lower bounds for the problem that eliminate the existences of an (exact) kernel of polynomial size and a PTAS.

Keywords: k-median clustering · parameterized approximation · kernelization · lossy kernels

1 Introduction

Lossy kernelization stems from *parameterized complexity*, a branch in theoretical computer science that studies complexity of problems as functions of multiple *parameters* of the input or output [27]. A central notion in parameterized complexity is *kernelization*, which is a generic technique for designing efficient algorithms availing a polynomial time preprocessing step that transforms a "large" instance of a problem into a smaller, equivalent instance. Naturally, the preprocessing step is called the *kernelization algorithm* and the smaller instance is called the *kernel*. One limitation of the classical kernelization technique is that kernels can only examine "lossless" preprocessing, in the sense that a kernel must be equivalent to the original instance. This is why most of the interesting problems arising from machine learning, e.g., clustering, are intractable from the perspective of kernelization. Lossy or approximate kernelization is a successful attempt of combining kernelization with approximation algorithms. Informally, in lossy kernelization, given an instance of the problem and a parameter, we would like the kernelization algorithm to output a reduced instance of size polynomial in

The research leading to these results have been supported by the Research Council of Norway via the project BWCA (grant no. 314528), European Research Council (ERC) via grant LOPPRE, reference 819416, and Austrian Science Fund (FWF) via project P31336 (New Frontiers for Parameterized Complexity).

A. S. Kulikov and S. Raskhodnikova (Eds.): CSR 2022, LNCS 13296, pp. 96–114, 2022.
https://doi.org/10.1007/978-3-031-09574-0_7

the parameter; however the notion of equivalence is relaxed in the following way. Given a c-approximate solution (i.e., one with the cost within c-factor of the optimal cost) to the reduced instance, it should be possible to produce in polynomial time an αc-approximate solution to the original instance. The factor α is the loss incurred while going from the reduced instance to the original instance. The notion of lossy kernelization was introduced by Lokshtanov et al. in [45]. However, most of the developments of lossy kernelization up to now are in graph algorithms [2,28,29,40,48], see also [35, Chapter 23] for an overview.

One of the actively developing areas of parameterized complexity concerns *fixed-parameter tractable-* or FPT-approximation. We refer to the survey [32] for an overview of the area. Several important advances on FPT-approximation concern clustering problems. It includes tight algorithmic and complexity results for k-means and k-median [18] and constant factor FPT-approximation for capacitated clustering [20]. The popular approach for data compression used for FPT-approximation of clustering is based on *coresets.* The notion of coresets originated from computational geometry. It was introduced by Har-Peled and Mazumdar [37] for k-means and k-median clustering. Informally, a coreset is a summary of the data that for every set of k centers, approximately (within $(1\pm\epsilon)$ factor) preserves the optimal clustering cost.

Lossy kernels and coresets have a lot of similarities. Both compress the space compared to the original data, and any algorithm can be applied on a coreset or kernel to efficiently retrieve a solution with guarantee almost the same as the one provided by the algorithm on the original input. The crucial difference is that coreset constructions result in a small set of weighted points. The weights could be up to the input size n. Thus a coreset of size polynomial in k/ϵ, is not a polynomial sized lossy kernel for parameters k, ϵ because of the $\log n$ bits required to encode the weights. Moreover, usually coreset constructions do not bound the number of coordinates or dimension of the points.

While the notion of lossy kernelization proved to be useful in the design of graph algorithms, we are not aware of its applicability in clustering. This brings us to the following question: *What can lossy kernelization offer to clustering?*

In this work, we make the first step towards the development of lossy kernels for clustering problems. Our main result is the design of a lossy kernel for a variant of the well-studied k-MEDIAN clustering with clusters of equal sizes. More precisely, consider a collection (multiset) of points from $\mathbb{Z}^d$ under the ℓ_p-norm. Thus every point is a d-dimensional vector with integer coordinates. For a nonnegative integer p, we use $\|\mathbf{x}\|_p$ to denote the ℓ_p-norm of a d-dimensional vector $\mathbf{x} = (x[1], \ldots, x[d]) \in \mathbb{R}^d$, that is, for $p \geq 1$, $\|\mathbf{x}\|_p = \left(\sum_{i=1}^{d} |x[i]|^p\right)^{1/p}$ and for $p = 0$, $\|\mathbf{x}\|_0$ is the number of nonzero elements of $\mathbf{x}$, i.e., the Hamming norm. For any $T \subseteq \mathbb{Z}^d$, we define $\mathsf{cost}_p(T) = \min_{\mathbf{c}\in\mathbb{R}^d} \sum_{\mathbf{x}\in T} \|\mathbf{c}-\mathbf{x}\|_p$. Then k-MEDIAN[1] clustering

[1] Traditionally this problem is studied with real input points, but because of the choice of the parameterization, it is natural for us to assume that points have integer coordinates. As the coordinates can be scaled, this does not lead to the loss of generality.

(without constraints) is the task of finding a partition $\{X_1, \ldots, X_k\}$ of a given family $\mathbf{X} \subseteq \mathbb{Z}^d$ of points minimizing the sum $\sum_{i=1}^{k} \mathsf{cost}_p(X_i)$.

In many real-life scenarios, it is desirable to cluster data into clusters of equal sizes. For example, to tailor teaching methods to the specific needs of various students, one would be interested in allocating k fair class sizes by grouping students with homogeneous abilities and skills [38]. In scheduling, the standard task is to distribute n jobs to k machines while keeping identical workloads on each machine and simultaneously reducing the configuration time. In the setting of designing a conference program, one might be interested in allocating n scientific papers according to their similarities to k "balanced" sessions [51].

The following model is an attempt to capture such scenarios.

EQUAL CLUSTERING

Input: A collection (multiset) $\mathbf{X} = \{\mathbf{x}_1, \ldots, \mathbf{x}_n\}$ of n points of $\mathbb{Z}^d$ and a positive integer k such that n is divisible by k.

Task: Find a partition $\{X_1, \ldots, X_k\}$ (k-clustering) of $\mathbf{X}$ with $|X_1| = \cdots = |X_k| = \frac{n}{k}$ minimizing $\sum_{i=1}^{k} \mathsf{cost}_p(X_i)$.

First, note that EQUAL CLUSTERING is a restricted variant of the capacitated version [20] of k-MEDIAN where the size of each cluster is required to be bounded by a given number U. Also note, that some points in $\mathbf{X}$ may be identical. (In the above examples, several students, jobs, or scientific papers can have identical features but could be assigned to different clusters due to the size limitations.) We refer to the multisets $X_1, \ldots, X_k$ as the *clusters.*

To describe the lossy-kernel result, we need to define the parameterized version of EQUAL CLUSTERING with the cost of clustering B (the budget) being the parameter. Following the framework of lossy kernelization [45], when the cost of an optimal clustering exceeds the budget, we assume it is equal to $B + 1$. More precisely, in PARAMETERIZED EQUAL CLUSTERING, we are given an additional integer B (budget parameter). The task is to find a k-clustering $\{X_1, \ldots, X_k\}$ with $|X_1| = \cdots = |X_k|$ and minimizing the value

$$\mathsf{cost}_p^B(X_1, \ldots, X_k) = \begin{cases} \sum_{i=1}^{k} \mathsf{cost}_p(X_i) & \text{if } \sum_{i=1}^{k} \mathsf{cost}_p(X_i) \leq B, \\ B + 1 & \text{otherwise.} \end{cases}$$

Before stating our results, let us first discuss some limitations and advantages of parameterization of DECISION EQUAL CLUSTERING by the budget B. First, parameterization by B is reasonable when the vectors are integer-valued, which is a common situation when the data is categorical, that is, can admit a fixed number of possible values. For example, it could be gender, blood type, or political orientation. A prominent example of categorical data is binary data, where the points are binary vectors. Binary data arise in several critical applications. For example, in electronic commerce, each transaction can be modeled as a binary vector (known as market basket data), each of whose coordinates denotes whether a particular item is purchased or not [44,52]. In document clustering, each document can be modeled as a binary vector, each of whose coordinates denotes whether a specific word is present or not in the document [44,52].

The most drastic effect of compression occurs when B is small. Intuitively, this means that many of the data points are the same. Such a condition is common in handling personal data that cannot be re-identified. For example, the k-anonymity property requires each person in the data set to be undistinguishable from at least k individuals whose information appears in the release [50].

Finally, comparing lossy kernelization from Theorem 1 and the coresets for k-MEDIAN and k-MEANS. The sizes of all known coreset constructions depend on the number of clusters k, and thus guarantee compression only for small values of k. On the other hand, the size of the lossy kernel is independent of k. In particular, such type of results are interesting when we have to identify many clusters of small size.

Our first main result is the following theorem providing a polynomial 2-approximate kernel.

Theorem 1. *For every nonnegative integer constant p,* PARAMETERIZED EQUAL CLUSTERING *admits a 2-approximate kernel when parameterized by B, where the output collection of points has $\mathcal{O}(B^2)$ points of $\mathbb{Z}^{d'}$ with $d' = \mathcal{O}(B^{p+2})$, where each coordinate of a point takes an absolute value of $\mathcal{O}(B^3)$.*

In other words, the theorem provides a polynomial-time algorithm that compresses the original instance $\mathbf{X}$ to a new instance whose size is bounded by a polynomial of B and such that any c-approximate solution in the new instance can be turned in polynomial time to a $2c$-approximate solution of the original instance.

A natural question is whether the approximation ratio of lossy kernel in Theorem 1 is optimal. While we do not have a complete answer to this question, we provide lower bounds supporting our study of the problem from the perspective of approximate kernelization. Our next result rules out the existence of an "exact" kernel for the problem. To state the result, we need to define the decision version of EQUAL CLUSTERING. In this version, we call it DECISION EQUAL CLUSTERING, the question is whether for a given budget B, there is a k-clustering $\{X_1, \ldots, X_k\}$ with clusters of the same size such that $\sum_{1 \le i \le k} \mathsf{cost}_p(X_i) \le B$.

Theorem 2. *For ℓ_0 and ℓ_1-norms,* DECISION EQUAL CLUSTERING *has no polynomial kernel when parameterized by B, unless* $\mathsf{NP} \subseteq \mathsf{coNP/poly}$*, even if the input points are binary, that is, are from $\{0,1\}^d$.*

On the other hand, we prove that DECISION EQUAL CLUSTERING admits a polynomial kernel when parameterized by k and B.

Theorem 3. *For every nonnegative integer constant p,* Decision Equal Clustering *admits a polynomial kernel when parameterized by k and B, where the output collection of points has $\mathcal{O}(kB)$ points of $\mathbb{Z}^{d'}$ with $d' = \mathcal{O}(kB^{p+1})$ and each coordinate of a point takes an absolute value of $\mathcal{O}(kB^2)$.*

When it comes to approximation in polynomial time, we show (Theorem 4) that it is NP-hard to obtain a $(1+\epsilon_c)$-approximation for Equal Clustering with ℓ_0 (or ℓ_1) distances for some $\epsilon_c > 0$. However, parameterized by k and ϵ, standard techniques yield $(1+\epsilon)$-approximation in FPT time. For ℓ_2 norm, there is a general framework for designing algorithms of this form for k-Median with additional constraints on cluster sizes, introduced by Ding and Xu [26]. The best-known improvements by Bhattacharya et al. [11] achieve a running time of $2^{\widetilde{\mathcal{O}}(k/\epsilon^{\mathcal{O}(1)})}n^{\mathcal{O}(1)}d$ in the case of Equal Clustering, where $\widetilde{\mathcal{O}}$ hides polylogarithmic factors. In another line of work, FPT-time approximation is achieved via constructing small-sized coresets of the input, and the work [8] guarantees an ϵ-coreset for Equal Clustering (in ℓ_2 norm) of size $(kd\log n/\epsilon)^{\mathcal{O}(1)}$, and consequently a $(1+\epsilon)$-approximation algorithm with running time $2^{\widetilde{\mathcal{O}}(k/\epsilon^{\mathcal{O}(1)})}(nd)^{\mathcal{O}(1)}$.

Moreover, specifically for Equal Clustering, simple $(1+\epsilon)$-approximations with similar running time can be designed directly via sampling. A seminal work of Kumar et al. [41] achieves a $(1+\epsilon)$-approximation for k-Median (in ℓ_2 norm) with running time $2^{\widetilde{\mathcal{O}}(k/\epsilon^{\mathcal{O}(1)})}nd$. The algorithm proceeds as follows. First, take a small uniform sample of the input points, and by guessing ensure that the sample is taken only from the largest cluster. Second, estimate the optimal center of this cluster from the sample. In the case of k-Median, Theorem 5.4 of [41] guarantees that from a sample of size $(1/\epsilon)^{\mathcal{O}(1)}$ one can compute in time $2^{(1/\epsilon)^{\mathcal{O}(1)}}d$ a set of candidate centers such that at least one of them provides a $(1+\epsilon)$-approximation to the cost of the cluster. Finally, "prune" the set of points so that the next largest cluster is at least $\Omega(1/k)$ fraction of the remaining points and continue the same process with one less cluster. One can observe that in the case of Equal Clustering, a simplification of the above algorithm suffices: one does not need to perform the "pruning" step, as we are only interested in clusterings where all the clusters have size exactly n/k. Thus, $(1/\epsilon)^{\mathcal{O}(1)}$-sized uniform samples from each of the clusters can be computed immediately in total time $2^{\widetilde{\mathcal{O}}(k/\epsilon^{\mathcal{O}(1)})}nd$. This achieves $(1+\epsilon)$-approximation for Equal Clustering with the same running time as the algorithm of Kumar et al. In fact, the same procedure works for ℓ_0 norm as well, where for estimating the cluster center it suffices to compute the optimal center of a sample of size $\mathcal{O}(1/\epsilon^2)$, as proven by Alon and Sudakov [4]. Thus, in terms of FPT approximation, Equal Clustering is surprisingly "simpler" than its unconstrained variant k-Median, however, our hardness result of Theorem 4 shows that the problems are similarly hard in terms of polynomial time approximation.

Related Work. Since the work of Har-Peled and Mazumdar [37] for k-means and k-median clustering, designing small coresets for clustering has become a flourishing research direction. For these problems, after a series of interesting works, the best-known upper bound on coreset size in general metric space is

$\mathcal{O}((k\log n)/\epsilon^2)$ [30] and the lower bound is known to be $\Omega((k\log n)/\epsilon)$ [6]. For the Euclidean space (i.e., ℓ_2-norm) of dimension d, it is possible to construct coresets of size $(k/\epsilon)^{\mathcal{O}(1)}$ [31,49]. Remarkably, the size of the coresets in this case does not depend on n and d. For Equal Clustering, the best known coreset size of $(kd\log n/\epsilon)^{O(1)}$ (for $p=2$) follows from coresets for the more general capacitated clustering problem [8,20].

Clustering is undoubtedly one of the most common procedures in unsupervised machine learning. We refer to the book [1] for an overview on clustering. Algorithms for k-median and k-means has been one of the most interesting problems in the area of approximation and led to a plethora of work [3,13,15,39,43]. For k-median, the best known polynomial time approximation factor is 2.675 [13] and for k-means, it is 6.356 [3]. Moreover, if one is allowed to use FPT time parameterized by k, then these two factors can be improved to $\approx (1+2/e) \le 1.736$ and $\approx (1+8/e) \le 3.944$, respectively [18]. Assuming the Gap-ETH [46], these factors are indeed tight [18]. PTASes are known for Euclidean version of k-median and k-means when the dimension is a constant [5,9,19,21,36]. Cohen-Addad et al. [22] obtained an $n^{o(k)}$ lower bound for k-median when $d \ge 4$. When the dimension d is arbitrary, one can obtain $(1+\epsilon)$-approximation in FPT(k) time where the dependency on n and d are only linear [41]. Feng et al. in [33] gave a unified framework to design FPT approximation algorithms for clustering.

Equal Clustering belongs to a wide class of clustering with constraints on the sizes of the clusters. In many applications of clustering, constraints come naturally [10]. In particular, there is a rich literature on approximation algorithms for various versions of capacitated clustering. While for the capacitated version of k-median and k-means in general metric space, no polynomial time $O(1)$-approximation is known, bicriteria constant-approximations violating either the capacity constraints or the constraint on the number of clusters, by an $O(1)$ factor can be obtained [12,14–16,25,42]. Cohen-Addad and Li [20] designed FPT $\approx$ 3- and $\approx$ 9-approximation with parameter k for the capacitated version of k-median and k-means, respectively. For these problems in the Euclidean plane, Cohen-Addad [17] obtained a true PTAS. Moreover, for higher dimensional spaces (i.e., $d \ge 3$), he designed a $(1+\epsilon)$-approximation that runs in time $n^{(\log n/\epsilon)^{O(d)}}$ [17]. Being a restricted version of capacitated clustering, Equal Clustering admits all the approximation results mentioned above.

Our Approach. We briefly sketch the main ideas behind the construction of our lossy kernel for Parameterized Equal Clustering. The lossy kernel's main ingredients are a) a polynomial algorithm based on an algorithm for computing a minimum weight perfect matching in bipartite graphs, b) preprocessing rules reducing the size and dimension of the problem, and c) a greedy algorithm. Each of the steps is relatively simple and easily implementable. However, the proof that these steps result in the lossy kernel with the required properties is not easy.

Recall that for a given budget B, we are looking for a k-clustering of a collection of points $\mathbf{X} = \{\mathbf{x}_1, \ldots, \mathbf{x}_n\}$ into k clusters of the same size minimizing the cost. We also assume that the cost is $B+1$ if the instance points do not admit a clustering of cost at most B. Informally, we are only interested in optimal clustering when its cost does not exceed the budget. First, if the cluster's size $s = \frac{n}{k}$ is sufficiently large (with respect to the budget), we can construct an optimal clustering in polynomial time. More precisely, we prove that if $s \geq 4B+1$, then the clusters' medians could be selected from $\mathbf{X}$. Moreover, we show how to identify the (potential) medians in polynomial time. In this case, constructing an optimal k-clustering could be reduced to the classical problem of computing a perfect matching of minimum weight in a bipartite graph.

The case of cluster's size $s \leq 4B$ is different. We apply a set of reduction rules. These rules run in polynomial time. After exhaustive applications of reduction rules, we either correctly conclude that the considered instance has no clustering of cost at most B or constructs an equivalent reduced instance. In the equivalent instance, the dimension is reduced to $\mathcal{O}(kB^{p+1})$ while the absolute values of the coordinates of the points are in $\mathcal{O}(kB^2)$.

Finally, we apply the only approximate reduction on the reduced instance. The approximation procedure is greedy: whenever there are s identical points, we form a cluster out of them. For the points remaining after the exhaustive application of the greedy procedure, we conclude that either there is no clustering of cost at most B or the number of points is $\mathcal{O}(B^2)$. This construction leads us to the lossy kernel. However the greedy selection of the clusters composed of identical points maybe not be optimal. In particular, the reductions used to obtain our algorithmic lower bounds given in Sects. 4 and 5 exploit the property that it may be beneficial to split a block of s identical points between distinct clusters.

Nevertheless, the greedy clustering of identical points leads to a 2-approximation. The proof of this fact requires some work. We evaluate the clustering cost obtained from a given optimal clustering by swapping some points to form clusters composed of identical points. Further, we upper bound the obtained value by the cost of the optimum clustering. For the last step, we introduce an auxiliary clustering problem formulated as a min-cost flow problem. This reduction allows to evaluate the cost and obtain the required upper bound.

Due to space constraints various proofs are omitted in this extended abstract. The full details are available in [7].

2 Preliminaries

In this section, we give basic definition and introduce notation used throughout the paper. We also state some useful auxiliary results.

Parameterized Complexity and Kernelization. We refer to the books [23, 35] for a formal introduction to the area. Here we only define the notions used in our paper.

Formally, a *parameterized problem* Π is a subset of $\Sigma^* \times \mathbb{N}$, where Σ is a finite alphabet. Thus, an instance of Π is a pair (I, k), where $I \subseteq \Sigma^*$ and k is a nonnegative integer called a *parameter*. It is said that a parameterized problem

Π is *fixed-parameter tractable* (FPT) if it can be solved in $f(k) \cdot |I|^{\mathcal{O}(1)}$ time for some computable function $f(\cdot)$.

A *kernelization* algorithm (or *kernel*) for a parameterized problem Π is an algorithm that, given an instance (I, k) of Π, in polynomial time produces an instance (I', k') of Π such that (i) $(I, k) \in \Pi$ if and only if $(I', k') \in \Pi$, and (ii) $|I'| + k' \leq g(k)$ for a computable function $g(\cdot)$. The function $g(\cdot)$ is called the *size* of a kernel; a kernel is *polynomial* if $g(\cdot)$ is a polynomial. Every decidable FPT problem admits a kernel. However, it is unlikely that all FPT problems have polynomial kernels and the parameterized complexity theory provide tools for refuting the existence of polynomial kernels up to some reasonable complexity assumptions. The standard assumption here is that $\mathsf{NP} \not\subseteq \mathsf{coNP/poly}$.

We also consider the parameterized analog of optimization problems. Since we only deal with minimization problems where the minimized value is nonnegative, we state the definitions only for optimization problems of this type. A *parameterized minimization* problem P is a computable function

$$P \colon \Sigma^* \times \mathbb{N} \times \Sigma^* \to \mathbb{R}_{\geq 0} \cup \{+\infty\}.$$

The instances of a parameterized minimization problem P are pairs $(I, k) \in \Sigma^* \times \mathbb{N}$, and a solution to (I, k) is simply a string $s \in \Sigma^*$, such that $|s| \leq |I| + k$. Then the function $P(\cdot, \cdot, \cdot)$ defines the *value* $P(I, k, s)$ of a solution s to an instance (I, k). The optimum value of an instance (I, k) is

$$\mathsf{Opt}_P(I, k) = \min_{s \in \Sigma^* \text{ s.t. } |s| \leq |I| + k} P(I, k, s).$$

A solution s is *optimal* if $\mathsf{Opt}_P(I, k) = P(I, k, s)$. A parameterized minimization problem P is said to be FPT if there is an algorithm that for each instance (I, k) of P computes an optimal solution s in $f(k) \cdot |I|^{\mathcal{O}(1)}$ time, where $f(\cdot)$ is a computable function. Let $\alpha \geq 1$ be a real number. An FPT α-approximation algorithm for P is an algorithm that in $f(k) \cdot |I|^{\mathcal{O}(1)}$ time computes a solution s for (I, k) such that $P(I, k, s) \leq \alpha \cdot \mathsf{Opt}_P(I, k)$, where $f(\cdot)$ is a computable function.

It is useful for us to make some comments about defining $P(\cdot, \cdot, \cdot)$ for the case when the considered problem is parameterized by the solution value. For simplicity, we do it informally and refer to [35] for details and explanations. If s is not a "feasible" solution to an instance (I, k), then it is convenient to assume that $P(I, k, s) = +\infty$. Otherwise, if s is "feasible" but its value is at least $k + 1$, we set $P(I, k, s) = k + 1$.

Lossy Kernels. Finally we define *α-approximate* or *lossy* kernels for parameterized minimization problems. Informally, an α-approximate kernel of size $g(\cdot)$ is a polynomial-time algorithm, that given an instance (I, k), outputs an instance (I', k') such that $|I'| + k' \leq g(k)$ and any c-approximate solution s' to (I', k') can be turned in polynomial time into a $(c \cdot \alpha)$-approximate solution s to the original instance (I, k). More precisely, let P be a parameterized minimization problem and let $\alpha \geq 1$. An *α-approximate* (or *lossy*) kernel for P is a pair of polynomial algorithms $\mathcal{A}$ and $\mathcal{A}'$ such that

(i) given an instance (I, k), $\mathcal{A}$ (called a *reduction algorithm*) computes an instance (I', k') with $|I'| + k' \leq g(k)$, where $g(\cdot)$ is a computable function,
(ii) the algorithm $\mathcal{A}'$ (called a *solution-lifting algorithm*), given the initial instance (I, k), the instance (I', k') produced by $\mathcal{A}$, and a solution s' to (I', k'), computes an solution s to (I, k) such that

$$\frac{P(I, k, s)}{\mathsf{Opt}_P(I, k)} \leq \alpha \cdot \frac{P(I', k', s')}{\mathsf{Opt}_P(I', k')}.$$

To simplify notation, we assume here that $\frac{P(I,k,s)}{\mathsf{Opt}_P(I,k)} = 1$ if $\mathsf{Opt}_P(I, k) = 0$ and use the same assumption for $\frac{P(I',k',s')}{\mathsf{Opt}_P(I',k')}$. As with classical kernels, $g(\cdot)$ is called the *size* of an approximate kernel, and an approximate kernel is polynomial if $g(\cdot)$ is a polynomial.

Vectors and Clusters. For a vector $\mathbf{x} \in \mathbb{R}^d$, we use $\mathbf{x}[i]$ to denote the i-th element of the vector for $i \in \{1, \ldots, d\}$. For a set of indices $R \subseteq \{1, \ldots, d\}$, $\mathbf{x}[R]$ denotes the vector of $\mathbb{R}^{|R|}$ composed by the elements of vector $\mathbf{x}$ from set R, that is, if $R = \{i_1, \ldots, i_r\}$ with $i_1 < \ldots < i_r$ and $\mathbf{y} = \mathbf{x}[R]$, then $\mathbf{y}[j] = \mathbf{x}[i_j]$ for $j \in \{1, \ldots, r\}$. In our paper, we consider collections $\mathbf{X}$ of points of $\mathbb{Z}^d$. We underline that some points of such a collection may be identical. However, to simplify notation, we assume throughout the paper that the identical points of $\mathbf{X}$ are distinct elements of $\mathbf{X}$ assuming that the points are supplied with unique identifiers. By this convention, we often refer to (sub)collections of points as (sub)sets and apply the standard set notation.

Let X be a collection of points of $\mathbb{Z}^d$. For a vector $\mathbf{c} \in \mathbb{R}^d$, we define the *cost of X with respect to* $\mathbf{c}$ as $\mathsf{cost}_p(X, \mathbf{c}) = \sum_{\mathbf{x} \in X} \|\mathbf{c} - \mathbf{x}\|_p$. Slightly abusing notation we often refer to $\mathbf{c}$ as a (given) *median* of X. We say that $\mathbf{c}^* \in \mathbb{R}^d$ is an *optimum median* of X if $\mathsf{cost}_p(X) = \mathsf{cost}_p(X, \mathbf{c}^*) = \min_{\mathbf{c} \in \mathbb{R}^d} \mathsf{cost}_p(X, \mathbf{c})$. Notice that the considered collections of points have integer coordinates but the coordinates of medians are not constrained to integers and may be real.

Let $\mathbf{X} = \{\mathbf{x}_1, \ldots, \mathbf{x}_n\}$ a collection of points of $\mathbb{Z}^d$ and let k be a positive integer such that n is divisible by k. We say that a partition $\{X_1, \ldots, X_k\}$ of $\mathbf{X}$ is an *equal k-clustering* of $\mathbf{X}$ if $|X_i| = \frac{n}{k}$ for all $i \in \{1, \ldots, k\}$. For an equal k-clustering $\{X_1, \ldots, X_k\}$ and given vectors $\mathbf{c}_1, \ldots, \mathbf{c}_k$, we define the *cost of clustering with respect to* $\mathbf{c}_1, \ldots, \mathbf{c}_k$ as

$$\mathsf{cost}_p(X_1, \ldots, X_k, \mathbf{c}_1, \ldots, \mathbf{c}_k) = \sum_{i=1}^{k} \mathsf{cost}_p(X_i, \mathbf{c}_i).$$

The *cost* of an equal k-clustering $\{X_1, \ldots, X_k\}$ is defined as $\mathsf{cost}_p(X_1, \ldots, X_k) = \mathsf{cost}_p(X_1, \ldots, X_k, \mathbf{c}_1, \ldots, \mathbf{c}_k)$, where $\mathbf{c}_1, \ldots, \mathbf{c}_k$ are optimum medians. For an integer $B \geq 0$,

$$\mathsf{cost}_p^B(X_1, \ldots, X_k) = \begin{cases} \mathsf{cost}_p(X_1, \ldots, X_k) & \text{if } \mathsf{cost}_p(X_1, \ldots, X_k) \leq B, \\ B + 1 & \text{otherwise.} \end{cases}$$

We define $\mathsf{Opt}(\mathbf{X}, k)$

$$= \min\{\mathsf{cost}_p(X_1, \ldots, X_k) \mid \{X_1, \ldots, X_k\} \text{ is an equal } k\text{-clustering of } \mathbf{X}\},$$

and given a nonnegative integer B, $\mathsf{Opt}(\mathbf{X}, k, B)$

$$= \min\{\mathsf{cost}_p^B(X_1, \ldots, X_k) \mid \{X_1, \ldots, X_k\} \text{ is an equal } k\text{-clustering of } \mathbf{X}\}.$$

We conclude this section by observing that, given vectors $\mathbf{c}_1, \ldots, \mathbf{c}_k \in \mathbb{R}^d$, we can find an equal k-clustering $\{X_1, \ldots, X_k\}$ that minimizes $\sum_{i=1}^{k} cost_p(X_i, \mathbf{c}_i)$ using a reduction to the classical Minimum Weight Perfect Matching problem on bipartite graphs that is well-known to be solvable in polynomial time.

Lemma 1 (⋆).[2] *Let $\mathbf{X} = \{\mathbf{x}_1, \ldots, \mathbf{x}_n\}$ be a collection of points of $\mathbb{Z}^d$ and k be a positive integer such that n is divisible by k. Let also $\mathbf{c}_1, \ldots, \mathbf{c}_k \in \mathbb{R}^d$. Then an equal k-clustering $\{X_1, \ldots, X_k\}$ of minimum $\mathsf{cost}(X_1, \ldots, X_k, \mathbf{c}_1, \ldots, \mathbf{c}_k)$ can be found in polynomial time.*

3 Lossy Kernel

In this section, we prove Theorem 1 by establishing a 2-approximate polynomial kernel for Parameterized Equal Clustering. Throughout this section we assume that $p \geq 0$ defining the ℓ_p-norm is a fixed constant.

We start by proving the following results about medians of clusters when their size is sufficiently big with respect to the budget.

Lemma 2 (⋆). *Let $\{X_1, \ldots, X_k\}$ be an equal k-clustering of a collection of points $\mathbf{X} = \{\mathbf{x}_1, \ldots, \mathbf{x}_n\}$ of $\mathbb{Z}^d$ of cost at most $B \in \mathbb{Z}_{\geq 0}$, and let $s = \frac{n}{k}$. Then each cluster X_i for $i \in \{1, \ldots, k\}$ contains at least $s - 2B$ identical points.*

Lemma 3 (⋆). *Let $\{X_1, \ldots, X_k\}$ be an equal k-clustering of a collection of points $\mathbf{X} = \{\mathbf{x}_1, \ldots, \mathbf{x}_n\}$ of $\mathbb{Z}^d$ of cost at most $B \in \mathbb{Z}_{\geq 0}$, and let $s = \frac{n}{k} \geq 4B+1$. Let also $\mathbf{c}_1, \ldots, \mathbf{c}_k \in \mathbb{R}^d$ be optimum medians for $X_1, \ldots, X_k$, respectively. Then for every $i \in \{1, \ldots, k\}$, $\mathbf{c}_i = \mathbf{x}_j$ for the unique $\mathbf{x}_j \in \mathbf{X}_i$ such that $\mathbf{X}_i$ contains at least $s - 2B$ points identical to $\mathbf{x}_j$.*

Using Lemma 3, we can identify optimum medians.

Lemma 4 (⋆). *Let $\{X_1, \ldots, X_k\}$ be an equal k-clustering of a collection of points $\mathbf{X} = \{\mathbf{x}_1, \ldots, \mathbf{x}_n\}$ of $\mathbb{Z}^d$ of cost at most $B \in \mathbb{Z}_{\geq 0}$, and let $s = \frac{n}{k} \geq 4B+1$. suppose that $Y \subseteq \mathbf{X}$ is a collection of at least $B+1$ identical points of $\mathbf{X}$. Then there is $i \in \{1, \ldots, k\}$ such that an optimum median of X_i coincides with $\mathbf{x}_j$ for $\mathbf{x}_j \in Y$.*

[2] The proofs of statements labeled (⋆) are omitted in the extended abstract and are available in [7].

We use our next lemma to upper bound the clustering cost if we collect $s = \frac{n}{k}$ identical points in the same cluster.

Lemma 5 (⋆). *Let* $\{X_1, \ldots, X_k\}$ *be an* equal k-clustering *of a collection of points* $\mathbf{X} = \{\mathbf{x}_1, \ldots, \mathbf{x}_n\}$ *of* $\mathbb{Z}^d$*, and let* $\mathbf{c}_1, \ldots, \mathbf{c}_k \in \mathbb{R}^d$*. Suppose that* S *is a collection of* $s = \frac{n}{k}$ *identical points of* $\mathbf{X}$ *and* $\mathbf{x}_j \in S$*. Then there is an equal* k*-clustering* $\{X'_1, \ldots, X'_k\}$ *of* $\mathbf{X}$ *with* $X'_1 = S$ *such that*

$$\mathsf{cost}_p(X'_1, \ldots, X'_k, \mathbf{c}'_1, \ldots, \mathbf{c}'_k) \leq \mathsf{cost}_p(X_1, \ldots, X_k, \mathbf{c}_1, \ldots, \mathbf{c}_k) + s||\mathbf{c}_1 - \mathbf{x}_j||_p,$$

where $\mathbf{c}'_1 = \mathbf{x}_j$ *and* $\mathbf{c}'_h = \mathbf{c}_h$ *for* $h \in \{2, \ldots, k\}$.

Our next lemma shows that we can solve PARAMETERIZED EQUAL CLUSTERING in polynomial time if the cluster size is sufficiently big with respect to the budget. To prove it, we exploit Lemmas 1, 3, 4, and 5.

Lemma 6 (⋆). *There is a polynomial-time algorithm that, given a collection* $\mathbf{X} = \{\mathbf{x}_1, \ldots, \mathbf{x}_n\}$ *of* n *points of* $\mathbb{Z}^d$*, a positive integer* k *such that* n *is divisible by* k*, and a nonnegative integer* B *such that* $\frac{n}{k} \geq 4B + 1$*, either computes* $\mathsf{Opt}(X, k) \leq B$ *and produces an equal* k*-clustering of minimum cost or correctly concludes that* $\mathsf{Opt}(\mathbf{X}, k) > B$.

Our next aim is to show that we can reduce the dimension and the absolute values of the coordinates of the points if $\mathsf{Opt}(X, k) \leq B$. To achieve this, we mimic some ideas of the kernelization algorithm of Fomin et al. in [34] for the related clustering problem. However, they considered only points from $\{0, 1\}^d$ and the Hamming norm. The proof uses Lemma 2.

Lemma 7 (⋆). *There is a polynomial-time algorithm that, given a collection* $\mathbf{X} = \{\mathbf{x}_1, \ldots, \mathbf{x}_n\}$ *of* n *points of* $\mathbb{Z}^d$*, a positive integer* k *such that* n *is divisible by* k*, and a nonnegative integer* B*, either correctly concludes that* $\mathsf{Opt}(\mathbf{X}, k) > B$ *or computes a collection of* n *points* $\mathbf{Y} = \{\mathbf{y}_1, \ldots, \mathbf{y}_n\}$ *of* $\mathbb{Z}^{d'}$ *such that the following holds:*

(i) For every partition $\{I_1, \ldots, I_k\}$ *of* $\{1, \ldots, n\}$ *such that* $|I_1| = \cdots = |I_k| = \frac{n}{k}$*, either* $\mathsf{cost}_p(X_1, \ldots, X_k) > B$ *and* $\mathsf{cost}_p(Y_1, \ldots, Y_k) > B$ *or* $\mathsf{cost}_p(X_1, \ldots, X_k) = \mathsf{cost}_p(Y_1, \ldots, Y_k)$*, where* $X_i = \{\mathbf{x}_h \mid h \in I_i\}$ *and* $Y_i = \{\mathbf{y}_h \mid h \in I_i\}$ *for every* $i \in \{1, \ldots, k\}$.
(ii) $d' = \mathcal{O}(kB^{p+1})$.
(iii) $|\mathbf{y}_i[h]| = \mathcal{O}(kB^2)$ *for* $h \in \{1, \ldots, d'\}$ *and* $i \in \{1, \ldots, n\}$.

Finally, we use Lemma 5 to upper bound the additional cost incurred by the greedy clustering of blocks of identical points.

Lemma 8 (⋆). *Let* $\mathbf{X} = \{\mathbf{x}_1, \ldots, \mathbf{x}_n\}$ *be a collection of* n *points of* $\mathbb{Z}^d$ *and set* k *be a positive integer such that* n *is divisible by* k*. Suppose that* $S_1, \ldots, S_t$ *are disjoint collections of identical points of* $\mathbf{X}$ *such that* $|S_1| = \cdots = |S_t| = \frac{n}{k}$ *and* $\mathbf{Y} = \mathbf{X} \setminus (S_1 \cup \cdots \cup S_t)$*. Then* $\mathsf{Opt}(\mathbf{Y}, k - t) \leq 2 \cdot \mathsf{Opt}(\mathbf{X}, k)$.

Now we are ready to show the result about approximate kernel.

Theorem 1. *For every nonnegative integer constant p,* Parameterized Equal Clustering *admits a 2-approximate kernel when parameterized by B, where the output collection of points has $\mathcal{O}(B^2)$ points of $\mathbb{Z}^{d'}$ with $d' = \mathcal{O}(B^{p+2})$, where each coordinate of a point takes an absolute value of $\mathcal{O}(B^3)$.*

Proof. Let $(\mathbf{X}, k, B)$ be an instance of Parameterized Equal Clustering with $\mathbf{X} = \{\mathbf{x}_1, \dots, \mathbf{x}_n\}$, where the points are from $\mathbb{Z}^d$ and n is divisible by k. Recall that a lossy kernel consists of two algorithms. The first algorithm is a polynomial time reduction producing an instance $(\mathbf{X}', k', B')$ of bounded size. The second algorithm is a solution-lifting and for every equal k'-clustering $\{X_1', \dots, X_k'\}$ of $\mathbf{X}'$, this algorithm produces in polynomial time an equal k-clustering $\{X_1, \dots, X_k\}$ of $\mathbf{X}$ such that[3]

$$\frac{\mathsf{cost}_p^B(X_1, \dots, X_k)}{\mathsf{Opt}(\mathbf{X}, k, B)} \le 2 \cdot \frac{\mathsf{cost}_p^{B'}(X_1', \dots, X_{k'}')}{\mathsf{Opt}(\mathbf{X}', k', B')}. \tag{1}$$

We separately consider the cases when $\frac{n}{k} \ge 4B + 1$ and $\frac{n}{k} \le 4B$.

Suppose that $\frac{n}{k} \ge 4B + 1$. Then we apply the algorithm from Lemma 6. If the algorithm returns the answer that $\mathbf{X}$ does no admit an equal k-clustering of cost at most B, then the reduction algorithm returns an trivial no-instance $(\mathbf{X}', k', B')$ of constant size, that is, an instance such that $\mathbf{X}'$ has no clustering of cost at most B'. For example, we set $\mathbf{X}' = \{(0), (1)\}$, $k' = 1$, and $B' = 0$. Here and in the further cases when the reduction algorithm returns a trivial no-instance, the solution-lifting algorithm returns an arbitrary equal k-clustering of $\mathbf{X}$. Since $\mathsf{cost}_p^B(X_1, \dots, X_k) = \mathsf{Opt}(\mathbf{X}, k, B) = B + 1$, (1) holds. Assume that the algorithm from Lemma 6 produced an equal k-clustering $\{X_1, \dots, X_k\}$ of minimum cost. Then the reduction returns an arbitrary instance of Parameterized Equal Clustering of constant size. For example, we can use $\mathbf{X}' = \{(0)\}$, $k' = 1$, and $B' = 0$. The solution-lifting algorithms always returns $\{X_1, \dots, X_k\}$. Clearly, $\mathsf{cost}_p^B(X_1, \dots, X_k) = \mathsf{Opt}(\mathbf{X}, k, B)$ and (1) is fulfilled.

From now on, we assume that $\frac{n}{k} \le 4B$, that is, $n \le 4Bk$. We apply the algorithm from Lemma 7. If this algorithm reports that there is no equal k-clustering of cost at most B, then the reduction algorithm returns a trivial no-instance and the solution-lifting algorithm outputs an arbitrary equal k-clustering of $\mathbf{X}$. Clearly, (1) is satisfied. Assume that this is not the case. Then we obtain a collection of $n \le 4Bk$ points $\mathbf{Y} = \{\mathbf{y}_1, \dots, \mathbf{y}_n\}$ of $\mathbb{Z}^{d'}$ satisfying conditions (i)–(iii) of Lemma 7. That is, (i) for every partition $\{I_1, \dots, I_k\}$ of $\{1, \dots, n\}$ such that $|I_1| = \dots = |I_k| = \frac{n}{k}$, either $\mathsf{cost}_p(X_1, \dots, X_k) > B$ and $\mathsf{cost}_p(Y_1, \dots, Y_k) > B$ or $\mathsf{cost}_p(X_1, \dots, X_k) = \mathsf{cost}_p(Y_1, \dots, Y_k)$, where $X_i = \{\mathbf{x}_h \mid h \in I_i\}$ and $Y_i = \{\mathbf{y}_h \mid h \in I_i\}$ for every $i \in \{1, \dots, k\}$, (ii) $d' = \mathcal{O}(kB^{p+1})$, and (iii) $|\mathbf{y}_i[h]| = \mathcal{O}(kB^2)$ for $h \in \{1, \dots, d'\}$ and $i \in \{1, \dots, n\}$. By (i), for given an

[3] Note that by our simplifying assumption, $\frac{\mathsf{cost}_p^B(X_1, \dots, X_k)}{\mathsf{Opt}(\mathbf{X}, k, B)} = 1$ if $\mathsf{Opt}(\mathbf{X}, k, B) = 0$, and the same assumption is used for $\frac{\mathsf{cost}_p^{B'}(X_1', \dots, X_{k'}')}{\mathsf{Opt}(\mathbf{X}', k', B')}$.

equal k-clustering clustering $\{Y_1, \ldots, Y_k\}$ of $\mathbf{Y}$, we can compute the corresponding clustering $\{X_1, \ldots, X_k\}$ by setting $X_i = \{\mathbf{x}_h \mid \mathbf{y}_h \in Y_i\}$ for $i \in \{1, \ldots, k\}$. Then $\mathsf{Opt}(\mathbf{X}, k, B) = \mathsf{Opt}(\mathbf{Y}, k, B)$ and

$$\frac{\mathsf{cost}_p^B(X_1, \ldots, X_k)}{\mathsf{Opt}(\mathbf{X}, k, B)} = \frac{\mathsf{cost}_p^B(Y_1, \ldots, Y_k)}{\mathsf{Opt}(\mathbf{Y}, k, B)}. \tag{2}$$

Hence the instances $(\mathbf{X}, k, B)$ and $(\mathbf{Y}, k, B)$ are equivalent. We continue with the compressed instance $(\mathbf{Y}, k, B)$.

Now we apply the greedy procedure that constructs clusters $S_1, \ldots, S_t$ composed by identical points. Formally, we initially set $\mathbf{X}' := Y$, $k' := k$, and $i := 0$. Then we do the following:

- while $\mathbf{X}'$ contains a collections S of s identical points, set $i := i + 1$, $S_i := S$, $\mathbf{X}' := \mathbf{X}' \backslash S$, and $k' := k' - 1$.

Denote by $\mathbf{X}'$ the set of points obtained by the application of the procedure and let $S_1, \ldots, S_t$ be the collections of identical points constructed by the procedure. Note that $k' = k - t$. We also define $B' = 2B$. Notice that it may happen that $\mathbf{X}' = \mathbf{Y}$ or $\mathbf{X}' = \emptyset$. The crucial property exploited by the kernelization is that by Lemma 8, $\mathsf{Opt}(\mathbf{X}', k') \leq 2 \cdot \mathsf{Opt}(\mathbf{Y}, k)$.

We argue that if $k' > B$, then we have no k-clustering of cost at most B. Suppose that $k' > B'$. Consider an arbitrary equal k'-clustering $\{X_1', \ldots, X_{k'}'\}$ of $\mathbf{X}'$. Because the construction of $S_1, \ldots, S_t$ stops when there is no collection of s identical points, each cluster X_i' contains at least two distinct points. Since all points have integer coordinates, we have that $\mathsf{cost}_p(X_i') \geq 1$ for every $i \in \{1, \ldots, k'\}$. Therefore, $\mathsf{cost}_p(X_1', \ldots, X_{k'}') = \sum_{i=1}^{k'} \mathsf{cost}_p(X_i') \geq k' > B' = 2B$. This means that $2 \cdot \mathsf{Opt}(Y, k) \geq \mathsf{Opt}(\mathbf{X}', k') > 2B$ and $\mathsf{Opt}(\mathbf{Y}, k) > B$. Using this, our reduction algorithm returns a trivial no-instance. Then the solution-lifting algorithm outputs an arbitrary equal k-clustering of $\mathbf{X}$ and this satisfies (1).

From now on we assume that $k' \leq B' = 2B$ and construct the reduction and solution lifting algorithms for this case.

If $k' = 0$, then $\mathbf{X}' = \emptyset$ and the reduction algorithm simply returns an arbitrary instance of constant size. Otherwise, our reduction algorithms returns $(\mathbf{X}', k', B')$. Observe that since $k' \leq B' = 2B$, $|\mathbf{X}'| \leq n \leq 4B^2$. Recall that $d' = \mathcal{O}(B^{p+2})$ and $|\mathbf{x}_i'[h]| = \mathcal{O}(B^3)$ for $h \in \{1, \ldots, d'\}$ for every point $\mathbf{x}_i' \in \mathbf{X}'$. We conclude that the instance $(\mathbf{X}', k', B')$ of Parameterized Equal Clustering satisfies the size conditions of the theorem.

Now we describe the solution-lifting algorithm and argue that (1) holds.

If $k' = 0$, then the solution-lifting algorithm ignores the output of the reduction algorithm which was arbitrary. It takes the equal k-clustering $\{S_1, \ldots, S_k\}$ of $\mathbf{Y}$ and outputs the equal k-clustering $\{X_1, \ldots, X_k\}$ of $\mathbf{X}$ by setting $X_i = \{\mathbf{x}_h \mid \mathbf{y}_h \in S_i\}$ for $i \in \{1, \ldots, k\}$. Clearly, $\mathsf{cost}_p(S_1, \ldots, S_k) = \mathsf{cost}_p(X_1, \ldots, X_p) = 0$. Therefore, (1) holds.

If $k' > 0$, we consider an equal k'-clustering $\{X_1', \ldots, X_{k'}'\}$ of $\mathbf{X}'$. The solution-lifting algorithm constructs an equal k-clustering $\{S_1, \ldots, S_t, X_1', \ldots, X_{k'}'\}$, that is, we just add the clusters constructed by our greedy procedure.

Since the points in each set S_i are identical, $\mathsf{cost}_p(S_i) = 0$ for every $i \in \{1, \dots, t\}$. Therefore,

$$\mathsf{cost}_p(S_1, \dots, S_t, X'_1, \dots, X'_{k'}) = \mathsf{cost}_p(X'_1, \dots, X'_{k'}).$$

Notice that since $\mathsf{Opt}(\mathbf{X}', k') \le 2 \cdot \mathsf{Opt}(\mathbf{Y}, k)$, we have that $\mathsf{Opt}(\mathbf{X}', k', B') \le 2 \cdot \mathsf{Opt}(\mathbf{Y}, k, B)$. Indeed, if $\mathsf{Opt}(\mathbf{Y}, k) \le B$, then $\mathsf{Opt}(\mathbf{X}', k') \le 2B = B'$. Hence, $\mathsf{Opt}(\mathbf{Y}, k, B) = \mathsf{Opt}(\mathbf{Y}, k)$, $\mathsf{Opt}(\mathbf{X}', k', B') = \mathsf{Opt}(\mathbf{X}', k')$, and $\mathsf{Opt}(\mathbf{X}', k', B') \le 2 \cdot \mathsf{Opt}(\mathbf{Y}, k, B)$. If $\mathsf{Opt}(\mathbf{Y}, k) > B$, then $\mathsf{Opt}(\mathbf{Y}, k, B) = B + 1$. In this case $2 \cdot \mathsf{Opt}(\mathbf{Y}, k, B) = 2B + 2 > \mathsf{Opt}(\mathbf{X}', k', B')$, because $\mathsf{Opt}(\mathbf{X}', k', B') \le B' + 1 = 2B + 1$. Finally, since $\mathsf{cost}_p(S_1, \dots, S_t, X'_1, \dots, X'_{k'}) = \mathsf{cost}_p(X'_1, \dots, X'_{k'})$ and $\mathsf{Opt}(\mathbf{X}', k', B') \le 2 \cdot \mathsf{Opt}(\mathbf{Y}, k, B)$, we conclude that

$$\frac{\mathsf{cost}_p^B(S_1, \dots, S_t, X'_1, \dots, X'_{k'})}{\mathsf{Opt}(\mathbf{Y}, k, B)} \le 2 \cdot \frac{\mathsf{cost}_p^B(X_1, \dots, X'_{k'})}{\mathsf{Opt}(\mathbf{X}', k', B')}. \tag{3}$$

Then the solution-lifting algorithm computes the k-clustering $\{X_1, \dots, X_k\}$ for the equal k-clustering $\{Y_1, \dots, Y_k\} = \{S_1, \dots, S_t, X'_1, \dots, X'_{k'}\}$ of $\mathbf{Y}$ by setting $X_i = \{\mathbf{x}_h \mid \mathbf{y}_h \in Y_i\}$ for $i \in \{1, \dots, k\}$. By (2) and (3), we obtain (1).

This concludes the description of the reduction and solution-lifting algorithms, as well as the proof of their correctness. To argue that the reduction algorithm is a polynomial-time algorithm, we observe that the algorithms from Lemmata 6 and 7 run in polynomial time. Trivially, the greedy construction of $S_1, \dots, S_t$, $\mathbf{X}$, and k' can be done in polynomial time. Therefore, the reduction algorithm runs in polynomial time. The solution-lifting algorithm is also easily implementable to run in polynomial time. This concludes the proof. □

4 Kernelization

In this section we study (exact) kernelization of clustering with equal sizes. First, we show that it is unlikely that Decision Equal Clustering admits a polynomial kernel when parameterized by B only. We prove this for ℓ_0 and ℓ_1-norms. Our lower bound holds even for points with binary coordinates, that is, for points from $\{0,1\}^d$. For this, we use the result of Dell and Marx [24] about kernelization lower bounds for the Perfect r-Set Matching problem.

Theorem 2 ($\star$). *For ℓ_0 and ℓ_1-norms,* Decision Equal Clustering *has no polynomial kernel when parameterized by B, unless $\mathsf{NP} \subseteq \mathsf{coNP/poly}$, even if the input points are binary, that is, are from $\{0,1\}^d$.*

Now we prove Theorem 3 that we restate here.

Theorem 3. *For every nonnegative integer constant p,* Decision Equal Clustering *admits a polynomial kernel when parameterized by k and B, where the output collection of points has $\mathcal{O}(kB)$ points of $\mathbb{Z}^{d'}$ with $d' = \mathcal{O}(kB^{p+1})$ and each coordinate of a point takes an absolute value of $\mathcal{O}(kB^2)$.*

Proof. Let $(\mathbf{X}, k, B)$ be an instance of DECISION EQUAL CLUSTERING with $\mathbf{X} = \{\mathbf{x}_1, \ldots, \mathbf{x}_n\}$, where the points are from $\mathbb{Z}^d$. Recall that n is divisible by k.

Suppose $\frac{n}{k} \geq 4B + 1$. Then we can apply the algorithm from Lemma 6. If the algorithm returns that there is no equal k-clustering of cost at most B, then the kernelization algorithm returns a trivial no-instance of DECISION EQUAL CLUSTERING. Otherwise, if $\mathsf{Opt}(X, k) \leq B$, then the algorithm returns a trivial yes-instance.

Assume that $\frac{n}{k} \leq 4B$, that is, $n \leq 4Bk$. Then we apply the algorithm from Lemma 7. If this algorithm reports that there is no equal k-clustering of cost at most B, then the kernelization algorithm returns a trivial no-instance of DECISION EQUAL CLUSTERING. Otherwise, the algorithm from Lemma 7 returns a collection of $n \leq 4Bk$ points $\mathbf{Y} = \{\mathbf{y}_1, \ldots, \mathbf{y}_n\}$ of $\mathbb{Z}^{d'}$ satisfying conditions (i)–(iii) of the lemma. By (i), we obtain that the instances $(\mathbf{X}, k, B)$ and $(\mathbf{Y}, k, B)$ of DECISION EQUAL CLUSTERING are equivalent. By (ii), we have that the dimension $d' = \mathcal{O}(k(B^{p+1}))$, and by (iii), each coordinate of a point takes an absolute value of $\mathcal{O}(kB^2)$. Thus, $(\mathbf{Y}, k, B)$ is a required kernel. □

5 APX-Hardness of EQUAL CLUSTERING

In this section, we prove APX-hardness of EQUAL CLUSTERING w.r.t. Hamming (ℓ_0) and ℓ_1 distances. The constructed hard instances consists of high-dimensional binary (0/1) points. As the ℓ_0 and ℓ_1 distances between any two binary points are the same, we focus on the case of ℓ_0 distances. Our reduction is from 3-DIMENSIONAL MATCHING (3DM) is based on the inapproximability result of Petrank [47].

Theorem 4 ($\star$). *There exists a constant $\epsilon_c > 0$, such that it is* NP*-hard to obtain a $(1 + \epsilon_c)$-approximation for* EQUAL CLUSTERING *with ℓ_0 (or ℓ_1) distances, even if the input points are binary, that is, are from $\{0, 1\}^d$.*

6 Conclusion

We initiated the study of lossy kernelization for clustering problems and proved that PARAMETERIZED EQUAL CLUSTERING admits a 2-approximation kernel. It is natural to ask whether the approximation factor may be improved. In particular, does the problem admit a *polynomial size approximate kernelization scheme* (PSAKS) that is a lossy kernelization analog of PTAS (we refer to [35] for the definition)? Note that we proved that EQUAL CLUSTERING is APX-hard and this refutes the existence of PTAS and makes it natural to ask the question about PSAKS. We also believe that it is interesting to consider the variants of the considered problems for means instead of medians. Here, the cost of a collection of points $\mathbf{X} \subseteq \mathbb{Z}^d$ is defined as $\min_{\mathbf{c} \in \mathbb{R}^d} \sum_{\mathbf{x} \in \mathbf{X}} \|\mathbf{c} - \mathbf{x}\|_p^p$ for $p \geq 1$. Clearly, if $p = 1$, that is, in the case of Manhattan norm, our results hold. However, for $p \geq 2$, we cannot translate our results directly, because our arguments rely on the triangle inequality. We would like to conclude the paper by underlining our belief that lossy kernelization may be natural tool for the lucrative area of approximation algorithms for clustering problems.

References

1. Aggarwal, C.C., Reddy, C.K. (eds.): Data Clustering: Algorithms and Applications. CRC Press, Boca Raton (2013)
2. Agrawal, A., Saurabh, S., Tale, P.: On the parameterized complexity of contraction to generalization of trees. In: 12th International Symposium on Parameterized and Exact Computation (IPEC). LIPIcs, vol. 89, pp. 1:1–1:12. Schloss Dagstuhl - Leibniz-Zentrum fuer Informatik (2017)
3. Ahmadian, S., Norouzi-Fard, A., Svensson, O., Ward, J.: Better guarantees for k-means and Euclidean k-median by primal-dual algorithms. In: 58th IEEE Annual Symposium on Foundations of Computer Science, FOCS 2017, pp. 61–72. IEEE Computer Society (2017)
4. Alon, N., Sudakov, B.: On two segmentation problems. J. Algorithms **33**(1), 173–184 (1999)
5. Arora, S., Raghavan, P., Rao, S.: Approximation schemes for Euclidean k-medians and related problems. In: Thirtieth Annual ACM Symposium on Theory of Computing, STOC 1998, pp. 106–113. ACM, New York (1998)
6. Baker, D., Braverman, V., Huang, L., Jiang, S.H.C., Krauthgamer, R., Wu, X.: Coresets for clustering in graphs of bounded treewidth. In: International Conference on Machine Learning, pp. 569–579. PMLR (2020)
7. Bandyapadhyay, S., Fomin, F.V., Purohit, N., Simonov, K.: Lossy kernelization of same-size clustering. CoRR abs/2107.07383 (2021)
8. Bandyapadhyay, S., Fomin, F.V., Simonov, K.: On coresets for fair clustering in metric and Euclidean spaces and their applications. In: 48th International Colloquium on Automata, Languages, and Programming (ICALP). LIPIcs, vol. 198, pp. 23:1–23:15. Schloss Dagstuhl - Leibniz-Zentrum für Informatik (2021)
9. Bandyapadhyay, S., Varadarajan, K.R.: On variants of k-means clustering. In: 32nd International Symposium on Computational Geometry, SoCG 2016. LIPIcs, Boston, MA, USA, 14–18 June 2016, vol. 51, pp. 14:1–14:15. Schloss Dagstuhl - Leibniz-Zentrum für Informatik (2016)
10. Basu, S., Davidson, I., Wagstaff, K.: Constrained Clustering: Advances in Algorithms, Theory, and Applications. CRC Press, Boca Raton (2008)
11. Bhattacharya, A., Jaiswal, R., Kumar, A.: Faster algorithms for the constrained k-means problem. Theory Comput. Syst. **62**(1), 93–115 (2018). https://doi.org/10.1007/s00224-017-9820-7
12. Byrka, J., Fleszar, K., Rybicki, B., Spoerhase, J.: Bi-factor approximation algorithms for hard capacitated k-median problems. In: Twenty-Sixth Annual ACM-SIAM Symposium on Discrete Algorithms, SODA 2015, pp. 722–736. SIAM (2015)
13. Byrka, J., Pensyl, T.W., Rybicki, B., Srinivasan, A., Trinh, K.: An improved approximation for k-median and positive correlation in budgeted optimization. ACM Trans. Algorithms **13**(2), 23:1–23:31 (2017)
14. Byrka, J., Rybicki, B., Uniyal, S.: An approximation algorithm for uniform capacitated k-median problem with $1+\epsilon$ capacity violation. In: Louveaux, Q., Skutella, M. (eds.) IPCO 2016. LNCS, vol. 9682, pp. 262–274. Springer, Cham (2016). https://doi.org/10.1007/978-3-319-33461-5_22
15. Charikar, M., Guha, S., Tardos, É., Shmoys, D.B.: A constant-factor approximation algorithm for the k-median problem. J. Comput. Syst. Sci. **65**(1), 129–149 (2002)
16. Chuzhoy, J., Rabani, Y.: Approximating k-median with non-uniform capacities. In: Sixteenth Annual ACM-SIAM Symposium on Discrete Algorithms, SODA 2005, pp. 952–958. SIAM (2005)

17. Cohen-Addad, V.: Approximation schemes for capacitated clustering in doubling metrics. In: ACM-SIAM Symposium on Discrete Algorithms, SODA 2020, pp. 2241–2259. SIAM (2020)
18. Cohen-Addad, V., Gupta, A., Kumar, A., Lee, E., Li, J.: Tight FPT approximations for k-median and k-means. In: 46th International Colloquium on Automata, Languages, and Programming (ICALP). LIPIcs, vol. 132, pp. 42:1–42:14. Schloss Dagstuhl - Leibniz-Zentrum für Informatik (2019)
19. Cohen-Addad, V., Klein, P.N., Mathieu, C.: Local search yields approximation schemes for k-means and k-median in Euclidean and minor-free metrics. SIAM J. Comput. **48**(2), 644–667 (2019)
20. Cohen-Addad, V., Li, J.: On the fixed-parameter tractability of capacitated clustering. In: 46th International Colloquium on Automata, Languages, and Programming (ICALP). LIPIcs, vol. 132, pp. 41:1–41:14. Schloss Dagstuhl - Leibniz-Zentrum für Informatik (2019)
21. Cohen-Addad, V., Mathieu, C.: Effectiveness of local search for geometric optimization. In: 31st International Symposium on Computational Geometry, SoCG 2015. LIPIcs, vol. 34, pp. 329–343. Schloss Dagstuhl - Leibniz-Zentrum für Informatik (2015)
22. Cohen-Addad, V., de Mesmay, A., Rotenberg, E., Roytman, A.: The bane of low-dimensionality clustering. In: Twenty-Ninth Annual ACM-SIAM Symposium on Discrete Algorithms (SODA), pp. 441–456. SIAM (2018)
23. Cygan, M., et al.: Parameterized Algorithms. Springer, Cham (2015). https://doi.org/10.1007/978-3-319-21275-3
24. Dell, H., Marx, D.: Kernelization of packing problems. CoRR abs/1812.03155 (2018)
25. Demirci, H.G., Li, S.: Constant approximation for capacitated k-median with $(1+\varepsilon)$-capacity violation. In: 43rd International Colloquium on Automata, Languages, and Programming (ICALP). LIPIcs, vol. 55, pp. 73:1–73:14. Schloss Dagstuhl-Leibniz-Zentrum für Informatik (2016)
26. Ding, H., Xu, J.: A unified framework for clustering constrained data without locality property. Algorithmica **82**(4), 808–852 (2020). https://doi.org/10.1007/s00453-019-00616-2
27. Downey, R.G., Fellows, M.R.: Fundamentals of Parameterized Complexity. Texts in Computer Science, Springer, London (2013). https://doi.org/10.1007/978-1-4471-5559-1
28. Dvořák, P., Feldmann, A.E., Knop, D., Masařík, T., Toufar, T., Veselý, P.: Parameterized approximation schemes for Steiner trees with small number of Steiner vertices. CoRR abs/1710.00668 (2017)
29. Eiben, E., Kumar, M., Mouawad, A.E., Panolan, F., Siebertz, S.: Lossy kernels for connected dominating set on sparse graphs. In: 34th International Symposium on Theoretical Aspects of Computer Science (STACS). LIPIcs, vol. 96, pp. 29:1–29:15. Schloss Dagstuhl - Leibniz-Zentrum fuer Informatik (2018)
30. Feldman, D., Langberg, M.: A unified framework for approximating and clustering data. In: 43rd Annual ACM Symposium on Theory of Computing (STOC), pp. 569–578. ACM (2011)
31. Feldman, D., Schmidt, M., Sohler, C.: Turning big data into tiny data: constant-size coresets for k-means, PCA, and projective clustering. SIAM J. Comput. **49**(3), 601–657 (2020)
32. Feldmann, A.E., Karthik, C.S., Lee, E., Manurangsi, P.: A survey on approximation in parameterized complexity: hardness and algorithms. Algorithms **13**(6), 146 (2020)

33. Feng, Q., Zhang, Z., Huang, Z., Xu, J., Wang, J.: A unified framework of FPT approximation algorithms for clustering problems. In: 31st International Symposium on Algorithms and Computation (ISAAC). LIPIcs, vol. 181, pp. 5:1–5:17. Schloss Dagstuhl - Leibniz-Zentrum für Informatik (2020)
34. Fomin, F.V., Golovach, P.A., Panolan, F.: Parameterized low-rank binary matrix approximation. Data Min. Knowl. Discov. **34**(2), 478–532 (2020). https://doi.org/10.1007/s10618-019-00669-5
35. Fomin, F.V., Lokshtanov, D., Saurabh, S., Zehavi, M.: Kernelization: Theory of Parameterized Preprocessing. Cambridge University Press, Cambridge (2019)
36. Friggstad, Z., Rezapour, M., Salavatipour, M.R.: Local search yields a PTAS for k-means in doubling metrics. SIAM J. Comput. **48**(2), 452–480 (2019)
37. Har-Peled, S., Mazumdar, S.: On coresets for k-means and k-median clustering. In: Proceedings of the 36th Annual ACM Symposium on Theory of Computing (STOC), pp. 291–300. ACM (2004)
38. Höppner, F., Klawonn, F.: Clustering with size constraints. In: Jain, L.C., Sato-Ilic, M., Virvou, M., Tsihrintzis, G.A., Balas, V.E., Abeynayake, C. (eds.) Computational Intelligence Paradigms, Innovative Applications. SCI, vol. 137, pp. 167–180. Springer, Heidelberg (2008). https://doi.org/10.1007/978-3-540-79474-5_8
39. Jain, K., Vazirani, V.V.: Approximation algorithms for metric facility location and k-median problems using the primal-dual schema and Lagrangian relaxation. J. ACM **48**(2), 274–296 (2001)
40. Krithika, R., Misra, P., Rai, A., Tale, P.: Lossy kernels for graph contraction problems. In: 36th IARCS Annual Conference on Foundations of Software Technology and Theoretical Computer Science (FSTTCS). LIPIcs, vol. 65, pp. 23:1–23:14. Schloss Dagstuhl - Leibniz-Zentrum fuer Informatik (2016)
41. Kumar, A., Sabharwal, Y., Sen, S.: Linear-time approximation schemes for clustering problems in any dimensions. J. ACM **57**(2), 5:1–5:32 (2010)
42. Li, S.: On uniform capacitated k-median beyond the natural LP relaxation. ACM Trans. Algorithms **13**(2), 22:1–22:18 (2017)
43. Li, S., Svensson, O.: Approximating k-median via pseudo-approximation. SIAM J. Comput. **45**(2), 530–547 (2016)
44. Li, T.: A general model for clustering binary data. In: KDD 2005, pp. 188–197 (2005)
45. Lokshtanov, D., Panolan, F., Ramanujan, M.S., Saurabh, S.: Lossy kernelization. In: 49th Annual ACM Symposium on Theory of Computing (STOC), pp. 224–237. ACM (2017)
46. Manurangsi, P., Raghavendra, P.: A birthday repetition theorem and complexity of approximating dense CSPs. In: 44th International Colloquium on Automata, Languages, and Programming (ICALP 2017). Schloss Dagstuhl-Leibniz-Zentrum fuer Informatik (2017)
47. Petrank, E.: The hardness of approximation: gap location. Comput. Complex. **4**, 133–157 (1994). https://doi.org/10.1007/BF01202286
48. Siebertz, S.: Lossy kernels for connected distance-r domination on nowhere dense graph classes. CoRR abs/1707.09819 (2017)
49. Sohler, C., Woodruff, D.P.: Strong coresets for k-median and subspace approximation: goodbye dimension. In: 59th Annual Symposium on Foundations of Computer Science (FOCS), pp. 802–813. IEEE (2018)
50. Sweeney, L.: k-anonymity: a model for protecting privacy. Int. J. Uncertain. Fuzziness Knowl. Based Syst. **10**(05), 557–570 (2002)

51. Vallejo-Huanga, D., Morillo, P., Ferri, C.: Semi-supervised clustering algorithms for grouping scientific articles. In: International Conference on Computational Science (ICCS) (2017). Procedia Comput. Sci. **108**, 325–334. Elsevier
52. Zhang, Z., Li, T., Ding, C., Zhang, X.: Binary matrix factorization with applications. In: ICDM 2007, pp. 391–400. IEEE (2007)

Output Sensitive Fault Tolerant Maximum Matching

Niranka Banerjee[1(✉)], Manoj Gupta[2], Venkatesh Raman[3], and Saket Saurabh[3,4]

[1] Research Institute for Mathematical Sciences, Kyoto University, Kyoto, Japan
niranka@gmail.com

[2] IIT Gandhinagar, Gandhinagar, Gujarat, India
gmanoj@iitgn.ac.in

[3] The Institute of Mathematical Sciences HBNI, Chennai, India
{vraman,saket}@imsc.res.in

[4] University of Bergen, Bergen, Norway

Abstract. We consider the problem of maintaining the size of a Maximum Matching in the presence of failures of vertices and edges. For a graph G, we use $\mu(G)$ to denote the size of a maximum matching of G. A subgraph H of G is an (α, f)-Fault Tolerant Matching Subgraph ((α, f)-FTMS) if it has the following property: For any set F of at most f vertices or edges in G, $\alpha \cdot \mu(G - F) \leq \mu(H - F)$. Assadi and Bernstein [SOSA 2019] showed that for any $\epsilon > 0$, there exists a $(\frac{2}{3} - \epsilon, f)$-FTMS of size $\mathcal{O}(n + f)$. In this paper we initiate a study of $(1, f)$-FTMS or f-FTMS in short.

In particular we obtain the following results,

- On bipartite graphs, there exists 1-FTMS, for one edge fault with $\mathcal{O}(\mu(G))$ vertices and edges. We complement this upper bound with the matching lower bound of $\Omega(\mu(G))$ on 1-FTMS for one edge fault.
- On general graphs, there exists f-FTMS for at most f edge faults with $\mathcal{O}(\mu(G)^2 + \mu(G)f)$ edges and $\mathcal{O}(\mu(G) \cdot f)$ vertices. We also provide a matching lower bound of $\Omega(\max\{\mu(G)^2, \mu(G)f\})$ edges and $\Omega(\mu(G)f)$ vertices for f-FTMS, $f \geq 2$ for at most f edge faults.

The same construction works for vertex faults, and they result in even tighter bounds for $f = 1$. Our algorithmic results exploit the structural properties of matchings and use tools from Parameterized Algorithms, such as Expansion Lemma. We leave open the question of existence of 1-FTMS for one edge fault, of linear size (in terms of $\mu(G)$) on general graphs.

Keywords: Fault Tolerant · Maximum Matching · Upper and Lower Bound

---

N. Banerjee—Supported by JSPS KAKENHI Grant No. JP20H05967.

A. S. Kulikov and S. Raskhodnikova (Eds.): CSR 2022, LNCS 13296, pp. 115–132, 2022.
https://doi.org/10.1007/978-3-031-09574-0_8

1 Introduction

Given a graph G with m edges and n vertices, a matching in G is a set of edges such that no two edges in the set share any common endpoint. The study of matching has been one of the important problems in graph theory [22,23]. In particular, the problem of finding maximum matching has interested many researchers and there is a huge body of work for this problem [15,17,20,21,24–26].

Graphs used to model real-life networks are prone to failures. Such networks are modeled as graphs where vertices communicate with each other through edges. A failure of an edge (edges) or vertex (vertices) of the network may lead to a breakdown in communication. This motivates us to build algorithms that are resilient to failures. Such algorithms are built in the *fault tolerant model.* A fault tolerant algorithm is expected to work inspite of failures in the network. Normally it is assumed that the number of failures in the network is much less than the size of the network. Thus, when we say that there are f edge or vertex faults, then $f \ll m$. Also, we assume that the faults are repaired readily, thus they are not permanent.

We now give a formal definition of our model, which is called the *fault tolerant subgraph model* in literature: Given a graph G, we want to find a subgraph H of G such that after any set of F failures, a property P in $G - F$ is maintained in $H - F$. In general, the solution of the fault tolerant subgraph problem is judged by the size of the subgraph H. Fault tolerant subgraphs have been developed for various problems like reachability [4,5], shortest path [9,18,28–30] and spanners [8,11,12,14,27].

In the fault tolerant model the set F of failures is picked adversarially. If instead, each edge or vertex of a graph fails independently at random with a probability p then this setting is known as the non-adaptive stochastic matching problem as defined in [10]. This problem has been extensively studied in literature [2,3,6,7,32].

Our Results and Techniques

We formally define our problem.

Definition 1. *((α, f)-FTMS) Given a graph G, let $\mu(G)$ denote the size of a maximum matching of G. An (α, f)-FTMS is a subgraph H of G such that for any set of edges or vertices F of cardinality at most f, $\alpha \cdot \mu(G-F) \leq \mu(H-F)$. When $\alpha = 1$, we simply drop α. Thus, $(1, f)$-FTMS is referred to as f-FTMS. For a graph G, we use $\Psi(G)$ to denote the minimum number of edges in an f-FTMS of G. That is,*

$$\Psi(G) = \min_{H \text{ is an } f\text{-FTMS of } G} |E(H)|$$

Let G' be a family of graphs, then for all $n \in N$, we define the following:

$$\text{FTMS}(G', n, f) = \max_{G \in G', |V(G)|=n} \Psi(G)$$

To the best of our knowledge, FTMS has only been studied by Assadi and Bernstein [1]. They showed that for any $\epsilon > 0$, there exists a $(\frac{2}{3} - \epsilon, f)$-FTMS of size $\mathcal{O}(n+f)$, while any $(\frac{2}{3} + \epsilon, f)$-FTMS, when $f = \Theta(n)$ requires $n^{1+\Omega(\frac{1}{\log \log n})}$ edges. Our study initiates the study of exact maximum matching in the fault tolerant setting. One of our results (see Theorem 8 in Sect. 4.2) show that there exist graphs where even 2-FTMS requires $\Omega(n^2)$ edges.

This seems to suggest that we have reached the end of the road for $f \geq 2$. However, we observe that for our example, $\mu(G) = \Omega(n)$. Thus, we can also express our lower bound as $\mu(G)^2$. This motivates us to look for a *fine-grained* definition of f-FTMS that not only take into account n and f, but also some parameter that captures the size of the maximum matching of the input graph. In particular, we can come up with the following new definitions.

Let G' be a family of graphs, then for all $n, \ell \in N$, we define the following:

$$\text{FTMS}(G', n, \ell, f) = \max_{G \in G', |V(G)|=n, \mu(G)=\ell} \Psi(G)$$

Henceforth, we refer to FTMS(G', n, ℓ, f) as f-FTMS. With respect to our new definition, when G' is a family of graphs as given in Theorem 8, we have that 2-FTMS is at most $\mathcal{O}(\ell^2)$. Thus, a natural question arises: Can we derive a similar upper bound even when G' denotes the family of all graphs? Indeed, we provide a matching upper and lower bound on these quantities in this paper.

Our first result gives a bound when $f = 1$ edge fault for bipartite graphs. We show the following,

Theorem 1. *For a bipartite graph G, there exists a* 1*-FTMS of G, for one edge fault of size $\mathcal{O}(\mu(G))$. Furthermore, there exist graphs G for which any* 1*-FTMS for one edge fault requires $\Omega(\mu(G))$ edges and vertices.*

The construction achieving 1-FTMS in Theorem 1 is based on "preserving augmenting paths". That is, we start with a maximum matching M, and construct H iteratively. Initially, H contains M and in each iteration for every edge $e \in M$, if there exists an augmenting path P in $G - \{e\}$, then we add an augmenting path P' to H. We can not add any augmenting path as this could blow up the size of H. Thus, we need to construct H carefully. Towards this, orient the matched edges in one direction and the unmatched edges in the opposite direction in G. Then each component of H is constructed such that it is a maximal strongly connected component (SCC) of the oriented graph. Observe that any SCC is a 1-FTMS for all edges of M in that SCC. This intuition is detailed in Sect. 3. The construction requires careful analysis both for size and its correctness. The analyses requires maintaining several invariants and updating them carefully.

In fact, we observe that almost the same construction yields the following result for vertex faults,

Theorem 2. *For any graph G, there exists a* 1*-FTMS of G, for one vertex fault, of size $\mathcal{O}(\mu(G))$. Furthermore, there exist graphs G for which any* 1*-FTMS for one vertex fault requires $\Omega(\mu(G))$ edges and vertices.*

In contrast to one edge fault where our results hold for only bipartite graphs, it is interesting to note that for one vertex fault our results can be extended to general graphs. This is due to the fact that due to a vertex fault certain types of augmenting paths from Theorem 1 do not need to be considered when constructing a 1−FTMS for one vertex fault. For the specific types of augmenting paths that we need to consider, Theorem 1 holds true even for general graphs. Hence, the theorem follows.

Our second result, gives tight bounds when $f \geq 2$ for general graphs. In this result the usage of the terms f−FTMS or f faults refer to both vertex or edge faults. Our proofs for both upper and lower bounds work for both vertex and edge faults simultaneously giving the same bounds. Specifically, we show,

Theorem 3. *For any graph G, there exists an f-FTMS of G of size $\mathcal{O}((\mu(G))^2 + \mu(G)f)$. Furthermore, there exist graphs G for $f \geq 2$ for which any f-FTMS requires $\Omega(\max\{\mu(G)^2, \mu(G)f\})$ edges and $\Omega(\mu(G)f)$ vertices.*

Note that the restriction on the bound $f \geq 2$ is only on the lower bound and not the upper bound. The algorithm that achieves the upper bound mentioned in Theorem 3 combines two efficient construction for f-FTMS. The first algorithm is a simple greedy algorithm. Let M be a maximum matching of G and $I = V(G) - V(M)$. We call the edges between $V(M)$ and I *cross edges*. We show that a graph induced on $V(M)$, together with at most $3f$ cross edges incident to each vertex in $V(M)$, is a valid f-FTMS subgraph H. The essence of the proof lies in the following structural claim: for any set of edges $F \subseteq E(G)$ of size at most f, there exists a matching M_F in $H - F$ such that $\mu(G - F) = |M_F|$ and it uses at most $2f$ cross edges. We further refine this construction making use of expansion lemma [16,31], a tool used in parameterized complexity, to further reduce the number of vertices in the f-FTMS. This construction gives the desired upper bound on f-FTMS, as claimed in Theorem 3.

2 Preliminaries

Given a graph $G = (V, E)$, a matching μ is a set of edges such that no two edges in μ are adjacent to each other. We also use $V(G)$ and $E(G)$ to denote the vertex and the edge set of G, respectively. An edge in μ is said to be matched. All other edges are said to be unmatched. We say a vertex is matched if it is incident to an edge in μ. Otherwise a vertex is unmatched. A maximum matching is a matching of largest cardinality. In the rest of the paper we define $\mu(G)$ to be the size of a maximum matching of graph G. We sometimes abuse notation and also refer to an edge $(a, b) \in \mu(G)$ or the set of edges of the maximum matching $\mu(G)$, which will be clear from the context. We define $\mu(V)$ to be the matched vertices in the matching $\mu(G)$. A path is called an augmenting path with respect to a matching μ if the two endpoints of the path are unmatched in μ and the edges of the path alternate between edges in μ and edges not in μ. $P[x, y]$ denotes the subpath of a path P starting from the vertex $x \in P$ and ending at the vertex $y \in P$.

3 1-FTMS

In this section, we show a construction of a 1-FTMS H of a bipartite graph in case of one edge fault and of a general graph for one vertex fault. Suppose an edge $e = (a, b)$ or a vertex a is removed from the graph G. As a result, let M^* be the new maximum matching in $G - e$ or in $G - a$. A maximum matching is not unique, hence our aim in creating a 1−FTMS H is not to compute the matching M^*, but some matching M' in H such that $|M'| = |M^*|$.

Let us look at the edges which should be kept in H. We compute the size of a maximum matching $\mu(G)$ in G and include the edges of this maximum matching in H. Let us look at the other edges that need to be included in H. A failed edge e may be a matched or an unmatched edge. Similarly, a failed vertex a may be a matched or an unmatched vertex. If e or a is unmatched then the matching $\mu(G-e) = \mu(G)$ or $\mu(G-a) = \mu(G)$. Since H contains $\mu(G)$, no new edges need to be included in H.

If e or a is matched, then we require more work to figure out the edges we need to add to H. Let a's matching endpoint be b. When an edge $e = (a, b)$ is deleted, a and b become newly unmatched vertices. When a matched vertex a is deleted, b becomes a newly unmatched vertex. We now need to add edges to H based on the following two cases:

(i) There is an augmenting path from a to b in $G - e$.
In this case, we will add edges in H such that there is an augmenting path from a to b in $H - e$. We will refer to these augmenting paths as *Type 1 augmenting paths.*

(ii) There is an augmenting path from a or b to an unmatched vertex in $G - e$ or there is an augmenting path from b to an unmatched vertex in $G - a$.
Again, we will add edges in H such that there is an augmenting path from a or b to an unmatched vertex in $H - e$ or there is an augmenting path from b to an unmatched vertex in $G - a$. We will refer to these augmenting paths as *Type 2 augmenting paths.*

3.1 1 FTMS for Bipartite Graphs

It would seem that we need to add an augmenting path for each edge $(a, b) \in \mu(G)$. Thus, the number of edges that needs to be added to H may be huge. However, we show the following theorem in this section which bounds the number of edges and vertices in 1-FTMS of a bipartite graph:

Theorem 4. *For a bipartite graph G, there exists a 1-FTMS of G for one edge fault, with $5\mu(G)$ edges and $3\mu(G)$ vertices.*

The proof of the above theorem will follow from the following sections. In Sect. 3.2, we show the construction and correctness of a 1-FTMS H. In Sect. 3.3, we give a bound on the size of this subgraph.

3.2 Construction of H

As an initial attempt to construct our subgraph H, let us try a greedy approach where for every matched edge $(a, b) \in \mu(G)$, we find an augmenting path starting from either a or b and keep the path in H. There is the following issue with this approach: let us assume that the augmenting paths picked for the first k matched edges are vertex disjoint. Then we have formed k disjoint components in H. However when the $(k+1)^{st}$ matched edge is processed, its augmenting path touches all the k components previously generated. Thus, for the $(k+1)^{st}$ edge, we need to add at least k unmatched edges in H. This turns out to be very bad if $k = \Omega(\mu(G))$. Indeed, one can create an example where the number of edges added to H are $\mathcal{O}(\mu(G)^2)$.

The above approach suggests that a construction would work if at any point of time, there are small number of components in H. Ideally we would like an augmenting path of the $(k+1)^{st}$ matched edge to extend a single component if possible and that is exactly what our construction of H_1 (the first part of the algorithm to construct H) does.

The algorithm is broken into two parts. In Algorithm 1, we construct a subgraph H_1 of G. H_1 has the following property: for a matched edge $(a, b) \in \mu(G)$, if there exists an augmenting path from a to b in $G - (a, b)$ then there exists an augmenting path from a to b in $H_1 - (a, b)$. In Algorithm 2, we construct a subgraph H_2 of G. H_2 has the following property: for a matched edge $(a, b) \in H_2$ if there exists an augmenting path from a or b to an unmatched vertex in $G - (a, b)$ then there exists an augmenting path from a or b to an unmatched vertex in $H_2 - (a, b)$. Our subgraph H is a union of subgraphs H_1, H_2 and $\mu(G)$. Initially both H_1 and H_2 are empty graphs. We denote P as an augmenting path starting from a or b in the graph $G - (a, b)$. We will start with the construction of H_1.

Algorithm 1: Constructing H_1 for 1-fault

$H_1 = \phi$;
for $(a, b) \in \mu(G) - H_1$ **do**
  if $\exists$ *an alternating path* P *from* a *to* b *in* $G - (a, b)$ **then**
    $H_1 = H_1 \cup P \cup (a, b)$;
    for $(p, q) \in \mu(G) - H_1$ **do**
      if $\exists$ *an alternating path* P *from* p *to* q *in* $G - (p, q)$ *that intersects with* H_1 **then**
        Let $x_i \in P$ be the vertex such that P hits H_1 for the first time;
        Let $x_j \in P$ be the vertex such that P hits H_1 for the last time;
        $P = P[p, x_i] \cup P[x_j, q]$;
        $H_1 = H_1 \cup P \cup (p, q)$;

Construction of H_1. Algorithm 1 gives a pseudocode description of the construction of H_1. In lines 2–4, the *outer for* loop finds a pair $(a, b) \in \mu(G) - H_1$ such that there is an augmenting path P in the graph $G - (a, b)$ from a to b. Once such a pair is found, we add $P \cup (a, b)$ to H_1. Next, from lines 5–10 in the *inner for* loop we go through all matching edges $(p, q) \in \mu(G) - H_1$, to check if there exists an augmenting path P from p to q that intersects with H_1 i.e. $P \cap H_1 \neq \phi$. We include a subset of edges of the path P in H_1, namely the edges of the paths $P[p, x_i]$ and $P[x_j, q]$. Here, P hits H_1 for the first time at x_i and the last time at x_j.

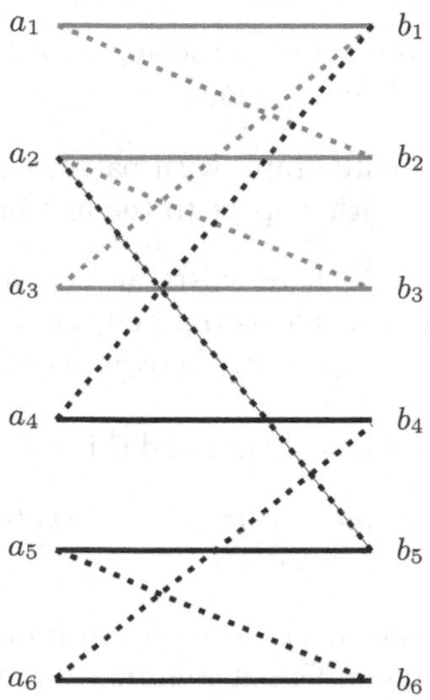

Fig. 1. Construction of H_1. $(a_1, b_1), (a_2, b_2)$ and (a_3, b_3) are the edges computed first in line 4 which generates the blue bold and dotted edges and are added to H_1. Line 5 (*inner for* loop) of the algorithm looks at an edge of the form $(a_6, b_6) \notin H_1$ currently. Here $P[p, x_i] = (a_6, b_4, a_4, b_1)$ and $P[x_j, q] = (b_6, a_5, b_5, a_2)$

See Fig. 1 for an illustration of the construction of H_1.

Correctness: We now prove the correctness of the above algorithm. To this end, we need to show that for any matched edge $e = (a, b)$, if there is an augmenting path from a to b in $G - e$, then there is an augmenting path from a to b in $H_1 - e$. We will first point a feature of the Algorithm 1.

For any matched edge (a, b), if there is an augmenting path in $G - (a, b)$ that intersects with the current H_1, then the algorithm detects it and inserts the portion of the augmenting path in $G - H_1$ along with the matched edge (a, b) in H_1. In the *outer for* loop Algorithm 1 only matched edges outside H_1 are considered. So after processing (a, b) and its augmenting path in $G - H_1$ none of the matched edges in this path is considered in the *outer for* loop again. Therefore, edges added to H_1 in any two iterations of the *outer for* loop

Algorithm 1 are vertex disjoint. For any matched edge (p, q), looked at by the algorithm in the *inner for* loop, the algorithm only adds the parts $P[p, x_i]$ and $P[x_j, q]$ which are not in the current H_1 to H_1. Therefore, the matched edges added by the algorithm in the *outer for* loop are disjoint to the matched edges added by the algorithm in the *inner for* loop.

Remark 1. The endpoints of the edges added to H_1 in any two different iterations of the *outer for* loop of Algorithm 1 are vertex disjoint. The endpoints of the matched edges processed and added by the algorithm in the *outer for* loop is vertex disjoint to the endpoints of the matched edges processed and added in the *inner for* loop.

We will use the above observations crucially in our subsequent proofs. Let us state one more useful remark and lemma.

Remark 2. Let G be a bipartite graph with partitions $\mathcal{A}$ and $\mathcal{B}$. If there exists an alternating cycle $\mathcal{C}$ in H with respect to the maximum matching $\mu(G)$ then,

1. $\forall\{u, v\} \in \mathcal{C}, u \in \mathcal{A}, v \in \mathcal{B}$, there exists an alternating path of odd length between the matched edge incident to u and the matched edge incident to v.
2. $\forall e = (a, b) \in \mathcal{C} \cap \mu(G), a \in \mathcal{A}, b \in \mathcal{B}$, there exists an augmenting path from a to b in $\mathcal{C} - e$ or vice versa.

This follows as G is a bipartite graph and $\mathcal{C}$ is an alternating cycle.

Lemma 1. *At any point of time during the construction of H_1, for any matched edge $(a, b) \in \mu(G)$ if $a \in H_1$ then $b \in H_1$.*

Proof. By Remark 1, we can focus on each iteration of the *outer for* loop of Algorithm 1 as edges added in different iterations are vertex disjoint. Before the inner for loop of Algorithm 1 starts, we just have an alternating cycle in H_1. Therefore, for each matched edge $(a, b) \in \mathcal{C}$, the observations holds.

If a is added to H_1 in the t-th iteration of the inner for loop, then there can be two cases:

(i) (a, b) is processed in line 5 in which case we add (a, b) in H_1 in line 10 or,
(ii) (a, b) is present in an augmenting path of some matched edge (c, d) processed in line 5. In this case, (a, b) belongs to either $P[c, x_i]$ or $P[x_j, d]$ and is thus added to H_1.

We will now prove our main lemma of this subsection which proves the correctness of H_1.

Lemma 2. *Given a bipartite graph G with partitions $\mathcal{A}$ and $\mathcal{B}$, let $\mu(G)$ be the maximum matching in G.*

(i) for any pair of vertices $u, v \in H_1$ such that $u \in \mathcal{A}, v \in \mathcal{B}$, there exists an alternating path of odd length between the matched edge incident to u and the matched edge incident to v.

(ii) *for all matched edges* (a, b) *in* H_1 *such that* $a \in \mathcal{A}, b \in \mathcal{B}$, *if there exists an augmenting path* P *with respect to* $\mu(G)$ *from* a *to* b *in* $G - e$ *then there exists an augmenting path* P' *with respect to* $\mu(G)$ *from* a *to* b *in* $H_1 - e$.

Proof. By Remark 1, we can focus on each iteration of the *outer for* loop of Algorithm 1 as edges added in different iterations are vertex disjoint.

Our proof uses induction on the number of iterations of the inner for loop in Algorithm 1. For the base case, we consider all edges processed by the algorithm before the first iteration of the inner for loop. Thus, H_1 just contains alternating cycle $\mathcal{C}$. So, $\forall\{u, v\} \in \mathcal{C}$ such that $u \in \mathcal{A}, v \in \mathcal{B}$, Remark 2(i) holds true. All matched vertex pairs $\{a, b\} \in \mu(G) \cap \mathcal{C}$ satisfy Remark 2(ii). Therefore, the lemma holds true for the base case.

By induction hypothesis, assume that for all matched edges processed by the algorithm until the tth iteration of the *inner for* loop, our lemma holds true. We will show that the lemma holds true for a matched edge $e = (p, q)$ processed by the algorithm at the $(t+1)^{th}$ iteration. Assume that the algorithm processes an augmenting path from p to q to extend H_1.

Let $P = \{x_0 = p, x_1, \ldots, x_\ell = q\}$ be the augmenting path in $G - e$ such that a subpath of P is then used to extend H_1. We follow the path P from p till we hit a vertex $x_i \in H_1$ for the first time. We also follow the path P from a vertex $x_j \in H_1$ to the vertex q, where x_j was the last vertex in the path P which hit H_1. $P[p, x_i]$ and $P[x_j, q]$ are added to H_1.

By Lemma 1, both edges (x_{i-1}, x_i) and (x_j, x_{j+1}) are unmatched edges. So we have $x_i \in \mathcal{B} \cap H_1$ and $x_j \in \mathcal{A} \cap H_1$. By induction hypothesis, there exists an alternating path P_c of odd length starting from the matched edge incident to x_i and ending with the matched edge incident to x_j. Thus, $P' = P[p, x_i] \cup P_c \cup P[x_j, q]$ is an augmenting path from p to q in $H_1 - e$ satisfying part (ii) of the lemma for p and q.

We need to show that our lemma holds true for all the newly added matched edges, that is, $(c, d) \in P[p, x_i] \cup P[x_j, q]$. We first prove the second part of the lemma. The path $P' \cup (p, q) - (c, d)$ is an augmenting path from c to d. Thus, all vertices in the path $P[p, x_i]$ and $P[x_j, q]$ satisfy part (ii).

To show part (i), observe that $P' \cup (p, q)$ forms an alternating cycle $\mathcal{C}'$. Consider the following three cases where $u \in \mathcal{A}$ and $v \in \mathcal{B}$:

1. $u \in \mathcal{C}'$ and $v \in \mathcal{C}'$
   (i) holds as $\mathcal{C}'$ is an alternating cycle.
2. $u \in \mathcal{C}'$ but $v \notin \mathcal{C}'$
   Let (u', v') be a matched edge in P_c where $u' \in \mathcal{A}$ and $v' \in \mathcal{B}$. Such a matched edge should exist as P_c is not empty. Since u and u' lie in $\mathcal{C}'$, there is an alternating path from u to u'. Since $u' \in H_1$ and $v \in H_1$, by induction hypothesis, there is an alternating path from u' to v. The concatenation of the above two paths gives us an alternating path from u to v, thus satisfying (*i*).
3. $u \notin \mathcal{C}'$ but $v \in \mathcal{C}'$
   Symmetric to the above case.

Remark 3. The construction of H_1 uses critically that the graph is bipartite, as otherwise, Remark 2 and subsequently Lemma 2 may not hold.

Construction of H_2. Algorithm 2 gives a pseudocode description of the construction of H_2. To this end, we introduce a new variable X which stores all vertices processed by Algorithm 2 that have an alternating path starting with an unmatched edge to an unmatched vertex. In lines 2–6, let us assume that we are processing an augmenting path P from a to an unmatched vertex. When P hits a vertex $q \in X$ for the first time, we add the path $P[a,p]$ in H_2 where $(p,q) \in \mu(G)$. Lines 7–9 then adds every alternate vertex from $P[a,p]$ to X.

Algorithm 2: Constructing H_2 for 1-fault

1 $H_2 = \phi, X = \phi$;
2 **for** $(a,b) \in \mu(G) - H_2$ **do**
3   **if** $\exists P_1$ *from* a *to an unmatched vertex* u *in* $G - (a,b)$ *or* $\exists P_2$ *from* b *to an unmatched vertex* v *in* $G - (a,b)$ **then**
4   **for** $P \in \{P_k | k \in \{1,2\}\}$ **do**
5   Let (p,q) be the first matched edge in P from the vertex a such that $q \in X$;
6             $H_2 = H_2 \cup P[a,p] \cup (a,b)$;
7   **for** $(u,v) \in P$ **do**
8   **if** $(u,v) \in \mu(G)$ **then**
9                     $X = X \cup v$;

Correctness: Next we will prove the correctness of H_2 using the following theorem.

Lemma 3. *Given a graph G, let $\mu(G)$ be the maximum matching in G. For all matched edges $e = (a,b)$, if there exists an augmenting path from a or b to an unmatched vertex in $G - e$, then there exists an augmenting path from a or b to an unmatched vertex in $H_2 - e$.*

Proof. Any matching edge that satisfies the statement of the lemma is processed by Algorithm 2. So we focus on the edges that are processed in the *for* loop of Algorithm 2. Our proof uses induction on the number of iterations of this *for* loop. Along with the statement of the lemma, we also prove by induction that after each iteration of the *for* loop, X contains all vertices in current H_2 that have an alternating path starting from an unmatched edge to an unmatched vertex.

For the base case, which is the first iteration of the *for* loop, for a matched edge (a,b), if there exists an augmenting path P from a or b to an unmatched vertex in $G-e$, then we insert the entire path P in H_2. In addition, in Algorithm 2, alternate vertices of P are inserted to X. This proves the base case.

Suppose for all matched edges until the tth iteration of the *for* loop, our lemma (and our assertion on X) holds. We will show that the lemma (and our assertion on X) holds true after an edge $e = (a, b)$ processed by the algorithm at the $(t+1)^{th}$ iteration. Assume that there is an augmenting path P from vertex a to an unmatched vertex in $G - e$. The proof for an augmenting path from vertex b is the same.

We follow P until we hit a matched edge (p, q) in the path such that $q \in X$. We add the truncated path $P[a, p]$ to H_2. Since $q \in X$, by induction hypothesis, there is an alternating path Q starting with an unmatched edge from q to a unmatched vertex. Therefore the path $P[a, p] \cup (p, q) \cup Q$ gives our required augmenting path from a to an unmatched vertex in the $(t+1)^{th}$ iteration. Thus, our lemma holds after the $(t+1)^{th}$ iteration.

Next, we add all the alternate vertices in the path $P[a, p]$ in X as all of them now have an alternating path starting from an unmatched edge to an unmatched vertex as well. After this update, X contains all vertices in current H_2 that have an alternating path starting from an unmatched edge to an unmatched vertex. Thus, our assertion on X also holds.

Lemmas 2 and 3 together show that H is a 1-FTMS of G.

Remark 4. Observe that the construction and proof of correctness of H_2 holds even for general graphs. This means that construction of all *Type 2 augmenting paths* hold for general graphs.

3.3 Bounding the Size of H

Lemma 1 implies that a matched edge (a, b) is added only once to H_1. Whenever such a matched edge is added it is part of a cycle (in line 4) or a path (in line 10). Therefore, for every matched edge added to H_1, there is at most two unmatched edge incident to it which is added in H_1. The matched edges contribute at most $\mu(G)$ edges to H_1. Thus, in this case H_1 contains $\mu(G)$ matched edges and $2\mu(G)$ unmatched edges for a total size of $3\mu(G)$ edges.

Let us now bound the size of H_2. Every time a vertex is added to the set X it contributes exactly one unmatched edge to H_2. As each vertex is added to X only once and there are at most $2\mu(G)$ such vertices this contributes $2\mu(G)$ edges to H_2. Thus, the total size of the number of edges of H is $5\mu(G)$.

Next, we calculate the number of vertices in H. H contains all $2\mu(G)$ matched vertices of G. H also contains at most one unmatched vertex adjacent to either a or b where $(a, b) \in \mu(G)$ but not both. This is because if there was an unmatched vertex from both a and b, then we could extend our initial maximum matching $\mu(G)$. Therefore H contains at most $\mu(G)$ unmatched vertices. Thus, the total size of H is $3\mu(G)$ vertices. Lemmas 2 and 3 together with the bound on the size of H give a proof of Theorem 4.

3.4 1 Vertex Fault for General Graphs

Surprisingly, for a vertex fault our above results can also be extended to general undirected graphs. As the following lemma shows, it is enough to consider just *Type 2* augmenting paths when constructing a 1-FTMS for one vertex fault.

Lemma 4. *To construct a 1-FTMS for one vertex fault, only augmenting paths of Type 2 have to be added.*

Proof. Let (a, b) be any arbitrary matched edge in $\mu(G)$. If a is deleted, there cannot be an augmenting path from b to a in $G - a$. Thus, *Type 1* augmenting paths do not need to be considered to construct a 1-FTMS for one vertex fault. Hence, for a vertex fault a, only augmenting paths of *Type 2* from b have to be added to the 1-FTMS H.

We directly get the following theorem for the construction of a 1-FTMS for one vertex fault.

Theorem 5. *For any graph G, there exists a 1-FTMS of G for one vertex fault with $2\mu(G)$ edges and $3\mu(G)$ vertices.*

Proof. Lemma 4 and Remark 4 together imply that the construction of *Type 2* augmenting paths as given by the subgraph H_2, gives a 1-FTMS for one vertex fault for any general undirected graph. The space bounds also follow directly from Sect. 3.3 as we simply need to consider the space used in the construction of H_2.

3.5 Lower Bound

In the following lower bound, 1-FTMS refers to both a single vertex or a single edge failure.

Theorem 6. $(\star)$[1] *For any positive integer n, there exists a graph $G = (V, E)$ on n vertices and a maximum matching $\mu(G)$ whose 1-FTMS requires at least $3\mu(G)$ vertices and $2\mu(G)$ edges.*

4 *f*-Fault Tolerant Subgraph for General Graphs

In this section we give an algorithm to find an f-FTMS with $\binom{2\mu(G)}{2} + 2\mu(G) \cdot 3f$ edges and $2\mu(G)(f+3)$ vertices in general graphs. Also, f-FTMS will mean both at most f vertex and edge faults as all proofs in this section work for both. The algorithm proceeds in two phases, we first construct a subgraph H' that has the desired number of edges, but the number of vertices could be larger than the claimed bound following the technique used in [19]. To improve the bound on the number of vertices, we run the second phase of our algorithm and obtain the desired f-FTMS, H, with the claimed number of vertices and edges. We conclude the section with a lower bound of $\Omega(\mu(G)^2)$ edges on 2-FTMS and $\Omega(\mu(G)f)$ vertices for f-FTMS.

[1] Results marked with $\star$ are deferred to the full version.

4.1 Construction of f-FTMS

Given an undirected graph G and a positive integer f our algorithm constructs an f-FTMS, H'. A similar construction to the following was also used in [19]. We give the construction and proof for completeness. Moreover, we also take care of constants in our bounds.

Construction 1: Let M be a maximum matching of G. Let $V(M)$ denote the vertices incident to the edges of M and $I = V(G) - V(M)$. Observe that I is an independent set. For every vertex $v \in V(M)$, let I_v denote the set of arbitrary $3f$ neighbors of v present in I. If v has less than $3f$ neighbors then I_v contains all the neighbors of v that are in I. Furthermore, let E_v denotes the edges between v and the vertices in I_v. The vertex set of subgraph H' is $V(M) \cup_{v \in V(M)} I_v$ and the edge set consists of $E(G[V(M)]) \cup_{v \in V(M)} E_v$.

In plain words, for H' we take the graph induced on $V(M)$ and for every vertex in $V(M)$ add arbitrary $3f$ neighbors of it (if they are present or take all the neighbors) that are in I.

Next we need to prove that H', as constructed above, is indeed an f-FTMS. Towards this we need to show that for any set F of at most f edges or vertices in $E(G)$, $\mu(G - F) \leq \mu(H' - F)$. Since, $H' - F$ is a subgraph of $G - F$ we have that $\mu(G - F) \geq \mu(H' - F)$. These two inequalities together would imply that $\mu(G - F) = \mu(H' - F)$. For the proof of correctness we show the following lemma.

Lemma 5. *($\star$) Let G be an undirected graph and f be a positive integer. Furthermore, let H' be the subgraph constructed as above. Then, for any set F of at most f edges or vertices in $E(G)$, $\mu(G - F) \leq \mu(H' - F)$.*

Using Lemma 5 we show that H' is an f-FTMS.

Lemma 6. *($\star$) For an undirected graph G and a positive integer f, there exists an f-FTMS with $(2\mu(G))(3f + 1)$ vertices and $\binom{2\mu(G)}{2} + 2\mu(G) \cdot 3f$ edges.*

In Lemma 6, the number of vertices in H can be a large as $2\mu(G)(3f + 1)$. We give another construction of f-FTMS, where the number of vertices is upper bounded by at most $2\mu(G)(f + 3)$. However, in this construction we are not able to upper bound the number of edges, as claimed. So to simultaneously achieve an upper bound on the number of vertices and edges, we first apply construction-1 and obtain an f-FTMS, H', with the required number of edges and then apply the second construction on H' to get the desired f-FTMS H. That is, we compose the two constructions to get the desired upper bound on the number of vertices and the edges.

Towards this we need *expansion lemma.* A q-star, $q \geq 1$, is a graph with $q + 1$ vertices, one vertex of degree q, called the *center*, and all other vertices of degree 1 adjacent to the center. Let G be a bipartite graph with bipartition A and B. For a positive integer q, a set of edges $M \subseteq E(G)$ is called a q-expansion of A into B if (a) every vertex of A is incident to exactly q edges of M; and (b)

M saturates exactly $q|A|$ vertices in B. Note that q-expansion saturates all the vertices of A and for every $u, v \in A$, $u \neq v$, the set of vertices E_u adjacent to u by edges of M does not intersect the set of vertices E_v adjacent to v via edges of M. Thus, every vertex $v \in A$ could be thought of as the center of star with q leaves in B, with all these $|A|$ stars being vertex-disjoint.

We now state the following lemma which is crucial in the second construction of f-FTMS.

Lemma 7 ([13]). *Let G be a bipartite graph with bipartitions (A, B) and $q > 0$ be a positive integer such that,*

- *$|B| \geq q|A|$,*
- *There are no isolated vertices in B.*

Then there exists non-empty vertex sets $X \subseteq A$ and $Y \subseteq B$ such that there is a q-expansion of X into Y and no vertex in Y has a neighbor outside X, that is, $N(Y) \subseteq X$. Moreover, the sets X and Y can be found in polynomial time.

The second construction is based on the following reduction rule. This rule removes a vertex that it deems irrelevant for the purpose. To get the final H, we apply the next rule until no longer possible.

Reduction Rule 1: Let M be a maximum matching of G. Let $V(M)$ denote the vertices incident to the edges of M and $I = V(G) - V(M)$. Observe that I is an independent set. We obtain a bipartite graph G' with vertex bipartitions $A := V(M)$ and $B := I$, and it contains all the *cross edges*. That is, all the edges with one endpoint in A and the other in B. We apply the first applicable rule below.

Case 1: If there is a vertex v that is isolated in B, then delete v and return $G - \{v\}$.

Case 2: Else, assume that B does not have any isolated vertex. Now, if $|B| \geq (f+2)|A|$, then by Lemma 7 there exist non-empty vertex sets $X \subseteq A$ and $Y \subseteq B$ such that there is a $(f+2)$-expansion of X into Y and $N(Y) \subseteq X$. Let v be a vertex in Y, then delete v and return $G - \{v\}$. If $|B| < (f+2)|A|$, then return G itself.

Next we show that our reduction rule is sound.

Lemma 8. ($\star$) *Let G be an undirected graph and f be a positive integer. Let $G' = G - \{v\}$ be the graph returned by an application of Reduction Rule 1. Then, G' is f-FTMS.*

Using Reduction Rule 1, we give our second construction of f-FTMS.

Construction 2: Let G be a graph and f be a positive integer. Apply Reduction Rule 1, until no longer possible. Let the resulting graph be H.

Lemma 9. ($\star$) *For an undirected graph G and a positive integer f, there exists an f-FTMS with $2\mu(G)(f+3)$ vertices.*

Next by composing two constructions we obtain the final f-FTMS.

Theorem 7. ⋆ *For an undirected graph G and a positive integer f, there exists an f-FTMS with $(2\mu(G))(f+3)$ vertices and $\binom{2\mu(G)}{2} + 2\mu(G) \cdot 3f$ edges.*

4.2 Lower Bounds

Let us look at the lower bound on the size of H in terms of the number of edges, when F is a set of at most f edge or vertex faults.

Theorem 8. *For any positive integers n, ℓ with $n \geq 2\ell$ and ℓ is even, there exists a bipartite graph G on n vertices with $\mu(G) = \ell$ and any f-FTMS of G has at least $\frac{\mu(G)^2}{4} + \mu(G)$ edges.*

Proof. See Fig. 2 for an illustration. We will prove that any 2−FTMS of G has at least $\frac{\mu(G)^2}{4} + \mu(G)$ edges. This will also imply that the theorem holds for any $f > 2$ as well, as we can simply add extra dummy edges in our constructed graph and treat those edges as faults. Let n, ℓ be two positive integers such that $n \geq 2\ell$. We first describe the construction of a bipartite graph G on n vertices. The vertex set $V(G)$ consists of 4 parts, A, B, C and D each part consisting of $q = \frac{\ell}{2}$ vertices. Finally, add $n - 2\ell$ isolated vertices in G, so that the total number of vertices of G becomes n. Let $Z = \{z_1, \ldots, z_q\}$ denote the vertices in part $Z \in \{A, B, C, D\}$. For $i \in [q]$, $a_i \in A$ is adjacent exactly to one vertex $b_i \in B$. Similarly, each vertex $c_i \in C$ is adjacent exactly to one vertex $d_i \in D$. Furthermore, each vertex $a_i \in A$ has edges to all vertices $d_i \in D$. That is, there is a complete bipartite graph between vertices of A and D and every vertex in B and C has degree exactly equal to one. To see that G is a bipartite graph, consider the bipartitions $\mathcal{A} = A \cup C$, and $\mathcal{B} = B \cup D$. Finally, add isolated vertices to either of the part.

The unique maximum matching in this graph is $M = \{(a_i, b_i), (c_i, d_i) \mid i \in [q]\}$. The size of $|M| = 2q = \ell$. Let H be a 2-FTMS of G. We will show that H must contain all the edges of G. Towards this we first note that H must contain all the edges of M, as M is a unique maximum matching of G.

Next we show that all the non-matching edges of G are also required. For contradiction, suppose an edge of the form (a_j, d_k) for a fixed $j, k \in [1, \ldots, q]$ is not present in H. Suppose that edges (a_j, b_j) and (c_k, d_k) are deleted in G. Then (a_j, d_k) must be included in the maximum matching of $G - \{(a_j, b_j), (c_k, d_k)\}$. Thus the size of maximum matching in $G - \{(a_j, b_j), (c_k, d_k)\}$ is $\ell - 1$. But the maximum matching size in $H - \{(a_j, b_j), (c_k, d_k)\}$ is equal to $\ell - 2$ as $(a_j, d_k) \notin H$. This contradicts our assumption that H was 2-FTMS of G. Therefore the subgraph H contains all $\ell^2/4 + \ell$ edges of G.

The above proof also works for 2 vertex faults. Instead of deleting the edges (a_j, b_j) and (c_k, d_k) from G, delete the vertices b_j and d_k from G. As b_j and d_k are of degree 1, edge faults and vertex faults are equivalent.

Theorem 8 shows that the upper bound achieved on the number of edges on f-FTMS of G in Theorem 7 is tight. In the next result, we show that in fact our upper bound on the number of vertices is also asymptotically tight.

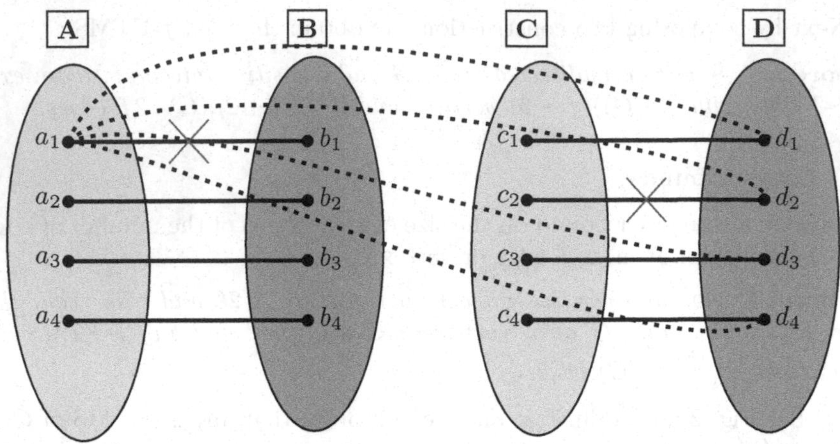

Fig. 2. The bipartite graph G where A and C are one partition and B and D the other partition. Each partition contains 8 vertices. If edges (a_1, b_1) and (c_2, d_2) are deleted, then the edge (a_1, d_2) must be included in 2-FTMS.

Theorem 9. ($\star$) *For any positive integers* n, ℓ, f *with* $n = \ell(f+2)$, *there exists a bipartite graph* G *on* n *vertices with* $\mu(G) = \ell$ *and any* f*-FTMS of* G *must contain at least* $\mu(G)(f+1)$ *vertices.*

References

1. Assadi, S., Bernstein, A.: Towards a unified theory of sparsification for matching problems. In: 2nd Symposium on Simplicity in Algorithms, 8–9 January 2019 - San Diego, CA, USA, pages 11:1–11:20 (2019)
2. Assadi, S., Khanna, S., Li, Y.: The stochastic matching problem with (very) few queries. In: Proceedings of the 2016 ACM Conference on Economics and Computation, EC 2016, Maastricht, The Netherlands, 24–28 July 2016, pp. 43–60 (2016). https://doi.org/10.1145/2940716.2940769
3. Assadi, S., Khanna, S., Li, Y.: The stochastic matching problem: beating half with a non-adaptive algorithm. In: Proceedings of the 2017 ACM Conference on Economics and Computation, EC 2017, Cambridge, MA, USA, 26–30 June 2017, pp. 99–116 (2017). https://doi.org/10.1145/3033274.3085146
4. Baswana, S., Chaudhury, S.R., Choudhary, K., Khan, S.: Dynamic DFS in undirected graphs: breaking the O(m) barrier. In: Proceedings of the Twenty-Seventh Annual ACM-SIAM Symposium on Discrete Algorithms, SODA 2016, Arlington, VA, USA, 10–12 January 2016, pp. 730–739 (2016)
5. Baswana, S., Choudhary, K., Roditty, L.: Fault tolerant reachability for directed graphs. In: Proceedings of the 29th International Symposium on istributed Computing - DISC 2015, Tokyo, Japan, 7–9 October 2015, pp. 528–543 (2015)
6. Behnezhad, S., Derakhshan, M., Hajiaghayi, M.: Stochastic matching with few queries: (1-ϵ) approximation. CoRR, abs/2002.11880 (2020). https://arxiv.org/abs/2002.11880

7. Behnezhad, S., Reyhani, N.: Almost optimal stochastic weighted matching with few queries. In: Proceedings of the 2018 ACM Conference on Economics and Computation, Ithaca, NY, USA, 18–22 June 2018, pp. 235–249 (2018). https://doi.org/10.1145/3219166.3219226
8. Bilò, D., Grandoni, F., Gualà, L., Leucci, S., Proietti, G.: Improved purely additive fault-tolerant spanners. In: Algorithms - ESA 2015–23rd Annual European Symposium, Patras, Greece, 14–16 September 2015, pp. 167–178 (2015)
9. Bilò, D., Gualà, L., Leucci, S., Proietti, G.: Multiple-edge-fault-tolerant approximate shortest-path trees. In: 33rd Symposium on Theoretical Aspects of Computer Science, STACS 2016, 17–20 February 2016, Orléans, France, pp. 18:1–18:14 (2016)
10. Blum, A., Dickerson, J.P., Haghtalab, N., Procaccia, A.D., Sandholm, T., Sharma, A.: Ignorance is almost bliss: Near-optimal stochastic matching with few queries. Oper. Res. **68**(1), 16–34 (2020). https://doi.org/10.1287/opre.2019.1856
11. Braunschvig, G., Chechik, S., Peleg, D., Sealfon, A.: Fault tolerant additive and (μ, α)-spanners. Theor. Comput. Sci. **580**, 94–100 (2015)
12. Chechik, S., Langberg, M., Peleg, D., Roditty, L.: Fault tolerant spanners for general graphs. SIAM J. Comput. **39**(7), 3403–3423 (2010)
13. Cygan, M., et al.: Parameterized Algorithms. Springer, Cham (2015). https://doi.org/10.1007/978-3-319-21275-3
14. Dinitz, M., Krauthgamer, R.: Fault-tolerant spanners: better and simpler. In: Proceedings of the 30th Annual ACM Symposium on Principles of Distributed Computing, PODC 2011, San Jose, CA, USA, 6–8 June 2011, pp. 169–178 (2011)
15. Edmonds, J.: Paths, trees, and flowers. Can. J. Math. **17**, 449–467 (1965)
16. Fomin, F.V., Lokshtanov, D., Saurabh, S., Zehavi, M.: Kernelization: Theory of Parameterized Preprocessing. Cambridge University Press, Cambridge (2019)
17. Gabow, H.N., Tarjan, R.E.: Faster scaling algorithms for general graph-matching problems. J. ACM **38**(4), 815–853 (1991)
18. Gupta, M., Khan, S.: Multiple source dual fault tolerant BFS trees. In: Chatzigiannakis, I., Indyk, P., Kuhn, F., Muscholl, A. (eds.) 44th International Colloquium on Automata, Languages, and Programming, ICALP 2017, 10–14 July 2017, Warsaw, Poland, volume 80 of LIPIcs, pp. 127:1–127:15. Schloss Dagstuhl - Leibniz-Zentrum für Informatik (2017). https://doi.org/10.4230/LIPIcs.ICALP.2017.127
19. Gupta, M., Peng, R.: Fully dynamic (1+ e)-approximate matchings. In: 54th Annual IEEE Symposium on Foundations of Computer Science, FOCS 2013, 26–29 October 2013, Berkeley, CA, USA, pp. 548–557. IEEE Computer Society (2013). https://doi.org/10.1109/FOCS.2013.65
20. Hopcroft, J.E., Karp, R.M.: An $n^{5/2}$ algorithm for maximum matchings in bipartite graphs. SIAM J. Comput. **2**(4), 225–231 (1973)
21. Huang, C.-C., Kavitha, T.: Efficient algorithms for maximum weight matchings in general graphs with small edge weights. In: SODA, pp. 1400–1412 (2012)
22. Lawler, E.: Combinatorial Optimization: Networks and Matroids. Holt Rinehart & Winston, Newyork (1976)
23. Lovasz, L., Plummer, M.D.: Matching Theory. AMS Chelsea Publishing, Amsterdam (1986)
24. Micali, S., Vazirani, V.V.: An $O(\sqrt{(|V|)}|E|)$ algorithm for finding maximum matching in general graphs. In: FOCS, pp. 17–27 (1980)
25. Motwani, R.: Average-case analysis of algorithms for matchings and related problems. J. ACM **41**(6), 1329–1356 (1994)
26. Mucha, M., Sankowski, P.: Maximum matchings via Gaussian elimination. In: FOCS, pp. 248–255 (2004)

27. Parter, M.: Vertex fault tolerant additive spanners. In: Distributed Computing - 28th International Symposium, DISC 2014, Austin, TX, USA, 12–15 October 2014, pp. 167–181 (2014)
28. Parter, M.: Dual failure resilient BFS structure. In: Proceedings of the 2015 ACM Symposium on Principles of Distributed Computing, PODC 2015, Donostia-San Sebastián, Spain, 21–23 July 2015, pp. 481–490 (2015)
29. Parter, M., Peleg, D.: Sparse fault-tolerant BFS trees. In: Algorithms - ESA 2013–21st Annual European Symposium, Sophia Antipolis, France, 2–4 September 2013, pp. 779–790 (2013)
30. Parter, M., Peleg, D.: Fault tolerant approximate BFS structures. In: Proceedings of the Twenty-Fifth Annual ACM-SIAM Symposium on Discrete Algorithms, SODA 2014, Portland, Oregon, USA, 5–7 January 2014, pp. 1073–1092 (2014)
31. Thomassé, S.: A $4k^2$ kernel for feedback vertex set. ACM Trans. Algorithms **6**(2), 32:1–32:8 (2010)
32. Yamaguchi, Y., Maehara, T.: Stochastic packing integer programs with few queries. In: Proceedings of the Twenty-Ninth Annual ACM-SIAM Symposium on Discrete Algorithms, SODA 2018, New Orleans, LA, USA, 7–10 January 2018, pp. 293–310 (2018). https://doi.org/10.1137/1.9781611975031.21

Bounds for Synchronizing Markov Decision Processes

Laurent Doyen[1(✉)] and Marie van den Bogaard[2]

[1] CNRS & LMF, ENS Paris-Saclay, Gif-sur-Yvette, France
doyen@lsv.fr

[2] LIGM, Université Gustave Eiffel, Marne-la-Vallée, France

Abstract. We consider Markov decision processes with synchronizing objectives, which require that a probability mass of $1 - \varepsilon$ accumulates in a designated set of target states, either once, always, infinitely often, or always from some point on, where $\varepsilon = 0$ for sure synchronizing, and $\varepsilon \to 0$ for almost-sure and limit-sure synchronizing.

We introduce two new qualitative modes of synchronizing, where the probability mass should be either *positive*, or *bounded* away from 0. They can be viewed as dual synchronizing objectives. We present algorithms and tight complexity results for the problem of deciding if a Markov decision process is positive, or bounded synchronizing, and we provide explicit bounds on ε in all synchronizing modes. In particular, we show that deciding positive and bounded synchronizing always from some point on, is coNP-complete.

1 Introduction

Markov decision processes (MDP) are finite-state probabilistic systems with controllable (non-deterministic) choices. They play a central role in several application domains for practical purpose [14,19], and in theoretical computer science as a basic model for the analysis of stochastic transition systems [2,9].

In the traditional state-based semantics, we consider the *sequences of states* that form a path in the underlying graph of the MDP. When a control policy (or strategy) for the non-deterministic choices is fixed, we obtain a purely stochastic process that induces a probability measure over sets of paths [2,7].

In the more recent distribution-based semantics, the outcome of a stochastic process is a sequence of distributions over states [3,18]. This alternative semantics has received some attention recently for theoretical analysis of probabilistic bisimulation [16] and is adequate to describe large populations of agents [8,12] with applications in system biology [1,18]. The behaviour of an agent is modeled as an MDP with some state space Q, and a large population of identical agents is described by a (continuous) distribution $d : Q \to [0, 1]$ that gives the fraction $d(q)$ of agents in the population that are in each state $q \in Q$. The control problem is to construct a strategy for the agents that guarantees a specified global outcome of the agents, defined in terms of *sequences of distributions.* Specifications of interest include safety objectives [1] and synchronization objectives [12].

A. S. Kulikov and S. Raskhodnikova (Eds.): CSR 2022, LNCS 13296, pp. 133–151, 2022.
https://doi.org/10.1007/978-3-031-09574-0_9

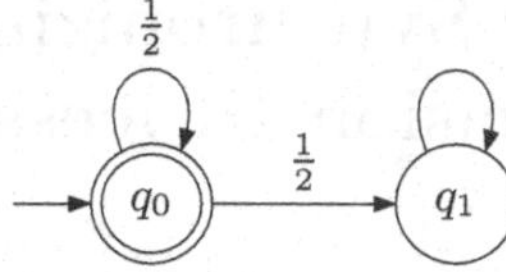

Fig. 1. A Markov chain that is positively but not boundedly synchronizing (for all modes except eventually).

A distribution is p-synchronized in a set T of states if it assigns to the states in T a mass of probability at least p. Synchronization objectives require that p-synchronized distributions occur in the outcome sequence, either, at some position (eventually), at all positions (always), infinitely often (weakly), or always from some point on (strongly), where synchronization is sure winning for $p = 1$, and almost-sure or limit-sure winning for p arbitrarily close to 1 [12].

Consider eventually synchronizing as an illustration. Formally, denoting by $d_i^\sigma(T)$ the probability mass in a set T under strategy σ at position i in a given MDP, the three winning modes for eventually synchronizing correspond to the following three possible orders of the quantifiers:

- $\forall \varepsilon > 0 \cdot \exists \sigma \cdot \exists i : d_i^\sigma(T) \geq 1 - \varepsilon$, for limit-sure winning,
- $\exists \sigma \cdot \forall \varepsilon > 0 \cdot \exists i : d_i^\sigma(T) \geq 1 - \varepsilon$, for almost-sure winning,
- $\exists \sigma \cdot \exists i \cdot \forall \varepsilon > 0 : d_i^\sigma(T) \geq 1 - \varepsilon$, for sure winning.

Note that the formula $\forall \varepsilon > 0 : d_i^\sigma(T) \geq 1 - \varepsilon$ is equivalent to $d_i^\sigma(T) = 1$ in the case of sure winning. Defining the value of a strategy σ as $\text{val}(\sigma) = \sup_i d_i^\sigma(T)$, the question for limit-sure winning is analogous to the cutpoint isolation problem for value 1, i.e. whether the value 1 can be approached arbitrarily closely [4,20]. Previous work [12] shows that the above three questions are PSPACE-complete, and presents a construction of the (existentially quantified) strategy σ when one exists.

In this paper, we consider dual synchronization objectives obtained either by taking the negation of the synchronization objectives, or by replacing the existential quantifier on strategies by a universal quantifier.

1. Taking the negation corresponds to the control player having no strategy to satisfy the synchronization objective. In that case, we show that a more precise information can be derived, namely bounds on the value of ε, which is existentially quantified, and we construct explicit values for the four synchronizing modes. These values give bounds on the isolation distance of the value 1. For instance, the negation of limit-sure eventually synchronizing in T is given by the formula:

$$\exists \varepsilon > 0 \cdot \forall \sigma \cdot \forall i : d_i^\sigma(T) \leq 1 - \varepsilon.$$

We show that the statement holds for a value $\varepsilon = \varepsilon_e(n, \alpha, \alpha_0)$ that depends on the number n of states of the MDP, the smallest positive probability α

Table 1. Positive and Bounded winning modes for always, strongly, weakly, and eventually synchronizing objectives.

	Always			Strongly		
Positively	$\exists\sigma$	$\forall i$	$d_i^\sigma(T) > 0$	$\exists\sigma$	$\exists N\, \forall i \geq N$	$d_i^\sigma(T) > 0$
Boundedly	$\exists\sigma$	$\inf_i$	$d_i^\sigma(T) > 0$	$\exists\sigma$	$\liminf_{i\to\infty}$	$d_i^\sigma(T) > 0$
	Weakly			Eventually		
Positively	$\exists\sigma$	$\forall N\, \exists i \geq N$	$d_i^\sigma(T) > 0$	$\exists\sigma$	$\exists i$	$d_i^\sigma(T) > 0$
Boundedly	$\exists\sigma$	$\limsup_{i\to\infty}$	$d_i^\sigma(T) > 0$	$\exists\sigma$	$\sup_i$	$d_i^\sigma(T) > 0$

in the transitions of the MDP, and the smallest positive probability α_0 in the initial distribution d_0 (see Theorem 1). The most interesting case is when limit-sure weakly synchronizing does not hold, that is:

$$\exists \varepsilon > 0 \cdot \forall \sigma \cdot \exists N \cdot \forall i \geq N : d_i^\sigma(T) \leq 1 - \varepsilon.$$

Given the value $\varepsilon = \varepsilon_w$ that satisfies this condition (see Theorem 2), the value of N can be arbitrarily large (depending on the strategy σ). Nevertheless, we can effectively construct a constant N_w such that, for all strategies σ, in the sequence $(d_i^\sigma)_{i\in\mathbb{N}}$ there are at most N_w distributions that are $(1 - \varepsilon_w)$-synchronized in T.

2. Replacing the existential strategy quantifier by a universal quantifier corresponds to an adversarial MDP where all strategies need to satisfy the requirement, or after taking the negation, to the existence of a strategy that violates a dual of the synchronizing requirement. Note that there is no more alternation of quantifiers on ε and on σ ($\forall\varepsilon \cdot \forall\sigma$ is the same as $\forall\sigma \cdot \forall\varepsilon$), which gives rise to only two new winning modes in existential form:
   - $\exists\sigma \cdot \exists\varepsilon > 0 \cdot \forall i : d_i^\sigma(T) \geq \varepsilon$, that we call *bounded* winning,
   - $\exists\sigma \cdot \forall i \cdot \exists\varepsilon > 0 : d_i^\sigma(T) \geq \varepsilon$, that we call *positive* winning (since this is equivalent to $\exists\sigma \cdot \forall i : d_i^\sigma(T) > 0$).

Table 1 presents the analogous definitions of bounded and positive winning for the four synchronizing modes. It is easy to see that for eventually synchronizing, the positive and bounded mode coincide, while for the other synchronizing modes the positive and bounded modes are distinct, already in Markov chains (see Fig. 1).

We establish the complexity of deciding bounded and positive winning in the four synchronizing modes, given an MDP and initial distribution (which we call the membership problem), and we also construct explicit values for ε. Adversarial MDPs are a special case of two-player stochastic games [7] in which only the second player (the adversary of the first player) is non-trivial. The results of this paper will be useful for the analysis of adversarial MDPs obtained from a game by fixing a strategy of the first player. The complexity results are summarized in Table 2. For positive winning, memoryless winning strategies exist (playing all actions uniformly at random is sufficient), and the problem

Table 2. Computational complexity of the membership problem (for eventually synchronizing, the positive and bounded modes coincide).

	Always	Eventually	Weakly	Strongly
Positively	coNP-C	NL-C	NL-C	coNP-C
Boundedly	coNP-C		NL-C	coNP-C

can be solved by graph-theoretic techniques on Markov chains. For bounded winning, the most challenging case is strongly synchronizing, where we show that a simple form of strategy with memory is winning, and that the decision problem is coNP-complete. We give a structural characterization of bounded strongly synchronizing MDPs, and show that it can be decided in coNP. Note that the coNP upper bound is not obtained by guessing a strategy, since the coNP lower bound holds in the case of Markov chains where strategies play no role. Omitted proofs and additional material can be found in an extended version of this paper [13].

Related works. The distribution-based semantics of MDPs [3,18] has received an increased amount of attention recently, with works on safety objectives [1] and synchronizing objectives [12] (see also references therein). Logic and automata-based frameworks express distribution-based properties, by allowing different order of the logical quantifiers, such as $\forall\sigma\exists i$ in standard reachability which becomes $\exists i\forall\sigma$ in synchronized reachability [3,6,17]. The bounded and positive winning modes introduced in this paper have not been considered before. They bear some similarity with the qualitative winning modes in concurrent games [11].

Applications are found in modeling of large populations of identical agents, such as molecules, yeast, bacteria, etc. [1,18] where the probability distributions represent concentrations of each agent in the system. Analogous models have been considered in a discrete setting where the number of agents is a parameter n, giving rise to control problems for parameterized systems, asking if there exists a strategy that brings all n agents synchronously to a target state [5,8].

2 Definitions

A *probability distribution* over a finite set Q is a function $d : Q \to [0,1]$ such that $\sum_{q\in Q} d(q) = 1$. The *support* of d is the set $\mathsf{Supp}(d) = \{q \in Q \mid d(q) > 0\}$. We denote by $\mathcal{D}(Q)$ the set of all probability distributions over Q. Given a set $T \subseteq Q$, let $d(T) = \sum_{s\in T} d(s)$.

A *Markov decision process* (MDP) is a tuple $\mathcal{M} = \langle Q, \mathsf{A}, \delta\rangle$ where Q is a finite set of states, A is a finite set of labels called actions, and $\delta : Q \times \mathsf{A} \to \mathcal{D}(Q)$ is a probabilistic transition function. A *Markov chain* is an MDP with singleton action set $|\mathsf{A}| = 1$. Given a state $q \in Q$ and an action $a \in \mathsf{A}$, the successor state of q under action a is q' with probability $\delta(q, a)(q')$.

Given $X, Y \subseteq Q$, let

$$\mathsf{APre}(Y, X) = \{q \in Q \mid \exists a \in \mathsf{A} : \mathsf{Supp}(\delta(q,a)) \subseteq Y \wedge \mathsf{Supp}(\delta(q,a)) \cap X \neq \varnothing\},$$

be the set of states from which there is an action to ensure that all successor states are in Y and that with positive probability the successor state is in X, and for $X = Q$, let $\mathsf{Pre}(Y) = \mathsf{APre}(Y, Q) = \{q \in Q \mid \exists a \in \mathsf{A} : \mathsf{Supp}(\delta(q,a)) \subseteq Y\}$ be the set of states from which there is an action to ensure (with probability 1) that the successor state is in Y. For $k > 0$, let $\mathsf{Pre}^k(Y) = \mathsf{Pre}(\mathsf{Pre}^{k-1}(Y))$ with $\mathsf{Pre}^0(Y) = Y$. Note that the sequence $\mathsf{Pre}^k(Y)$ of iterated predecessors is ultimately periodic, precisely there exist $k_1 < k_2 \leq 2^{|Q|}$ such that $\mathsf{Pre}^{k_1}(Y) = \mathsf{Pre}^{k_2}(Y)$.

Strategies. A (randomized) *strategy* in $\mathcal{M}$ is a function $\sigma : (Q\mathsf{A})^* Q \to \mathcal{D}(\mathsf{A})$ that, given a finite sequence $\rho = q_0 a_0 q_1 a_1 \dots q_k$, chooses the next action a_k with probability $\sigma(\rho)(a_k)$. We write $\sigma_1 \subseteq \sigma_2$ if $\mathsf{Supp}(\sigma_1(\rho)) \subseteq \mathsf{Supp}(\sigma_2(\rho))$ for all $\rho \in (Q\mathsf{A})^* Q$. A strategy σ is *pure* if for all $\rho \in (Q\mathsf{A})^* Q$, there exists an action $a \in \mathsf{A}$ such that $\sigma(\rho)(a) = 1$. In all problems considered in this paper, it is known that pure strategies are sufficient [12]. However, the bounds we provide in case there is no winning strategy hold for all strategies, pure or randomized.

Given an initial distribution $d_0 \in \mathcal{D}(Q)$ and a strategy σ in $\mathcal{M}$, the probability of a finite sequence $\rho = q_0 a_0 q_1 a_1 \dots q_k$ is defined by $\Pr^{\sigma}_{d_0}(\rho) = d_0(q_0) \cdot \prod_{j=0}^{k-1} \sigma(q_0 a_0 \dots q_j)(a_j) \cdot \delta(q_j, a_j)(q_{j+1})$. For an initial distribution d_0 such that $d_0(q_0) = 1$, we sometimes write $\Pr^{\sigma}_{q_0}(\cdot)$ and say that q_0 is the initial state. We say that ρ is *compatible* with σ and d_0 if $\Pr^{\sigma}_{d_0}(\rho) > 0$. By extension, an infinite sequence $\pi \in (Q\mathsf{A})^\omega$ is compatible with σ and d_0 if all prefixes of π that end in a state are compatible. It is standard to extend (in a unique way) $\Pr^{\sigma}_{d_0}$ over Borel sets of infinite paths in $(Q\mathsf{A})^\omega$ (called events), by assigning probability $\Pr^{\sigma}_{d_0}(\rho)$ to the basic cylinder set containing all infinite paths with prefix ρ [2,22]. Given a set $T \subseteq Q$ of target states, and $k \in \mathbb{N}$, we define the following events (sometimes called objectives):

- $\Box T = \{q_0 a_0 q_1 \dots \in (Q\mathsf{A})^\omega \mid \forall i : q_i \in T\}$ the safety event of staying in T;
- $\Diamond T = \{q_0 a_0 q_1 \dots \in (Q\mathsf{A})^\omega \mid \exists i : q_i \in T\}$ the event of reaching T;
- $\Diamond^k T = \{q_0 a_0 q_1 \dots \in (Q\mathsf{A})^\omega \mid q_k \in T\}$ the event of reaching T after exactly k steps;

A distribution d_0 is *almost-sure winning* for an event Ω if there exists a strategy σ such that $\Pr^{\sigma}_{d_0}(\Omega) = 1$, and *limit-sure winning* if $\sup_\sigma \Pr^{\sigma}_{d_0}(\Omega) = 1$, that is the event Ω can be realized with probability arbitrarily close to 1. Finally d_0 is *sure winning* for Ω if there exists a strategy σ such that all paths compatible with σ and d_0 belong to Ω.

Safety and reachability events are dual, in the sense that $\Diamond T$ and $\Box(Q \setminus T)$ form a partition of $(Q\mathsf{A})^\omega$. It is known for safety objectives $\Box T$ that the three winning regions (sure, almost-sure winning, and limit-sure winning) coincide in MDPs, and for reachability objectives $\Diamond T$, almost-sure and limit-sure winning coincide [10]. It follows that if the negation of almost-sure reachability holds, that is $\mathrm{Pr}^{\sigma}_{d_0}(\Diamond T) < 1$ for all strategies σ, then equivalently $\inf_\sigma \mathrm{Pr}^{\sigma}_{d_0}(\Box(Q \setminus T)) > 0$ (note the strict inequality), the probability mass that remains always outside T can be bounded. An explicit bound can be obtained from the classical characterization of the winning region for almost-sure reachability [9].

Lemma 1. *If a distribution d_0 is not almost-sure winning for a reachability objective $\Diamond T$ in an MDP $\mathcal{M}$, then for all strategies σ, for all $i \geq 0$, we have $Pr^{\sigma}_{d_0}(\Diamond^i T) \leq 1 - \alpha_0 \cdot \alpha^n$ where $n = |Q|$ is the number of states and α the smallest positive probability in $\mathcal{M}$, and $\alpha_0 = \min\{d_0(q) \mid q \in \mathsf{Supp}(d_0)\}$ is the smallest positive probability in the initial distribution d_0.*

In Lemma 1 it is crucial to notice that the bound $\alpha_0 \cdot \alpha^n$ is independent of the number i of steps.

Synchronizing objectives. We consider MDPs as generators of sequences of probability distributions over states [18]. Given an initial distribution $d_0 \in \mathcal{D}(Q)$ and a strategy σ in $\mathcal{M}$, the sequence $\mathcal{M}^\sigma = (\mathcal{M}^\sigma_i)_{i \in \mathbb{N}}$ of probability distributions (from d_0, which we assume is clear from the context) is defined by $\mathcal{M}^\sigma_i(q) = Pr^{\sigma}_{d_0}(\Diamond^i \{q\})$ for all $i \geq 0$ and $q \in Q$. Hence, $\mathcal{M}^\sigma_i$ is the probability distribution over states after i steps under strategy σ. Note that $\mathcal{M}^\sigma_0 = d_0$.

Informally, synchronizing objectives require that the probability of some set T of states tends to 1 in the sequence $(\mathcal{M}^\sigma_i)_{i \in \mathbb{N}}$, either always, once, infinitely often, or always after some point [12]. Given a target set $T \subseteq Q$, we say that a probability distribution d is *p-synchronized* in T if $d(T) \geq p$ (and strictly p-synchronized in T if $d(T) > p$), and that a sequence $d_0 d_1 \dots$ of probability distributions is:

(*a*) *always p-synchronizing* if d_i is p-synchronized (in T) for all $i \geq 0$;
(*b*) *event(ually) p-synchronizing* if d_i is p-synchronized (in T) for some $i \geq 0$;
(*c*) *weakly p-synchronizing* if d_i is p-synchronized (in T) for infinitely many i's;
(*d*) *strongly p-synchronizing* if d_i is p-synchronized (in T) for all but finitely many i's.

Given an initial distribution d_0, we say that for the objective of {always, eventually, weakly, strongly} synchronizing from d_0, the MDP $\mathcal{M}$ is:

- *sure winning* if there exists a strategy σ such that the sequence $\mathcal{M}^\sigma$ from d_0 is {always, eventually, weakly, strongly} 1-synchronizing in T;
- *almost-sure winning* if there exists a strategy σ such that for all $\varepsilon > 0$ the sequence $\mathcal{M}^\sigma$ from d_0 is {always, eventually, weakly, strongly} $(1-\varepsilon)$-synchronizing in T;
- *limit-sure winning* if for all $\varepsilon > 0$, there exists a strategy σ such that the sequence $\mathcal{M}^\sigma$ from d_0 is {always, eventually, weakly, strongly} $(1-\varepsilon)$-synchronizing in T;

For $\lambda \in \{always, event, weakly, strongly\}$, we denote by $\langle\langle 1 \rangle\rangle^{\lambda}_{sure}(T)$ the *winning region* defined as the set of initial distributions d_0 such that $\mathcal{M}$ is sure winning for λ-synchronizing in T (in this notation, we assume that $\mathcal{M}$ is clear

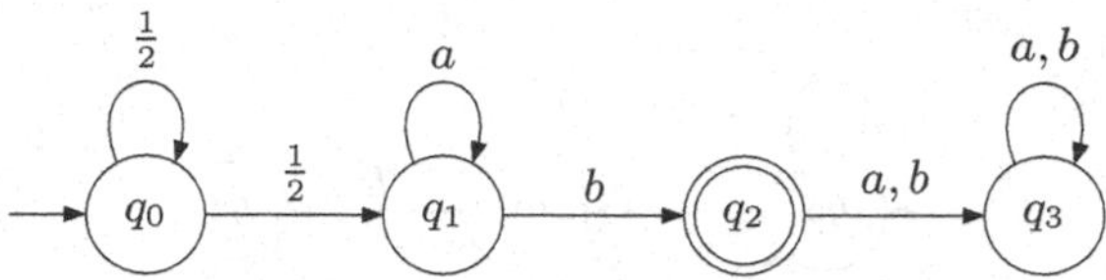

Fig. 2. An MDP where $\{q_0\} \in \langle\langle 1 \rangle\rangle^{event}_{limit}(\{q_2\})$.

from the context). We define analogously the winning regions $\langle\langle 1 \rangle\rangle^{\lambda}_{almost}(T)$ and $\langle\langle 1 \rangle\rangle^{\lambda}_{limit}(T)$ of almost-sure and limit-sure winning distributions.

It is known that for all winning modes, only the support of the initial distributions is relevant, that is for every winning region $W = \langle\langle 1 \rangle\rangle^{\lambda}_{\mu}(T)$ (where $\mu \in \{sure, almost, limit\}$), for all distributions d, d', if $\mathsf{Supp}(d) = \mathsf{Supp}(d')$, then $d \in W$ if and only if $d' \in W$ [12]. Therefore, in the sequel we sometimes write $S \in \langle\langle 1 \rangle\rangle^{\lambda}_{\mu}(T)$, which can be read as any distribution d with support S is in $\langle\langle 1 \rangle\rangle^{\lambda}_{\mu}(T)$. For each synchronizing mode λ and winning mode μ, the membership problem asks to decide, given an MDP $\mathcal{M}$, a target set T, and a set S, whether $S \in \langle\langle 1 \rangle\rangle^{\lambda}_{\mu}(T)$.

Consider the MDP in Fig. 2, with initial state q_0 and target set $T = \{q_2\}$. The probability mass cannot loop through q_2 and therefore, it is immediate that the MDP is neither always, nor weakly, nor strongly $(1-\varepsilon)$-synchronizing, thus $\{q_0\} \notin \langle\langle 1 \rangle\rangle^{\lambda}_{almost}(T)$ for $\lambda = always, weakly, strongly$, and thus also $\{q_0\} \notin \langle\langle 1 \rangle\rangle^{\lambda}_{sure}(T)$.

For eventually synchronizing in q_2, at every step, half of the probability mass in q_0 stays in q_0 while the other half is sent to q_1. Thus, the probability mass in q_0 tends to 0 but is strictly positive at every step, and the MDP is not sure eventually synchronizing, $\{q_0\} \notin \langle\langle 1 \rangle\rangle^{event}_{sure}(T)$. In state q_1, action a keeps the probability mass in q_1, while action b sends it to the target state q_2. If action b is never chosen, then q_2 is never reached, and whenever b is chosen, a strictly positive probability mass remains in q_0, thus the MDP is not almost-sure eventually synchronizing, $\{q_0\} \notin \langle\langle 1 \rangle\rangle^{event}_{almost}(T)$. On the other hand, for every $\varepsilon > 0$, the strategy that plays a in q_1 for k steps such that $\frac{1}{2^k} < \varepsilon$, and then plays b, is winning for eventually $(1-\varepsilon)$-synchronizing in T. Thus the MDP is limit-sure eventually synchronizing, $\{q_0\} \in \langle\langle 1 \rangle\rangle^{event}_{limit}(T)$.

The MDP in Fig. 3 is also limit-sure eventually synchronizing in $\{q_2\}$. As the probability mass is sent back to q_0 from q_2, the MDP is even almost-sure weakly (and eventually) synchronizing, using a strategy that plays action a in q_1 for k steps to accumulate probability mass $1 - \frac{1}{2^k}$ in q_1, then plays action b and repeats the same pattern for increasing values of k.

End-Components. Given a state $q \in Q$ and a set $S \subseteq Q$, let $\mathsf{A}_S(q)$ be the set of all actions $a \in \mathsf{A}$ such that $\mathsf{Supp}(\delta(q,a)) \subseteq S$. A *closed* set in an MDP is a set $S \subseteq Q$ such that $\mathsf{A}_S(q) \neq \varnothing$ for all $q \in S$. A set $S \subseteq Q$ is an *end-component* [2,10] if (i) S is closed, and (ii) the graph (S, E_S) is strongly connected where $E_S = \{(q,q') \in S \times S \mid \delta(q,a)(q') > 0$ for some $a \in \mathsf{A}_S(q)\}$ denote the set

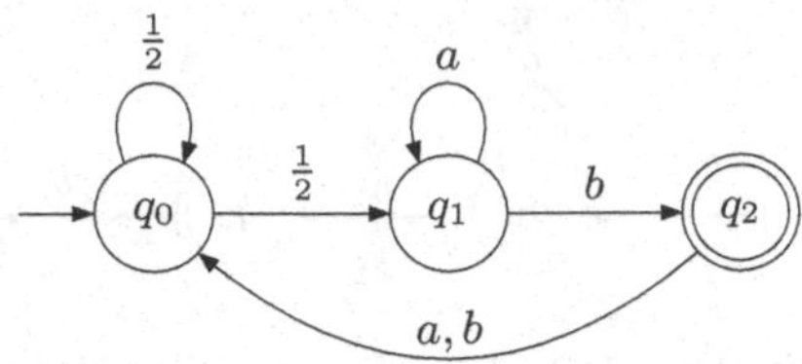

Fig. 3. An MDP where $\{q_0\} \in \langle\langle 1 \rangle\rangle^{weakly}_{almost}(\{q_2\})$.

of edges given the actions. In the sequel, end-components should be considered *maximal*, that is such that no strict superset is an end-component. We denote by $\mathcal{E}$ the union of all end-components, and for $q \in \mathcal{E}$, we denote by $\mathcal{E}(q)$ the maximal end-component containing q. A fundamental property of end-components is that under arbitrary strategies, with probability 1 the set of states visited infinitely often along a path is an end-component.

Lemma 2 ([9,10]). *Let $\mathcal{M}$ be an MDP. For all strategies σ, we have* $\liminf_{i\to\infty} \mathcal{M}_i^\sigma(\mathcal{E}) = 1$.

Tracking Counter in MDPs. It will be useful to track the number of steps (modulo a given number r) in MDPs. Given a number $r \in \mathbb{N}$, define the MDP $\mathcal{M} \times [r] = \langle Q_r, \mathsf{A}, \delta_r \rangle$ where $Q_r = Q \times \{r-1, \dots, 1, 0\}$ and δ_r is defined as follows, for all $\langle q, i \rangle, \langle q', j \rangle \in Q_r$ and $a \in \mathsf{A}$:

$$\delta_r(\langle q, i \rangle, a)(\langle q', j \rangle) = \begin{cases} \delta(q, a)(q') & \text{if } j = i - 1 \mod r, \\ 0 & \text{otherwise.} \end{cases}$$

For a distribution $d \in \mathcal{D}(Q)$ and $0 \le t < r$, we denote by $d \times \{t\}$ the distribution defined, for all $q \in Q$, by $d \times \{t\}(\langle q, i \rangle) = d(q)$ if $t = i$, and $d \times \{t\}(\langle q, i \rangle) = 0$ otherwise. Given a finite sequence $\rho = q_0 a_0 q_1 a_1 \dots q_n$ in $\mathcal{M}$, and $0 \le t < r$, there is a corresponding sequence $\rho' = \langle q_0, k_0 \rangle a_0 \langle q_1, k_1 \rangle a_1 \dots \langle q_n, k_n \rangle$ in $\mathcal{M} \times [r]$ where $k_0 = t$ and $k_{i+1} = k_i - 1 \mod r$ for all $0 \le i < n$. Since the sequence ρ' is uniquely defined from ρ and t, there is a clear bijection between the paths in $\mathcal{M}$ starting in q_0 and the paths in $\mathcal{M} \times [r]$ starting in $\langle q_0, t \rangle$. In the sequel, we freely omit to apply and mention this bijection. In particular, we often consider that a strategy σ in $\mathcal{M}$ can be played directly in $\mathcal{M} \times [r]$.

Consider the MDP in Fig. 4 (which is in fact a Markov chain), with initial state q_0 and target set $T = \{q_2, q_3\}$. There are two end-components, $S_1 = \{q_1, q_2\}$ and $S_2 = \{q_3, q_4\}$. Although both S_1 and S_2 are sure eventually synchronizing in T (from q_1 and q_3 respectively), the uniform distribution over $\{q_1, q_3\}$ is not even limit-sure eventually synchronizing in T.

3 Eventually Synchronizing

In the rest of this paper, fix an MDP $\mathcal{M} = \langle Q, \mathsf{A}, \delta \rangle$ and let $n = |Q|$ be the size of $\mathcal{M}$, and let α be the smallest positive probability in the transitions of $\mathcal{M}$.

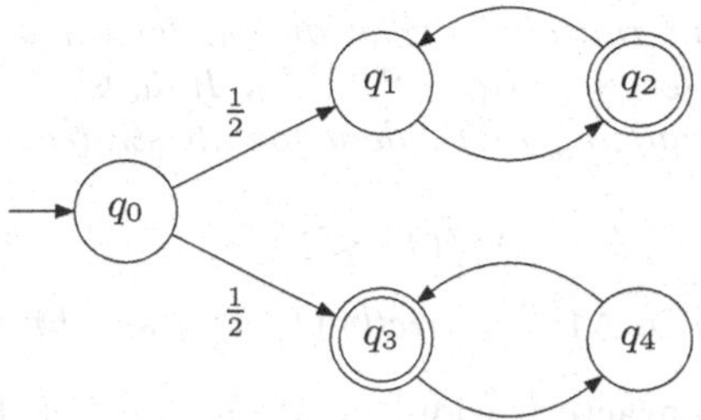

Fig. 4. A Markov chain with two periodic end-components.

We first consider eventually synchronizing, that is synchronization must happen once.

3.1 Sure Winning

We recall the following characterization of the sure-winning region for eventually synchronizing [12, Lemma 7]: $d \in \langle\langle 1 \rangle\rangle_{sure}^{event}(T)$ if and only if there exists $k \geq 0$ such that $\mathsf{Supp}(d) \subseteq \mathsf{Pre}^k(T)$. Intuitively, from all states in $\mathsf{Pre}^i(T)$, there exists an action to ensure that the successor is in $\mathsf{Pre}^{i-1}(T)$ (for all $i > 0$), and therefore there exists a strategy to ensure that the probability mass in $\mathsf{Pre}^k(T)$ reaches T in exactly k steps. Now, if $q_0 \notin \mathsf{Pre}^k(T)$, then for all sequences of actions $a_0, \dots, a_{k-1}$ there is a path $q_0 a_0 q_1 a_1 \dots q_k$ of length k that ends in $q_k \in Q \setminus T$. It is easy to derive the following result from this characterization.

Lemma 3. *If $d_0 \notin \langle\langle 1 \rangle\rangle_{sure}^{event}(T)$ is not sure eventually synchronizing in T, then for all strategies σ, for all $i \geq 0$, we have:*

$$\mathcal{M}_i^\sigma(T) \leq 1 - \alpha_0 \cdot \alpha^i$$

where α_0 is the smallest positive probability in d_0.

Note that the bound $1 - \alpha_0 \cdot \alpha^i$ tends to 1 as $i \to \infty$, which is unavoidable since MDPs that are not sure eventually synchronizing may be almost-sure eventually synchronizing [12]. The following variant of Lemma 3 will be useful in the sequel.

Remark 1. If $\{q_0\} \notin \langle\langle 1 \rangle\rangle_{sure}^{event}(T)$ and we take $\alpha_0' = d_0(q_0)$, then from the initial distribution d_0 we have, for all strategies σ, for all $i \geq 0$:

$$\mathcal{M}_i^\sigma(T) \leq 1 - \alpha_0' \cdot \alpha^i.$$

3.2 Limit-Sure Winning

If the MDP $\mathcal{M}$ is not limit-sure winning for eventually synchronizing in T, then the probability in $Q \setminus T$ is bounded away from 0 in all distributions in $\mathcal{M}^\sigma$ (for all strategies σ). We give an explicit bound ε_e as follows.

Theorem 1. *Given an initial distribution d_0, let α_0 be the smallest positive probability in d_0, and let $\varepsilon_e = \alpha_0 \cdot \alpha^{(n+1)\cdot 2^n}$. If $d_0 \notin \langle\langle 1\rangle\rangle^{event}_{limit}(T)$ is not limit-sure eventually synchronizing in T, then for all strategies σ, for all $i \geq 0$, we have:*

$$\mathcal{M}^{\sigma}_i(T) \leq 1 - \varepsilon_e,$$

that is, no distribution in $\mathcal{M}^{\sigma}$ is strictly $(1-\varepsilon_e)$-synchronizing in T.

Proof. We recall the characterization[1] of [12, Lemma 11] for limit-sure synchronizing in an arbitrary set T. For all $k \geq 0$, we have

$$\langle\langle 1\rangle\rangle^{event}_{limit}(T) = \langle\langle 1\rangle\rangle^{event}_{sure}(T) \cup \langle\langle 1\rangle\rangle^{event}_{limit}(R),$$

where $R = \mathsf{Pre}^k(T)$.

We use this characterization with a specific k (and R) as follows. Consider the sequence of predecessors $\mathsf{Pre}^i(T)$ (for $i = 1, 2, \dots$), which is ultimately periodic. Let $0 \leq k < 2^n$ and $1 \leq r < 2^n$ be such that $\mathsf{Pre}^k(T) = \mathsf{Pre}^{k+r}(T)$, and let $R = \mathsf{Pre}^k(T)$. Thus $R = \mathsf{Pre}^{k+r}(T) = \mathsf{Pre}^r(R)$.

Since $d_0 \notin \langle\langle 1\rangle\rangle^{event}_{limit}(T)$, we have:

$$(a)\ d_0 \notin \langle\langle 1\rangle\rangle^{event}_{sure}(T), \quad \text{and} \quad (b)\ d_0 \notin \langle\langle 1\rangle\rangle^{event}_{limit}(R).$$

By (a), it follows from Lemma 3 that $\mathcal{M}^{\sigma}_i(T) \leq 1 - \alpha_0 \cdot \alpha^i$ for all strategies σ and all $i \geq 0$, which establishes the bound in the lemma for the first 2^n steps, since $\alpha_0 \cdot \alpha^i \geq \varepsilon_e$ for all $i \leq 2^n$.

We now recall the characterization(See footnote 1) of [12, Lemma 12] for limit-sure synchronizing in the set R, which has the property that $R = \mathsf{Pre}^r(R)$: $d_0 \in \langle\langle 1\rangle\rangle^{event}_{limit}(R)$ if and only if there exists $0 \leq t < r$ such that $d_0 \times \{t\}$ is almost-sure winning for the reachability objective $\Diamond(R \times \{0\})$ in the MDP $\mathcal{M} \times [r]$. By (b), it follows that for all $0 \leq t < r$, the distribution $d_0 \times \{t\}$ is *not* almost-sure winning for the reachability objective $\Diamond(R \times \{0\})$ in the MDP $\mathcal{M} \times [r]$.

Let $\mathcal{N} = \mathcal{M} \times [r]$. By Lemma 1, from all distributions $d_0 \times \{t\}$ (for all $0 \leq t < r$), for all strategies σ and all $i \geq 0$, we have:

$$\mathcal{N}^{\sigma}_i(R \times \{0\}) \leq 1 - \alpha_0 \cdot \alpha^{|Q_r|} = 1 - \alpha_0 \cdot \alpha^{n\cdot 2^n}.$$

Since this holds for all $t = 0, \dots, r-1$, we conclude that $\mathcal{M}^{\sigma}_i(Q \setminus R) \geq \alpha_0 \cdot \alpha^{n\cdot 2^n}$ in the original MDP $\mathcal{M}$ from d_0, for all strategies σ and all $i \geq 0$.

Since $R = \mathsf{Pre}^k(T)$, it follows from Lemma 3 and Remark 1 that, if at step i a mass of probability p is outside R, then at step $i+k$ a mass of probability at least $p \cdot \alpha^k$ is outside T. Hence we have $\mathcal{M}^{\sigma}_{i+k}(Q \setminus T) \geq \alpha_0 \cdot \alpha^{n\cdot 2^n} \cdot \alpha^k \geq \alpha_0 \cdot \alpha^{(n+1)\cdot 2^n}$ for all strategies σ and for all $i \geq 0$, which implies $\mathcal{M}^{\sigma}_i(Q \setminus T) \geq \alpha_0 \cdot \alpha^{(n+1)\cdot 2^n}$ for all $i \geq 2^n$ (since $k < 2^n$).

[1] The results of [12, Lemma 11 & 12] consider a more general definition of limit-sure synchronizing, where the support of the $(1-\varepsilon)$-synchronizing distribution is required to have its support contained in a given set Z. We release this constraint by taking $Z = Q$.

Combining the results for $i \leq 2^n$ and for $i \geq 2^n$, we get $\mathcal{M}_i^\sigma(T) \leq 1 - \varepsilon_e$ for all $i \geq 0$, which concludes the proof. □

Theorem 1 also gives a sufficient condition that can be used as an alternative to [12, Lemma 11] to show that an MDP is limit-sure eventually synchronizing. This will be useful in the proof of our main result (Theorem 2).

A variant of Theorem 1 is obtained by observing that if $d_0 \notin \langle\langle 1 \rangle\rangle_{limit}^{event}(T)$, there exists a set $S_0 \subseteq \mathsf{Supp}(d_0)$ such that $S_0 \notin \langle\langle 1 \rangle\rangle_{limit}^{event}(T)$. It may be that S_0 is a strict subset of $\mathsf{Supp}(d_0)$, and then it is sufficient to consider α_0 as the smallest positive probability of d_0 on S_0.

Remark 2. If $S_0 \notin \langle\langle 1 \rangle\rangle_{limit}^{event}(T)$ and $S_0 \subseteq \mathsf{Supp}(d_0)$, then we can define α_0 by $\min\{d_0(q) \mid q \in S_0\}$ in the bound ε_e of Theorem 1.

3.3 Almost-Sure Winning

A simple argument shows that the almost-sure winning region for eventually synchronizing consists of the union of the sure winning region for eventually synchronizing and the almost-sure winning region for weakly synchronizing [21, Section 5.1.2], that is $\langle\langle 1 \rangle\rangle_{almost}^{event}(T) = \langle\langle 1 \rangle\rangle_{sure}^{event}(T) \cup \langle\langle 1 \rangle\rangle_{almost}^{weakly}(T)$.

It follows that if $d_0 \notin \langle\langle 1 \rangle\rangle_{almost}^{event}(T)$, then both $d_0 \notin \langle\langle 1 \rangle\rangle_{sure}^{event}(T)$ and $d_0 \notin \langle\langle 1 \rangle\rangle_{almost}^{weakly}(T)$, and we can use both the results of Lemma 3 and Theorem 2.

4 Weakly Synchronizing

We now consider weakly synchronizing, which intuitively requires that synchronization happens infinitely often.

4.1 Sure Winning

We recall the following characterization of the sure-winning region for weakly synchronizing [12, Lemma 18]: for all distributions $d_0 \in \mathcal{D}(Q)$, we have $d_0 \in \langle\langle 1 \rangle\rangle_{sure}^{weakly}(T)$ if and only if there exists a set $S \subseteq T$ such that $\mathsf{Supp}(d) \subseteq \mathsf{Pre}^k(S)$ for some $k \geq 0$, and $S \subseteq \mathsf{Pre}^r(S)$ for some $r \geq 1$.

Lemma 4. *If $d_0 \notin \langle\langle 1 \rangle\rangle_{sure}^{weakly}(T)$ is not sure weakly synchronizing in T, then for all strategies σ, in the sequence $\mathcal{M}^\sigma$ there are at most 2^n distributions that are 1-synchronized in T, that is $\mathcal{M}_i^\sigma(T) = 1$ for at most 2^n values of i.*

4.2 Limit-Sure and Almost-Sure Winning

The winning region for limit-sure and almost-sure weakly synchronizing coincide [12, Theorem 7]. Therefore, in the sequel we treat them interchangeably. We recall the following characterization of almost-sure weakly synchronizing.

Lemma 5 ([12, Lemma 23,Theorem 7]). *For all distributions d_0, the following equivalence holds: $d_0 \in \langle\!\langle 1 \rangle\!\rangle^{weakly}_{almost}(T)$ if and only if there exists a set $T' \subseteq T$ such that:*

$$d_0 \in \langle\!\langle 1 \rangle\!\rangle^{event}_{limit}(T') \quad \text{and} \quad T' \in \langle\!\langle 1 \rangle\!\rangle^{event}_{limit}(\mathsf{Pre}(T')).$$

The condition in Lemma 5 ensures that from d_0 almost all the probability mass (namely $1 - \varepsilon$ for arbitrarily small $\varepsilon > 0$) can be injected in a set T' of target states in 0 or more steps, and that from T' almost all the probability mass can be injected in $\mathsf{Pre}(T')$, thus also in T' (but, in at least 1 step). Intuitively, by successively halving the value of ε one can construct a strategy that ensures almost all the probability mass loops through T', thus a limit-sure weakly synchronizing strategy (which is equivalent to the existence of an almost-sure weakly synchronizing strategy).

If $d_0 \notin \langle\!\langle 1 \rangle\!\rangle^{weakly}_{almost}(T)$ is not almost-sure weakly synchronizing, we use Lemma 5 to show that for all sets $T' \subseteq T$, if $d_0 \in \langle\!\langle 1 \rangle\!\rangle^{event}_{limit}(T')$ is limit-sure eventually synchronizing in T', then T' is not limit-sure eventually synchronizing in $\mathsf{Pre}(T')$ (i.e., $T' \notin \langle\!\langle 1 \rangle\!\rangle^{event}_{limit}(\mathsf{Pre}(T'))$). This implies that a bounded number of distributions in the sequence $\mathcal{M}^\sigma$ can be $(1-\varepsilon)$-synchronized in T (for sufficiently small ε). We now state the main result of this section.

Theorem 2. *Given an initial distribution d_0, let α_0 be the smallest positive probability in d_0, and let $\varepsilon_w = \alpha_0 \cdot \frac{\alpha^{(n+2)\cdot 4^n}}{n^{2^n+1}}$ and $N_w = 2^n$.*

If $d_0 \notin \langle\!\langle 1 \rangle\!\rangle^{weakly}_{almost}(T)$ is not almost-sure weakly synchronizing in T, then for all strategies σ, in the sequence $\mathcal{M}^\sigma$ at most N_w distributions are strictly $(1-\varepsilon_w)$-synchronized in T, that is $\mathcal{M}^\sigma_i(T) > 1 - \varepsilon_w$ for at most N_w values of i.

Proof. Given the assumption of the lemma, we show the following statement by induction on $k = 0, 1, \ldots, 2^n$: if there are k distributions in $\mathcal{M}^\sigma$ that are strictly $(1 - \varepsilon_w)$-synchronized in T, then there exist k *distinct* nonempty sets $T_1, \ldots, T_k \subseteq T$ such that no distribution after those k distributions in $\mathcal{M}^\sigma$ is strictly $(1-\varepsilon_w)$-synchronized in T_j (for all $1 \leq j \leq k$).

For $k = 2^n$, one of the sets T_j is equal to T and it follows that at most 2^n distributions in $\mathcal{M}^\sigma$ can be $(1 - \varepsilon_w)$-synchronized in T, which concludes the base case. For the proof by induction, we use the bound ε_e of Theorem 1. Let $F = (n+1)\cdot 2^n$ (thus $\varepsilon_e = \alpha_0 \cdot \alpha^F$) and for $k = 0, 1, \ldots$ define $z_k = \frac{\alpha_0}{n} \cdot \left(\frac{\alpha^{F+1}}{n}\right)^k$. We prove a slightly stronger statement: for $k = 0, 1, \ldots, 2^n$, if there are k positions $i_1 < i_2 < \ldots < i_k$ such that the distributions $\mathcal{M}^\sigma_{i_j}$ $(j = 1, \ldots, k)$ are strictly $(1 - \varepsilon_w)$-synchronized in T, then there exist k distinct nonempty sets $T_1, \ldots, T_k \subseteq T$ such that no distribution after position i_j in $\mathcal{M}^\sigma$ is strictly $(1 - z_j \cdot \alpha^{F+1})$-synchronized in T_j (for all $1 \leq j \leq k$).

This statement is indeed stronger since the sequence z_k is decreasing, and ε_w was chosen such that $\varepsilon_w \leq z_{2^n}$, from which it follows that $1 - \varepsilon_w \geq 1 - z_k$ for all $k \leq 2^n$.

The base case for $k = 0$ holds trivially. For the induction case, assume that the statement holds for a given $k < 2^n$, and show that it holds for $k+1$ as follows. If there are $k+1$ positions $i_1 < i_2 < \ldots < i_{k+1}$ such that all distributions $d_j = \mathcal{M}^{\sigma}_{i_j}$ ($j = 1, \ldots, k+1$) are strictly $(1 - \varepsilon_w)$-synchronized in T, then by the induction hypothesis, no distribution after position i_j in $\mathcal{M}^{\sigma}$ is strictly $(1 - z_j \cdot \alpha^{F+1})$-synchronized in T_j (for all $1 \leq j \leq k$).

Now consider the distribution d_{k+1} at position i_{k+1}, which is $(1 - \varepsilon_w)$-synchronized in T and appears after position i_k in $\mathcal{M}^{\sigma}$. We construct the set $T_{k+1} = \{q \in T \cap \mathsf{Supp}(d_{k+1}) \mid d_{k+1}(q) > z_{k+1}\}$, which contains the states in T that carry enough probability mass (namely z_{k+1}) according to d_{k+1}.

Note that not all states in $T \cap \mathsf{Supp}(d_{k+1})$ carry a probability mass less than z_{k+1}: otherwise, the total mass of T in d_{k+1} would be at most $n \cdot z_{k+1} \leq 1 - \varepsilon_w$ (this inequality holds thanks to $n \geq 2$), in contradiction with d_{k+1} being $(1-\varepsilon_w)$-synchronized in T. Therefore T_{k+1} is nonempty. Hence the set T_{k+1} can be obtained from T by removing at most $n - 1$ states and we have

$$\begin{cases} d_{k+1}(T_{k+1}) > 1 - \varepsilon_w - (n-1) \cdot z_{k+1} \geq 1 - n \cdot z_{k+1} = 1 - z_k \cdot \alpha^{F+1} \\ d_{k+1}(q) > z_{k+1} \text{ for all } q \in T_{k+1} \end{cases}$$

So d_{k+1} is strictly $(1 - z_k \cdot \alpha^{F+1})$-synchronized in T_{k+1}, and therefore also strictly $(1 - z_j \cdot \alpha^{F+1})$-synchronized in T_{k+1} (for all $1 \leq j \leq k$). Then, the induction hypothesis implies that the set T_{k+1} is distinct from $T_1, \ldots, T_k$. Since $1 - z_k \cdot \alpha^{F+1} \geq 1 - z_0 \cdot \alpha^{F+1} > 1 - \varepsilon_e$, it follows that $d_{k+1} = \mathcal{M}^{\sigma}_{i_{k+1}}$ is strictly $(1 - \varepsilon_e)$-synchronized in T_{k+1}, and by Theorem 1, that the initial distribution d_0 is limit-sure eventually synchronizing in T_{k+1}, that is $d_0 \in \langle\langle 1 \rangle\rangle^{event}_{limit}(T_{k+1})$.

By Lemma 5, this entails that T_{k+1} is not limit-sure eventually synchronizing in $\mathsf{Pre}(T_{k+1})$ (i.e., $T_{k+1} \notin \langle\langle 1 \rangle\rangle^{event}_{limit}(\mathsf{Pre}(T_{k+1}))$), and by Theorem 1, for all distributions d in $\mathcal{M}^{\sigma}$ that occur at or after position i_{k+1}, we have $d(\mathsf{Pre}(T_{k+1})) \leq 1 - z_{k+1} \cdot \alpha^F$ where $z_{k+1} < \min\{d_{k+1}(q) \mid q \in T_{k+1} \cap \mathsf{Supp}(d_{k+1})\}$ is a lower bound on the smallest positive probability of a state of T_{k+1} in the distribution d_{k+1}, taken as the initial distribution (see Remark 2). It follows that for all distributions d in $\mathcal{M}^{\sigma}$ that occur (strictly) after position i_{k+1}, we have $d(T_{k+1}) \leq 1 - z_{k+1} \cdot \alpha^{F+1}$. Hence no distribution in $\mathcal{M}^{\sigma}$ after d_{k+1} is strictly $(1 - z_{k+1} \cdot \alpha^{F+1})$-synchronized, which concludes the proof of the induction case. □

5 Always and Strongly Synchronizing

The anaysis of always and strongly synchronizing modes is relatively straightforward, and we present the bounds in Theorem 3.

Theorem 3. *Given an initial distribution d_0, let α_0 be the smallest positive probability in d_0, and let $\varepsilon_a = \alpha_0 \cdot \frac{\alpha^n}{n}$ and $\varepsilon_s = \alpha_0 \cdot \frac{\alpha^{2n}}{n^2}$.*

- *if $d_0 \notin \langle\langle 1 \rangle\rangle^{always}_{sure}(T)$ is not sure always synchronizing in T, then for all strategies σ, in the sequence $\mathcal{M}^{\sigma}$ there exists a position $i \leq n$ such that $\mathcal{M}^{\sigma}_i$ is not $(1 - \varepsilon_a)$-synchronized in T,*

- *if* $d_0 \notin \langle\langle 1 \rangle\rangle_{sure}^{strongly}(T)$ *is not sure strongly synchronizing in* T*, then for all strategies* σ*, in the sequence* $\mathcal{M}^\sigma$ *there exist infinitely many positions* $i_0 < i_1 < i_2 < \ldots$ *where* $i_0 \leq n$ *and* $i_{j+1} - i_j \leq n$ *for all* $j \geq 0$ *such that* $\mathcal{M}^\sigma_{i_j}$ *is not* 1*-synchronized in* T*.*
- *if* $d_0 \notin \langle\langle 1 \rangle\rangle_{almost}^{strongly}(T)$ *is not almost-sure strongly synchronizing in* T*, then for all strategies* σ*, in the sequence* $\mathcal{M}^\sigma$ *there exist infinitely many positions* $i_0 < i_1 < i_2 < \ldots$ *where* $i_0 \leq n$ *and* $i_{j+1} - i_j \leq n$ *for all* $j \geq 0$ *such that* $\mathcal{M}^\sigma_{i_j}$ *is not* $(1 - \varepsilon_s)$*-synchronized in* T*.*

6 Adversarial Synchronizing Objectives

In an adversarial MDP the strategies are universally quantified, which corresponds to satisfying an objective regardless of the choice of strategies by an adversary. Replacing $\exists\sigma$ by $\forall\sigma$ in the definition of the three winning modes gives, after taking the negation to get existentially quantified strategies, the following new winning modes.

Given a set $T \subseteq Q$, we say that a sequence $d_0 d_1 \ldots$ of probability distributions is:

- *positively* {always, eventually, weakly, strongly} winning if $d_i(T) > 0$ for, respectively, all $i \geq 0$, some $i \geq 0$, infinitely many i's, all but finitely many i's.
- *boundedly* {always, eventually, weakly, strongly} winning if there exists $\varepsilon > 0$ such that $d_i(T) > \varepsilon$ for, respectively, all $i \geq 0$, some $i \geq 0$, infinitely many i's, all but finitely many i's.

For $\lambda \in \{always, event, weakly, strongly\}$, we denote by $\langle\langle 1 \rangle\rangle_{positive}^{\lambda}(T)$ (resp., $\langle\langle 1 \rangle\rangle_{bounded}^{\lambda}(T)$) the set of initial distributions d_0 from which there exists a strategy σ such that the sequence $\mathcal{M}^\sigma$ is positively (resp., boundedly) λ-synchronizing in T, and we say that σ is positively (resp., boundedly) λ-synchronizing in T from d_0.

Table 1 summarizes the new definitions. Note that replacing the existential quantification on strategies in boundedly winning mode by a supremum gives the same question, since $\exists\sigma : f(\sigma) > 0$ is equivalent to $\sup_\sigma f(\sigma) > 0$. For the same reason, we have the identity $\langle\langle 1 \rangle\rangle_{positive}^{event}(T) = \langle\langle 1 \rangle\rangle_{bounded}^{event}(T)$. It is easy to show that the definitions imply the identity $\langle\langle 1 \rangle\rangle_{bounded}^{always}(T) = \langle\langle 1 \rangle\rangle_{positive}^{always}(T) \cap \langle\langle 1 \rangle\rangle_{bounded}^{strongly}(T)$, which we also obtain as a corollary of Lemma 6 below.

Remark 3. It immediately follows from the definitions that for all synchronizing modes $\lambda \in \{always, event, weakly, strongly\}$, and $\mu \in \{positive, bounded\}$:

- $\langle\langle 1 \rangle\rangle_{\mu}^{always}(T) \subseteq \langle\langle 1 \rangle\rangle_{\mu}^{strongly}(T) \subseteq \langle\langle 1 \rangle\rangle_{\mu}^{weakly}(T) \subseteq \langle\langle 1 \rangle\rangle_{\mu}^{event}(T)$,
- $\langle\langle 1 \rangle\rangle_{bounded}^{\lambda}(T) \subseteq \langle\langle 1 \rangle\rangle_{positive}^{\lambda}(T)$,

and moreover,

- $\langle\langle 1\rangle\rangle^{event}_{positive}(T) = \langle\langle 1\rangle\rangle^{event}_{bounded}(T)$, and
- $\langle\langle 1\rangle\rangle^{always}_{bounded}(T) = \langle\langle 1\rangle\rangle^{always}_{positive}(T) \cap \langle\langle 1\rangle\rangle^{strongly}_{bounded}(T)$.

It is easy to see that if there exists a strategy σ that is positively λ-synchronizing in T, then the strategy σ_{u} that plays at every round all actions uniformly at random is also positively λ-synchronizing in T, because the condition $d_i(T) > 0$ is equivalent to $\mathsf{Supp}(d_i) \cap T \neq \varnothing$, and because we have $\sigma \subseteq \sigma_{\mathsf{u}}$, which implies that $\mathsf{Supp}(\mathcal{M}^{\sigma}_i) \subseteq \mathsf{Supp}(\mathcal{M}^{\sigma_{\mathsf{u}}}_i)$ for all $i \geq 0$.

Hence, in all four synchronization modes, the question is equivalent to the same question in Markov chains (obtained from the given MDP by fixing the strategy σ_{u}) which can be solved as follows. Given a Markov chain, consider the underlying directed graph $\langle Q, E\rangle$ where $(q, q') \in E$ if $\delta(q, a)(q') > 0$ (where $\mathsf{A} = \{a\}$). For positive eventually synchronizing, it suffices to find a state in T that is reachable in that graph, and for positive weakly synchronizing, it suffices to find a state in T that is both reachable and can reach itself. These questions are NL-complete. For positive always and strongly synchronizing, the question is equivalent to the model-checking problem for the formulas $G\exists T$ and $FG\exists T$ in the logic CTL+Sync, which are both coNP-complete [6, Lemma 2 & Section 3].

For boundedly winning, we show that one strategy is good enough in all four synchronization modes, like for positive winning. The strategy plays like σ_{u} for the first 2^n rounds, and then switches to a strategy $\sigma_{\mathcal{E}}$ that, in the states $q \in \mathcal{E}$, plays uniformly at random all actions that stay in the end-component $\mathcal{E}(q)$ of q (thus all actions in $\mathsf{A}_{\mathcal{E}(q)}$), and in the transient states $q \notin \mathcal{E}$, plays all actions uniformly at random. We call this strategy the *freezing* strategy. Intuitively we use σ_{u} to scatter the probability mass in all end-components of the MDP, and then $\sigma_{\mathcal{E}}$ to maintain a bounded probability in each end-component.

Lemma 6. *Let $\mathcal{M}$ be an MDP with n states and initial distribution d_0, and let T be a target set. Consider the following conditions:*

(1) $\forall i \geq 0 : \mathcal{M}^{\sigma_{\mathsf{u}}}_i(T) > 0$ *(2)* $\forall i \geq 2^n : \mathcal{M}^{\sigma_{\mathsf{u}}}_i(\mathcal{E} \cap T) > 0$

Then, the following equivalences hold:

(a) $d_0 \in \langle\langle 1\rangle\rangle^{always}_{positive}(T)$ *if and only if Condition* (1) *holds;*
(b) $d_0 \in \langle\langle 1\rangle\rangle^{strongly}_{bounded}(T)$ *if and only if Condition* (2) *holds;*
(c) $d_0 \in \langle\langle 1\rangle\rangle^{always}_{bounded}(T)$ *if and only if Conditions* (1) *and* (2) *hold;*

Proof. Equivalence (a) follows from the definition of positive always synchronizing, and from the fact that the uniform strategy σ_{u} is sufficient for positive winning.

We show Equivalence (b) as follows. First, if Condition (2) does not hold, then $\mathcal{M}^{\sigma_{\mathsf{u}}}_i(\mathcal{E} \cap T) = 0$ for some $i \geq 2^n$, and thus also for infinitely many i's (since the sequence $\mathsf{Supp}(\mathcal{M}^{\sigma_{\mathsf{u}}}_i)$ is ultimately periodic, after at most 2^n steps). For arbitrary strategy σ, we have $\mathsf{Supp}(\mathcal{M}^{\sigma}_i) \subseteq \mathsf{Supp}(\mathcal{M}^{\sigma_{\mathsf{u}}}_i)$ for all $i \geq 0$, therefore

$\mathcal{M}_i^\sigma(\mathcal{E} \cap T) = 0$ for infinitely many i's. By Lemma 2, we have $\liminf_{i\to\infty} \mathcal{M}_i^\sigma(\mathcal{E}) = 1$ which entails that $\limsup \mathcal{M}_i^\sigma(\mathcal{E} \setminus T) = 1$ and $\limsup \mathcal{M}_i^\sigma(Q \setminus T) = 1$, that is $\liminf \mathcal{M}_i^\sigma(T) = 0$. Since this holds for arbitrary strategy σ, it follows that $d_0 \notin \langle\langle 1 \rangle\rangle_{bounded}^{strongly}(T)$.

For the converse direction, assuming Condition (2) holds, we show that $d_0 \in \langle\langle 1 \rangle\rangle_{bounded}^{strongly}(T)$, witnessed by the freezing strategy σ_f (which plays like σ_{u} for the first 2^n rounds, and then switches to the strategy $\sigma_{\mathcal{E}}$).

We show the key property that

$$\mathsf{Supp}(\mathcal{M}_i^{\sigma_{\mathsf{u}}}) \cap \mathcal{E} = \mathsf{Supp}(\mathcal{M}_i^{\sigma_f}) \cap \mathcal{E} \text{ for all } i \geq 2^n.$$

Fix an arbitrary $i \geq 2^n$ and let p be a period of the sequence $\mathsf{Supp}(\mathcal{M}^{\sigma_{\mathsf{u}}})$ such that $i - p \leq 2^n$ and $\mathsf{Supp}(\mathcal{M}_i^{\sigma_{\mathsf{u}}}) = \mathsf{Supp}(\mathcal{M}_{i-p}^{\sigma_{\mathsf{u}}})$. Consider the Markov chain $\mathcal{M}_{\mathcal{E}}$ obtained by fixing the strategy $\sigma_{\mathcal{E}}$ in $\mathcal{M}$. From the basic theory of Markov chains, each end-component C in $\mathcal{M}$ is a recurrent class in $\mathcal{M}_{\mathcal{E}}$. For each $i \geq 2^n$, either all or none of the states in a periodic class of C are in the support of $\mathcal{M}_i^{\sigma_{\mathsf{u}}}$.

To show the key property, first consider a state $q \in \mathsf{Supp}(\mathcal{M}_i^{\sigma_{\mathsf{u}}}) \cap \mathcal{E}$ for $i \geq 2^n$, and show that $q \in \mathsf{Supp}(\mathcal{M}_i^{\sigma_f}) \cap \mathcal{E}$. Let S be the periodic class of $\mathcal{E}(q)$ containing q (in $\mathcal{M}_{\mathcal{E}}$), and thus

$$S \subseteq \mathsf{Supp}(\mathcal{M}_i^{\sigma_{\mathsf{u}}}) \cap \mathcal{E}, \text{ and thus } S \subseteq \mathsf{Supp}(\mathcal{M}_{i-p}^{\sigma_{\mathsf{u}}}) \cap \mathcal{E}.$$

Since σ_{u} and σ_f coincide on the first 2^n rounds, we have $S \subseteq \mathsf{Supp}(\mathcal{M}_{i-p}^{\sigma_f}) \cap \mathcal{E}$.

Now consider the strategy $\sigma_{\mathcal{E}}$ and an initial distribution with support S, and denote by $S + j$ the support of the probability distribution after playing $\sigma_{\mathcal{E}}$ for j steps. Then, since $\sigma_{\mathcal{E}} \subseteq \sigma_f \subseteq \sigma_u$,

$$S + p \subseteq \mathsf{Supp}(\mathcal{M}_i^{\sigma_f}) \cap \mathcal{E}, \text{ and } S + p \subseteq \mathsf{Supp}(\mathcal{M}_i^{\sigma_u}) \cap \mathcal{E}.$$

We can repeat the same argument with $S + p$ instead of S, and show by induction that $S + j \cdot p \subseteq \mathsf{Supp}(\mathcal{M}_i^{\sigma_f}) \cap \mathcal{E}$ for all $j \geq 1$. In particular, by taking j the period of the end-component containing q, we get $S + j \cdot p = S$ and thus $S \subseteq \mathsf{Supp}(\mathcal{M}_i^{\sigma_f}) \cap \mathcal{E}$, which establishes one direction of the key property (the converse direction follows from $\sigma_f \subseteq \sigma_{\mathsf{u}}$).

From the theory of Markov chains, in every end-component state $q \in \mathcal{E}$, the positive probability mass is bounded away from 0 in $\mathcal{M}^{\mathcal{E}}$, that is there exists a bound $\varepsilon > 0$ such that for all $i \geq 2^n$, for all $q \in \mathcal{E}$, if $\mathcal{M}_i^{\sigma_f}(q) \neq 0$, then $\mathcal{M}_i^{\sigma_f}(q) \geq \varepsilon$. By the key property and Condition (2), for all $i \geq 2^n$, there exists $q \in \mathcal{E} \cap T$ such that $\mathcal{M}_i^{\sigma_f}(q) \neq 0$, which implies that $\liminf_{i\to\infty} M_i^{\sigma_f}(T) \geq \varepsilon > 0$ and thus $d_0 \in \langle\langle 1 \rangle\rangle_{bounded}^{strongly}(T)$.

Finally, the proof for Equivalence (c) follows the same steps as above to show that Conditions (1) and (2) imply $d_0 \in \langle\langle 1 \rangle\rangle_{bounded}^{always}(T)$, where Condition (1) is used to bound $M_i^{\sigma_f}(T)$ for the first 2^n rounds, and thus to ensure that $M_i^{\sigma_f}(T) \geq B > 0$ for all $i \geq 0$, hence $d_0 \in \langle\langle 1 \rangle\rangle_{bounded}^{always}(T)$. The converse direction immediately follows from the first part of Remark 3 and Equivalences (a) and (b). □

We extract explicit bounds from the proof of Lemma 6. All end-components are reached within a most n steps (under σ_{u}), and further all states in (a periodic class of) a recurrent class are reached (synchronously) within a most n^2 steps [15, Theorem 4.2.11], thus all states in the periodic class have probability mass at least $\varepsilon_a = \alpha_0 \cdot \left(\frac{\alpha}{|\mathsf{A}|}\right)^{n+n^2}$ where α_0 is the smallest positive probability in the initial distribution d_0 (note that $\alpha/|\mathsf{A}|$ is the smallest probability in the Markov chain $\mathcal{M}_{\mathcal{E}}$). It follows that the freezing strategy ensures probability at least ε_a in T at every step (if $\mathcal{M}$ is boundedly always synchronizing), and probability at least ε_a in T at every step after $N = n + n^2$.

The conditions (1) and (2) in Lemma 6 can be decided in coNP as follows. For Condition (1) we guess an index $i \leq 2^n$ (in binary) and compute the i-th power of the Boolean transition matrix $M \in \{0,1\}^{n^2}$ where $M(q,q') = 1$ if there is a transition from state q to state q' in the Markov chain obtained from the given MDP $\mathcal{M}$ by fixing the strategy σ_{u}. The matrix M^i can be computed in polynomial time by successive squaring of M. Then it suffices to check whether $M^i(q_0, q) = 0$ for all $q_0 \in \mathsf{Supp}(d_0)$ and $q \in T$. For Condition (2), since the sequence $\mathsf{Supp}(\mathcal{M}_i^{\sigma_{\mathsf{u}}})$ is ultimately periodic, we guess two indices $i, p \leq 2^n$ $(p \geq 1)$ and check that $\mathsf{Supp}(\mathcal{M}_i^{\sigma_{\mathsf{u}}}) = \mathsf{Supp}(\mathcal{M}_{i+p}^{\sigma_{\mathsf{u}}})$ and $\mathsf{Supp}(\mathcal{M}_i^{\sigma_{\mathsf{u}}}) \cap \mathcal{E} \cap T = \varnothing$, using the same approach by successive squaring. Note that the union $\mathcal{E}$ of all end-components can be computed in polynomial time [9,10].

Conditions (1) and (2) are also coNP-hard, using the same reduction that established coNP-hardness of the positive always and positive bounded synchronizing [6, Lemma 2 & Section 3], in which positive and bounded winning mode coincide. It follows that the membership problem for bounded always and bounded strongly synchronizing is coNP-complete.

We now show the solution for bounded weakly synchronizing. It suffices to find a state in $T \cap \mathcal{E}$ that is reachable in the underlying graph of the Markov chain $\mathcal{M}_{\sigma_{\mathsf{u}}}$, which is a NL-complete problem (like for positive weakly synchronizing, except we require a reachable state in $T \cap \mathcal{E}$, not just in T). Indeed, if all reachable end-components are contained in $Q \setminus T$, then by Lemma 2 we have $\liminf_{i\to\infty} \mathcal{M}_i^{\sigma}(Q \setminus T) = 1$, that is $\limsup_{i\to\infty} \mathcal{M}_i^{\sigma}(T) = 0$. For the converse direction, if a state $\hat{q} \in T \cap \mathcal{E}$ is reachable, then by a similar argument as above based on the theory of Markov chains, as the probability mass in the states of the periodic classes (that contain some probability mass) is bounded away from 0 in $\mathcal{M}^{\sigma_{\mathcal{E}}}$, it follows that within every p steps, where p is the period of the recurrent class $\mathcal{E}(\hat{q})$ the probability mass in $\hat{q}$ is at least $\alpha_0 \cdot (\alpha/|\mathsf{A}|)^{n+n^2}$. Therefore, $\mathcal{M}$ is boundedly weakly synchronizing in T. For the sake of completeness, note that for eventually synchronizing MDPs, the probability mass $\varepsilon_e = \alpha_0 \cdot (\alpha/|\mathsf{A}|)^n$ in T can be ensured within n steps (using σ_{u}).

Theorem 4. *The complexity of the membership problem for positive and bounded synchronizing objectives is summarized in Table 2.*

In Table 2, the merged cells for eventually synchronizing reflect the fact that the winning regions coincide (see Remark 3). The winning regions for the other synchronizing modes do not coincide, already in Markov chains (see Fig. 1).

Acknowledgment. The authors are grateful to Jean-François Raskin for logistical support, and to Mahsa Shirmohammadi for interesting discussions about adversarial objectives.

References

1. Akshay, S., Genest, B., Vyas, N.: Distribution-based objectives for Markov decision processes. In: Proceedings of LICS, pp. 36–45. ACM (2018)
2. Baier, C., Katoen, J.-P.: Principles of Model Checking. MIT Press, Cambridge (2008)
3. Beauquier, D., Rabinovich, A., Slissenko, A.: A logic of probability with decidable model-checking. In: Bradfield, J. (ed.) CSL 2002. LNCS, vol. 2471, pp. 306–321. Springer, Heidelberg (2002). https://doi.org/10.1007/3-540-45793-3_21
4. Bell, P.C., Semukhin, P.: Decidability of cutpoint isolation for probabilistic finite automata on letter-bounded inputs. In: Proceedings of CONCUR, vol. 171 of LIPIcs, pp. 22:1–22:16. Schloss Dagstuhl - Leibniz-Zentrum für Informatik (2020)
5. Bertrand, N., Dewaskar, M., Genest, B., Gimbert, H.: Controlling a population. In: Proceedings of CONCUR: Concurrency Theory, volume 85 of LIPIcs, pp. 12:1–12:16. Schloss Dagstuhl - Leibniz-Zentrum fuer Informatik (2017)
6. Chatterjee, K., Doyen, L.: Computation tree logic for synchronization properties. In: Proc. of ICALP: Automata, Languages, and Programming, volume 55 of LIPIcs, pp. 98:1–98:14. Schloss Dagstuhl - Leibniz-Zentrum fuer Informatik (2016)
7. Chatterjee, K., Henzinger, T.A.: A survey of stochastic ω-regular games. J. Comput. Syst. Sci. **78**(2), 394–413 (2012)
8. Colcombet, T., Fijalkow, N., Ohlmann, P.: Controlling a random population. In: FoSSaCS 2020. LNCS, vol. 12077, pp. 119–135. Springer, Cham (2020). https://doi.org/10.1007/978-3-030-45231-5_7
9. Courcoubetis, C., Yannakakis, M.: The complexity of probabilistic verification. J. ACM **42**(4), 857–907 (1995)
10. de Alfaro, L.: Formal verification of probabilistic systems. Ph.D. thesis, Stanford University (1997)
11. de Alfaro, L., Henzinger, T.A.: Concurrent omega-regular games. In: Proceedings. of LICS: Logic in Computer Science, pp. 141–154. IEEE (2000)
12. Doyen, L., Massart, T., Shirmohammadi, M.: The complexity of synchronizing Markov decision processes. J. Comput. Syst. Sci. **100**, 96–129 (2019)
13. Doyen, L., van den Bogaard, M.: Bounds for synchronizing Markov decision processes. CoRR, abs/2204.12814 (2022)
14. Feinberg, E., Shwartz, A. (eds.) Handbook of Markov Decision Processes - Methods and Applications. Kluwer, Boston (2002)
15. Gallager, R.G.: Stochastic Processes: Theory for Applications. Cambridge University Press, New York (2013)
16. Hermanns, H., Krčál, J., Křetínský, J.: Probabilistic Bisimulation: naturally on distributions. In: Baldan, P., Gorla, D. (eds.) CONCUR 2014. LNCS, vol. 8704, pp. 249–265. Springer, Heidelberg (2014). https://doi.org/10.1007/978-3-662-44584-6_18
17. Jancar, P., Sawa, Z.: A note on emptiness for alternating finite automata with a one-letter alphabet. Inf. Process. Lett. **104**(5), 164–167 (2007)
18. Korthikanti, V.A., Viswanathan, M., Agha, G., Kwon, Y.: Reasoning about MDPs as transformers of probability distributions. In: Proceedings of QEST: Quantitative Evaluation of Systems, pp. 199–208. IEEE Computer Society (2010)

19. Puterman. M.L.: Markov Decision Processes. John Wiley and Sons, New York (1994)
20. Rabin, M.O.: Probabilistic automata. Inf. Control **6**, 230–245 (1963)
21. Shirmohammadi, M.: Qualitative analysis of probabilistic synchronizing systems. Ph.D. thesis, U. Libre de Bruxelles & École Normale Supérieure de Cachan (2014)
22. Vardi, M.Y.: Automatic verification of probabilistic concurrent finite-state programs. In: Proceedings of FOCS, pp. 327–338. IEEE Computer Society (1985)

Parameterized Complexity of Set-Restricted Disjoint Paths on Chordal Graphs

Petr A. Golovach[1], Fahad Panolan[2], Ashutosh Rai[3(✉)], and Saket Saurabh[1,4]

[1] University of Bergen, Bergen, Norway
Petr.Golovach@uib.no
[2] Indian Institute of Technology Hyderabad, Hyderabad, India
fahad@iith.ac.in
[3] Department of Mathematics, IIT Delhi, New Delhi, India
ashutosh.rai@maths.iitd.ac.in
[4] The Institute of Mathematical Sciences, Chennai, India
saket@imsc.res.in

Abstract. The Disjoint Paths problem takes as input a graph and pairs of terminals, and asks whether all the terminal pairs can be connected by paths that are vertex disjoint. It is known to be NP-complete even on interval graphs. On general graphs, the framework of Robertson and Seymour can be used to get an FPT result parameterized by the number of terminals, but the running time is very high. Considering this, there has been a lot of work on Disjoint Paths on restricted graph classes like planar graphs, chordal graphs, etc.

In this work, we look at a generalization of the Disjoint Paths problem, namely Set-Restricted Disjoint Paths (SRDP), where in addition to terminal pairs, we are also given subsets of vertices as *domains* for each pair, and we want to connect the terminal pairs by vertex disjoint paths that use the vertices only from their respective domains. This problem is known to be in XP on chordal graphs. We show that the FPT result of Disjoint Paths on chordal graphs can be generalized to SRDP. In particular, we show that SRDP can be solved in time $\mathcal{O}^*(2^{\mathcal{O}(k \log k)})$ on chordal graphs (here the $\mathcal{O}^*$ notation hides the polynomial factors in the running time), where k is the number of terminal pairs. We complement this result by showing that SRDP does not have a polynomial kernel on interval graphs, a subclass of chordal graphs.

Keywords: chordal graphs · disjoint paths · set restricted disjoint paths · fpt · kernel

1 Introduction

Disjoint Paths is a well studied problem in the theory of algorithms. The input to the problem is a graph, and a set of k terminal pairs $\{(s_1, t_1), \ldots, (s_k, t_k)\}$. The objective is to test whether there exists k vertex disjoint paths $P_1, \ldots, P_k$

A. S. Kulikov and S. Raskhodnikova (Eds.): CSR 2022, LNCS 13296, pp. 152–169, 2022.
https://doi.org/10.1007/978-3-031-09574-0_10

such that P_i is a path from s_i to t_i for all $i \in \{1, \ldots, k\}$. DISJOINT PATHS is NP-Complete even on interval graphs [14]. In the seminal work on the graph minor theory, Robertson and Seymour [15] designed an algorithm for DISJOINT PATHS running in time $f(k)n^3$ where f is a computable function and n is the number of vertices in the input graph. This work introduced the irrelevant vertex technique which was used later to design many FPT algorithms [1,8,11]. Here, when the input graph has *large* treewidth, an irrelevant vertex can be found and safely deleted. Then, finally the treewidth of the graph will be bounded by a function of k. But here the function f in the running time is a highly growing function and because of that there were attempts to design fast FPT algorithms for the problem on many graph classes. Adler et al. [1] proved that DISJOINT PATHS on planar graphs can be solved in time $2^{2^{\mathcal{O}(k)}} n^2$. Towards proving this result, the authors showed that if a planar graph has *large* treewidth, then an *irrelevant* vertex can be found and deleted. Thus, to prove the result authors reduce the problem to planar graphs with bounded treewidth. Very recently, Lokshtanov et al. [13] designed a fast FPT algorithm for the problem on planar graphs running in time $2^{\mathcal{O}(k^2)} n^{\mathcal{O}(1)}$. Their algorithm is based on the treewidth reduction technique and an algebraic co-homology based technique.

Kammer and Tholey [12] studied DISJOINT PATHS on chordal graphs. They proved that the problem can be solved in time $\mathcal{O}(2^{\mathcal{O}(k \log k)} n + m)$ by reducing the treewidth of the input graph and utilizing the fact that every bag in the tree decomposition of the chordal graph is a clique. In this work we study a generalization of DISJOINT PATHS, called SET-RESTRICTED DISJOINT PATHS which is defined below. The problem SET-RESTRICTED DISJOINT PATHS was introduced by Belmonte et al. [3].

SET-RESTRICTED DISJOINT PATHS (SRDP)	
Input:	A graph $G = (V, E)$, a set of pairs of vertices $T = \{(s_i, t_i) \mid i \in [k]\}$ and a set of respective domains $\mathcal{U} = \{U_1, \ldots, U_k\} \subseteq 2^{V(G)}$.
Parameter:	k
Question:	Do there exist k internally vertex disjoint paths $P_1, \ldots, P_k$ such that for each $i \in [k]$, P_i is a path between s_i and t_i and $V(P_i) \subseteq U_i$?

Here, the terminal pairs can overlap, and hence the paths are required to be vertex disjoint *internally*). SRDP is NP-complete on interval graphs (a subclass of chordal graphs) since DISJOINT PATHS is NP-complete on interval graphs[14]. In contrast to DISJOINT PATHS, Belmonte et al. [3] proved that SRDP is para-NP-hard on general graphs even when $k = 2$. Also, they show that SRDP on chordal graphs is in XP, i.e., it can be solved in time $n^{f(k)}$, for some function f. Recently, this problem was considered by Ahn et al. [2] and designed an FPT algorithm on well-partitioned chordal graphs, a subclass of chordal graphs that generalizes split graphs.

In this work we prove that SRDP on chordal graphs is FPT and the problem does not admit a polynomial kernel even on interval graph, a subclass of chordal graphs. So this implies that SRDP does not admit a polynomial kernel on chordal graphs as well.

Theorem 1. SRDP *can be solved in time* $\mathcal{O}^*(2^{\mathcal{O}(k \log k)})$ *on chordal graphs.*

Theorem 2. SRDP *does not admit a polynomial kernel on interval graphs unless* $NP \subseteq coNP/poly$.

The existence of a polynomial kernel for Disjoint Paths on chordal graphs still remains an open problem. In this work, we show that while the algorithm for Disjoint Path on chordal graphs can be generalized to work for SRDP, SRDP not admitting a polynomial kernel even on interval graphs adds a nice twist to the tale of Disjoint Paths on chordal graphs. Our hardness result relies crucially on the domains, and it is not obvious how it can be generalized to get a similar hardness for Disjoint Paths on chordal or interval graphs.

Our Methods. For our positive results, we borrow from the techniques of Kammer and Tholey [12] which they used to solve the Disjoint Paths problem, by extending them to SRDP. The algorithm for bounded treewidth chordal graphs remains essentially the same, by exploiting the fact that not more than two vertices from any clique would be used by a minimal solution of SRDP. Hence, guessing these $2k+2$ vertices and their colors would give us a coloring analogous to one defined in [12]. We just need to be careful about the domains while looking at the configurations. For the treewidth reduction part, our approach is same in spirit as that of [12], but we have tried to do the reduction arguably more systematically, by considering the bags in groups depending on their degrees.

Finally, the kernelization lower bound result makes use of the technique of AND-cross-composition introduced by Bodlaender et al. [5]. For this, we start with instances of the Disjoint Paths problem on interval graphs, which is known to be NP-hard, to arrive at an instance of SRDP on interval graphs with small parameter, which is a Yes instance if and only if all the Disjoint Paths instances were Yes instances.

2 Preliminaries

In this section, we first give the notations and definitions which are used in the paper. Then we state some known results which will be used later in the paper.

Notations and Definitions: We use $[n]$ to denote the set of first n positive integers $\{1, 2, 3, \ldots n\}$. For a graph G, we denote the set of vertices of the graph by $V(G)$ and the set of edges of the graph by $E(G)$. We denote $|V(G)|$ and $|E(G)|$ by n and m respectively, where the graph is clear from context. We abbreviate an edge $\{u, v\}$ as uv sometimes. For a set $S \subseteq V(G)$, the *subgraph of* G *induced by* S is denoted by $G[S]$ and it is defined as the subgraph of G with vertex set S and edge set $\{\{u, v\} \in E(G) : u, v \in S\}$ and the subgraph obtained after deleting S (and the edges incident to the vertices in S) is denoted as $G - S$. For $v \in V(G)$, we will use $G - v$ to denote $G - \{v\}$ for ease of notation. All vertices adjacent to a vertex v are called neighbours of v and the set of all such vertices is called *open* neighbourhood of v, denoted by $N_G(v)$. For a set of vertices $S \subseteq V(G)$, we define $N_G(S) = (\cup_{v \in S} N(v)) \setminus S$. We define the *closed* neighbourhood of a vertex v in the graph G to be $N_G[v] := N(G) \cup \{v\}$ and closed neighbourhood of a set of vertices $S \subseteq V(G)$ to be $N_G(S) := N(S) \cup S$. We drop the subscript G when the graph is clear from the context. We say a vertex v is *simplicial* in G if $N(v)$ forms a clique in G. For $C \subseteq V(G)$, if $G[C]$ is connected and $N(C) = \emptyset$, then we say that $G[C]$ is a connected component of G.

A *path* P in a graph G is a subgraph of G where $V(P) = \{x_1, x_2, \ldots, x_\ell\} \subseteq V(G)$ and $E(P) = \{\{x_1, x_2\}, \{x_2, x_3\}, \ldots, \{x_{\ell-1}, x_\ell\}\} \subseteq E(G)$ for some $\ell \in [n]$. We denote it by $P := x_1 x_2 \ldots x_\ell$. The vertices x_1 and x_ℓ are called endpoints of the path P and the remaining vertices in $V(P)$ are called internal vertices of P. We also say that P is an x_1-x_ℓ path. The *length* of a path is the number of vertices in it. Let P be a path in the graph G on at least three vertices. We say that $\{u, v\} \in E(G)$ is a chord of P if $u, v \in V(P)$ but $\{u, v\} \notin E(P)$. A path P is chordless if it has no chords. We also use P to denote the set of vertices or edges of the path P sometimes, when it is clear from the context.

Definition 1. *Let G be a graph. A* tree-decomposition *of a graph G is a pair (F, β), where F is a tree and and $\beta : V(F) \to 2^{V(G)}$ such that*

1. $\cup_{x \in V(F)} \beta(x) = V(G)$,
2. *for every edge $uv \in E(G)$ there is a $x \in V(F)$ such that $\{u, v\} \subseteq \beta(x)$, and*
3. *for every vertex $v \in V(G)$ the subgraph of F induced by the set $\beta^{-1}(v) := \{x \mid v \in \beta(x)\}$ is connected.*

For $x \in V(F)$, we call $\beta(x)$ the *bag* of v, and for the sake of clarity of presentation, we sometimes use x and $\beta(x)$ interchangeably. We refer to the vertices in $V(F)$ as *nodes* or *bags*.

Chordal Graphs and Interval Graphs. A graph G is called *chordal* if it does not contain any chordless cycle of length at least four. It is well known that the set of chordal graphs is closed under the operation of taking induced subgraphs and contracting edges [10]. A *clique-tree* of G is a tree-decomposition of G where every bag is a maximal clique. We further insist that every bag of the clique-tree is distinct. The following lemma shows that the class of chordal graphs is exactly the class of graphs that have a clique-tree.

Lemma 1 ([10]). *A graph G is a chordal graph if and only if G has a clique-tree.*

Even though the maximal cliques of a chordal graph define the nodes of its clique-tree, they can be connected in different ways to get different clique-trees for the same graph. Observe that since every bag is a maximal clique, not only the bags are distinct in the clique-tree (F, β), but also for any $x, y \in V(F)$, we have that none of $\beta(x)$ and $\beta(y)$ is a subset of the other, i.e., $\beta(x) \nsubseteq \beta(y)$ and $\beta(y) \nsubseteq \beta(x)$.

Given a tree F and a surjective function $\beta : V(F) \to \mathcal{S}$ where $\mathcal{S} \subseteq 2^V$, such that it satisfies property 3 of Definition 1, we can associate a graph H with

$V(H) = \cup_{S \in \mathcal{S}} S$ and $E(H)$ defined by $uv \in E(H)$ if and only if there exists $x \in V(F)$ such that $\{u, v\} \subseteq \beta(x)$. It is easy to see that in this case the graph H is chordal and that the bags of (F, β) correspond to the maximal cliques of H and we say that H is the chordal graph associated with the clique-tree (F, β).

A graph G is an *interval* graph if it is isomorphic to an intersection graph of intervals of the real line. Equivalently, an interval graph G is a chordal graph having a clique-tree (F, β), where F is a path; we say that (F, β) is a *clique-path.* We refer the book of Golumbic [10] for this property.

3 FPT Algorithm

In this section we show that SRDP is FPT on chordal graphs. First we give an algorithm for SRDP on chordal graphs of bounded treewidth, and in the next subsection we show how the treewidth can be reduced. For an SRDP instance $(G, T, \mathcal{U})$, we assume the graph G to be connected. The case when G is disconnected can be easily reduced to this. For an SRDP instance $(G, T, \mathcal{U})$, we sometimes use T to also denote the set $\cup_{i \in [k]} \{s_i, t_i\}$.

3.1 Algorithm for Bounded Treewidth Graphs

In this section, we show that SRDP is FPT on chordal graphs of bounded treewidth, when treewidth is also a parameter in addition to the number of terminal pairs.

Theorem 3. SRDP *can be solved in* $\mathcal{O}^*(\mathbf{tw}^{\mathcal{O}(k)})$ *time on chordal graphs of treewidth* $\mathbf{tw}$.

We say that a set of paths $\mathcal{P} = \{P_1, \ldots, P_k\}$ is a solution to $(G, T, \mathcal{U})$ if for all $i \in [k]$, P_i is a path between s_i and t_i and $V(P_i) \subseteq U_i$. We say that a solution $\mathcal{P} = \{P_1, \ldots, P_k\}$ is *minimal* if for all $i \in [k]$, there does not exist a path P_i' between s_i and t_i of length smaller than that of P_i such that $V(P_i') \subseteq U_i$ and $(\mathcal{P} \setminus P_i) \cup P_i'$ is also a solution. We start with a simple lemma.

Lemma 2. *Let* $(G, T = \{(s_i, t_i) \colon i \in [k]\}, \mathcal{U})$ *be an instance of* SRDP. *Let* (F, β) *be a clique-tree of* G *and let* $\mathcal{P} = \{P_1, \ldots, P_k\}$ *be a minimal solution. Then, for any* $x \in V(F)$ *and* $i \in [k]$, $|V(P_i) \cap \beta(x)| \leq 2$. *Moreover, for any* $x \in V(F)$ *and* $i \in [k]$, *if* $|V(P_i) \cap \beta(x)| = 2$, *then* $uv \in E(P_i)$, *where* $\{u, v\} = V(P_i) \cap \beta(x)$.

Proof. For the sake of contradiction suppose there exist $x \in V(F)$ and $i \in [k]$ such that $|V(P_i) \cap \beta(x)| \geq 3$. Let $P_i := v_1 v_2 \ldots v_\ell$. Let j, r, s be the indices in $[k]$ such that $j < r < s$ and $v_j, v_r, v_s \in \beta(x)$. Since $v_j v_s \in E(G)$ (because $\beta(x)$ is a clique in G), we have that $P_i' := v_1 \ldots v_{j-1} v_j v_s v_{s+1} v_\ell$ is a path from v_1 to v_ℓ and $V(P_i') \subsetneq V(P_i)$. This is a contradiction to the assumption that $\mathcal{P}$ is a minimal solution.

Suppose there exist $x \in V(F)$ and $i \in [k]$ such that $|V(P_i) \cap \beta(x)| = 2$. Let $P_i := v_1 v_2 \ldots v_\ell$. Let j, r be two distinct indices in $[k]$ such that $j < r$ and

$v_j, v_r \in V(P_i) \cap \beta(x)$. We claim that $r = j+1$ and hence $v_j v_r \in E(P_i)$. If $r > j+1$, then $P_i' = v_1 \ldots v_j v_r v_{r+1} \ldots v_\ell$ is a path from v_1 to v_ℓ such that $V(P_i') \subset V(P_i)$. This is a contradiction to the assumption that $\mathcal{P}$ is a minimal solution. □

Now we are ready to prove Theorem 3.

Proof sketch of Theorem 3. A dynamic programming algorithm for k-DISJOINT PATHS on a clique-tree is designed by Kammer and Tholey [12]. Notice that here we have one additional condition that for each $i \in [k]$, $V(P_i) \subseteq U_i$ for the s_i-t_i path P_i in a solution. Thus, our algorithm is an extension the algorithm of Kammer and Tholey [12] where we have an additional constraint. So here we give a proof sketch. Let $(G, T = \{\{s_i, t_i\} : i \in [k]\}, \mathcal{U} = \{U_1, \ldots, U_k\})$ be the input instance of SRDP. First we compute a clique-tree (F, β) of G using a linear time algorithm mentioned in [4]. In [12], a solution to k-DISJOINT PATHS is viewed as coloring function. Here the objective is to find a coloring $c : U \mapsto [k]$ on a subset U of vertices of G using k colors $[k]$ such that the following holds.

- $\{s_i, t_i : i \in [k]\} \subseteq U$.
- For each $i \in [k]$, $c(s_i) = c(t_i)$. Moreover, for any $j \in [k] \setminus \{i\}$, $c(s_i) \neq c(s_j)$.
- For each $i \in [k]$, there is a path from s_i to t_i in the subgraph of G induced on $c^{-1}(j)$, where $j = c(s_i) = c(t_i)$.

For our problem we will have one additional constraint as follows.

- For each $i \in [k]$, $c^{-1}(j) \subseteq U_j$, where $j = c(s_i) = c(t_i)$.

By Lemma 2, we get that for each node x in F and for each color j, there is at most two vertices in $\beta(x)$ colored j. This implies that the number of states with respect to a bag in a dynamic programming algorithm is bounded by $\mathbf{tw}^{\mathcal{O}(k)}$. The steps of the algorithm is similar to the one in [12] where we make sure that the additional constraint is satisfied. Hence, the running time of the algorithm is $\mathcal{O}^*(\mathbf{tw}^{\mathcal{O}(k)})$. □

3.2 Treewidth Reduction and FPT Algorithm

In this section, given an instance of SRDP where the input graph is chordal, we will show how to reduce the treewidth to a polynomial function of the parameter. This is achieved by reducing the clique sizes in the clique-tree of the input graph. For that, we first apply some simple reduction rules that would provide more structure to the instance.

Reduction Rule 1. *Let $(G, T, \mathcal{U})$ be an instance of* SRDP *such that $s_i = s_j$ for some $i, j \in [k]$, $i \neq j$. Then we add a new vertex s^* to the graph and add edges such that $N(s^*) = N[s_i]$, and replace the pair (s_j, t_j) by (s^*, t_j) to obtain a new instance $(G', T', \mathcal{U})$.*

Lemma 3. *Reduction Rule 1 is correct.*

Proof. If $(G,T,\mathcal{U})$ is a YES instance, then let $\mathcal{P} = \{P_1,\ldots,P_k\}$ be a solution for it. Then we get a solution for $(G',T',\mathcal{U})$ by replacing s_j with s^* in P_j. This can be done since $N(s^*) = N[s_j]$. The converse follows from replacing s^* by s_j in a solution for $(G',T',\mathcal{U})$. □

Observe that even though the reduction rule has been stated in terms of $s_i = s_j$, we can also apply it if some $t_i = t_j$ or $s_i = t_j$, and the same proof of correctness works. It is also easy to see that it can be applied in polynomial time. So now onwards, we will assume that Reduction Rule 1 has been applied exhaustively, and all the terminals in all the terminal pairs are distinct.

Reduction Rule 2. *Let $(G,T,\mathcal{U})$ be an instance of* SRDP *such that $s_it_i \in E(G)$, then output a new instance $(G-\{s_i,t_i\}, T\setminus\{(s_i,t_i)\}, \mathcal{U}\setminus\{U_i\})$.*

The correctness of the reduction rule follows from the fact that if the instance is a YES instance then there exists a solution with $P_i = s_it_i$. After applying this reduction rule exhaustively, we can assume that $s_it_i \notin E(G)$ for all $i \in [k]$. Since all the bags in the clique-tree of G induce cliques, this means that no bag in the clique-tree of G contains both s_i and t_i. Now we give the following reduction rule that makes each terminal belong to only one bag of the clique-tree. We would need the following notation for that. Let $(G,T,\mathcal{U})$ be an instance of SRDP where G is a chordal graph and let (F,β) be a clique-tree of G. For each $i \in [k]$, let B_{s_i} be the set of nodes in $V(F)$ that contain s_i and let B_{t_i} be the set of nodes that contain t_i. We denote by $\Pi_G(s_i,t_i)$ be the shortest length path between a node in B_{s_i} and B_{t_i} in F. We will drop the subscript G if the graph is clear from context.

Reduction Rule 3. *Let $(G,T,\mathcal{U})$ be an instance of* SRDP *such that G is a chordal graph and let (F,β) be a clique-tree of G. Let x and y be the endpoints of $\Pi_G(s_i,t_i)$. Delete s_i from all the nodes of the clique-tree except from x and delete t_i from all the nodes of the clique-tree except from y. Let G' be the graph corresponding to the new clique-tree. Output $(G',T,\mathcal{U})$.*

Lemma 4. *Reduction Rule 3 is correct.*

Proof. Let $(G,T,\mathcal{U})$ be a YES instance and let $\mathcal{P} = \{P_1,\ldots.P_k\}$ be a minimal solution for it. We claim that in P_i, the vertex adjacent to s_i is in $\beta(x)$ and the vertex adjacent to t_i is in $\beta(y)$. This would prove the correctness, since removing s_i and t_i from other bags is equivalent to reducing their adjacency to $\beta(x)$ and $\beta(y)$ respectively. Now, since $\Pi_G(s_i,t_i)$ is the shortest path between bags containing s_i and t_i, we know that s_i is not in any other bag of $\Pi_G(s_i,t_i)$ except x. So if s_i is adjacent to a vertex $u \notin \beta(x)$ in P_i, deleting $\beta(x)$ disconnects s_i from t_i. This means that the path has to contain a vertex v from $\beta(x)$. But we know that $s_iv \in E(G)$ as $s_i, v \in \beta(x)$ and $\beta(x)$ induces a clique. This means that the path P_i contains a chord and hence is not induced, which is a contradiction to minimality of $\mathcal{P}$.

For the other direction, any solution to $(G',T,\mathcal{U})$ is a solution to $(G,T,\mathcal{U})$ as G' is a subgraph of G. □

Since we can find the clique-tree of chordal graph in linear time [4], Reduction Rule 3 can be applied in polynomial time. After exhaustive application of the reduction rule, all the terminals belong to unique bags in the clique-tree of G. For a terminal s_i (or t_i), let x_{s_i} (or x_{t_i}) be the unique bag in $V(F)$ that contains it. Observe that $\Pi_G(s_i, t_i)$ is the path between x_{s_i} and x_{t_i}.

Reduction Rule 4. *Let* $(G,T,\mathcal{U})$ *be an instance of* SRDP *where* G *is a chordal graph and let* $v \in V(G) \setminus T$ *be a simplicial vertex in* G. *Output the instance* $(G - v, T, \mathcal{U}')$ *where* $\mathcal{U}'$ *is obtained from* $\mathcal{U}$ *by deleting* v *from all the domains.*

Lemma 5. *Reduction Rule 4 is correct.*

Proof. Let $G' = G - v$. As G' is an induced subgraph of G, it is chordal, and any solution to $(G',T,\mathcal{U})$ remains a solution to $(G,T,\mathcal{U})$. For the converse, let $\mathcal{P} = \{P_1, \ldots, P_k\}$ be a minimal solution to $(G',T,\mathcal{U})$. Suppose, for the sake of contradiction that $\mathcal{P}$ is not a solution to G. Then there exist $(s_i, t_i) \in T$ such that P_i is not a path between s_i and t_i such that $V(P_i) \subseteq U_i$. That means P_i must pass through v. Let u and w be the neighbours of v on this path, and let P_i' be the path obtained by deleting v from P_i and using the edge between u and w, which exists because v is a simplicial vertex. Since $V(P_i') \subsetneq V(P_i)$, we have that $\mathcal{P}$ is not a minimal solution, which is a contradiction. □

Now we can show that each leaf bag in the clique-tree must contain a terminal.

Lemma 6. *Let* $(G,T,\mathcal{U})$ *be an instance of* SRDP, *where* G *is a chordal graph. Suppose Reduction Rule 4 is not applicable on* $(G,T,\mathcal{U})$. *Let* (F,β) *be a clique-tree of* G. *Then for each leaf node* $x \in V(F)$, $\beta(x) \cap T \neq \emptyset$ *(as mentioned earlier, in a slight abuse of notation, here we take* $T = \cup_{i \in [k]} \{s_i, t_i\}$*).*

Proof. Let us suppose, for the sake of contradiction, that there exists a leaf $x \in V(F)$, such that $\beta(x) \cap T = \emptyset$. Let $N_F(x) = \{x_1\}$. Since all the bags are distinct and also maximal cliques, we must have a vertex $v \in V(G) \setminus T$ such that $v \in \beta(x) \setminus \beta(x_1)$. But then $N[v] = \beta(x)$ which is a clique and hence v is simplicial in G. It is a contradiction to that fact that Reduction Rule 4 does not apply and proves the statement of the lemma. □

Let $(G,T,\mathcal{U})$ be an instance of SRDP and let (F,β) be a clique-tree of G. We divide the vertex set of F into three parts as following. Let $V(F) = F_1 \cup F_2 \cup F_{\geq 3}$, where F_1 is set of leaves of F, F_2 is the set of nodes of F with degree exactly 2 and $F_{\geq 3}$ is the set of nodes of degree at least three. Let F_T be the set of nodes that contain terminals, and let $F_B := F_T \cup F_{\geq 3}$. We refer to the set F_B as the set of *branching* nodes. Lemma 6 has already shown that $F_1 \subseteq F_T$, so bounding the size of F_B would bound the sizes of F_1, F_3, and F_T together.

Lemma 7. *Let* $(G,T,\mathcal{U})$ *be an instance obtained after applying Reduction Rule 4 exhaustively, and let* (F,β) *be a clique-tree of* G. *Then,* $|F_B| \leq 4k$.

Proof. We know from Lemma 6 that after applying Reduction Rule 4, each leaf bag contains a terminal. This gives us $F_1 \subseteq F_T$. The number of terminals is $2k$. We also know that because of Reduction Rule 3, each terminal occurs in exactly one bag of (F, β). This gives us $|F_T| \leq 2k$. As the number of vertices with degree at least three in a tree is at most the number of leaves, we also get $|F_{\geq 3}| \leq 2k$. Since $F_B = F_T \cup F_{\geq 3}$, we get $|F_B| \leq 4k$ as desired. □

Now, we will describe a marking procedure that would reduce the size of the branching nodes. For that, we will make use the notion of $\Pi_G(s_i, t_i)$ defined earlier. Let $(s_i, t_i) \in T$ be a pair of terminals in an instance $(G, T, \mathcal{U})$ of SRDP and let (F, β) be a clique-tree of G. Let $\Pi(s_i, t_i) := x_1 x_2 \ldots x_d$ where $s_i \in \beta(x_1)$ and $t_i \in \beta(x_d)$. For each $i \in [k]$ and $p \in [d]$, we define two orderings $\leq_{(s_i,t_i)}$ and $\leq_{(t_i,s_i)}$ on vertices of $\beta(x_p) \cap U_i$ as following. For $u, v \in \beta(x) \cap U_i$, $u \leq_{(s_i,t_i)} v$ if and only if, for all $q \geq p$, $q \in [d]$, if $u \in \beta(x_q)$ then $v \in \beta(x_q)$. Similarly, for defining $\leq_{(t_i,s_i)}$, we say that $u \leq_{(t_i,s_i)} v$ if and only if, for all $q \leq p$, $q \in [d]$, if $u \in \beta(x_q)$ then $v \in \beta(x_q)$. In other words, the ordering represents how far along $\Pi(s_i, t_i)$ the vertices of $\beta(x_p) \cap U_i$ go, ranking the ones that go the farthest on either side as the highest.

Now we describe what we call *marking procedure (I)*. For each bag $x \in F_B$, for each $(s_i, t_i) \in T$ for which $x \in \Pi(s_i, t_i)$, we mark $2k+1$ vertices in $\beta(x) \cap U_i$ which are largest in the ordering $\leq_{(s_i,t_i)}$ and call the set $M_x(s_i, t_i)$. We also mark $2k+1$ vertices in $\beta(x) \cap U_i$ which are largest in the ordering $\leq_{(t_i,s_i)}$ and call that set $M_x(t_i, s_i)$. If $|\beta(x) \cap U_i| \leq 2k+1$, then we mark all the vertices in $\beta(x) \cap U_i$ as $M_x(t_i, s_i)$. Let the set of all marked vertices inside a bag $\beta(x)$, such that $x \in F_B$ be $M(x) := \bigcup_{(s_i,t_i) \in T} (M_x(s_i, t_i) \cup M_x(t_i, s_i))$ and let $M := \cup_{x \in F_B} M(x)$.

Now we are ready to give the next reduction rule which will help us bound the size of nodes in F_B.

Reduction Rule 5. *Let $(G, T, \mathcal{U})$ be an instance of* SRDP *where G is a chordal graph and let (F, β) be a clique-tree of G. If there exists a node $x \in F_B$ such that $\beta(x) \setminus M$ is nonempty, then delete an arbitrary vertex $v \in \beta(x) \setminus M$ from G and output $(G - v, T, \mathcal{U}')$, where $\mathcal{U}'$ is obtained from $\mathcal{U}$ by deleting v from all the domains.*

Lemma 8. *Reduction Rule 5 is correct.*

Proof. Let $G' := G - v$. As G' is an induced subgraph of G, G' is chordal and any solution for $(G', T, \mathcal{U}')$ is a solution for $(G, T, \mathcal{U})$. For the other direction, let $\mathcal{P} = \{P_1, \ldots, P_k\}$ be a minimal solution for $(G, T, \mathcal{U})$. Let us assume, for the sake of contradiction that $(G', T, \mathcal{U}')$ is a No instance. Since P_is are vertex disjoint, at most one of them can pass through v, and all others still exist in G'. Without loss of generality, let P_1 pass through v in G.

Let $P_1 := s_1 v_1 v_2 \ldots v_{p-1} v_p v_{p+1} \ldots v_q t_1$ and let $v_p := v$ for some $p \in [q]$. Since $P_1 \in \mathcal{P}$, we have that $v_r \in U_1$ for all $r \in [q]$. Also, let $\Pi(s_1, t_1) := x_1 x_2 \ldots x_d$ where $s_1 \in \beta(x_1)$ and $t_1 \in \beta(x_d)$. Since P_1 has to be chordless due to minimality of $\mathcal{P}$, v has to occur in some bag in $\Pi(s_1, t_1)$, otherwise P_1 would have a chord. Now we look at the following two cases.

Case 1: There exists $x_v \in F_B \cap \{x_2, \ldots, x_{d-1}\}$ **such that** $v \in \beta(x_v)$**.** Clearly, $v \notin M(x_v)$ as otherwise v would not be deleted. We know that marking procedure (I) marked $2k+1$ vertices in $\beta(x_v)$ as $M_{x_v}(s_1, t_1)$ such that for each $u \in M_{x_v}(s_1, t_1)$, $v \leq_{(s_1,t_1)} u$. Since $\mathcal{P}$ is a minimal solution, we have that any P_i uses at most two vertices from $\beta(x_v)$ due to Lemma 2. We get that at least one vertex from $M_{x_v}(s_1, t_1)$ is not being used by any P_i for $i \in [k]$. Let w_2 be an arbitrary vertex in $M_{x_v}(s_1, t_1) \setminus \cup_{i \in [k]} V(P_i)$. By the same logic, let w_1 be an arbitrary vertex in $M_{x_v}(t_1, s_1) \setminus \cup_{i \in [k]} V(P_i)$. Observe that it might be the case that $w_1 = w_2$.

We claim that $P_1' := s_i v_1 v_2 \ldots v_{p-1} w_1 w_2 v_{p+1} \ldots v_q t_i$ is a path in G' such that $V(P_1') \subseteq U_1$ (there is a slight abuse of notation, as it might be the case that $w_1 = w_2$). Since $w_1, w_2 \notin \cup_{i \in [k]} V(P_i)$ and $w_1, w_2 \in U_1$ by definition of $M_{x_v}(s_1, t_1)$ and $M_{x_v}(t_1, s_1)$, all we need to show is that the edges $w_1 w_2$ (in case $w_1 \neq w_2$), $v_{p-1} w_1$, and $w_2 v_{p+1}$ exist in G' (or in G, as G' is an induced subgraph of G). Since $w_1, w_2 \in \beta(x_v)$, that induces a clique in G, we have that $w_1 w_2 \in E(G')$.

We have that $P_1 := s_1 v_1 v_2 \ldots v_{p-1} v v_{p+1} \ldots v_q t_1$. Let y be a bag on the path $\Pi(s_1, t_1)$ such that $v v_{p+1} \in \beta(y)$. Such a bag exists due to Lemma 2 and P_1 being chordless (due to minimality of $\mathcal{P}$). Now, from the definition of $\leq_{(s_1,t_1)}$ we have the following. Since $v \leq_{(s_1,t_1)} w_2$, w_2 is present in all the bags after x, along the path $\Pi(s_1, t_1)$ towards x_d (that contains t_1), wherever v is present. In particular, $w_2 \in \beta(y)$, and hence $w_2 v_{p+1} \in E(G')$. Similarly we can show that $v_{p-1} w_1 \in E(G')$ by traversing $\Pi(s_1, t_1)$ in the other direction, and making use of the ordering $\leq_{(t_1,s_1)}$.

Case 2: There does not exist $x_v \in F_B \cap \{x_2, \ldots, x_{d-1}\}$ **such that** $v \in \beta(x_v)$**.** Since the bags in $V(F)$ that contain v induce a connected subgraph and v has to occur in a bag in F_B to be deleted, we conclude that in this case either $v \in \beta(x_1)$ or $v \in \beta(x_d)$. We look at the case when $v \in \beta(x_1)$, the case when $v \in \beta(x_d)$ is similar. Now, since $x_1 \in \Pi(s_1, t_1)$, marking procedure (I) marked $2k+1$ vertices in $\beta(x_1) \cap U_1$ as $M_{x_1}(s_1, t_1)$ such that for each $u \in M_{x_1}(s_1, t_1)$, $v \leq_{(s_1,t_1)} u$. Now, we can replace v by a vertex in $M_{x_1}(s_1, t_1)$ which is not used by any other path, following the same procedure as in Case 1. This finishes the proof of the lemma. □

Lemma 9. *Let* $(G, T, \mathcal{U})$ *be an instance of* SRDP *after applying Reduction Rule 5 exhaustively, and let* (F, β) *be a clique-tree of* G*. Let* F_B *be set of branching nodes as defined above. Then,* $|\beta(x)| = \mathcal{O}(k^3)$ *for all* $x \in F_B$*.*

Proof. For any $x \in F_B$, we know that $|\beta(x)| \leq |M|$, since otherwise Reduction Rule 5 would apply. We know by definition of M that $M = \cup_{x \in F_B} M(x)$ and from Lemma 7 that $|F_B| \leq 4k$. So, to prove the lemma, all we need to show is that $M(x) = \mathcal{O}(k^2)$ for each $x \in F_B$. This is true because we have k terminal pairs, and for each of them we mark at most $4k+2$ vertices in $\beta(x)$. This gives $|M(x)| \leq 2k(k+1)$ as desired. □

Now, to decrease the treewidth of the graph, all we need to do is to bound the bag sizes for degree 2 bags in a clique-tree of G. For that, we will be looking at paths in the clique-tree of G such that all the internal nodes of the paths are degree 2 nodes, and the endpoints are branching nodes. Let $V_B = \cup_{x \in F_B} \beta(x)$. We will be marking some vertices in the nodes in F_2 which are not in V_B.

Let $(G, T, \mathcal{U})$ be an instance of SRDP where G is a chordal graph and (F, β) be a clique-tree of G. We also take two fixed orderings $f : V(G) \to [n]$ and $g : V(F) \to [|V(F)|]$. Let $Q := x_1 x_2 \dots x_q$ be a path in F such that $x_1, x_q \in F_B$, $g(x_1) < g(x_q)$, $x_\gamma \notin F_B$ for all $\gamma \in \{2, 3, \dots, q-1\}$. For each x_j such that $j \in \{2, \dots, q-2\}$ (such a j does not exist if $q < 4$) and for each $i \in [k]$, we define an ordering $<_i$ on the vertices of $(\beta(x_j) \cap U_i) \setminus V_B$ as follows. For $u, v \in (\beta(x_j) \cap U_i) \setminus V_B$, we say that $u <_i v$, if one of the following two is true.

1. There exists $r \in \{j+1, \dots q-1\}$ such that $v \in \beta(x_r)$ and $u \notin \beta(x_r)$, or
2. For all $r \in \{j+1, \dots q-1\}$, $v \in \beta(x_r)$ if and only if $u \in \beta(x_r)$, and $f(u) < f(v)$.

We also define these orderings $<_i$ for vertices of $(\beta(x_{q-1}) \cap U_i) \setminus V_B$, as following. For $u, v \in (\beta(x_{q-1}) \cap U_i) \setminus V_B$, we say that $u <_i v$ if and only if $f(u) < f(v)$. Observe that $<_i$ is a total ordering on the vertices of $(\beta(x_j) \cap U_i) \setminus V_B$ for all $j \in \{2, \dots, q-1\}$.

Now, *marking procedure (II)* considers all paths $Q := x_1 x_2 \dots x_q$ in F such that $x_1, x_q \in F_B$, $g(x_1) < g(x_q)$, and $x_\gamma \notin F_B$ for all $\gamma \in \{2, 3, \dots, q-1\}$, and does the following. The first step of marking procedure (II), for every bag x_j such that $j \in \{2, \dots, q-1\}$ and for every $i \in [k]$, marks $2k+1$ vertices in $\beta(x_j) \cap U_i$ that are highest in the ordering $<_i$. If $|\beta(x_j) \cap U_i| \le 2k+1$, then all the vertices in $\beta(x_j) \cap U_i$ are marked. Let $D^1(x_j, i)$ denote the set of vertices in $\beta(x_j)$ marked by the first step of marking procedure (II) according to the ordering $<_i$. In addition to that, for $j \in \{3, \dots, q-1\}$ and for each $i \in k$, the second step of marking procedure (II) marks the vertices $D^2(x_j, i) := D^1(x_{j-1}, i) \cap \beta(x_j)$. Let $D(x_j) := \bigcup_{i \in k} (D^1(x_j, i) \cup D^2(x_j, i))$ be the set of all marked vertices in x_j by both the steps of the marking procedure (II). Before we give the final reduction rule, we prove the following lemma.

Lemma 10. *Let $(G, T, \mathcal{U})$ be an instance of* SRDP *where G is a chordal graph and (F, β) be a clique-tree of G. Let $Q := x_1 x_2 \dots x_q$ be a path in F such that $x_1, x_q \in F_B$, $x_\gamma \notin F_B$ for all $\gamma \in \{2, 3, \dots, q-1\}$. Let $v \notin V_B$ such that v is marked for some internal node of Q by marking procedure (II). Then, the graph induced by all the internal nodes of Q where v is marked is connected.*

Proof. Without loss of generality, let $g(x_1) < g(x_q)$. Let us assume for the sake of contradiction that the graph induced by all the internal nodes of Q where v is marked is not connected. This means that there exists a subpath $Q' = y_1 y_2 \dots y_r$ of Q (with the vertices taken in the same order as in Q) such that $v \in D(y_1) \cap D(y_r)$ but $v \notin D(y_j)$ for $j \in \{2, \dots, r-1\}$. Let us look at y_{r-1}. Since v is not marked there, for all $i \in [k]$ such that $v \in U_i$, there is a set of $2k+1$ vertices W_i in $(\beta(y_{r-1}) \cap U_i) \setminus V_B$ such that $v <_i w$ for all $w \in W_i$. But by definition of $<_i$, since $v \in \beta(y_r)$ this would mean that $W_i \subseteq \beta(y_r)$ for all $i \in [k]$ such that $v \in U_i$. Since $v <_i w$ for all $w \in W_i$, this implies that $v \notin D^1(y_r, i)$ for any $i \in [k]$ such that $v \in U_i$. Now, the only way for v to be marked in y_r is if $v \in D^2(y_r, i)$ for some $i \in [k]$. But for that, we need to have that $v \in D^1(y_{r-1}, i)$, and hence we get that v is marked for y_{r-1}, which is the desired contradiction. □

Now we are ready to give our final reduction rule.

Reduction Rule 6. *Let* $(G, T, \mathcal{U})$ *be an instance of* SRDP *where* G *is a chordal graph and let* (F, β) *be a clique-tree of* G. *Let* $Q := x_1x_2 \ldots x_q$ *be a path in* F *such that* $g(x_1) < g(x_q)$, $x_1, x_q \in F_B$, $x_\gamma \notin F_B$ *for all* $\gamma \in \{2, 3, \ldots, q-1\}$. *Suppose there exists* $v \notin V_B$ *such that there exists* $j \in \{2, \ldots, q-1\}$ *and* $v \notin D(x_j)$. *Delete* v *from all the bags* x_j *such that* $v \notin D(x_j)$ *to get a clique-tree* (F, β'). *Output* $(G', T, \mathcal{U})$, *where* G' *is the graph corresponding to* (F, β').

Before we show the correctness of the reduction rule, let us first observe that due to Lemma 10, what we get is indeed a clique-tree, and hence G' is a chordal graph.

Lemma 11. *Reduction Rule 6 is correct.*

Proof. For the forward direction, let $(G, T, \mathcal{U})$ be a YES instance and let $\mathcal{P} = \{P_1, \ldots, P_k\}$ be a minimal solution to it. Suppose that $(G', T, \mathcal{U})$ is a NO instance. If none of the paths in $\mathcal{P}$ use v, then $\mathcal{P}$ remains a solution to $(G', T, \mathcal{U})$, a contradiction. Without loss of generality, let P_1 go through v. Let $P_1 := s_1v_1v_2 \ldots v_{p-1}v_pv_{p+1} \ldots v_qt_1$, which has length $q+1$ and let $v_p := v$ for some $p \in [q]$. Let $Q := x_1x_2 \ldots x_q$ be the path in F such that $g(x_1) < g(x_q)$, $x_1, x_q \in F_B$, $x_\gamma \notin F_B$ for all $\gamma \in \{2, 3, \ldots, q-1\}$ and v appears in some internal node(s) of Q. Clearly, $v \notin \beta(x_1) \cup \beta(x_q)$ as then we would have $v \in V_B$ and Reduction Rule 6 would not apply.

We know that $v_{p-1}v_{p+1} \notin E(G)$ as that would give rise to a chord in P_1 and violate the minimality of $\mathcal{P}$. This means that there does not exist $x \in V(F)$ such that $v_{p-1}, v_{p+1} \in \beta(x)$. On the other hand, since $v_{p-1}v, vv_{p+1} \in E(G)$, there exist x_i and x_j such that $v_{p-1}, v \in \beta(x_i)$ and $v, v_{p+1} \in \beta(x_j)$. If $i = j$, then we would have that v_{p-1}, v_{p+1} appear in the same bag in G, and would give rise to a chord in P_1, a contradiction. Hence we have $i \neq j$. Since $v \notin \beta(x_1) \cup \beta(x_q)$, x_i, x_j are internal vertices of Q. We consider the case when $i < j$. The case when $j < i$ is symmetric, and exactly the same proof works by considering the $t_1 - s_1$ path.

Let $P^* := s_1v_1v_2 \ldots v_{p-1}u_1 \ldots u_r$ be a minimum length path in G' that minimizes the distance between bags containing u_r and x_j in (F, β'), such that $u_1, \ldots, u_r \in U_1$ and $\{u_1, \ldots, u_r\} \cap P_z = \emptyset$ for all $z \in \{2, \ldots, k\}$. In other words, we try to extend the path $P_p := s_1v_1v_2 \ldots v_{p-1}$ in G' along Q towards x_j using only the vertices from U_1 that are not used by any other path in $\mathcal{P}$. Note that there is a slight abuse of notation and it might be the case that $u_r = v_{p-1}$ in case the path cannot be extended beyond v_{p-1}.

Let the bag that minimizes the distance between bags containing u_r and x_j (the last bag that contains u_r) in (F, β') be $x_{i'}$. Clearly, $i' < j$, otherwise we would have that v_{p+1} is adjacent to some vertex in P^*, and that would give us the desired replacement path for P_1. So we have that for P^*, the distance between bags containing u_r and x_j in (F, β') is $j - i' \geq 1$. Also, we have that $i' \geq i$ as P^* by definition contains P_p. We know that $v \in \beta(x_i) \cap \beta(x_j)$, and $i \leq i' < j$, using the connectivity property of tree-decomposition, this gives us that $v \in \beta(x_{i'})$ and $v \in \beta(x_{i'+1})$.

Now, if v is marked by the first step of marking procedure (II) as a vertex in $D^1(x_{i'}, 1)$, we would have that $v \in D^2(x_{i'+1}, 1)$. We also see that $u_r v \in E(G')$ as $u_r, v \in \beta'(x_{i'})$. This gives us that for the path $P^{**} := s_1 v_1 v_2 \dots v_{p-1} u_1 \dots u_r v$, the distance between bags containing v and x_j in (F, β') is less than $j - i'$, a contradiction to the definition of P^*. So, $v \notin D^1(x_{i'}, 1)$. This means that there is a set of $2k+1$ vertices $W_1 := D^1(x_{i'}, 1)$ in $\beta(x_{i'}) \setminus V_B$ such that $v <_1 w$ for all $w \in W_1$. By definition of $<_i$, this would imply that $W_1 \subseteq \beta(x_{i'+1})$ as $v \in \beta(x_{i'+1})$ and $v <_1 w$ for all $w \in W_1$. This gives us that $W_1 = D^1(x_{i'}, 1) \cap \beta(x_{i'+1})$ and hence $W_1 = D^2(x_{i'+1}, 1)$. This lets us conclude that $W_1 \subseteq \beta'(x_{i'+1})$.

If there exists $w \in W_1 \cap \{v_{p+1}, \dots, v_q\}$, then we obtain the desired path P_1' by using w to concatenate P_p and $P_r := v_{p+1} \dots v_q t_1$. This is possible as $w \in P_1$ and hence w cannot be used by any other path in $\mathcal{P}$. So, no vertex of W_1 is used by P_r. Now, since all the paths $P_2, P_3, \dots, P_k$ and P^* are minimal in G', they do not use more than two vertices from the bag $x_{i'+1}$ due to Lemma 2. This means that there exists $w \in \beta'(x_{i'+1})$ such that w is not used by the paths $P_2, P_3, \dots, P_k$, and P^*. Since $W_1 \subseteq \beta'(x_{i'})$, we also have that $u_r w \in E(G')$. Hence the path P^* can be extended to get a new path $P^{**} := s_1 v_1 v_2 \dots v_{p-1} u_1 \dots u_r w$, such that distance between bags containing w and x_j in (F, β') is smaller than $j - i'$. Since $w \in U_1$ and $w \notin P_z$ for all $z \in \{2, \dots, k\}$, this gives us the desired contradiction to the definition of P^*, and finishes the proof for the forward direction.

For the other direction, if $(G', T, \mathcal{U})$ is a YES instance then $(G, T, \mathcal{U})$ is a YES instance because G' is a subgraph of G. □

Now we are ready to prove the lemma that bounds the treewidth of the graph.

Lemma 12. *Let* $(G, T, \mathcal{U})$ *be an instance of* SRDP *obtained after applying reductions Rules 1–6 exhaustively. Then* $\mathbf{tw}(G) = \mathcal{O}(k^3)$.

Proof. Let (F, β) be a clique tree of G. Since G is reduced with respect to reduction Rules 1–5, we know from Lemma 7 that for each $x \in F_B$, we have $\beta(x) = \mathcal{O}(k^3)$. Since $F_3, F_1 \subseteq F_B$, we only need to bound $\beta(x)$ for $x \in F_2$ to bound the treewidth of G.

The first step of marking procedure (II) marks at most $2k + 1$ vertices as $D^1(x, i)$ for each $i \in k$ for a bag $x \in F_2$. So the total number of vertices marked in the first step for a bag $x \in F_2$ is at most $k(2k + 1)$. Similarly, for the second step, again for each $i \in [k]$, there as at most $2k + 1$ vertices marked as $D^2(x, i)$ for a bag $x \in F_2$. So the total number of vertices marked in the second step for a bag $x \in F_2$ is at most $k(2k + 1)$. In total, this gives us $D(x) \leq 2k(2k + 1)$ for all $x \in F_2$. Since G is reduced with respect to Reduction Rule 6, this means that $|\beta(x)| \leq |V_B| + 2k(2k+1)$ as otherwise Reduction Rule 6 would apply. This gives us that $\beta(x) = \mathcal{O}(k^3)$ for all $x \in V(F)$, and hence $\mathbf{tw}(G) = \mathcal{O}(k^3)$. □

Now we are ready to prove the main result (Theorem 1) of this section.

Proof of Theorem 1. Given an instance $(G, T, \mathcal{U})$, we reduce it using reductions Rules 1–6 exhaustively. We have already shown the correctness of reductions Rules 1–6, so that gives us that the output instance is a YES instance if and only if the original instance is a YES instance. It is easy to see that the reduction rules can be applied in polynomial time. Lemma 12 gives that after exhaustive application of the reduction rules, the treewidth of the resulting graph is bounded by $\mathcal{O}(k^3)$. Then we use the algorithm from Theorem 3 to solve the instance in time $\mathcal{O}^*((k^3)^{\mathcal{O}(k)})$ which is $\mathcal{O}^*(2^{\mathcal{O}(k \log k)})$ as desired. □

4 Kernelization Lower Bound for Interval Graphs

In this section, we show that SRDP does not admit a polynomial kernel on interval graph up to reasonable complexity assumptions. This is done by making use the *cross-composition* technique introduced by Bodlaender, Jansen and Kratsch [5] (see also [7,9] for the introduction to the technique). To apply the cross-composition technique, we need the following additional definitions. Since we are using an AND-cross-composition, we are giving definitions tailored for this case.

We remind that a decision problem L is a language $L \subseteq \Sigma^*$ where Σ^* is the set of strings over a finite alphabet Σ, and a parameterized problem is defined as $P \subseteq \Sigma^* \times \mathbb{N}$. An equivalence relation $\mathcal{R}$ on the set of strings Σ^* is called a *polynomial equivalence relation* if the following two conditions hold:

(i) there is an algorithm that given two strings $x, y \in \Sigma^*$ decides whether x and y belong to the same equivalence class in time polynomial in $|x| + |y|$,
(ii) for any finite set $S \subseteq \Sigma^*$, the equivalence relation $\mathcal{R}$ partitions the elements of S into a number of classes that is polynomially bounded in the size of the largest element of S.

Let $L \subseteq \Sigma^*$ be a problem and let $\mathcal{R}$ be a polynomial equivalence relation on Σ^*. Let also $P \subseteq \Sigma^* \times \mathbb{N}$ be a parameterized problem. An *AND-cross-composition of L into P* (with respect to $\mathcal{R}$) is an algorithm that, given p instances $I_1, I_2, \dots, I_p \in \Sigma^*$ of L belonging to the same equivalence class of $\mathcal{R}$, takes time polynomial in $\sum_{i=1}^{p} |x_i|$ and outputs an instance $(I', k) \in \Sigma^* \times \mathbb{N}$ such that:

(i) the parameter value k is polynomially bounded in $\max\{|I_1|, \dots, |I_p|\} + \log p$,
(ii) the instance (I', k) is a YES-instance for P if and only if I_i is a YES-instance of L for every $i \in [p]$.

It is said that L *AND-cross-composes into P* if an AND-cross-composition algorithm exists for a suitable relation $\mathcal{R}$. We use the following result of Bodlaender, Jansen and Kratsch [5].

Theorem 4 ([5]). *If an NP-hard language L AND-cross-composes into a parameterized problem P, then P does not admit a polynomial kernel unless NP $\subseteq$ coNP/poly.*

We use this theorem to show that SRDP has no polynomial kernel on interval graph assuming $\mathsf{NP} \not\subseteq \mathsf{coNP/poly}$ by demonstrating an AND-cross-composition from Disjoint Paths that was shown to be NP-complete on interval graph by Natarajan and Sprague [14].

Proof of Theorem 2. We consider instances (G, T) of Disjoint Paths such that the terminal vertices in distinct pairs in T are distinct and for every $(s_i, t_i) \in T$, $s_i \neq t_i$ and $\{s_i, t_i\} \notin E(G)$. Clearly, Disjoint Paths remains NP-complete when constrained to such instances [14]. We say that two instances (G_1, T_1) and (G_2, T_2) are equivalent if $|T_1| = |T_2|$, that is, the number of required paths is the same in both instances.

Let $(G_1, T_1), \ldots, (G_p, T_p)$ be equivalent instances of Disjoint Paths, where $G_1, \ldots, G_p$ are interval graphs. For every $i \in [p]$, let $T_i = \{(s_1^i, t_1^i), \ldots, (s_k^i, t_k^i)\}$ and denote by (Q_i, β_i) a clique path of G_i. We assume that $Q_i = x_1^i \ldots x_{q_i}^i$ for $i \in [k]$. Notice that a clique-path of an interval graph or, equivalently, its interval representation can be found in linear time using, e.g., the classical algorithm of Booth and Lueker [6].

Because $s_j^i \neq t_j^i$ and $\{s_j^i, t_j^i\} \notin E(G_i)$ for all $i \in [p]$ and $j \in [k]$, we can assume without loss of generality that if $s_j^i \in \beta_i(x_\ell)$ and $t_j^i \in \beta_i(x_r)$, then $\ell < r$. In words, for every pair of terminals $(s_j^i, t_j^i) \in T_i$, s_j^i occurs before t_j^i in the bags of the clique-path. Otherwise, we can swap s_j^i and t_j^i in the terminal pair. For every $i \in [p]$ and $j \in [k]$, let $\ell_j^i = \max\{\ell \in [q_i] \mid s_j^i \in \beta_i(\ell)\}$ and $r_j^i = \min\{r \in [q_i] \mid t_j^i \in \beta_i(r)\}$. By our assumption, $\ell_j^i < r_j^i$ for all $j \in [p]$ and $i \in [k]$.

For every $i \in [p]$, we modify the graph G_i and its clique-path (Q_i, β_i) as follows:

- for every $j \in [k]$ and every $h \in \{1, \ldots, \ell_i^j\}$, set $\beta_i(x_h^i) := \beta_i(x_h^i) \cup \{s_j^i\}$,
- for every $j \in [k]$ and every $h \in \{r_j^i, \ldots, q_i\}$, set $\beta_i(x_h^i) := \beta_i(x_h^i) \cup \{t_j^i\}$.

Denote the obtained graph by G_i' and let (Q_i, β') be its clique-path. In words, G_i' is constructed by including every terminal s_j^i in the first ℓ_j^i bags and including each terminal t_j^i in the last $q_i - r_j^i + 1$ bags (see Fig. 1). Notice that now $s_1^i, \ldots, s_k^i$ are in the first bag and $t_1^i, \ldots, t_k^i$ are in the last bag. By the construction, each G_i' is an interval graph and we have the following property that immediately follows from the fact that each bag is a clique.

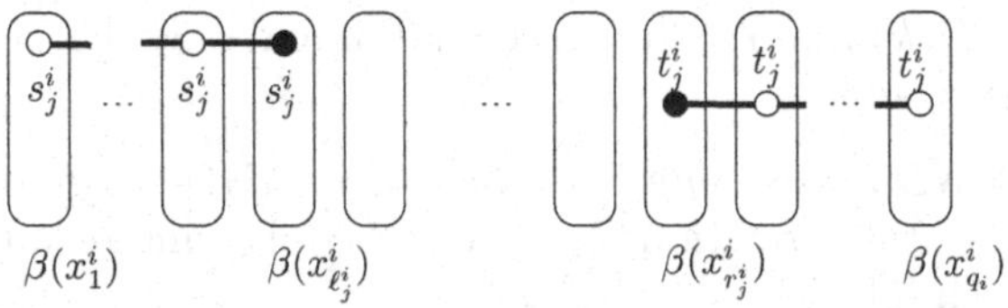

Fig. 1. Construction of G_i'.

Claim. For every $i \in [p]$, (G_i, T_i) is a YES-instance of DISJOINT PATHS if and only if (G'_i, T_i) is a YES-instance.

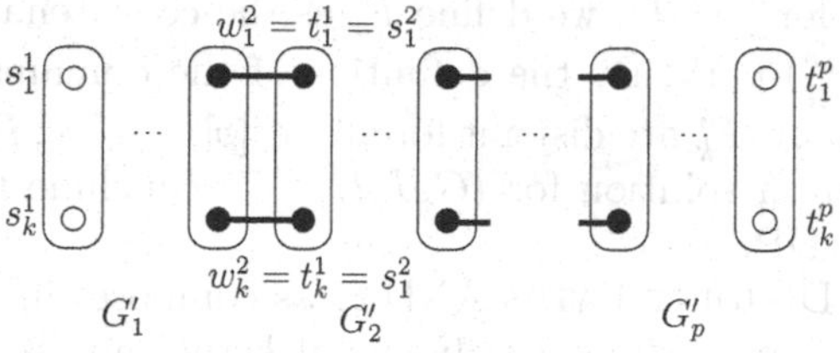

Fig. 2. Construction of G.

We construct the instance $(G, T, \mathcal{U})$ of SRDP, where $|T| = |\mathcal{U}| = k$ as follows. To construct G, we

- construct disjoint copies of $G'_1, \ldots, G'_p$,
- for each $i \in \{2, \ldots, p\}$ and for every $j \in [k]$, identify t_j^{i-1} and s_j^i, and denote the obtained vertex w_j^i.

For $i \in \{2, \ldots, p\}$, we define $W_i = \{w_1^i, \ldots, w_k^i\}$. Notice that G is an interval graph and its clique-path can be obtained by the concatenation of the clique-paths of $G'_1, \ldots, G'_p$ (see Fig. 2). We set $T = \{(s_1^1, t_1^p), \ldots, (s_k^1, t_k^p)\}$. We define $\mathcal{U} = \{U_1, \ldots, U_k\}$ as follows: for every $j \in [k]$,

$$U_j = \Big(\bigcup_{i=1}^{p} (V(G'_i) \setminus (\{s_1^i, \ldots, s_k^i\} \cup \{t_1^i, \ldots, t_k^i\}))\Big) \cup \{s_j^1, t_j^p\} \cup \{w_j^1, w_j^2, \ldots, w_j^p\}.$$

Because $G'_1, \ldots, G'_p$ can be constructed in polynomial time, the time taken for the construction of the instance $(G, T, \mathcal{U})$ is polynomial. Note that the parameter k is upper bounded by $\max\{|V(G_1), \ldots, |V(G_p)|\}$. We claim that $(G, T, \mathcal{U})$ is a YES-instance of SRDP if and only if (G_i, T_i) is a YES-instance of DISJOINT PATHS for every $i \in [p]$.

Suppose that $(G, T, \mathcal{U})$ is a YES-instance of SRDP and denote by $P_1, \ldots, P_k$ the paths forming a solution, where P_j is an (s_j^1, t_j^p)-path for every $j \in [k]$. Consider $j \in [k]$. By the construction of G' (see Fig. 2), the sets $W_2, \ldots, W_p$ are (s_j^1, t_j^p)-separators. Hence, P_j contains a unique vertex from W_i for each $i \in \{2, \ldots, p\}$. Let $w_1^j = s_j^1$ and $w_{p+1}^j = t_j^p$. Since for each $i \in \{1, \ldots, p+1\}$, only $w_j^i \in W_i$ is in the domain U_j, we have that $w_j^1, \ldots, w_j^{p+1} \in V(P_j)$. Moreover, for every $i \in \{1, \ldots, p\}$, the (w_j^i, w_j^{i+1})-subpath P_j^i of P_i is, in fact, an (s_j^i, t_j^i)-path in G'_i. Thus, for every $i \in [p]$, $P_1^i, \ldots, P_k^i$ are disjoint paths in G'_i and for every $j \in [k]$, P_j^i is an (s_j^i, t_j^i)-path. This means that (G'_i, T_i) is a YES-instance of DISJOINT PATHS for every $i \in [p]$. By Claim 4, we conclude that (G_i, T_i) is a YES-instance of DISJOINT PATHS for every $i \in [p]$.

Assume that (G_i, T_i) is a YES-instance of DISJOINT PATHS for every $i \in [p]$. Then each (G'_i, T_i) is a YES-instance as well by Claim 4. For every $i \in [p]$, denote by $P^i_1, \dots, P^i_k$ disjoint path in G'_i, where P^i_j is an (s^i_j, t^i_j)-path for $j \in [k]$. Recall that in the construction of G, t^{i-1}_j and s^i_j are identified for $i \in \{2, \dots, p\}$ and $j \in [k]$. Using this, for $j \in [k]$, we define P_j as the concatenation of $P^1_j, \dots, P^p_j$ and obtain an (s^1_j, t^p_j)-path. By the definition of the domains, $V(P_j) \subseteq U_j$ for $j \in [k]$. Because $P^i_1, \dots, P^i_k$ are disjoint for all $i \in [p]$, $P_1, \dots, P_k$ are also disjoint. Therefore, they form a solution for $(G, T, \mathcal{U})$. We conclude that $(G, T, \mathcal{U})$ is a YES-instance of SRDP.

We obtain that DISJOINT PATHS AND-cross-composes into SRDP. By Theorem 4, SRDP does not admit a polynomial kernel unless $\mathsf{NP} \subseteq \mathsf{coNP/poly}$. This concludes the proof. □

References

1. Adler, I., Kolliopoulos, S.G., Krause, P.K., Lokshtanov, D., Saurabh, S., Thilikos, D.M.: Irrelevant vertices for the planar disjoint paths problem. J. Comb. Theory Ser. B **122**, 815–843 (2017). https://doi.org/10.1016/j.jctb.2016.10.001
2. Ahn, J., Jaffke, L., Kwon, O., Lima, P.T.: Well-partitioned chordal graphs: obstruction set and disjoint paths. In: Adler, I., Müller, H. (eds.) WG 2020. LNCS, vol. 12301, pp. 148–160. Springer, Cham (2020). https://doi.org/10.1007/978-3-030-60440-0_12
3. Belmonte, R., Golovach, P.A., Heggernes, P., van 't Hof, P., Kaminski, M., Paulusma, D.: Detecting fixed patterns in chordal graphs in polynomial time. Algorithmica **69**(3), 501–521 (2014). https://doi.org/10.1007/s00453-013-9748-5
4. Blair, J.R., England, R.E., Thomason, M.G.: Cliques and their separators in triangulated graphs. University of Tennessee, USA (1988)
5. Bodlaender, H.L., Jansen, B.M.P., Kratsch, S.: Kernelization lower bounds by cross-composition. SIAM J. Discret. Math. **28**(1), 277–305 (2014)
6. Booth, K.S., Lueker, G.S.: Testing for the consecutive ones property, interval graphs, and graph planarity using PQ-tree algorithms. J. Comput. Syst. Sci. **13**(3), 335–379 (1976)
7. Cygan, M., et al.: Parameterized Algorithms. Springer, Cham (2015). https://doi.org/10.1007/978-3-319-21275-3
8. Fomin, F.V., Lokshtanov, D., Panolan, F., Saurabh, S., Zehavi, M.: Hitting topological minors is FPT. In: Makarychev, K., Makarychev, Y., Tulsiani, M., Kamath, G., Chuzhoy, J. (eds.) Proceedings of the 52nd Annual ACM SIGACT Symposium on Theory of Computing, STOC 2020, Chicago, IL, USA, 22–26 June 2020, pp. 1317–1326. ACM (2020). https://doi.org/10.1145/3357713.3384318
9. Fomin, F.V., Lokshtanov, D., Saurabh, S., Zehavi, M.: Kernelization: Theory of Parameterized Preprocessing. Cambridge University Press, Cambridge (2019). https://doi.org/10.1017/9781107415157
10. Golumbic, M.C.: Algorithmic Graph Theory and Perfect Graphs. Academic Press, New York (1980)
11. Grohe, M., Kawarabayashi, K.I., Marx, D., Wollan, P.: Finding topological subgraphs is fixed-parameter tractable. In: Proceedings of the Forty-Third Annual ACM Symposium on Theory of Computing, STOC 2011, pp. 479–488. Association for Computing Machinery, New York (2011). https://doi.org/10.1145/1993636.1993700

12. Kammer, F., Tholey, T.: The k-disjoint paths problem on chordal graphs. In: Paul, C., Habib, M. (eds.) WG 2009. LNCS, vol. 5911, pp. 190–201. Springer, Heidelberg (2010). https://doi.org/10.1007/978-3-642-11409-0_17
13. Lokshtanov, D., Misra, P., Pilipczuk, M., Saurabh, S., Zehavi, M.: An exponential time parameterized algorithm for planar disjoint paths. In: Proceedings of the 52nd Annual ACM SIGACT Symposium on Theory of Computing, STOC 2020, pp. 1307–1316. Association for Computing Machinery, New York (2020). https://doi.org/10.1145/3357713.3384250
14. Natarajan, S., Sprague, A.P.: Disjoint paths in circular arc graphs. Nordic J. Comput. **3**(3), 256–270 (1996)
15. Robertson, N., Seymour, P.: Graph minors. XIII. The disjoint paths problem. J. Comb. Theory Ser. B **63**(1), 65–110 (1995). https://doi.org/10.1006/jctb.1995.1006. https://www.sciencedirect.com/science/article/pii/S0095895685710064

Discrete Versions of the KKM Lemma and Their PPAD-Completeness

Alexander Grishutin[1] and Daniil Musatov[1,2,3](✉)

[1] Moscow Institute of Physics and Technology, Dolgoprudny, Russia
{grishutin.ai,musatov.dv}@phystech.edu

[2] Russian Presidential Academy of National Economy and Public Administration, Moscow, Russia

[3] Caucasus Mathematical Center at Adyghe State University, Maykop, Russia

Abstract. PPAD is the class of computational search problem that are equivalent to the EndOfALine problem: given a succinct representation of a directed graph consisting of chains and cycles and a source in this graph, find a sink or another source. It turns out that this class contains many problems of searching for a fixed point in various frameworks. The complete problems in **PPAD** include Sperner's lemma, discrete analogues of Brouwer and Kakutani theorems, Nash equilibrium, market equilibria, cake-cutting and many other models in mathematical economics.

In this paper we analyze the Knaster–Kuratowski–Mazurkievicz (KKM) lemma: if an n-dimensional simplex is covered by $n+1$ closed sets and every face of the simplex is covered by the union of the respective sets, then the intersection of all sets is non-empty. We elaborate a discrete analogue of a covering by closed sets, base on it several discrete analogues of the KKM lemma and prove that the corresponding search problems are **PPAD**-complete.

Keywords: Fixed points · Discrete topology · Sperner's lemma · KKM lemma · PPAD-completeness

1 Introduction

Many models in mathematical economics define some sort of an equilibrium and prove that such equilibrium always exists. There is an extended discussion whether an equilibrium is a good prediction of what actually happens. In classical paradigm, the system should achieve an equilibrium, but an alternative point of view says that external conditions change faster than the system ends up in an equilibrium, so actually the system is always out of the equilibrium. In any case, to apply such kind of a model, one needs to compute an equilibrium. Thus it becomes important to design algorithms that find an equilibrium and to estimate the computational complexity of the problem. Complexity is itself an argument about applicability of the model. According to Kamal Jain's quote [25]: "If your laptop cannot find it, neither can the market". This is why many particular economic models are analyzed from a complexity-theoretic point of view.

A. S. Kulikov and S. Raskhodnikova (Eds.): CSR 2022, LNCS 13296, pp. 170–189, 2022.
https://doi.org/10.1007/978-3-031-09574-0_11

Existence of an equilibrium in many models stands on a small number of basic mathematical facts about fixed points, especially Brouwer and Kakutani theorems. This is why the complexity of the respective computational problems was analyzed already in the pioneering work [28]. In some cases, another fixed-point theorem is employed: the KKM lemma. As far as we know, it was never analyzed from a computational point of view, probably because one straightforward way of discretizing it yields a proposition that is clearly equivalent to Sperner's lemma. In this paper we introduce and analyze other discrete versions that better represent the spirit of the original KKM lemma.

1.1 Overview and Discussion of the Main Results

Originally, Knaster, Kuratowski and Mazurkievicz proved the following lemma [20]:

Lemma 1. *Suppose that a simplex*

$$\Delta_d = \left\{(x_0, x_1, \ldots, x_d) \mid x_i \geq 0, \sum_{j=0}^{d} x_j = 1\right\}$$

is covered by the union of closed sets $S_0, S_1, \ldots, S_d$. Moreover, a face of the simplex with $x_i = 0$ is covered by the union of all sets without S_i. (If several coordinates are zero on a low-dimensional face, then all the respective sets need not be used to cover this face.) Then there exists a point that belongs to all S_i.

But a simplex is poorly suitable for discretization, because in higher dimensions it does not have a regular tiling by equal figures. On the other hand, a cube can be split into equal cubelets. This is why we restate the lemma on a cube:

Lemma 2. *Suppose that a cube $[0,1]^d = \{(x_1, \ldots, x_d) \mid 0 \leq x_i \leq 1\}$ is covered by the union of closed sets $S_0, S_1, \ldots, S_d$. Moreover, a face of the cube with $x_i = 0$ is covered by the union of all sets without S_i and all faces with $x_j = 1$ are covered by all sets without S_0. (If several conditions hold simultaneously on a low-dimensional face, then all the respective sets may be excluded from the coverage of this face.) Then there exists a point that belongs to all S_i.*

A sinple idea of discretization would be to split the cube into cubelets (or, probably, some other polyhedral cells) and add a condition that all sets S_i must include any cell as a whole. We can say that every cell is colored in one or more colors and we are looking for a cell that is colored in all colors. Later we use "cover sets" and "colors" interchangeably. The question is what to take as an analogue of the closedness condition. We consider the following variants:

1. No discrete analogue of closedness: just consider closed cells. In this case it is true that there must exist a point (not a cell) colored in all colors, but this claim is just equivalent to Sperner's lemma. This discretization does not fully capture the spirit of the closedness condition. The latter implies that a border point of one set must also belong to another set. In the discrete version we color not points, but cells, so we would like to have a similar condition that a border cell of one set must also belong to another set.

2. Add the above mentioned condition: say that a cell is on the border of a set if it belongs to the set and one of its neighbors does not. Require any border cell to belong to at least one other set. Unfortunately, it is insufficient for having a cell that belongs to all sets. In two dimensions it can be proved that there is either a multicolored cell, or three neighboring two-colored cells with three different color pairs. In higher dimensions no analogue is true.
   This condition has a drawback: in the continuous setting, if we consider intersections of different sets with the border of one particular set, then a border point of one intersection must still lie in some other intersection. But our discrete condition does not imply a similar property.
3. Finally, add explicitly the property mentioned above. Require that it is impossible that one cell is colored in i, but not j, and an adjacent one is colored in j, but not i. It turns out that this condition is sufficient for obtaining a multicolored cell. For the quadratic tiling in 2D it is sufficient to pose this condition only on cells neighboring by an edge, but in higher dimensions or for general tilings the condition must be required for neighbors by at least one vertex. So, our first main result is the following discrete KKM theorem.

Theorem 1 (For the full statement see Theorem 6**).** *Suppose that a d-dimensional cube is split into cells that are colored in $d+1$ colors satisfying the usual KKM border conditions. Suppose that the cells sharibg at least one point are not colored in such a way that the first one has color i, but not j, and the second one has color j, but not i. Then there exists at least one cell colored in all colors.*

Since a multicolored cell does always exist, one can ask how to find it. More precisely, one need to find either a multicolored cell or a violation of the coloring assumptions. If a coloring is described explicitly by the colors of all cells, then a multicolored cell or a violated condition may be found efficiently by exhaustive search. A more interesting problem arises when a coloring of an exponential number of cells is succinctly described by a polynomial number of bits and the colors of any particular cell may be found in polynomial time. In this case exhaustive search is intractable, so the question is whether there exists a polynomial algorithm that finds either a multicolored cell or a violated condition. Our second result estimates the complexity of this problem.

As usual for total search problems, **NP**-hardness does not capture the complexity of this problem. Moreover, **NP**-hardness of such problem would imply **NP** = **coNP** [21]. On the other hand, the class of all total search problems, **TFNP**, does not have known complete problems because of its "semantic" nature. A usual approach is to specify "syntactic" subclasses of **TFNP** and analyze completeness in these subclasses. One of the most important classes that contains many problems about fixed points and economic equilibria is **PPAD**. We classify discrete KKM into this class and show its completeness.

Theorem 2 (For the full statement see Theorem 10**).** *Suppose that an d-dimensional cube is regularly split into 2nd equal cubelets. Suppose that a coloring of these cubelets is described by a polynomial-size circuit C_n. Consider a problem* *of finding either a multicolored cell or a cubelet where the condition of Theorem 1 is violated. Then this problem lies in* **PPAD** *and is* **PPAD***-complete for* $d \geq 2$.

1.2 Related Work

Fixed-point analysis is a classical area lying between calculus, topology, combinatorics, game theory and theoretical economics. The most celebrated results include Sperner's lemma about multicolored simplices [34], Brouwer theorem about fixed points of continuous mappings on a convex compact [5], Kakutani theorem about fixed points of point-set mappings [18], Nash theorem about equilibria in non-cooperative games [23,24], Arrow–Debreu theorem about competitive equilibrium [1], Scarf theorem about the core [30,32], Simmons–Su theorems about envy-free cake-cutting [35] and consensus halving [33], among many others. A classical exposition of the subject is presented by Border in [4].

Complexity analysis of fixed points was initiated in the seminal work by Papadimitriou [28], where the class **PPAD** was introduced among other search classes. It was proved there that computational problems SPERNER (in 3D), BROUWER, KAKUTANI and some others are **PPAD**-complete. Later Daskalakis et al. [11] and Chen and Deng [8] obtained the celebrated result about **PPAD**-completeness of finding a Nash equilibrium, even for 2 players. The latter authors also proved [9] that SPERNER is complete even in 2D. One difference between 2-player and 3-player Nash is that for 2 players an equlibrium can be found exactly and for 3 players only approximately: there exists an example [6] of a 3-player game with rational outcomes but only irrational equilibria. This is why approximation factor is very important. It was analyzed in [10,12,29]. Many economics models were treated from complexity point of view, inluding Fisher and Arrow-Debreu market equlibria [7,14,36], fractional core allocations [19], approximate envy-free cake-cutting [26], equilibria in public good [27] and congestion games [2], clearing payments in financial networks [31] and stable jurisdiction partitions [22], to name a few. A good survey may be found in [15].

1.3 Roadmap

The remaining part of the paper is organized as follows. In Sect. 2 we give formal definitions of computational search problems and reductions among them, present the class **PPAD** and several important problems inside it and discuss the original KKM lemma. In Sect. 3 we present our discrete variants of the KKM lemma and prove them. In Sect. 4 we prove that the respective computational problems belong to **PPAD** and are complete in this class. Section 5 presents a conclusion and some open questions.

2 Preliminaries

2.1 Search Problems and Reductions

In this subsection we briefly describe the main notions in the theory of computational search problems.

Definition 1. *Suppose that* $V : \{0,1\}^* \times \{0,1\}^* \to \{0,1\}$ *is a computable predicate. Then the corresponding search problem is the following: given* x*, either find* y *such that* $V(x,y) = 1$ *or indicate that there is no such* y*.*

If V is computable in polynomial time of $|x|$, then we may assume that $|y|$ is also polynomial: a standard Turing machine would not be able to read more bits. This motivates the following definition:

Definition 2. FNP *is the class of all search problems where* V *is computable in polynomial time. In other words,* V *maps* $\{0,1\}^n \times \{0,1\}^{p(n)}$ *to* $\{0,1\}$ *and is computable in time* $q(n)$ *for some polynomials* $p(n)$ *and* $q(n)$*. The problem is to find* y *such that* $V(x,y) = 1$ *or indicate that there is no such* y*, on input* x*.*

A very important subclass is the class of total problems, where $\forall x \exists y\, V(x,y)$. The existence of y may be obtained by different kinds of reasoning, like the pigeonhole principle, the parity argument, the gradient descent method, the existence of a prime divisor etc.

Definition 3. TFNP *is the subclass of total search problems in* **FNP**. *That is, for any* x *it is guaranteed that there exists* y *such that* $V(x,y) = 1$ *and the task is to find such* y*.*

Reduction of one computational problem to another is a very important concept in complexity theory. In the context of search problems the no-solution case must be handled. We employ the following definition:

Definition 4. *A search problem* V *is polynomially reducible to* W *if there are polynomially computable functions* $f\colon \{0,1\}^* \to \{0,1\}^*$ *and* $g\colon \{0,1\}^* \times \{0,1\}^* \to \{0,1\}^* \cup \{\bot\}$ *such that the following is true:*

1. *If* $\exists y\, V(x,y) = 1$*, then* $\exists z\, W(f(x),z) = 1$*;*
2. *If* $W(f(x),z) = 1$ *and* $g(x,z) \neq \bot$*, then* $V(x, g(x,z)) = 1$*;*
3. *If* $W(f(x),z) = 1$ *and* $g(x,z) = \bot$*, then* $\forall y\, V(x,y) = 0$*.*

Thus f reduces an instance of V to an instance of W and g restores a solution for V from a solution for W. Note that the definition captures the case when W always has a solution and V does not: in this case $g(x,z)$ returns $\bot$.

It is a routine to check that this reduction is transitive and that a problem reducible to a polynomially solvable one is also polynomially solvable. As usual, the notion of reducibility yields the notion of completeness: a problem is complete in some class if it belongs to this class and any other problems from the class is reducible to this problem. **FNP**-complete problems are closely connected to **NP**-complete ones, but Megiddo and Papadmitriou have shown [21] that problems from **TFNP** cannot be **FNP**-complete, unless **NP** = **coNP**. On the other hand, there are no known **TFNP**-complete problems: standard generic constructions do not work due to the "semantic" nature of **TFNP**. This is why "syntactic" subclasses of **TFNP** are considered.

2.2 The Class PPAD and Its Complete Problems

Subclasses of **TFNP** are defined by the main idea that implies existence of a solution. **PPAD** means "Polynomial parity argument, directed version" and the idea behind it is very basic: if there is an unbalanced vertex in a directed graph, that is, a vertex with different indegree and outdegree, then there must exist another unbalanced vertex. Informally, **PPAD** consists of all total search problems, where a solution exists due to this principle. Formally, one basic problem is chosen and the class is defined as the set of all problems that are reducible to it. Usually the main principle is applied to a graph where all indegrees and outdegrees are bounded by 1.

Definition 5. *An instance of the problem* EndOfALine *is described by two polynomial-size circuits N and P with n inputs and n outputs. This pair defines a directed graph with 2^n vertices: an edge (x, y) for $x \neq y$ belongs to the graph if simultaneously $y = N(x)$ and $x = P(y)$. A* source *is a vertex s such that $N(s) \neq s$, $P(N(s)) = s$ and $N(P(s)) \neq s$. A* sink *is a vertex t such that $P(t) \neq t$, $N(P(t)) = t$ and $P(N(t)) \neq t$. In the search problem, the circuits N and P are given, as well as a source s. The task is to find either a sink t, or another source s'.*

In the graph defined by N and P any vertex has both indegree and outdegree at most one. Thus the graph must consist of chains, cycles and isolated vertices. Since a source is given, there must exist a sink, so the problem always has a solution.

A similar problem Imbalance may be defined if N and P return not one vertex but a polynomial list of vertices. In this case an edge (x, y) belongs to the graph if $y \in N(x)$ and $x \in P(y)$. Thus N and P define a graph with exponential number of vertices but only polynomial degree. In the search problem, the circuits N and P are given, as well as an unbalanced vertex v. The task is to find another unbalanced vertex. It is clear that EndOfALine is a particular case of Imbalance. Papadimitriou [28] and Beame et al. [3] claimed that there exists a reduction in the opposite way. Unfortunately, there construction was incorrect and a correct one was constructed only recently by Goldberg and Hollender [16,17].

The class **PPAD** is defined in the following way:

Definition 6. *A search problem belongs to* **PPAD** *if it is polynomially reducible to* EndOfALine. *It is* **PPAD***-complete if, moreover, any other problem in* **PPAD** *is polynomially reducible to it.*

It is easy to see that **PPAD**-completeness may be defined solely through EndOfALine: a problem W is **PPAD**-complete if W and EndOfALine are polynomially reducible to each other. Thus both EndOfALine and Imbalance are **PPAD**-complete. Some other **PPAD**-complete problems are mentioned in Sect. 1.2. The most important for us would be the Sperner's lemma in 2D. Unlike the classical Sperner's lemma where the vertices of a triangulation are colored, we would like to take the dual approach and color the cells.

Definition 7. *Search problem* 2D-Sperner *is the following one. A square* $[0, 2^n] \times [0, 2^n]$ *is split into cells* $[x, x+1] \times [y, y+1]$ *for integer* x *and* y*. Denote the set of cells by* Q*. A coloring* $\mathrm{col}\colon Q \to \{0, 1, 2\}$ *is specified by a* $\mathrm{poly}(n)$*-size circuit. It is guaranteed that the bottom row is colored in* 0 *and* 1*, the left column is colored in* 0 *and* 2 *and the top and right sides are colored in* 1 *and* 2*. The task is to find an integer point such that among the four adjacent cells all colors are present.*

Existence of such node follows from the standard Sperner's lemma. Chen and Deng proved [9] that this problem is **PPAD**-complete. Thus **PPAD**-completeness of W follows from a mutual reduction between W and 2D-Sperner.

2.3 Sperner's and KKM Lemmas

In this section we briefly discuss why Sperner's and KKM lemmas follow from each other. We employ "cubic" versions of each lemma. For the KKM lemma, it is precisely Lemma 2. For Sperner's lemma, consider the following one:

Lemma 3. *Suppose that a cube* $[0, 1]^d$ *is split into* N^d *equal cubelets of the form* $\left[\frac{x_1}{N}, \frac{x_1+1}{N}\right] \times \cdots \times \left[\frac{x_d}{N}, \frac{x_d+1}{N}\right]$ *for integer* $x_1, \ldots, x_d$*. Denote by* Q *the set of cubelets and index the cubelets by* $\mathbf{x} = (x_1, \ldots, x_d)$*. Suppose that a coloring function* $\mathrm{col}\colon Q \to \{0, 1, \ldots, d\}$ *is specified in such way that:*

1. *The cubelets adjacent to a "zero" face of the cube are not colored in the index of this face. Formally, if* $x_i = 0$*, then* $\mathrm{col}(\mathbf{x}) \neq i$*. If several coordinates are zero, then all respective colors are excluded.*
2. *The cubelets adjacent to a "one" face of the cube are not colored in* 0*. Formally, if* $x_i = N - 1$*, then* $\mathrm{col}(\mathbf{x}) \neq 0$*. This condition is combined with the previous one, if applicable.*

Then there exists a node of the lattice $\left(\frac{x_1}{N}, \ldots, \frac{x_d}{N}\right)$ *such that among* 2^d *cubelets adjacent to this node all values of* col *are present.*

Here we do not present a full proof of either lemma, but we need to show the connection between them.

Claim. Lemmas 2 and 3 are equivalent.

Proof. Firstly, show how the KKM lemma implies Sperner's lemma. Take the closures of all cubelets of a particulat color, unite them and treat the result as a respective set in the assumption of the KKM lemma. It can be routinely checked that the border conditions are satisfied. Then there must exist a point covered by all sets. Since any cubelet have only one color, this point must be on the border of a cell. Even if it is not in the corner, it must be on a face and every corner of this face will suit.

Secondly, show how Sperner's lemma implies the KKM lemma. Consider a KKM coloring of a cube and its splitting into N^d cubelets. Color every cubelet in some color of some point inside it. For border cubelets, choose a color satisfying the border conditions of Sperner's lemma. The border conditions of the KKM lemma guarantee that it is possible. Thus, by Sperner's lemma, there must be a node adjacent to cells of all colors. This means that in a $O\left(\frac{1}{\sqrt{N}}\right)$-vicinity of this node there exist points covered by all sets. Let N go to the infinity and consider a limit point of the constructed nodes. There are elements of all sets arbitrarily close to this point. Because all sets are closed, the limit point itself belongs to all of them. This is exactly the conclusion of the KKM lemma, so we are done.

3 Discrete Analogues of the KKM Lemma

Here we present three ways to discretize the KKM lemma and argue that the last one is the most natural. For simplicity, we will talk about regular cubic tilings, but in the last subsection we will expand the result to arbitrary ones.

3.1 General Framework

We consider a d-dimensional cube $[0, 2^n]^d$ that is split into 2nd regular unit cubelets of the form $[x_1, x_1 + 1] \times \cdots \times [x_d, x_d + 1]$ for integer $x_1, \ldots, x_d$. We characterize a cubelet by $\mathbf{x} = (x_1, \ldots, x_d)$. Denote the set of cubelets by $Q = \{0, \ldots, 2^n - 1\}^d$. In all variants we consider a multivalued function $\mathrm{col}\colon Q \rightrightarrows \{0, 1, \ldots, d\}$ that satisfies the conditions specified below.

Definition 8. *A multivalued function* $\mathrm{col}\colon Q \rightrightarrows \{0, 1, \ldots, d\}$ *is called* normal *if the following conditions hold:*

1. *Every cell is colored in at least one color. Formally,* $\mathrm{col}(\mathbf{x})$ *is non-empty.*
2. *If* $\mathbf{x}$ *is adjacent to a face of the cube where some coordinate is minimal, then* $\mathbf{x}$ *is not colored in this coordinate. Formally, if* $x_i = 0$*, then* $\mathrm{col}(\mathbf{x}) \not\ni i$.
3. *If* $\mathbf{x}$ *is adjacent to a face of the cube where some coordinate is maximal, then* $\mathbf{x}$ *is not colored in* 0. *Formally, if* $x_i = 2^n - 1$*, then* $\mathrm{col}(\mathbf{x}) \not\ni 0$.

These conditions resemble coloring conditions of the original KKM lemma. The main question is how to replace the condition of closedness of all sets.

3.2 The First Variant: Closed Cells

The first idea is just to expand the coloring of cells to the coloring of points and assume all cells to be closed. In this case there icould be no multicolored cell, but there must exist a node with adjacent cells of all colors.

Theorem 3. *Suppose that a normal coloring is defined on a cube* $[0, 2^n]^d$*. Then there exists a point with integer coordinates such that among the colors of the adjacent cells all possible colors occur.*

Proof. This is a simple corollary of Sperner's lemma as stated in Lemma 3. Indeed, for each cell take a single value such that the border conditions are satisfied. Sperner's lemma implies that there exists a node with adjacent cells of all colors. For the initial coloring it will be true all the more.

This theorem is almost equivalent to Sperner's lemma and thus is of low interest. We would like to have assumptions that would yield a multicolored cell, not just a multicolored point. To this end, we should more closely analyze what does the closedness condition mean.

3.3 The Second Variant: Several Colors on the Border

Recall the continuous variant of the KKM lemma: a cube K is covered by closed sets. Consider a point x on the border of some set S_i. Then there are points from $K \setminus S_i$ arbitrarily close to x. They must be covered by other sets. Since the number of sets is finite, there exists some S_j, $j \neq i$, that contains points arbitrarily close to x. Since S_j is closed, x must belong to S_j. Thus we get the following property: if x lies on the border of S_i, then it must also belong to some other S_j. Try to repeat this property in the discrete framework straightforwardly: if a cell is on the border of some color, then it must be colored in some other color. Formally, say that $\mathrm{adj}(x, y)$ is true if cells x and y have at least one point in common. Then we impose the following condition:

$$\forall i \forall x \forall y \; ((\mathrm{adj}(x, y) \wedge \mathrm{col}(x) \ni i \wedge \mathrm{col}(y) \not\ni i) \rightarrow \exists j \neq i \; \mathrm{col}(x) \ni j) \qquad (*)$$

Unfortunately, this does not guarantee that there exists a multicolored cell. Here is an example (the numbers indicate the colors, a 2-colored cell is divided diagonally):

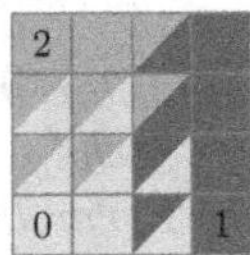

Note that in this example the central node is adjacent to cells of all possible color pairs. It turns out that in 2 dimensions it holds in general:

Theorem 4. *Suppose that a normal coloring* col *with condition* (*) *is defined on a square* $[0, 2^n]^2$. *Then at least one of the two facts hold:*

- *There exists a multicolored cell, that is,* $\mathrm{col}(x) = \{0, 1, 2\}$ *for some* x,
- *There exist three cells* x, y *and* z *that have a corner point in common such that* $\mathrm{col}(x) = \{0, 1\}$, $\mathrm{col}(y) = \{1, 2\}$ *and* $\mathrm{col}(z) = \{1, 2\}$.

Proof. Here we present a beautiful and direct but not very short proof. In Theorem 8 we present a shorter proof that uses Sperner's lemma.

Firstly we present an intuitive exposition and then formally clarify it. The conditions on col imply that the bottom left cell is colored in 0, the bottom right cell is colored in 1 and the top left one is colored in 2. Somewhere in the bottom row there must be a border cell of color 0. Due to (*), it must be colored in some other color, and due to the normality condition it must be color 1. Similarly, some cell in the left column is colored in 0 and 2. There must be a way between these two cells passing through border cells of color 0 (this assertion is clarified below in Lemma 4). All these cells must have at least one other color, again due to (*), see Fig. 1(a). Since the additional color is different on the two ends of the way, there must be two adjacent cells colored differently: x with colors $\{0, 1\}$ and y with colors $\{0, 2\}$. Adjacent to them, there must be a cell z not colored in 0 (this assertion is also clarified below). W.l.o.g., it is colored in 1. Then there are two cases. If z is a border cell of color 1, then there must be another color. Since z does not have color 0, the other color must be 2 and we have three adjacent cells with all color pairs, as claimed. If z is not a border cell of color 1, then all its adjacent cells must be colored in 1. Since y is adjacent to z, y must have all colors, as claimed. The two cases are illustrated on Fig. 1.

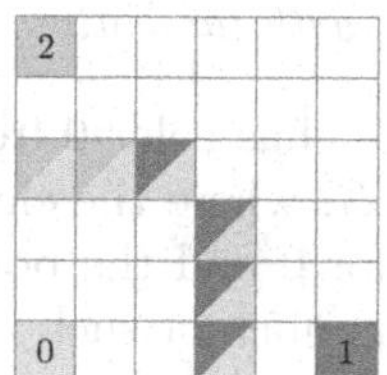

(a) A way of 2-colored cells

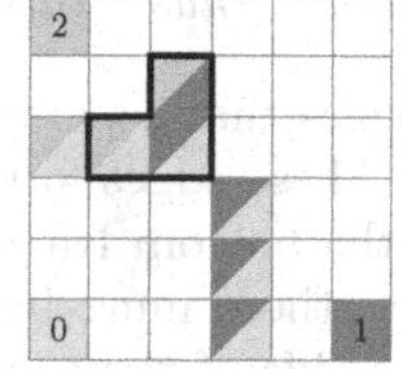

(b) 3 adjacent color pairs

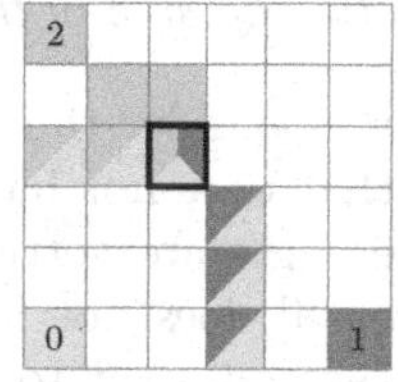

(c) A multicolored cell

Fig. 1. Two cases of Theorem 4.

Now we clarify our topological assertions. In fact, we cannot take an arbitrary way made of border cells and arbitrary neighboring cells with different color pairs on it. On Fig. 2(a), there is a unique pair of such cells on the way, but the cells adjacent to them also lie on the border. The reason is that the way takes an accidental "shortcut". The argument works if the way on Fig. 2(b) is considered instead.

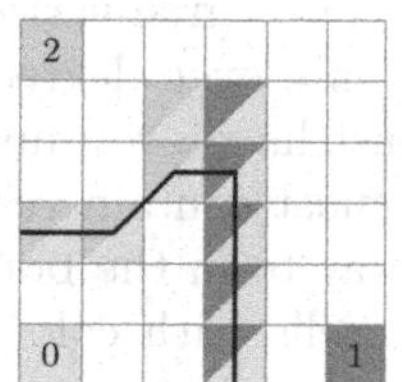

(a) An accidental shortcut

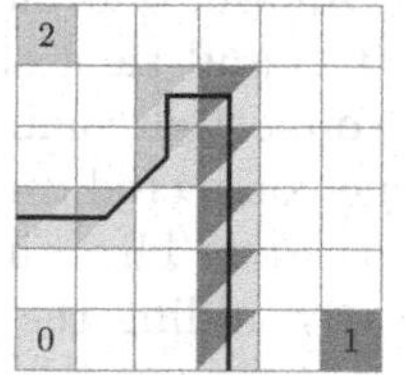

(b) The correct way

Fig. 2. Choosing the right way.

Now we show how to construct a suitable way in general. We start by defining what we mean by "way" and by "suitable".

Definition 9. *Call a* border way *a sequence of pairs* (x, e) *where* x *is a cell and* e *is its edge such that the following holds:*

- $\text{col}(x) \ni 0$ *and* $\text{col}(w) \not\ni 0$ *for* w *that borders* x *by* e.
- *If* (x_2, e_2) *follows* (x_1, e_1) *in the sequence, then* e_1 *and* e_2 *have one common point. Hence* x_1 *and* x_2 *either have a common corner, or have a common edge, or are equal to each other.*

Note that a border way is completely defined by the sequence of edges: since every edge must separate two cells with different colors, the sequence of cells may be completely restored. Adding the cells to the definition simplifies the subsequent analysis.

Now let us prove that a suitable way exists:

Lemma 4. *Suppose that* col *is a normal coloring satisfying* (*). *Then there exists a border way* $((x_1, e_1), \ldots, (x_m, e_m))$ *such that* e_1 *has a common point with the left side of the square and* e_m *has a common point with the bottom one.*

Proof. Consider the set of all edges that separate a cell that has color 0 from a cell that does not have color 0. These edges form a graph G, where the ends of these edges are vertices. Since the bottom left cell has color 0 and the bottom right cell does not have color 0, there must be an odd number of such edges that are adjacent to the bottom side of the square. All these edges correspond to vertices of degree 1 in graph G. Similarly, there must be an odd number of edges that are adjacent to the left side of the square.

Note that all nodes strictly inside the square have an even degree. Indeed, if an edge is incident to such node, then among four adjacent cells one has color 0 and another does not have. For the remaining 2 cells there are 4 options and for each of them the degree of the central node is either 2 or 4:

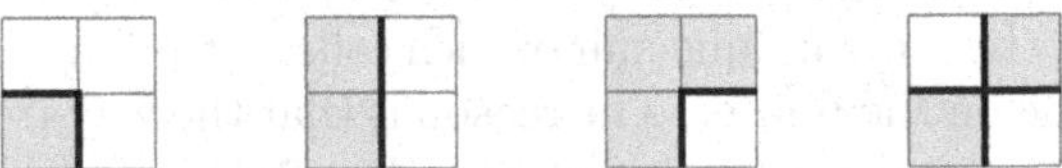

Thus we have a graph with an odd number of odd-degree vertices on the bottom side of the square, odd number of odd-degree vertices on the left side, no vertices on the top and right sides and only even-degree vertices inside the square. Since any connected component must have even number of odd-degree vertices, at least one connected component must contain vertices from both the bottom and the left sides. Thus there is a way from the bottom side to the left side in this graph. By adding the adjacent cells with color 0, we get a border way, as claimed.

Let us proceed with the proof of the theorem. Consider the border way $((x_1, e_1), \ldots, (x_m, e_m))$ that goes from the left to the bottom. Since all x_i are border cells of color 0, they must have at least one other color. Since the coloring is normal and x_1 lies on the left, its other color must be 2. Similarly, the other color of x_m is 1. Thus there exists i such that x_i is colored in 0 and 2 and x_{i+1} is colored in 0 and 1. Consider w_i that borders x_i through e_i. Since e_i has a common point with e_{i+1}, w_i must also have a common point with e_{i+1} and hence with x_{i+1}. Thus w_i may be taken as z from the initial exposition of the proof. Indeed, w_i does not have color 0, so w.l.o.g. it has color 2. If it is its only color, then all its neighbors must also have color 2, including x_{i+1}. Thus x_{i+1} has all three colors. Otherwise w_i has both colors 1 and 2 and thus x_i, x_{i+1} and w_i are mutually adjacent and have all three possible color pairs.

Theorem 4 has two drawbacks. Firstly, we do not obtain a multicolored cell, instead we have two variants. Secondly, it is hardly generalizable to higher dimensions. Natural generalizations like existence of adjacent cells that have all color sets of size d or all possible color pairs are wrong. The reason is that condition (*) does not fully capture the effect of closed sets in the original lemma. In particular, the condition is no longer valid if we narrow it to the cells that have a particular color, while in the continuous case the property that border points of a set belong to some other set remains valid if we take intersections with one particular set. This is why we propose another variant.

3.4 The Third Variant: No Distinct Colors on Adjacent Cells

In this subsection we present a framework that guarantees existence of a multicolored cell in any dimension. Now we want to discretize the following property of closed sets: if x lies on the border of closed set S, then either x also lies in closed set T, or the distance between x and T is strictly positive. In other words, if x lies in S but not in T, then all points sufficiently close to x do not lie in T either. Of course, this property cannot be repeated literally: somewhere cells in T and not in T must be neighbors. We impose the following condition (the framework is as before):

$$\forall x \forall y (\mathrm{adj}(x,y) \to \neg \exists i \exists j (i \in \mathrm{col}(x) \setminus \mathrm{col}(y) \wedge j \in \mathrm{col}(y) \setminus \mathrm{col}(x))). \qquad (**)$$

It is a simple exercise to check that it is equivalent to the following:

$$\forall x \forall y (\mathrm{adj}(x,y) \to (\mathrm{col}(x) \subset \mathrm{col}(y) \vee \mathrm{col}(y) \subset \mathrm{col}(x))). \qquad (1)$$

Later we employ (**) and (1) interchangeably.

We proceed with another discrete version of the KKM lemma in 2D.

Theorem 5. *Let* col *be a normal coloring of a square that satisfies condition* (**) *where adjacency is understood as having a common edge. Then there exists a cell colored in all three colors.*

Proof. Firstly show that (**) implies (*). Indeed, suppose that cell x is a border cell of color i. It must have a neighbor y that is not colored in i. It must be colored in some j. If i is the only color of x, then (**) is violated. Thus x must be colored in some other color, namely, j.

Now we can apply Theorem 4. If there is a multicolored cell, then we are done. Otherwise there are three adjacent cells with all color pairs. In any case two of them would be adjacent by an edge and thus violate (**). Thus only the multicolored case is possible, as claimed.

In the high-dimensional case we have to weaken the adjacency condition and thus to strengthen the assumption.

Theorem 6. *Let* col *be a normal coloring of a hypercube that satisfies condition* (**) *where adjacency is understood as having at least one common point. Then there exists a cell colored in all colors.*

Proof. Here we adopt a much simpler approach that works due to strengthening of the assumption. Just take the cells that are colored in particular colors and apply the original KKM lemma to the respective sets. The normality of col implies that the border conditions of the KKM lemma are satisfied. Then there exists a point p that is colored in all colors. This point may be adjacent to several cells. Note that all these cells are also adjacent to each other, since they have p in common. If one of these cells is also colored in all colors, then we are done. Otherwise consider the cell x that is colored in the maximum number of colors. Suppose that x is not colored in i. Then some other cell y must be colored in i. If y is not colored in some $j \in \text{col}(x)$, then (**) is violated. Otherwise $\text{col}(y)$ contains all $\text{col}(x)$ and also i, then x does not have the maximum number of colors. This contradiction shows that a multicolored cell always exists, as claimed.

3.5 Non-regular Tilings

Note that the proof of Theorem 6 did not use the fact that all cells are equal. Neither it used that the cells are cubelets. The same methods may yield a theorem for a general tiling:

Theorem 7. *Suppose that a hypercube* $[0,1]^d$ *is split into polytopes such that no polytope touches opposite faces of the hypercube. Denote the set of polytopes by* Q*. Suppose that there is a multivalued function* $\text{col}\colon Q \to \{0, 1, \ldots, d\}$ *such that the following conditions hold:*

- *For any cell* x *the set* $\text{col}(x)$ *is non-empty;*
- *If cell* x *is adjacent to a face of the hypercube with* $x_i = 0$*, then* $\text{col}(x) \not\ni i$*;*
- *If cell* x *is adjacent to a face of the hypercube with* $x_i = 1$*, then* $\text{col}(x) \not\ni 0$*;*
- *The condition* (**) *holds where adjacency of polytopes means that they have at least one point in common.*

Then there exists a cell colored in all colors.

The proof of Theorem 6 works almost without any change, so we do not repeat it. Note that for non-quadratic tilings Theorem 5 is no longer valid. Figure 3 shows s counterexample for a triangular grid. It can be easily modified for a square.

4 Computational Problems and Their PPAD-Completeness

In this section we analyze the computational complexity of the search problems that correspond to different versions of the KKM lemma. Meanwhile, we present alternative proofs that employ Sperner's lemma.

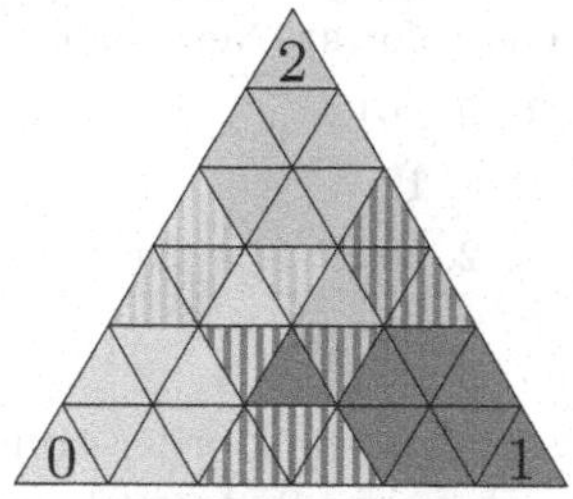

Fig. 3. A counterexample to Theorem 5 for a non-quadratic tiling.

4.1 Two Dimensions

We start from the 2-dimensional case that is more vivid and has stronger theorems. We consider the following computational problems:

Definition 10. *A computational search problem* 2D-KKM *is the following: the algorithm gets a polynomial-size circuit C that defines a multi-valued function* col *on a $2^n \times 2^n$ table. Suppose that C is interpreted in such way that normality (as in Definition 8) of* col *is guaranteed. Consider two variants of the problem:*

- 2D-KKM-A*: find a multicolored cell, or three adjacent cells with all possible color pairs, or a cell where condition (*) is violated.*
- 2D-KKM-B*: find a multicolored cell, or two cells adjacent by edge where condition (**) is violated.*

Firstly we show that both these problems lie in **PPAD** and then demonstrate their completeness. In fact we describe a cycle of 3 reductions between these two problems and 2D-Sperner, as in Definition 7.

Theorem 8. *Both* 2D-KKM-A *and* 2D-KKM-B *lie in* **PPAD**.

Proof. We show the reductions 2D-KKM-B $\leq$ 2D-KKM-A $\leq$ 2D-Sperner.

The first reduction uses the proof idea of Theorem 5. Indeed, we take the same coloring and while solving 2D-KKM-A find either a multicolored cell, or three adjacent cells with all color pairs, or a cell where (*) is violated. In the first case, the found solution is also suitable for 2D-KKM-B. In the latter two cases, condition (**) is violated for the found cells, so 2D-KKM-B is solved, too.

Now describe a reduction from 2D-KKM-A to 2D-Sperner, which gives an alternative proof of Theorem 4. In a coloring given as the input of 2D-KKM-A, every cell may have one of the seven possible colorings: 0, 1, 2, 01, 12, 20 and 012. We transform it to a single-valued coloring in 3 colors by the following rule:

Old color(s)	New color
0, 01, 012	01
1, 12	12
2, 20	20

Note that the new coloring satisfies the border condition of Sperner's lemma. Indeed, the bottom row was colored in 0, 1 or 01, so the new color must be 01 or 12, and similarly for the other sides. Thus, by Sperner's lemma, in the new coloring there must exist a node with adjacent cells colored in 01, 12 and 20.

If color 01 comes from 012 in the initial coloring, then a multicolored cell is found (see Fig. 4(a)). Suppose that 01 comes from 0. Then, by the contraposition to (*), it cannot be a border cell of color 0 (otherwise we found a place where (*) is violated). Then the cell now colored in 12 must have been colored also in 0. But this contradicts our construction. Hence 01 must come from also 01. Similarly 12 and 20 cannot come from 1 and 2, respectively, so they must come from 12 and 20. Thus three adjacent cells with all color pairs are found (see Fig. 4(b)).

In any case, a solution to 2D-Sperner leads to a solution of 2D-KKM-A and thus a reduction is justified. Meanwhile, we obtained an alternative proof of Theorem 4. Despite it seems to be much shorter, in fact a similar topological argument is hidden inside Sperner's lemma.

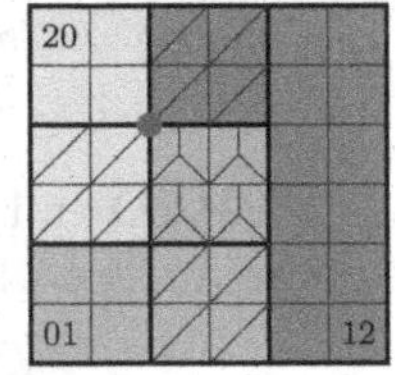

(a) The case of a multicolored cell. The red dot adjacent to a multicolored cell in the initial coloring

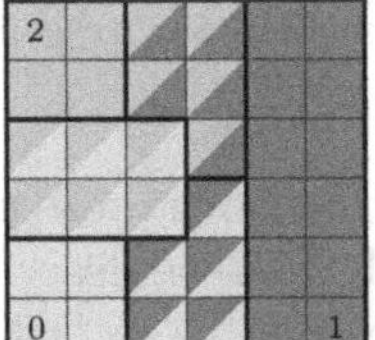

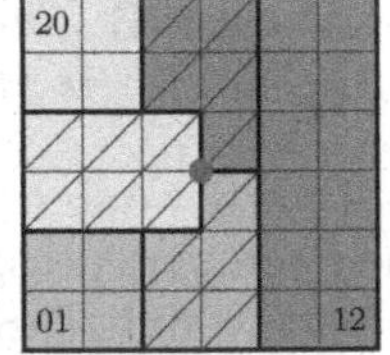

(b) The case of three different color pairs. The red dot is adjacent to to three cells of different color pairs.

Fig. 4. Proof of Theorem 8. The left part in each pair shows the initial coloring: color 0 is yellow, color 1 is blue, color 2 is red. The right parts shows the new coloring for Sperner's lemma: color 01 is green, color 12 is magenta, color 20 is orange. The red dot shows a multicolored node in Sperner's lemma. (Color figure online)

Theorem 9. *Both* 2D-KKM-A *and* 2D-KKM-B *are* **PPAD**-*complete.*

Proof. Since 2D-KKM-B is reducible to 2D-KKM-A and 2D-Sperner is **PPAD**-complete, it is sufficient to show that 2D-Sperner is reducible to 2D-KKM-B.

The idea is the following: take a refined grid where the new cells correspond to cells, edges and nodes of the initial grid. Formally if the initial grid had size $N \times N$, then the new grid has size $(2N+1) \times (2N+1)$. A cell (p, q) is colored in i if some cell adjacent to $\left(\frac{p}{2}, \frac{q}{2}\right)$ was colored in i in the initial table. In other words, cell (p, q) is colored in the colors of:

- $(\frac{p-1}{2}, \frac{q-1}{2})$ if both p and q are odd;
- $(\frac{p-1}{2}, \frac{q}{2}-1)$ and $(\frac{p-1}{2}, \frac{q}{2})$ if p is odd and q is even;
- $(\frac{p}{2}-1, \frac{q-1}{2})$ and $(\frac{p}{2}, \frac{q-1}{2})$ if p is even and q is odd;
- $(\frac{p}{2}-1, \frac{q}{2}-1)$, $(\frac{p}{2}-1, \frac{q}{2})$, $(\frac{p}{2}, \frac{q}{2}-1)$ and $(\frac{p}{2}, \frac{q}{2})$ if both p and q are even.

The procedure is illustrated on Fig. 5.

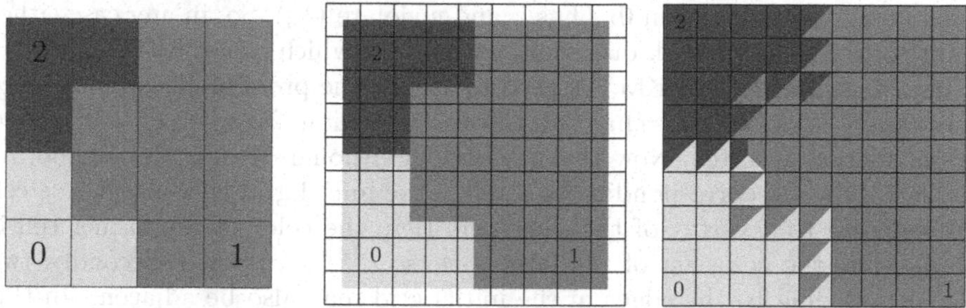

Fig. 5. Reducing 2D-Sperner to 2D-KKM-B.

Let us show that it is indeed a reduction. Firstly, it can be routinely checked that border conditions of Sperner's lemma imply normality of the resulting coloring. Now let us check (**) for edge adjacency. The pair of neighboring cells may have two types: one corresponds to a cell of the initial grid and the other corresponds to an edge, or one corresponds to an edge of the initial grid and the other corresponds to a node. In the first case the cell is incident to the edge, so the color of the first cell belongs to the color set of the second cell. In the second case the edge is incident to the node, so all cells incident to the edge are also incident to the node. Thus the color set of the first cell must be included in the color set of the second cell. So, (**) is also justified.

Due to Theorem 5, there must exist a multicolored cell in the new coloring. It must correspond to a node in the initial grid, since cells and edges have at most two colors. This node is a solution for 2D-Sperner, so the reduction is justified.

4.2 Higher Dimensions

Finally, estimate the search complexity of Theorem 6. Define the respective computational problem:

Definition 11. *Search problem* KKM *is the following: the input is a* poly(n)*-size circuit* C *that defines a point-set function* col *from* $\{0, \dots, 2^n - 1\}^d$ *to* $\{0, \dots, d\}$. *Suppose that normality (as in Definition 8) of* col *is guaranteed by the way* C *is interpreted. The task is to find either a multicolored cell, or a violation of* (**).

Theorem 10. *The problem* KKM *is* **PPAD***-complete.*

Proof. The reduction from KKM to Sperner works in any dimension and proves that KKM $\in$ **PPAD**. In the other direction we show how to reduce KKM in a lower dimension to that in a higher one.

To reduce KKM to Sperner, we need to produce a single-valued coloring from a multi-valued one. Unlike the construction for Theorem 8, define the new color as the minimal among the old ones. Sperner's border conditions can be routinely checked. Thus in the new coloring there must exist a node with adjacent cells of all colors. Among them, the cell x colored in 0 must have been a multicolored one. Indeed, suppose that color i was missed. Take the adjacent cell y colored in i in the new coloring. Since the new color is the minimal old color, y must have been colored in i, but not in 0. Thus x and y violate (**). So, in any case either a multicolored cell is found, or a violation of (**), which solves KKM.

To reduce Sperner to KKM, we need to modify the proof of Theorem 9, since the notion of adjacency was changed. Check the claim in 2D when (**) is applied to cells sharing a vertex. Now there are two additional cases with neighboring cells. Firstly, a cell corresponding to a cell in the initial grid is adjacent to a cell corresponding to a vertex of the same cell. Here the color of the former cell is included into the color set of the latter one, so (**) is satisfied. Secondly, two cells correspoding to the edges in the initial grid may also be adjacent. In this case (**) may be violated. But it happens in one possible case: one of the cells is colored in i and j and the other is colored in i and k, like in this figure:

Such configuration means that the original edges belong to a cell of color i which is adjacent to cells of colors j and k. They must be also adjacent to each other, so there must be a node in the original grid adjacent to cells of all colors. Thus, both a multicolored cell and violation of (**) yield a solution of Sperner.

Unfortunately, this argument does not work in higher dimensions. Instead, we reduce a problem in dimension d to a problem in dimension $d+1$. Since the base case is obtained, we just use induction. The caveat is that it is not trivial to satisfy (**) (and thus Theorem 6 is weaker than we would like it to be). For instance, it is not satisfied for a simple configuration on Fig. 6(a), but a small shift shown on Fig. 6(b) restores the property.

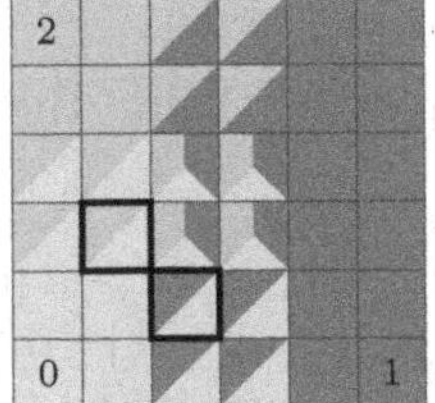

(a) Violation of $(**)$

(b) Restoration of $(**)$ by a small change

Fig. 6. Construction of a coloring with (**)

Let us describe how to generalize such shift. Suppose that a coloring col of a d-dimensional grid is normal and satisfies (**). Construct a coloring col′ of a $(d+1)$-dimensional grid. Let us denote by $(\mathbf{x}, z)$ the cell with first d coordinates $\mathbf{x}$ and last coordinate z. Replicate col in the bottom $d+1$ layers. That is, $\mathrm{col}'(\mathbf{x}, z) \supset \mathrm{col}(\mathbf{x})$ if $z \le d$. All upper cells are colored only in $d+1$. That is, $\mathrm{col}'(\mathbf{x}, z) = \{d+1\}$ if $z > d$. Also if $|\mathrm{col}(\mathbf{x})| = k$, then cells $(\mathbf{x}, d)$, $(\mathbf{x}, d-1)$, ..., $(\mathbf{x}, d-k+1)$ are also colored in $d+1$. Summarizing, we have the following:

$$\mathrm{col}'(\mathbf{x}, z) = \begin{cases} \mathrm{col}(\mathbf{x}), & \text{if } z \le d - |\mathrm{col}(\mathbf{x})|; \\ \mathrm{col}(\mathbf{x}) \cup \{d+1\}, & \text{if } d - |\mathrm{col}(\mathbf{x})| < z \le d; \\ \{d+1\}, & \text{if } z > d. \end{cases} \tag{2}$$

A routine check shows that this coloring is normal. Let us check (**).

Case 1: let $(\mathbf{x}, z)$ be adjacent to $(\mathbf{y}, z)$. Then $\mathbf{x}$ must be adjacent to $\mathbf{y}$. By induction hypothesis, w.l.o.g., $\mathrm{col}(\mathbf{x}) \subset \mathrm{col}(\mathbf{y})$. Hence $|\mathrm{col}(\mathbf{x})| \le |\mathrm{col}(\mathbf{y})|$ and thus $d - |\mathrm{col}(\mathbf{x})| \ge d - |\mathrm{col}(\mathbf{y})|$. So, if $(d+1) \in \mathrm{col}'(\mathbf{x}, z)$, then also $(d+1) \in \mathrm{col}'(\mathbf{y}, z)$ and $\mathrm{col}'(\mathbf{x}, z) \subset \mathrm{col}'(\mathbf{y}, z)$. Thus (**) is satisfied.

Case 2: let $(\mathbf{x}, z)$ be adjacent to $(\mathbf{y}, z+1)$. Then $\mathbf{x}$ must be adjacent to $\mathbf{y}$. Here the subcases $\mathrm{col}(\mathbf{x}) \subset \mathrm{col}(\mathbf{y})$ and $\mathrm{col}(\mathbf{y}) \subset \mathrm{col}(\mathbf{x})$ are not symmetric, so consider them one by one. Firstly, note that if $z = d$, then $\mathrm{col}'(\mathbf{y}, z+1) = \{d+1\}$ and $\mathrm{col}'(\mathbf{x}, z) \ni (d+1)$, so (**) is true. If $z > d$, then $\mathrm{col}'(\mathbf{y}, z+1) = \mathrm{col}'(\mathbf{x}, z) = \{d+1\}$, so (**) is also true. Now, let $z < d$ and $\mathrm{col}(\mathbf{x}) \subset \mathrm{col}(\mathbf{y})$. In this case the argument from case 1 is valid. Finally, let $z < d$ and $\mathrm{col}(\mathbf{y}) \subsetneq \mathrm{col}(\mathbf{x})$. Then $|\mathrm{col}(\mathbf{y})| \le |\mathrm{col}(\mathbf{x})| - 1$. Then if $(d+1) \in \mathrm{col}'(\mathbf{y}, z+1)$, then $z+1 > d - |\mathrm{col}(\mathbf{y})|$. Hence $z > d - |\mathrm{col}(\mathbf{y})| - 1 \ge d - |\mathrm{col}(\mathbf{x})|$ and $(d+1) \in \mathrm{col}(\mathbf{x}, z)$. Thus $\mathrm{col}'(\mathbf{y}, z+1) = \mathrm{col}(\mathbf{y}) \cup \{d+1\} \subset \mathrm{col}(\mathbf{x}) \cup \{d+1\} = \mathrm{col}'(\mathbf{x}, z)$. In all cases (**) is justified.

Since $\rfloor\wr\updownarrow'$ satisfies (**), there must be a multicolored cell $(\mathbf{x}, z)$. It can occur only if $\mathrm{col}(\mathbf{x}) = \{0, \ldots, d\}$. Thus, a multicolored cell in dimension d is found and it completes the reduction.

5 Conclusion

In this paper, we introduced a discrete analogue of covering with closed sets, applied it to the KKM lemma and analyzed complexity of the respective search problems. We want to specify some open questions and future directions:

- Is this approach applicable to other existence theorems that deal with coverings with closed sets? For instance, one can analyze Lesbegue theorem: if the cube $[0,1]^n$ is covered by M closed sets such that no point is included in more than n sets, then one of the sets must contain points from two opposite faces of the cube.
- Could Theorem 6 be strengthened by weakening the adjacency condition in (**)? Our hypothesis is that in dimension 3 it is sufficient to require (**) for cells adjacent by an edge.
- Can our **PPAD**-completeness results be applied to some economic model? One possible candidate is Gale's lemma from [13].

Acknowledgments. The authors thank attendants of the 3rd Hungarian-Russian Combinatorics workshop, Kolmogorov seminar at Moscow State university and 4th conference "Autumn mathematical readings at Adyghea" for their attention and discussion of preliminary versions of this work.

References

1. Arrow, K.J., Debreu, G.: Existence of an equilibrium for a competitive economy. Econometrica **22**(3), 265–90 (1954)
2. Babichenko, Y., Rubinstein, A.: Settling the complexity of Nash equilibrium in congestion games. In: Proceedings of the 53rd Annual ACM SIGACT Symposium on Theory of Computing, pp. 1426–1437 (2021)
3. Beame, P., Cook, S., Edmonds, J., Impagliazzo, R., Pitassi, T.: The relative complexity of NP search problems. J. Comput. Syst. Sci. **57**(1), 3–19 (1998)
4. Border, K.C.: Fixed Point Theorems With Applications to Economics and Game Theory. Cambridge University Press, Cambridge (1985)
5. Brouwer, L.E.J.: Über abbildung von mannigfaltigkeiten. Math. Ann. **71**(1), 97–115 (1911)
6. Bubelis, V.: On equilibria in finite games. Int. J. Game Theory **8**(2), 65–79 (1979)
7. Chen, X., Dai, D., Du, Y., Teng, S.H.: Settling the complexity of Arrow-Debreu equilibria in markets with additively separable utilities. In: 50th Annual IEEE Symposium on Foundations of Computer Science, pp. 273–282 (2009)
8. Chen, X., Deng, X.: Settling the complexity of 2-player Nash-equilibrium. Electronic Colloquium on Computational Complexity (ECCC), 140 (2005). http://eccc.hpi-web.de/eccc-reports/2005/TR05-140/index.html
9. Chen, X., Deng, X.: On the complexity of 2D discrete fixed point problem. Theoret. Comput. Sci. **410**(44), 4448–4456 (2009)
10. Chen, X., Deng, X., Teng, S.H.: Settling the complexity of computing two-player Nash equilibria. J. ACM (JACM) **56**(3), 14 (2009)
11. Daskalakis, C., Goldberg, P.W., Papadimitriou, C.H.: The complexity of computing a Nash equilibrium. SIAM J. Comput. **39**(1), 195–259 (2009). https://doi.org/10.1137/070699652
12. Etessami, K., Yannakakis, M.: On the complexity of Nash equilibria and other fixed points. SIAM J. Comput. **39**(6), 2531–2597 (2010)
13. Gale, D.: Equilibrium in a discrete exchange economy with money. Int. J. Game Theory **13**(1), 61–64 (1984)
14. Garg, J., Mehta, R., Vazirani, V.V., Yazdanbod, S.: Settling the complexity of Leontief and PLC exchange markets under exact and approximate equilibria. In: Proceedings of the 49th STOC, pp. 890–901. ACM (2017)
15. Goldberg, P.W.: A survey of PPAD-completeness for computing Nash equilibria. CoRR abs/1103.2709 (2011). http://arxiv.org/abs/1103.2709
16. Goldberg, P.W., Hollender, A.: The hairy ball problem is PPAD-complete. J. Comput. Syst. Sci. **122**, 34–62 (2021)
17. Hollender, A., Goldberg, P.: The complexity of multi-source variants of the end-of-line problem, and the concise mutilated chessboard. In: Electronic Colloquium on Computational Complexity, vol. 25, p. 120 (2018)
18. Kakutani, S.: A generalization of Brouwer's fixed point theorem. Duke Math. J. **8**(3), 457–459 (1941)
19. Kintali, S., Poplawski, L.J., Rajaraman, R., Sundaram, R., Teng, S.H.: Reducibility among fractional stability problems. SIAM J. Comp. **42**(6), 2063–2113 (2013)

20. Knaster, B., Kuratowski, C., Mazurkiewicz, S.: Ein beweis des fixpunktsatzes für n-dimensionale simplexe. Fundam. Math. **14**(1), 132–137 (1929). https://doi.org/10.4064/fm-14-1-132-137
21. Megiddo, N., Papadimitriou, C.H.: On total functions, existence theorems and computational complexity. Theoret. Comput. Sci. **81**(2), 317–324 (1991). https://doi.org/10.1016/0304-3975(91)90200-L, http://dx.doi.org/10.1016/0304-3975(91)90200-L
22. Musatov, D., Yakunin, A.: How hard is to find a stable jurisdiction structure? (2022). (forthcoming)
23. Nash, J.: Non-cooperative games. Ann. Math. **1**, 286–295 (1951)
24. Nash, J.F.: Equilibrium points in n-person games. Proc. Natl. Acad. Sci. **36**(1), 48–49 (1950)
25. Nisan, N., Roughgarden, T., Tardos, E., Vazirani, V.V.: Algorithmic Game Theory. Cambridge University Press, Cambridge (2007)
26. Othman, A., Papadimitriou, C., Rubinstein, A.: The complexity of fairness through equilibrium. ACM Trans. Econ. Comput. **4**(4), 20 (2016)
27. Papadimitriou, C., Peng, B.: Public good games in directed networks. arXiv preprint arXiv:2106.00718 (2021)
28. Papadimitriou, C.H.: On the complexity of the parity argument and other inefficient proofs of existence. J. Comput. Syst. Sci. **48**(3), 498–532 (1994). https://doi.org/10.1016/S0022-0000(05)80063-7
29. Rubinstein, A.: Settling the complexity of computing approximate two-player Nash equilibria. In: 2016 IEEE 57th Annual Symposium on Foundations of Computer Science (FOCS), pp. 258–265. IEEE (2016)
30. Scarf, H.E.: The core of an N person game. Econom. J. Econom. Soc. **1**, 50–69 (1967)
31. Schuldenzucker, S., Seuken, S., Battiston, S.: Finding clearing payments in financial networks with credit default swaps is PPAD-complete. In: LIPIcs-Leibniz International Proceedings in Informatics, vol. 67 (2017)
32. Shapley, L.S.: On balanced games without side payments. In: Mathematical Programming, pp. 261–290. Elsevier (1973)
33. Simmons, F.W., Su, F.E.: Consensus-halving via theorems of Borsuk-Ulam and Tucker. Math. Soc. Sci. **45**(1), 15–25 (2003)
34. Sperner, E.: Neuer beweis für die invarianz der dimensionszahl und des gebietes. Abh. Math. Semi. Univ. Hamb. **6**, 265–272 (1928)
35. Su, F.E.: Rental harmony: Sperner's lemma in fair division. Am. Math. Monthly **106**(10), 930–942 (1999)
36. Vazirani, V.V., Yannakakis, M.: Market equilibrium under separable, piecewise-linear, concave utilities. J. ACM (JACM) **58**(3), 10 (2011)

The Fast Algorithm for Online k-server Problem on Trees

Kamil Khadiev(✉) and Maxim Yagafarov

Kazan Federal University, Kazan, Russia
kamilhadi@gmail.com

Abstract. We consider online algorithms for the k-server problem on trees. There is a k-competitive algorithm for this problem, and it is the best competitive ratio. M. Chrobak and L. Larmore provided it. At the same time, the existing implementation has $O(n)$ time complexity for processing a query and $O(n)$ for prepossessing, where n is the number of nodes in a tree. Another implementation of the algorithm has $O(k^2 + k\log n)$ time complexity for processing a query and $O(n\log n)$ for prepossessing. We provide a new time-efficient implementation of the algorithm. It has $O(n)$ time complexity for preprocessing and $O\left(k(\log n)^2\right)$ for processing a query.

Keywords: online algorithms · k-server problem · tree · time complexity

1 Introduction

Online optimization is a field of optimization theory that deals with optimization problems not knowing the future [27]. The most standard method to define the effectiveness of an online algorithm is a competitive ratio [18,30]. The competitive ratio is the worst-case ratio between the cost of a solution found by the algorithm and the cost of an optimal solution. In the general setting, online algorithms have unlimited computational power. Nevertheless, many papers consider them with different restrictions. Some of them are restrictions on memory [1,4,7,10,14,19–24,26], other ones are restrictions on time complexity [13,29]. This paper focuses on efficient online algorithms in terms of time complexity. One of the well-known online minimization problems is the k-server problem on trees [11]. Other related well-known problems are the matching problem, r-gathering problem, facility assignment problem [2,3,16]. There is a k-competitive deterministic algorithm for the k-server problem on trees, and the algorithm has the best competitive ratio. Expected competitive ratio for a best-known randomized algorithm [5,6] is $O(\log^3 n \log^2 k)$, where n is the number of nodes in a tree. In this paper, we are focused on the deterministic one. So, the competitive ratio of

This paper has been supported by the Kazan Federal University Strategic Academic Leadership Program ("PRIORITY-2030").

A. S. Kulikov and S. Raskhodnikova (Eds.): CSR 2022, LNCS 13296, pp. 190–208, 2022.
https://doi.org/10.1007/978-3-031-09574-0_12

the deterministic algorithm is the best one. At the same time, the naive implementation has $O(n)$ time complexity for each query and preprocessing. There is a time-efficient algorithm for general graphs [29] that uses a min-cost-max-flow algorithm, but it is too slow in the case of a tree. In the case of a tree, there exists an algorithm with time complexity $O(n \log n)$ for preprocessing and $O\left(k^2 + k \log n\right)$ for each query [17].

We suggest a new time-efficient implementation of the algorithm from [11]. It has $O(n)$ time complexity for preprocessing and $O\left(k(\log n)^2\right)$ for processing a query. It is based on data structures and techniques like a segment tree [28], heavy-light decomposition (heavy path decomposition) [15,31] for a tree and fast algorithms for computing Lowest Common Ancestor (LCA) [8,9]. Let us compare our algorithm with the implementation from [17]. Our prepossessing procedure is more efficient, and we obtain speed-up for the query processing procedure in the case of $k = \omega\left((\log n)^2\right)$. The algorithm is more efficient than the naive algorithm in the case of $k = o\left(n/(\log n)^2\right)$.

The structure of the paper is as follows. Preliminaries are presented in Sect. 2. Section 4 contains a subproblem on a segment tree that is used in the main algorithm. The main algorithm is discussed in Sect. 3. Section 5 concludes the paper.

2 Preliminaries

An online minimization problem consists of a set $\mathcal{I}$ of inputs and a cost function. An input is $I = (x_1, \ldots, x_n)$, where n is a length of an input $|I| = n$. Furthermore, a set of feasible outputs (or solutions) $\mathcal{O}(I)$ is associated with each I; an output is $O = (y_1, \ldots, y_n)$. The cost function assigns a positive real value $cost(I, O)$ to $I \in \mathcal{I}$ and $O \in \mathcal{O}(I)$. The optimal solution for $I \in \mathcal{I}$ is $O_{opt}(I) = argmin_{O \in \mathcal{O}(I)} cost(I, O)$.

Let us define an online algorithm for this problem. **A deterministic online algorithm** A computes an output sequence $A(I) = (y_1, \ldots, y_n)$ such that y_i is computed based on $x_1, \ldots, x_i$. We say that A is *c-competitive* if there exists a constant $\alpha \geq 0$ such that, for every n and for any input I of size n, we have: $cost(I, A(I)) \leq c \cdot cost(I, O_{Opt}(I)) + \alpha$. Here, c is the minimal number that satisfies the inequality. Also we call c the **competitive ratio** of A.

2.1 Graph Theory

Let us consider a rooted tree $G = (V, E)$, where V is a set of nodes (vertices), and E is a set of edges. Let $n = |V|$ be the number of nodes, and $V = \{v^1, \ldots, v^n\}$. Let the root of the tree be the v^1 node.

A path P is a sequence of nodes $(v_1, \ldots, v_h)$ that are connected by edges, i.e. $(v_i, v_{i+1}) \in E$ for all $i \in \{1, \ldots, h-1\}$. Note, that there are no duplicates among $v_1, \ldots, v_h$. Here, h is the length of the path. We use $v \in P$ notation if there is j such that $v_j = v$. The notation is reasonable, because there is no duplicates in a path. Note that for any two nodes u and v the path between them is unique because G is a tree.

The distance $dist(v,u)$ between two nodes v and u is the length of the path between them. A height of a node v is the distance from the root that is $dist(v^1,v)$. For each node v except the root node we can define a parent node $\textsc{Parent}(v)$, it is a node such that $dist(v^1,\textsc{Parent}(v))+1 = dist(v^1,v)$ and it belongs to the path from v^1 to v. We assume that for the root node, $\textsc{Parent}(v^1) = NULL$. Additionally, we can define a set of children $\textsc{Children}(v) = \{u : \textsc{Parent}(u) = v\}$.

Distance. For each node v we compute the distance from the v^1 (root) node to the node v. We call it $dist(v^1,v)$. We can do it using Depth-first search algorithm [12]. There is a well-known simple algorithm for computing of $dist(v^1,v)$, we present it for completeness in the arXiv version [25]. Let ComputeDistance be a subroutine that computes distances. After invocation of this procedure, we can obtain $dist(v^1,v)$ in $O(1)$ time complexity.

Heavy-Light Decomposition. Heavy-light decomposition is a decomposition of the tree to a set of paths $\mathcal{P}$. The technique is presented in [15,31]. It has the following properties:

- Each node v of the tree belongs to exactly one path from $\mathcal{P}$, i.e., all paths have no intersections, and they cover all nodes of the tree.
- For any node v, a path from v to the root of the tree contains nodes of at most $\log_2 n$ paths from $\mathcal{P}$.
- Let us consider a node v and a path $P \in \mathcal{P}$ such that $v \in P$. Then, $beg(v)$ is the node that belongs to P and has the minimal height, i.e. $beg(v)$ is such that $dist(v^1, beg(v)) = \min_{u\in P} dist(v^1,u)$.
- For a node v of the tree, let $P(v)$ be the path from $\mathcal{P}$ that contains v.
- For a node v of the tree, let $index_P(v)$ be an index of an element of the path P. For an index i of an element in the path P, let $node_P(i)$ be the node v. In other words, if $P = (v_1,\dots,v_h)$, then $v_{index_P(v)} = v$, and $v_i = node_P(i)$
- We can construct the set $\mathcal{P}$ with $O(n)$ time complexity.

Lowest Common Ancestor. Given two nodes u and v of a rooted tree, the Lowest Common Ancestor is a node w such that w is an ancestor of both u and v, and w is the closest one to u and v among all such ancestors. The following result is well-known.

Lemma 1 ([8,9]). *There is an algorithm for the LCA problem with the following properties: (i) The time complexity of the preprocessing step is $O(n)$ (ii)The time complexity of computing LCA for two nodes is $O(1)$.*

Let LCA_Preprocessing() be the subroutine for the preprocessing step. Let $\mathrm{LCA}(u,v)$ be the procedure for computing LCA of two nodes u and v. We can compute the distance $dist(v,q)$ between nodes v and q using LCA in $O(1)$. Let $l = \mathrm{LCA}(v,q)$ be a lowest common ancestor of v and q. Then, $dist(v,q) = dist(v^1,q) + dist(v^1,v) - 2\cdot dist(v^1,l)$.

2.2 k-server Problem on a Tree

We have a rooted tree $G = (V, E)$. We are also given k servers that can move among nodes of G. At each time slot, a query $q \in V$ appears, and we have to "serve" it, that is, choose one of our servers and move it to q. Other servers are also allowed to move. Our measure of cost is the distance by which we move our servers. In other words, if before the query positions of servers are $v_1, \ldots, v_k$ and after the query they are $v'_1, \ldots, v'_k$, then $q \in \{v'_1, \ldots, v'_k\}$ and the cost of the move is $\sum_{i=1}^{k} dist(v_i, v'_i)$. The problem is to design a strategy that minimizes the cost of serving a sequence of queries given online.

2.3 Coloration Problem

Let us present the coloration problem used as a sub-task in the main algorithm for the k-server problem. It is used in the following way. In a tree, we color a node v by a color j if the server j visits the node. More detailed motivation is presented in the next section.

Coloration Problem. Assume that we have a sequence of d nodes $v_1, \ldots, v_d$ of the tree G. We associate a color c_i with a node v_i of the tree G, where $0 \leq c_i \leq Z$ for some positive integer Z. Initially, all nodes are not colored, i.e. $c_i = 0$. We should be able to do several operations. Each operation can be one of three types:

- **Update.** For three integers l, r, c $(1 \leq l \leq r \leq d,\ 1 \leq c \leq Z)$, we should color all elements of segment $[l, r]$ by c, i.e. $c_i \leftarrow c$ for $l \leq i \leq r$.
- **Request.** For an integer x $(1 \leq x \leq d)$, we should return c_x.
- **Request Closest Colored.** For two integers l, r $(1 \leq l \leq r \leq d)$, we should return the minimal and the maximal indexes of colored elements from the segment, i.e. the maximal and the minimal i such that $c_i > 0$ and $l \leq i \leq r$.

We can implement these operations using the segment tree data structure [28]. The definition of the Segment Tree data structure is presented in Sect. 4. Assume that we have several procedures. The procedure CONSTRUCTST$(1, d)$ constructs a segment tree. This procedure is used by the initialization process for the coloration problem solution (Lemma 5). The procedure returns the root of the segment tree. The time complexity is $O(d)$. The procedure COLORREQUEST$(x, root)$ implements the **Request** operation for c_x and a segment tree with a root node *root* (Lemma 6). It has $O(\log d)$ time complexity. The procedure COLORUPDATE$(l, r, c, root)$ implements the **Update** operation for a segment $[l, r]$, a color c and a segment tree with a root node *root* (Lemma 7). It has $O(\log d)$ time complexity. The procedure GETCLOSESTCOLORRIGHT$(l, r, root)$ implements the **Request Closest Colored** operation for a segment $[l, r]$ and a segment tree with a root node *root* (Lemma 8). It returns the minimal index from the segment and has $O(\log d)$ time complexity. The GETCLOSESTCOLORLEFT$(l, r, root)$ procedure has similar properties and returns the maximal index. The more detailed discussion is presented in Sect. 4.

3 The Fast Online Algorithm for k-server Problem on Trees

Let us describe a k-competitive algorithm for the k-server problem on trees from [11].

Chrobak-Larmore's k-competitive Algorithm for the k-server Problem from [11]. Let us have a query q, and let servers be in nodes $v_1, \ldots, v_k$. Let a server i be *active* if there is no other servers on the path from v_i to q. If several severs in a node, then the server with the smallest index is active. Formally, let us consider a path $P = (w_1, \ldots, w_h)$, where $w_1 = v_i$ and $w_h = q$. Then, $v_{i'} \notin P$ for $i' \neq i$. If there is $v_{i'} = v_i$, then the server i is active if $i' > i$. In each phase, we move each *active* server one step towards the node q. After each phase, the set of *active* servers can be changed. We repeat phases (moves of servers) until one of the servers reaches the query node q. The naive implementation of the algorithm has time complexity $O(n)$ for each query. It can be the following. Firstly, we run the Depth-first search algorithm with time labels [12]. Using it, we can put labels to each node that allows us to check for any two nodes u and v, whether u is an ancestor of v in $O(1)$. After that, we can move each active server to the query step by step. Together all active servers cannot visit more than $O(n)$ nodes.

Here, we present an effective implementation of Chrobak-Larmore's algorithm. The algorithm contains two parts that are preprocessing and query processing. The preprocessing part is done once and has $O(n)$ time complexity (Theorem 1). The query processing part is done for each query and has $O\left(k(\log n)^2\right)$ time complexity (Theorem 2).

3.1 Preprocessing

We do the following steps for the preprocessing:

- We construct a Heavy-light decomposition $\mathcal{P}$ for the tree. Properties of decomposition are described in Sect. 2.1. Assume that, for construction $\mathcal{P}$, we have ConstructingHLD() subroutine.
- We do the required preprocessing for the LCA algorithm that is discussed in Sect. 2.1. Assume that we have LCA_Preprocessing() subroutine for this procedure.
- For each path $P \in \mathcal{P}$ we construct a segment tree that will be used for the coloration problem that is described in Sect. 2.3 and Sect. 4. Let ConstructingSegemntTree(P) be a subroutine for construction a segment tree for the path P. Let ST_P be a segment tree for the path P.
- Additionally, for each node v we compute the distance from the v^1 (root) node to the node v using ComputeDistance subroutine from Sect. 2.1.

Finally, we have Algorithm 1 for the preprocessing.

Algorithm 1. PREPROCESSING. Preprocessing procedure.

```
𝒫 ← ConstructHLD()
LCA_Preprocessing()
for P ∈ 𝒫 do
    ST_P ← ConstructST(P)
end for
dist(v^1, v^1) ← 0, ComputeDistance()
```

Theorem 1. *Algorithm 1 for the preprocessing has time complexity* $O(n)$.

Proof. As it was mentioned in Sect. 2.1 the time complexity of Heavy-light decomposition $\mathcal{P}$ construction is $O(n)$. Due to Lemma 5, time complexity of CONSTRUCTST(P) is $O(|P|)$. The total time complexity of constructing all segment trees is $O\left(\sum_{P\in\mathcal{P}}|P|\right) = O(n)$ because of property of the decomposition. Time complexity of COMPUTEDISTANCE is $O(n)$. Therefore, the total time complexity is $O(n)$. □

3.2 Query Processing

Let us have a query on a node q, and servers are in nodes $v_1,\dots,v_k$. We make the following steps:

Step 1. Let us sort all servers by the distance to the node q. We assume that if two servers have the same distance to the node q, then the server with a smaller index should precede the server with a bigger index. Let SORT$(q, v_1,\dots,v_k)$ be a sorting procedure. On the following steps we assume that $dist(v_i, q) \le dist(v_{i+1}, q)$ for $i \in \{1,\dots,k-1\}$.

Step 2. The first server from v_1 processes the query. We move them to the node q and color all nodes of a path from v_1 to q to color 1. The node's color shows the number of a server that visited the node. Let the coloring process be implemented as a procedure COLORPATH$(v_1, q, 1)$. The procedure and detailed description of this step is presented in the end of this section.

Step 3. For $i \in \{2,\dots k\}$ we consider a server that stays in the v_i node. It becomes inactive when some other server j becomes closer to the query than i-th server. It is easy to see that $j < i$ because the distance from v_j to the target q is smaller than v_i to the same target q. When i-th server becomes inactive, the server j is active. Therefore, the node where j-th server was in that moment should have color j.

To obtain the index j, we search a colored node closest to v_i on the path from v_i to q. The color of this node is j. Let the search of the closest colored node be implemented as a procedure GETCLOSESTCOLOR(v_i, q). It is described in the end of this section. Let the obtained node be w and its color is j. The j-th server reaches the node w in $z = dist(v_j, w)$ steps. After that the i-th server becomes inactive. So, we should move the i-th server to a node v_i' to z steps on the path from v_i to w. Let the moving process be implemented as a procedure MOVE(v_i, w, z). It is described in the end of this section. Then, we color all nodes on the path from v_i to v_i' to the color i. Let us describe the procedure as Algorithm 2.

Algorithm 2. QUERY(q). Query procedure.

```
SORT(q, v_1, ..., v_k)
COLORPATH(v_1, q, 1)
v'_1 ← q
for i ∈ {2, ..., k} do
    (w, j) ← GETCLOSESTCOLOR(v_i, q)
    z ← dist(v_j, w)
    v'_i ← MOVE(v_i, w, z)
    COLORPATH(v_i, v'_i, i)
end for
```

Coloring of a Path. Let us consider the problem of coloring nodes on a path from a node v to a node u. The color is c.

Let $l = LCA(v, u)$ be an LCA of v and u. Let $P_1, \dots, P_t \in \mathcal{P}$ be paths that contain nodes of the path from v to l and let $P_1', \dots, P_{t'}' \in \mathcal{P}$ be paths that contain nodes of the path from l to u. Let $w_0 = v$, $w_0 \in P_1$; $w_1 = beg(P_1)$, $\text{PARENT}(w_1) \in P_2$; $w_2 = beg(P_2)$, $\text{PARENT}(w_2) \in P_3; \dots w_{t-1} = beg(P_{t-1})$, $\text{PARENT}(w_{t-1}) \in P_t$; $w_t = l$; and $w_0' = u$, $w_0' \in P_1'$; $w_1' = beg(P_1')$, $\text{PARENT}(w_1') \in P_2'$; $w_2' = beg(P_2')$, $\text{PARENT}(w_2') \in P_3'; \dots w_{t-1}' = beg(P_{t'-1}')$, $\text{PARENT}(w_{t'-1}') \in P_t'$; $w_{t'}' = l$. Then, the coloring process is two steps:

- COLORUPDATE$(index_{P_i}(\text{PARENT}(w_{i-1})), index_{P_i}(w_i), c, ST_{P_i})$ for $i \in \{2, \dots, t\}$, and COLORUPDATE$(index_{P_i}(w_0), index_{P_i}(w_1), c, ST_{P_1})$;
- COLORUPDATE$(index_{P_i'}(\text{PARENT}(w_{i-1}')), index_{P_i'}(w_o'), c, ST_{P_i'})$ for $i \in \{2, \dots, t'\}$, and COLORUPDATE$(index_{P_i'}(w_0'), index_{P_i'}(w_1'), c, ST_{P_1'})$. The procedure is presented as Algorithm 3.

Algorithm 3. ColorPath(v, u, c). Coloring the path between v and u.

```
l ← LCA(v,u),   w ← v,   P ← P(v)
while P ≠ P(l) do
    bw ← beg(P)
    ColorUpdate(index_P(w), index_P(bw), c, ST_P)
    w ← Parent(bw),   P ← P(w)
end while
ColorUpdate(index_P(w), index_P(l), c, ST_P)
w ← u,   P ← P(u)
while P ≠ P(l) do
    bw ← beg(P)
    ColorUpdate(index_P(w), index_P(bw), c, ST_P)
    w ← Parent(bw),   P ← P(w)
end while
ColorUpdate(index_P(w), index_P(l), c, ST_P)
```

Lemma 2. *Time complexity of Algorithm 3 is* $O\left((\log n)^2\right)$.

Proof. Due to properties of Heavy-light decomposition from Sect. 2.1, $t, t' = O(\log n)$. Due to Lemma 7, each invocation of ColorUpdate for P has time complexity $O(\log |P|) = O(\log n)$. So, the total time complexity is $O\left((\log n)^2\right)$. □

The Search of the Closest Colored Node. Let us consider the problem of searching the closest colored node on the path from v to u. The idea is similar to the idea from the previous section. Let $l = LCA(v, u)$ be a LCA of v and u. Let $P_1, \dots, P_t \in \mathcal{P}$ be paths that contain nodes of a path from v to l and let $P'_1, \dots, P'_{t'} \in \mathcal{P}$ be paths that contain nodes of a path from l to u. Let $w_0 = v$, $w_0 \in P_1$; $w_1 = beg(P_1)$, $\textsc{Parent}(w_1) \in P_2$; $w_2 = beg(P_2)$, $\textsc{Parent}(w_2) \in P_3; \dots; w_{t-1} = beg(P_{t-1})$, $\textsc{Parent}(w_{t-1}) \in P_t$; $w_t = l$; and $w'_0 = u$, $w'_0 \in P'_1$; $w'_1 = beg(P'_1)$, $\textsc{Parent}(w'_1) \in P'_2$; $w'_2 = beg(P'_2)$, $\textsc{Parent}(w'_2) \in P'_3; \dots; w'_{t-1} = beg(P'_{t'-1})$, $\textsc{Parent}(w'_{t'-1}) \in P'_t$; $w'_{t'} = l$. For the searching process, firstly, we invoke the procedure GetClosestColorRight$(index_{P_i}(w_0), index_{P_i}(w_i), ST_{P_i})$. Assume that the procedure returns $NULL$ if there are no colored nodes in the segment. If the procedure returns $NULL$, then we invoke the procedure GetClosestColorRight$(index_{P_i}(\textsc{Parent}(w_{i-1})), index_{P_i}(w_i), ST_{P_i})$ for $i \in \{2, \dots, t\}$. We stop on the minimal i such that the result is not $NULL$. If all of them are $NULL$, then we continue. Then, we invoke the procedure

GetClosestColorLeft$(index_{P'_i}(\textsc{Parent}(w'_{i-1})), index_{P'_i}(w_i), ST_{P'_i})$ for $i \in \{t', \dots, 2\}$. We stop on the maximal i such that a result is not $NULL$. If all of them $NULL$, then we invoke GetClosestColorLeft$(index_{P'_1}(w'_0))$, $index_{P'_1}(w_1), ST_{P'_1})$. The procedure is presented as Algorithm 4.

Algorithm 4. GetClosestColor(v, u). Getting the closest colored vertex on the path between v and u.

```
l ← LCA(v,u),   w ← v,   P ← P(v),   g ← NULL
while g = NULL and P ≠ P(l) do
    bw ← beg(P)
    g ← GetClosestColorRight(index_P(w), index_P(bw), ST_P)
    if g = NULL then
        w ← Parent(bw),   P ← P(w)
    end if
end while
if g = NULL then
    g ← GetClosestColorRight(index_P(w), index_P(l), ST_P)
end if
if g = NULL then
    i ← 0,   w'_i ← u,   P ← P(u)
    while P ≠ P(l) do
        i ← i + 1,   w'_i ← beg(P),   bw ← Parent(w'_i),   P ← P(bw)
    end while
    g ← GetClosestColorLeft(index_P(Parent(w'_i)), index_P(l), ST_P)
    while g = NULL do
        P ← P(w_i),   bw ← Parent(w'_{i-1})
        g ← GetClosestColorLeft(index_P(bw), index_P(w'_i), ST_P)
        i ← i − 1
    end while
end if
resW ← node_P(g),   j ← ColorRequest(g, ST_P)
return (resW, j)
```

Let us discuss time complexity of the algorithm.

Lemma 3. *Time complexity of Algorithm 4 is* $O\left((\log n)^2\right)$.

Proof. Due to properties of Heavy-light decomposition from Sect. 2.1, we have $t, t' = O(\log n)$. Due to results from Sect. 2.3, each invocation of the procedure GetClosestColorLeft or GetClosestColorRight for P has time complexity $O(\log |P|) = O(\log n)$. So, the total time complexity is $O\left((\log n)^2\right)$. □

Moving of a Server. Let us consider a moving of a server from v to a distance g on a path from v to u. The idea is similar to the idea from the previous section. Let $l = LCA(v, u)$ be a LCA of v and u. Let $P_1, \dots, P_t \in \mathcal{P}$ be paths that contains nodes of a path from v to l and let $P'_1, \dots, P'_{t'} \in \mathcal{P}$ be paths that contains nodes of a path from l to u. Let $w_0 = v$, $w_0 \in P_1$; $w_1 = beg(P_1)$, $\textsc{Parent}(w_1) \in P_2$; $w_2 = beg(P_2)$, $\textsc{Parent}(w_2) \in P_3; \dots; w_{t-1} = beg(P_{t-1})$, $\textsc{Parent}(w_{t-1}) \in P_t$; $w_t = l$; and $w'_0 = u$, $w'_0 \in P'_1$; $w'_1 = beg(P'_1)$, $\textsc{Parent}(w'_1) \in P'_2$; $w'_2 = beg(P'_2)$, $\textsc{Parent}(w'_2) \in P'_3; \dots; w'_{t-1} = beg(P'_{t'-1})$, $\textsc{Parent}(w'_{t'-1}) \in P'_t$; $w'_{t'} = l$. Then, the moving process is the following. We check whether the distance $dist(\textsc{Parent}(w_{i-1}), w_i) \leq g$. If $dist(\textsc{Parent}(w_{i-1}), w_i)) \leq g$, then we can return the node $node_{P_i}(index_{P_i}(\textsc{Parent}(w_{i-1})) + g)$ as a result and stop the process. Otherwise, we reduce $g \leftarrow g - dist(\textsc{Parent}(w_{i-1}), w_i) - 1$ and move to the next i, i.e. $i \leftarrow i + 1$. We do it for $i \in \{1, \dots, t\}$.

If $g > 0$, then we continue with the path from l to u. We check whether $dist(\textsc{Parent}(w'_{i-1}), w'_i) \leq g$. If $dist(\textsc{Parent}(w'_{i-1}), w'_i)) \leq g$, then we can return the node $node_{P'_i}(index_{P'_i}(w'_i) - g)$ as a result and stop the process. Otherwise, we reduce $t \leftarrow t - dist(\textsc{Parent}(w'_{i-1}), w'_i) - 1$ and move to the previous i, i.e. $i \leftarrow i - 1$. We do it for $i \in \{t', \dots, 1\}$.

Lemma 4. *Time complexity of the moving is* $O(\log n)$.

Proof. Due to properties of Heavy-light decomposition from Sect. 2.1, we have $t, t' = O(\log n)$. The time complexity for processing of each path is $O(1)$. So, the total time complexity is $O(\log n)$. □

Correctness and Complexity of the Query Processing

Theorem 2. *The query processing Algorithm 2 has time complexity* $O\left(k(\log n)^2\right)$.

Proof. The complexity of servers sorting by distance is $O(k \log k)$. Due to Lemma 2, Lemma 3 and Lemma 4, the complexity for processing one server is $O\left(\log n + (\log n)^2 + (\log n)^2\right) = O\left((\log n)^2\right)$. So, the total complexity of processing all servers is $O\left(k \log k + k(\log n)^2\right) = O\left(k(\log n)^2\right)$ because $k < n$. □

4 Segment Tree with Range Updates for Coloration Problem

In the paper, we use a segment tree with range updates for Coloration Problem (Sect. 2.3) as one of the main tools for the main algorithm. The data structure allows us to do the main operations for the coloration problem with logarithmic time complexity. As a book with a description of the data structure [28] can be used.

Firstly, let us describe the segment tree data structure. It is the full binary tree of height h such that $2^{h-1} < d \leq 2^h$. The data structure works with the sequence of elements of the length 2^h, but we are care only about the first d elements. Each node of the tree is associated with some segment $[a, b]$ such that $1 \leq a \leq b \leq 2^h$. Each leaf is associated with elements of the sequence or we can say that it is associated with a segment of size 1. i-th node of the last level is associated with a segment $[i, i]$. Let us consider an internal node v and its two children u and w. Then, u is associated with a segment $[a, q]$, w is associated with a segment $[q + 1, b]$, and v is associated with a segment $[a, b]$ for some $1 \leq a \leq q < b \leq 2^h$. Note that because of the structure of the tree, we have $q = (a + b)/2$.

Each node v of the segment tree is labeled by a color $C(v)$, where $0 \leq C(v) \leq Z$. Assume that v is associated with a segment $[a, b]$. If $C(v) = 0$, then the segment $[a, b]$ is not colored at all or it has not a single color. If $1 \leq C(v) \leq Z$, then the segment has a single color $C(v)$, i.e. $c_a = C(v), \dots, c_b = C(v)$. Additionally, we add two labels $Max(v)$ and $Min(v)$. $a \leq Max(v) \leq b$ is the maximal index of a colored element of the segment. $a \leq Min(v) \leq b$ is the minimal index of a colored element of the segment. Initially, $Max(v) \leftarrow -1$, $Min(v) \leftarrow 2^h + 1$.

For a node v and the associated segment $[a, b]$, we use the following notation.

- LEFT(v) is the left border of the segment. LEFT$(v) = a$
- RIGHT(v) is the right border of the segment. RIGHT$(v) = b$
- LEFTCHILD(v) is the left child of v.
- RIGHTCHILD(v) is the right child of v.

Let CONSTRUCTST(a, b) be a procedure that returns the root of a segment tree for a segment $[a, b]$. The procedure is standard and has a property that described in Lemma 5. Let us present the description and the proof of the lemma in the arXiv version [25] for completeness.

Lemma 5. *Time complexity of* CONSTRUCTST$(1, d)$ *the segment tree constructing procedure is* $O(d)$.

Let us describe the processing of three types of operations.

Request. The operation is requesting c_x for some $1 \leq x \leq 2^h$. We start with the root node of the segment tree. Assume that we observe a node v. If $C(v) = 0$, then we go to the child that is associated with a segment $[a, b]$, where $a \leq x \leq b$. We continue this process until we meet v such that $C(v) \geq 1$ or v is a leaf. If $C(v) \geq 1$, then the result is $C(v)$. If $C(v) = 0$ and v is a leaf, then c_x is not assigned yet. Let a name of the procedure be COLORREQUEST$(x, root)$. It is a request for a color c_x from a segment tree with *root* node as the root. If the color is not assigned, then the procedure returns 0. The implementation of the procedure is presented in the arXiv version [25] and properties are presented in the following lemma.

Lemma 6. *The request color procedure* COLORREQUEST *is correct and has* $O(\log d)$ *time complexity.*

Proof. If the segment tree stores correct colors for segments, then the correctness of the algorithm follows from the description. The algorithm returns a color only if x belongs to a segment that has a single color. On each step, we change a node to a node on the next level. The tree is a full binary tree. Therefore, it has h levels. Hence, the time complexity is $O(h) = O(\log d)$ because $2^{h-1} \leq d \leq 2^h$. □

Update. Assume that we want to color a segment $[l, r]$ in a color c, where $1 \leq c \leq Z$, $1 \leq l \leq r \leq 2^h$. Let us describe two specific cases. The first one is the coloring of a prefix and the second one is the coloring of a suffix. Let us have a segment tree with the root node *root*. Let us consider the general case, where a segment $[q, t]$ is associated with the node *root*.

Firstly, assume that $[l, r]$ is a prefix of $[q, t]$, i.e. $q = l$ and $q \le r \le t$. Let us observe a node v and an associated segment $[a, b]$. If v is a leaf, then we assign $C(v) \leftarrow c$ and stop. Otherwise, we continue. We use a variable c' for an existing color. Initially $c' \leftarrow 0$. If on some step $C(v) \ge 1$ and $c' = 0$, then we assign $c' \leftarrow C(v)$. If $c' \ge 1$ or $C(v) = 0$, then we do not change c' because we already have a color for the segment from an ancestor.

Let u be the left child of v, and let w be the right child of v. We update $Max(v) \leftarrow \max(Max(v), r)$, $Min(v) \leftarrow \textsc{Left}(v)$ because $[l, r]$ is a prefix. Then, we do the following action.

- If $r \in [a, (a+b)/2]$, then we go to the left child u. Additionally, if $c' \ge 1$, then we color $C(w) \leftarrow c'$ because a segment of w has no intersection with $[l, r]$ and keeps its color c'.
- If $r \in [(a+b)/2+1, b]$, then we go to the right child w. Additionally, we color $C(u) \leftarrow c$ and update $Min(u) \leftarrow \textsc{Left}(u)$, $Max(u) \leftarrow \textsc{Right}(u)$ because $[a, (a+b)/2]$ of u is a subsegment of $[l, r]$. Additionally, we update $l \leftarrow (a + b)/2 + 1$ because the segment $[a, (a + b)/2]$ is colored and the segment $[(a + b)/2 + 1, r]$ is left. The new segment is a prefix of the segment tree with the root node w.

Let us call the procedure ColorUpdatePrefix and present it in Appendix A.

Secondly, assume that $[l, r]$ is a suffix of $[q, t]$, i.e. $t = r$ and $q \le l \le t$. This function is similar to the previous one. The difference is the following. Let u be the left child of v, and let w be the right child of v. We update $Min(v) \leftarrow \min(Min(v), l)$, $Max(v) \leftarrow \textsc{Right}(v)$ because $[l, r]$ is a suffix. Then, we do the following action.

- If $l \in [(a+b)/2+1, b]$, then we go to the right child w. Additionally, if $c' \ge 1$, then we color $C(u) \leftarrow c'$ because a segment of u has no intersection with $[l, r]$ and we keep its color c'.
- If $l \in [a, (a + b)/2]$, then we go to the left child u. Additionally, we color $C(w) \leftarrow c$ and update $Min(w) \leftarrow \textsc{Left}(w)$, $Max(w) \leftarrow \textsc{Right}(w)$ because $[(a + b)/2 + 1, b]$ of w is a subsegment of $[l, r]$. Additionally, we update $r \leftarrow (a + b)/2$ because the segment $[(a + b)/2 + 1, b]$ is colored and the segment $[l, (a + b)/2]$ is left. The new segment is a suffix of the segment tree with the root node u.

Let us call this procedure ColorUpdateSuffix and present it in Appendix A.

Finally, let us consider a general case for $[l, r]$, i.e. $q \le l \le r \le t$. Assume that we observe a node v and an associated segment $[a, b]$. If v is a leaf, then we assign $C(v) \leftarrow c$ and stop. Otherwise, we continue. We use a variable c' for an existing color. Initially $c' \leftarrow 0$. If on some step $C(v) \ge 1$ and $c' = 0$, then we assign $c' \leftarrow C(v)$. If $c' \ge 1$ or $C(v) = 0$, then we do not change c'. We update $Min(v) \leftarrow \min(Min(v), l)$, $Max(v) \leftarrow \max(Max(v), r)$.

- If $(a+b)/2+1 \le l \le r \le b$, then we go to the right child w. Additionally, if $c' \ge 1$, then we color $C(u) \leftarrow c'$ because a segment of u has no intersection with $[l,r]$ and keeps its color c'.
- If $a \le l \le r \le (a+b)/2$, then we go to the left child u. Additionally, if $c' \ge 1$, then we color $C(w) \leftarrow c'$ because a segment of w has no intersection with $[l,r]$ and we keep its color c'.
- If $a \le l \le (a+b)/2 \le r \le b$, then we split our segment to $[l,(a+b)/2]$ and $[(a+b)/2+1,r]$. The segment $[l,(a+b)/2]$ is a suffix of the segment tree with the root u. For coloring it, we invoke ColorUpdateSuffix$(l,(a+b)/2,c,c',u)$. The segment $[(a+b)/2+1,r]$ is a prefix of the segment tree with the root w. For coloring it, we invoke ColorUpdatePrefix$((a+b)/2+1,r,c,c',w)$.

Let us call the procedure ColorUpdate and present it in Appendix A.

Lemma 7. *The update procedure* ColorUpdate *is correct and has* $O(\log d)$ *time complexity.*

Proof. If the segment tree stores correct colors for segments, then the correctness of the algorithm follows from the description. The algorithm colors a required segment and keeps the color of the rest part. Procedures ColorUpdatePrefix and ColorUpdateSuffix on each step change a node to a node on the next level. The tree is a full binary tree. Therefore, the tree has h levels. Hence, the time complexity of these two algorithms is $O(h)=O(\log d)$ because $2^{h-1} \le d \le 2^h$. The procedure ColorUpdate on each step changes a node to a node on the next level, then, stops and invokes the procedure ColorUpdatePrefix and the procedure ColorUpdateSuffix. Its time complexity is $O(h)=O(\log d)$ also. We can say that procedures run consistently. Therefore, the total time complexity is $O(\log d)$. □

Request the Closest Colored Element. Assume that we want to get the minimal index of a colored element from a segment $[l,r]$, where $1 \le l \le r \le 2^h$. Let $[q,t]$ be a segment of the root of the segment tree. Let us describe two specific cases that are requesting from a prefix of $[q,t]$ and requesting from a suffix of $[q,t]$.

Firstly, assume that $[l,r]$ is a prefix of $[q,t]$, i.e. $q=l$ and $q \le r \le t$. Assume that we observe a node v and an associated segment $[a,b]$. Let u be the left child of v, and let w be the right child of v. We do the following action.

- If $r \le (a+b)/2$, then we go to the left child u.
- If $r > (a+b)/2$ and $Min(u)$ is assigned (i.e. there are colored elements in the left child u), then the result is $Min(u)$ and we stop the process.
- If $r > (a+b)/2$ and $Min(u)$ is not assigned (i.e. there is no colored element in the left child u), then we go to the right child w.

If there is no colored elements in v, then the algorithm returns $NULL$. We call the procedure GetClosestColorRightPrefix$(l,r,root)$ and present it in Appendix A.

Secondly, assume that $[l, r]$ is a suffix of $[q, t]$, i.e. $t = r$ and $q \leq l \leq t$. Assume that we observe a node v and an associated segment $[a, b]$. Let u be the left child of v, and let w be the right child of v. We do the following action.

- If $l \geq (a+b)/2+1$, then we go to the right child w.
- If $l \leq (a+b)/2$ and $Min(u)$ is assigned (i.e. there are colored elements in the left child u), then we go to the left child u.
- If $l \leq (a+b)/2$ and $Min(u)$ is not assigned (i.e. there is no colored element in the left child u), then the result is $Min(w)$ and we stop the process.

If there is no colored elements in v, then the algorithm returns $NULL$. We call the procedure GETCLOSESTCOLORRIGHTSUFFIX($l, r, root$) and present it in Appendix A.

Finally, let us consider the general case, i.e. $q \leq l \leq r \leq t$. Assume that we observe a node v and an associated segment $[a, b]$. Let u be the left child of v, and let w be the right child of v. We do the following action.

- If $(a+b)/2+1 \leq l \leq r \leq b$, then we go to the right child w.
- If $a \leq l \leq r \leq (a+b)/2$, then we go to the left child u.
- If $a \leq l \leq (a+b)/2 \leq r \leq b$, then we split our segment to $[l, (a+b)/2]$ and $[(a+b)/2+1, r]$. The segment $[l, (a+b)/2]$ is a suffix of the segment tree with the root u. We invoke GETCLOSESTCOLORRIGHTSUFFIX($l, (a+b)/2, u$). If the result is not $NULL$, then there is a colored element in the left child, and we return the result of the procedure. If the result is $NULL$, then there is no colored element in the left children, and only the right children can have the minimal colored element. So, we invoke GETCLOSESTCOLORRIGHTPREFIX($(a+b)/2+1, r, u$) and we return the result of the procedure.

If there are no colored elements in v, then the algorithm returns $NULL$.

We call this function GETCLOSESTCOLORRIGHT($l, r, root$). We can define the function that returns the maximal index of a colored element symmetrically. We call it GETCLOSESTCOLORLEFT($l, r, root$).

Lemma 8. *The request the closest colored element procedures* GETCLOSEST COLORLEFT *and* GETCLOSESTCOLORRIGHT *are correct and have* $O(\log d)$ *time complexity.*

Proof. The proof is similar to the proof of Lemma 7. □

5 Conclusion

We discuss the time-efficient implementation of online algorithms for the k-server problem on trees. Here we present an algorithm with $O(n)$ time complexity for preprocessing and $O(k(\log n)^2)$ time complexity for processing a query. It process a query faster than existing implementations of [11] (the naive implementation and [17]) in a case of $\omega\left((\log n)^2\right) = k = o\left(n/(\log n)^2\right)$. This case is reasonable in practice. An open problem is an analysis of time complexity for the randomized algorithm [5,6].

A Algorithms for Coloration Problem on a Segment Tree

Algorithm 5. COLORUPDATEPREFIX$(l, r, c, c', root)$. An operation of update color of a prefix segment $[l, r]$ by a color c. The operation is for a segment tree with the *root* node as a root. c' is a color for rest part of the segment of *root*. If c' is not assigned, then $c' = 0$

```
v ← root
while v is not a leaf do
    if c' = 0 and C(v) ≥ 1 then
        c' ← C(v)
    end if
    Max(v) ← max(Max(v), r), Min(v) ← LEFT(v)
    u ← LEFTCHILD(v), w ← RIGHTCHILD(v)
    if r ≤ RIGHT(u) then
        if c' ≥ 1 then
            C(w) ← c'
        end if
        v ← u
    else
        C(u) ← c, Min(u) ← LEFT(u), Max(u) ← RIGHT(u), v ← w
    end if
end while
C(v) ← c, Min(v) ← LEFT(v), Max(v) ← RIGHT(v)
```

Algorithm 6. COLORUPDATESUFFIX$(l, r, c, c', root)$. An operation of update color of a suffix segment $[l, r]$ by a color c. The operation is for a segment tree with *root* node as a root. c' is a color for rest part of the segment of *root*. If c' is not assigned, then $c' = 0$

```
v ← root
while v is not a leaf do
    if c' = 0 and C(v) ≥ 1 then
        c' ← C(v)
    end if
    Min(v) ← min(Min(v), l), Max(v) ← RIGHT(v)
    u ← LEFTCHILD(v), w ← RIGHTCHILD(v)
    if l ≥ LEFT(w) then
        if c' ≥ 1 then
            C(u) ← c'
        end if
        v ← w
    else
        C(w) ← c, Min(w) ← LEFT(w), Max(w) ← RIGHT(w), v ← u
    end if
end while
C(v) ← c, Min(v) ← LEFT(v), Max(v) ← RIGHT(v)
```

Algorithm 7. COLORUPDATE($l, r, c, root$). An operation of update color of a segment $[l, r]$ by a color c. The operation is for a segment tree with $root$ node as a root.

```
v ← root
c' ← 0
Split ← False
while v is not a leaf and Split = False do
    if c' = 0 and C(v) ≥ 1 then
        c' ← C(v)
    end if
    Min(v) ← min(Min(v), l), Max(v) ← max(Max(v), r)
    u ← LeftChild(v)
    w ← RightChild(v)
    if l ≥ Left(w) then
        if c' ≥ 1 then
            C(u) ← c'
        end if
        v ← w
    end if
    if r ≤ Right(u) then
        if c' ≥ 1 then
            C(w) ← c'
        end if
        v ← u
    end if
    if l ≤ Right(u) and r ≥ Left(w) then
        Split ← True
        ColorUpdateSuffix(l, Right(u), c, c', u)
        ColorUpdatePrfix(Left(w), r, c, c', w)
    end if
end while
if v is a leaf then
    C(v) ← c
end if
```

Algorithm 8. GETCLOSESTCOLORRIGHTPREFIX($l, r, root$). A request for the minimal index of a colored element of a prefix segment $[l, r]$. It returns $NULL$ if there is no such elements

```
v ← root, Result ← NULL
if Min(v) ≠ 2^h + 1 then
    Found ← False
    while v is not a leaf and Found = False do
        u ← LeftChild(v), w ← RightChild(v)
        if r ≤ Right(u) then
            v ← u
        end if
        if r ≥ Left(w) and Min(u) ≠ 2^h + 1 then
            Result ← Min(u), Found ← True
        end if
        if r ≥ Left(w) and Min(u) = 2^h + 1 then
            v ← w
        end if
    end while
    if Found = False and Min(v) ≠ 2^h + 1 then
        Result = Min(v)
    end if
end if
return Result
```

Algorithm 9. GETCLOSESTCOLORRIGHTSUFFIX($l, r, root$). A request for the minimal index of a colored element of a suffix segment $[l, r]$. It returns $NULL$ if there is no such elements

```
v ← root, Result ← NULL
if Min(v) ≠ 2^h + 1 then
    Found ← False
    while v is not a leaf and Found = False do
        u ← LeftChild(v), w ← RightChild(v)
        if l ≥ Left(w) then
            v ← w
        end if
        if l ≤ Right(u) and Min(u) ≠ 2^h + 1 then
            v ← u
        end if
        if l ≤ Right(u) and Min(u) = 2^h + 1 then
            Result ← Min(w), Found ← True
        end if
    end while
    if Found = False and Min(v) ≠ 2^h + 1 then
        Result = Min(v)
    end if
end if
return Result
```

References

1. Ablayev, F., Ablayev, M., Khadiev, K., Vasiliev, A.: Classical and quantum computations with restricted memory. In: Böckenhauer, H.-J., Komm, D., Unger, W. (eds.) Adventures Between Lower Bounds and Higher Altitudes. LNCS, vol. 11011, pp. 129–155. Springer, Cham (2018). https://doi.org/10.1007/978-3-319-98355-4_9
2. Ahmed, A.R., Rahman, M.S., Kobourov, S.: Online facility assignment. Theoret. Comput. Sci. **806**, 455–467 (2020)
3. Akagi, T., Nakano, S.: On r-gatherings on the line. In: Wang, J., Yap, C. (eds.) FAW 2015. LNCS, vol. 9130, pp. 25–32. Springer, Cham (2015). https://doi.org/10.1007/978-3-319-19647-3_3
4. Baliga, G.R., Shende, A.M.: On space bounded server algorithms. In: Proceedings of ICCI 1993: 5th International Conference on Computing and Information, pp. 77–81. IEEE (1993)
5. Bansal, N., Buchbinder, N., Madry, A., Naor, J.: A polylogarithmic-competitive algorithm for the k-server problem. In: 2011 IEEE 52nd Annual Symposium on Foundations of Computer Science, pp. 267–276. IEEE (2011)
6. Bansal, N., Buchbinder, N., Madry, A., Naor, J.: A polylogarithmic-competitive algorithm for the k-server problem. J. ACM (JACM) **62**(5), 1–49 (2015)
7. Becchetti, L., Koutsoupias, E.: Competitive analysis of aggregate max in windowed streaming. In: Albers, S., Marchetti-Spaccamela, A., Matias, Y., Nikoletseas, S., Thomas, W. (eds.) ICALP 2009. LNCS, vol. 5555, pp. 156–170. Springer, Heidelberg (2009). https://doi.org/10.1007/978-3-642-02927-1_15
8. Bender, M.A., Farach-Colton, M.: The LCA problem revisited. In: Gonnet, G.H., Viola, A. (eds.) LATIN 2000. LNCS, vol. 1776, pp. 88–94. Springer, Heidelberg (2000). https://doi.org/10.1007/10719839_9
9. Berkman, O., Vishkin, U.: Recursive star-tree parallel data structure. SIAM J. Comput. **22**(2), 221–242 (1993)

10. Boyar, J., Larsen, K.S., Maiti, A.: The frequent items problem in online streaming under various performance measures. Int. J. Found. Comput. Sci. **26**(4), 413–439 (2015)
11. Chrobak, M., Larmore, L.L.: An optimal on-line algorithm for k servers on trees. SIAM J. Comput. **20**(1), 144–148 (1991)
12. Cormen, T.H., Leiserson, C.E., Rivest, R.L., Stein, C.: Introduction to Algorithms. McGraw-Hill, New York (2001)
13. Flammini, M., Navarra, A., Nicosia, G.: Efficient offline algorithms for the bicriteria k-server problem and online applications. J. Discret. Algorithms **4**(3), 414–432 (2006)
14. Giannakopoulos, Y., Koutsoupias, E.: Competitive analysis of maintaining frequent items of a stream. Theoret. Comput. Sci. **562**, 23–32 (2015)
15. Harel, D., Tarjan, R.E.: Fast algorithms for finding nearest common ancestors. SIAM J. Comput. **13**(2), 338–355 (1984)
16. Kalyanasundaram, B., Pruhs, K.: Online weighted matching. J. Algorithms **14**(3), 478–488 (1993)
17. Kapralov, R., Khadiev, K., Mokut, J., Shen, Y., Yagafarov, M.: Fast classical and quantum algorithms for online k-server problem on trees. In: CEUR Workshop Proceedings, vol. 3072, pp. 287–301 (2022)
18. Karlin, A.R., Manasse, M.S., Rudolph, L., Sleator, D.D.: Competitive snoopy caching. In: 27th Annual Symposium on FOCS, 1986, pp. 244–254. IEEE (1986)
19. Khadiev, K.: Quantum request-answer game with buffer model for online algorithms. Application for the most frequent keyword problem. In: CEUR Workshop Proceedings, vol. 2850, pp. 16–27 (2021)
20. Khadiev, K., Khadieva, A.: Two-way quantum and classical automata with advice for online minimization problems. In: Sekerinski, E., et al. (eds.) FM 2019. LNCS, vol. 12233, pp. 428–442. Springer, Cham (2020). https://doi.org/10.1007/978-3-030-54997-8_27
21. Khadiev, K., Khadieva, A.: Quantum online streaming algorithms with logarithmic memory. Int. J. Theor. Phys. **60**(2), 608–616 (2019). https://doi.org/10.1007/s10773-019-04209-1
22. Khadiev, K., Khadieva, A., Mannapov, I.: Quantum online algorithms with respect to space and advice complexity. Lobachevskii J. Math. **39**(9), 1210–1220 (2018)
23. Khadiev, K., Khadieva, A.: Quantum and classical log-bounded automata for the online disjointness problem. Mathematics **10**(1), 143 (2022). https://doi.org/10.3390/math10010143
24. Khadiev, K., et al.: Two-way and one-way quantum and classical automata with advice for online minimization problems. Theoret. Comput. Sci. (2022). https://doi.org/10.1016/j.tcs.2022.02.026
25. Khadiev, K., Yagafarov, M.: A fast algorithm for online k-servers problem on trees. arXiv preprint arXiv:2006.00605 (2020)
26. Khadiev, K., Lin, D.: Quantum online algorithms for a model of the request-answer game with a buffer. Uchenye Zapiski Kazanskogo Universiteta. Seriya Fiziko-Matematicheskie Nauki **162**(3), 367–382 (2020)
27. Komm, D.: An Introduction to Online Computation: Determinism, Randomization, Advice. Springer, Cham (2016). https://doi.org/10.1007/978-3-319-42749-2
28. Laaksonen, A.: Guide to Competitive Programming. Springer, Cham (2020). https://doi.org/10.1007/978-3-319-72547-5

29. Rudec, T., Baumgartner, A., Manger, R.: A fast work function algorithm for solving the k-server problem. CEJOR **21**(1), 187–205 (2013)
30. Sleator, D.D., Tarjan, R.E.: Amortized efficiency of list update and paging rules. Commun. ACM **28**(2), 202–208 (1985)
31. Sleator, D.D., Tarjan, R.E.: A data structure for dynamic trees. J. Comput. Syst. Sci. **26**(3), 362–391 (1983)

Finite Ambiguity and Finite Sequentiality in Weighted Automata over Fields

Peter Kostolányi([✉])

Department of Computer Science, Comenius University in Bratislava, Mlynská dolina, 842 48 Bratislava, Slovakia
kostolanyi@fmph.uniba.sk

Abstract. Infinite hierarchies of rational series realised by finitely ambiguous and finitely sequential weighted automata over fields, classifying them according to the ambiguity or sequentiality degree of realising automata, are examined. It is shown that both these hierarchies are strict if and only if the field under consideration is not locally finite; in that case, the hierarchies are strict already for series over a unary alphabet. Relations between finitely ambiguous and finitely sequential unary weighted automata are explored. It is also readily observed that polynomially ambiguous weighted automata over a field of characteristic zero are more powerful than finitely ambiguous weighted automata over the same field, again already over a unary alphabet. On the other hand, it is proved that unary alphabets are insufficient to separate the series realised by polynomially and finitely ambiguous weighted automata over algebraically closed fields of positive characteristic.

Keywords: Weighted automaton · Rational series · Degree of ambiguity · Degree of sequentiality · Hierarchy

1 Introduction

Weighted automata of *restricted ambiguity* have recently attracted significant research attention. This was often motivated by the idea that certain problems undecidable – or not known to be decidable – for general weighted automata might admit reasonable decision algorithms when their scope is restricted to, e.g., finitely or polynomially ambiguous automata. Such questions have been studied for tropical automata in connection to their determinisation [14–16], as well as in the setting of probabilistic automata [4,12]. Unary weighted automata of restricted ambiguity were also studied over the field of rational numbers [3], with motivation coming from the research dealing with decision problems for linear recurrences such as the Skolem problem. Moreover, classes of weighted automata with restricted ambiguity arise in connection with the weighted first-order logic of M. Droste and P. Gastin [8].

The work was supported by the grant VEGA 1/0601/20.

A. S. Kulikov and S. Raskhodnikova (Eds.): CSR 2022, LNCS 13296, pp. 209–223, 2022.
https://doi.org/10.1007/978-3-031-09574-0_13

Various observations about the expressive power of weighted automata with restricted ambiguity have recently crystallised into its more systematic study. The so-called *ambiguity hierarchy*, composed by the classes of series realised by the unambiguous, finitely ambiguous, polynomially ambiguous, and unrestricted weighted automata, is observed to be strict over tropical semirings by A. Chattopadhyay et al. [6]. The same observation over the rational numbers is due to C. Barloy et al. [3] and is established already over unary alphabets; some of their results also follow, to some extent, from the findings of [8,21]. Moreover, it is noted in [3] that the infinite hierarchy of series realised by k-ambiguous unary weighted automata over the rationals, for $k = 0, 1, 2, \ldots$, is strict.

Another restriction studied in the context of weighted finite automata is that of *finite sequentiality* [2] or *multisequentiality* [7]. Both terms have been used interchangeably, basically to describe deterministic weighted automata with possibly more than one initial state. A normal form of such automata, given by finite unions of deterministic automata, has been used as their definition as well. Every finitely sequential automaton is finitely ambiguous, but a finitely ambiguous automaton might not even admit a finitely sequential equivalent [2].

There has also been research on restricted ambiguity and finite sequentiality in weighted tree automata [20,23–26].

The power of restricted ambiguity in weighted automata has thus mainly been examined over tropical semirings. On the contrary, its study for weighted automata over fields has so far been limited to the research dealing with the particular case of automata over the rationals. This is relatively surprising, as weighted automata over fields are particularly well explored and known for richness of their theory and abundance of appealing properties [5,27]. The study of such automata has a long history going back to M.-P. Schützenberger [29]. To the author's knowledge, finite sequentiality in weighted automata has been studied neither over fields in general, nor over any specific field such as the rationals.

The aim of this article is to explore some of the basic relations between classes of series realised by weighted automata with restricted ambiguity over general fields, in hope of later leading to a full understanding of ambiguity hierarchies over fields. In this respect, the article follows the same direction as the manuscript [17] examining relations between *polynomially ambiguous* and unrestricted weighted automata over fields. In particular, it is shown in [17] that unrestricted weighted automata over fields of characteristic zero that are not algebraically closed are more powerful than polynomially ambiguous weighted automata over the same field – already over unary alphabets. On the contrary, *unary* weighted automata over algebraically closed fields always admit polynomially ambiguous equivalents, regardless of the field's characteristic.

The questions asked in this article are in a sense complementary to those considered in [17]. We mostly focus on *finitely ambiguous* weighted automata over fields – we study the hierarchy of series realised by k*-ambiguous* automata for $k = 0, 1, 2, \ldots$, as well as the relations between finitely ambiguous and polynomially ambiguous automata. In addition, we initiate the study of *finitely sequential* weighted automata over fields by examining the hierarchy of series realised by

k-sequential automata for $k = 0, 1, 2, \ldots$, and observe some connections between finitely ambiguous and finitely sequential *unary* weighted automata.

In particular, we first observe that finitely ambiguous *unary* weighted automata over *commutative semirings* always admit finitely sequential equivalents, while the sequentiality degree of an equivalent automaton is linked to a structural measure of the original finitely ambiguous automaton. We next prove that the hierarchies of series realised by the k-ambiguous and k-sequential weighted automata over a *field* $\mathbb{F}$ for $k = 0, 1, 2, \ldots$ are strict whenever $\mathbb{F}$ is not locally finite; this also trivially is a necessary condition. Unary alphabets are sufficient to establish these results. Finally, we consider the relations between finitely and polynomially ambiguous weighted automata over fields. While it is essentially trivial to observe that already the unary polynomially ambiguous weighted automata over fields of characteristic zero are strictly more powerful than their finitely ambiguous counterparts, the case of a positive characteristic is far more interesting. We show that polynomially ambiguous *unary* weighted automata over algebraically closed fields of characteristic $p > 0$ always admit finitely ambiguous equivalents. Unary alphabets are thus insufficient to separate the series realised by finitely and polynomially ambiguous automata over such fields.

2 Preliminaries

Fields are understood to be commutative, and alphabets finite and nonempty. We denote by $\mathbb{N}$ the set of all *nonnegative* integers and write $[n] = \{1, \ldots, n\}$ for each $n \in \mathbb{N}$. The set of all $m \times n$ matrices over a set S is denoted by $S^{m \times n}$, and the identity $n \times n$ matrix over any *semiring* by $\mathbf{I}_n$. A field (a semiring) is *locally finite* if its finitely generated subfields (subsemirings) are all finite. A field is locally finite if and only if it is locally finite as a semiring.

Consult, e.g., [5,9,10,27,28] for a reference on weighted automata and formal power series. We now briefly recall the most important concepts needed.

A (noncommutative) *formal power series* over a semiring S and alphabet Σ is a mapping $r \colon \Sigma^* \to S$ interpreted as follows: the value of r upon $w \in \Sigma^*$ is denoted by (r, w) and called the *coefficient* of w in r; we then write

$$r = \sum_{w \in \Sigma^*} (r, w)\, w.$$

The set of all formal power series over S and Σ is denoted by $S\langle\langle \Sigma^* \rangle\rangle$.

A *weighted (finite) automaton* over a semiring S and over an alphabet Σ is a quadruple $\mathcal{A} = (Q, \sigma, \iota, \tau)$ with Q being a finite set of states, $\sigma \colon Q \times \Sigma \times Q \to S$ a transition weighting function, $\iota \colon Q \to S$ an initial weighting function, and $\tau \colon Q \to S$ a terminal weighting function.

A *transition* in the automaton $\mathcal{A}$ is a triple $(p, c, q) \in Q \times \Sigma \times Q$ such that $\sigma(p, c, q) \neq 0$. A *run* of $\mathcal{A}$ is a word $\gamma = q_0 c_1 q_1 c_2 q_2 \ldots q_{t-1} c_t q_t \in (Q\Sigma)^* Q$ with $q_0, \ldots, q_t \in Q$ and $c_1, \ldots, c_t \in \Sigma$ such that (q_{k-1}, c_k, q_k) is a transition for $k = 1, \ldots, t$. We also say that γ is a *run on the word* $c_1 \ldots c_t$ *from* q_0 *to* q_t.

We say that γ is *successful* if $\iota(q_0) \neq 0$ and $\tau(q_t) \neq 0$. The *pure value* of γ is the element $\sigma(\gamma) = \sigma(q_0, c_1, q_1)\sigma(q_1, c_2, q_2) \ldots \sigma(q_{t-1}, c_t, q_t)$, and the *complete value* of γ is given by $\overline{\sigma}(\gamma) = \iota(q_0)\sigma(\gamma)\tau(q_t)$. The *length* of γ is given by $|\gamma| = t$. The set of all runs of $\mathcal{A}$ on w is denoted by $\mathcal{R}(\mathcal{A}, w)$ and the set of all successful runs of $\mathcal{A}$ on w by $\mathcal{R}_s(\mathcal{A}, w)$. We then also write

$$\mathcal{R}(\mathcal{A}) = \bigcup_{w \in \Sigma^*} \mathcal{R}(\mathcal{A}, w) \qquad \text{and} \qquad \mathcal{R}_s(\mathcal{A}) = \bigcup_{w \in \Sigma^*} \mathcal{R}_s(\mathcal{A}, w).$$

The *behaviour* of a weighted automaton $\mathcal{A} = (Q, \sigma, \iota, \tau)$ over S and Σ is a formal power series $\|\mathcal{A}\| \in S\langle\langle \Sigma^* \rangle\rangle$ given by

$$(\|\mathcal{A}\|, w) = \sum_{\gamma \in \mathcal{R}_s(\mathcal{A}, w)} \overline{\sigma}(\gamma) = \sum_{\gamma \in \mathcal{R}(\mathcal{A}, w)} \overline{\sigma}(\gamma)$$

for all $w \in \Sigma^*$, both sums being obviously finite. We also say that the series $\|\mathcal{A}\|$ is *realised* by $\mathcal{A}$. A series $r \in S\langle\langle \Sigma^* \rangle\rangle$ is *rational* over S if it is realised by a weighted finite automaton over S and Σ.

A weighted automaton $\mathcal{A}$ over S and Σ is said to be *k-sequential* for $k \in \mathbb{N}$ if there are at most k distinct states $q \in Q$ satisfying $\iota(q) \neq 0$, and if $\sigma(p, c, q) \neq 0$ with $\sigma(p, c, q') \neq 0$ imply $q = q'$ for all $p, q, q' \in Q$ and $c \in \Sigma$. In particular, 1-sequential automata are typically termed *deterministic* or *sequential* [19].[1] The automaton $\mathcal{A}$ is *finitely sequential* [2] if it is k-sequential for some $k \in \mathbb{N}$.[2]

The *ambiguity degree* of $\mathcal{A}$ is given by a function $\mathrm{amb}_{\mathcal{A}} \colon \Sigma^* \to \mathbb{N}$ counting successful runs of $\mathcal{A}$ on words over Σ; that is, $\mathrm{amb}_{\mathcal{A}}(w) = |\mathcal{R}_s(\mathcal{A}, w)|$ for all $w \in \Sigma^*$. The automaton $\mathcal{A}$ is said to be *k-ambiguous* for $k \in \mathbb{N}$ if $\mathrm{amb}_{\mathcal{A}}(w) \leq k$ for all $w \in \Sigma^*$, while 1-ambiguous automata are called *unambiguous*. An automaton $\mathcal{A}$ is *finitely ambiguous* if it is k-ambiguous for some $k \in \mathbb{N}$ and *polynomially ambiguous* if there exists a polynomial function $p \colon \mathbb{N} \to \mathbb{N}$ such that $\mathrm{amb}_{\mathcal{A}}(w) \leq p(|w|)$ for all $w \in \Sigma^*$.

A weighted automaton $\mathcal{A} = (Q, \sigma, \iota, \tau)$ over S and Σ is *accessible* if for each $q \in Q$, there exists a run of $\mathcal{A}$ from some p with $\iota(p) \neq 0$ to q; *coaccessible* if for each $p \in Q$, there exists a run of $\mathcal{A}$ from p to some q with $\tau(q) \neq 0$; and *trim* if it is both accessible and coaccessible.

In what follows, we often without loss of generality confine ourselves to automata with state sets $[n]$ for $n \in \mathbb{N}$ – we then write $\mathcal{A} = (n, \sigma, \iota, \tau)$ instead of $\mathcal{A} = ([n], \sigma, \iota, \tau)$. Moreover, we apply the standard graph-theoretic terminology to weighted automata. This refers to a directed multigraph whose vertices are states of the automaton, while for each pair of states p, q, the transitions of the form (p, c, q) correspond bijectively to directed edges from p to q.

Weighted automata over a semiring S and alphabet Σ can also be viewed as *linear S-representations* over Σ, *i.e.*, quadruples $\mathcal{P} = (n, \mathbf{i}, \mu, \mathbf{f})$, where $n \in \mathbb{N}$,

[1] Some authors also call such automata *subsequential*, while they reserve the term *sequential* for a more restricted class of automata. See S. Lombardy and J. Sakarovitch [19] for more information.

[2] Note that C. Allauzen and M. Mohri [1] use the term *finitely subsequential transducer* in a completely different sense.

$\mathbf{i} \in S^{1\times n}$ is a vector of initial weights, $\mu\colon (\Sigma^*, \cdot, \varepsilon) \to (S^{n\times n}, \cdot, \mathbf{I}_n)$ is a monoid homomorphism, and $\mathbf{f} \in S^{n\times 1}$ is a vector of terminal weights. The *series* $\|\mathcal{P}\|$ *realised by* $\mathcal{P}$ is given by $(\|\mathcal{P}\|, w) = \mathbf{i}\mu(w)\mathbf{f}$ for all $w \in \Sigma^*$. A series $r \in S\langle\langle \Sigma^* \rangle\rangle$ is *recognisable* over S if it is realised by a linear S-representation.

The classes of recognisable and rational series *over words* coincide by a well-known classical result [27]. In fact, every weighted automaton $\mathcal{A} = (n, \sigma, \iota, \tau)$ over S and Σ corresponds to a linear S-representation $\mathcal{P}_\mathcal{A} = (n, \mathbf{i}, \mu, \mathbf{f})$, where $\mathbf{i} = (\iota(1), \ldots, \iota(n))$, the matrix $\mu(c) = (c_{i,j})_{n\times n}$ is given by $c_{i,j} = \sigma(i, c, j)$ for every $c \in \Sigma$ and $i, j = 1, \ldots, n$, and $\mathbf{f} = (\tau(1), \ldots, \tau(n))^T$. Clearly $\|\mathcal{P}_\mathcal{A}\| = \|\mathcal{A}\|$.

Consider in addition a mapping $\nu\colon S \to \mathbb{N}$ given for all $a \in S$ by

$$\nu(a) = \begin{cases} 1 & \text{if } a \neq 0, \\ 0 & \text{if } a = 0. \end{cases} \tag{1}$$

Applying this mapping componentwise to vectors and matrices, it is clear that $\mathrm{amb}_\mathcal{A}(c_1 \ldots c_t) = \nu(\mathbf{i})\nu(\mu(c_1)) \ldots \nu(\mu(c_t))\nu(\mathbf{f})$ for all $t \in \mathbb{N}$ and $c_1, \ldots, c_t \in \Sigma$.

We mostly work with linear representations over *unary alphabets* in what follows. We usually write a linear representation $\mathcal{P} = (n, \mathbf{i}, \mu, \mathbf{f})$ over $\Sigma = \{c\}$ as $\mathcal{P} = (n, \mathbf{i}, A, \mathbf{f})$, where $A = \mu(c)$ is the only matrix needed to specify the homomorphism μ. This means that given a weighted automaton $\mathcal{A}$ over a semiring S and unary alphabet $\Sigma = \{c\}$ with $\mathcal{P}_\mathcal{A} = (n, \mathbf{i}, A, \mathbf{f})$,

$$(\|\mathcal{A}\|, c^t) = \mathbf{i}A^t\mathbf{f}$$

holds for all $t \in \mathbb{N}$. The automaton $\mathcal{A}$ can thus also be interpreted as an initial value problem for the system of difference equations (*i.e.*, recurrences)

$$\mathbf{x}_{t+1} = A\mathbf{x}_t \qquad \text{for all } t \in \mathbb{N},$$

the initial conditions being given by $\mathbf{x}_0 = \mathbf{f}$. When $S = \mathbb{F}$ is a *field*, the theory of difference equations [11] allows us to express the components of $\mathbf{x}_t$, and thus also $(\|\mathcal{A}\|, c^t)$, in closed form over the *algebraic closure* $\overline{\mathbb{F}}$ of $\mathbb{F}$. Indeed, by similarity of A to a matrix over $\overline{\mathbb{F}}$ in the Jordan canonical form, it follows that for all $t \in \mathbb{N}$,

$$(\|\mathcal{A}\|, c^t) = \sum_{\lambda\in\sigma} \sum_{j=0}^{\alpha(\lambda)-1} a_{\lambda,j} \binom{t}{j} \lambda^{t-j}, \tag{2}$$

where σ denotes the spectrum of A over $\overline{\mathbb{F}}$, the algebraic multiplicity of each eigenvalue λ of A is denoted by $\alpha(\lambda)$, and $a_{\lambda,j} \in \overline{\mathbb{F}}$ are constants for $\lambda \in \sigma$ and $j = 0, \ldots, \alpha(\lambda) - 1$. Recall that the spectrum σ contains precisely the roots over $\overline{\mathbb{F}}$ of the characteristic polynomial $\mathrm{ch}_A(x) = \det(x\mathbf{I}_n - A)$ of A, and that the algebraic multiplicity of $\lambda \in \sigma$ is its multiplicity as a root of $\mathrm{ch}_A(x)$.

The constants $a_{\lambda,j}$ of (2) are always *uniquely* determined as a solution to a linear system of equations given by (2) for $t = 0, \ldots, n-1$, in which they are the only unknowns. In particular, *every* choice of initial values on the left-hand sides uniquely determines the constants $a_{\lambda,j}$ and conversely, every choice of the constants $a_{\lambda,j}$ gives different initial values [11]. This observation can be established, e.g., as a consequence of the fact that the matrix of the above-mentioned linear system is the so-called Casorati matrix [11] of the functions $\binom{t}{j}\lambda^{t-j}$ for $\lambda \in \sigma$ and $j = 0, \ldots, \alpha(\lambda) - 1$. This is a generalised Vandermonde matrix [11,13], so it is necessarily invertible. The linear system thus always has a unique solution. Moreover, any finite set of pairwise distinct functions of the form $\binom{t}{j}\lambda^{t-j}$ with $\lambda \in \overline{\mathbb{F}}$ and $j \in \mathbb{N}$ is linearly independent.

Similarly, consider a weighted automaton $\mathcal{A}$ over any semiring S and unary alphabet $\Sigma = \{c\}$, with $\mathcal{P}_{\mathcal{A}} = (n, \mathbf{i}, A, \mathbf{f})$. Let $\nu \colon S \to \mathbb{N}$ be given by (1). Then

$$\mathrm{amb}_{\mathcal{A}}(c^t) = \nu(\mathbf{i})\nu(A)^t\nu(\mathbf{f})$$

for all $t \in \mathbb{N}$, so that $\mathrm{amb}_{\mathcal{A}}(c^t)$ admits a closed form analogous to (2) over $\mathbb{C}$:

$$\mathrm{amb}_{\mathcal{A}}(c^t) = \sum_{\lambda \in \sigma'} \sum_{j=0}^{\alpha'(\lambda)-1} a'_{\lambda,j} \binom{t}{j} \lambda^{t-j}, \tag{3}$$

where σ' denotes the spectrum of $\nu(A)$, the algebraic multiplicity of an eigenvalue λ of $\nu(A)$ is denoted by $\alpha'(\lambda)$, and $a'_{\lambda,j} \in \mathbb{C}$ for $\lambda \in \sigma'$ and $j = 0, \ldots, \alpha'(\lambda) - 1$. We call $\nu(A)$ the *enumeration matrix* of $\mathcal{A}$ in what follows.

3 Finite Ambiguity and Sequentiality in Unary Automata

We now make some preliminary remarks on finitely ambiguous and finitely sequential unary weighted automata. First, let us note that the ambiguity degree of a weighted automaton does not at all depend on its weights. This means that weights can be forgotten and the known criteria [30] for nondeterministic finite automata without weights can be applied in order to determine whether a given weighted automaton is, say, finitely or polynomially ambiguous.

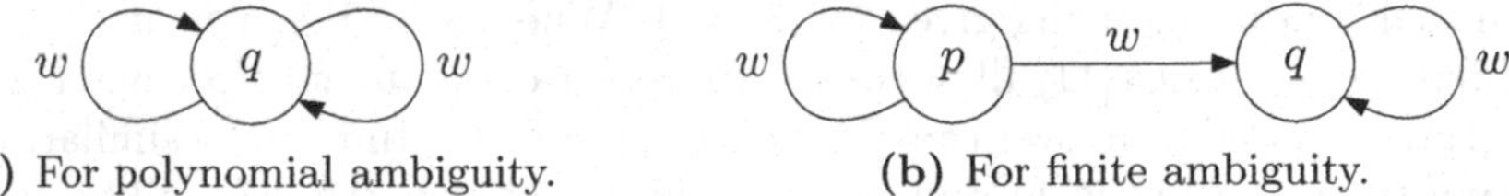

(a) For polynomial ambiguity. **(b)** For finite ambiguity.

Fig. 1. The "forbidden configurations" for polynomially and finitely ambiguous trim finite automata, as identified by A. Weber and H. Seidl [30]. Distinct arrows represent distinct *runs*, as opposed to transitions.

Let us recall these criteria, as described by A. Weber and H. Seidl [30]. A trim finite automaton $\mathcal{A}$ with state set Q over an alphabet Σ is polynomially ambiguous if and only if there does not exist a state q with at least two distinct runs from q to q upon some word $w \in \Sigma^*$. Moreover, $\mathcal{A}$ is finitely ambiguous if and only if there is no pair of distinct states p, q such that for some $w \in \Sigma^*$, there are runs upon w from p to p, from p to q, as well as from q to q. These "forbidden configurations" for polynomially and finitely ambiguous automata are schematically depicted in Fig. 1.

These criteria admit a particularly simple form for unary automata, which we now make explicit.

Theorem 1. *Let S be a semiring and $\mathcal{A}$ a trim unary weighted automaton over S and $\Sigma = \{c\}$. The automaton $\mathcal{A}$ is:*

(i) Polynomially ambiguous *if and only if its strongly connected components are all either single vertices, or directed cycles.*
(ii) Finitely ambiguous *if and only if, in addition to (i), there is no run of $\mathcal{A}$ passing through two distinct directed cycles.*

The characterisations of Theorem 1 can also be obtained, for a unary weighted automaton $\mathcal{A}$ with $\mathcal{P}_{\mathcal{A}} = (n, \mathbf{i}, A, \mathbf{f})$, with a little help of the Perron-Frobenius theory [22] applied to the enumeration matrix $\nu(A)$. Indeed, the condition (i) is equivalent to all eigenvalues of $\nu(A)$ being of absolute value 0 or 1. If this is the case, (3) reduces to a polynomial function and $\mathcal{A}$ is polynomially ambiguous. Otherwise, the Perron-Frobenius theory gives us existence of an eigenvalue $\lambda > 1$ with at least one nonzero coefficient $a'_{\lambda,j}$ in (3) – the automaton $\mathcal{A}$ is not polynomially ambiguous. Given (i), the equivalence of (ii) with finite ambiguity can be easily established by noting that a possibility of passing through two different cycles in a single run is equivalent to unboundedness of $\mathrm{amb}_{\mathcal{A}}$.

Given these characterisations of polynomially and finitely ambiguous trim unary weighted automata, the number of strongly connected components taking the form of cycles becomes a natural measure of their structural complexity.

Definition 2. *Let S be a semiring, $\mathcal{A}$ a trim polynomially ambiguous unary weighted automaton over S and $\Sigma = \{c\}$, and $k \in \mathbb{N}$. We say that $\mathcal{A}$ is a k-*cycle automaton *if it contains at most k directed cycles.*

It is easy to see that $\mathcal{A}$ as above is a k-cycle automaton if and only if the algebraic multiplicity of 1 as an eigenvalue of its enumeration matrix is at most k. We mostly apply this measure to *finitely ambiguous* automata in what follows; nevertheless, note that this measure is incomparable with the ambiguity degree in general.

We now note that every trim finitely ambiguous k-cycle automaton $\mathcal{A}$ over a unary alphabet decomposes, for $k \geq 1$, into k finitely ambiguous 1-cycle automata. The construction is intuitively obvious: for each of the cycles, we make use of the criterion (ii) of Theorem 1, and alter the original automaton $\mathcal{A}$ in order to obtain a 1-cycle automaton, whose successful runs are exactly the successful runs of $\mathcal{A}$ visiting at least one state on the cycle in question. Then we only need to take care of the runs of $\mathcal{A}$ that do not visit any cycle – but these can clearly be realised by a 0-cycle automaton, which may be "adjoined" to any of the k automata without spoiling their 1-cycle property.

Proposition 3. *Let S be a semiring, $k \in \mathbb{N} \setminus \{0\}$, and $\mathcal{A}$ a trim finitely ambiguous k-cycle automaton over S and $\Sigma = \{c\}$. Then there are trim 1-cycle automata $\mathcal{A}_1, \ldots, \mathcal{A}_k$ over S and Σ such that $\mathcal{R}_s(\mathcal{A}) = \mathcal{R}_s(\mathcal{A}_1) \uplus \ldots \uplus \mathcal{R}_s(\mathcal{A}_k)$, the values of successful runs of $\mathcal{A}_1, \ldots, \mathcal{A}_k$ being the same as in the original automaton $\mathcal{A}$. This in particular implies that for all $t \in \mathbb{N}$,*

$$(\|\mathcal{A}\|, c^t) = \sum_{j=1}^{k} (\|\mathcal{A}_j\|, c^t)$$

and

$$\mathrm{amb}_{\mathcal{A}}(c^t) = \sum_{j=1}^{k} \mathrm{amb}_{\mathcal{A}_j}(c^t).$$

Proof. Without loss of generality, assume that $\mathcal{A}$ contains *precisely* k cycles.[3] Let $\mathcal{A} = (Q, \sigma, \iota, \tau)$ and let the k cycles of $\mathcal{A}$ correspond to state sets $C_1, \ldots, C_k \subseteq Q$, respectively. Thus, denoting by $Q_0 \subseteq Q$ the set of states that do not belong to any cycle, we obtain $Q = Q_0 \uplus C_1 \uplus \ldots \uplus C_k$. For $j = 1, \ldots, k$, denote by $\mathcal{R}_s^{(j)}(\mathcal{A})$ the set of all successful runs of $\mathcal{A}$ visiting at least one state of C_j, *i.e.*,

$$\mathcal{R}_s^{(j)}(\mathcal{A}) = \{\gamma \in \mathcal{R}_s(\mathcal{A}) \mid Q(\gamma) \cap C_j \neq \emptyset\},$$

where $Q(\gamma)$ is the set of states passed by γ, *i.e.*, $Q(\gamma) = \{q_0, \ldots, q_t\}$ for each $\gamma = q_0 c q_1 c q_2 \ldots q_{t-1} c q_t \in \mathcal{R}(\mathcal{A})$ with $q_0, \ldots, q_t \in Q$. For

$$\mathcal{R}_s^{(0)}(\mathcal{A}) = \{\gamma \in \mathcal{R}_s(\mathcal{A}) \mid Q(\gamma) \cap C_j = \emptyset \text{ for } j = 1, \ldots, k\},$$

we clearly obtain $\mathcal{R}_s(\mathcal{A}) = \mathcal{R}_s^{(0)}(\mathcal{A}) \uplus \mathcal{R}_s^{(1)}(\mathcal{A}) \uplus \ldots \uplus \mathcal{R}_s^{(k)}(\mathcal{A})$.

For $j = 1, \ldots, k$, we may also decompose Q as $Q = Q_\rightarrow \uplus C_j \uplus Q_\leftarrow \uplus Q_\times$, where $Q_\rightarrow$ consists of all $q \in Q \backslash C_j$ *from which* there exists a run to a state in C_j, $Q_\leftarrow$ consists of all $q \in Q \setminus C_j$ *to which* there exists a run from some state in C_j, and $Q_\times = Q \setminus (Q_\rightarrow \cup C_j \cup Q_\leftarrow)$. Denote by Q_0' the set of all states $q \in Q_0$ such that $q \in Q(\gamma)$ for some run $\gamma \in \mathcal{R}_s^{(0)}(\mathcal{A})$. Let $Q_j = Q_0' \cup Q_\rightarrow \cup C_j \cup Q_\leftarrow$ if $j = 1$ and $Q_j = Q_\rightarrow \cup C_j \cup Q_\leftarrow$ otherwise. Let $\mathcal{A}_j = (Q_j, \iota_j, \sigma_j, \tau_j)$ be a weighted automaton over S and $\Sigma = \{c\}$ such that for all $p, q \in Q_j$,

$$\iota_j(q) = \begin{cases} \iota(q) & \text{if } q \in Q_\rightarrow \cup C_j \text{ or } j = 1, \\ 0 & \text{otherwise,} \end{cases}$$

$$\sigma_j(p, c, q) = \begin{cases} \sigma(p, c, q) & \text{if } p \notin Q_\rightarrow, q \notin Q_\leftarrow, \text{or } j = 1 \\ 0 & \text{otherwise,} \end{cases}$$

$$\tau_j(q) = \begin{cases} \tau(q) & \text{if } q \in C_j \cup Q_\leftarrow \text{ or } j = 1, \\ 0 & \text{otherwise.} \end{cases}$$

Then $\mathcal{A}_j$ is clearly a trim 1-cycle automaton for $j = 1, \ldots, k$. Moreover, obviously $\mathcal{R}_s(\mathcal{A}_1) = \mathcal{R}_s^{(0)}(\mathcal{A}) \uplus \mathcal{R}_s^{(1)}(\mathcal{A})$ and $\mathcal{R}_s(\mathcal{A}_j) = \mathcal{R}_s^{(j)}(\mathcal{A})$ for $j = 2, \ldots, k$, so that indeed $\mathcal{R}_s(\mathcal{A}) = \mathcal{R}_s(\mathcal{A}_1) \uplus \ldots \uplus \mathcal{R}_s(\mathcal{A}_k)$, the values of these runs in $\mathcal{A}_1, \ldots, \mathcal{A}_k$ being clearly the same as in $\mathcal{A}$. □

Let us now turn our attention to unary weighted automata over *commutative* semirings, for which we relate finite ambiguity with finite sequentiality.

[3] If $\mathcal{A}$ contains ℓ cycles with $1 \leq \ell < k$, then we obtain in this way a decomposition into ℓ automata $\mathcal{A}_1, \ldots, \mathcal{A}_\ell$, and a decomposition into k automata follows by taking $\mathcal{A}_{\ell+1}, \ldots, \mathcal{A}_k$ empty. If $\ell = 0$, then $\mathcal{A}$ itself can be taken for a 1-cycle automaton $\mathcal{A}_1$, while $\mathcal{A}_2, \ldots, \mathcal{A}_k$ can be empty.

Lemma 4. *Let S be a commutative semiring, and $\mathcal{A}$ a trim finitely ambiguous 1-cycle automaton over S and unary alphabet $\Sigma = \{c\}$. Then there is a deterministic weighted automaton $\mathcal{B}$ over S and Σ such that $\|\mathcal{B}\| = \|\mathcal{A}\|$.*

Proof. The observation is trivial when $\mathcal{A}$ contains no cycle. We may thus assume that there is *precisely one* cycle in $\mathcal{A} = (Q, \sigma, \iota, \tau)$. Let $\ell \in \mathbb{N} \setminus \{0\}$ be its length, and $\gamma_C = q_1 c q_2 \dots q_\ell c q_1$, for some $q_1, \dots, q_\ell \in Q$, a run of $\mathcal{A}$ on c^ℓ that goes around the cycle exactly once. Then there is $t_0 \in \mathbb{N}$ such that for all $t \geq t_0$, each run γ of $\mathcal{A}$ upon c^t visits q_1 and goes around the cycle from q_1 to q_1 at least $\lfloor (t - t_0)/\ell \rfloor$ times.[4] Such γ first follows some run γ_1 until it visits q_1 for the first time, then goes $\lfloor (t - t_0)/\ell \rfloor$ times around γ_C, and finally follows some run γ_2 from q_1 (the run γ_2 may revisit q_1). Setting $M = \sigma(\gamma_C)$, we get $\sigma(\gamma) = (\sigma(\gamma_1)\sigma(\gamma_2))\, M^{\lfloor (t-t_0)/\ell \rfloor}$.

Now, $|\gamma_1| + |\gamma_2| = t - \ell \lfloor (t - t_0)/\ell \rfloor = t - ((t - t_0) - s) = t_0 + s$, where $s \in \{0, \dots, \ell - 1\}$ is the remainder after dividing $t - t_0$ by ℓ – in other words, we have $t - t_0 \equiv s \pmod{\ell}$. The set of all possible pairs (γ_1, γ_2) is thus finite for all $s \in \{0, \dots, \ell - 1\}$ and depends only on s. It thus follows that there are $b_0, \dots, b_{\ell-1} \in S$ such that for $s = 0, \dots, \ell-1$ and all $t \geq t_0$ with $t - t_0 \equiv s \pmod{\ell}$,

$$(\|\mathcal{A}\|, c^t) = b_s M^{\lfloor (t-t_0)/\ell \rfloor}.$$

Moreover, for $t = 0, \dots, t_0 - 1$, denote by a_t the value $(\|\mathcal{A}\|, c^t)$.

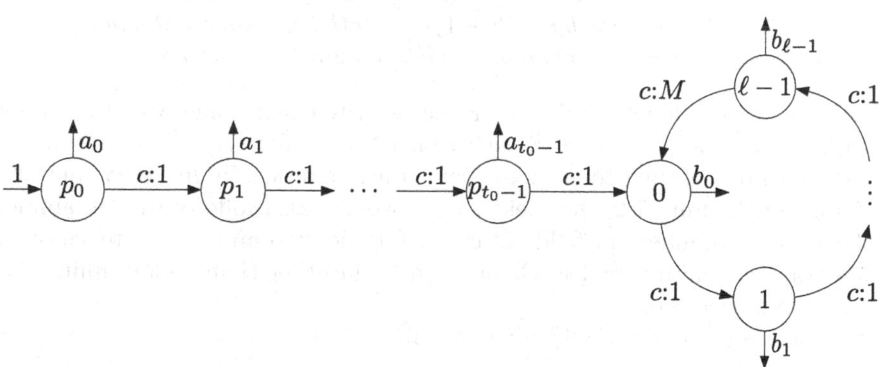

Fig. 2. The equivalent deterministic weighted automaton $\mathcal{B}$.

The automaton $\mathcal{A}$ is then obviously equivalent to the deterministic weighted automaton $\mathcal{B}$ over S and $\Sigma = \{c\}$ in Fig. 2. □

Theorem 5. *Let S be a commutative semiring, $k \in \mathbb{N} \setminus \{0\}$, and $\mathcal{A}$ a trim finitely ambiguous k-cycle automaton over S and unary alphabet $\Sigma = \{c\}$. Then there is a k-sequential weighted automaton $\mathcal{B}$ over S and Σ such that $\|\mathcal{B}\| = \|\mathcal{A}\|$.*

[4] One can take, e.g., $t_0 = |Q|$.

Proof. Decompose $\mathcal{A}$ into trim finitely ambiguous 1-cycle automata $\mathcal{A}_1, \ldots, \mathcal{A}_k$ as in Proposition 3, so that $\mathcal{A}_j$ has a deterministic equivalent $\mathcal{B}_j = (Q_j, \sigma_j, \iota_j, \tau_j)$ for $j = 1, \ldots, k$ by Lemma 4. Then $\|\mathcal{A}\| = \|\mathcal{B}\|$ for $\mathcal{B}$ the *union* of $\mathcal{B}_1, \ldots, \mathcal{B}_k$, *i.e.*, a k-sequential automaton $\mathcal{B} = (Q, \sigma, \iota, \tau)$ with $Q = (Q_1 \times \{1\}) \cup \ldots \cup (Q_k \times \{k\})$, $\iota(q, j) = \iota_j(q)$, $\sigma((p, j), c, (q, j)) = \sigma_j(p, c, q)$, and $\tau(q, j) = \tau_j(q)$ for all $p, q \in Q$, $j \in [k]$, and $c \in \Sigma$, while $\sigma(p, c, q) = 0$ for all other $(p, c, q) \in Q \times \Sigma \times Q$. □

Corollary 6. *Every finitely ambiguous unary weighted automaton $\mathcal{A}$ over a commutative semiring S admits a finitely sequential equivalent* (*and* vice versa).

4 Infinite Hierarchies

We now consider weighted automata *over fields* and first focus on the infinite hierarchies of formal power series realised, for $k = 0, 1, 2, \ldots$, by the k-ambiguous and k-sequential weighted automata. Our aim is to show that these hierarchies are strict if and only if the underlying field is not locally finite, while unary alphabets are sufficient to establish this observation. C. Barloy et al. [3] have noted that the finite ambiguity hierarchy *over the rationals* is strict, describing a counterexample witnessing this fact. We provide a similar counterexample that works over all other than locally finite fields and note that strictness of the finite sequentiality hierarchy is implied by this counterexample as well.

Lemma 7. *Let $\mathbb{F}$ be a field that is not locally finite and $k \in \mathbb{N}$. Then there exists a series $r \in \mathbb{F}\langle\langle c^* \rangle\rangle$ realised by a $(k+1)$-sequential weighted automaton over $\mathbb{F}$ and $\Sigma = \{c\}$, but by no k-ambiguous weighted automaton over $\mathbb{F}$.*

Proof. As $\mathbb{F}$ is not locally finite, there necessarily exists some $\alpha \in \mathbb{F}$ of infinite multiplicative order, *i.e.*, $\alpha \in \mathbb{F}$ such that $\alpha^s = \alpha^t$ for $s, t \in \mathbb{N}$ implies $s = t$. In fact, such α is known to exist in every other than locally finite commutative semiring [18, Lemma 7.2]; for fields, its existence also follows by containment of the rational numbers in fields of characteristic zero and by existence of elements transcendental over the Galois field $\mathbb{F}_p$ in other than locally finite fields of characteristic $p > 0$.

Consider a series $r \in \mathbb{F}\langle\langle c^* \rangle\rangle$ given for all $t \in \mathbb{N}$ by

$$\left(r, c^t\right) = \alpha^t + \alpha^{2t} + \ldots + \alpha^{(k+1)t}. \tag{4}$$

Then r is clearly realised by a $(k+1)$-sequential weighted automaton.

Suppose for contradiction that r is realised by some k-ambiguous weighted automaton $\mathcal{A}$ over $\mathbb{F}$ and $\Sigma = \{c\}$. Without loss of generality, assume $\mathcal{A}$ is trim; moreover, let $\mathcal{P}_{\mathcal{A}} = (n, \mathbf{i}, A, \mathbf{f})$. The spectrum of A then allows us to uniquely express (r, c^t), as a function of $t \in \mathbb{N}$, in the form (2). It thus follows by (4), together with the linear independence of pairwise distinct functions $\binom{t}{j}\lambda^{t-j}$ with $\lambda \in \overline{\mathbb{F}}$ and $j \in \mathbb{N}$, that $\alpha, \alpha^2, \ldots, \alpha^{k+1}$ are eigenvalues of A.[5]

[5] Note that $\alpha^{dt} = \binom{t}{0}\left(\alpha^d\right)^{t-0}$ for $d = 1, \ldots, k+1$.

As $\mathcal{A}$ is finitely ambiguous, Theorem 1 tells us that its strongly connected components are all either directed cycles, or single vertices (without a loop). Nonzero eigenvalues of A are thus precisely the roots of characteristic polynomials of matrices corresponding to the directed cycles, each taking the form $x^\ell - b$ for some $\ell \in \mathbb{N} \setminus \{0\}$ and $b \in \mathbb{F} \setminus \{0\}$.

For each $a \in \overline{\mathbb{F}}$, let $\xi(a)$ be the set of all multiples of a by roots of unity in $\overline{\mathbb{F}}$, *i.e.*, $\xi(a) = \{\kappa a \mid \kappa \in \overline{\mathbb{F}};\ \exists t \in \mathbb{N}\setminus\{0\} : \kappa^t = 1\}$. The roots of each polynomial $x^\ell - b$ are then contained in $\xi(a)$ for any of its roots $a \in \overline{\mathbb{F}}$: indeed, if $a, a' \in \overline{\mathbb{F}}$ are roots of $x^\ell - b$, then they are both nonzero and

$$\left(\frac{a'}{a}\right)^\ell = \frac{b}{b} = 1,$$

so that

$$a' = \left(\frac{a'}{a}\right) a \in \xi(a).$$

On the other hand, the sets $\xi(\alpha), \xi(\alpha^2), \ldots, \xi(\alpha^{k+1})$ are pairwise disjoint – if this was not a case, there would exist $x < y \in [k+1]$ such that $\kappa\alpha^x = \nu\alpha^y$ for some roots of unity $\kappa, \nu \in \overline{\mathbb{F}}$; this would imply that $\alpha^{y-x} = \kappa/\nu$ is a root of unity, contradicting the infinite multiplicative order of α. In particular, none of the polynomials $x^\ell - b$ can have two distinct roots among $\alpha, \alpha^2, \ldots, \alpha^{k+1}$. It follows that $\mathcal{A}$ contains $K \geq k+1$ cycles.

Decompose the K-cycle automaton $\mathcal{A}$ into 1-cycle automata $\mathcal{A}_1, \ldots, \mathcal{A}_K$ as in Proposition 3. For $j = 1, \ldots, K$, let $\mathcal{P}_{\mathcal{A}_j} = (n_j, \mathbf{i}_j, A_j, \mathbf{f}_j)$. Then, by what has been said, $[K] = J_0 \uplus J_1 \uplus \ldots \uplus J_{k+1}$, where J_d consists, for $d = 1, \ldots, k+1$, of precisely all $j \in [K]$ such that the eigenvalues of A_j are in $\xi(\alpha^d) \cup \{0\}$, while they are not all zero; the nonzero eigenvalues of A_j for $j \in J_0$ do not belong to any $\xi(\alpha^d)$ with $d \in [k+1]$. It thus follows by uniqueness of the form (2) that there exists some $t_0 \in \mathbb{N}$ such that for all $t \geq t_0$,

$$\sum_{j \in J_d} (\|\mathcal{A}_j\|, c^t) = \alpha^{dt} \qquad \text{for } d = 1, \ldots, k+1.$$

As these values are always nonzero, we find out that the set $\bigcup_{j\in J_d} \mathcal{R}_s(\mathcal{A}_j, c^t)$ is nonempty for $d = 1, \ldots, k+1$, the decomposition of Proposition 3 guaranteeing that $\mathcal{R}_s(\mathcal{A}, c^t) = \mathcal{R}_s(\mathcal{A}_1, c^t) \uplus \ldots \uplus \mathcal{R}_s(\mathcal{A}_K, c^t)$. There are thus at least $k+1$ successful runs of $\mathcal{A}$ on c^t, so $\mathcal{A}$ cannot be k-ambiguous: a contradiction. □

For $\mathbb{F}$ a field, Σ an alphabet, and $k \in \mathbb{N}$, let $\mathrm{AMB}_k(\mathbb{F}, \Sigma)$ and $\mathrm{SEQ}_k(\mathbb{F}, \Sigma)$ denote, respectively, the sets of series realised by the k-ambiguous and k-sequential automata over $\mathbb{F}$ and Σ. The following theorem is obtained directly by Lemma 7.

Theorem 8. *Let $\mathbb{F}$ be a field and Σ an alphabet. If $\mathbb{F}$ is not locally finite, then* $\mathrm{AMB}_k(\mathbb{F}, \Sigma) \subsetneq \mathrm{AMB}_{k+1}(\mathbb{F}, \Sigma)$ *and* $\mathrm{SEQ}_k(\mathbb{F}, \Sigma) \subsetneq \mathrm{SEQ}_{k+1}(\mathbb{F}, \Sigma)$ *for all $k \in \mathbb{N}$.*

As all weighted automata over locally finite semirings are determinisable [19], both hierarchies collapse over locally finite fields: $\mathrm{AMB}_k(\mathbb{F}, \Sigma) = \mathrm{AMB}_{k+1}(\mathbb{F}, \Sigma)$ and $\mathrm{SEQ}_k(\mathbb{F}, \Sigma) = \mathrm{SEQ}_{k+1}(\mathbb{F}, \Sigma)$ for $\mathbb{F}$ locally finite and $k \geq 1$.

5 Separation of Finite and Polynomial Ambiguity

We now examine the relations between finitely and polynomially ambiguous weighted automata over fields. C. Barloy et al. [3] have proved that polynomially ambiguous unary weighted automata *over the rationals* are more powerful than their finitely ambiguous counterparts. Let us first observe that their observation directly generalises to all fields of characteristic zero.

Theorem 9. *Let $\mathbb{F}$ be a field of characteristic zero. Then there exists a series $r \in \mathbb{F}\langle\langle c^* \rangle\rangle$ realised by a polynomially ambiguous weighted automaton over $\mathbb{F}$ and $\Sigma = \{c\}$, but by no finitely ambiguous weighted automaton over $\mathbb{F}$.*

Proof. Let $(r, c^t) = t$ for all $t \in \mathbb{N}$. Then r is clearly realised by a polynomially ambiguous automaton. Suppose for contradiction that there is a finitely ambiguous automaton realising r. Then it can be decomposed into 1-cycle automata by Proposition 3. As $\mathbb{F}$ is of characteristic zero, all polynomials $x^\ell - b$ with $\ell \in \mathbb{N} \setminus \{0\}$ and $b \in \mathbb{F} \setminus \{0\}$ are separable. The nonzero eigenvalues of A are thus of algebraic multiplicity 1 for every 1-cycle automaton $\mathcal{A}$ with $\mathcal{P}_\mathcal{A} = (n, \mathbf{i}, A, \mathbf{f})$. By uniqueness of the expression (2) for (r, c^t), it follows that it cannot contain the term $\binom{t}{1}1^{t-1}$, so that (r, c^t) cannot equal t for all $t \in \mathbb{N}$. □

The situation for fields of positive characteristic seems to be slightly different. We make just a single step towards its understanding, by showing that polynomially and finitely ambiguous automata over algebraically closed fields of positive characteristic are equally powerful when restricted to unary alphabets.

Theorem 10. *Let $\mathbb{F}$ be an algebraically closed field of characteristic $p > 0$ and $\mathcal{A}$ a polynomially ambiguous* unary *weighted automaton over $\mathbb{F}$ and $\Sigma = \{c\}$. Then there is a finitely ambiguous weighted automaton $\mathcal{B}$ over $\mathbb{F}$ such that $\|\mathcal{B}\| = \|\mathcal{A}\|$.*

Proof. Without loss of generality, let us assume that $\mathcal{A}$ with $\mathcal{P}_\mathcal{A} = (n, \mathbf{i}, A, \mathbf{f})$ is trim. By Theorem 1, the strongly connected components of $\mathcal{A}$ are all directed cycles or single vertices, so that

$$\mathrm{ch}_A(x) = x^{\ell_0} \prod_{k=1}^{s} \left(x^{\ell_k} - b_k\right)$$

for some $\ell_0, s \in \mathbb{N}$, $\ell_1, \ldots, \ell_s \in \mathbb{N} \setminus \{0\}$, and $b_1, \ldots, b_s \in \mathbb{F} \setminus \{0\}$. For $k = 1, \ldots, s$, let $\sigma_k \subseteq \mathbb{F}$ consist of all roots of $x^{\ell_k} - b_k$ that are not in $\sigma_1 \uplus \ldots \uplus \sigma_{k-1}$.[6] Let $\sigma_0 = \{0\}$ if 0 is a root of $\mathrm{ch}_A(x)$, and $\sigma_0 = \emptyset$ otherwise. Moreover, given a root $\lambda \in \mathbb{F}$ of $\mathrm{ch}_A(x)$, let $\alpha(\lambda)$ denote its multiplicity. Then (2) can be rewritten as

$$(\|\mathcal{A}\|, c^t) = \sum_{k=0}^{s} (r_k, c^t)\,, \tag{5}$$

[6] The field $\mathbb{F}$ is algebraically closed, so all roots of $\mathrm{ch}_A(x)$ are indeed in $\mathbb{F}$.

where $r_k \in \mathbb{F}\langle\!\langle c^* \rangle\!\rangle$ is given, for $k = 0, \ldots, s$ and all $t \in \mathbb{N}$, by

$$(r_k, c^t) = \sum_{\lambda \in \sigma_k} \sum_{j=0}^{\alpha(\lambda)-1} a_{\lambda,j} \binom{t}{j} \lambda^{t-j} \tag{6}$$

for some constants $a_{\lambda,j} \in \mathbb{F}$ for $\lambda \in \sigma_k$ and $j = 0, \ldots, \alpha(\lambda) - 1$.

Now, the series r_0 can clearly be realised by a finitely ambiguous automaton. For $k = 1, \ldots, s$, let $m \in \mathbb{N} \setminus \{0\}$ satisfy $p^m \geq \alpha(\lambda)$ for all $\lambda \in \sigma_k$. Let $M = \ell_k p^m$ and $B = b_k^{p^m}$, and let us consider a deterministic 1-cycle weighted automaton $\mathcal{A}_k = (M, \sigma, \iota, \tau)$ with $\sigma(t, c, t+1) = 1$ for $t = 1, \ldots, M-1$, $\sigma(M, c, 1) = B$, $\sigma(t, c, t') = 0$ for all remaining $(t, t') \in [M]^2$, $\iota(1) = 1$, $\iota(t) = 0$ for $t = 2, \ldots, M$, and $\tau(t) = (r_k, c^{t-1})$ for $t = 1, \ldots, M$. If $\mathcal{P}_{\mathcal{A}_k} = (M, \mathbf{i}_k, A_k, \mathbf{f}_k)$, then

$$\mathrm{ch}_{A_k}(x) = x^M - B = \left(x^{\ell_k}\right)^{p^m} - b_k^{p^m} = \left(x^{\ell_k} - b_k\right)^{p^m},$$

as $\mathbb{F}$ is of characteristic p. The eigenvalues of A_k thus form a superset of σ_k and the algebraic multiplicity of every eigenvalue $\lambda \in \sigma_k$ of A_k is at least $\alpha(\lambda)$. The constants in the expression (2) for the series $(\|\mathcal{A}_k\|, c^t)$ are uniquely determined by $(\|\mathcal{A}_k\|, c^t) = (r_k, c^t)$ for $t = 0, \ldots, M-1$. It follows that the expression (2) for $(\|\mathcal{A}_k\|, c^t)$ is the same as in (6). In other words, $\|\mathcal{A}_k\| = r_k$.

Each of the series r_k for $k = 0, \ldots, s$ is thus realised by a finitely ambiguous automaton. Existence of $\mathcal{B}$ thus follows by (5). □

Note that the property that we have just established holds trivially – and regardless of the alphabet considered – for weighted automata over finite fields and their algebraic extensions, which are always locally finite. It would thus be interesting to know whether there exists a field of positive characteristic, over which the series realised by polynomially ambiguous and finitely ambiguous weighted automata can be separated, and how the answer to this question depends on the size of the alphabet.

References

1. Allauzen, C., Mohri, M.: Finitely subsequential transducers. Int. J. Found. Comput. Sci. **14**(6), 983–994 (2003)
2. Bala, S.: Which finitely ambiguous automata recognize finitely sequential functions? In: Chatterjee, K., Sgall, J. (eds.) MFCS 2013. LNCS, vol. 8087, pp. 86–97. Springer, Heidelberg (2013). https://doi.org/10.1007/978-3-642-40313-2_10
3. Barloy, C., Fijalkow, N., Lhote, N., Mazowiecki, F.: A robust class of linear recurrence sequences. In: Computer Science Logic, CSL 2020, pp. 9:1–9:16 (2020)
4. Bell, P.C.: Polynomially ambiguous probabilistic automata on restricted languages. In: Automata, Languages and Programming, ICALP 2019. pp. 105:1–105:14 (2019)
5. Berstel, J., Reutenauer, C.: Noncommutative Rational Series with Applications. Cambridge University Press, Cambridge (2011)
6. Chattopadhyay, A., Mazowiecki, F., Muscholl, A., Riveros, C.: Pumping lemmas for weighted automata. Logical Methods Comput. Sci. **17**(3), 7:1–7:21 (2021)

7. Daviaud, L., Jecker, I., Reynier, P.-A., Villevalois, D.: Degree of Sequentiality of weighted automata. In: Esparza, J., Murawski, A.S. (eds.) FoSSaCS 2017. LNCS, vol. 10203, pp. 215–230. Springer, Heidelberg (2017). https://doi.org/10.1007/978-3-662-54458-7_13
8. Droste, M., Gastin, P.: Aperiodic weighted automata and weighted first-order logic. In: Mathematical Foundations of Computer Science, MFCS 2019. pp. 76:1–76:15 (2019)
9. Droste, M., Kuich, W., Vogler, H. (eds.): Handbook of Weighted Automata. Springer-Verlag. Heidelberg (2009). https://doi.org/10.1007/978-3-642-01492-5
10. Droste, M., Kuske, D.: Weighted automata. In: Pin, J.E. (ed.) Handbook of Automata Theory, Vol. 1, chap. 4, pp. 113–150. European Mathematical Society (2021)
11. Elaydi, S.: An Introduction to Difference Equations, 3rd edn. Springer, New York (2005). https://doi.org/10.1007/0-387-27602-5
12. Fijalkow, N., Riveros, C., Worrell, J.: Probabilistic automata of bounded ambiguity. Inf. Comput. **282**, 104648 (2022)
13. Kalman, D.: The generalized Vandermonde matrix. Math. Mag. **57**(1), 15–21 (1984)
14. Kirsten, D.: A Burnside approach to the termination of Mohri's algorithm for polynomially ambiguous min-plus-automata. RAIRO Theoret. Inform. Appl. **42**(3), 553–581 (2008)
15. Kirsten, D., Lombardy, S.: Deciding unambiguity and sequentiality of polynomially ambiguous min-plus automata. In: Symposium on Theoretical Aspects of Computer Science, STACS 2009, pp. 589–600 (2009)
16. Klimann, I., Lombardy, S., Mairesse, J., Prieur, C.: Deciding unambiguity and sequentiality from a finitely ambiguous max-plus automaton. Theoret. Comput. Sci. **327**(3), 349–373 (2004)
17. Kostolányi, P.: Polynomially ambiguous unary weighted automata over fields, submitted
18. Kostolányi, P., Mišún, F.: Alternating weighted automata over commutative semirings. Theoret. Comput. Sci. **740**, 1–27 (2018)
19. Lombardy, S., Sakarovitch, J.: Sequential? Theoret. Comput. Sci. **356**, 224–244 (2006)
20. Maletti, A., Nasz, T., Stier, K., Ulbricht, M.: Ambiguity hierarchies for weighted tree automata. In: Maneth, S. (ed.) CIAA 2021. LNCS, vol. 12803, pp. 140–151. Springer, Cham (2021). https://doi.org/10.1007/978-3-030-79121-6_12
21. Mazowiecki, F., Riveros, C.: Copyless cost-register automata: Structure, expressiveness, and closure properties. J. Comput. Syst. Sci. **100**, 1–29 (2019)
22. Minc, H.: Nonnegative Matrices. Wiley, New York (1988)
23. Paul, E.: On finite and polynomial ambiguity of weighted tree automata. In: Brlek, S., Reutenauer, C. (eds.) DLT 2016. LNCS, vol. 9840, pp. 368–379. Springer, Heidelberg (2016). https://doi.org/10.1007/978-3-662-53132-7_30
24. Paul, E.: Finite sequentiality of unambiguous max-plus tree automata. In: Symposium on Theoretical Aspects of Computer Science, STACS 2019, pp. 55:1–55:17 (2019)
25. Paul, E.: Finite sequentiality of finitely ambiguous max-plus tree automata. In: Automata, Languages and Programming, ICALP 2020, pp. 137:1–137:15 (2020)
26. Paul, E.: Finite sequentiality of unambiguous max-plus tree automata. Theory Comput. Syst. **65**(4), 736–776 (2021)
27. Sakarovitch, J.: Elements of Automata Theory. Cambridge University Press, New York (2009)

28. Salomaa, A., Soittola, M.: Automata-Theoretic Aspects of Formal Power Series. Springer, New York (1978). https://doi.org/10.1007/978-1-4612-6264-0
29. Schützenberger, M.P.: On the definition of a family of automata. Inf. Control **4**(2–3), 245–270 (1961)
30. Weber, A., Seidl, H.: On the degree of ambiguity of finite automata. Theoret. Comput. Sci. **88**(2), 325–349 (1991)

New Bounds for the Flock-of-Birds Problem

Alexander Kozachinskiy(✉)

Steklov Mathematical Institute of Russian Academy of Sciences,
8 Gubkina St., Moscow 119991, Russia
akozachinskiy@mi-ras.ru

Abstract. In this paper, we continue a line of work on obtaining succinct population protocols for Presburger-definable predicates. We focus on threshold predicates. These are predicates of the form $n \geq d$, where n is a free variable and d is a constant.

For every d, we establish a 1-aware population protocol for this predicate with $\log_2 d + \min\{e, z\} + O(1)$ states, where e (resp., z) is the number of 1's (resp., 0's) in the binary representation of d (resp., $d-1$). This improves upon an upper bound $4\log_2 d + O(1)$ due to Blondin et al. We also show that any 1-aware protocol for our problem must have at least $\log_2(d)$ states. This improves upon a lower bound $\log_3 d$ due to Blondin et al.

Keywords: Population protocols · Presburger arithmetic · Threshold predicates

1 Introduction

Population protocols were initially introduced as a model of distributed computation in large networks of low-memory sensors [2]. There are also similarities between population protocols and some models of social networks [10] and chemical reactions [11], see a discussion in [5]. Perhaps, population protocols are most known for their deep connection to logic, namely, to Presburger arithmetic. More specifically, there is a theorem that a predicate over the set of natural numbers is definable in Presburger arithmetic if and only if it can be computed by some population protocol [4]. In this paper, we continue a line of work on the *minimization* of population protocols [6–8]: given a Presburger-definable predicate, what is the minimal size of a population protocol computing it? More specifically, we obtain some new upper and lower bounds for *threshold* predicates.

We start by describing the model of population protocols in more detail.

This work was performed at the Steklov International Mathematical Center and supported by the Ministry of Science and Higher Education of the Russian Federation (agreement no. 075-15-2022-265). A part of this work was done during the Theoretical Foundations of Computer Systems (TFCS 2021) program at the Simons Institute.

A. S. Kulikov and S. Raskhodnikova (Eds.): CSR 2022, LNCS 13296, pp. 224–237, 2022.
https://doi.org/10.1007/978-3-031-09574-0_14

The Model. In this paper, we only consider population protocols for unary predicates. On a high level, population protocols are a sort of finite-state distributed algorithms. A population protocol can have an arbitrary natural number n on input. A population protocol *computes* a unary predicate $R\colon \mathbb{Z}^+ \to \{0,1\}$ if for every $n \in \mathbb{Z}^+$, having n on input, this protocol in some sense "converges" to $R(n)$.

In this framework, natural numbers are represented as *populations* of indistinguishable agents (or, in other words, as piles of indistinguishable items). Namely, a natural number n corresponds to a population with n agents. It turns out that this way of representing natural numbers is quite convenient for Presburger arithmetic. Intuitively, this is because to add two numbers in this model, we just have to join the corresponding piles.

A population protocol Π is specified by a finite set of states, a transition function mapping pairs of states into pairs of states, and a partition of the set of states into "0-states" and "1-states". Having a population of n agents on input, Π works as follows. First, it puts every agent into an initial state (which is specified in the description of the protocol and is the same for all n). Then agents start to *encounter* each other. We assume that the time is discrete and that a single encounter of 2 agents happens in each unit of time. This process is infinite and is not controlled by Π. However, when two agents meet, their states are updated according to the transition function of Π (given a pair of their states before the encounter, it gives a pair of their states after the encounter).

Recall that states of Π are partitioned into 1-states and 0-states. This partition is responsible for the opinions of the agents on the value of a predicate. Namely, agents in 1-states (resp., 0-states) "think" that n belongs to a predicate (resp., does not belong to a predicate).

Finally, we clarify what does it mean that Π converges to 1 (resp., 0) on n. We want all agents to be in 1-states (resp., in 0-states) forever after some finite time. However, it is meaningless to require this for all possible infinite sequences of encounters. For example, it might be that the same two agents meet each other over and over again. There is no chance agents will learn anything about n in this way. So will only consider sequences of encounters that form *fair executions* of our protocol.

To define this, we first need a notion of a *configuration*. An n-size configuration of Π is a function from the set of n agents to the set of states of Π. In turn, an execution of Π is an infinite sequence of configurations such that ***(a)*** in the first configuration all agents are in the initial state; ***(b)*** every configuration, except the first one, is obtained from the previous one via some encounter. In turn, an execution is fair if for any two configurations C_1 and C_2 the following holds: if C_1 appears infinitely often in our execution, and if C_2 is reachable from C_1 via some finite sequence of encounters, then C_2 also appears infinitely often in our execution. Finally, we say that Π converges to 1 (resp., 0) on n if all fair executions have this property: all but finitely many configurations of this execution include only agents in 1-states (resp., 0-states).

Threshold Predicates. In this paper, we are interested in *threshold predicates*, that is, predicates of the form:

$$R(n) = \begin{cases} 1 & n \geq d, \\ 0 & \text{otherwise}, \end{cases}$$

where $d \in \mathbb{Z}^+$. For brevity, below we use the following notation for these predicates: $R(n) = \mathbb{I}\{n \geq d\}$.

The problem of computing this family of predicates by population protocols is called sometimes the *flock-of-birds problem.* This is because of the following analogy due to Angluin et al. [2]. Imagine a flock of birds, where each bird is equipped with a temperature sensor. Some birds are sick due to the elevated temperature. Our sensors have very low action radius: two sensors can interact with each other only if they are, say, at most 1 m apart. Let there be n sick birds. From time to time, two sick birds approach each other sufficiently close so that their sensors can interact. We want to know whether n (the number of sick birds) is at least some threshold d. This turns into a problem of computing the predicate $R(n) = \mathbb{I}\{n \geq d\}$ by a population protocol.

The first population protocol computing this predicate was given in [2] (in fact, this was the first population protocol ever considered in the literature). It works as follows. Imagine that initially every agent has 1 coin. An agent can hold up to $d - 1$ coins. Consider an arbitrary encounter of two agents. If two agents meet and have less than d coins in total, one of them gets all the coins of the other one. In turn, if they have at least d coins in total, they both become "converted". That is, they start to think to $n \geq d$ (initially everybody thinks that $n < d$). Finally, any agent who meets a converted agent also becomes converted.

Let us see why this protocol computes the predicate $R(n) = \mathbb{I}\{n \geq d\}$. First, assume that $n < d$. Then in the beginning we have less than d coins. The total number of coins is preserved throughout the protocol. In particular, no two agents can have at least d coins in total. Thus, everybody will always think that $n < d$, as required.

Assume now that $n \geq d$. After any sequence of encounters it is still possible to reach a configuration in which everybody is converted. Indeed, go to a configuration with the least possible number of non-bankrupt agents (bankrupt agents are agents with 0 coins). In this minimal configuration, any two non-bankrupt agents must have at least d coins in total (otherwise, one could reduce the number of such agents). Thus, it is possible to convert somebody. It remains to pair all the agents one by one with a converted agent.

To finish the argument, consider any fair execution with $n \geq d$ agents. Let C be any configuration which appears infinitely often in this execution. There is a configuration D which is reachable from C and in which everybody is converted. Thus, D must belong to our execution in some place. Starting from this place, everybody will always think that $n \geq d$.

1-Awareness. The protocol which we just described has the following feature. If $n < d$, then no agent will ever think that $n \geq d$. In other words, to start thinking that $n \geq d$, an agent must obtain some proof of this fact. In our case, a proof is a physical presence of d coins.

Blondin et al. [7] call this kind of protocols *1-aware protocols.* Formally, they are defined as follows. Let $R\colon \mathbb{Z}^+ \to \{0,1\}$ be a predicate. We say that a protocol computing this predicate is *1-aware* if the following holds: for every n with $R(n) = 0$, no execution of n agents ever contains an agent thinking that $R(n) = 1$.

It is not hard to see that 1-aware protocols can only compute threshold predicates and the all-zero predicate. Indeed, if it is possible to make one of n agents think that $R(n) = 1$, then the same is possible for all populations with more than n agents. Hence, any predicate R which can be computed by a 1-aware population protocol is monotone: if $R(n) = 1$, then $R(m) = 1$ for every $m > n$.

Thus, 1-aware population protocols are a quite natural model for computing threshold predicates. In this paper, for every d we study the following question: what is the minimal number of states in a 1-aware population protocol, computing the predicate $R(n) = \mathbb{I}\{n \geq d\}$?

Our Results. Observe first that the protocol of Angluin et al., described above, requires $d + 1$ states. Indeed, in this protocol, agents just memorize how many coins they hold. This is a number from 0 to $d - 1$. We also need one more state for converted agents.

This can be drastically improved when d is a power of 2. Consider the same protocol, but forbid any "transfers" of coins unless two agents have the *same number of coins.* Then an agent can hold either 0 coins or a power of 2 of them. Thus, this modified protocol requires only about $\log_2 d$ states.

When $n \geq d$, it works for the same reasons as before – minimize the number of non-bankrupt agents and observe that there must 2 of them holding at least d coins (because otherwise they must hold different powers of 2 whose sum is smaller than d). In fact, this protocol also works when d is the sum of two powers of 2, but for other d it does not. A problem is that it might be impossible to get two agents with d coins in total (for example, when there are $d = 4 + 2 + 1 = 7$ coins, two agents can hold at most $4 + 2 = 6$ coins).

Nevertheless, for every d, Blondin et al. [7] have constructed a 1-aware protocol with $O(\log d)$ states, computing the predicate $R(n) = \mathbb{I}\{n \geq d\}$. Their construction has two steps. First, they solve the problem with a protocol in which encounters can involve not only 2 but up to $\log_2 d$ agents. Second, they show a general result, transforming any protocol with "crowded" encounters into a standard protocol. The second part of their argument is rather technical. As a result, they get a protocol with $4 \log_2 d + O(1)$ states. Our first result is the following improvement of this upper bound.

Theorem 1. *For any $d \in \mathbb{Z}^+$ the following holds: there exists a deterministic 1-aware population protocol with $\log_2 d + \min\{e, z\} + O(1)$ states, computing the predicate $R(n) = \mathbb{I}\{n \geq d\}$. Here e (resp., z) is the number of 1's (resp., 0's) in the binary representation of d (resp., $d - 1$).*

This upper bound never exceeds $\frac{3}{2}\log_2 d + O(1)$. Indeed, the number of 1's in the binary representation of d is larger at most by one than the number of 1's in the binary representation of $d-1$. Hence, $e+z$ does not exceed the length of the binary representation of $d-1$ plus one. This implies that $\min\{e, z\} \leq \frac{1}{2}\log_2 d + O(1)$.

In fact, we devise two different protocols for Theorem 1: one with $\log_2 d + e + O(1)$ states, and the other with $\log_2 d + z + O(1)$ states. The first one is given in Sect. 4 and the second one is given in Sect. 5. These two protocols require different ideas. Unlike the construction of Blondin et al., our constructions are direct.

Additionally, Blondin et al. in [7] show that any 1-aware protocol computing $R(n) = \mathbb{I}\{n \geq d\}$ must have at least $\log_3 d$ states. Our second result is an improvement of this lower bound.

Theorem 2. *For any $d \in \mathbb{Z}^+$ the following holds: any 1-aware population protocol computing the predicate $R(n) = \mathbb{I}\{n \geq d\}$ has at least $\log_2 d + 1$ states.*

Theorem 2 is proved in Sect. 3.

Other Related Works. In this paper we only deal with 1-aware protocols. For general population protocols, the gap between upper and lower bounds is much wider. A simple counting argument shows that for infinitely many d, the minimal size of a population protocol computing $R(n) = \mathbb{I}\{n \geq d\}$ is $\Omega(\log^{1/4} d)$. We are not aware of any explicit sequence of d's on which this lower bound is attained. Recently, Czerner and Esparza [8] have shown that for *every* d, the minimal size of a population protocol computing $R(n) = \mathbb{I}\{n \geq d\}$ is $\Omega(\log\log\log d)$.

Similar questions have been studied for other predicates. Namely, Blondin et al. [6] obtained the following general result. Assume that a predicate R is definable in Presburger arithmetic via some quantifier-free formula of length l (where all constants are written in binary; for example, the predicate $R(n) = \mathbb{I}\{n \geq d\}$ can be given by a formula of length $\log_2 d + O(1)$). Then there is a population protocol with $l^{O(1)}$ states computing R.

Let us mention a related line of research which aims to minimize another parameter of population protocols – *the time of convergence* [3]. It is defined as the expected number of encounters until all agents stably have the right opinion on the value of a predicate. We refer the reader to [1,9] for the recent results in this area.

2 Preliminaries

We only consider population protocols for unary predicates. Moreover, we only define 1-aware population protocols. For more detailed introduction to population protocols, see [5].

Notation. By $\mathbb{Z}^+$ we denote the set of positive integers. For $n \in \mathbb{Z}^+$, we write $[n] = \{1, 2, \ldots, n\}$. We also write $A = B \sqcup C$ for three sets A, B, C if $A = B \cup C$ and $B \cap C = \varnothing$. By 2^A we mean the power set of a set A.

Definition 1. *A* ***population protocol*** *Π is a tuple $\langle Q, Q_0, Q_1, q_{init}, \delta\rangle$, where*

- *Q is a finite set of states of Π;*
- *$Q_0, Q_1 \subseteq Q$ are such that $Q = Q_0 \sqcup Q_1$.*
- *$q_{init} \in Q$ is the initial state of Π;*
- *$\delta\colon Q^2 \to 2^{Q^2} \setminus \{\varnothing\}$ is the transition function of Π.*

We say that Π is ***deterministic*** *if $|\delta(q_1, q_2)| = 1$ for every $q_1, q_2 \in Q$.*

Let $\Pi = \langle Q, Q_0, Q_1, q_{init}, \delta\rangle$ be a population protocol. Consider any $n \in \mathbb{Z}^+$. An n-size *configuration* of Π is a function $C\colon [n] \to Q$. Intuitively, elements of $[n]$ are agents, and the function C maps every agent to the state this agent in. Define the initial n-size configuration as $I_n\colon [n] \to Q$, $I_n(i) = q_{init}$ for all $i \in [n]$. A pair of two n-size configurations (C_1, C_2) is called a *transition* if there exist $i, j \in [n]$, $i \neq j$ such that

$$(C_2(i), C_2(j)) \in \delta\big((C_1(i), C_1(j))\big) \text{ and } C_2(k) = C_1(k) \text{ for all } k \in [n] \setminus \{i, j\}.$$

That is, C_2 must be obtained from C_1 via an encounter of two distinct agents i and j. These agents update their states according to δ, and other agents do not change their states.

We stress that 2 agents participating in an encounter are ordered. It is convenient to imagine that one of the agents "initiates" the encounter and the other agent "responds" to it. This is why δ is defined over ordered pairs of states and not over 2-element subsets of Q.

Next, let C and D be two n-size configurations. We say that D is *reachable* from C if for some $k \geq 1$ and for some sequence $C_1, C_2, \ldots, C_k$ of configuration we have:

- $C_1 = C, C_k = D$;
- for every $1 \leq i < k$ we have that (C_i, C_{i+1}) is a transition.

An execution is an infinite sequence $\{C_i\}_{i=1}^{\infty}$ of configurations such that $C_1 = I_n$ for some n and (C_i, C_{i+1}) is a transition for every $i \in \mathbb{Z}^+$. We call an execution $E = \{C_i\}_{i=1}^{\infty}$ *fair* if for every two configurations C, D the following holds: if, first, C occurs infinitely often in E, and second, D is reachable from C, then D also occurs infinitely often in E.

Definition 2. *Let $R\colon \mathbb{Z}^+ \to \{0, 1\}$ be some predicate. We say that a population protocol $\Pi = \langle Q, Q_0, Q_1, q_{init}, \delta\rangle$ is a 1-aware population protocol computing R if for any $n \in \mathbb{Z}^+$ the following holds:*

- *if $R(n) = 0$, then for every configuration C which is reachable from I_n we have $C([n]) \subseteq Q_0$.*
- *if $R(n) = 1$, then for every fair execution $\{C_i\}_{i=1}^{\infty}$ which start from $C_1 = I_n$ there exists i_0 such that for every $i \geq i_0$ we have $C_i([n]) \subseteq Q_1$.*

3 Proof of Theorem 2

Assume that $\Pi = \langle Q, Q_0, Q_1 q_{init}, \delta \rangle$ is a 1-aware population protocol computing the predicate $R(n) = \mathbb{I}\{n \geq d\}$. Let $C\colon [n] \to Q$ be a configuration of Π and $q \in Q$ be a state. We say that q *can occur* from C if there exists a configuration D of Π such that ***(a)*** D is reachable from C; ***(b)*** $D(i) = q$ for some $i \in [n]$. Additionally, by a q-agent we mean an agent whose state is q.

For $q \in Q$, let $f(q)$ denote the minimal $n \in \mathbb{Z}^+$ such that q can occur from I_n. If there is no such n at all, set $f(q) = +\infty$. Obviously, $|Q| \geq |f(Q)|$, so it is sufficient to prove that $|f(Q)| \geq \log_2 d + 1$.

Observe that $1 = f(q_{init})$. Hence, $1 \in f(Q)$. By definition of 1-awareness, there exists a state $q \in Q_1$ which can occur from I_d (just consider any fair execution starting from I_d). On the other hand, no state from Q_1 can occur from I_n for $n < d$. Hence, $f(q) = d$ and $d \in f(Q)$. It remains to establish the following lemma.

Lemma 1. *Let $a < b$ be two consecutive elements of $f(Q)$. Then $b \leq 2a$.*

Loosely speaking, this lemma asserts that $f(Q)$ does not contain large gaps. Since $1, d \in f(Q)$, it shows that between 1 and d there must be about $\log_2(d)$ elements of $f(Q)$. In more detail, let $1 = i_1 < i_2 < \ldots < i_k = d$ be elements of $f(Q)$ up to d, in the increasing order. By Lemma 1, we have:

$$i_2 \leq 2i_1, \ldots, i_k \leq 2i_{k-1}.$$

By taking the product of these inequalities, we obtain:

$$d = i_k \leq 2^{k-1} \cdot i_1 = 2^{k-1}.$$

Hence, $|f(Q)| \geq k \geq \log_2(d) + 1$.

Proof (of Lemma 1). Consider the minimal k such that some $q \in Q$ with $f(q) = b$ can occur from I_b after k encounters. Note that $k \geq 1$. Indeed, if $k = 0$, then $q = q_{init}$. However, $f(q) = b > a \geq 1$, so $q \neq q_{init}$.

Due to minimality of k, a q-agent occurs in the last of these k encounters. Consider this agent and also the second agent participating in this encounter. Let their states prior to the encounter be q_1 and q_2. We conclude that a q-agent can occur whenever we have a q_1-agent and a q_2-agent in a population (these agents have to be distinct, even when $q_1 = q_2$).

Since q_1 and q_2 can occur from I_b, we have that $f(q_1), f(q_2) \leq b$. In turn, since q_1, q_2 can occur from I_b in less than k encounters, we have $f(q_1) \neq b$ and $f(q_2) \neq b$, by minimality of k. Hence, $f(q_1), f(q_2) \leq a$, because a is the predecessor of b in $f(Q)$. To finish the proof, it is sufficient to show that $f(q) \leq f(q_1) + f(q_2)$. In other words, we have to show that q can occur from $I_{f(q_1)+f(q_2)}$. By definition, a q_1-agent can occur from $I_{f(q_1)}$ and a q_2-agent can occur from $I_{f(q_2)}$. Hence, if we have $f(q_1) + f(q_2)$ agents in the initial state, the first $f(q_1)$ of them are able to produce a q_1-agent, while the last $f(q_2)$ of them are able to produce a q_2-agent. In turn, these two agents are able to produce a q-agent. □

4 Proof of Theorem 1: The First Protocol

In this section we establish a 1-aware population protocol with $\log_2(d)+e+O(1)$ states, computing the predicate $R(n) = \mathbb{I}\{n \geq d\}$. Here, e is the number of 1's in the binary representation of d.

Let $i_1 > i_2 > \ldots > i_e$ be such that

$$d = 2^{i_1} + 2^{i_2} + \ldots + 2^{i_e}.$$

Imagine that initially every agent holds 1 coin. During the protocol, some agents may run out of coins; we will call these agents *bankrupts*. At each moment of time, a non-bankrupt agent can hold $1, 2, 4, \ldots, 2^{i_1-1}$ or 2^{i_1} coins. Additionally, every bankrupt maintains a counter $k \in \{0, 1, \ldots, e-1\}$. Under some circumstances, an agent can come into a special *final* state (informally, this happens when this agent becomes convinced that $n \geq d$). When an agent comes into the final state, it forgets the number of coins it had (this will not be problematic because everything will be decided at this point). So, some agents in the final state might be bankrupt, while the others not. In total, besides the final state, we have $i_1 + 1 \leq \log_2(d) + 1$ states for non-bankrupt agents and e states for bankrupt agents; this is at most $\log_2(d) + e + 2$ states.

We now describe the transitions of our protocol. First, assume that two non-bankrupt agents both having 2^i coins meet. If $i = i_1$, then both agents come into the final state. If $i < i_1$, then one of the agents gets all the coins of the other one. That is, one of the agents is left with 2^{i+1} coins, and the other one becomes a bankrupt with $k = 0$. Now, if an agent with 2^i coins meets an agent with 2^j coins and $j \neq i$, nothing happens.

Next, we describe transitions that involve bankrupts. If two bankrupts meet, nothing happens. Now, assume that a bankrupt whose counter equals k meets an agent with 2^i coins. There are four cases:

1. if $k < e - 1$ and $i = i_{k+1}$, then k increments by 1;
2. if $k = e - 1$ and $i = i_e$, then the bankrupt comes into the final state;
3. if $k > 0$ and $i_k > i > i_{k+1}$, then the bankrupt comes into the final state;
4. in any other case, the bankrupt sets $k = 0$.

Finally, if an agent is already in the final state, then everybody this agent meets also comes into the final state.

The description of the protocol is finished. To show that this protocol is a 1-aware protocol computing the predicate $R(n) = \mathbb{I}\{n \geq d\}$, it is sufficient to show the following two things:

- *(soundness)* if $n < d$, then no agent can come into the final state;
- *(completeness)* if $n \geq d$, then, after any finite sequence of encounters, it is still possible to bring one of the agents into the final state.

Here n is the number of agents in a population. Indeed, soundness ensures that our protocol satisfies the definition of 1-awareness for $n < d$. Now, consider any $n \geq d$. Take any fair execution E of n agents. We have to show that there exists a moment in E, starting from which all agents are always in the final state. Let C be any configuration which occurs infinitely often in E. By definition of an execution, C is reachable from I_n. Hence, by completeness, there is a configuration D which is reachable from C and which has an agent in the final state. Now, let this agent meet all the other agents. We obtain a configuration D' which is reachable from D and in which all agents are in the final state. By definition of fairness, D' occurs in E. Finally, note that once all agents are in the final state, they will always be in this state.

We start by showing the soundness. Assume for contradiction that there are $n < d$ agents, but one of them came into the final state. First, it could happen if two agents with 2^{i_1} coins met. However, the total number of coins is preserved throughout the protocol, and initially there are $n < d = 2^{i_1}+2^{i_2}+\ldots+2^{i_e} < 2\cdot 2^{i_1}$ coins, contradiction.

Second, it might be that some bankrupt came into the final state. This can happen after an encounter with a non-bankrupt agent. Assume that this non-bankrupt agent held 2^i coins. Then there are two options: if k was the value of the counter of our bankrupt agent, then either $k = e - 1$ and $i = i_e$ or $k > 0$ and $i_k > i > i_{k+1}$. Note that in both cases we have $2^{i_1} + \ldots + 2^{i_k} + 2^i \geq d$. We will show that there must be at least $2^{i_1} + \ldots + 2^{i_k} + 2^i$ distinct coins, and this would be a contradiction.

Consider the counter of our bankrupt. Its current value is k. It cannot increase by more than 1 at once. So the last k changes of the counter were as follows: it became equal to 1, then it became equal to 2 and so on, up to a moment when it reached its current value. At the moment when it became equal to 1, our bankrupt saw an agent with 2^{i_1} coins. After that, when it became equal to 2, our bankrupt saw an agent with 2^{i_2} coins, and so on. In the end, when the counter reached its current value, our bankrupt saw 2^{i_k} coins. Additionally, in the very last encounter, it saw 2^i coins. We claim these $2^{i_1} + 2^{i_2} + \ldots + 2^{i_k} + 2^i$ are distinct. To see this, fix any coin. At each moment of time, it belongs to some group of coins. A point it that the size of this group can only increase over time. Now, recall that $2^{i_1} > 2^{i_2} > \ldots > 2^{i_k} > 2^i$. Since our bankrupt first saw a group of 2^{i_1} coins, then a smaller group of 2^{i_2} coins and so on, none of these coins were seen twice. The soundness is proved.

We now show the completeness. Assume that there are $n \geq d$ agents. Consider any configuration C which is reachable from the initial one. Let D be a configuration which is reachable from C and has the least number of non-bankrupt agents. If in D there are two agents that both have 2^{i_1} coins, then we can bring them into the final state. Assume from now on that in D there is at most one agent with 2^{i_1} coins. Then no two non-bankrupt agents have the same number of coins in D – otherwise, one could decrease the number of non-bankrupt agents.

Assume that in D there are t non-bankrupt agents, the first one with 2^{j_1} coins, the second one with 2^{j_2} coins, and so on. Here $0 \leq j_1, \ldots, j_t \leq i_1$. W.l.o.g. $j_1 > j_2 > \ldots > j_t$. Note that

$$n = 2^{j_1} + 2^{j_2} + \ldots + 2^{j_t} \geq d = 2^{i_1} + 2^{i_2} + \ldots + 2^{i_e}.$$

In particular, $i_1 = j_1$. Moreover, either $t = e$ and $j_1 = i_1, \dots j_e = i_e$, or there exists $1 \le k < e$ such that $j_1 = i_1, \dots j_k = i_k$ and $i_k > j_{k+1} > i_{k+1}$.

Now, take any bankrupt (there will be at least one bankrupt already after the first transition). If its counter is not 0, we reset it to 0 by pairing our bankrupt with the agent holding $2^{j_1} = 2^{i_1}$ coins. It is now easy to bring this bankrupt into the final state. Indeed, if $t = e$ and $j_1 = i_1, \dots j_e = i_e$, pair our bankrupt with the agent holding 2^{i_1} coins, then with the agent holding 2^{i_2} coins, and so on, up to the agent holding 2^{i_e} coins. Now, if there exists $1 \le k < e$, such that $j_1 = i_1, \dots j_k = i_k$ and $i_k > j_{k+1} > i_{k+1}$, pair our bankrupt with the agent holding $2^{j_1} = 2^{i_1}$ coins, then with the agent holding $2^{j_2} = 2^{i_2}$ coins, and so on, up to the agent holding $2^{j_{k+1}}$ coins.

5 Proof of Theorem 1: The Second Protocol

In this section we establish a 1-aware population protocol with $\log_2(d)+z+O(1)$ states computing the predicate $R(n) = \mathbb{I}\{n \ge d\}$. Here, z is the number of 0's in the binary representation of $d - 1$.

As a warm-up, we first consider $d = 2^{k+1} - 1$. In this case, $z = 1$. The protocol from the previous section requires about $2\log_2 d$ states for such d. We present a simple protocol which only needs $\log_2 d + O(1)$ states for such d.

5.1 Warm-up: Case $d = 2^{k+1} - 1$

Again, initially each agent holds 1 coin. As before, we distinguish between bankrupt and non-bankrupt agents. A non-bankrupt agent can hold $1, 2, \dots,$ 2^{k-1} or 2^k coins. Thus, there are $k+1$ possible states of non-bankrupt agents, 1 state indicating bankrupts, and also 1 final state – in total, $k+3 = \log_2 d + O(1)$ states.

We now describe the transitions of the protocol. Assume that two agents both having 2^i coins for some $0 \le i < k - 1$ meet. Then, as in the previous section, one of them gets 2^{i+1} coins and the other one becomes bankrupt. Now, when two agents both having 2^{k-1} coins meet, one of them gets 2^k coins and the other one gets 1 coin "out of nowhere". When two agents with 2^k coins meet, both of them come into the final state. Finally, if an agent is already in the final state, then everybody this agent meets also comes into the final state. All the other encounters do not change states of agents.

The rest of the argument has the same two parts – "soundness" and "completeness". "Soundness" means that if n, the total number of agents, is smaller than d, then no agent can come into the final state. "Completeness" means that if $n \ge d$, then, after any sequence of encounters, it is still possible to bring one of the agents into the final state. Similarly to the argument from the previous section, "soundness" and "completeness" imply that our protocol is a 1-aware protocol computing $R(n) = \mathbb{I}\{n \ge d\}$.

Let us start with the soundness. Assume that $n < d$. We claim that an "out of nowhere" coin may occur at most once. Indeed, consider the first time it occurs.

At this moment, one of the agents gets 2^k coins. Nothing happens with these 2^k coins unless we get one more agent with 2^k coins. However, all the other agents in total have $(n - 2^k) + 1 < (2^{k+1} - 1 - 2^k) + 1 = 2^k$ coins. Thus, from now on it is impossible to get two agents with 2^{k-1} coins. In particular, it is impossible to get a coin "out of nowhere". This means that the total number of coins never exceeds $n + 1 < 2^{k+1}$. However, to bring somebody into the final state, we must have at least 2^{k+1} coins. The soundness is proved.

Let us now show the completeness. Assume that $n \geq d$. Let C be any configuration, reachable from the initial configuration of n agents. Assume for contradiction that no configuration with an agent in the final state is reachable from C. Let D be a configuration which is reachable from C and has the most coins in total (as any agent can hold up to 2^k coins, the total number of coins is bounded by $n2^k$). Next, let D' be a configuration which is reachable from D and has the least number of non-bankrupts. We have at most 1 agent with 2^k coins in D' – otherwise we could reach the final state. Also, in D' there is at most one agent with 2^{k-1} coins – otherwise we could increase the total number of coins. Similarly, for every $0 \leq i < k - 1$, there is at most one agent with 2^i coins – otherwise one could decrease the number of non-bankrupts. Thus, we have at most $1 + 2 + \ldots + 2^k = d$ coins in total. Initially, there are $n \geq d$ coins. The total number of coins does not decrease in our protocol. Hence, in D' there must be exactly $d = 1 + 2 + \ldots + 2^k$ coins. In particular, in D' there must be an agent with 2^k coins. When an agent with 2^k coins occurs, we also get a coin "out of nowhere". This means that in D' the total number of coins is bigger than in the initial configuration. That is, initially there were at most $d - 1$ coins, contradiction.

5.2 General Case

We assume that d is not a power of 2 (otherwise we could use the protocol from Sect. 4). Let 2^k be the largest power of 2 below d. Define $a = 2^{k+1} - d$. Observe that:

$$2^{k+1} - 1 = \underbrace{11\ldots1}_{k+1} = (d - 1) + a$$

Since $2^k < d < 2^{k+1}$, there are $k + 1$ digits in the binary representation of $d - 1$. Hence, the number of 1's in the binary representation of a equals the number of 0's in the binary representation of $d - 1$ (that is, equals z).

Assume that

$$a = 2^{b_1} + 2^{b_2} + \ldots + 2^{b_z}, \tag{1}$$

where $b_1 > b_2 > \ldots > b_z$. Note that $a = 2^{k+1} - d < 2^{k+1} - 2^k = 2^k$. Hence, $b_1 < k$.

The protocol in the general is essentially the same as for the case $d = 2^{k+1} - 1$, except that instead of just 1 coin "out of nowhere" we get a coins "out of nowhere" every time two agents with 2^{k-1} coins meet. However, there will be additional technical difficulties, as a might not be a power of 2.

In more detail, a non-bankrupt agent may have

$$s \in \{1, 2, \dots, 2^k, 2^{b_1} + 2^{b_2}, 2^{b_1} + 2^{b_2} + 2^{b_3}, \dots, 2^{b_1} + 2^{b_2} + \dots + 2^{b_z} = a\} \text{ coins.}$$

Thus, a non-bankrupt agent can be in one of the $k + z$ states. Taking into the account the state indicating bankrupts and the final state, in total we have $k+z+2 \leq \log_2 d+z+O(1)$ states. We will call agents that hold $2^{b_1}+2^{b_2}+\dots+2^{b_i}$ coins for some $i > 1$ *non-standard.*

Let us now describe transitions of the protocol. When two agents with 2^i coins meet, where $0 \leq i < k - 1$, one of them gets 2^{i+1} coins and the other one becomes bankrupt. When two agents with 2^{k-1} coins meet, one of them gets 2^k coins and the other one gets a coins "out of nowhere". When two agents with 2^k coins meet, both of them come into the final state. Now, when a non-standard agent with $2^{b_1} + \dots + 2^{b_i}$ meets a bankrupt, this bankrupt gets 2^{b_i} coins, and the non-standard agent is left with $2^{b_1} + \dots + 2^{b_{i-1}}$ coins (if $i = 2$, the non-standard agent becomes standard). Finally, if an agent is already in the final state, then everybody this agent meets also comes into the final state. All the other encounters do not change the states of agents.

Let us now show the soundness of our protocol. Assume that the number of agents is $n < d$. We show that no agent can be brought into the final state. For that, we first show that we can get a coins out of nowhere at most once. Indeed, consider the first time this happened. We get one agent with 2^k coins. Other agents have $n - 2^k + a = n - 2^k + (2^{k+1} - d) < 2^k$ coins in total (the inequality holds because $n < d$). Thus, we will never have two agents with 2^{k-1} coins again. Thus, in any execution, the total number of coins never exceeds $n + a = n + (2^{k+1} - d) < 2^{k+1}$. However, to bring somebody into the final state, we must have two agents with 2^k coins.

Let us now show the completeness of our protocol. Assume that $n \geq d$. Let C be any configuration, reachable from the initial one. Assume for contradiction that no configuration with an agent in the final state is reachable from C. Let C_1 be a configuration which is reachable from C and has the most coins in total (as before, this number is bounded by $n2^k$). Next, let C_2 be a configuration which is reachable from C_1 and minimizes the following parameter:

$$\begin{aligned} p = &\text{ the number of standard non-bankrupt agents} \\ &+ 3 \times \text{the number of coins belonging to non-standard agents.} \end{aligned}$$

In C_2 there is at most one agent with 2^k coins – otherwise, we could reach the final state. There is also at most one agent with 2^{k-1} coins – otherwise, one could increase the total number of coins. Similarly, for any $0 \leq i < k - 1$, there is at most one agent in C_2 with 2^i coins (otherwise, by pairing two agents with 2^i coins, one could decrease p).

If there is no agent with 2^k coins in C_2, then we never got a coins out of nowhere on our path to C_2. Indeed, when we get a coins out of nowhere, we get an agent with 2^k coins, and nothing happens with this agent unless the final state is reached. So there are 0 non-standard agents in C_2 (they are created only when we get coins out of nowhere). Hence, there are at most $1+2+\ldots+2^{k-1} < 2^k < d$ coins in C_2, contradiction.

Hence, in C_2 there is exactly one agent with 2^k coins. Clearly, this also means that on our path to C_2 we got a coins out of nowhere exactly once. This is because the only transition creating an agent with 2^k coins is the transition creating a coins out of nowhere. Indeed, other transitions with standard agents create smaller power of 2, and transitions with non-standard agents involve at most $a < 2^k$ coins. We conclude that, first, in C_2 there is exactly one agent with 2^k coins, second, there are $n + a$ coins in total, and third, there is at most 1 non-standard agent (it could be created only once, when we got a coins out of nowhere).

Assume first that all agents in C_2 are standard. Then $n+a \le 1+2+\ldots+2^k = 2^{k+1} - 1$. Hence, $n \le 2^{k+1} - 1 - a = d - 1$, contradiction.

Now, assume that in C_2 there is exactly one non-standard agent who holds $2^{b_1} + \ldots + 2^{b_i}$ coins, $i > 1$. Let us show that in C_2 there exists a bankrupt agent. Indeed, assume for contradiction that all agents in C_2 are non-bankrupt. Now, leave every agent with exactly one coin. There will be exactly n coins. That is, exactly a coins were taken. However, from the agent with 2^k coins we took $2^k - 1$ coins. Additionally, we took at least 1 coin from the non-standard agent. Hence, we took at least 2^k coins. Since $a < 2^k$, we obtain a contradiction.

Now, pair the non-standard agent with any bankrupt agent. We claim that the parameter p will decrease (this will be a contradiction with the definition of C_2). Indeed, as a result, we get at most 2 new standard non-bankrupt agents. However, the number of coins belonging to the non-standard agent decreases by at least 1. Therefore, p decreases.

Acknowledgements. I would like to thank Karoliina Lehtinen and K. S. Thejaswini for discussions on population protocols.

References

1. Alistarh, D., Aspnes, J., Eisenstat, D., Gelashvili, R., Rivest, R.L.: Time-space trade-offs in population protocols. In: Proceedings of the Twenty-eighth Annual ACM-SIAM Symposium on Discrete Algorithms, pp. 2560–2579. SIAM (2017)
2. Angluin, D., Aspnes, J., Diamadi, Z., Fischer, M.J., Peralta, R.: Computation in networks of passively mobile finite-state sensors. Distrib. Comput. **18**(4), 235–253 (2006)
3. Angluin, D., Aspnes, J., Eisenstat, D.: Fast computation by population protocols with a leader. Distrib. Comput. **21**(3), 183–199 (2008)
4. Angluin, D., Aspnes, J., Eisenstat, D., Ruppert, E.: The computational power of population protocols. Distrib. Comput. **20**(4), 279–304 (2007)
5. Aspnes, J., Ruppert, E.: An introduction to population protocols. Middlew. Netw. Eccen. Mobile App. 97–120 (2009)
6. Blondin, M., Esparza, J., Genest, B., Helfrich, M., Jaax, S.: Succinct population protocols for presburger arithmetic. In: STACS (2020)

7. Blondin, M., Esparza, J., Jaax, S.: Large flocks of small birds: on the minimal size of population protocols. In: Niedermeier, R., Vallée, B. (eds.) 35th Symposium on Theoretical Aspects of Computer Science (STACS 2018). Leibniz International Proceedings in Informatics (LIPIcs), vol. 96, pp. 16:1–16:14. Schloss Dagstuhl-Leibniz-Zentrum fuer Informatik, Dagstuhl, Germany (2018). https://doi.org/10.4230/LIPIcs.STACS.2018.16, http://drops.dagstuhl.de/opus/volltexte/2018/8511
8. Czerner, P., Esparza, J.: Lower bounds on the state complexity of population protocols. In: Proceedings of the 2021 ACM Symposium on Principles of Distributed Computing, pp. 45–54. PODC 2021, Association for Computing Machinery, New York, NY, USA (2021). https://doi.org/10.1145/3465084.3467912, https://doi.org/10.1145/3465084.3467912
9. Czerner, P., Guttenberg, R., Helfrich, M., Esparza, J.: Fast and succinct population protocols for presburger arithmetic. In: Aspnes, J., Michail, O. (eds.) 1st Symposium on Algorithmic Foundations of Dynamic Networks (SAND 2022). Leibniz International Proceedings in Informatics (LIPIcs), vol. 221, pp. 11:1–11:17. Schloss Dagstuhl - Leibniz-Zentrum für Informatik, Dagstuhl, Germany (2022). https://drops.dagstuhl.de/opus/volltexte/2022/15953
10. Diamadi, Z., Fischer, M.J.: A simple game for the study of trust in distributed systems. Wuhan Univ. J. Nat. Sci. **6**(1), 72–82 (2001)
11. Gillespie, D.T.: Exact stochastic simulation of coupled chemical reactions. J. Phys. Chem. **81**(25), 2340–2361 (1977)

Heterogeneous Multi-commodity Network Flows over Time

Yifen Li[1,4], Xiaohui Bei[2(✉)], Youming Qiao[3], Dacheng Tao[4], and Zhiya Chen[1]

[1] School of Traffic and Transportation Engineering, Central South University, Changsha, China
{yifen.li,chzy}@csu.edu.cn

[2] School of Physical and Mathematical Sciences, Nanyang Technological University, Singapore, Singapore
xhbei@ntu.edu.sg

[3] Centre for Quantum Software and Information, University of Technology Sydney, Ultimo, Australia

[4] UBTECH Sydney AI Centre, School of Computer Science, Faculty of Engineering, The University of Sydney, Darlington, NSW 2008, Australia
dacheng.tao@sydney.edu.au

Abstract. In the 1950's, Ford and Fulkerson introduced dynamic flows by incorporating the notion of time into the network flow model (*Oper. Res.*, 1958). In this paper, motivated by real-world applications including route planning and evacuations, we extend the framework of multi-commodity dynamic flows to the heterogeneous commodity setting by allowing different transit times for different commodities along the same edge.

We first show how to construct the time-expanded networks, a classical technique in dynamic flows, in the heterogeneous setting. Based on this construction, we give a pseudopolynomial-time algorithm for the quickest flow problem when there are two heterogeneous commodities. We then present a fully polynomial-time approximation scheme when the nodes have storage for any number of heterogeneous commodities. The algorithm is based on the condensed time-expanded network technique introduced by Fleischer and Skutella (*SIAM J. Comput.*, 2007).

Keywords: Multi-Commodity Network Flow · Dynamic Flow

1 Introduction

Network flows form a well-studied and hugely successful area in optimisation, with many deep theorems and efficient algorithms. Still, in some real-world applications, it is natural to augment the basic network flow model further. One such example, described in [13], is to consider scheduling cars in a traffic network. In this setting, it is clear that *time* is an essential factor to take into consideration. Therefore, it is natural to associate each edge in the network a *transit time*, and consider flows that can vary with time. It is not hard to come up with other

A. S. Kulikov and S. Raskhodnikova (Eds.): CSR 2022, LNCS 13296, pp. 238–255, 2022.
https://doi.org/10.1007/978-3-031-09574-0_15

examples in production systems, communication networks, and financial flows, where time plays a key role in the corresponding network flow problems.

A formal study of network flows where flows vary with time was initiated in the 1950's by Ford and Fulkerson in their seminal works [7,8]. It has now become a rather mature area with many basic questions answered. We refer the reader to [15] for an excellent introduction. There are also several nice surveys [1,2,13,14], and the thesis of Hoppe [11], where the reader can find an abundance of information. In the literature, several names have been used for network flows with flow transit times, including flows over time [5], dynamic flows [13], and time-dependent flows [3]. In this paper we adopt flows over time, following works of e.g. Fleischer and Skutella [5,15].

In this paper, we consider a further augmentation to the multi-commodity network flows over time model. *The key assumption is that various commodities can have different speeds when traveling along the same edge.* We shall call such commodities as *heterogeneous*, as opposed to the *homogeneous* commodities in previous models where commodities have the same speed along a fixed edge.

To see the motivation of doing so, consider the following setting. Suppose a factory needs two types of raw materials, material A and material B, for production. Each of the materials A and B needs to be transported by special trucks in a common road network. When traveling along the same road, these two types of trucks can have different speed limits. To make things more interesting, it is possible that different roads have different speed limits for even the same truck. It is also not hard to come up with other situations in say emergency evacuation, where different commodities or agents have different speeds when traveling along the same edge.

1.1 An Overview of the Heterogeneous Model and Our Results

In this subsection, we outline our model, review some results from literature, and briefly introduce our results.

The Heterogeneous Model. The above discussions motivate us to study the *multi-commodity network flows over time* problem with heterogeneous commodities. Recall that, compared to the homogeneous commodities that have been studied previously, heterogeneous commodities may have different speeds when traveling along the same edge. This amounts to setting different transit times for different commodities for each edge.

A key new feature of the heterogeneous model is that, because of the differences in speeds, it is possible for a faster commodity to catch up with a slower one in the middle of an edge, therefore causing a violation of the capacity constraint. We shall refer to such event as a *collision*, where flows of multiple commodities sent at different times meet at the same point within an edge. A concrete example is shown in Fig. 1.

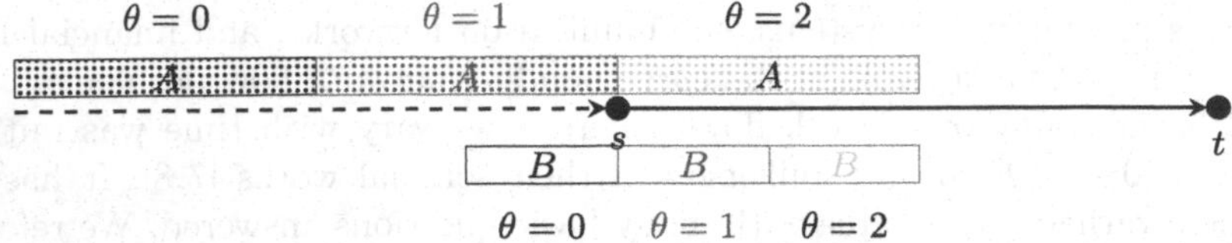

Fig. 1. An example of an edge $e = (s, t)$ of capacity 1, and two heterogeneous commodities A and B, where commodity A flows twice as fast as commodity B. Suppose one unit of B flows into edge e in the time interval $[0, 1)$, and one unit of B flows into e in the time interval $[1, 2)$. The two flow packets never overlap at point s. However, because commodity A flows faster than B, its packet would catch up and collide with the packet of B, hence causing a capacity violation in the middle of edge (s, t).

How to handle collisions will be the key technical problem in this model. To the best of our knowledge, no studies on such collision issues have yet addressed these issues adequately.

For network flows over time, the time can be either discrete or continuous, and the nodes may have storage or cannot – if nodes have storage, then the flow can be held at this node and only released later if needed. In this paper, we work in the *continuous-time* model, and most of our results *require node storage.* For a detailed description of the model, see Sect. 3.

In the *Heterogeneous Multi-commodity Flows over Time* problem (HeteroMFT for short), we are given a network with capacities and transit times, a time horizon, and for each commodity a source node, a sink node, and a demand. The goal is to obtain a multi-commodity flow over time within the time horizon satisfying the demands, if there exists one. For a formal definition of the problem, see Definition 2. Clearly, HeteroMFT is closely related to the *quickest* version of the heterogeneous multi-commodity flow over time problem, which asks to find a multi-commodity flow that satisfies the demands of all commodities from their sources to their respective destinations within the minimal time horizon.

Review of Some Works in the Homogeneous Setting. Since the heterogeneous model is a generalisation of the homogeneous model, it is necessary to review some results from the homogeneous multi-commodity dynamic network flow problem (HomoMFT).

Using the classical technique of time-expanded networks [7], HomoMFT can be solved in pseudo-polynomial time, i.e. polynomial in the time horizon. (A true polynomial-time algorithm needs to run in time polynomial in the logarithm of the time horizon.) From the perspective of approximation algorithms for HomoMFT, a breakthrough result is a fully polynomial-time approximation scheme (FPTAS) in the setting of bounded costs and with storage [5]. In [9], the HomoMFT problem is shown to be weakly NP-hard for two or more commodities, and it is also NP-hard to design fully polynomial-time approximation scheme (FPTAS) for the quickest HomoMFT with simple paths and without storage.

Since the HeteroMFT problem is a generalisation of the HomoMFT problem, the NP-hardness results for HomoMFT apply to HeteroMFT as well. Therefore, we focus on designing approximation algorithms for the HeteroMFT problem.

Our First Result: Time-Expanded Networks in the Heterogeneous Setting. We first examine the classical time-expanded network technique. Briefly speaking, in the homogeneous setting, given a network $G = (V, E)$, a time-expanded network $\tilde{G}$ with time horizon T is built by replicating T copies of V, with each copy called a layer. Then for each edge in the original graph with transit time τ, connect the corresponding nodes in ith layer and the $(i + \tau)$th layer.

In the heterogeneous setting, the construction of time-expanded networks is trickier. Suppose the number of commodities is k. As the transit times are different for different commodities on a fixed arc in the heterogeneous setting, it is natural to split an arc in the original network into k arcs in the time-expanded network, one for each commodity. Figure 2 gives such an example.

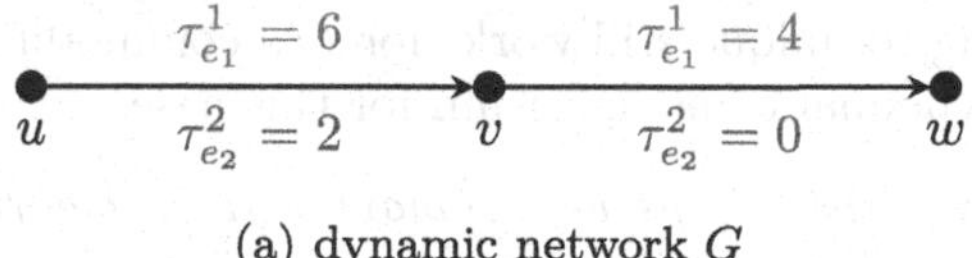

(a) dynamic network G

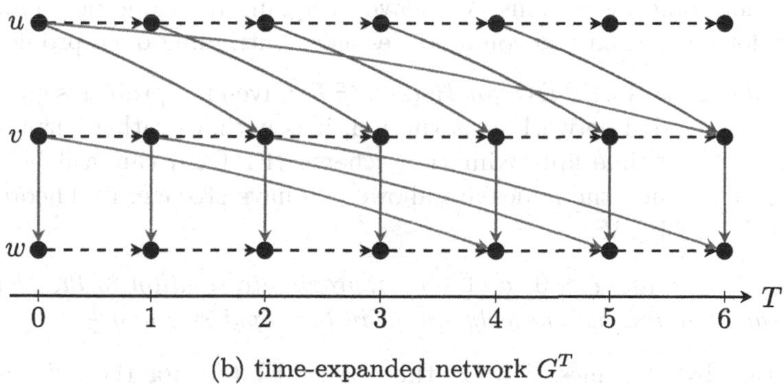

(b) time-expanded network G^T

Fig. 2. A dynamic network with two commodities and its corresponding time-expanded network with time horizon $T = 6$.

Here, we come across the first difficulty caused by the heterogeneity regarding the capacity constraints. First, note that the capacities of these k arcs starting from the same layer need to be considered altogether as not to exceed the capacity. However, this just suggests that the flows on this arc in the original network do not exceed the capacity at the tail of the arc. In order to avoid *collison*, we also need to examine the capacities of several arcs starting from different layers. At first sight, this seems to involve enumerating every point in e, leading to possibly exponentially many constraints. Fortunately, Proposition 1 indicates that only a polynomial number of additional capacity constraints need to be considered.

While the above gives a proper definition of time-expanded networks in the heterogeneous setting, there is a more serious problem which prevents it from yielding a pseudo-polynomial time algorithm for the HeteroMFT problem. This is because, the key observation for using time-expanded networks in the homogeneous setting is the following (see e.g. [15, Lemma 4.4]): A feasible flow over time in G with time horizon T yields a feasible static flow in $\tilde{G}$ (by averaging according to each time interval), and the inverse direction is also true (by a straightforward construction). However, in the heterogeneous setting, while we can still construct a feasible flow over time from a feasible static flow, the inverse direction does not necessarily hold, as the averaging technique no longer works due to the collision issue.

Despite the above difficulty, we show that by incorporating a further observation, the averaging technique still works for *two* commodities (Proposition 2), giving a pseudopolynomial-time algorithm for this case.

Theorem 1. *There exists a pseudopolynomial-time algorithm for the HeteroMFT problem when the number of commodities is* 2.

The proof for Theorem 1 does not apply to more than two commodities; see Remark 1 for some discussions. We leave designing a pseudo-polynomial time algorithm for more than two commodities as an intriguing open problem.

Our Second Result: An FPTAS for HeteroMFT. Given the problems encountered in the time-expanded network construction, it is perhaps rather surprising that a fully polynomial-time approximation scheme (FPTAS) can still be achieved for HeteroMFT, when the nodes are allowed to have storage. In Theorem 2, we present such an FPTAS.

Theorem 2. *For any $\epsilon > 0$, a $(1+\epsilon)$-approximate solution to the HeteroMFT problem can be found in time polynomial in the input size and $\frac{1}{\epsilon}$.*

Note that by [9], unless P=NP, there is no FPTAS for the quickest multicommodity flow problem when node storage is prohibited and flows are only sent on simple paths, even in the homogeneous setting. So allowing node storage is unavoidable.

An FPTAS for the homogeneous version of the problem was given in [5], and our algorithm builds upon and generalises that algorithm. More specifically, we utilize the *condensed time-expanded network* technique introduced there, which are time-expanded networks with longer time intervals. Figure 3 gives an illustration of this idea, following the example in Fig. 2.

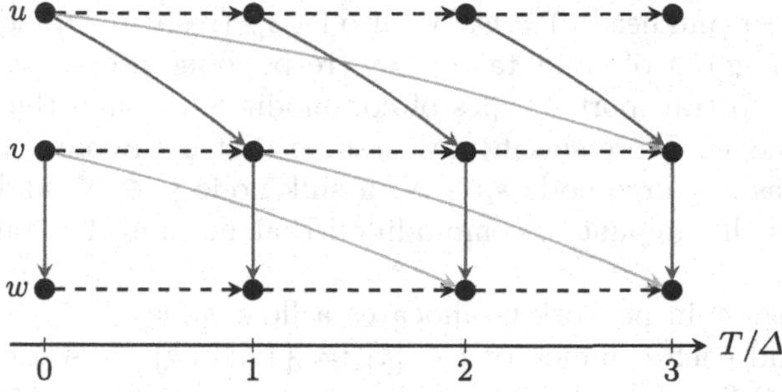

Fig. 3. Δ-condensed time-expanded network G^T/Δ with $\Delta = 2$

Overcoming the difficulties brought by the heterogeneity of the commodities requires some non-trivial technical works. Indeed, in the construction of time expanded networks, we need to adjust existing constraints and introduce new constraints on the static flow network to ensure that the solution corresponds to a feasible flow over time, and that the static network problem is of polynomial size. This means that the analysis in [5] cannot be directly applied to prove the correctness of this algorithm. More specifically, the averaging step there no longer yields a feasible flow in the time expanded network in the heterogeneous setting. Our main technical contribution is to show that the feasibility is still approximately preserved thanks to a previous flow smoothing step , which is a key step for the FPTAS.

1.2 Structure of the Paper

In the following, we give a detailed account of our results. In Sect. 2, to prepare for introducing our model, we review the static and homogeneous dynamic network flow models. In Sect. 3, we formally define the heterogeneous multi-commodity flow over time model. In Sect. 4, we describe the time-expanded network construction in the heterogeneous setting. In Sect. 5, we present the FPTAS for the HeteroMFT problem. Due to space constraints, some proofs are omitted and can be found in the full version of this paper.

2 Review of Static and Homogeneous Flows over Time

In this section we review the classic static multi-commodity network flow model, and the homogeneous multi-commodity network flow over time model.

Static Flows in Networks. In a static network flow problem, we are given a network (directed graph) $G = (V, E)$ with $|V| = n$ nodes and $|E| = m$ edges. Each edge $e \in E$ has a capacity $u_e : E \to \mathbb{R}_{\geq 0}$, which bounds the total amount of flow allowed to go through this edge at any time. For each edge $e = (v, w)$, we denote $\mathsf{tail}(e) = v$ and $\mathsf{head}(e) = w$. We also let δ_v^+ (resp. δ_v^-) to denote the set of edges $e \in E$ going out of v, i.e. $\mathsf{tail}(e) = v$ (resp. going into v, i.e. $\mathsf{head}(e) = v$).

Our goal is to transport k types of commodities through the same network G by sharing edges. More specifically, assume that each commodity $i \in [k] := \{1, 2, \ldots, k\}$ has a source node $s_i \in N$, a sink node $t_i \in N$, and a demand d_i that represents the amount of commodity i that needs to be transported from s_i to t_i.

A *static flow* x in network G allocates a flow value $x_e^i : E \to \mathbb{R}_{\geq 0}$ to each edge $e \in E$ and each commodity $i \in [k] := \{1, \ldots, k\}$. A static flow is called *feasible* if it satisfies the following constraints.

$$\forall e \in E, \quad 0 \leq \sum_{i \in [k]} x_e^i \leq u_e \qquad \text{(capacity constraints)} \tag{1}$$

$$\forall i \in [k], v \in V \backslash \{s_i, t_i\}, \quad \sum_{e \in \delta_v^-} x_e^i - \sum_{e \in \delta_v^+} x_e^i = 0 \qquad \text{(flow conservation constraints)} \tag{2}$$

$$\forall i \in [k], \quad \sum_{e \in \delta_{t_i}^-} x_e^i - \sum_{e \in \delta_{t_i}^+} x_e^i = d_i \qquad \text{(demand constraints)} \tag{3}$$

Network Flows over Time. When taking *time* into consideration, we arrive at the network flow over time problem. There are two main approaches to model time. The first one is the discrete-time model, first studied by Ford and Fulkersen [7,8]. The second one is the continuous model. Fleischer and Tardos showed strong connections between these two models [6]. In this paper, we focus on a continuous-time model, mostly following notations in [5,15].

Another feature of the flow over time model is that storing flows in the intermediate nodes becomes possible. That is, we may assume that intermediate nodes have storage that could hold inventory of (any amount of) flow before sending it forward. Allowing storage is a common assumption in most previous works on flows over time. On the other hand, to fit certain applications such as telecommunications, one could also consider a model in which storage is limited, or even no storage is allowed, at any intermediate node. Then the flow conservation constraints simply change the inequality condition to equality. Flows over time with no storage or restricted storage were studied in several works [4,10–12]. In this paper we will adopt the model *with* intermediate storage.

For network flows over time, apart from capacity u_e, every edge $e \in E$ also has a transit time $\tau_e \geq 0$ that specifies the time it takes for a unit of flow of a commodity to travel from $\mathsf{tail}(e)$ to $\mathsf{head}(e)$. That is, the flow for a commodity sent at time θ from $\mathsf{tail}(e)$ will reach $\mathsf{head}(e)$ at time $\theta + \tau_e$.

The following definition of dynamic flows (named *flows over time* in this paper) is standard (cf. e.g. [15, Definition 2.1]).

Definition 1. *A flow over time f with time horizon $T \geq 0$ is a Lebesgue-integrable function $f_e^i : \mathbb{R} \to \mathbb{R}^{\geq 0}$ for each edge $e \in E$ and $i \in [k]$.*

We will only consider flows that can arrive at its destination by time T, that is, we require that $f_e^i(\theta) = 0$ for all $\theta \geq T - \tau_e$ or $\theta < 0$.

That is, for any $\theta \in [0, T)$ and any commodity i, $f_e^i(\theta)$ denotes the flow *rate* of commodity i going into the tail of edge e at time θ.

We now discuss on feasibility constraints for a multi-commodity flow over time $f = (f_e^i)$ with time horizon T. Let $G = (V, E)$ be the underlying directed graph. Suppose that there are k types of commodities, and each commodity has a source node s_i and a sink node t_i.

- The *capacity constraint* is

$$\forall e \in E, \theta \in [0, T), 0 \leq \sum_{i=1}^{k} f_e^i(\theta) \leq u_e. \tag{4}$$

- *Flow conservation constraints.* Recall that storing flows in the intermediate nodes may be allowed. This leads to the following weak flow conservation constraints.

$$\forall v \in V \backslash \{s_i, t_i\}, i \in [k], \theta \in [0, T], \sum_{e \in \delta_v^-} \int_0^{\theta - \tau_e} f_e^i(\xi) d\xi - \sum_{e \in \delta_v^+} \int_0^{\theta} f_e^i(\xi) d\xi \geq 0 \tag{5}$$

  In the above equation, when $\geq$ is replaced by $=$, the conservation constraint is called strict.
- *Demand constraints.* Finally, demand constraints state that for each commodity i, the net flow that has reached sink t_i by time T should equal its demand d_i.

$$\forall i \in [k], \sum_{e \in \delta_{t_i}^-} \int_0^{T - \tau_e} f_e^i(\xi) d\xi - \sum_{e \in \delta_{t_i}^+} \int_0^{T} f_e^i(\xi) d\xi = d_i \tag{6}$$

3 Our Model: Heterogeneous Multi-commodity Dynamic Flow

In this paper, we generalise the above multi-commodity network flow over time model by introducing speed heterogeneity among different commodities. In the previous network flow over time model, on each edge all commodities are assumed to have the same speed, i.e., the flows are *homogeneous*. We propose a model in which commodities may have different speeds on the same edge, and we refer to this as the *heterogeneous multi-commodity flow over time* model. This is achieved by allowing an edge e to have k transit times $\{\tau_e^1, \tau_e^2, \ldots, \tau_e^k\}$, for which τ_e^i is the time needed for one unit of flow of commodity i to go through edge e. In this paper, we also assume that the transit times τ_e^i are *integral*, which is a realistic assumption for most potential applications.

Flow Feasibility. We now define the feasibility constraints of a heterogeneous multi-commodity flow over time.

The flow conservation constraint 5 and the demand constraint 6 are defined with regard to each commodity. So they carry over from homogeneous to heterogeneous setting, after changing τ_e to τ_e^i, namely:

$$\forall v \in V \setminus \{s_i, t_i\}, i \in [k], \theta \in [0, T], \quad \sum_{e \in \delta_v^-} \int_0^{\theta - \tau_e^i} f_e^i(\xi) d\xi - \sum_{e \in \delta_v^+} \int_0^{\theta} f_e^i(\xi) d\xi \geq 0. \tag{7}$$

$$\forall i \in [k], \quad \sum_{e \in \delta_{t_i}^-} \int_0^{T - \tau_e^i} f_e^i(\xi) d\xi - \sum_{e \in \delta_{t_i}^+} \int_0^{T} f_e^i(\xi) d\xi = d_i, \tag{8}$$

We need to pay special attention to the capacity constraints. Because of the heterogeneity of commodity speeds, it no longer suffices to only require capacity constraints only at the entrance of each edge. That is, when k commodities move in a common pipeline at various speeds, some fast commodity may catch up with the slower commodities to create congestion in the middle of the edge. Figure 1 above shows a concrete example.

Therefore, we need to require that at any moment, *at any point* of any edge, the sum of the rates of all flows together must not exceed the capacity of that edge. The capacity constraint is then the following.

$$\forall e \in E, \theta \in [0, T), \alpha \in [0, 1] : \quad \sum_{i=1}^{k} f_e^i(\theta - \alpha \cdot \tau_e^i) \leq u_e. \tag{9}$$

The Heterogeneous Multi-commodity Flow over Time Problem. In this paper, we focus on the problem of transporting each commodity to their respective destinations within a pre-set time horizon.

Definition 2. *An instance of the* heterogeneous multi-commodity flow over time *problem, denoted by* HeteroMFT, *consists of the following.*

Input: *A network $G = (V, E)$. For every edge $e \in E$, a capacity $u_e \geq 0$. There are k commodities. For every commodity $i \in [k]$, a source node $s_i \in V$, a sink node $t_i \in V$, and a demand $d_i \geq 0$. For every $e \in E$ and $i \in [k]$, the transit time of commodity i on e is $\tau_e^i \geq 0$. A time horizon $T \geq 0$.*

Output: *A feasible multi-commodity flow over time with time horizon T satisfying the given demands, if there exists one.*

Correspondingly, the homogeneous multi-commodity flow over time Problem, studied in e.g. [5,9], is denoted by HomoMFT.

Approximations. In Sect. 5, we will focus on FPTAS for HeteroMFT. Here, a $(1+\epsilon)$-approximate solution to HeteroMFTmeans that the output is a feasible multi-commodity flow over time with time horizon $(1+\epsilon)T$ satisfying the given demands.

4 Time-Expanded Networks in the Heterogeneous Setting

4.1 Time-Expanded Networks: From Homogeneous to Heterogeneous

As already mentioned in Sect. 1.1, a classical technique for tackling flows over time problem is to construct time-expanded networks. The underlying principle for using time-expanded networks lies in the conversions between feasible static flows in the time-expanded network and feasible flows over time in the original network. To convert feasible flows over time in the original network to feasible static flows in the time-expanded network, we need the averaging technique. That is, by averaging the flows in each time unit, we can start from any feasible flow over time, to obtain a "stair-case" like flow which is also feasible and completes within the same time horizon.

A surprising feature of the heterogeneous setting is that the averaging technique does not result in a feasible flow, when the number of commodities is larger than 2. Even for the case of two commodities, some subtle argument is needed. In the following, we first define time-expanded networks in the heterogeneous setting. As the readers will see, the time-expanded networks need to be adjusted to accommodate different speeds, and the feasibility condition is also more complicated due to the need to avoid collisions in the middle of the edges.

4.2 Heterogeneous Time-Expanded Networks

We now present a construction of time-expanded static networks in the heterogeneous setting. Let $G = (V, E)$ be a network with capacities u_e^i, transit times τ_e^i, and time horizon T. We assume T and τ_e^i are integers.

First, we construct a static network $G^T = (N^T, E^T)$ as follows.

- The set of nodes N^T consists of $T + 1$ copies of the set of vertices N, labeled from N_0 to N_T. For any $v \in N$ and $\zeta = 0, 1, \ldots, T$, v_ζ in G^T is the ζth copy of node v.
- For every commodity i and every edge $e = (v, w) \in E$ and $\zeta = 0, 1, \ldots, T - \tau_e^i$, there is an edge $e_\zeta^i = (v_\zeta, w_{\zeta+\tau_e^i})$ in E^T.
- For each $v \in N$ and $\zeta = 0, 1, \ldots, T - 1$, there is an edge $(v_\zeta, v_{\zeta+1})$. It is used to model storage at the node.
- Finally, for each commodity i, its source node is s_0^i, and its sink node is t_T^i.

The following table summarizes the correspondences of the network structures.

	Dynamic network	Time-expanded network
Network	$G = (N, E)$	$G^T = (N^T, E^T)$ $N^T = N_0 \cup \cdots \cup N_\zeta \cup \cdots \cup N_{T-1}$ $E^T = \bigcup_{e \in E} \{e_0^i, \ldots, e_\zeta^i, \ldots, e_{T-\tau_e^i}^i \mid i = 1, 2, \ldots, k\}$ $\bigcup_{v \in N} \{(v_\zeta, v_{\zeta+1}) \mid \zeta = 0, 1, \ldots, T\}$
Nodes	$v \in N$	$v_i \in N_i$
Edges	$e = (v, w) \in E$	$e_\zeta^i = (v_\zeta, w_{\zeta+\tau_e^i})$

See also Fig. 2 (a) and (b) for an instance of a dynamic network and its corresponding time-expanded network.

Next, let us define flow feasibility in this situation. The constraints for feasibility will be closely related to the construction of flows over time, so let us first illustrate the desired static-to-dynamic conversion here.

Definition 3 (Static to flow over time conversion). *Let x be a static flow in G^T in which $x^i(e)$ denotes the flow of commodity i on edge e. For $e^i_\zeta = (v_\zeta, w_{\zeta+\tau^i_e})$, we interpret the value of $x^i(e^i_\zeta)$ as the flow rate of commodity i entering edge (v, w) in the time interval $[\zeta, \zeta+1)$. This gives a flow f_x in the original dynamic network.*

Our goal now is to introduce appropriate constraints on the static flow in the time-expanded network, so that the above procedure can convert it into a feasible flow over time.

1. (Flow conservation.) This constraint is the same as for static network flows; see Eq. 2.
2. (Each edge is exclusive to a specific commodity.) Note that for problem HeteroMFT, for $v_\zeta \in N^T$, every edge $e = (v, w)$ in G is converted into k different edges $(v_\zeta, v_{\zeta+\tau^i_e})$ in E^T, where k is the number of commodities. Since each edge e^i_ζ is G^T is now catered only for the specific commodity i, we need to add further constraints to the feasible static flow conditions to forbid other commodities to travel along this edge.
   We therefore add the following constraints
   $$x^i(e^j_\zeta) = 0 \qquad \forall \zeta \in \{0, 1, \ldots, T-1\}, i \neq j. \tag{10}$$
3. (Capacity constraints at edge tails.) Again, since we split an edge e at time ζ into k edges e^i_ζ, we need to impose
   $$\sum_{i \in [k]} x^i(e^i_\zeta) \leq u_e.$$
4. (Capacity constraints along the edges.) The above capacity constraints at edge tails, when interpreted in the context of the flow over time f_x as defined in Definition 3, only impose the flows not to exceed the edge capacity at the entrance of each edge. However, the capacity constraints for a feasible flow over time in G, as shown in Eq. 9, are defined not only at the entrance of each edge, but also at *every point* along the edge; see Fig. 1 for an example where collision happens in the middle of an edge.
   To take care of that issue, let us first focus on the set of edges $\{e^i_\zeta : i \in [k], \zeta \in \{0, 1, \ldots, T-1\}\}$ which are derived from the edge $e \in E$. To analyze collisions happening in the middle of edges, we need to identify those $(\zeta_1, \ldots, \zeta_k)$, $\zeta_i \in \{0, 1, \ldots, T\}$, such that there exist $\chi_i \in [\zeta_i, \zeta_i + 1)$, and the flows sending commodity i at time χ_i arrive at the same point along the edge e at the same time. For such $(\zeta_1, \ldots, \zeta_k)$, we need to ensure that the sum of static flows along $e^i_{\zeta_i}$ is within the capacity u_e.

At first sight, this seems to involve enumerating every point in e, leading to infinitely many constraints. Fortunately, this can be reduced to finitely many points in e. Thanks to the following Propostion 1, we can first compute, for each pair of commodities $j, j' \in [k]$, every two time points $\zeta_j, \zeta_{j'} \in \{0, \ldots, T-1\}$, and every edge e, whether flow of commodity j at time ζ_j meets with flow of commodity j' at time $\zeta_{j'}$, or catches up with commodity j' at time $\zeta_{j'}+1$, at some point $\alpha \in [0,1]$ along e at time t. If so, for every $i \neq j, j'$, compute ζ_i such that $[\zeta_i, \zeta_i + 1)$ covers α at time t. After computing such ζ_i's, $i \in [k]$, we set up the constraint that

$$\sum_{i\in[k]} x^i(e^i_{\zeta_i}) \le u_e. \tag{11}$$

Proposition 1. *Suppose flows only change rate at integral time steps. Given $\alpha \in [0,1]$ and time θ. For every commodity $i \in [k]$, let χ_i be the point in time such that $\chi_i + \alpha\tau^i_e = \theta$, and let $\zeta_i = \lfloor \chi_i \rfloor$.*

Then there exists another set of times $\{\chi'_i \in [\zeta_i, \zeta_i+1]\}$, $\alpha' \in [0,1]$, and time θ', such that we have $\chi'_i + \alpha'\tau^i_e = \theta'$ for each $i \in [k]$, and one of the following cases hold:

1. *$\alpha' = 0$, and $\forall i, j \in [k]$, $\zeta_i = \zeta_j$;*
2. *there exist $\ell \neq j \in [k]$, such that $\chi'_\ell = \zeta_\ell$, $\chi'_j = \zeta_j$;*
3. *there exist $\ell \neq j \in [k]$, such that $\chi'_\ell = \zeta_\ell$, $\chi'_j = \zeta_j + 1 - \epsilon$ for any small $\epsilon > 0$.*

Proof. If $\alpha = 0$, then we have $\chi_i = \chi_j$ for any $i, j \in [k]$. Since $\chi_i \in [\zeta_i, \zeta_i + 1)$, we have $\zeta_i = \lfloor \chi_i \rfloor = \lfloor \chi_j \rfloor = \zeta_j$.

If $\alpha \neq 0$, then take $\ell \in [k]$ such that $\chi_\ell - \zeta_\ell$ is the minimum among $\chi_j - \zeta_j$, $j \in [k]$. For any $j \in [k]$, let $\chi'_j = \chi_j - (\chi_\ell - \zeta_\ell)$, so $\chi'_\ell = \zeta_\ell$. Note that for any $i, j \in [k]$, we still have $\chi'_i + \alpha\tau^i_e = \chi'_j + \alpha\tau^j_e$.

If there exists $j \in [k]$ and $j \neq \ell$, such that $\chi'_j = \zeta_j$, then case (b) holds. Otherwise, we have $\chi'_j > \zeta_j$ for any $j \neq \ell$.

For any $\delta > 0$ and $j \in [k]$, we have

$$\zeta_\ell + \alpha\tau^\ell_e - \delta = \chi'_j + \alpha\tau^j_e - \delta.$$

Note that the left-hand side is $\zeta_\ell + (\alpha - \delta/\tau^\ell_e)\tau^\ell_e$, and the right-hand side is $\chi'_j + \frac{\tau^j_e - \tau^\ell_e}{\tau^\ell_e} \cdot \delta + (\alpha - \delta/\tau^\ell_e)\tau^j_e$, and we need to ensure that (1) $\alpha - \delta/\tau^\ell_e > 0$, (2) for any $j \neq \ell$, $\zeta_j < \chi'_j + \frac{\tau^j_e - \tau^\ell_e}{\tau^\ell_e} \cdot \delta$, and (3) for any $j \neq \ell$, $\chi'_j + \frac{\tau^j_e - \tau^\ell_e}{\tau^\ell_e} \cdot \delta < \zeta_j + 1 - \epsilon$ for arbitrarily small $\epsilon > 0$. We now increase δ, and take $\chi'_j + \frac{\tau^j_e - \tau^\ell_e}{\tau^\ell_e} \cdot \delta$ to be the new χ'_j for each j, until one of (1), (2), and (3) is violated.

- If (1) is violated, then we are back to the $\alpha = 0$ setting.
- If (2) is violated, then we are in case (b). This means $\tau^j_e < \tau^\ell_e$, i.e. ℓ is slower than j.
- If (3) is violated, then we are in case (c). This means $\tau^j_e > \tau^\ell_e$, i.e. ℓ is faster than j.

This concludes the proof.

After the above adjustments, we can ensure that any static flow in the time-expanded network satisfying all the above constraints corresponds to a feasible flow over time in the original network.

4.3 A Pseudo-Polynomial-Time Algorithm for Two Commodities

In the homogeneous setting, a well-known application of time-expanded networks is a pseudo-polynomial-time algorithm to decide whether a feasible flow exists with time horizon T (cf. e.g. [15, Theorem 4.2]). The key is to realise that a flow over time can be converted to a static flow using the averaging technique, and a static flow can be converted to a flow over time using the obvious transformation in Definition 3.

However, it is not clear that the averaging technique can be applied to the heterogeneous setting in general, due to the possible violations of the capacity constraint due to heterogeneity. Interestingly, when the number of commodities is 2, a simple argument ensures that the averaging technique still works. This will also suggest why the averaging technique cannot work, at least not directly, for three or more commodities.

Given an instance of the HeteroMFT problem, suppose f^i, $i = 1, 2$, are feasible flows over time with time horizon T. We also assume that all transit times are integral. By averaging f^i in $[\zeta, \zeta+1)$ for $\zeta \in \{0, 1, \ldots, T-1\}$, we obtain a static flow x^i on G^T:

$$\forall e \in E, x(e^i_\zeta) := \int_\zeta^{\zeta+1} f^i_e(\xi) d\xi.$$

Proposition 2. *Let f^i and x^i, $i = 1, 2$, be as above. Then x^i's form a feasible flow on G^T.*

Proof. Note that feasible flows on G^T correspond exactly to those feasible, staircase like, flows over time in the original network. So we need to show that the flow over time f_x corresponding to x as defined in Definition 3 form a feasible flow over time. The flow conservation constraint clearly holds. We then examine the capacity constraint. Fix an edge e, and suppose commodity 1 is faster than commodity 2, i.e. $\tau^1_e < \tau^2_e$. Consider two flow intervals, f^1_e in $[\zeta_1, \zeta_1 + 1)$ and f^2_e in $[\zeta_2, \zeta_2 + 1)$. Suppose the first interval catches up with the second. Then there exists a time $\theta \in [0, T]$, $0 \leq \alpha \leq 1$, and $\chi_2 \in [\zeta_2, \zeta_2+1)$, such that $\theta - \alpha \cdot \tau^1_e = \zeta_1$, and $\theta - \alpha \cdot \tau^2_e = \chi_2$. It follows that $\alpha = (\zeta_1 - \chi_2)/(\tau^2_e - \tau^1_e)$. Note that τ^i_e, $i = 1, 2$, and ζ_1 are integers. So if χ_2 is not an integer, α cannot be 1. We then also have that $(\zeta_1 - \zeta_2)/(\tau^2_e - \tau^1_e) \leq 1$. Let $\alpha' = (\zeta_1 - \zeta_2)/(\tau^2_e - \tau^1_e)$. Because $\alpha' \leq 1$, the flow sent by f^1_e at time ζ_1 also catches up with the flow sent by f^2_e at time ζ_2 at the α' fraction of e. We can then use the capacity constraint 9 at the α'-fraction of e to conclude that the averaged flows also satisfy the capacity constraint.

Proposition 2 immediately gives the following.

Proof (Proof of Theorem 1). By a binary search, we can determine the optimal time T^* for which there exists a solution to the given instance of HeteroMFT in poly(T^*) rounds. For each time T' guessed during this procedure, we construct the time expanded network, solve the corresponding static flow problem in time polynomial in the input size and T', and convert that static flow (if it is solvable) to a dynamic one using the procedure in Definition 3. Proposition 2 ensures that for T no less than the optimal value in the dynamic network, there exists a feasible flow in G^T. This concludes the proof.

Remark 1. When the number of commodities is more than 2, the argument to prove Proposition 2 does not work, at least directly, due to the following. Suppose the intervals of f_e^i sent at $[\zeta_i, \zeta_i + 1)$, $i = 1, 2, 3$, do overlap at some point. Then we cannot ensure that the flows sent at time ζ_i meet at some time, which causes difficulty as we then cannot use the dynamic capacity constraints.

5 An FPTAS for HeteroMFT

In [5], Fleischer and Skutella designed a fully polynomial-time approximation scheme (FPTAS) for the HomoMFT problem. The key idea in their algorithm is to convert the dynamic network into a static *Δ-condensed time-expanded network*, whose definition we will discuss in detail later, and find a static flow in that network to approximate the optimal flow over time.

In this section we design an FPTAS for the more general HeteroMFT problem and any number of commodities. The main ideas supporting our FPTAS for HeteroMFT are drawn from [5]. However, because of the heterogeneity of the commodity speeds and the possible failure of the averaging technique for more than 2 commodities (see Sect. 4.3), it is not clear that any feasible flow over time can be converted to a feasible static flow in the condensed time-expanded network, which does hold in the homogeneous setting [5, Lemma 4.1]. Therefore, though our techniques are mostly already in [5], new analyses are needed to show that the best static flow produced by our algorithm is indeed a good approximation to the optimal dynamic problem for HeteroMFT.

Below we first present some preliminaries that support our algorithm, and then explain our algorithm and its analysis.

5.1 Preliminaries

Δ-Condensed Time-Expanded Network. The size of the static time-expanded network is linear in the value of time horizon T. Therefore, even though one can find a static flow in that network in polynomial time, it will be polynomial in T and therefore pseudo-polynomial in the input-size. To overcome this issue, Fleischer and Skutella introduced in [5] the *Δ-condensed time-expanded network.* More specifically, when the transit time of each commodity on each edge is always a multiple of $\Delta > 0$, then the time-expanded network G^T can be rescaled to a Δ-condensed time expanded network, denoted by G^T/Δ, in which each unit time interval now has length Δ. The new network contains only T/Δ copies of N, as depicted in Fig. 3. All capacities are also multiplied by Δ because each edge in G^T corresponds to a time interval of length Δ in G^T/Δ.

Paths with Delays. In the static flow setting, the well-known flow decomposition theorem states that a flow can be decomposed into a sum of path and cycle flows. In the flow over time setting, such a nice decomposition may not exist in general. Still, every infinitesimal unit of flow can be viewed as following a particular path. Since we allow node storage, we also need to record how long it stays at each node. This leads to the notion of paths with delays from [5, Sec. 4.6]. Let $P = (v_0, \ldots, v_\ell)$ be a path in G, and let $\iota = (\iota_1, \ldots, \iota_\ell)$, $\iota_i \in \mathbb{R}^{\geq 0}$, be a sequence of non-negative numbers. A *path with delays* P^ι is understood as indicating that a flow along P needs to stop at v_j for exactly ι_j time, $j \in \{1, \ldots, \ell\}$. The flow for commodity i along P^ι is then denoted by $f^i_{P^\iota}$.

Given this notion, a flow over time f with time horizon T can be decomposed into (possibly infinitely many) flows over time f_{P^ι} along paths with delays. In particular, the total flow of commodity i entering $e = (v_j, v_{j+1})$ at time θ is

$$f^i_e(\theta) = \sum_{P^\iota : e \in P} f^i_{P^\iota}(\theta - \tau(P^\iota, e)),$$

where

$$\tau(P^\iota, e) := \sum_{s=1}^{j} (\tau^i_{(v_{s-1}, v_s)} + \iota_s) \tag{12}$$

for $e = (v_j, v_{j+1})$. In addition, one can assume without loss of generality that all paths in the decomposition are simple. This is because the flow traveling along a cycle that visits some node v twice can also just wait at node v. Conversely, any flow over time given in the form of f_{P^ι} along paths with delays corresponds to a flow over time f defined on edges. Throughout the remainder of this section, we will discuss a flow over time both in its paths with delays representation f_{P^ι} and in its standard representation f.

5.2 Algorithm and Proof Outline

The idea of our approximation scheme is to first round up the transit times of each commodity on each edge to the nearest multiple of Δ, for some carefully selected Δ. Then we convert the dynamic network problem into a static Δ-condensed time-expanded network, and solve the quickest static flow problem on that network with the additional set of constraints 10 and 11. Finally we convert the static flow to a feasible flow over time.

We restate Theorem 2 as below here.

Theorem 2. For any $\epsilon > 0$, a $(1 + \epsilon)$-approximate solution to the HeteroMFT problem can be found in time polynomial in the input size and $\frac{1}{\epsilon}$.

The key to Theorem 2 is the following lemma.

Lemma 1. *For any constant $\epsilon > 0$, let $\Delta = \frac{\epsilon^2}{2n}T$. Let f be a heterogeneous multi-commodity flow over time f in a dynamic network G with demand $D = (d_1, \ldots, d_k)$ and time horizon T. Let $T' = (1+\epsilon)^4 \cdot T$.*

Then there exists another dynamic network G', obtained from G by modifying transit and delay times, satisfying the following property: in the time-expanded network $G'^{T'}/\Delta$, there exists a feasible static flow x such that the flow over time f_x constructed from x by Definition 3 is a feasible flow in G with time horizon at most $(1+\epsilon)^4 \cdot T$.

Furthermore, the parameters of G' can be computed in polynomial time.

The remaining of this section is devoted to the proof of Lemma 1.

5.3 Proof of Lemma 1

Let $\epsilon > 0$, and set $\Delta = \frac{\epsilon^2}{2n}T$. Starting from a flow over time f with time horizon T in a network G, our goal is to devise a static flow x in the Δ-condensed time-expanded network with time horizon $(1+\epsilon) \cdot T$. The construction of x goes through the following four steps.

Step 1: Flow Smoothening. Briefly speaking, given any heterogeneous multi-commodity flow over time f in network G with demand D and time horizon T, we can get a smoothened heterogeneous multi-commodity flow over time $\hat{f}$ with the same demand D within time horizon $(1+\epsilon) \cdot T$ and still obeys the capacity constraints in G. Here, smooth means that the rate changes are not drastic. The flow smoothening procedure applies to flows along paths with delays.

Definition 4. *Let f be a flow over time in a network G with time horizon T, and f_{P^ι} be a path decomposition of f. Given $\epsilon > 0$, the* smoothed flow *$\hat{f}$ is defined by*

$$\hat{f}^i_{P^\iota}(\theta) = \frac{1}{\epsilon T} \int_{\theta - \epsilon T}^{\theta} f^i_{P^\iota}(\xi) d\xi \tag{13}$$

for all $\theta \in [0, (1+\epsilon)T]$ and P^ι appears in the path decomposition of f.

The smoothed flow $\hat{f}$ enjoys the following property.

Proposition 3. *Let f be a flow over time in a network G with time horizon T. For any $\epsilon > 0$, the smoothed flow $\hat{f}$ is also a feasible flow over time with time horizon $(1+\epsilon)T$, and for any $\theta \in [0, (1+\epsilon)T]$, $\mu > 0$ and commodity i,*

$$|\hat{f}^i_{P^\iota}(\theta) - \hat{f}^i_{P^\iota}(\theta - \mu)| \leq \frac{\mu}{\epsilon T} u_P$$

where $u_P = \min_{e \in P} u_e$.

Step 2: Rounding up the Transit Times. After smoothing the flow, the next step is to round up the transit time of each commodity on each edge to the nearest multiple of Δ, such that the dynamic network can be feasibly converted to a Δ-condensed time-expanded network. We need to ensure that this rounding procedure will not jeopardize the feasibility and optimality of the solution. Fortunately this can be guaranteed by the smoothness property of the flow over time.

Proposition 4. *Let $\epsilon > 0$ and $\Delta \leq \frac{\epsilon^2}{2n}T$. Let $\tilde{G}$ be the network where the transit time of each commodity on each edge is rounded up to the nearest multiple of Δ. We think of the smoothed flow $\hat{f}$ from Definition 4 as a flow over time in $\tilde{G}$ with the delay on each node also rounded up to the nearest multiple of Δ. Then this flow satisfies the demand of each commodity and finishes with the time horizon $\tilde{T} \leq (1+\epsilon)^2 \cdot T$, and the capacity constraint on each edge is violated by at most a factor of $(1+\epsilon)$.*

Step 3: Construct a Condensed Time-Expanded Network. After Step 2, by averaging the flow over time $\tilde{f}$ over the time intervals $[i\Delta, (i+1)\Delta]$ in $\tilde{G}$, we get a corresponding static flow x in the Δ-condensed time-expanded network $\tilde{G}^{\tilde{T}}/\Delta$. Because $\tilde{f}$ is constructed from $\hat{f}$ which has been smoothened in Step 1, this static flow x achieves demand D within time $(1+\epsilon)^2 \cdot T$, and exceeds the capacity of edges by at most a factor of $(1+\epsilon)^2$.

Proposition 5. *The flow over time $\bar{f}$ constructed by Definition 3 from the static flow x in $\tilde{G}^{\tilde{T}}/\Delta$ achieves demand at least $D = (d_1, \ldots, d_k)$ with time horizon at most $(1+\epsilon)^2 \cdot T$, and the capacity constraint on each edge is violated by at most a factor of $(1+\epsilon)^2$.*

At this point, we have constructed a Δ-condensed time-expanded network $\tilde{G}^{\tilde{T}}/\Delta$ and have found a static flow x in it, such that the flow over time f_x constructed from x by Definition 3 achieves demand at least D with time horizon at most $(1+\epsilon)^2 T$, and the capacity constraint on each edge is violated by at most a factor of $(1+\epsilon)^2$.

Step 4: Remove the Capacity Violations. The last step is to remove the capacity violations. To achieve this, we apply the following two procedures:

1. First if we keep the structure of the time-expanded network intact, but change the unit time interval length from Δ to $(1+\epsilon)^2\Delta$, it will correspond to a new dynamic network in which all transit times and the time horizon are increased by a factor of $(1+\epsilon)^2$. The static flow x still corresponds to a flow over time f_x in this new network with the supply and demand of each commodity also increased by a factor of $(1+\epsilon)^2$. That is, f_x has time horizon $(1+\epsilon)^4 T$ and achieves demand $(1+\epsilon)^2 D$. But the capacity constraint on each edge is still violated by at most a factor of $(1+\epsilon)^2$.

2. Next, we reduce the flow values of x on all edges by a factor of $(1+\epsilon)^2$. The resulting static flow x will achieve demand $\frac{(1+\epsilon)^2 D}{(1+\epsilon)^2} = D$, with all capacity constraints strictly satisfied. The timespan of f_x is still $(1+\epsilon)^4 T$.

The above four steps complete the proof of Lemma 1. □

With the help of Lemma 1, the proof of our main theorem becomes rather straightforward.

Proof (Proof of Theorem 2). This proof follows the same structure of the proof of Theorem 1. That is, we use binary search to find the smallest T, such that in the Δ-condensed time-expanded network $G'^{T'}/\Delta$ constructed from Lemma 1, there exists a feasible static flow, which in turn implies the desired flow over time in G.

References

1. Ahuja, R.K., Magnanti, T.L., Orlin, J.B., Weihe, K.: Network flows: theory, algorithms and applications. ZOR-Methods Models Oper. Res. **41**(3), 252–254 (1995)
2. Aronson, J.E.: A survey of dynamic network flows. Ann. Oper. Res. **20**(1), 1–66 (1989)
3. Dhamala, T.N.: A survey on models and algorithms for discrete evacuation planning network problems. J. Indust. Manage. Optim. **11**(1), 265–289 (2015)
4. Fleischer, L., Skutella, M.: Minimum cost flows over time without intermediate storage. In: Proceedings of the Fourteenth Annual ACM-SIAM Symposium on Discrete Algorithms, pp. 66–75. Society for Industrial and Applied Mathematics (2003)
5. Fleischer, L., Skutella, M.: Quickest flows over time. SIAM J. Comput. **36**(6), 1600–1630 (2007)
6. Fleischer, L., Tardos, É.: Efficient continuous-time dynamic network flow algorithms. Oper. Res. Lett. **23**(3–5), 71–80 (1998)
7. Ford, L.R., Fulkerson, D.R.: Constructing maximal dynamic flows from static flows. Oper. Res. **6**(3), 419–433 (1958)
8. Ford, L.R., Fulkerson, D.R.: Flows in Networks. Princeton University Press, Princeton (1962)
9. Hall, A., Hippler, S., Skutella, M.: Multicommodity flows over time: efficient algorithms and complexity. Theoret. Comput. Sci. **379**(3), 387–404 (2007)
10. Halpern, J.: A generalized dynamic flows problem. Networks **9**(2), 133–167 (1979)
11. Hoppe, B.: Efficient dynamic network flow algorithms. Cornell University, Technical report (1995)
12. Hoppe, B., Tardos, É.: The quickest transshipment problem. Math. Oper. Res. **25**(1), 36–62 (2000)
13. Kotnyek, B.: An annotated overview of dynamic network flows. Ph.D. thesis, INRIA (2003)
14. Powell, W.B., Jaillet, P., Odoni, A.: Stochastic and dynamic networks and routing. Handbooks Oper .Res. Manage. Sci. **8**, 141–295 (1995)
15. Skutella, M.: An introduction to network flows over time. In: Cook, W., Lovasz, L., Vygen, J. (eds) Research Trends in Combinatorial Optimization, pp. 451–482. Springer, Heidelberg (2009). https://doi.org/10.1007/978-3-540-76796-1_21

On the Determinization of Event-Clock Input-Driven Pushdown Automata

Mizuhito Ogawa[1] and Alexander Okhotin[2](✉)

[1] Japan Advanced Institute of Science and Technology, Nomi, Japan
mizuhito@jaist.ac.jp
[2] Department of Mathematics and Computer Science, St. Petersburg State University, Saint Petersburg, Russia
alexander.okhotin@spbu.ru

Abstract. A timed extension of input-driven pushdown automata (also known as visibly pushdown automata and as nested word automata) under the event-clock model was introduced by Nguyen and Ogawa ("Event-clock visibly pushdown automata", 2009), who showed that this model can be determinized using the method of region construction. This paper proposes a new, direct determinization procedure for these automata: an n-state nondeterministic automaton with k different clock constraints is transformed to a deterministic automaton with 2^{n^2} states, 2^{n^2+k} stack symbols and the same clock constraints as in the original automaton. The construction is shown to be asymptotically optimal with respect to both the number of states and the number of stack symbols.

Keywords: Timed systems · input-driven pushdown automata · visibly pushdown automata · determinization · state complexity

1 Introduction

Timed automata (TA), introduced by Alur and Dill [2], are finite automata operating in real time. These automata enjoy decidability of the emptiness problem (equivalently, the state reachability problem) and are implemented as UPPAAL [7] for safety checking. The decidability of emptiness holds under various extensions of the model equipped with a pushdown store, such as the *Dense-Timed Pushdown Automata* (DTPDA) of Abdulla et al. [1] with *ages* (representing local clocks), which are further analyzed by Clemente and Lasota [11].

Although the emptiness problem for timed automata is decidable, timed automata are not closed under complementation, and their nondeterministic case cannot generally be determinized. Their inclusion problem is decidable only in the case of a single clock [18], and becomes undecidable for two clocks [2].

As an alternative timed device, the class of *event-clock automata* (ECA) was introduced by Alur et al. [3] and further studied by Geeraerts et al. [12]: this

Supported by the Russian Foundation for Basic Research under grant 20-51-50001.

A. S. Kulikov and S. Raskhodnikova (Eds.): CSR 2022, LNCS 13296, pp. 256–268, 2022.
https://doi.org/10.1007/978-3-031-09574-0_16

class allows determinization and complementation, and hence it enjoys decidable inclusion problem. An ECA is defined with a "prophecy clock" and a "history clock" bound to each input symbol. The history clock $\overleftarrow{x_a}$ associated with an input symbol a is always reset when a is read, and the prophecy clock $\overrightarrow{x_a}$ predicts the next occurrence of a.

In general, when a stack is introduced, this often destroys the decidability of the inclusion problem, since asynchronous behavior of two stacks disrupts a direct product of two devices. Even starting from finite automata, adding the stack makes the inclusion undecidable.

To remedy this, a constraint on the synchronous behaviour of stacks is imposed upon the model. The resulting *input-driven pushdown automata* [10, 14] (IDPDA), also known as *visibly pushdown automata* [5] and as *nested word automata* [6], are defined over an alphabet split into three parts: *left brackets* Σ_{+1}, on which the automaton must push one stack symbol, *right brackets* Σ_{-1}, on which the automaton must pop one stack symbol, and *neutral symbols* Σ_0, on which the automaton ignores the stack. Unlike the standard pushdown automata, IDPDA are closed under all Boolean operations, and they can be determinized [10]. An extensive study of this model was initiated by Alur and Madhusudan [5,6], who, in particular, established a lower bound on the determinization complexity, accordingly starting a line of research on the succinctness of description for this model [16], and also defined a Büchi-like extension for infinite strings, which has also received further attention [13, 17].

Event-clock visibly pushdown automata, which combine the ideas of input-driven pushdown and event-clock automata, were proposed by Nguyen and Ogawa [19], who proved that this model can be determinized. Their work was followed and extended by Bhave et al. [8] and Bozzelli et al. [9]. This paper revisits this model, with the aim to improve the determinization procedure. In addition, the model is further extended by introducing special event clocks recording the duration of the call/return relation. The resulting model is called *event-clock input-driven pushdown automata* (ECIDPDA).

The proposed determinization procedure is *direct*, in the sense that it *does not rely on the classical discretization* or "untime translation" method, and *is not based on the region construction*, which handles the extension by the age of a stack symbol in Bhave et al. [8]. Even though direct determization was once used by Alur and Madhusudan [4] for determinizing event-clock finite automata with only history clocks ($\overleftarrow{x_a}$), this idea, up to the authors' knowledge, did not receive any further development in the literature; in particular, all the existing work on input-driven/visibly pushdown event-clock automata relies on more sophisticated determinization constructions.

As per the proposed construction, presented in Sect. 3, any given n-state nondeterministic automaton with k different clock constraints and with any number of stack symbols is transformed to a deterministic automaton with 2^{n^2} states, 2^{n^2+k} stack symbols and the same clock constraints as in the original automaton. Furthermore, in Sect. 4, this construction is shown to be asymptotically optimal both with respect to the number of states and with respect to the number of stack symbols.

2 Definitions

Event-clock automata operate on *timed strings* over an alphabet Σ, that is, sequences of the form $w = (a_1, t_1) \dots (a_n, t_n)$, where $a_1 \dots a_n \in \Sigma^*$ is a string, and $t_1 < \dots < t_n$ are real numbers indicating the time of the symbols' appearance.

For input-driven pushdown automata, the alphabet Σ is split into three disjoint classes: $\Sigma = \Sigma_{+1} \cup \Sigma_{-1} \cup \Sigma_0$, where symbols in Σ_{+1} are called *left brackets*, symbols in Σ_{-1} are *right brackets*, and Σ_0 contains *neutral symbols.* An input-driven pushdown automaton always pushes one stack symbol upon reading a left bracket, pops one stack symbol upon reading a right bracket, and does not access the stack on neutral symbols. Typically, a string over such an alphabet is assumed to be *well-nested* with respect to its left and right brackets, but Alur and Madhusudan [5] adapt the definition to handle ill-nested inputs.

The proposed *event-clock input-driven pushdown automata* (ECIDPDA) operate on timed strings over an alphabet $\Sigma = \Sigma_{+1} \cup \Sigma_{-1} \cup \Sigma_0$. These automata operate like input-driven pushdown automata, and additionally can evaluate certain constraints upon reading each input symbol. These constraints refer to the following *clocks*, each evaluating to a real number:

- a symbol history clock $\overleftarrow{x_a}$, with $a \in \Sigma$, provides the time elapsed since the symbol a was last encountered;
- a symbol prediction clock $\overrightarrow{x_a}$, with $a \in \Sigma$, foretells the time remaining until the symbol a will be encountered next time;
- a stack history clock $\overleftarrow{x_{\text{push}}}$, defined on a right bracket, evaluates to the time elapsed since the matching left bracket;
- a stack prediction clock $\overrightarrow{x_{\text{pop}}}$, defined on a left bracket, foretells the time remaining until the matching right bracket.

These values are formally defined as follows.

Definition 1. *Let $\Sigma = \Sigma_{+1} \cup \Sigma_{-1} \cup \Sigma_0$ be an alphabet. The set of clocks over Σ is $\mathcal{C}(\Sigma) = \{\, \overleftarrow{x_a} \mid a \in \Sigma \,\} \cup \{\, \overrightarrow{x_a} \mid a \in \Sigma \,\} \cup \{\overleftarrow{x_{\text{push}}}, \overrightarrow{x_{\text{pop}}}\}$. Then the value of a clock from $\mathcal{C}(\Sigma)$ on a timed string $w = (a_1, t_1) \dots (a_n, t_n)$ at position $i \in \{1, \dots, n\}$ is defined as follows.*

$$\begin{aligned}
\overleftarrow{x_a} &= t_i - t_j, && \textit{for greatest } j < i \textit{ with } a_j = a \\
\overrightarrow{x_a} &= t_j - t_i, && \textit{for least } j > i \textit{ with } a_j = a \\
\overleftarrow{x_{\text{push}}} &= t_i - t_j, && \textit{if } a_j \in \Sigma_{+1} \textit{ and} a_i \in \Sigma_{-1} \textit{ match each other} \\
\overrightarrow{x_{\text{pop}}} &= t_j - t_i, && \textit{if } a_i \in \Sigma_{+1} \textit{ and } a_j \in \Sigma_{-1} \textit{ match each other}
\end{aligned}$$

In each case, if no such j exists, then the value of the clock is undefined.

The original model by Nguyen and Ogawa [19] used only symbol history clocks $\overleftarrow{x_a}$ and symbol prediction clocks $\overrightarrow{x_a}$. Stack history clocks $\overleftarrow{x_{\text{push}}}$ were first introduced by Bhave et al. [8], who called them *the age of stack symbols.* As

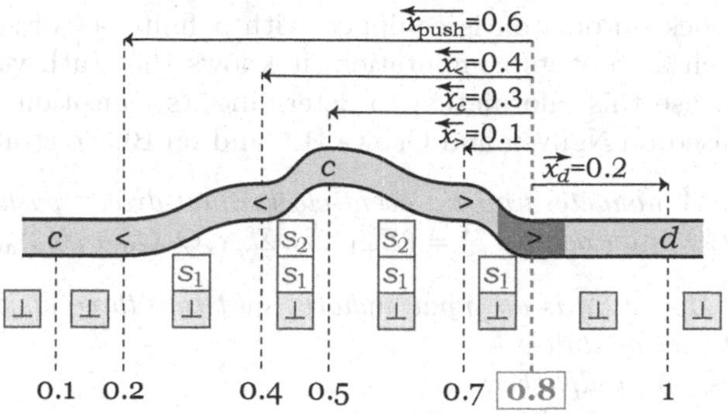

Fig. 1. Clock values for the string $w = (0.1, c)(0.2, <)(0.4, <)(0.5, c)(0.7, >)\mathbf{(0.8, >)}$ $(1, d)$, at the last right bracket, as in Example 1.

compared to the definition of Bhave et al. [8], another clock type, the stack prediction clock $\overrightarrow{x_{\text{pop}}}$, has been added to the model for symmetry.

A clock constraint is a logical formula that restricts the values of clocks at the current position: clock values can be compared with constants, and any Boolean combination of such conditions can be expressed.

Definition 2. *Let $\Sigma = \Sigma_{+1} \cup \Sigma_{-1} \cup \Sigma_0$ be an alphabet. The set of clock constraints over Σ, denoted by $\Phi(\Sigma)$, consists of the following formulae.*

- *For every clock $C \in \mathcal{C}(\Sigma)$ and for every non-negative constant $\tau \in \mathbb{R}$, the following are atomic clock constraints: $C \leqslant \tau$; $C \geqslant \tau$.*
- *If φ and ψ are clock constraints, then so are $(\varphi \vee \psi)$, $(\varphi \wedge \psi)$ and $\neg\varphi$.*

Let $w = (a_1, t_1) \dots (a_n, t_n)$ be a timed string, let $i \in \{1, \dots, n\}$ be a position therein. Each clock constraint can be either true or false on w at position i.

- *$C \leqslant \tau$ is true if the value of C on w at position i is defined and is at most τ.*
- *$C \geqslant \tau$ is true if the value of C on w at i is defined and is at least τ.*
- *$(\varphi \vee \psi)$ is true on w at i, if so is φ or ψ;*
- *$(\varphi \wedge \psi)$ is true on w at i, if so are both φ and ψ;*
- *$\neg\varphi$ is true on w at i, if φ is not.*

The following abbreviations are used: $C = \tau$ stands for $(C \leqslant \tau \wedge C \geqslant \tau)$; $C < \tau$ stands for $(C \leqslant \tau \wedge \neg(C \geqslant \tau))$; $C > \tau$ stands for $(C \geqslant \tau \wedge \neg(C \leqslant \tau))$.

Example 1. Let $\Sigma = \Sigma_{+1} \cup \Sigma_{-1} \cup \Sigma_0$, with $\Sigma_{+1} = \{<\}$, $\Sigma_{-1} = \{>\}$ and $\Sigma_0 = \{c, d\}$. Let $w = (0.1, c)(0.2, <)(0.4, <)(0.5, c)(0.7, >)\mathbf{(0.8, >)}(1, d)$ be a well-nested timed string over Σ, illustrated in Fig. 1. Then, the values of the clocks at position 6 (the last right bracket) are: $\overleftarrow{x_{\text{push}}} = 0.8 - 0.2 = 0.6$, $\overleftarrow{x_<} = 0.4$, $\overleftarrow{x_c} = 0.3$, $\overleftarrow{x_>} = 0.1$, $\overrightarrow{x_d} = 1 - 0.8 = 0.2$, and $\overleftarrow{x_d}$, $\overrightarrow{x_<}$, $\overrightarrow{x_c}$, $\overrightarrow{x_>}$, $\overrightarrow{x_{\text{pop}}}$ are undefined. Accordingly, the clock constraint $\overleftarrow{x_{\text{push}}} > 0.1 \vee \overrightarrow{x_c} \geqslant 0$ is true, whereas $\overleftarrow{x_c} > 0.1 \wedge \overrightarrow{x_d} < 0.2$ is false.

An event-clock automaton is equipped with a finite set of such clock constraints. At each step of its computation, it knows the truth value of each of them, and can use this information to determine its transition. The following definition is based on Nguyen and Ogawa [19] and on Bhave et al. [8].

Definition 3. *A nondeterministic event-clock input-driven pushdown automaton (ECIDPDA) is an octuple* $\mathcal{A} = (\Sigma_{+1}, \Sigma_0, \Sigma_{-1}, Q, Q_0, \Gamma, \langle\delta_a\rangle_{a\in\Sigma}, F)$, *where:*

- $\Sigma = \Sigma_{+1} \cup \Sigma_{-1} \cup \Sigma_0$ *is an input alphabet split into three disjoint classes;*
- Q *is a finite set of states;*
- Γ *is the pushdown alphabet;*
- $Q_0 \subseteq Q$ *is the set of initial states;*
- *for each neutral symbol* $c \in \Sigma_0$, *the state change is described by a partial function* $\delta_c \colon Q \times \Phi(\Sigma) \to 2^Q$;
- *the transition function by each left bracket symbol* $< \in \Sigma_{+1}$ *is* $\delta_< \colon Q \times \Phi(\Sigma) \to 2^{Q\times\Gamma}$, *which, for a given current state and the truth value of clock constraints, provides zero or more transitions of the form (next state, symbol to be pushed);*
- *for every right bracket symbol* $> \in \Sigma_{-1}$, *there is a partial function* $\delta_> \colon Q \times (\Gamma \cup \{\perp\}) \times \Phi(\Sigma) \to 2^Q$ *specifying possible next states, assuming that the given stack symbol is popped from the stack, or the stack is empty* ($\perp$)*;*
- $F \subseteq Q$ *is the set of accepting states.*

The domain of the transition function by each symbol must be finite.

An accepting computation of $\mathcal{A}$ *on a timed string* $w = (a_1, t_1) \ldots (a_n, t_n)$ *is any sequence* (q_0, α_0), (q_1, α_1), $\ldots$, (q_n, α_n), *with* $q_0, \ldots, q_n \in Q$, *and* $\alpha_0, \ldots, \alpha_n \in \Gamma^*$, *that satisfies the following conditions.*

- *It begins in an initial state* $q_0 \in Q_0$ *with the empty stack,* $\alpha_0 = \varepsilon$.
- *For each* $i \in \{1, \ldots, n\}$, *with* $a_i = c \in \Sigma_0$, *there exists a clock constraint* φ_i *that is true on* w *at position* i, *with* $q_i \in \delta_c(q_{i-1}, \varphi_i)$ *and* $\alpha_i = \alpha_{i-1}$.
- *For each* $i \in \{1, \ldots, n\}$, *with* $a_i = < \in \Sigma_{+1}$, *there exists a clock constraint* φ_i *that is true on* w *at position* i, *with* $(q_i, s) \in \delta_<(q_{i-1}, \varphi_i)$ *and* $\alpha_i = s\alpha_{i-1}$ *for some* $s \in \Gamma$.
- *For each* $i \in \{1, \ldots, n\}$, *with* $a_i = > \in \Sigma_{-1}$, *if* $\alpha_{i-1} = s\beta$ *for some* $s \in \Gamma$ *and* $\beta \in \Gamma^*$, *then there exists a clock constraint* φ_i *that is true on* w *at position* i, *with* $q_i \in \delta_>(q_{i-1}, s, \varphi_i)$ *and* $\alpha_i = \beta$
- *For each* $i \in \{1, \ldots, n\}$, *with* $a_i = > \in \Sigma_{-1}$, *if* $\alpha_{i-1} = \varepsilon$, *then there exists a clock constraint* φ_i *that is true on* w *at position* i, *with* $q_i \in \delta_>(q_{i-1}, \perp, \varphi_i)$ *and* $\alpha_i = \varepsilon$.
- *The computation ends in an accepting state* $q_n \in F$ *with any stack contents.*

The language recognized by $\mathcal{A}$, *denoted by* $L(\mathcal{A})$, *is the set of all timed strings, on which* $\mathcal{A}$ *has at least one accepting computation.*

Definition 4. *A nondeterministic event-clock input-driven pushdown automaton* $\mathcal{A} = (\Sigma_{+1}, \Sigma_0, \Sigma_{-1}, Q, Q_0, \Gamma, \langle\delta_a\rangle_{a\in\Sigma}, F)$ *is said to be deterministic if the following conditions hold.*

1. *There is a unique initial state:* $|Q_0| = 1$.
2. *Every transition function* δ_a, *with* $a \in \Sigma_0 \cup \Sigma_{+1}$, *satisfies* $|\delta_a(q, \varphi)| \leqslant 1$ *for all* $q \in Q$ *and* $\varphi \in \Phi(\Sigma)$, *and whenever* $\delta_a(q, \varphi)$ *and* $\delta_a(q, \varphi')$, *with* $\varphi \neq \varphi'$, *are both non-empty, the clock constraints* φ *and* φ' *cannot both be true at the same position of the same string.*
3. *Similarly, every transition function* $\delta_>$, *with* $> \in \Sigma_{-1}$, *satisfies* $|\delta_>(q, s, \varphi)| \leqslant 1$ *for all* $q \in Q$, $s \in \Gamma \cup \{\perp\}$ *and* $\varphi \in \Phi(\Sigma)$, *and whenever* $\delta_c(q, s, \varphi)$ *and* $\delta(q, s, \varphi')$, *with* $\varphi \neq \varphi'$, *are both non-empty, the clock constraints* φ *and* φ' *cannot both be true at the same position of the same string.*

The first result of this paper is that nondeterministic event-clock input-driven pushdown automata can be determinized. Determinization results for a very similar model were earlier given by Nguyen and Ogawa [19] and by Bhave et al. [8]. However, their constructions relied on the method of *region construction*, in which the space of clock values is discretized. On the other hand, the construction in the present paper has the benefit of being *direct*, in the sense that the transition function for a deterministic automaton directly simulates the transitions of a nondeterministic automaton. Later it will be proved that this easier construction is also optimal with respect to the number of states and stack symbols. The proposed construction is not much more difficult than the construction for standard input-driven pushdown automata, without time.

3 Direct Determinization of Event-Clock IDPDA

The classical construction for determinizing a standard (untimed) input-driven pushdown automaton [6,10], is based upon considering a nondeterministic automaton's behaviour on a left bracket and on a matching right bracket at the same time, while reading the right bracket. This is achieved by computing a *behaviour relation* $R \subseteq Q \times Q$ of the original automaton inside brackets, and then using it to simulate these two moments in the computation at once. In this way, the stack symbol pushed while reading the left bracket is matched to the symbol popped while reading the right bracket, and all possible computations of this kind can be considered at once.

In the event-clock case, the nondeterministic decisions made on a left bracket are based upon the clock values at that time, and if the simulation of these decisions were deferred until reading the matching right bracket, then those clock values would no longer be available. Since event-clock automata cannot manipulate clock values explicitly, they, in particular, cannot push the clock values onto the stack for later use. What can be done is to *test all elementary clock constraints while reading the left bracket*, store their truth values in the stack, and later, upon reading the right bracket, use this information to simulate the behaviour of the original automaton on the left bracket. This idea is implemented in the following construction, which uses the same set of states as the classical construction [6,10], but requires more complicated stack symbols.

Theorem 1. *Let* $\mathcal{A} = (\Sigma_{+1}, \Sigma_0, \Sigma_{-1}, Q, Q_0, \Gamma, \langle\delta_a\rangle_{a\in\Sigma}, F)$ *be a nondeterministic event-clock input-driven pushdown automaton. Let* Ψ *be the set of atomic constraints used in its transitions. Then there exists a deterministic event-clock input-driven pushdown automaton with the set of states* $Q' = 2^{Q\times Q}$*, and with the pushdown alphabet* $\Gamma' = 2^{Q\times Q} \times \Sigma_{+1} \times 2^{\Psi}$*, which recognizes the same set of timed strings as* $\mathcal{A}$*.*

Proof. States of the deterministic automaton $\mathcal{B}$ are sets of pairs $(p, q) \in Q \times Q$, with each pair meaning that there is a computation of the original automaton $\mathcal{A}$ on the longest well-nested suffix of the input that begins in the state p and ends in the state q. The initial state of $\mathcal{B}$ is $q_0' = \{\, (q_0, q_0) \mid q_0 \in Q_0 \,\}$.

For a **neutral symbol** $c \in \Sigma_0$ and a state $P \in Q'$, the transition $\delta_c'(P)$ advances all current computations traced in P by the next symbol c. Each computation continues by its own transition, which requires a certain clock constraint to be true. Whether each clock constraint $\varphi \in \Phi(\Sigma)$ is true or false, can be deduced from the truth assignment to the atomic constraints. For every set of atomic constraints $S \subseteq \Psi$, let $\xi_S = \bigwedge_{C\in S} C \wedge \bigwedge_{C\in\Psi\setminus S} \neg C$ be a clock constraint asserting that among all atomic constraints, exactly those belonging to S are true. Then, for every set S, the new automaton has the following transition.

$$\delta_c(P, \xi_S) = \{\, (p, q') \mid \exists (p, q) \in P,\ \exists \varphi \in \Phi(\Sigma) : q' \in \delta_c(q, \varphi),\ \varphi \text{ is true under } S \,\}$$

On a **left bracket** $< \in \Sigma_{+1}$, the transition of $\mathcal{B}$ in a state $P \in Q'$ pushes the current context of the simulation onto the stack, and starts the simulation afresh at the next level of brackets, where it will trace the computations beginning in different states $p' \in Q$. A computation in a state p' is started only if any computations of $\mathcal{A}$ actually reach that state. In addition, $\mathcal{B}$ pushes the current left bracket ($<$), as well as the truth value of all atomic constraints at the present moment, $S \subseteq \Psi$. This is done in the following transitions, defined for all $S \subseteq \Psi$.

$$\delta'_<(P, \xi_S) = \big(\{\, (p', p') \mid \exists (p, q) \in P,\ \exists \varphi \in \Phi(\Sigma) : \varphi \text{ is true under } S,\\ p' \in \delta_<(q, \varphi) \},\ (P, <, S)\big)$$

If a matching right bracket ($>$) is eventually read, then $\mathcal{B}$ shall pop $(P, <, S)$ from the stack and reconstruct what has happened to each of the computations of $\mathcal{A}$ in P at this point and further on. On the other hand, if this left bracket ($<$) is unmatched, then the acceptance shall be determined on the basis of the computations traced on the inner level of brackets.

When $\mathcal{B}$ encounters a **matched right bracket** $> \in \Sigma_{-1}$ in a state $P' \subseteq Q \times Q$, it pops a stack symbol $(P, <, S) \in \Gamma'$ containing the matching left bracket ($< \in \Sigma_{+1}$), the data on all computations on the current level of brackets simulated up to that bracket ($P \subseteq Q \times Q$), and the truth value of all atomic clock constraints at the moment of reading that bracket ($S \subseteq \Psi$).

Then, each computation in P is continued by simulating the transition by the left bracket ($<$), the behaviour inside the brackets stored in P', and the transition by the right bracket ($>$), all at once. Let $u{<}v{>}$ be the longest well-nested suffix of the string read so far. Every computation of $\mathcal{A}$ on u, which begins in a state p and ends in a state q, is represented by a pair (p, q). Upon reading

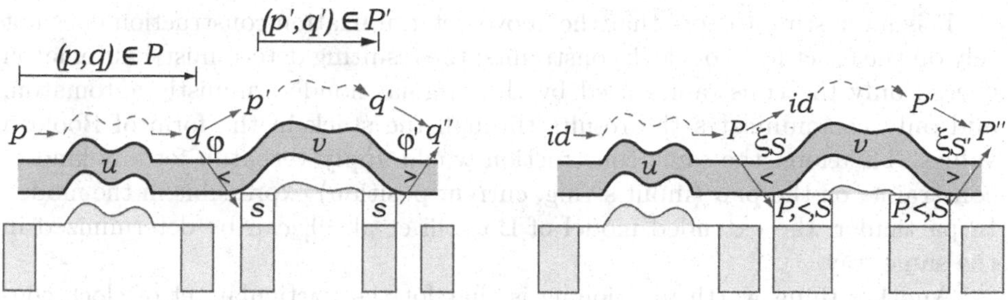

Fig. 2. (left) A computation of a nondeterministic event-clock IDPDA; (right) Its simulation by a deterministic event-clock IDPDA.

the left bracket (<), the automaton $\mathcal{A}$ makes a transition to a state p', pushing a stack symbol s, along with checking a clock constraint φ. The automaton $\mathcal{B}$ can now check the same clock constraint by using the set S of atomic clock constraints that held true at the earlier left bracket (<). For every set of atomic constraints $S' \subseteq \Psi'$, the following transition is defined (Fig. 2).

$$\begin{aligned}\delta'_{>}(P', (P, <, S), \xi_{S'}) = \{\, (p, q'') \mid\\ \exists (p, q) \in P, \exists (p', q') \in P', \exists s \in \Gamma, \exists \varphi, \varphi' \in \Phi(\Sigma) : \varphi \text{ is true under } S,\\ (p', s) \in \delta_{<}(q, \varphi),\ \varphi' \text{ is true under } S',\ q'' \in \delta_{>}(q', s, \varphi')\}\end{aligned}$$

When $\mathcal{B}$ reads an **unmatched right bracket** $> \in \Sigma_{-1}$ while in a state $P \subseteq Q \times Q$, it continues the existing computations on the new bottom level of brackets.

$$\delta_{>}(P, \bot, \xi_S) = \{\, (p', p') \mid \exists (p, q) \in P,\ \exists \varphi : p' \in \delta_{>}(q, \bot, \varphi),\ \varphi \text{ is true under } S \,\}$$

The set of **accepting states** reflects all computations of $\mathcal{A}$ ending in an accepting state.

$$F' = \{\, P \subseteq Q \times Q \mid \text{there is a pair } (p, q) \text{ in } P, \text{ with } q \in F \,\}$$

A formal correctness claim for this construction reads as follows.

Claim. Let uvw be a timed string, where v is the longest well-nested suffix of uv, and let $P \subseteq Q \times Q$ be the state reached by $\mathcal{B}$ on uvw after reading uv. Then a pair (p, q) is in P if and only if there is a computation of $\mathcal{A}$ on uvw that passes through the state p right after reading u, and later, after reading the following v, enters the state q.

The claim can be proved by induction on the bracket structure of an input string.

Applying the claim to the whole input string shows that $\mathcal{B}$ accepts this string if and only if one of the computations of $\mathcal{A}$ on the same input string is accepting.

□

It is interesting to note that the above determinization construction does not rely on the exact form of clock constraints: the resulting deterministic automaton checks only the constraints used by the original nondeterministic automaton, and only communicates the results through the stack in the form of Boolean values. Therefore, the same construction would apply verbatim for any kind of constraints on the pair (input string, current position) expressible in the model. In particular, the extended model of Bozzelli et al. [9] can be determinized in the same way.

Another thing worth mentioning is that for the particular set of clock constaints assumed in this paper, the determinization construction in Theorem 1 can be improved to eliminate all references to the stack prediction clock ($\overrightarrow{x_{\text{pop}}}$), at the expense of using more states. This construction shall be presented in the upcoming full version of this paper.

4 A Lower Bound on the Determinization Complexity

The timed determinization construction in Theorem 1 produces 2^{n^2} states and 2^{n^2+k} stack symbols, where n is the number of states in the nondeterministic automaton and k is the number of atomic clock constraints. It shall now be proved that this construction is asymptotically optimal. The following theorem, proved in the rest of this section, is a timed extension of a result by Okhotin, Piao and Salomaa [15, Thm. 3.2].

Theorem 2. *For every n and for every k, there is an $O(n)$-state nondeterministic ECIDPDA over an alphabet of size $k + O(1)$, with nk stack symbols and k atomic constraints referring only to symbol history clocks, such that every deterministic ECIDPDA recognizing the same timed language must have at least 2^{n^2} states and at least $2^{n^2-O(n)+k}$ stack symbols.*

The automaton is defined over the following alphabet: $\Sigma_{+1} = \{<\}$, $\Sigma_{-1} = \{>\}$, $\Sigma_0 = \{a, b, c, \#\} \cup \{ e_i \mid 1 \leqslant i \leqslant k \}$. For a set of pairs $R = \{(i_1, j_1), \ldots, (i_\ell, j_\ell)\} \subseteq \{1, \ldots, n\}^2$, let $u_R \in \{a, b, \#\}^*$ be the string that lists all pairs in R in the lexicographical order, under the following encoding.

$$u_R = \#ab\#a^{i_1}b^{j_1}\#a^{i_2}b^{j_2}\ldots\#a^{i_\ell}b^{j_\ell}\#ab$$

For every set of symbols $X = \{e_{i_1}, \ldots, e_{i_\ell}\} \subseteq \{e_1, \ldots, e_k\}$, let $v_X = e_1 \ldots e_k e_{i_1} \ldots e_{i_\ell}$ be the string that first lists all the symbols in $\{e_1, \ldots, e_k\}$, and then only the symbols in X.

Now, let $m \geqslant 1$ be the number of levels in the string to be constructed, let $s_1, \ldots, s_m, s_{m+1} \in \{1, \ldots, n\}$ be numbers, let $R_1, \ldots, R_m \subseteq \{1, \ldots, n\}^2$ be relations, and let $X_1, Y_1, \ldots, X_m, Y_m \subseteq \{e_1, \ldots, e_k\}$ be $2m$ sets of symbols. This information is encoded in the following string.

$$w = \underbrace{v_{X_1}{<}u_{R_1}v_{X_2}{<}u_{R_2}\cdots v_{X_m}{<}u_{R_m}}_{w_1}\underbrace{c^{s_{m+1}}v_{Y_m}{>}c^{s_m}\ldots v_{Y_2}{>}c^{s_2}v_{Y_1}{>}c^{s_1}}_{w_2}$$

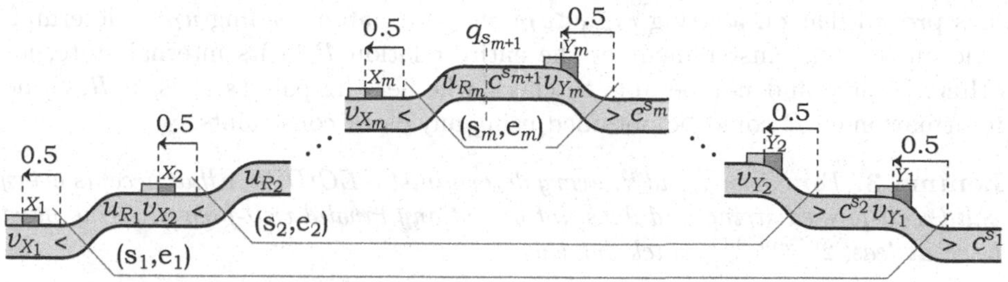

Fig. 3. A nondeterministic event-clock IDPDA checking the validity of a well-formed string.

The string is made timed by saying that the duration of each named substring is 1 time unit, and in each substring v_{X_i}, its first k symbols occur more than 0.5 time units earlier than the subsequent left bracket ($<$), whereas its remaining symbols representing the elements of X_i occur less than 0.5 time units earlier than the left bracket. Similarly, in each string v_{Y_i}, its first k symbols occur more than 0.5 time units earlier than the next right bracket ($>$), while its remaining symbols occur less than 0.5 time units earlier than the bracket. This allows an event-clock automaton to *see* the set X_i using clock constraints while reading the left bracket ($<$), and to see Y_i while at the right bracket ($>$). For the clock constraints not to see anything else, the first k symbols of v_X, and the first and the last three symbols u_R, occur at predefined time independent of X and R.

A timed string is said to be *well-formed* if it is defined as above, for some m, s_i, R_i, X_i and Y_i. A well-formed string is *valid*, if $(s_i, s_{i+1}) \in R_i$ and $X_i \cap Y_i \neq \varnothing$ for each i.

Lemma 1. *For every n and k, there exists a nondeterministic ECIDPDA using $O(n)$ states, nk stack symbols and k clock constraints, which accepts every valid well-formed string and does not accept any invalid well-formed string.*

Proof (a sketch). The automaton operates as in Fig. 3. At the left bracket following each v_{X_i}, it guesses s_i and e_i, using a clock constraint $\overleftarrow{x_{e_i}} < 1$ to check that $e_i \in X_i$, pushes the pair (s_i, e_i) and remembers s_i in its state. While reading u_{R_i}, it guesses any s_{i+1} with $(s_i, s_{i+1}) \in R_i$ and remembers s_{i+1} in its state. On each $c^{s_{i+1}}$, the automaton checks that the current state is s_{i+1} and forgets its value. On the following right bracket, the automaton pops the pair (s_i, e_i), verifies that $e_i \in Y_i$ using a constraint $\overleftarrow{x_{e_i}} < 1$, and keeps s_i in its current state. □

Lemma 2. *For every n and k, every deterministic ECIDPDA that accepts every valid well-formed string and does not accept any invalid well-formed string must have at least 2^{n^2} states.*

Although the bound is the same as in the untimed case [15], an event-clock automaton could potentially use its clocks to reduce the number of states. Still, it is proved that on a string $v_{\{e_1\}}{<}u_R c^t v_{\{e_1\}}{>}c^s$, after reading u_R, a deterministic automaton must remember the entire relation R in its internal state, for otherwise it would not be able to check whether the pair (s,t) is in R, as no information on R could be obtained using any clock constraints.

Lemma 3. *For every n and k, every deterministic ECIDPDA that accepts every valid well-formed string and does not accept any invalid well-formed string must have at least $2^{n^2-o(1)+k}$ stack symbols.*

Proof. The proof is modelled on the proof by Okhotin, Piao and Salomaa [15, Lemma 3.4], with the clock constraints added. The argument uses binary relations that are both left-total and right-total: that is, relations $R \subseteq \{1,\ldots,n\}^2$ in which, for every $x \in \{1,\ldots,n\}$, there is an element y with $(x,y) \in R$, and, symmetrically, for every y, there is an element x with $(x,y) \in R$. There are at least $2^{n^2} - 2n \cdot 2^{n(n-1)} = 2^{n^2-O(n)}$ such relations.

Fix the number of levels $m \geqslant 1$, let $R_1,\ldots,R_m \subseteq \{1,\ldots,n\}^2$ be left- and right-total relations, and let $X_1,\ldots,X_m \subseteq \{e_1,\ldots,e_k\}$ be non-empty sets of symbols. These parameters define the first part w_1 of a well-formed string. It is claimed that, after reading w_1, a deterministic automaton somehow has to store all relations $R_1,\ldots,R_m$ and all sets $X_1,\ldots,X_m$ in the available memory: that is, in m stack symbols and in one internal state.

Suppose that, for some $R_1,\ldots,R_m,R'_1,\ldots,R'_m \subseteq \{1,\ldots,n\}^2$ and $X_1,\ldots,X_m,X'_1,\ldots,X'_m \subseteq \{e_1,\ldots,e_k\}$, with $(R_1,\ldots,R_m,X_1,\ldots,X_m) \neq (R'_1,\ldots,R'_m,X'_1,\ldots,X'_m)$, the automaton, after reading the corresponding first parts w_1 and w'_1, comes to the same state with the same stack contents.

$$w_1 = v_{X_1}{<}u_{R_1}v_{X_2}{<}u_{R_2}\cdots v_{X_m}{<}u_{R_m}$$
$$w'_1 = v_{X'_1}{<}u_{R'_1}v_{X'_2}{<}u_{R'_2}\cdots v_{X'_m}{<}u_{R'_m}$$

First, as in the argument by Okhotin, Piao and Salomaa [15, Lemma 3.4], assume that these parameters differ in an i-th relation, with $(s,t) \in R_i \setminus R'_i$. Let $s_i = s$. Since all relations $R_{i-1},\ldots,R_1$ are right-total, there exists a sequence of numbers $s_{i-1},\ldots,s_1$, with $(s_j,s_{j+1}) \in R_j$ for all $j \in \{1,\ldots,i-1\}$. Similarly, let $s_{i+1} = t$. Since the relations $R_{i+1},\ldots,R_m$ are left-total, there is a sequence $s_{i+2},\ldots,s_{m+1}$, with $(s_j,s_{j+1}) \in R_j$ for all $j \in \{i+1,\ldots,m\}$. Construct the following continuation for w_1 and w'_1.

$$w_2 = c^{s_{m+1}}v_{X_m}{>}c^{s_m}\ldots v_{X_2}{>}c^{s_2}v_{X_1}{>}c^{s_1}$$

The concatenation w_1w_2 is then well-formed and valid, whereas the concatenation w'_1w_2 is well-formed and invalid, because $(s_i,s_{i+1}) \notin R'_i$. But, while reading w_2, the automaton cannot tell w_1 from w'_1 using history clocks, and thus the automaton either accepts both concatenations or rejects both of them, which is a contradiction.

Now assume that the prefixes w_1 and w'_1 use the same relations $R_1,\ldots,R_m$ and differ in an i-th set, with $e \in X_i \setminus X'_i$. Since all relations are left-total, there exists a sequence of numbers $s_1,\ldots,s_m,s_{m+1}$, with $(s_j,s_{j+1}) \in R_j = R'_j$ for all

$j \in \{1, \ldots, m\}$. This time, the continuation includes the sequence of numbers and takes all sets X_j from w_1, except for X_i, which is replaced by $\{e\}$.

$$w_2 = c^{s_{m+1}} v_{X_m} {>} c^{s_m} \ldots v_{X_{i+1}} {>} c^{s_{i+1}} v_{\{e\}} {>} c^{s_i} v_{X_{i-1}} {>} c^{s_{i-1}} \ldots v_{X_1} {>} c^{s_1}$$

Then, both concatenations $w_1 w_2$ and $w_1' w_2$ are well-formed. However, the concatenation $w_1 w_2$ is valid, whereas $w_1' w_2$ is invalid, because $X_i' \cap \{e\} = \varnothing$. Hence the automaton again either accepts or rejects both strings, and a contradiction is obtained.

This shows that, for each $m \geqslant 1$, the automaton must be able to reach at least $(2^{n^2} - 2n \cdot 2^{n(n-1)})^m (2^k - 1)^m$ distinct configurations after reading different strings of the given form. Then, $|\Gamma|^m \cdot |Q|$ cannot be less than this number, and for m large enough this inequality holds only if $|\Gamma| \geqslant 2^{n^2 - o(1) + k}$. □

The proof of Theorem 2 follows from Lemmata 1–3. It implies that the determinization construction in Theorem 1 is asymptotically optimal both with respect to the number of states and to the number of stack symbols.

Acknowledgement. The authors are grateful to the anonymous reviewers for pointing out numerous shortcomings of the original submission.

References

1. Abdulla, P.A., Atig, M.F., Stenman, J.: Dense-timed pushdown automata. In: Proceedings of the 27th Annual IEEE Symposium on Logic in Computer Science, LICS 2012, Dubrovnik, Croatia, June 25–28, 2012, pp. 35–44. IEEE Computer Society (2012). https://doi.org/10.1109/LICS.2012.15
2. Alur, R., Dill, D.L.: A theory of timed automata. Theor. Comput. Sci. **126**(2), 183–235 (1994). https://doi.org/10.1016/0304-3975(94)90010-8
3. Alur, R., Fix, L., Henzinger, T.A.: Event-clock automata: a determinizable class of timed automata. Theor. Comput. Sci. **211**(1–2), 253–273 (1999). https://doi.org/10.1016/S0304-3975(97)00173-4
4. Alur, R., Madhusudan, P.: Decision problems for timed automata: a survey. In: Bernardo, M., Corradini, F. (eds.) SFM-RT 2004. LNCS, vol. 3185, pp. 1–24. Springer, Heidelberg (2004). https://doi.org/10.1007/978-3-540-30080-9_1
5. Alur, R., Madhusudan, P.: Visibly pushdown languages. In: Babai, L. (ed.) Proceedings of the 36th Annual ACM Symposium on Theory of Computing, Chicago, IL, USA, June 13–16, 2004, pp. 202–211. ACM (2004). https://doi.org/10.1145/1007352.1007390
6. Alur, R., Madhusudan, P.: Adding nesting structure to words. J. ACM **56**(3), 16:1–16:43 (2009). https://doi.org/10.1145/1516512.1516518
7. Bengtsson, J., Larsen, K., Larsson, F., Pettersson, P., Yi, W.: UPPAAL—a tool suite for automatic verification of real-time systems. In: Alur, R., Henzinger, T.A., Sontag, E.D. (eds.) HS 1995. LNCS, vol. 1066, pp. 232–243. Springer, Heidelberg (1996). https://doi.org/10.1007/BFb0020949
8. Bhave, D., Dave, V., Krishna, S.N., Phawade, R., Trivedi, A.: A logical characterization for dense-time visibly pushdown automata. In: Dediu, A.-H., Janoušek, J., Martín-Vide, C., Truthe, B. (eds.) LATA 2016. LNCS, vol. 9618, pp. 89–101. Springer, Cham (2016). https://doi.org/10.1007/978-3-319-30000-9_7

9. Bozzelli, L., Murano, A., Peron, A.: Event-clock nested automata. In: Klein, S.T., Martín-Vide, C., Shapira, D. (eds.) LATA 2018. LNCS, vol. 10792, pp. 80–92. Springer, Cham (2018). https://doi.org/10.1007/978-3-319-77313-1_6
10. von Braunmühl, B., Verbeek, R.: Input driven languages are recognized in log n space. In: Karplnski, M., van Leeuwen, J. (eds.) Topics in the Theory of Computation, North-Holland Mathematics Studies, vol. 102, pp. 1–19. North-Holland (1985). https://doi.org/10.1016/S0304-0208(08)73072-X
11. Clemente, L., Lasota, S.: Timed pushdown automata revisited. In: 30th Annual ACM/IEEE Symposium on Logic in Computer Science, LICS 2015, Kyoto, Japan, 6–10 July 2015, pp. 738–749. IEEE Computer Society (2015). https://doi.org/10.1109/LICS.2015.73
12. Geeraerts, G., Raskin, J.-F., Sznajder, N.: On regions and zones for event-clock automata. Formal Methods Syst. Des. **45**(3), 330–380 (2014). https://doi.org/10.1007/s10703-014-0212-1
13. Löding, C., Madhusudan, P., Serre, O.: Visibly pushdown games. In: Lodaya, K., Mahajan, M. (eds.) FSTTCS 2004. LNCS, vol. 3328, pp. 408–420. Springer, Heidelberg (2004). https://doi.org/10.1007/978-3-540-30538-5_34
14. Mehlhorn, K.: Pebbling mountain ranges and its application to DCFL-recognition. In: de Bakker, J., van Leeuwen, J. (eds.) ICALP 1980. LNCS, vol. 85, pp. 422–435. Springer, Heidelberg (1980). https://doi.org/10.1007/3-540-10003-2_89
15. Okhotin, A., Piao, X., Salomaa, K.: Descriptional complexity of input-driven pushdown automata. In: Bordihn, H., Kutrib, M., Truthe, B. (eds.) Languages Alive. LNCS, vol. 7300, pp. 186–206. Springer, Heidelberg (2012). https://doi.org/10.1007/978-3-642-31644-9_13
16. Okhotin, A., Salomaa, K.: Complexity of input-driven pushdown automata. SIGACT News **45**(2), 47–67 (2014). https://doi.org/10.1145/2636805.2636821
17. Okhotin, A., Selivanov, V.L.: Input-driven pushdown automata on well-nested infinite strings. In: Santhanam, R., Musatov, D. (eds.) CSR 2021. LNCS, vol. 12730, pp. 349–360. Springer, Cham (2021). https://doi.org/10.1007/978-3-030-79416-3_21
18. Ouaknine, J., Worrell, J.: On the language inclusion problem for timed automata: closing a decidability gap. In: 19th IEEE Symposium on Logic in Computer Science (LICS 2004), 14–17 July 2004, Turku, Finland, Proceedings, pp. 54–63. IEEE Computer Society (2004). https://doi.org/10.1109/LICS.2004.1319600
19. Van Tang, N., Ogawa, M.: Event-clock visibly pushdown automata. In: Nielsen, M., Kučera, A., Miltersen, P.B., Palamidessi, C., Tůma, P., Valencia, F. (eds.) SOFSEM 2009. LNCS, vol. 5404, pp. 558–569. Springer, Heidelberg (2009). https://doi.org/10.1007/978-3-540-95891-8_50

The GKK Algorithm is the Fastest over Simple Mean-Payoff Games

Pierre Ohlmann[(✉)]

University of Warsaw, Warsaw, Poland
pohlmann@mimuw.edu.pl

Abstract. We study the algorithm of Gurvich, Karzanov and Khachyian (GKK algorithm) when it is ran over mean-payoff games with no simple cycle of weight zero. We propose a new symmetric analysis, lowering the $O(n^2N)$ upper-bound of Pisaruk on the number of iterations down to $N + E^+ + E^- \leq nN$, where n is the number of vertices, N is the largest absolute value of a weight, and E^+ and E^- are respectively the largest finite energy and dual-energy values of the game. Since each iteration is computed in $O(m)$, this improves on the state of the art pseudopolynomial $O(mnN)$ runtime bound of Brim, Chaloupka, Doyen, Gentilini and Raskin, by taking into account the structure of the game graph. We complement our result by showing that the analysis of Dorfman, Kaplan and Zwick also applies to the GKK algorithm, which is thus also subject to the state of the art combinatorial runtime bound of $O(m2^{n/2})$.

Keywords: Mean-payoff games · Symmetric algorithm · GKK algorithm · Pseudopolynomial

1 Introduction

Mean-Payoff and Energy Games. In the games under study, two players, Min and Max, take turns in moving a token over a sinkless finite directed graph whose edges are labelled by (potentially negative) integers, interpreted as payoffs from Min to Max. In a mean-payoff game, the players aim to optimise the average payoff in the long run. When playing an energy game, Min and Max optimise the profile upper-bound which takes values in $[0, +\infty]$; in a dual-energy game, the profile lower-bound in $[-\infty, 0]$ comes under scrutiny.

These three games are determined [12]: for each initial vertex v, there is a value x such that starting from v, the minimiser can ensure an outcome $\leq x$ whereas the maximiser can ensure a least x. They are moreover uniformly positionally determined [2,7] which means that the players can achieve the optimal values from every vertex even when restricted to a single strategy with no memory. We refer to Fig. 1 for a complete example.

In this paper, we are interested in solving the threshold problem for mean-payoff games: given a game and an initial vertex, decide whether its value is ≤ 0.

A. S. Kulikov and S. Raskhodnikova (Eds.): CSR 2022, LNCS 13296, pp. 269–288, 2022.
https://doi.org/10.1007/978-3-031-09574-0_17

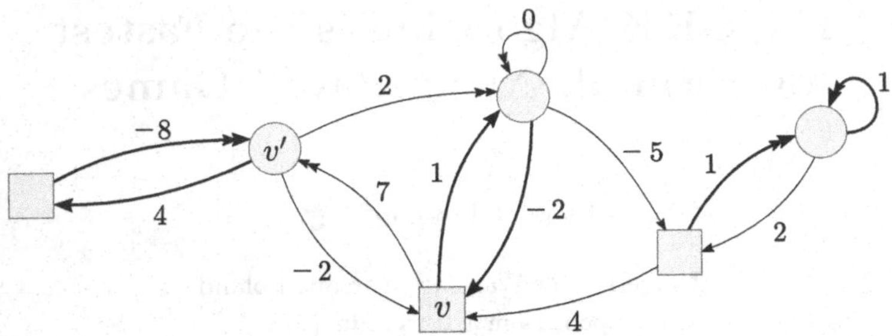

Fig. 1. Example of a game; circles and squares represent vertices which respectively belong to Min and Max. Mean-payoff values from left to right are $-2, -2, -\frac{1}{2}, -\frac{1}{2}, 1$ and 1, and mean-payoff-optimal positional strategies for both players are identified in bold. Energy values are $0, 2, 9, 0, \infty$ and ∞, and energy-optimal strategies are given by arrows with double heads. Dual energy values are $-\infty, -\infty, -\infty, -\infty, 0$ and 0; the bold strategy also gives an optimal strategy in the dual-energy game.

As a consequence of positional determinacy, the mean-payoff value of a vertex is non-positive if and only if the energy value is finite [3]. In fact, all state of the art algorithms [1,3,6] for the threshold problem – further discussed below – actually go through computing the energy values. The best algorithms for the more general problems of computing the exact values or synthesising optimal strategies in the mean-payoff game also rely on solving many auxiliary energy games [5].

Positional strategies achieving positive or non-positive values can be checked in polynomial time, and therefore the problem belongs to NP $\cap$ coNP. Despite numerous efforts, no polynomial algorithm is known. Mean-payoff games are known [15] to be more general than parity games [8,13] which enjoy a similar complexity status but were recently shown to be solvable in quasipolynomial time [4]. It is however unlikely that algorithms for solving parity games in quasipolynomial time generalise to mean-payoff games [9].

We use n for the number of vertices, $m \geq n$ for the number of edges, and N for the maximal absolute value of a weight. We will say that a runtime bound (or an algorithm) is combinatorial if it does not depend on N, and that it is pseudopolynomial if it is polynomial in n and N.

Although such a terminology was not introduced at that time, the first algorithm for solving energy games is due to Gurvich, Karzanov and Khachyian [11]. They used such an algorithm, which we will call the GKK algorithm, as a subroutine in a dichotomy for computing the values in the mean-payoff game. The GKK algorithm is based on iterating *potential transformations*, each of which require $O(m)$ operations. From their proof of termination, one can immediately extract an upper bound of $O(n2^n)$ on the number of iterations, which is easily improved to $O(2^n)$ with a slightly refined analysis. The results of Pisaruk [14] in a more general setting imply a pseudopolynomial bound of $O(n^2N)$ on the number of iterations of the GKK algorithm, aligning its worst case runtime bound with that of Zwick and Paterson [17].

The current state-of-the-art combinatorial algorithm is the randomised strategy improvement algorithm of Björklund and Vorobiov [1] which has runtime $\min(O(mn^2N), 2^{O(\sqrt{n \log n})})$. The pseudopolynomial bound was later improved by Brim, Chaloupka, Doyen, Gentilini and Raskin [3] by reduction to energy games to $O(mnN)$ with a deterministic value iteration algorithm. This technique was recently refined by Dorfman, Kaplan and Zwick [6] who proposed an acceleration of the algorithm which runs in time $O(\min(mnN, m2^{n/2}))$. Currently, this is the best known deterministic algorithm for the threshold problem, both in terms of combinatorial and pseudopolynomial bounds; in particular, no deterministic subexponential algorithm is known to this day.

Our Contribution. We propose to analyse the GKK algorithm when it is ran over a *simple* mean-payoff game, meaning, one which has no simple cycle of weight zero. Simple mean-payoff games arise directly when translating from parity games; moreover one can reduce in general to a simple game with a multiplicative blow-up of n on the largest weight N. We give a completely symmetric presentation of the GKK algorithm in this case, and a novel symmetric analysis based on energy and dual-energy values.

Our main result is a novel bound of $N+E^++E^-$ on the number of iterations of the GKK algorithm over simple games, where E^+ and E^- are respectively the maximal finite energy and dual-energy values among vertices. This quantity is always smaller than[1] nN, and therefore the GKK algorithm is at least as efficient in this case as the state of the art value iteration algorithms [3,6].

In practice however, $N+E^++E^-$ may be much smaller than nN; for instance in the game of Fig. 1, we have $N+E^++E^- = 8+9+0 = 17$ whereas $nN = 48$. It is very easy to forge examples where the difference is much higher; we believe that for many natural classes of games it holds that $N+E^++E^- = o(nN)$. Moreover, the value iteration algorithms rely on using nN as a threshold beyond which energy values are considered to be infinite, and therefore they often display runtime $\Omega(nN)$ when there are vertices with positive mean-payoff value. Our result indicates that the GKK algorithm avoids this drawback, all the while retaining (and often improving, as explained above) the state of the art pseudopolynomial runtime bound, at least for simple games.

We complement our main bound by showing that the analysis of [6] can also be applied to the GKK algorithm, establishing a combinatorial $O(2^{n/2})$ bound on the number of iterations. Hence the GKK algorithm also matches the combinatorial state of the art for deterministic algorithms (here, the fact that simple arenas are used is not a restriction, since the reduction only blows up the size of the weights). We also believe that the analysis of Dorfman, Kaplan and Zwick is conceptually simpler (and completely symmetric) when instantiated to the GKK algorithm.

1 To achieve this bound, let n^+ and n^- be respectively the number of vertices with positive and negative mean-payoff value (in a simple game, there is no vertex with value 0). It is a standard fact (see also Corollary 1) that $E^+ \leq (n^+ - 1)N$, and likewise $E^- \leq (n^- - 1)N$; the bound follows.

In Sect. 2, we formally introduce the necessary definitions and concepts. Section 3 presents the GKK algorithm over simple games, and Sect. 4 provides the novel pseudopolynomial bound. In Sect. 5, the combinatorial bound is derived.

2 Preliminaries

In this preliminary section, we introduce mean-payoff and energy games, potential reductions, and discuss simple games.

Mean-Payoff and Energy Games. In this paper, a game is a tuple $\mathcal{G} = (G, w, V_{\text{Min}}, V_{\text{Max}})$, where $G = (V, E)$ is a finite directed graph with no sink, $w : E \to \mathbb{Z}$ is a labelling of its edges by integer weights, and $V_{\text{Min}}, V_{\text{Max}}$ is a partition of V. As in the introduction, we use n, m and N respectively for $|V|, |E|$ and $\max_e |w(e)|$; we say that vertices in V_{Min} belong to Min while those in V_{Max} belong to Max. We now fix a game $\mathcal{G} = (G, w, V_{\text{Min}}, V_{\text{Max}})$.

A path is a (possibly empty, possibly infinite) sequence of edges $\pi = e_0 e_1 \dots$ with matching endpoints: if $e_{i+1} = v_{i+1}v_{i+2}$ is defined then its first component v_{i+1} matches the second component of e_i. For convenience, we often write $v_0 \to v_1 \to v_2 \to \dots$ for the path $e_0 e_1 \dots = (v_0v_1)(v_1v_2)\dots$. Given a finite or infinite path $\pi = e_0 e_1 \dots$ we let $w(\pi) = w(e_0)w(e_1)\dots$ denote the sequence of weights appearing on π. The sum of a finite path π is the sum of the weights appearing on it, we denote it by $\text{sum}(\pi)$.

Given a finite or infinite path $\pi = e_0 e_1 \dots = v_0 \to v_1 \to \dots$ and an integer $k \geq 0$, we let $\pi_{<k} = e_0 e_1 \dots e_{k-1} = v_0 \to v_1 \to \dots \to v_k$, and we let $\pi_{\leq k} = \pi_{<k+1}$. Note that $\pi_{<0}$ is the empty path, and that $\pi_{<k}$ has length k in general: it belongs to E^k. We say that π starts in v_0, and when it is finite and of length k that it ends in v_k. By convention, the empty path starts and ends in all vertices. A cycle is a finite path which starts and ends in the same vertex. A finite path $v_0 \to v_1 \to \dots \to v_k$ is simple if there is no repetition in $v_0, v_1, \dots, v_{k-1}$; note that a cycle may be simple. We let Π_v^ω denote the set of infinite paths starting in v.

We use $\mathbb{R}^{\pm\infty}$ and $\mathbb{Z}^{\pm\infty}$ to denote respectively $\mathbb{R} \cup \{-\infty, +\infty\}$ and $\mathbb{Z} \cup \{-\infty, \infty\}$. A valuation is a map $\text{val} : \mathbb{Z}^\omega \to \mathbb{R}^{\pm\infty}$ which assigns a potentially infinite real number to infinite sequences of weights. The three valuations which are studied in this paper are the mean-payoff, energy, and dual-energy valuations, respectively given by

$$\begin{aligned}
\text{MP}(w_0 w_1 \dots) &= \limsup_k \tfrac{1}{k} \textstyle\sum_{i=0}^{k-1} w_i && \in \mathbb{R} \\
\text{En}^+(w_0 w_1 \dots) &= \sup_k \textstyle\sum_{i=0}^{k-1} w_i && \in [0, \infty] \\
\text{En}^-(w_0 w_1 \dots) &= \inf_k \textstyle\sum_{i=0}^{k-1} w_i && \in [-\infty, 0].
\end{aligned}$$

A strategy for Min is a map $\sigma : V_{\text{Min}} \to E$ such that for all $v \in V_{\text{Min}}$, it holds that $\sigma(v)$ is an edge outgoing from v. We say that a (finite or infinite) path $\pi = e_0 e_1 \dots = v_0 \to v_1 \to \dots$ is consistent with σ if whenever $e_i = v_i v_{i+1}$

is defined and such that $v_i \in V_{\text{Min}}$, it holds that $e_i = \sigma(v_i)$. We write in this case $\pi \models \sigma$. Strategies for Max are defined similarly and written $\tau : V_{\text{Max}} \to E$. Paths consistent with Max strategies are defined analogously and also denoted by $\pi \models \tau$.

Theorem 1 ([2,7]). *For each* val $\in \{\text{MP}, \text{En}^+, \text{En}^-\}$, *there exist strategies* σ_0 *for Min and* τ_0 *for Max such that for all* $v \in V$ *we have*

$$\sup_{\pi \models \sigma_0} \text{val}(w(\pi)) = \inf_{\sigma} \sup_{\pi \models \sigma} \text{val}(w(\pi)) = \sup_{\tau} \inf_{\pi \models \tau} \text{val}(w(\pi)) = \inf_{\pi \models \tau_0} \text{val}(w(\pi)),$$

where σ, τ *and* π *respectively range over strategies for Min, strategies for Max, and infinite paths from* v.

The quantity defined by the equilibrium above is called the value of v in the val game, and we denote it by $\text{val}_{\mathcal{G}}(v) \in \mathbb{R}^{\pm\infty}$; the strategies σ_0 and τ_0 are called val-optimal, note that they do not depend on v. The following result relates the values in the mean-payoff and energy games; this direct consequence of Theorem 1 was first stated in [3].

Corollary 1 ([3]). *For all* $v \in V$ *it holds that*

$$\text{MP}_{\mathcal{G}}(v) \leq 0 \iff \text{En}^+_{\mathcal{G}}(v) < \infty \iff \text{En}^+_{\mathcal{G}}(v) \leq (n-1)N,$$

and likewise,

$$\text{MP}_{\mathcal{G}}(v) \geq 0 \iff \text{En}^-_{\mathcal{G}}(v) > -\infty \iff \text{En}^-_{\mathcal{G}}(v) \geq -(n-1)N.$$

Therefore computing En^+ values of the games is harder than the threshold problem. As explained in the introduction, all state-of-the-art algorithms for the threshold problem actually compute En^+ values, and so does the GKK algorithm (in fact, it even computes En^- values, while algorithms of [1,3,6] do not). This shifts our focus from mean-payoff to energy games.

Potential Reductions. Fix a game $\mathcal{G} = (G = (V, E), w, V_{\text{Min}}, V_{\text{Max}})$. A potential is a map $\phi : V \to \mathbb{Z}$. Potentials are partially ordered coordinatewise. Given an edge $e = vv' \in E$, we define its ϕ-modified weight to be

$$w_\phi(e) = w(e) + \phi(v') - \phi(v).$$

The ϕ-modified game $\mathcal{G}_\phi$ is simply the game $(G, w_\phi, V_{\text{Min}}, V_{\text{Max}})$; informally, all weights are replaced by the modified weights. Note that the underlying graph does not change, in particular paths in $\mathcal{G}$ and $\mathcal{G}_\phi$ are the same. Observe that for a finite path $\pi = v_0 \to v_1 \to \ldots \to v_k$, its sum in $\mathcal{G}_\phi$ is given by

$$\text{sum}_\phi(v) = \text{sum}(\pi) + \phi(v_k) - phi(v_0).$$

We let 0 denote the constant zero potential; note that $\mathcal{G}_0 = \mathcal{G}$. For convenience, we use val_ϕ to denote $\text{val}_{\mathcal{G}_\phi}$ for val $\in \{\text{MP}, \text{En}^+, \text{En}^-\}$. Since $\mathcal{G}$ is always fixed, we thus write val_0 for $\text{val}_{\mathcal{G}}$.

Moving from $\mathcal{G}$ to $\mathcal{G}_\phi$ for a given potential ϕ is called a potential reduction; these were introduced by Gallai [10] for studying network related problems such as shortest-paths problems. In the context of mean-payoff or energy games, they were introduced in [11] and later rediscovered numerous times. The result below describes the effect of potential reductions over mean-payoff and energy values.

Theorem 2. – *For any potential ϕ we have $\mathrm{MP}_0 = \mathrm{MP}_\phi$ over V.*
– *If ϕ satisfies $0 \leq \phi \leq \mathrm{En}_0^+$, then it holds that $\mathrm{En}_0^+ = \phi + \mathrm{En}_\phi^+$ over V.*
– *If ϕ satisfies $\mathrm{En}_0^- \leq \phi \leq 0$, then it holds that $\mathrm{En}_0^- = \phi + \mathrm{En}_\phi^-$ over V.*

The first item in the Theorem follows directly from the fact that the mean-payoffs of any infinite path are the same in $\mathcal{G}$ and in $\mathcal{G}_\phi$. We focus on proving the second item, illustrated in Fig. 2; the third one follows by symmetry.

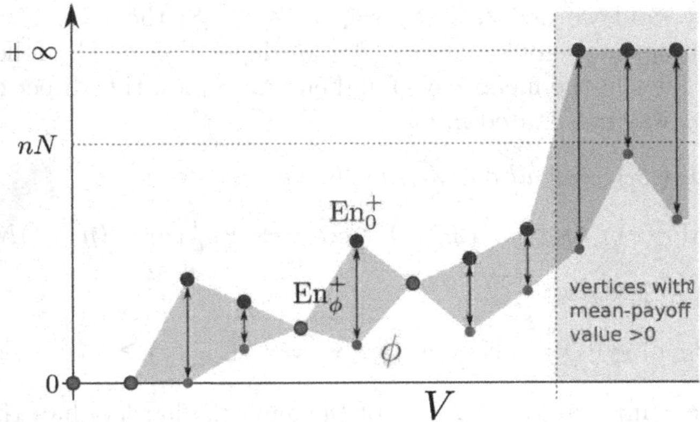

Fig. 2. An illustration of the second item in Theorem 2. For vertices on the right, energy values in both games are ∞.

Towards proving the second item in Theorem 2, we first establish a technical result.

Lemma 1. *Let σ_0 be an En^+-optimal Min strategy in $\mathcal{G}$ and $\pi = v_0 \to v_1 \to \ldots \to v_k$ be a finite path consistent with σ_0 such that $\mathrm{En}_0^+(v_k) < \infty$. Then we have $\mathrm{sum}(\pi) \leq \mathrm{En}_0^+(v_0) - \mathrm{En}_0^+(v_k)$.*

Proof. Let π' be an infinite path from v_k consistent with σ_0 and such that $\mathrm{En}_0^+(v_k) = \mathrm{En}^+(w(\pi'))$. Then $\pi\pi'$ is consistent with σ_0 and therefore $\mathrm{En}_0^+(v_0) \geq \mathrm{En}^+(w(\pi\pi'))$. We thus obtain

$$\begin{aligned}\mathrm{En}^+(v_0) \;\geq\; \mathrm{En}^+(w(\pi\pi')) &= \sup_{k'\geq 0}(\mathrm{sum}((\pi\pi')_{<k'}) \\ &\geq \sup_{k'\geq k}(\mathrm{sum}((\pi\pi')_{<k'}) \\ &= \mathrm{sum}(\pi) + \sup_{k'\geq 0}\mathrm{sum}(\pi'_{<k'}) \\ &= \mathrm{sum}(\pi) + \mathrm{En}^+(w(\pi')) \;=\; \mathrm{sum}(\pi) + \mathrm{En}_0^+(v_k),\end{aligned}$$

concluding the proof.

We now derive the second item of Theorem 2.

Proof. Let $\phi : V \to \mathbb{Z}$ be a potential such that $0 \leq \phi \leq \mathrm{En}_0^+$; we aim to prove that $\mathrm{En}_0^+ = \phi + \mathrm{En}_\phi^+$ over V. Over vertices with mean-payoff value > 0 (which coincide over both games by the first item), both terms are infinite thanks to Corollary 1. Let v be such a vertex with mean-payoff value ≤ 0 (or equivalently, finite energy value).

Consider an En^+-optimal Min strategy $\sigma_0 : V_{\mathrm{Min}} \to E$ in $\mathcal{G}$ and let $\pi = v_0 \to v_1 \to \dots$ be an infinite path consistent with σ_0. Note that for any $k \geq 0$, v_k has finite energy value, and thus we obtain thanks to Lemma 1

$$\begin{aligned}\mathrm{sum}_\phi(\pi_{<k}) &= \mathrm{sum}(\pi_{<k}) + \phi(v_k) - \phi(v_0)\\ &\leq \mathrm{En}_0^+(v_0) \underbrace{-\mathrm{En}_0^+(v_k) + \phi(v_k)}_{\leq 0} - \phi(v_0) \quad \leq \quad \mathrm{En}_0^+(v_0) - \phi(v_0),\end{aligned}$$

hence $\mathrm{En}_\phi^+(v_0) \leq \sup_{\pi \models \sigma_0} \sup_{k \geq 0} \mathrm{sum}_\phi(\phi_{<k}) \leq \mathrm{En}_0^+(v_0) - \phi(v_0)$.

For the other inequality, consider an optimal Min strategy σ_ϕ in $\mathcal{G}_\phi$, and take $\pi \models \sigma_\phi$. By applying Lemma 1 in $\mathcal{G}_\phi$ we now get

$$\begin{aligned}\mathrm{sum}(\pi_{<k}) &= \mathrm{sum}_\phi(\pi_{<k}) - \phi(v_k) + \phi(v_0)\\ &\leq \mathrm{En}_\phi^+(v_0) - \underbrace{\mathrm{En}_\phi^+(v_k)}_{\geq 0} - \underbrace{\phi(v_k)}_{\geq 0} + \phi(v_0) \quad \leq \quad \mathrm{En}_\phi^+(v_0) + \phi(v_0),\end{aligned}$$

and again the wanted result follows by taking a supremum.

We say that a potential ϕ is positively safe if it satisfies the hypothesis of the second item, $0 \leq \phi \leq \mathrm{En}_0^+$.

Note that potential reductions are invariant under shifts: we have $\mathcal{G}_\phi = \mathcal{G}_{\phi+c}$ if c is a constant potential. For convenience, we prefer to work with non-negative potentials, even though our approach will be completely symmetric; one could also work with equivalence classes of potentials up to shifts.

To apply the third item in Theorem 2, given a potential ϕ we define

$$\phi^- = \phi - \max \phi \leq 0,$$

and we say that ϕ is negatively safe if ϕ^- satisfies the hypothesis of the third item, $\mathrm{En}_0^- \leq \phi^- \leq 0$. We say that ϕ is bi-safe if it is both positively and negatively safe.

Observe that $(\mathcal{G}_\phi)_{\phi'} = \mathcal{G}_{\phi+\phi'}$: sequential applications of potential reductions correspond to reducing with respect to the sum of the potentials. The following is easily derived as a consequence of Theorem 2; the proof is detailed below for completeness.

Lemma 2. *If ϕ is positively (or negatively, or bi-) safe for $\mathcal{G}$, and ϕ' is positively (or negatively, or bi-) safe for $\mathcal{G}_\phi$, then $\phi + \phi'$ is positively (or negatively, or bi-) safe for $\mathcal{G}$.*

Proof. We first show the result for positively safe. Clearly $\phi + \phi'$ is non-negative since both are. Now Theorem 2 gives

$$\mathrm{En}_0^+ = \mathrm{En}_\phi^+ + \phi \geq \phi' + \phi,$$

the sought inequality.

For negatively safe, again non-positivity of $(\phi + \phi')^-$ is direct. Using the fact that $\max(\phi + \phi') \leq \max(\phi) + \max(\phi')$ in general we obtain similarly

$$\begin{aligned}(\phi + \phi')^- &= \phi + \phi' - \max(\phi + \phi') \geq \phi - \max \phi + \phi' - \max \phi' \\ &= \phi^- + \phi'^- = \mathrm{En}_0^- - \mathrm{En}_{\phi^-}^- + \phi'^- \geq \mathrm{En}_0^-.\end{aligned}$$

This also gives compositionality of bi-safe potentials by conjunction.

Simple and Reduced Games. The lemma above justifies the following approach for computing En_0^+: apply successive positively safe potential reductions $\phi_0, \phi_1, \ldots$ until reaching a game whose energy values are only 0 and ∞; then by Theorem 2 it holds that $\mathrm{En}_0^+ = \phi_0 + \phi_1 + \ldots$. We will present the GKK algorithm as one iterating potential reductions that are actually bi-safe. For this to hold however, we need to restrict to simple games.

A game is simple if all simple cycles have nonzero sum. The following result is folklore and states that one may reduce to a simple game at the cost of a linear blow up on N. It holds thanks to the fact that positive mean-payoff values are $\geq 1/n$, which is a well-known consequence of Theorem 1.

Lemma 3. *Let $\mathcal{G} = (G, w, V_{\mathrm{Min}}, V_{\mathrm{Max}})$ be an arbitrary game. The game $\mathcal{G}' = (G, (n+1)w - 1, V_{\mathrm{Min}}, V_{\mathrm{Max}})$ is simple and has the same vertices of positive mean-payoff values as $\mathcal{G}$.*

As another direct consequence of Theorem 1, it holds that in a simple game, mean-payoff values of the vertices are $\neq 0$. Energy and dual energy values in such a game are depicted in Fig. 3. Moreover, sums of cycles are preserved by potential reductions, and therefore if $\mathcal{G}$ is simple then so is $\mathcal{G}_\phi$, whatever the potential ϕ.

We say that a simple game is reduced if the vertices are partitioned between P^* and N^* such that

- vertices in $V_{\mathrm{Min}} \cap N^*$ have a non-positive edge towards N^*;
- all edges outgoing from vertices in $V_{\mathrm{Max}} \cap N^*$ are non-positive and towards N^*;
- vertices in $V_{\mathrm{Max}} \cap P^*$ have a non-negative edge towards P^*; and
- all edges outgoing from vertices in $V_{\mathrm{Min}} \cap P^*$ are non-negative and towards P^*.

These requirements are illustrated in Fig. 4.

Intuitively, a reduced game is a simple one in which Min can ensure that no positive edge is ever seen from any vertex of mean-payoff value < 0, and vice-versa. We have the following easy result.

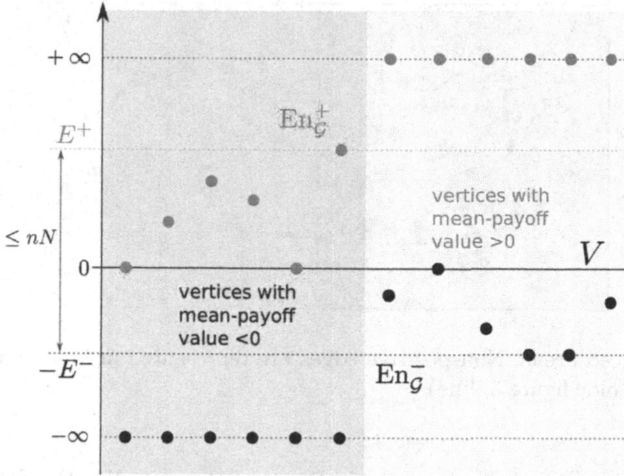

Fig. 3. Representation of energy and dual energy values when no vertex has mean-payoff value zero; this is always the case for simple arenas.

Lemma 4. *In a reduced game, vertices in* N^* *have mean-payoff value* < 0 *and those in* P^* *have mean-payoff value* > 0*. Moreover, a simple game is reduced if and only if energy values belong to* $\{0, \infty\}$ *and dual energy values belong to* $\{-\infty, 0\}$.

3 The GKK Algorithm

Fix a simple game $\mathcal{G} = (G = (V, E), w, V_{\mathrm{Min}}, V_{\mathrm{Max}})$. The GKK algorithm iterates bi-safe potential reductions until a reduced arena is obtained. The runtime for computing each reduction is $O(m)$, therefore the overall runtime is $O(m\ell)$, where ℓ is the number of iterations. In this section we present how the reduction is performed, and prove that it is bi-safe. Upper bounds on ℓ are the focus of Sects. 4 and 5.

Each iteration relies on a bipartition of the set of vertices, which is completely symmetric thanks to our simplicity assumption. Observe that since there are no simple cycles of sum zero in $\mathcal{G}$, any infinite path visits a non-zero weight. The arena is therefore partitioned into the set of vertices N^* from which Min can ensure that the first visited non-zero weight is negative, and the set of vertices P^* from which Max can ensure that the first visited non-zero weight is positive.

Note that the partition N^*, P^* depends only on the signs (and zeroness) of the weights, and not on their precise values. It is computable in linear time; in a standard terminology which is not formally introduced here, N^* is the Min-attractor to negative edges over non-positive edges. The GKK algorithm is in fact akin to Zielonka's algorithm for parity games [16]: both are based on computing relevant attractors.

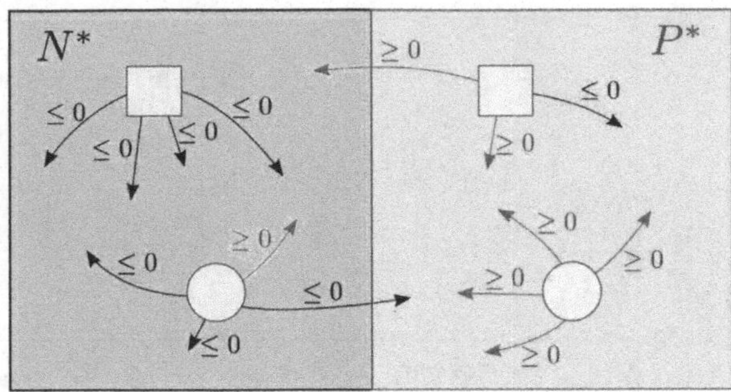

Fig. 4. A reduced arena. Non-positive edges are represented in blue and non-negative ones in red. (Color figure online)

We focus on the point of view of Min, and thus on N^*. By definition, from N^* Min is able to force that a negative edge is seen. The algorithm computes the worst possible (maximal) negative value that Min can ensure from N^*, which we now describe.

Consider a Max vertex v in N^*: any edge towards P^* is necessarily negative otherwise v would belong to P^*. Therefore Max may choose to switch to P^*, but at the cost of seeing a negative weight. We let

$$\delta^-_{\text{Max}} = \max\{w(e) \mid e \in E \cap (N^* \cap V_{\text{Max}}) \times P^*\} < 0$$

denote the largest such weight that Max can achieve. It may be that there is no such edge, in which case we have $\delta^-_{\text{Max}} = \max \varnothing = -\infty$.

From a Min vertex v in N^* if Min has a non-positive edge towards N^* she can follow this path and avoid to switch to P^*. Otherwise all edges outgoing from v towards N^* are positive, and we let

$$SN = \{v \in V_{\text{Min}} \cap N^* \mid \forall v' \in N^*, vv' \in E \implies w(vv') > 0\}$$

be the set of Min vertices in N^* from which she is forced to switch to P^* or see a positive edge. Note that a vertex $v \in SN$ necessarily has negative outgoing edges, which must therefore point towards P^*, otherwise v would not belong to N^*. Therefore we let

$$\delta^-_{\text{Min}} = \max_{v \in SN} \min\{w(vv') \mid vv' \in E\} < 0,$$

and we now put

$$\delta^- = \max(\delta^-_{\text{Min}}, \delta^-_{\text{Max}}) \in [-\infty, 0).$$

The following result (and the dual one) is crucial for our pseudopolynomial bound. We prove it now since it refers to the definitions just above.

Lemma 5. *It holds that* En_0^- *takes values* $\leq \delta^-$ *over* N^*.

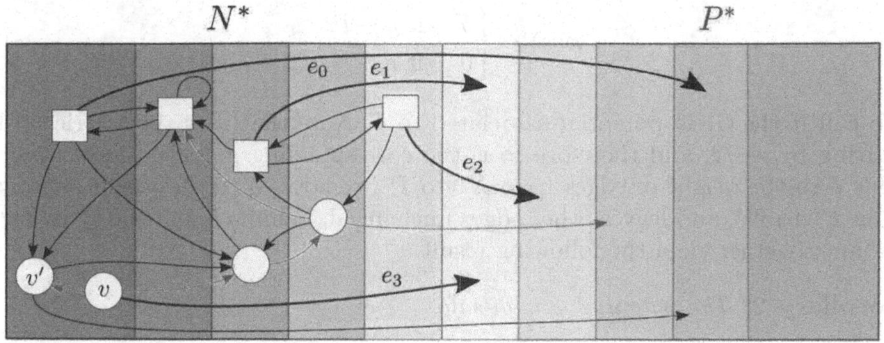

Fig. 5. An example of the partition of the vertices into N^* and P^*; for clarity, no details are given with respect to P^* where the situation is symmetric. Blue, black and red arrows respectively represent negative, zero, and positive edges. The layers depicted in N^* correspond to the Min-attractor over non-positive edges to negative ones. With regards to the explanation below: here three edges participate to the maximum defining δ^-_{Max} namely e_0, e_1 and e_2. Only e_3 participates to the maximum defining δ^-_{Min}; v' has a non-positive edge towards N^* and thus does not belong to SN. (Color figure online)

Proof. Consider a positional strategy σ for Min which assigns to $v \in (V_{\text{Min}} \cap N^*)\backslash SN$ a non-positive edge towards N^*, and to $v \in SN$ an edge of weight $\leq \delta^-_{\text{Min}}$ (which therefore necessarily leads to P^*). Consider an infinite path $\pi : v_0 \to v_1 \to \dots$ from $v_0 \in N^*$ which is consistent with σ.

If π remains in N^* then all weights are non-positive, and since moreover $\mathcal{G}$ is simple it must be that $\text{En}^-(\pi) = -\infty$. Otherwise, let $i_0 \geq 0$ be the first index such that $v_{i_0+1} \in P^*$. If $v_{i_0} \in V_{\text{Min}}$ then necessarily $v_{i_0} \in SN$ and thus $w(v_{i_0}v_{i_0+1}) \leq \delta^-_{\text{Min}} \leq \delta^-$. If $v_{i_0} \in V_{\text{Max}}$ then likewise $w(v_{i_0}v_{i_0+1}) \leq \delta^-_{\text{Max}} \leq \delta^-$. Since moreover $\pi_{<i_0}$ remains in N^* and is consistent with σ, it only sees non-positive weights, and therefore $\text{En}^-(\pi) \leq w(v_0v_1)+w(v_1v_2)+\dots+w(v_{i_0}v_{i_0+1}) \leq w(v_{i_0}v_{i_0+1}) \leq \delta^-$, the wanted result.

Symmetrically, one may define a relevant minimal positive weight for Max from P^* by setting

$$\delta^+_{\text{Min}} = \min\{w(e) \mid e \in E \cap (P^* \cap V_{\text{Min}}) \times N^*\}, \text{ and}$$
$$\delta^+_{\text{Max}} = \min_{v \in SP} \max\{w(vv') \mid vv' \in E\},$$

where $SP = \{v \in V_{\text{Max}} \cap P^* \mid \forall v' \in P^*, vv' \in E \implies w(vv') < 0\}$, and then

$$\delta^+ = \min(\delta^+_{\text{Min}}, \delta^+_{\text{Max}}) \in (0, \infty].$$

The symmetric version of Lemma 5 states that En^+_0 takes values $\geq \delta^+$ over P^*.

We now finally let $\delta = \min(-\delta^-, \delta^+) \in (0, \infty]$. If $\delta = +\infty$ then $\delta^- = -\infty$ and $\delta^+ = +\infty$ which implies that $\mathcal{G}$ is reduced and the iteration stops. Otherwise we have $0 < \delta < \infty$ and we consider the non-negative potential given by

$$\phi(v) = \begin{cases} \delta & \text{if } v \in P^* \\ 0 & \text{if } v \in N^*. \end{cases}$$

We call it the GKK potential associated to $\mathcal{G}$. Note that it is symmetric up to shifting by $-\delta/2$, and therefore so is the corresponding potential reduction; it adds δ to the weight of edges from N^* to P^*, removes δ to the weight of edges from P^* to N^*, and leaves other edges unchanged. Lemma 5 and the symmetric variant together yield the following result.

Corollary 2. *The potential ϕ is bi-safe.*

Without the simplicity assumption over $\mathcal{G}$, one has to deal with vertices from which neither player can attract to a weight of corresponding sign. In [11], such vertices are put in N^*, and therefore the obtained potential ϕ remains positively-safe, but it is no longer negatively safe. It is thus unclear how to generalise our approach to non-simple games: as it will appear in the next section, bi-safety is crucial to derive our novel upper bound.

The GKK algorithm iterates the potential reduction corresponding with the GKK potential ϕ, until the obtained game is reduced (or equivalently, $\delta = \infty$), with partition P^*, N^*. Let Φ denote the sum of all GKK potentials computed throughout the iteration. Energy values over N^* in the original game then coincide with Φ, while energy values over P^* are infinite. Likewise, dual energy values over P^* are given by Φ^-, and are $-\infty$ over N^*.

4 Improved Pseudopolynomial Bound

Following [11], we say that extremal edges of a vertex v are those with minimal weight if $v \in V_{\text{Min}}$ and of maximal weight if $v \in V_{\text{Max}}$. The extremal weight of v is the weight of its extremal edges. We say that a vertex is negative, zero, or positive according to the sign of its extremal weight, and let[2] N, Z and P denote the corresponding subsets of vertices. Note that $N \subseteq N^*$ and $P \subseteq P^*$, while Z is split between both. The following was already observed in [11], we give a proof for completeness.

Lemma 6 ([11]). *Let $\mathcal{G}' = \mathcal{G}_\phi$ where ϕ is the GKK potential associated to $\mathcal{G}$, and let N' and P' respectively denote the sets of negative and positive vertices in $\mathcal{G}'$. We have $N' \subseteq N$ and $P' \subseteq P$.*

Proof. We let $\text{ext}(v), \text{ext}'(v) \in \mathbb{Z}$ denote the extremal weights of v in $\mathcal{G}$ and $\mathcal{G}'$. We prove that

$$\forall v \in N^*, \qquad \text{ext}(v) \leq \text{ext}'(v) \leq 0$$
$$\forall v \in P^*, \qquad \text{ext}(v) \geq \text{ext}'(v) \geq 0.$$

[2] We apologise for the clash in notations with our notation N for the maximal absolute value of a weight; it is easily resolved thanks to context.

This implies the lemma: if $\text{ext}'(v) < 0$ then necessarily $\text{ext}(v) < 0$ so v, therefore $N' \subseteq N$; likewise, $P' \subseteq P$. We only prove the first line since the second follows by symmetry.

For the left inequality it suffices to observe that the weight of edges outgoing from N^* can only increase: edges pointing to N^* keep the same weight while those pointing towards P^* are increased by δ. For the inequality on the right we make a quick case disjunction.

- Let $v \in N^* \cap V_{\text{Max}}$. Then all extremal edges are non-positive, and those which point towards P^* are even $\leq -\delta$ by definition of δ hence they all remain non-positive.
- Let $v \in N^* \cap V_{\text{Min}}$. The result follows directly if v has a non-positive outgoing edge towards N^* since it is left unchanged. Otherwise $v \in SN$ hence v has an outgoing edge of weight $\leq -\delta$ which therefore remains non-positive.

This concludes the proof.

We now let $\mathcal{G} = \mathcal{G}^0, \mathcal{G}^1, \mathcal{G}^2, \ldots$ denote the sequence of games encountered throughout the iteration, inductively defined by $\mathcal{G}^{j+1} = \mathcal{G}^j_{\phi^j}$, where ϕ^j is the GKK potential associated to $\mathcal{G}^j$ (if it is defined). We use obvious notations such as $N^j, P^{*,j}$ or δ^j; in particular, $\mathcal{G}^{j+1}$ is defined if and only if $\delta^j < \infty$. Given j such that $\mathcal{G}^j$ is defined we moreover let $\Delta^j = \sum_{j'=0}^{j} \delta^{j'}$ and $\Phi^j = \sum_{j'=0}^{j} \phi^{j'}$. Note that we have $\mathcal{G}^{j+1} = \mathcal{G}^0_{\Phi^j}$ for all $j \geq 0$. The following is a direct consequence of Lemma 6.

Corollary 3. *For all $j \geq 0$, it holds that Φ^j takes value 0 over N^j and Δ^j over P^j.*

Proof. Thanks to Lemma 6 we have $N^0 \supseteq N^1 \supseteq \cdots \supseteq N^j$, therefore if $v \in N^j$ then for all $j' \leq j$, v belongs to $N^{j'} \subseteq N^{*,j'}$ and thus $\phi^{j'}(v) = 0$; the first result follows. Likewise, if $v \in P^j$ then for all $j' \leq j$ we have $\phi^{j'}(v) = \delta^{j'}$ therefore $\Phi^j(v) = \Delta^j$.

With this in hands we are ready to prove the announced result.

Theorem 3. *The iteration terminates in at most $N + E^+ + E^- + 1$ steps, where E^+ is the maximal finite energy value in $\mathcal{G}$, and E^- is minus the minimal finite dual energy value.*

The proof is illustrated in Fig. 6.

Proof. We let $N^{\infty,*}$ and $P^{\infty,*}$ respectively denote the sets of vertices with negative and positive mean-payoff values, which partition V. Since Φ^j is positively safe by Corollary 2 and Lemma 2 (and the quantities below are finite), we have thanks to Theorem 2 for all j that over $v \in N^{\infty,*}$,

$$\Phi^j(v) = \text{En}^+_{\mathcal{G}}(v) - \text{En}^+_{\mathcal{G}^j}(v) \leq E^+.$$

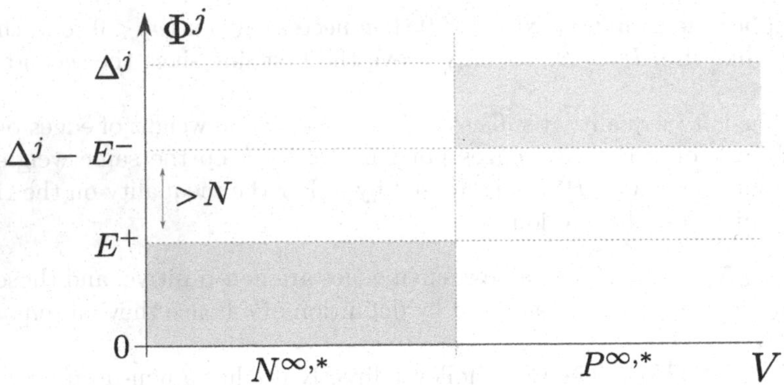

Fig. 6. An illustration for the proof of Theorem 3, where $j = N + E^+ + E^-$. Since Φ^j it is positively safe, vertices with finite En^+ value (denoted $N^{\infty,*}$) must be mapped to the blue region, and symmetrically; by our choice of j, this implies that edges from $N^{\infty,*}$ to $P^{\infty,*}$ are positive, and those from $P^{\infty,*}$ to $N^{\infty,*}$ are negative, which is key to the proof. (Color figure online)

Likewise, over $v \in P^{\infty,*}$ we obtain $(\Phi^j)^-(v) = \mathrm{En}^-_{\mathcal{G}}(v) - \mathrm{En}^+_{\mathcal{G}^j}(v) \geq -E^-$, which rewrites as

$$\Phi^j(v) \geq \Delta^j - E^-.$$

We now assume that the $j = N + E^+ + E^-$-th iteration is defined, and for contradiction that $\delta^j < \infty$. Note that $\Delta^j \geq j+1$ as a sum of $j+1$ positive integers. Note that N^j (and symmetrically, P^j) is non-empty: if $N^j = \varnothing$ then $P^j = V$ therefore $\delta^j = \infty$. (Intuitively, Max could then ensure that no negative weight is ever seen.)

By Corollary 3, Φ^j takes value 0 over N^j therefore $N^j \subseteq N^{\infty,*}$ thanks to the above since $0 < \Delta^j - E^-$ (see Fig. 6; vertices of value zero cannot belong to the red zone). Likewise, we have $P^j \subseteq P^{\infty,*}$ since $\Delta^j > E^+$.

Note that any edge vv' from $N^{\infty,*}$ to $P^{\infty,*}$ has weight

$$w_{\Phi^j}(vv') = w(vv') + \Phi^j(v') - \Phi^j(v) \geq -N + \Delta^j - E^- - E^+ \geq 1$$

in $\mathcal{G}^j$. Likewise, any edge from $P^{\infty,*}$ to $N^{\infty,*}$ has weight < 0 in $\mathcal{G}^j$, therefore zero edges cannot lead from $N^{\infty,*}$ to $P^{\infty,*}$ or vice-versa.

Now observe that by definition vertices in $N^{j,*}$ have a path to $N^j \subseteq N^{\infty,*}$ comprised only of zero weights in $\mathcal{G}^j$, and therefore it must be that $N^{j,*} \subseteq N^{\infty,*}$. Similarly, we have $P^{j,*} \subseteq P^{\infty,*}$ and thus the two partitions are equal:

$$N^{j,*} = N^{\infty,*} \qquad \text{and} \qquad P^{j,*} = P^{\infty,*}.$$

Since all edges from $N^{j,*}$ to $P^{j,*}$ are positive, we have $\delta^- = -\infty$. Likewise $\delta^+ = \infty$ and therefore $\delta = \infty$, a contradiction.

5 Combinatorial Bound

We now concentrate on establishing the following result.

Theorem 4. *The number of iterations of the GKK algorithm is $O(2^{n/2})$.*

It implies that the GKK algorithm also matches the state of the art combinatorial bound of [6]; we actually believe that the two algorithms are very similar in essence. Note that the simplicity assumption can be lifted without loss of generality here: there is no combinatorial blow up in the reduction stated in Lemma 3. The algorithm of [6] has the advantage of benefiting in general from the $O(nmN)$ upper bound inherited from that of [3], regardless of simplicity. Inversely, it is not clear whether our improved pseudopolynomial bound holds for the algorithm of [6], even when it is ran over simple arenas.

Our proof of Theorem 4 is directly based on that of [6], which we break into two steps. First, we partition N^* into non-empty layers $A_1, A_2, \dots$ and prove that the sequence $-|A_1|, |A_2|, -|A_3|, |A_4|, \dots$ strictly grows lexicographically. Establishing lexicographical growth of the sequence turns out to be quite technical, already in [6]; we believe that our argumentation is essentially the same, although conceptually simpler (and symmetrical) for the GKK algorithm. The second step is an ingenious encoding into integers which exploits the symmetry to lower the obtained upper bound from the naive 2^n to $2^{n/2}$.

Step one relies on so-called alternating layers, which are defined with respect to minimal number of alternations between V_{Min} and V_{Max} for zero paths in N^* towards N. A similar result is derived in [11] directly for the attracting layers, with a simpler proof. It is required however for the second step to apply that nonzero integers appearing in the sequence alternate between positive and negative, which is not the case for attracting layers in general. Assuming that the game is bipartite however (this incurs no loss of generality), one may combine the result of [11] with the encoding of [6] and obtain the same result; here, we prefer to follow the two steps of [6] which allows to establish Theorem 4 in general.

Step One: Layers and Their Dynamics. Again, we focus on N^*, but will later use the main result together with its dual to obtain the wanted bound. Given a finite path $\pi : v_0 \to v_1 \to \dots \to v_k$ in $\mathcal{G}$ we define its number of alternations (towards N) $\text{alt}(\pi) \in [0, \infty]$ to be the minimal ℓ such that there exist a decreasing sequence of $\ell + 1$ indices $k \geq i_0 \geq i_1 \geq \dots \geq i_\ell$ such that

- $v_{i_0}, \dots, v_k \in N$,
- for all $j \in [1, \ell]$, $v_{i_j}, \dots, v_{i_{j-1}-1}$ all belong to V_{Max} if j is odd and to V_{Min} if j is even.

In particular a path has finite alternation number if and only if it ends in N and it has alternation number 0 if and only if it is contained in N. Moreover note that a path from $v \notin N$ towards N has even alternation number if and only if $v \in V_{\text{Min}}$. The choice of the first layer being comprised of Max vertices is arbitrary, the proof below also goes through with the inverse convention.

We say that a path is zero if it visits only zero edges. We define the alternation depth $\mathrm{alt}(v)$ over vertices in N^* by

$$\mathrm{alt}(v) = \min\{\mathrm{alt}(\pi) \mid \pi \text{ is a zero path from } v \text{ to } N \text{ which remains in } N^*\}.$$

An example is given in Fig. 7. We say that a path from $v \in N^*$ is optimal if it is a zero path from v to N which remains in N^* and achieves the above minimum. Note that by definition of N^*, vertices in N^* have a simple zero path towards N hence $\mathrm{alt}(v)$ is finite and bounded by n.

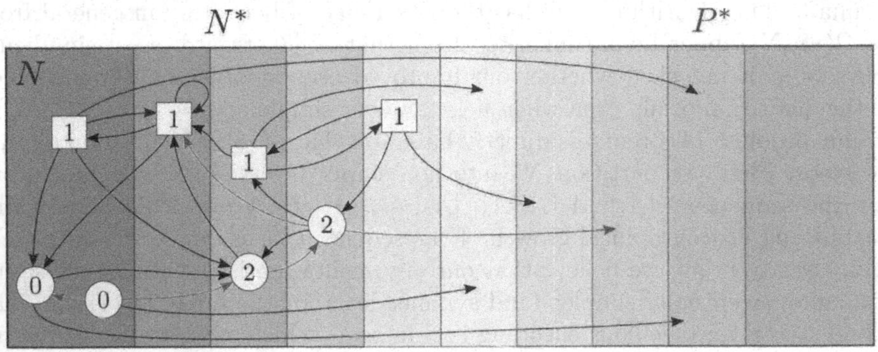

Fig. 7. The alternating layers, indicated by the green numbers, in the example of Fig. 5. Notice that alternating layers (green numbers) and attractor layers (in blue) are completely different; however – and quite surprisingly – a close variant of Theorem 5 holds for attractor layers (see [11] for details). (Color figure online)

We will study the dynamics of the sets

$$A_i = \{v \in N^* \mid \mathrm{alt}(v) = i\}.$$

We assume that the iteration is not over, $\delta < \infty$. We use the notation $\mathcal{G}'$ for $\mathcal{G}_\phi$, where ϕ is the GKK potential and use primes for sets and quantities relative to $\mathcal{G}'$. The following is the main result for the first step.

Theorem 5. *If $N = N'$ and $P = P'$, then the sequence*

$$-|A_1|, |A_2|, -|A_3|, |A_4|, \ldots$$

strictly grows lexicographically.

Towards proving the theorem, we define two relevant indices i_D and i_A which we respectively call the departure index and arrival index. As their names suggest the first is relevant to vertices which leave N^*, that is, those in $N^* \cap P'^*$, while the second is relevant to arriving vertices, those in $P^* \cap N'^*$. We let

$$\begin{aligned} i_D &= \min\{\mathrm{alt}(v) \mid v \in V_{\mathrm{Max}} \cap N^* \text{ and } v \in P'^*\}, \\ i_A &= \min\{\mathrm{alt}(e_0\pi_1) \mid e_0 \in E \cap [(P^* \cap V_{\mathrm{Min}}) \times N^*], w(e_0) = \delta, \\ &\qquad \text{and } \pi_1 \text{ is optimal from } v_1 \text{ in } \mathcal{G}\} \end{aligned}$$

Note that if finite, i_D is odd and i_A is even. We now provide a sequence of incremental results that eventually give the theorem.

Lemma 7. *Assume that* $N' = N$ *and* $P' = P$.

(i) *For all* $v \in N^*$, *if* $\text{alt}(v) < i_D$ *then* $v \in N'^*$ *and* $\text{alt}'(v) \leq \text{alt}(v)$.
(ii) *For any path* π' *which is optimal in* $\mathcal{G}'$ *but is not zero in* $\mathcal{G}$, *it holds that* $\text{alt}'(\pi') \geq i_A$.
(iii) *For all* $v \in P^* \cap N'^*$ *it holds that* $\text{alt}'(v) \geq i_A$.
(iv) *For all* $i \leq \min(i_D - 1, i_A)$ *we have* $A_i \subseteq A'_i$ *and for all* $i \leq \min(i_D, i_A - 1)$ *we have* $A'_i \subseteq A_i$.
(v) *If* $i_A < i_D$ *then* $|A'_{i_A}| > |A_{i_A}|$.
(vi) *We have* $\delta_E^- < -\delta$ *and likewise* $\delta_A^+ > \delta$.
(vii) *If* $i_A = \infty$ *then* $i_D < \infty$.
(viii) *Theorem 5 holds.*

Items (i), (ii) and (iii) build towards item (iv) which is the main intermediate result. Items (v) and (vii) have a similar proof (although (vii) also relies on (vi)) and build up to the conclusion.

Proof. (i) We prove the claim by induction on the length k of the smallest optimal path $\pi = v_0 \to \ldots \to v_k$ from $v_0 = v$. Note that π is zero in $\mathcal{G}$ and remains in N^* hence it is also zero in $\mathcal{G}'$. If π has length zero then $v \in N = N'$ hence $v \in N'^*$ and $\text{alt}'(v) = 0 \leq \text{alt}(v)$, so we now assume $k > 0$ and that the result is known for vertices with an optimal path of length $\leq k - 1$.
It holds by induction that $v_1, v_2, \ldots, v_k \in N'^*$ hence it suffices to prove that $v \in N'^*$ since it implies that π is a zero path in $\mathcal{G}'$ which remains in N'^*. If $v \in V_{\text{Min}}$ then v has a zero edge in $\mathcal{G}'$ towards $v' \in N'^*$ hence $v \in N'^*$. Otherwise it holds that $v \in N'^*$ because $v \in P'^*$ would contradict that $\text{alt}(v) < i_D$.

(ii) Let $\pi' : v_0 \to \ldots \to v_k$ be such a path. It cannot be that π' is included in N^* otherwise it would be zero in $\mathcal{G}$, and we let i_0 be the largest index such that $v_{i_0} \in P^*$. Since $w'(v_{i_0}v_{i_0+1}) = 0$ we have $w(v_{i_0}v_{i_0+1}) = \delta > 0$ hence it must be that $v_{i_0} \in V_{\text{Min}}$ otherwise we would have $v_{i_0} \in P = P'$ which contradicts that $v_{i_0} \in N'^*$. We now let π be an optimal path from v_{i_0+1}. Then we have $\text{alt}(\pi') \geq \text{alt}((v_{i_0}v_{i_0+1})\pi) \geq i_A$.

(iii) Let $v \in P^* \cap N'^*$ and let $\pi' : v_0 \to \ldots \to v_k$ be an optimal path from $v = v_0$ in $\mathcal{G}'$. We assume for contradiction that $\text{alt}'(v) < i_A$, which thanks to the previous item implies that π' is zero in $\mathcal{G}$. Since $v_k \in N' = N$ and $v = v_0 \in P^*$ there is an index i_0 such that $v_{i_0} \in P^*$ and $v_{i_0+1} \in N^*$. This contradicts the fact that $w(v_{i_0}v_{i_0+1}) = w'(v_{i_0}v_{i_0+1}) = 0$.

(iv) We prove the two results together by induction on i. For $i = 0$ we have $A_0 = N = N' = A'_0$ hence we let $i \geq 1$ and assume that both results hence the equality are known for smaller values.
By item (i) if $i < i_D$ and $v \in A_i$ then $v \in N'^*$ and $\text{alt}'(v) \leq i$, but our induction hypothesis tells us that $\text{alt}'(v)$ cannot be $< i$ hence $A_i \subseteq A'_i$.

Conversely let $v \in A'_i$, assume $i < i_A$, let $\pi : v_0 \to \ldots \to v_k$ be an optimal path from $v_0 = v$ in $\mathcal{G}'$, and let $j_0 > 0$ be the smallest index such that $v_{j_0} \notin A'_i$. We assume that π is chosen such that v_{j_0} is minimal, and prove the result by an inner induction on j_0. Since $\text{alt}'(v) = i < i_A$ we know by item (iii) that $v \in N^*$.
If $j_0 = 1$, that is if $v_1 \in A'_{i-1}$, then thanks to the (outer) induction hypothesis for all $j \geq 1$ we have $v_j \in A'_{k_j} = A_{k_j}$ for some $k_j < i$, hence for all $j \geq 0$ we have $v_j \in N^*$. Hence π' remains in N^* and is zero in $\mathcal{G}'$ thus it is also zero in $\mathcal{G}$ and $\text{alt}(v) \leq \text{alt}(\pi) = i$. We conclude thanks to the (outer) induction that $\text{alt}(v) = i$.
If $j_0 \geq 2$ then the inner induction hypothesis gives $v_j \in N^*$ for $j \in [1, j_0]$ and the outer induction hypothesis gives $v_j \in N^*$ for $j \in [j_0 + 1, k]$, and we repeat the same argument.

(v) Assume that $i_A < i_D$. By item (iv) it holds that $A_{i_A} \subseteq A'_{i_A}$ hence it suffices to find $v_0 \in A'_{i_A} \setminus A_{i_A}$ and we take v_0 given by the definition of i_A: $v_0 \in P^* \cap V_{\text{Min}}$ is such that there is $v_1 \in N^*$ with $v_0v_1 \in E$, $w(v_0v_1) = \delta$ (which implies $w'(v_0v_1) = 0$) and $\text{alt}(v_1) \leq i_A$.
Again by (iv) it holds that $v_1 \in N'^*$ and $\text{alt}'(v_1) \leq \text{alt}(v_1)$, thus $v_0 \in V_{\text{Min}}$ has a zero edge in $\mathcal{G}'$ towards a vertex of N'^* and therefore $v_0 \in N'^*$. Now $\text{alt}'(v_0) \leq \text{alt}((v_0v_1)\pi'_1)$, where π'_1 is an optimal path from v_1 in $\mathcal{G}'$ and hence $\text{alt}'(v_0) \leq i_A$. Yet again thanks to (iv) it cannot be that $\text{alt}'(v_0) < i_A$ since $A'_i \subseteq A_i$ for $i < i_A$ and $v_0 \in P^*$, therefore we conclude that $v_0 \in A'_i$.

(vi) Assume for contradiction that $\delta_{N,2} = -\delta$. Then there is $v \in SN$ such that $\text{ext}(v) = -\delta$, hence $\text{ext}'(v) = 0$ which contradicts $N' = N$. The proof of the second statement is symmetric.

(vii) If $i_A = \infty$ then there is no edge with weight δ in $\mathcal{G}$ from $P^* \cap V_{\text{Min}}$ to N^* hence $\delta_{P,1} > \delta$ therefore it must be by item (vi) that $\delta = -\delta^-_A$. We let $e_0 = v_0v_1$ be an edge with weight $-\delta$ from $v_0 \in V_{\text{Max}} \cap N^*$ to $v_1 \in P^*$. We claim that $P'^* \supseteq P^*$ which proves the result since then $v_0 \in V_{\text{Max}}$ has an edge e_0 which is zero (hence non-negative) in $\mathcal{G}'$ towards P'^*, hence $v_0 \in P'^*$ and $i_D \leq \text{alt}(v_0)$.
This follows from a quick induction over attractor-layers towards $P = P'$ over zero edges in $\mathcal{G}$: a vertex $v \in V_{\text{Max}} \cap (P^* \setminus P)$ has a zero edge, which remains zero, in $\mathcal{G}$ towards a vertex in the previous layer, and by assumption vertices $v \in V_{\text{Min}} \cap (P^* \setminus P)$ have all their edges towards N^* which are $\geq \delta_{P,1} > \delta$ hence remain positive.

(viii) By item (vii) $m = \min(i_D, i_A)$ is finite, and by item (iv) we have $A_i = A'_i$ for all $i < m$. If $m = i_A \leq i_D - 1$ then moreover $A_m \subseteq A'_m$ and the inclusion is strict by item (v), which concludes. Otherwise $m = i_D \leq i_A - 1$ hence $A_m \supseteq A'_m$ and the inclusion is strict by definition of i_D.

Even broken in elementary steps the proof above remains very tedious, we are not aware unfortunately of simplifications that could be made.

Step Two: Encoding into Integers. We now present the second step for the proof of Theorem 4, due to [6]. We let k denote $|P| + |N|$, which can only decrease throughout the iteration thanks to Lemma 6. Note that there exists $r \in [1, n-k]$ such that the layers $A_1, \ldots, A_r$ are non-empty and $A_{r+1}, A_{r+2}, \ldots$ are empty. We let $s_r = 1$ if r is even and 0 otherwise.

The argument relies on the following $n-k+1$-bit integer

$$\alpha^- = \underbrace{0\ldots0}_{|A_1|}\underbrace{1\ldots1}_{|A_2|}\underbrace{0\ldots0}_{|A_3|}\ldots\underbrace{s_r\ldots s_r}_{|A_r|}1\ \underbrace{0\ldots0}_{|P^*|-|P|},$$

and its symmetric counterpart α^+, which is defined in exactly the same way with respect to layers in P^*.

Lemma 8. *If $k = k'$ then $\alpha'^- > \alpha^- + 2^{|P^*|-|P|}$ and likewise $\alpha'^+ > \alpha^+ + 2^{|N^*|-|N|}$.*

Proof. By Theorem 5 the leftmost bit to switch from α^- to α'^- switches from 0 to 1, and occurs before the rightmost block of the form $10\ldots0$ with $|P^*|-|P|$ zeros, hence the result.

We are finally ready to prove the announced $O(2^{n/2})$ bound.

Proof. Consider $\alpha = \alpha^- + \alpha^+$, which is $\le 2^{n-k+2}$. Note that $|N^*|-|N|+|P^*|-|P| = n-k$, hence $\max(|N^*|-|N|, |P^*|-|P|) \ge \frac{n-k}{2}$. By the above lemma, if $k' = k$ then

$$\alpha' > 2^{\max(|N^*|-|N|,|P^*|-|P|)} \ge 2^{\frac{n-k}{2}}.$$

Hence, there are at most $2^{n-k+2}/2^{\frac{n-k}{2}} = 4 \cdot 2^{\frac{n-k}{2}}$ consecutive iterations with the same k. The bound follows since

$$\sum_{k=0}^{n-1} 4 \cdot 2^{\frac{n-k}{2}} = O(2^{n/2}).$$

References

1. Björklund, H., Vorobyov, S.G.: Combinatorial structure and randomized subexponential algorithms for infinite games. Theor. Comput. Sci. **349**(3), 347–360 (2005)
2. Bouyer, P., Fahrenberg, U., Larsen, K.G., Markey, N., Srba, J.: Infinite runs in weighted timed automata with energy constraints. In: Cassez, F., Jard, C. (eds.) FORMATS 2008. LNCS, vol. 5215, pp. 33–47. Springer, Heidelberg (2008). https://doi.org/10.1007/978-3-540-85778-5_4
3. Brim, L., Chaloupka, J., Doyen, L., Gentilini, R., Raskin, J.: Faster algorithms for mean-payoff games. Formal Methods Syst. Des. **38**(2), 97–118 (2011). https://doi.org/10.1007/s10703-010-0105-x
4. Calude, C.S., Jain, S., Khoussainov, B., Li, W., Stephan, F.: Deciding parity games in quasi-polynomial time. In: STOC, pp. 252–263 (2017)
5. Comin, C., Rizzi, R.: Improved pseudo-polynomial bound for the value problem and optimal strategy synthesis in mean payoff games. Algorithmica **77**(4), 995–1021 (2017). https://doi.org/10.1007/s00453-016-0123-1
6. Dorfman, D., Kaplan, H., Zwick, U.: A faster deterministic exponential time algorithm for energy games and mean payoff games. In: ICALP, pp. 114:1–114:14 (2019)

7. Ehrenfeucht, A., Mycielski, J.: Positional strategies for mean payoff games. Int. J. Game Theory **8**, 109–113 (1979). https://doi.org/10.1007/BF01768705
8. Emerson, E.A., Jutla, C.S.: Tree automata, μ-calculus and determinacy. In: FOCS, pp. 368–377. IEEE Computer Society (1991)
9. Fijalkow, N., Gawrychowski, P., Ohlmann, P.: Value iteration using universal graphs and the complexity of mean payoff games. In: MFCS. LIPIcs, vol. 170, pp. 34:1–34:15. Schloss Dagstuhl - Leibniz-Zentrum für Informatik (2020)
10. Gallai, T.: Maximum-minimum sätze über graphen. Acta Math. Acad. Sci. Hung. **9**(3–4), 395–434 (1958)
11. Gurvich, V.A., Karzanov, A.V., Khachiyan, L.G.: Cyclic games and an algorithm to find minimax cycle means in directed graphs. USSR Comput. Math. Math. Phys. **28**, 85–91 (1988)
12. Martin, D.A.: Borel determinacy. Ann. Math. **102**(2), 363–371 (1975)
13. Mostowski, A.W.: Games with forbidden positions. Technical report 78, University of Gdansk (1991)
14. Pisaruk, N.N.: Mean cost cyclical games. Math. Oper. Res. **24**(4), 817–828 (1999)
15. Puri, A.: Theory of hybrid systems and discrete event systems. Ph.D. thesis, EECS Department, University of California, Berkeley, December 1995
16. Zielonka, W.: Infinite games on finitely coloured graphs with applications to automata on infinite trees. Theor. Comput. Sci. **200**(1–2), 135–183 (1998)
17. Zwick, U., Paterson, M.: The complexity of mean payoff games on graphs. Theor. Comput. Sci. **158**(1–2), 343–359 (1996)

Partial Vertex Cover on Graphs of Bounded Degeneracy

Fahad Panolan[1] and Hannane Yaghoubizade[2(✉)]

[1] Department of Computer Science and Engineering, IIT Hyderabad, Sangareddy, India
fahad@cse.iith.ac.in

[2] Department of Mathematical Sciences, Sharif University of Technology, Tehran, Iran
h.yaghoubizade99@sharif.ir
https://iith.ac.in/~fahad

Abstract. In the Partial Vertex Cover (PVC) problem, we are given an n-vertex graph G and a positive integer k, and the objective is to find a vertex subset S of size k maximizing the number of edges with at least one end-point in S. This problem is W[1]-hard on general graphs, but admits a parameterized subexponential time algorithm with running time $2^{O(\sqrt{k})}n^{O(1)}$ on planar and apex-minor free graphs [Fomin et al. (FSTTCS 2009, IPL 2011)], and a $k^{O(k)}n^{O(1)}$ time algorithm on bounded degeneracy graphs [Amini et al. (FSTTCS 2009, JCSS 2011)]. Graphs of bounded degeneracy contain many sparse graph classes like planar graphs, H-minor free graphs, and bounded tree-width graphs (see Fig. 1). In this work, we prove the following results:

- There are algorithms for PVC on graphs of degeneracy d with running time $2^{O(dk)}n^{O(1)}$ and $(e+ed)^k 2^{o(k)}n^{O(1)}$ which are improvements on the previous $k^{O(k)}n^{O(1)}$ time algorithm by Amini et al. [2]
- PVC admits a polynomial compression on graphs of bounded degeneracy, resolving an open problem posed by Amini et al. [2].

Keywords: Parameterized Algorithms · Partial Vertex Cover · Bounded Degeneracy · Planar Graphs

1 Introduction

In a covering problem, we are given a family $\mathcal{F}$ of subsets of a universe U, and the objective is to find a minimum size subfamily of $\mathcal{F}$ covering all the elements in U. Well known examples of covering problems are Set Cover, Vertex Cover, Dominating Set, Facility Location, k-Median, k-Center, etc. Covering problems are fundamental in combinatorial optimization and they are very well studied in all areas of algorithms and complexity.

Another variant of covering problems is partial covering problems. In a partial covering problem, the input is a family $\mathcal{F}$ of subsets of a universe U and a positive integer k. The objective is to find a k size subset of $\mathcal{F}$ that covers the maximum

A. S. Kulikov and S. Raskhodnikova (Eds.): CSR 2022, LNCS 13296, pp. 289–301, 2022.
https://doi.org/10.1007/978-3-031-09574-0_18

number of elements in U. Two prominent examples of partial covering problems on graphs are Partial Vertex Cover (PVC) and Partial Dominating Set (PDS), which has got considerable attention in the field of parameterized complexity[1].

Partial Vertex Cover (PVC) **Parameter:** k
Input: An undirected graph G and a positive integer k
Objective: Find a vertex subset S of size k such that the number of edges with at least one end-point in S is maximized

Partial Dominating Set (PDS) **Parameter:** k
Input: An undirected graph G and a positive integer k
Objective: Find a vertex subset S of size k such that the size of the closed neighborhood of S is maximized

Even though there are many works on PVC and PDS in the realm of parameterized complexity, there are still some open questions about these problems. It is previously known that PVC is W[1]-hard [10] and PDS, as a more general problem of Dominating Set, is W[2]-hard. Amini et al. [2] proved that PVC can be solved in time $k^{O(k)}n^{O(1)}$ in bipartite graphs, triangle free graphs, planar graphs, H-minor free graphs (for a fixed H), and bounded degeneracy graphs. On planar graphs, they gave faster algorithms with running time $2^{O(k)}n^{O(1)}$ for PVC and PDS. Later, Fomin et al. [5] gave parameterized subexponential time algorithms with running time $2^{O(\sqrt{k})}n^{O(1)}$ for PVC and PDS on planar graphs and apex-minor free graphs. Also, unlike Dominating Set, which is known to be FPT [1] on bounded degeneracy graphs, PDS is W[1]-hard [9] in this class.

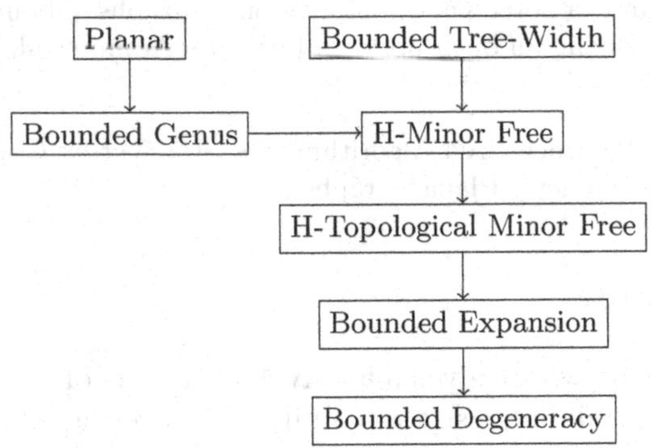

Fig. 1. Inclusion relation between various sparse graph classes.

[1] For basic definitions related to parameterized algorithms and complexity we refer to Sect. 2.1.

In this work, we give a parameterized single exponential time algorithm for PVC on d-degenerate graphs. Our algorithm also works for the more general weighted version of the problem.

Theorem 1.1. *Given $G = (V, E)$, a d-degenerate graph with edge weights $w : E \to \mathbb{R}^+$, and an integer $k > 0$, there is an algorithm that runs in time $2^{kd+k}(kd)^{O(\log(kd))}n^{O(1)}$ and finds a subset $S \subseteq V$ of size k, with maximum possible $E_G(S)$, i.e., the total weight of edges with at least one end-point in S.*

It is also possible to apply a slight change in the algorithm of Theorem 1.1 to get a faster running time.

Theorem 1.2. *Given $G = (V, E)$, a d-degenerate graph with edge weights $w : E \to \mathbb{R}^+$, and an integer $k > 0$, there is an algorithm that runs in time $(e + ed)^k\, 2^{o(k)}n^{O(1)}$ and finds a subset $S \subseteq V$ of size k, with maximum possible $E_G(S)$, i.e., the total weight of edges with at least one end-point in S.*

In [2], Amini et al. asked whether PVC and PDS admit polynomial kernels on planar graphs. We prove that PVC admits a polynomial compression on d-degenerate graphs, a more general class of sparse graphs. To get a better size bound for planar graphs, we prove the following general theorem.

Theorem 1.3. *Given a d-degenerate graph $G = (V, E)$ that does not contain any $K_{p,p}$ as a subgraph, and an integer $k > 0$, there is a polynomial-time algorithm that outputs a subgraph $H = (V' \subseteq V, E' \subseteq E)$ of G with $O(pd^2(2dk)^p)$ vertices and a weight function $\rho\colon V' \to \{0, \dots, 2^{dk}\}$ on the vertex set V' with the following properties.*

- *For any vertex subset $S' \subseteq V' \subseteq V$, $E_G(S')$ is equal to $E_H(S') + \sum_{v \in S'} \rho(v)$.*
- *Let S be a partial vertex cover of size k in G covering at least t edges. Then there is a vertex set $S' \subseteq V'$ of size k such that $E_H(S') + \sum_{v \in S'} \rho(v)$ is at least t.*

Since planar graphs are 5-degenerate and do not contain $K_{3,3}$ as a subgraph, we get the following corollary from Theorem 1.3.

Corollary 1.3.1. *There is a polynomial compression for* PVC *on planar graphs. Here, the compressed instance is a graph H with $O(k^3)$ vertices and a weight function on the vertex set of H where the weight of each vertex can be encoded using $O(k)$ bits.*

Because no d-degenerate graph contains $K_{d+1,d+1}$ as a subgraph, we also have the following corollary.

Corollary 1.3.2. *There is a polynomial compression for* PVC *on d-degenerate graphs. Here, the compressed instance is a graph H with $O(k^{d+1})$ vertices and a weight function on the vertex set of H, where the weight of each vertex can be encoded using at most kd bits.*

Independent of our work, Koana et al. [12] recently showed that PVC on d-degenerate graphs admits a kernel of size $k^{O(d)}$ and unless coNP $\subseteq$ NP\poly, it does not admit any kernel of size $O(k^{d-2-\epsilon})$.

Our Methods. First, we explain the overview of our FPT algorithm mentioned in Theorem 1.1, which is based on the following randomized process. Notice that for a d-degenerate graph, there is a sequence of vertices such that for any vertex v, the number of v's neighbors at the right of it in the sequence is at most d. Let S be a solution for PVC and let S' be the set of vertices that are not in S, but they are a "right neighbor" of a vertex in S. Clearly, $|S \cup S'| \leq k + kd$. If we color each vertex red or blue uniformly at random, with probability at least $\frac{1}{2^{k+kd}}$, all the vertices in S would get red, and all the vertices in S' would get blue. Now we assign a value $val(v)$ to any vertex v, which is $|N_G(v)|$ minus the number of red "right neighbors" of v. This assignment of values ensures that each edge incident on a red vertex contributes to the value of exactly one red vertex. Observing that for every vertex in S all of its red "right neighbors" are also in S, the solution will be the k most valuable red vertices, and the number of edges covered by them will be the sum of their values. This algorithm can be derandomized using universal sets. In Sect. 3, we present the deterministic version of the algorithm.

Next, we give a high-level idea of our polynomial compression algorithm. We prove that a "large" d-degenerate graph without any $K_{p,p}$ as a subgraph, has an independent set I of size $k+1$ and a vertex subset $\mathcal{C}$ such that for any distinct $x, y \in I$, $N_G(x) \cap N_G(y) = \mathcal{C}$. Then, we prove that there is a solution that does not contain the least degree vertex of I. This leads to a simple reduction rule as long as the number of vertices is not polynomially bounded in k. This algorithm is explained in Sect. 4.

Other Related Works. In [16] some generalization of vertex cover (e.g. PVC) parameterizing by tree-width is studied. Also, PVC parameterized by the number of covered edges is studied in [11]. There are also extensive works on the approximability of PVC on general graphs [13–15]. For example, Manurangsi in [14] presents a simple FPT approximation scheme that runs in $(1/\epsilon)^{O(k)} n^{O(1)}$ as well as an approximation kernelization scheme of $O(k/\epsilon)$ vertices for weighted PVC.

2 Preliminaries

For a graph $G = (V, E)$, we denote the number of vertices and edges by n and m, respectively. For a vertex $v \in V$ we denote the set of neighbors of v by $N_G(v)$ and the degree of v by $|N_G(v)|$. For $A \subseteq V$, we use $E_G(A)$ to denote the total number (weight) of edges with at least one end-point in A. We denote a complete bipartite graph with partitions of size p and q by $K_{p,q}$. We use $[n]$ to denote the set $\{1, 2, \ldots, n\}$.

Definition 2.1 (d-degenerate graph). *An undirected graph G is said to be d-degenerate if every subgraph of G contains a vertex of degree at most d. The degeneracy of a graph is the smallest value of d for which it is d-degenerate.*

We use the following proposition to derive Corollary 1.3.1 from Theorem 1.3.

Proposition 1. *Planar graphs are 5-degenerate.*

Proof. By Euler's formula, we know $m \leq 3n - 6$ for all $n \geq 3$. Therefore, $\sum_{v \in V} |N_G(v)| \leq 6n - 12$, and there is a vertex of a degree at most 5 in any planar graph. Since every subgraph of a planar graph is also planar, planar graphs are 5-degenerate. □

For a graph $G = (V, E)$, let λ be an ordering of vertices of G; i.e. $\lambda : [n] \to V$ is a bijective function. We say λ is *d-posterior*, if $\lambda(i)$ has at most d neighbors among $\lambda(i+1), \lambda(i+2), \ldots, \lambda(n)$. Also, for $v = \lambda(i)$, we call $N_G(v) \cap \{\lambda(i+1), \lambda(i+2), \ldots, \lambda(n)\}$ *posterior neighbors* of v and we denote them by $PN_\lambda(v)$. Note that since λ is a d-posterior ordering, we have $PN_\lambda(v) \leq d$ for all $v \in V$. Next, we will state some useful propositions about d-degenerate graphs.

Proposition 2. *There exists a d-posterior ordering for vertices of any d-degenerate graph G.*

Proof. Let $G_1 = G$, and for $2 \leq i \leq n$ construct G_i by removing the minimum degree vertex from G_{i-1}. Set $\lambda(i)$ to be a minimum degree vertex in G_i. □

Proposition 3. *For a d-degenerate graph $G = (V, E)$, we have $m \leq nd$.*

Proof. Consider a d-posterior ordering λ and note that $m = \sum_{v \in V} PN_\lambda(v) \leq nd$ because $PN_\lambda(v) \leq d$ for any $v \in V$. □

Proposition 4. *Let $G = (V, E)$ be a d-degenerate graph. Then, there is a $(d+1)$-coloring for V such that for any $(u, v) \in E$, u and v get different colors; i.e., $f : V \to [d+1]$ such that $f(u) \neq f(v)$ for all $(u, v) \in E$. Furthermore, one can construct this coloring in time $n^{O(1)}$.*

Proof. Let λ be a d-posterior ordering of V and for each i from n to 1, choose a color for $\lambda(i)$ which does not occur in $PN_\lambda(\lambda(i))$. □

2.1 Parameterized Complexity

We state the following definitions slightly modified from the Kernelization book [8].

Definition 2.2 (FPT optimization problem). *A parameterized optimization problem Π is fixed parameter tractable (FPT) if there is an algorithm (called FPT algorithm) that solves Π, such that the running time of the algorithm on instances of size n with parameter k is upper bounded by $f(k) \cdot n^{O(1)}$ for a computable function f.*

Definition 2.3 (Polynomial-time preprocessing algorithm). *A polynomial-time preprocessing algorithm $\mathcal{A}$ for a parameterized optimization problem Π is a pair of polynomial-time algorithms. The first one is called the* ***reduction algorithm****, and given an instance (I, k) of Π, the reduction algorithm outputs an instance $(I', k') = \mathcal{R}_\mathcal{A}(I, k)$ of a problem Π'. The second algorithm* *is called the* **solution lifting** *algorithm. This algorithm takes an instance* (I, k) *of* Π*, the output instance* (I', k') *of the reduction algorithm, and a solution* s' *to the instance* (I', k')*. The solution lifting algorithm works in time polynomial in* $|I|, k, |I'|, k'$ *and* $|s'|$*, and outputs a solution* s *to* (I, k) *such that if* s' *is an optimal solution to* (I', k') *then* s *is an optimal solution to* (I, k)*.*

Definition 2.4 (Compression, Kernelization). *A polynomial time preprocessing algorithm* $\mathcal{A}$ *is called a compression, if* $size_{\mathcal{A}}$ *is upper bounded by a computable function* $g : \mathbb{N} \to \mathbb{N}$ *where* $size_{\mathcal{A}}$ *is defined as follows:*

$$size_{\mathcal{A}}(k) = \sup\{|I'| + k' : (I', k') = \mathcal{R}_{\mathcal{A}}(I, k) \text{ for any instance } (I, k) \text{ of the problem}\}$$

If the upper bound $g(.)$ *is a polynomial function of* k*, we say* $\mathcal{A}$ *is a polynomial compression. A compression (polynomial compression) is called a kernelization (polynomial kernelization) if the input and output of the reduction algorithm are instances of the same problem, i.e.,* $\Pi = \Pi'$*.*

3 FPT Algorithm for Weighted Partial Vertex Cover

In this section, we show that PVC can be solved in parameterized single exponential time on d-degenerate weighted graphs. That is, we prove Theorem 1.1.

We will use a *universal set* in our algorithm defined as follows (see also section 5.6.1 of [4]).

Definition 3.1 ((n, l)-universal set). *An* (n, l)*-universal set is a family* $\mathcal{U}$ *of subsets of* $[n]$ *such that for any* $A \subseteq [n]$ *of size* l*, the family* $\{U \cap A : U \in \mathcal{U}\}$ *contains all* 2^l *subsets of* A*.*

Lemma 3.1 (Naor et al. [17]). *For any* $n, l \geq 1$*, one can construct an* (n, l)*-universal set of size* $2^l l^{O(\log l)} \log n$ *in time* $2^l l^{O(\log l)} n \log n$*.*

We now describe our FPT algorithm for solving PVC in the given d-degenerate weighted graph $G = (V, E)$. To give a better intuition, we first state the algorithm informally. Consider a d-posterior ordering for the vertices. Suppose we have an oracle that paints the vertices with blue and red, such that all vertices in the solution get red, all vertices that are not in the solution but are a posterior neighbor of a vertex in the solution get blue, and other vertices get either red or blue. Observe that the solution is a subset of red vertices such that for any vertex in the solution, its red posterior neighbors are also in the solution. Then we will assign a value to each vertex, such that the solution will be the set of k most valuable red vertices. In the algorithm, we use a universal set instead of the oracle. The following is the exact description of the algorithm.

Let λ be a d-posterior ordering of V and $l = \min(n, k{+}kd)$. First, we construct an (n, l)-universal set $\mathcal{U}$ of subsets of V, and for each $U \in \mathcal{U}$ with size $\geq k$ and $v \in V$, we define the *value* of v with respect to U as:

$$val_U(v) = \sum_{u \in N_G(v) \setminus (PN_\lambda(v) \cap U)} w(u, v)$$

And we define $sol(U) \subseteq U$ as the set of k most valuable vertices in U, and we set the value of U to be $val(U) = \sum_{v \in sol(U)} val_U(v)$. Finally, we return $sol(U)$ for the most valuable U.

To prove Theorem 1.1, first we show the following lemmas.

Lemma 3.2. *For any $U \in \mathcal{U}$ and $A \subseteq U$, we have $\sum_{v \in A} val_U(v) \leq E_G(A)$.*

Proof. Recall that $E_G(A)$ is the total weight of edges with at least one end-point in A.

Any edge $e = (u, v)$ with exactly one end-point, say v, in A is counted at most once in $val_U(v)$ and since $u \notin A$, it is also counted at most once in $\sum_{v \in A} val_U(v)$.

For an edge $e' = (u', v')$ with both end-points in A, without loss of generality, suppose u' is later than v' in the ordering λ, i.e., $\lambda^{-1}(u') > \lambda^{-1}(v')$. Therefore, $u' \in PN_\lambda(v')$ and since $A \subseteq U$, $u' \in PN_\lambda(v') \cap U$ and e is not counted in $val_U(v')$. On the other hand, $v' \notin PN_\lambda(u')$, and e is counted in $val_U(u')$. Therefore, e is counted exactly once in $\sum_{v \in A} val_U(v)$.

Since the weights of edges are positive and all edges counted exactly once in $E_G(A)$ are counted at most once in $\sum_{v \in A} val_U(v)$, we have $\sum_{v \in A} val_U(v) \leq E_G(A)$. □

Now, let S be a hypothetical solution, and define $\tilde{S} = S \cup \left(\bigcup_{v \in S} PN_\lambda(v)\right)$. Note that:

$$|\tilde{S}| \leq |S| + \left|\bigcup_{v \in S} PN_\lambda(v)\right| \leq k + k.d \qquad (\text{since } |S| = k \text{ and } PN_\lambda(v) \leq d)$$

Therefore we have $|\tilde{S}| \leq l$. Consider a subset $T \subseteq V$ with size l such that $\tilde{S} \subseteq T$. According to Definition 3.1, there is a set $\tilde{U} \in \mathcal{U}$ such that $S = \tilde{U} \cap T$. Note that since $|S| = k$, size of $\tilde{U}$ is $\geq k$, and $val_{\tilde{U}}$ and $sol(\tilde{U})$ are defined.

Lemma 3.3. $E_G(S) = \sum_{v \in S} val_{\tilde{U}}(v)$.

Proof. It is enough to show that each edge with at least one end-point in S is counted exactly once in $\sum_{v \in S} val_{\tilde{U}}(v)$.

Consider any $e = (u, v)$ with exactly one end-point, say v, in S. Note that $u \notin S$ and

$$\left(PN_\lambda(v) \cap \tilde{U}\right) \subseteq (\tilde{S} \cap \tilde{U}) \subseteq (T \cap \tilde{U}) = S$$

Therefore, $u \notin \left(PN_\lambda(v) \cap \tilde{U}\right)$ and e is counted in $val_{\tilde{U}}(v)$. Since $u \notin S$, e is counted in $\sum_{v \in S} val_{\tilde{U}}(v)$ exactly once. For edges with two end-points in S, the proof is the same as the proof of Lemma 3.2. □

We finally prove Theorem 1.1. For convenience, we restate the theorem here.

Theorem 1.1. *Given $G = (V, E)$, a d-degenerate graph with edge weights $w : E \to \mathbb{R}^+$, and an integer $k > 0$, there is an algorithm that runs in time $2^{kd+k}(kd)^{O(\log(kd))}n^{O(1)}$ and finds a subset $S \subseteq V$ of size k, with maximum possible $E_G(S)$, i.e., the total weight of edges with at least one end-point in S.*

Proof. By Lemma 3.2 and optimality of S, $val(U) = \sum_{v \in sol(U)} val_U(v) \leq E_G(sol(U)) \leq E_G(S)$ for all $U \in \mathcal{U}$ with size $\geq k$. Also, note:

$$\begin{aligned} val(\tilde{U}) &= \sum_{v \in sol(\tilde{U})} val_{\tilde{U}}(v) && \text{(definition of } val(\tilde{U})\text{)} \\ &\geq \sum_{v \in S} val_{\tilde{U}}(v) && \text{(definition of } sol(\tilde{U}) \text{ and since } S \subseteq \tilde{U}\text{)} \\ &= E_G(S) && \text{(Lemma 3.3)} \end{aligned}$$

Therefore, for the most valuable U, $val(U) = E_G(S)$. Since $val(U) \leq E_G(sol(U)) \leq E_G(S)$, $sol(U)$ is also a solution and $E_G(sol(U)) = val(U)$. This implies the algorithm's correctness and shows that the weight of the edges covered by the solution is equal to $val(U)$.

Finally, the running time of constructing the family $\mathcal{U}$ is

$$2^{kd+k}(kd+k)^{O(\log(kd+k))}n^{O(1)}.$$

Moreover, we only have a polynomial process for each $U \in \mathcal{U}$. Since, the size of $\mathcal{U}$ is $2^{kd+k}(kd+k)^{O(\log(kd+k))}\log n$, the total running time is

$$2^{kd+k}(kd+k)^{O(\log(kd+k))}n^{O(1)}.$$

□

3.1 Improved Running Time Using Lopsided Universal Sets

One can use lopsided universal sets instead of universal sets in the above algorithm to get the running time $(e+ed)^k\, 2^{o(k)}n^{O(1)}$. In the following we briefly introduce lopsided universal sets.

Definition 3.2 ((n,p,q)-lopsided universal set). *An (n,p,q)-lopsided universal set is a family $\mathcal{U}$ of subsets of $[n]$ such that for any $A \subseteq [n]$ of size p and $B \subseteq [n] \backslash A$ of size q, there is a $U \in \mathcal{U}$ that $A \subseteq U$ and $B \cap U = \emptyset$.*

Lemma 3.4 (Fomin et al. [6]). *There is an algorithm that given n, p and q constructs an (n,p,q)-lopsided universal set $\mathcal{U}$ of size $\binom{p+q}{p} \cdot 2^{o(p+q)} \log n$ in time $O\left(\binom{p+q}{p} \cdot 2^{o(p+q)} n \log n\right)$.*

Now, let $p = k$ and $q = \min(n-k, kd)$ and follow the same steps as the aforementioned algorithm using an (n,p,q)-lopsided universal set $\mathcal{U}$ instead of an (n,l)-universal set. The proof of the correctness is also the same, except that for Lemma 3.3, $\tilde{U} \in \mathcal{U}$ should be such that $S \subseteq \tilde{U}$ and $\left(\tilde{S} \backslash S\right) \cap \tilde{U} = \emptyset$. Finally, for the running time, we have the following:

Proposition 5. *For any r and n such that $1 \leq r \leq n$ we have $\binom{n}{r} \leq \left(\frac{en}{r}\right)^r$.*

Using the same analysis as the first algorithm, the running time of this algorithm would be $\binom{k+kd}{k} \cdot 2^{o(k)} n^{O(1)}$ which by the Proposition 5 is $(e+ed)^k\, 2^{o(k)} n^{O(1)}$. This proves Theorem 1.2.

4 Polynomial Compression for Partial Vertex Cover

In this section, we present a polynomial compression for PVC in families of graphs with bounded degeneracy. That is, we prove Theorem 1.3.

For convenience we will allow self-loops for this part, but not parallel edges. For a vertex v with self-loops, we will not count v in $N_G(v)$ so $v \notin N_G(v)$, and we will use $L_G(v)$ to denote the number of self-loops of v. Therefore, the given graph $G = (V, E)$ is undirected, unweighted and any $v \in V$ might have several self-loops. Also, G does not contain $K_{p,p}$ and without considering self-loops, it is d-degenerate.

We say a subset $U \subseteq V$ of size $k + 1$ is *nice* if U is an independent set and there is a subset $\mathcal{C} \subseteq V$ such that for any $u, u' \in U$, $N_G(u) \cap N_G(u') = \mathcal{C}$. For each $u \in U$, we call $N_G(u) \backslash \mathcal{C}$ *private neighbors* of u with respect to U, and we denote it by $PV_U(u)$. Figure 2 shows a *nice* subset.

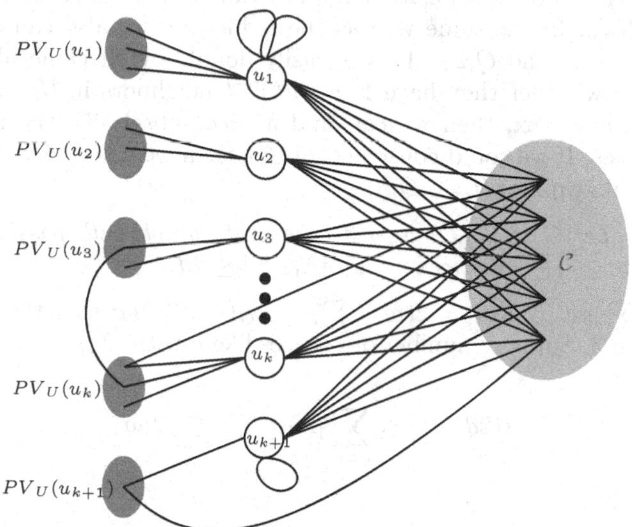

Fig. 2. A *nice* subset $U = \{u_1, u_2, \dots, u_{k+1}\}$

Lemma 4.1. *Let $G = (V, E)$ be an undirected graph with possible self-loops. For integers $h, p \geq 1$, suppose $I \subseteq V$ is an independent set of size $t > p \cdot (hk)^p$, such that $|N_G(v)| \leq h$ for all $v \in I$. Then either there is a nice $U \subseteq I$ or G contains a $K_{p,p}$. Furthermore, having G and I, we can find a nice subset or a $K_{p,p}$ in polynomial time.*

Proof. First, we show by induction that for each $0 \leq i \leq p$, either (a) there is a *nice* subset $U \subseteq I$, or (b) there is a $U_i \subseteq I$ of size $t_i > p \cdot (hk)^{p-i}$ such that $Q_i = \bigcap_{u \in U_i} N_G(u)$ has size $\geq i$.

For $i = 0$, clearly $U_0 = I$. If $i \geq 1$, by induction we know one of (a) or (b) is true for $i-1$. If (a) is true, then we are done. So there is a $U_{i-1} \subseteq I$ with conditions as mentioned earlier. If there was a vertex $v \in V \backslash Q_{i-1}$ with $> p \cdot (hk)^{p-i}$ neighbors in U_{i-1}, let U_i be $U_{i-1} \cap N_G(v)$ and (b) will be true for i. Otherwise, all vertices in $V \backslash Q_{i-1}$ have $\leq p \cdot (hk)^{p-i}$ neighbors in U_{i-1}, and we do the following:

As long as there is an unmarked vertex in U_{i-1}, we pick an unmarked vertex $u \in U_{i-1}$ and mark all vertices in U_{i-1} that have a neighbor in $N_G(u) \backslash Q_{i-1}$.

Since $N_G(u) \leq h$ and each vertex in $V \backslash Q_{i-1}$ has $\leq p \cdot (hk)^{p-i}$ neighbors in U_{i-1}, at most $ph^{p-i+1}k^{p-i}$ vertices would get marked after picking u. Therefore, we would pick at least $\frac{|U_{i-1}|}{ph^{p-i+1}k^{p-i}} > \frac{p \cdot (hk)^{p-i+1}}{ph^{p-i+1}k^{p-i}} = k$ vertices. Since these vertices are independent, their number is at least $k+1$, they are neighbors of Q_{i-1}, and they do not have common neighbors out of Q_{i-1}, each of their subsets of size $k+1$ forms a *nice* subset and (a) will be true.

If $i = p$, the above proposition implies that either there is a *nice* subset $U \subseteq I$ or a $K_{p,p}$. In the same way as the induction, we also can construct U_i and Q_i using U_{i-1} and Q_{i-1}. This is easily doable by checking all vertices in $V \backslash Q_{i-1}$ to see whether they have $> p \cdot (hk)^{p-i}$ neighbors in U_{i-1}. If we could not find such a vertex, then we can find a *nice* subset like the induction by marking vertices. If we could construct all U_is, then we can easily find a $K_{p,p}$ in the induced subgraph of $(U_p \cup Q_p)$. □

Lemma 4.2. *Let $G = (V, E)$ be a d-degenerate graph with possible self-loops. Then there are $\geq \frac{n}{2d+1}$ vertices v with $|N_G(v)| \leq 2d$.*

Proof. Note $\sum_{v \in V} |N_G(v)| = 2(m - \sum_{v \in V} L_G(v)) \leq 2nd$ that the inequality is by Proposition 3. Suppose number of vertices like v with $|N_G(v)| > 2d$ is t. Then we have:

$$t(2d+1) \leq \sum_{v \in V} |N_G(v)| \leq 2nd$$

This implies that

$$t \leq \frac{2nd}{2d+1}, \quad \text{and}$$
$$n - t \geq \frac{n}{2d+1}$$

This completes the proof of the lemma. □

Lemma 4.3. *Any d-degenerate graph $G = (V, E)$ with possible self-loops has an independent set I with size $\geq \frac{n}{(d+1)(2d+1)}$ such that $|N_G(v)| \leq 2d$ for all $v \in I$ and one can find such an independent set in time $(n+m)^{O(1)}$.*

Proof. First, construct a $(d+1)$-coloring for V in $n^{O(1)}$ using Proposition 4. By Lemma 4.2 there are $\geq \frac{n}{(2d+1)}$ vertices with $|N_G| \leq 2d$ and therefore, there are $\geq \frac{n}{(2d+1)(d+1)}$ vertices with $|N_G| \leq 2d$ and the same color, which means they form an independent set. □

Now, we are ready to describe the kernel. As long as, $n > p(d+1)(2d+1)(2dk)^p$, we apply the following reduction rule.

Reduction PVC 1. *Use Lemma 4.3 to find an independent set I of size $\geq \frac{n}{(d+1)(2d+1)} > p \cdot (2dk)^p$ such that $|N_G(v)| \leq 2d$ for all $v \in I$. Then, since the given graph G does not contain any $K_{p,p}$, by setting $h = 2d$ and using Lemma 4.1, find a nice subset $U \subseteq I$. Then remove $u \in U$ that minimizes $|N_G(u)| + L_G(u)$ and add a self-loop to each vertex of $N_G(u)$.*

To show the soundness of the reduction rule, we prove the following lemma.

Lemma 4.4. *Suppose $G = (V, E)$ is a graph with possible self-loops, and $U \subseteq V$ is nice. Then, for any $u \in U$ with the minimum $|N_G(u)| + L_G(u)$, there is a solution for* PVC *which does not contain u.*

Proof. Consider any solution S containing u. Since $|S| = k$, there is a $u' \in U$ such that (i) $(\{u'\} \cup PV_U(u')) \cap S = \emptyset$. Therefore, we have:

$$\begin{aligned} E_G(S \backslash \{u\} \cup \{u'\}) &\geq E_G(S) - (|N_G(u)| + L_G(u)) + (|N_G(u')| + L_G(u')) \\ &\qquad \text{(by } (i)\text{)} \\ &\geq E_G(S) \quad (\text{since } |N_G(u)| + L_G(u) \leq |N_G(u')| + L_G(u')) \end{aligned}$$

This implies that $S \backslash \{u\} \cup \{u'\}$ is a solution that does not contain u. □

We finally prove Theorem 1.3. For convenience, we restate the theorem here.

Theorem 1.3. *Given a d-degenerate graph $G = (V, E)$ that does not contain any $K_{p,p}$ as a subgraph, and an integer $k > 0$, there is a polynomial-time algorithm that outputs a subgraph $H = (V' \subseteq V, E' \subseteq E)$ of G with $O(pd^2(2dk)^p)$ vertices and a weight function $\rho \colon V' \to \{0, \ldots, 2^{dk}\}$ on the vertex set V' with the following properties.*

- *For any vertex subset $S' \subseteq V' \subseteq V$, $E_G(S')$ is equal to $E_H(S') + \sum_{v \in S'} \rho(v)$.*
- *Let S be a partial vertex cover of size k in G covering at least t edges. Then there is a vertex set $S' \subseteq V'$ of size k such that $E_H(S') + \sum_{v \in S'} \rho(v)$ is at least t.*

Proof. The running time of the described algorithm is polynomial by Lemma 4.1 and 4.3, and the reduction rule is safe by Lemma 4.4. The number of vertices in the kernel is $\leq p(d+1)(2d+1)(2dk)^p$, which is $O(pd^2(2dk)^p)$. Although the number of self-loops may be large, notice that the number of self-loops on a vertex will be at most n. We may remove the self-loops and add it as a weight on the vertex. Thus, each weight can be represented using at most $\log n$ bits. Since we have an algorithm for the problem with running time $2^{O(kd)} n^{O(1)}$, i.e., Theorem 1.1, when $kd \leq \log n$ the algorithm runs in polynomial time and thereby, it would be a compression itself. Otherwise, we have that $\log n \leq kd$ that guarantees the weight function ρ mentioned in the theorem statement. □

5 Conclusion

In this work we gave a single exponential parameterized algorithm and a polynomial compression for PVC on graphs of bounded degeneracy that include many sparse graph classes like planar graphs and H-minor free graphs. Is it possible to get similar results on biclique free graphs, a superclass of bounded degeneracy graphs? Notice that there is a linear kernel for DOMINATING SET on planar graphs, H-minor free graphs, and apex-minor free graphs [3, 7]. Can we get a linear kernel or compression for PVC on planar graphs?

References

1. Alon, N., Gutner, S.: Linear time algorithms for finding a dominating set of fixed size in degenerated graphs. Algorithmica **54**, 544–556 (2008). https://doi.org/10.1007/s00453-008-9204-0
2. Amini, O., Fomin, F.V., Saurabh, S.: Implicit branching and parameterized partial cover problems. J. Comput. Syst. Sci. **77**(6), 1159–1171 (2011). https://doi.org/10.1016/j.jcss.2010.12.002. https://www.sciencedirect.com/science/article/pii/S0022000010001431
3. Bodlaender, H.L., Fomin, F.V., Lokshtanov, D., Penninkx, E., Saurabh, S., Thilikos, D.M.: (Meta) kernelization. J. ACM **63**(5), 44:1–44:69 (2016). https://doi.org/10.1145/2973749.
4. Cygan, M., et al.: Parameterized Algorithms. Springer, Cham (2015). https://doi.org/10.1007/978-3-319-21275-3
5. Fomin, F., Lokshtanov, D., Raman, V., Saurabh, S.: Subexponential algorithms for partial cover problems. Inf. Process. Lett. **111**, 814–818 (2011). https://doi.org/10.1016/j.ipl.2011.05.016
6. Fomin, F.V., Lokshtanov, D., Panolan, F., Saurabh, S.: Efficient computation of representative families with applications in parameterized and exact algorithms. J. ACM **63**(4), 1–60 (2016). https://doi.org/10.1145/2886094
7. Fomin, F.V., Lokshtanov, D., Saurabh, S., Thilikos, D.M.: Bidimensionality and kernels. In: Proceedings of the 2010 Annual ACM-SIAM Symposium on Discrete Algorithms (SODA), pp. 503–510 (2010). https://doi.org/10.1137/1.9781611973075.43
8. Fomin, F.V., Lokshtanov, D., Saurabh, S., Zehavi, M.: Kernelization: Theory of Parameterized Preprocessing. Cambridge University Press, Cambridge (2019). https://doi.org/10.1017/9781107415157
9. Golovach, P.A., Villanger, Y.: Parameterized complexity for domination problems on degenerate graphs. In: Broersma, H., Erlebach, T., Friedetzky, T., Paulusma, D. (eds.) WG 2008. LNCS, vol. 5344, pp. 195–205. Springer, Heidelberg (2008). https://doi.org/10.1007/978-3-540-92248-3_18
10. Guo, J., Niedermeier, R., Wernicke, S.: Parameterized complexity of vertex cover variants. Theory Comput. Syst. **41**, 501–520 (2007). https://doi.org/10.1007/s00224-007-1309-3
11. Kneis, J., Langer, A., Rossmanith, P.: Improved upper bounds for partial vertex cover. In: Broersma, H., Erlebach, T., Friedetzky, T., Paulusma, D. (eds.) WG 2008. LNCS, vol. 5344, pp. 240–251. Springer, Heidelberg (2008). https://doi.org/10.1007/978-3-540-92248-3_22

12. Koana, T., Komusiewicz, C., Nichterlein, A., Sommer, F.: Covering many (or few) edges with k vertices in sparse graphs. In: Berenbrink, P., Monmege, B. (eds.) 39th International Symposium on Theoretical Aspects of Computer Science, STACS 2022. LIPIcs, Marseille, France, 15–18 March 2022 (Virtual Conference), vol. 219, pp. 42:1–42:18. Schloss Dagstuhl - Leibniz-Zentrum für Informatik (2022). https://doi.org/10.4230/LIPIcs.STACS.2022.42
13. Lokshtanov, D., Panolan, F., Ramanujan, M.S., Saurabh, S.: Lossy kernelization. CoRR abs/1604.04111 (2016). http://arxiv.org/abs/1604.04111
14. Manurangsi, P.: A note on max k-vertex cover: faster FPT-AS, smaller approximate kernel and improved approximation. In: SOSA (2019)
15. Marx, D.: Parameterized complexity and approximation algorithms. Comput. J. **51**, 60–78 (2008). https://doi.org/10.1093/comjnl/bxm048
16. Moser, H., Niedermeier, R., Guo, J.: Exact algorithms for generalizations of vertex cover (2005)
17. Naor, M., Schulman, L., Srinivasan, A.: Splitters and near-optimal derandomization. In: Proceedings of IEEE 36th Annual Foundations of Computer Science, pp. 182–191 (1995). https://doi.org/10.1109/SFCS.1995.492475

Abelian Repetition Threshold Revisited

Elena A. Petrova and Arseny M. Shur(✉)

Ural Federal University, Ekaterinburg, Russia
{elena.petrova,arseny.shur}@urfu.ru

Abstract. In combinatorics on words, *repetition thresholds* are the numbers separating avoidable and unavoidable repetitions of a given type in a given class of words. For example, the meaning of the "classical" repetition threshold $\mathsf{RT}(k)$ is "every infinite k-ary word contains an α-power of a nonempty word for some $\alpha \geq \mathsf{RT}(k)$ but some infinite k-ary words contain no such α-powers with $\alpha > \mathsf{RT}(k)$". It is well known that $\mathsf{RT}(k) = \frac{k}{k-1}$ with the exceptions for $k = 3, 4$.

For *Abelian* repetition threshold $\mathsf{ART}(k)$, avoidance of fractional Abelian powers of words is considered. The exact values of $\mathsf{ART}(k)$ are unknown; the lower bound $\mathsf{ART}(2) \geq \frac{11}{3}$, $\mathsf{ART}(3) \geq 2$, $\mathsf{ART}(4) \geq \frac{9}{5}$, $\mathsf{ART}(k) \geq \frac{k-2}{k-3}$ for all $k \geq 5$ was proved by Samsonov and Shur in 2012 and conjectured to be tight. We present a method of study of Abelian power-free languages using random walks in prefix trees and some experimental results obtained by this method. On the base of these results, we suggest that the lower bounds for $\mathsf{ART}(k)$ by Samsonov and Shur are not tight for all k except $k = 5$. We prove $\mathsf{ART}(k) > \frac{k-2}{k-3}$ for $k = 6, 7, 8, 9, 10$ and state a new conjecture on the Abelian repetition threshold.

Keywords: Abelian-power-free language · repetition threshold · prefix tree · random walk

1 Introduction

Two words are *Abelian equivalent* (A-equivalent) if they have the same multiset of letters; in other terms, if they are anagrams of each other, like English words *knee* and *keen*. *Abelian repetition* (A-repetition) is a pair of A-equivalent factors in a word. The study of A-repetitions originated from the question of Erdős [11]: does there exist an infinite finitary word having no consecutive pair of A-equivalent factors? The factors of the form uu', where u and u' are A-equivalent, are now called *Abelian squares* (A-squares). In modern terms, Erdős's question can be phrased as "are A-squares avoidable over some finite alphabet?" This question was answered in the affirmative by Evdokimov [12]; the smallest possible alphabet has cardinality 4, as was proved by Keränen [14]. In a similar way, kth A-powers are defined for arbitrary $k \geq 2$. Dekking [9] constructed infinite

E. A. Petrova—Supported by the Ministry of Science and Higher Education of the Russian Federation, project FEUZ-2020-0016.
A. M. Shur—Supported by Ural Mathematical Center, project 075-02-2022-877.

A. S. Kulikov and S. Raskhodnikova (Eds.): CSR 2022, LNCS 13296, pp. 302–319, 2022.
https://doi.org/10.1007/978-3-031-09574-0_19

ternary words without A-cubes and infinite binary words without 4th A-powers. The results by Dekking and Keränen form an Abelian analog of the seminal result by Thue [23]: there exist an infinite ternary word containing no squares (factors of the form uu) and an infinite binary word containing no cubes (factors of the form uuu).

Thue's result is considered as the origin of combinatorics on words and, in particular, of avoidability theory. Later this result was strengthened using *fractional* powers of a word: given a word u of length n, take a length-m prefix v of the infinite word $uuu\cdots$; then v is the $(\frac{m}{n})$th power of u ($m > n$ is assumed). Usually, v is referred to as an $(\frac{m}{n})$-power. A word is said to be α-*free* if it contains no $(\frac{m}{n})$-powers with $\frac{m}{n} \geq \alpha$. Fractional powers gave rise to the notion of *repetition threshold* which is the function

$$\mathsf{RT}(k) = \inf\{\alpha : \text{there exists an infinite } k\text{-ary } \alpha\text{-free word}\}.$$

The value $\mathsf{RT}(2) = 2$ is due to Thue [24]. Dejean [8] showed that $\mathsf{RT}(3) = 7/4$ and conjectured the remaining values $\mathsf{RT}(4) = 7/5$ (proved by Pansiot [16]) and $\mathsf{RT}(k) = \frac{k}{k-1}$ for $k \geq 5$ (proved by efforts of many authors [1,3,15,20]). Since the proof of Dejean's conjecture, a number of related results appeared, conjecturing and establishing similar thresholds for stronger or weaker restrictions on repetitions [4,6,25], for restricted classes of words [7,10,19,22], and for different models of words [5,13].

An extension of the notions of fractional power and repetition threshold to the case of A-powers was proposed by Cassaigne and Currie [2] for the case $m < 2n$ and by Samsonov and Shur [21] for the general case. Integral A-powers can be generalized to fractional ones in several ways; however, for the case $m < 2n$, one definition of an $(\frac{m}{n})$-A-power is preferable due to its symmetric nature. According to this definition, a word vuv' is an $(\frac{m}{n})$th A-power of the word vu if $|vu| = n$, $|vuv'| = m$, and v' is A-equivalent to v (in [21], such A-powers were called *strong*). Note that the reversal of an $(\frac{m}{n})$-A-power is also an $(\frac{m}{n})$-A-power. In this paper, we consider *only* strong A-powers; see Sect. 2 for the definition in the case $m > 2n$. Given the definition of fractional A-powers, one naturally defines α-A-free words and *Abelian repetition threshold*

$$\mathsf{ART}(k) = \inf\{\alpha : \text{there exists an infinite } k\text{-ary } \alpha\text{-A-free word}\}.$$

In [2], it was shown that for any $\varepsilon > 0$ there exists a $(1+\varepsilon)$-A-free word over an alphabet of size $2^{\mathrm{poly}(\varepsilon^{-1})}$. This bound is very loose but proves that $\lim_{k\to\infty} \mathsf{ART}(k) = 1$. In [21], the lower bound $\mathsf{ART}(k) \geq \frac{k-2}{k-3}$ for $k \geq 5$ was proved and conjectured to be tight; in full, this conjecture is as follows.

Conjecture 1 ([21]). $\mathsf{ART}(2) = 11/3$; $\mathsf{ART}(3) = 2$; $\mathsf{ART}(4) = 9/5$; $\mathsf{ART}(k) = \frac{k-2}{k-3}$ for $k \geq 5$.

No exact values of $\mathsf{ART}(k)$ are known, and no new bounds have appeared since [21]. One reason for the lack of progress in estimating $\mathsf{ART}(k)$ is the fact that the language $\mathsf{AF}(k,\alpha)$ of all k-ary α-A-free words can be finite but so huge that it cannot be enumerated by exhaustive search.

In the present study, we propose the following approach. The language $\mathsf{AF}(k,\alpha)$ is viewed as the *prefix tree* $\mathcal{T}_{k,\alpha}$: the elements of $\mathsf{AF}(k,\alpha)$ are nodes of the tree and u is an ancestor of v in the tree iff u is a prefix of w. In the same way we treat the languages $\mathsf{AF}(k,\alpha^+) = \bigcap_{\beta>\alpha} \mathsf{AF}(k,\beta)$. Hence it suffices to decide the (in)finiteness of $\mathcal{T}_{k,\alpha}$ and $\mathcal{T}_{k,\alpha^+}$ to compare α to $\mathsf{ART}(k)$. We construct random walks in such trees, using random depth-first search from the root (empty word). Analysing the statistics of such walks, we conjecture (in)finiteness of the studied trees. Our contribution can be summarized as follows:

- to speed up the search in prefix trees, we developed several algorithms to decide whether a word ua is α-A-free for a given α-A-free word u and a letter a; for all algorithms, we proved correctness and complexity guarantees;
- we ran multiple experiments for each of about 20 languages with unknown finiteness status and gathered the statistics;
- depending on statistics of constructed random walks, we classified most of the studied languages either as "finite-like" or as "infinite-like";
- we proved by an optimized exhaustive search that the finite-like languages $\mathsf{AF}(k, \frac{k-2}{k-3}^+)$ for $k = 6, 7, 8, 9, 10$ are finite, thus disproving Conjecture 1;
- we replaced Conjecture 1 with the following conjecture:

Conjecture 2. $\mathsf{ART}(2) > 11/3$; $2 < \mathsf{ART}(3) \leq 5/2$; $\mathsf{ART}(4) > 9/5$; $\mathsf{ART}(5) = 3/2$; $4/3 < \mathsf{ART}(6) < 3/2$; $\mathsf{ART}(k) = \frac{k-3}{k-4}$ for $k \geq 7$.

2 Definitions and Notation

We study finite words over finite alphabets, using the standard notation Σ for a (linearly ordered) alphabet, σ for its size, Σ^* for the set of all finite words over Σ, including the empty word λ. For a length-n word $u \in \Sigma^*$ we write $u = u[1..n]$; the elements of the range $[1..n]$ are *positions* in u, and the length of u is denoted by $|u|$. A word w is a *factor* of u if $u = vwz$ for some (possibly empty) words v and z; the condition $v = \lambda$ (resp., $z = \lambda$) means that w is a *prefix* (resp., *suffix*) of u. Any factor w of u can be represented as $w = u[i..j]$ for some i and j ($j < i$ means $w = \lambda$). A factor w of u can have several such representations; we say that $u[i..j]$ specifies the *occurrence of w at position i*.

A *k-power* of a word u is the concatenation of k copies of u, denoted by u^k. This notion can be extended to *α-powers* for an arbitrary rational $\alpha > 1$. The α-power of u is the word $u^\alpha = u \cdots uu'$ such that $|u^\alpha| = \alpha|u|$ and u' is a prefix of u. A word is *α-free* (resp., *α^+-free*) if no one of its factors is a β-power with $\beta \geq \alpha$ (resp., $\beta > \alpha$).

The *Parikh vector* $\Psi(u)$ of a word $u \in \Sigma^*$ is an integer vector of length σ whose coordinates are the numbers of occurrences of the letters from Σ in u. Thus, the word *acabac* over the alphabet $\Sigma = \{a < b < c < d\}$ has the Parikh vector $(3, 1, 2, 0)$. Two words u and v are A-equivalent (denoted by $u \sim v$) iff $\Psi(u) = \Psi(v)$. The *reversal* of a word $u = u[1..n]$ is the word $u^R = u[n]u[n-1] \cdots u[1]$. Clearly, $u \sim u^R$. A nonempty word u is a (*k-A-power*) if $u = w_1 \cdots w_k$, where $w_i \sim w_j$ for all indices i, j. A 2-A-power is an *A-square*, and a 3-A-power is an *A-cube*. Thus, k-A-powers generalize k-powers by relaxing the equality of factors to their A-equivalence. However, there are many ways to generalize the notion of an α-power to the Abelian case, and all of them have certain drawbacks. The reason is that $u \sim v$ implies $u[i..j] \sim v[i..j]$ for *no* pair of proper factors of u and v. If $1 < \alpha \leq 2$, we define an α-A-power as a word vuv' such that $\frac{|vuv'|}{|vu|} = \alpha$ and $v \sim v'$. The advantage of this definition is that the reversal of an α-A-power is an α-A-power as well. For $\alpha > 2$ the situation is worse: no natural definition compatible with the definition of k-A-power is symmetric with respect to reversals (see [21] for more details). So we give a definition which is compatible with the case $\alpha \leq 2$: an α-A-power is a word $u_1 \cdots u_k u'$ such that $\frac{|u_1 \cdots u_k u'|}{|u_1|} = \alpha$, $k = \lfloor \alpha \rfloor$, $u_1 \sim \cdots \sim u_k$, and u' is A-equivalent to a prefix of u_1. In [21], such words are called *strong* α-A-powers. For a given α, *α-A-free* and *α^+-A-free* words are defined in the same way as α-free (α^+-free) words. It is convenient to extend the set of rationals with "numbers" of the form α^+, postulating the equivalence of the inequalities $\beta > \alpha$ and $\beta \geq \alpha^+$.

A *language* is any subset of Σ^*. The *reversal* L^R of a language L consists of the reversals of all words in L. The α-A-free language over Σ (where α belongs to extended rationals) consists of all α-A-free words over Σ and is denoted by $\mathsf{AF}(\sigma, \alpha)$. These languages are the main objects of the studies aimed at finding the *Abelian repetition threshold* $\mathsf{ART}(k) = \inf\{\alpha : \mathsf{AF}(k, \alpha) \text{ is infinite}\}$. The languages $\mathsf{AF}(k, \alpha)$ are closed under permutations of the alphabet: if π is a permutation of Σ, then the words $u, \pi(u) \in \Sigma^*$ are α-A-free for exactly the same values of α. Hence the words in a language $\mathsf{AF}(\sigma, \alpha)$ can be enumerated by considering only lexicographically minimal (*lexmin*) words: a word $u \in \Sigma^*$ is lexmin if $u < \pi(u)$ for any permutation π of Σ.

Suppose that a language L is *factorial* (i.e., closed under taking factors of its words); for example, all languages $\mathsf{AF}(k, \alpha)$ are factorial. Then L can be represented by its *prefix tree* $\mathcal{T}_L$, which is a rooted labeled tree whose nodes are elements of L and edges have the form $u \xrightarrow{a} ua$, where a is a letter. Thus u is an ancestor of v iff u is a prefix of v. We study the languages $\mathsf{AF}(\sigma, \alpha)$ through different types of search in their prefix trees.

3 Algorithms

In this section we present the algorithms we develop for use in experiments. First we describe the random depth-first search in the prefix tree $\mathcal{T} = \mathcal{T}_L$ of an arbitrary factorial language L. Given a number N, the algorithm visits N distinct nodes of $\mathcal{T}$ following the depth-first order and returns the maximum level of a visited node. The search can be easily augmented to return the word corresponding to the node of maximum level, or to log the sequence of levels of visited nodes. Algorithm 1 below describes one iteration of the search. In the algorithm, $u = u[1..n]$ is the word corresponding to the current node; $\mathsf{Set}[u]$ is the set of all letters a such that the search has not tried the node ua yet; ml is the maximum level reached so far; count is the number of visited nodes; $\mathcal{L}(u)$ is the predicate returning true if $u \in L$ and false otherwise. The lines 3 and 8 refer to the updates of data structures used to compute $\mathcal{L}(u)$. The search starts with $u = \lambda$, $\mathsf{ml} = 0$, $\mathsf{count} = 1$. A variant of this search algorithm was used in [17] to numerically estimate the entropy of some α-free and α-A-free languages.

Algorithm 1. Random depth-first search in $\mathcal{T}_L$: one iteration

1: **if** $\mathsf{count} = N$ **then** break ▷ search finished
2: **if** $\mathsf{Set}[u] = \varnothing$ **then** ▷ all children of u were visited
3:     [update data structures]
4:     $u \leftarrow u[1..|u|-1]$ ▷ return to the parent of u
5: **else**
6:     $a \leftarrow \mathrm{random}(\mathsf{Set}[u])$; $\mathsf{Set}[u] \leftarrow \mathsf{Set}[u] - a$ ▷ take random unused letter
7:     **if** $\mathcal{L}(ua)$ **then** ▷ the node ua is in $\mathcal{T}(L)$
8:         [update data structures]
9:         $u \leftarrow ua$; $\mathsf{Set}[u] \leftarrow \Sigma$; $\mathsf{count} \leftarrow \mathsf{count} + 1$ ▷ visit ua next
10:         **if** $|u| > \mathsf{ml}$ **then** $\mathsf{ml} \leftarrow |u|$ ▷ update the maximum level

The key to an efficient search is a fast algorithm computing the predicate $\mathcal{L}(ua)$ (line 7); note that $\mathcal{L}(u) = \mathsf{true}$ as the search reached u. In the rest of the section we present such algorithms for $L = \mathsf{AF}(\sigma, \alpha)$. The summary of the algorithms is given in Table 1. As the search calls $\mathcal{L}()$ at least N times, the expected query time (computed for the uniformly random word u) is more informative than the worst-case time. Throughout the paper, we treat σ as a constant.

Table 1. Time and space usage of the algorithms detecting A-powers. Update time refers to a single data structure update (line 3 or 8 of Algorithm 1), query time refers to the computation of $\mathcal{L}$ (line 7 of Algorithm 1); n is the length of the processed word.

Algorithm	Powers	Update time	Expected query time	Space
Algorithm 2	$\alpha < 2$	$O(1)$	$O(n^{3/2})$	$O(n)$
Algorithm 3	$\alpha \leq 3/2$	$O(n)$	$O(n)$	$O(n^2)$
Algorithm 4	$\alpha > 2$	$O(1)$	$O(n^{3/2})$	$O(n)$
Algorithm 5	$\alpha > 2$, dual	$O(1)$	$O(n^{1/2})$	$O(n)$

3.1 Avoiding Small Powers

Let $\alpha < 2$ and u be a word of length n such that all proper prefixes of u are α-A-free. To prove u to be α-A-free, it is necessary and sufficient to show that

($\star$) no suffix of u can be written as xyz such that $|z| > 0$, $x \sim z$, and $\frac{|xyz|}{|xy|} \geq \alpha$.

Remark 1. Since A-equivalence is not closed under taking any sort of factors of words, the ratio $\frac{|xyz|}{|xy|}$ in ($\star$) can significantly exceed α. For example, all proper prefixes, and even all proper factors, of the word $u = abcde\,bdaec$ are $\frac{3}{2}$-A-free, while u is an A-square. Hence for each suffix z of u one should check multiple candidates for the factor x in $(\star)$. The number of such candidates can be as big as $\Theta(n)$; in total, $\Theta(n^2)$ candidates for the pair (x, z) should be analysed.

Remark 1 suggests a simple algorithm with $O(n^2)$ query time, which stores Parikh vectors of all prefixes of u and checks each candidate pair (x, z) directly. Let us describe a more efficient procedure. We store two length-n arrays for each letter $a \in \Sigma$: $c_a[i] = \Psi(u[1..i])(a)$ is the number of occurrences of a in $u[1..i]$ and $d_a[i]$ is the position of ith from the left letter a in the word u. The arrays are updated (lines 3,8 of Algorithm 1) as follows: in line 3, we delete $\Psi(u)$ from c-arrays and delete the last element of $d_{u[|u|]}$; in line 8, we add $\Psi(ua)$ to c-arrays and add a new element $|ua|$ to d_a. Hence each update takes $O(1)$ time. We use two auxiliary functions: $\mathsf{Parikh}(i, j)$ returns $\Psi(u[i..j])$; $\mathsf{cover}(\vec{P}, j)$ returns the biggest number i such that $\Psi(u[i..j]) \geq \vec{P}$ or zero if no such number exists.

Lemma 1. *Functions* $\mathsf{Parikh}(i, j)$ *and* $\mathsf{cover}(\vec{P}, j)$ *are computable in* $O(1)$ *time.*

Proof. Coordinates of $\mathsf{Parikh}(i, j)$ are the differences $c_a[j] - c_a[i-1]$. Further, if $c_a[j] < \vec{P}[a]$ holds for some letter a, then $\Psi(u[1..j]) \ngeq \vec{P}$ and $\mathsf{cover}(\vec{P}, j) = 0$; if all these inequalities fail, then $i = \min_{a \in \Sigma}\{d_a[c_a[j] - \vec{P}[a] + 1]\}$. □

Algorithm 2. A-powers detection (case $\alpha < 2$)

```
function alphafree(u)                                   ▷ u=word; n = |u|
free ← true                                             ▷ α-A-freeness flag
for i = n downto 1+⌈n/2⌉ do                             ▷ z = u[i..n]
    right ← i − 1
    len ← n − i + 1; P⃗ ← Parikh(i, n)                   ▷ length and Parikh vector of z
    left ← cover(P⃗, right)                              ▷ v = u[left..right], Ψ(v) ≥ Ψ(z)
    if left = 0 then break                              ▷ Ψ(u[1..right]) ≱ Ψ(z)
    while left ≥ max{1, ⌈(αi−1−n)/(α−1)⌉} do            ▷ guarantees |xyz|/|xy| ≥ α
        if right − left + 1 = len then                  ▷ x = u[left..right] ~ z
            free ← false; break
        else                    ▷ shift right leftwards, skip redundant comparisons
            right ← left + len − 1
        left ← cover(P⃗, right)
    if free = false then break
return free                                             ▷ the answer to "is u α-A-free?"
```

Proposition 1. *Let* α *be a number such that* $1 < \alpha < 2$ *and* u *be a word all proper prefixes of which are* α*-A-free. Then Algorithm 2 correctly detects whether* u *is* α*-A-free.*

Proof. Let us show that Algorithm 2 verifies the condition $(\star)$. The outer cycle of the algorithm fixes the first position i of the suffix z of u; the suffixes are analysed in the order of increased length $len = |z|$. If a forbidden suffix xyz is detected

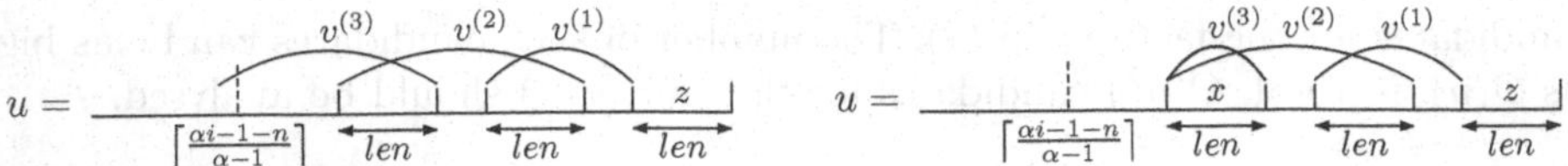

Fig. 1. Illustrating the proof of Proposition 1. Processing the suffix z, Algorithm 2 successively finds three words v satisfying $\Psi(v) \geq \Psi(z)$. On the left picture, the position *left* of $v^{(3)}$ is smaller than the bound in line 8, so the verification of $(\star)$ for z is finished. On the right picture, $|v^{(3)}| = |z|$, so a forbidden suffix, starting with $v^{(3)}$, is detected.

during the iteration, then the algorithm breaks the outer cycle in line 14 and returns false. Thus at the current iteration of the outer cycle the condition $(\star)$ is already verified for all shorter suffixes. The iteration uses a simple observation: if $x \sim z$, then every word v, containing x, satisfies $\Psi(v) \geq \Psi(z)$. Respectively, we fix the rightmost position *right* where a factor x satisfying $x \sim z$ can end. Initially $right = i - 1$ as x can immediately precede z (see Remark 1). Then we compute the shortest factor $v = u[left..right]$ such that $\Psi(v) \geq \Psi(z)$. If $v = x$, the suffix xz of u violates $(\star)$. Otherwise x cannot begin later than at the position *left* by the construction of v. Hence we decrease *right* by setting $right = left + |z| - 1$ and repeat the above procedure in a loop. The verification of $(\star)$ for z ends successfully either if v does not exist (i.e., $\Psi(u[1..right]) \not\geq \Psi(z)$ for the current value of *right*) or *left* is too small (i.e., $xyz = u[left..n]$ with $|x| = |z|$ means $\frac{|xyz|}{|xy|} < \alpha$). The described process is illustrated by Fig. 1.

Details are as follows. In lines 4–6 the algorithm calls Parikh to compute $\Psi(z)$ and cover to find $v = u[left..right]$ for $right = i - 1$. If $left = 0$, then $\Psi(u[1..i-1]) \not\geq \Psi(u[i..n])$ and hence no suffix xyz of u satisfies $x \sim z$. Moreover, one has $\Psi(u[1..j-1]) \not\geq \Psi(u[j..n])$ for each $j < i$ which immediately verifies $(\star)$ for all longer suffixes of u. Hence in this case the verification of $(\star)$ is finished; respectively, the algorithm breaks the outer cycle in line 7 and returns true. If no break happened, the algorithm enters the inner cycle, checks whether $v = x$ (line 9) and breaks with the output false if this condition holds. If it does not, the algorithm decreases *right* as described above (line 12) and computes the new factor v (line 13). If v does not exist, *left* gets 0, which results in the immediate exit from the inner cycle. If v is computed but its position is too small, then the cycle is also exited. The exit means the end of the ith iteration.

Thus, Algorithm 2 returns false only if it finds a suffix xyz of u which violates $(\star)$. For the other direction, let $xyz = u[j..n]$ violate $(\star)$ such that $|z|$ is minimal over all suffixes violating it. Then Algorithm 2 cannot stop before the iteration which checks z. During this iteration, *left* cannot become smaller than j by the definition of the factor v. As *right* decreases at each iteration of the inner cycle, eventually x will be found. Thus the algorithm indeed verifies $(\star)$ and thus detects the α-A-freeness of u. □

Remark 2. By Lemma 1, Algorithm 2 processes a length-n word u in $O(K + n)$ time, where K is the number of the inner cycle iterations during the course of the algorithm. Clearly, $K = O(n^2)$. If u is random, the expected length of a word

v built by Algorithm 2 when processing a suffix z is $|z| + \Omega(\sqrt{|z|})$, as follows from a technical Lemma 2 below. This means $K = O(n^{3/2})$ on expectation, and this is exactly what we have seen in the experiments.

Lemma 2. *Suppose that finite word z and an infinite word $\mathbf{w}$ are chosen uniformly at random over a finite alphabet Σ, and v is the shortest prefix of $\mathbf{w}$ such that $\Psi(v) \geq \Psi(z)$. Then the expected length of v is $|z| + \Omega(\sqrt{|z|})$.*

Proof. Let $\ell = |z|$, $\delta = |v| - |z|$. First consider $\Sigma = \{0, 1\}$. Then the process is as follows: z is generated by ℓ tosses of a fair coin; another ℓ tosses generate some prefix x of v; then tosses are made one by one until the result $\Psi(v) \geq \Psi(z)$ is reached after δ tosses. The Parikh vector of a binary word is determined by its length and the number of 1's. Hence $\Psi(z)$ and $\Psi(x)$ are random variables ξ, η with the binomial distribution $\mathsf{bin}(\ell, \frac{1}{2})$. The vector $\Psi(z) - \Psi(x)$ has the form $(-m, m)$ for some integer m. To obtain v, we should make $|m|$ "successful" tosses with the probability of success being $1/2$; hence the expectation of δ equals $2|m|$. Thus it remains to find the expectation of $|m| = |\xi - \eta|$. Since $E(\xi - \eta) = 0$, we see that $E(|\xi - \eta|)$ is the standard deviation of $\xi - \eta$ by definition.

By symmetry, η and $\ell - \eta$ have the same distribution. Hence we can replace $\xi - \eta$ by $\xi + \eta - \ell$. The random variable $\xi + \eta$ has the distribution $\mathsf{bin}(2\ell, \frac{1}{2})$, so its standard deviation is $\sqrt{\ell/2}$. Thus $E(\delta) = 2E(|\xi - \eta|) = \sqrt{2\ell} = \Omega(\sqrt{\ell})$.

Over larger alphabets the expectation of δ can only increase. The easiest way to see this is to split Σ arbitrarily into two subsets K_1 and K_2 of equal size. Then x with respect to z has a deficiency of letters from one of these subsets, say, K_1. By the argument for the binary alphabet, $\sqrt{2\ell}$ additional letters is needed, on expectation, to cover this deficiency. This is a necessary (but not sufficient) condition to obtain the word v. Hence $E(\delta) = \Omega(\sqrt{\ell})$. □

For the case $\alpha \leq 3/2$ we present a much faster dictionary-based Algorithm 3. Recall that a dictionary contains a set of pairs (key, value), where all keys are unique, and supports fast lookup, addition and deletion by key ($O(1)$ expected time per operation with the help of hash tables). For the dictionary *dict* used in Algorithm 3, the keys are Parikh vectors and the values are lists of positions, in the increasing order, of the factors having this Parikh vector. The algorithm accesses only the last (maximal) element of the list. The updates of the dictionary (lines 3,8 of Algorithm 1) are as follows. At line 3, we delete all suffixes of u from the dictionary. For a suffix z, this means the deletion of the last element from the list $dict[\Psi(z)]$; if the list becomes empty, the entry for $\Psi(z)$ is also deleted. At line 8, all suffixes of ua are added to the dictionary. For a suffix z, if $\Psi(z)$ was not in the dictionary, an entry is created; then the position $|ua| - |z| + 1$ is added to the end of the list $dict[\Psi(z)]$. Thus when answering the query for $u = u[1..n]$, Algorithm 3 has in the dictionary all factors of $u[1..n{-}1]$ up to the A-equivalence, at the expense of $O(n)$ update time and $O(n^2)$ space.

Proposition 2. *Let α be a number such that $1 < \alpha \leq 3/2$ and u be a word all proper prefixes of which are α-A-free. Then Algorithm 3 correctly detects whether u is α-A-free.*

Algorithm 3. Dictionary-based A-powers detection ($\alpha \leq 3/2$)

1: **function** alphafreedict(u) ▷ u=word; $n = |u|$
2: $\quad$ *free* ← true ▷ α-A-freeness flag
3: $\quad$ $\vec{P} \leftarrow \vec{0}$
4: $\quad$ **for** $i = n$ downto $1+\lceil n/2 \rceil$ **do** ▷ $z = u[i..n]$
5: $\quad\quad$ $len \leftarrow n - i + 1$ ▷ length of z
6: $\quad\quad$ $\vec{P}[u[i]] \leftarrow P[u[i]] + 1$ ▷ get $\Psi(z)$ from $\Psi(u[i{+}1..n])$
7: $\quad\quad$ $pos \leftarrow dict[\vec{P}].last$ ▷ position of last occurrence of some $x \sim z$, if exists
8: $\quad\quad$ **if** $pos \leq i - len$ **and** $pos \geq \lceil \frac{\alpha i - 1 - n}{\alpha - 1} \rceil$ **then** ▷ xyz is forbidden
9: $\quad\quad\quad$ *free* ← false; break
10: return *free* ▷ the answer to "is u α-A-free?"

Proof. Let us show that Algorithm 3 verifies ($\star$). First suppose that the algorithm returned false. Then it broke from the **for** cycle (line 9); let z be the last suffix processed. The lookup by the key $\Psi(z)$ returned the position *pos* of a factor $x \sim z$, and the condition in line 8 was true. The first inequality in line means that x and z do not overlap in u; the second inequality is equivalent to $\frac{|xyz|}{|xy|} \geq \alpha$. Therefore, the suffix $xyz = u[pos..n]$ violates ($\star$).

Now suppose that the algorithm returned true. Aiming at a contradiction, assume that u has a suffix violating ($\star$). Let xyz ($x \sim z$) be the shortest such suffix. Consider the iteration of the **for** cycle where z was processed. The key $\Psi(z)$ was present in the dictionary because $x \sim z$. If *pos* (line 7) corresponded to the x from our "bad" suffix, i.e., $xyz = u[pos..n]$, then both inequalities in line 8 held because x and z do not overlap in u and $\frac{|xyz|}{|xy|} \geq \alpha$. But then the algorithm would have returned false, contradicting our assumption. Hence *pos* was the position of some other $x' \sim z$ which occurs in u later than x. By the choice of the suffix xyz, u cannot have shorter suffix $x'y'z$ with $x' \sim z$. This means that the occurrences of x' and z overlap (see Fig. 2).

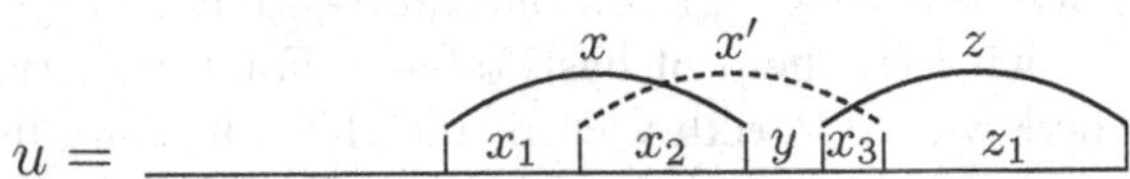

Fig. 2. Location of Abelian equivalent factors (Proposition 2).

Note that x' and x also overlap. Otherwise, xyz has a prefix of the form $x\hat{y}x'$ and $\frac{|x\hat{y}x'|}{|x'\hat{y}|} \geq \frac{|xyz|}{|xy|} \geq \alpha$, contradicting the condition that all proper prefixes of u are α-A-free. Then $x = x_1x_2$, $x' = x_2yx_3$, $z = x_3z_1$, as shown in Fig. 2, and x_1, x_2, x_3, z_1 are nonempty. We observe that $x \sim x' \sim z$ imply $x_1 \sim yx_3$ and $x_2y \sim z_1$. By the condition on the prefixes of u, $\frac{|x_1x_2yx_3|}{|x_1x_2|} < \alpha \leq 3/2$. Hence $|yx_3| < |x_2|$ and then $|x_3| < |x_2y| = |z_1|$. Therefore $\frac{|x_2yx_3z_1|}{|x_2yx_3|} > 3/2 \geq \alpha$, so the suffix $x'z_1 = x_2yx_3z_1$ of u violates ($\star$). But $|x'z_1| < |xyz|$, contradicting the choice of xyz. This contradiction proves that u satisfies ($\star$). □

As Algorithm 3 consists of a single cycle, the next statement is immediate.

Proposition 3. *For a word of length n, Algorithm 3 performs $O(n)$ operations, including dictionary operations.*

Remark 3. A slight modification of Algorithm 3 allows one to process the important case $\alpha = (3/2)^+$ within the same complexity bound. The argument from the proof of Proposition 2 remains valid for $\alpha = (3/2)^+$ except for one specific situation: in Fig. 2 it is possible that y is empty and $|x_1| = |x_2| = |x_3| = |x_4|$. Here Algorithm 3 misses the A-square xz. To fix this, we add a patch after line 7:

7.5: **if** $pos = i - len/2$ **then** $pos \leftarrow pos.next$

As an example, consider $u = abcdbadc$. Processing the suffix $z = badc$, Algorithm 3 retrieves $pos = 3$ from the dictionary by the key $\Psi(z)$. The corresponding factor $x' = cdba$ overlaps z and the condition in line 8 would fail for pos. However, pos satisfies the condition in the inserted line 7.5 and thus the factor $x = abcd$ at $pos = 1$ will be reached. The condition in line 8 holds for $pos = 1$ and the A-square is detected.

Remark 4. Algorithm 3 can be further modified to work for all $\alpha < 2$. If we replace the patch from Remark 3 with the following one:

7.5: **while** $pos > i - len$ **do** $pos \leftarrow pos.next$

the algorithm will find the closest factor $x \sim z$ which does not overlap with z. This new patch introduces an inner cycle and thus affects the time complexity but the algorithm remains faster in practice than Algorithm 2.

3.2 Avoiding Big Powers

Let $\alpha > 2$. The case $2 < \alpha < 3$ for ternary words and the case $3 < \alpha < 4$ for binary words are relevant to the studies of Abelian repetition threshold. We provide here the algorithms for the first case; the algorithms for the second case are very similar (the only difference is that one should check for A-cubes instead of A-squares). A β-A-power with $\alpha \le \beta \le 3$ has the form $ZZ'z$, where $Z \sim Z'$, z is equivalent to a prefix of Z, and $\frac{|ZZ'z|}{|Z|} \ge \alpha$. We write the A-square ZZ' as xy where $|x| \le |y|$ and $x \sim z$. Consequently, if all proper prefixes of a word u are α-A-free, then u is α-A-free iff the following analog of ($\star$) holds:

($*$) no suffix of u can be written as xyz such that $|y| \ge |x| > 0$, $x \sim z$, $\frac{2|xyz|}{|xy|} \ge \alpha$, and xy is an Abelian square.

Verifying ($*$) for u, we process its suffix z as follows. Within the range determined by α, we search for all factors $x = u[left..right]$ such that $x \sim z$ (see Fig. 1). For each x we consider the corresponding suffix xyz of u and check whether xy is an Abelian square. If yes, xyz violates ($*$). Algorithm 4 below, as well as the next Algorithm 5, uses the same data structure and auxiliary functions as Algorithm 2 and thus has $O(1)$ update time and use $O(n)$ space.

Proposition 4. *Let α be a number such that $2 < \alpha < 3$ and u be a word all proper prefixes of which are α-A-free. Then Algorithm 4 correctly detects whether u is α-A-free.*

Algorithm 4. A-powers detection (case $2 < \alpha < 3$)

```
1: function ALPHAfree(u)                                          ▷ u=word; n = |u|
2: free ← true                                                    ▷ α-A-freeness flag
3: for i = n downto 1+⌈2n/3⌉ do                                   ▷ z = u[i..n]
4:     right ← i − 1
5:     len ← n − i + 1; P⃗ ← Parikh(i, n)                          ▷ length and Parikh vector of z
6:     left ← cover(P⃗, right)
7:     if left = 0 then break                                     ▷ Ψ(u[1..right]) ≱ Ψ(z)
8:     while left ≥ max{1, ⌈(αi−1−2n)/(α−2)⌉} do                  ▷ guarantees 2|xyz|/|xy| ≥ α
9:         if left + len − 1 = right then                          ▷ x = u[left..right] ∼ z
10:            if 2 | (i − left) and Σ_{a∈Σ} |c_a[i−1] + c_a[left−1] − 2c_a[(i+left)/2 −1]| = 0 then
11:                free ← false; break                             ▷ xy = u[left..i−1] is an Abelian square
12:            else
13:                right ← right − 1                               ▷ right bound for the next search
14:        else
15:            right ← left + len − 1                              ▷ right bound for the next search
16:        left ← cover(P⃗, right)
17:    if free = false then break
18: return free                                                    ▷ the answer to "is u α-A-free?"
```

Proof. Algorithm 4 is similar to Algorithm 2, so we focus on their difference. If some suffix xyz violates $(*)$, then $|z| \leq |xyz|/3 \leq n/3$; hence the range for the outer cycle in line 3. For a fixed z we repeatedly seek for the shortest factor $v = u[\mathit{left}..\mathit{right}]$ with the given right bound and the property $\Psi(v) \geq \Psi(z)$. If $|v| = |z|$ (condition in line 9 holds), then v is a candidate for x in the suffix xyz violating $(*)$. The initial value for *right* (line 4) is set to ensure $|x| \leq |y|$. The candidate found in line 9 is checked in line 10 for the remaining condition: xy is an Abelian square. Namely, we check that $|xy|$ is even and its left and right halves have the same Parikh vector. If this condition holds, the algorithm breaks both inner and outer cycles and returns false. If the condition fails, we decrease *right* by 1 and compute the factor v for this new right bound. The rest is the same as in Algorithm 2. So we can conclude that Algorithm 4 verifies $(*)$. □

Remark 5. As Algorithm 4 shares the structure with Algorithm 2, it has the same time complexity $O(K + n)$; see Remark 2 for details.

Algorithm 4 is rather slow. But it appears that the reversals of A-powers can be detected by a much faster Algorithm 5 below. We call u a *dual α-A-power* if u^R is an α-A-power; then dual α-A-free words are exactly the reversals of α-A-free words. As a language and its reversal have equal numbers of words of each length, we use Algorithm 5 in the studies of Abelian repetition threshold instead of Algorithm 4.

Assume that all proper prefixes of a word u are dual α-A-free, where $2 < \alpha < 3$. Then u is dual α-A-free iff the following analog of $(*)$ holds:

(†) no suffix of u can be written as xyz such that $y \sim z$, $\frac{|xyz|}{|z|} \geq \alpha$, and x is equivalent to a suffix of z.

Algorithm 5. Dual A-powers detection ($2 < \alpha < 3$)

1: **function** dualALPHAfree(u) ▷ u=word; $n = |u|$
2: *free* ← true ▷ α-A-freeness flag
3: $i \leftarrow n$
4: **while** $i \geq 1 + \lceil \frac{\alpha-1}{\alpha} n \rceil$ **do** ▷ $z = u[i..n]$
5: $len \leftarrow n - i + 1$; $\vec{P} \leftarrow$ Parikh(i, n) ▷ length and Parikh vector of z
6: $left \leftarrow$ cover$(\vec{P}, i-1)$ ▷ computing v
7: **if** $left + len = i$ **then** ▷ $|v| = |z| \Rightarrow v = y \sim z$
8: $j = \lceil (\alpha - 2) \cdot len \rceil$ ▷ minimal length of x
9: **while** $j \leq len$ **do** ▷ possible lengths of x
10: $\vec{P_1} \leftarrow$ Parikh$(n-j+1, n)$ ▷ Parikh vector of the length-j suffix of z
11: $left_1 \leftarrow$ cover$(\vec{P_1}, left - 1)$ ▷ computing v_1 for x
12: **if** $left_1 + j = left$ **then** ▷ x is found
13: *free* ← false; break
14: **else**
15: $j \leftarrow left - left_1$
16: $i \leftarrow i - 1$
17: **else**
18: $i \leftarrow \lceil (n + left)/2 \rceil$
19: **if** *free* = false **then** break
20: return *free* ▷ the answer to "is u dual α-A-free?"

Proposition 5. *Let α be a number such that $2 < \alpha < 3$ and u be a word all proper prefixes of which are dual α-A-free. Then Algorithm 5 correctly detects whether u is dual α-A-free.*

Proof. If some suffix xyz violates (†), then $|z| \leq |xyz|/\alpha \leq n/\alpha$; hence the range for the outer cycle in line 3. The general scheme is as follows. For each processed suffix z, the algorithm first checks if u ends with an Abelian square yz ($y \sim z$); if yes, it checks whether yz is preceded by some x which is equivalent to a suffix of z. If such an x is found, the algorithm detects a violation of (†) and stops. If either x or y is not found, the algorithm moves to the next appropriate suffix.

Let us consider the details. In line 6, the shortest $v = u[left..i{-}1]$ such that vz is a suffix of u and $\Psi(v) \geq \Psi(z)$ is computed. If $|v| = |z|$ (the condition in line 7), then $y = v$ is found and we enter the inner cycle to find x. If $|v| > |x|$, the suffixes of u of lengths between $2|z|$ and $|vz| - 1$ cannot be A-squares; then the next suffix to be considered has the length $\lceil \frac{|vz|}{2} \rceil$, as is set in line 18. In the inner cycle, a similar idea is implemented: for each processed suffix z_1 of z the algorithm finds the shortest word $v_1 = u[left_1..left{-}1]$ satisfying $\Psi(v_1) \geq \Psi(z_1)$ (line 11). If $|v_1| = |z_1|$ (line 12), then x is found; consequently, the algorithm returns false. Otherwise, the next suffix of z to be checked is of length $|v_1|$ (line 15). The inner cycle breaks if this length exceeds the length of z. If the algorithm finishes the check of the suffix z without breaking or skips this suffix at all, then u has no suffix xyz, violating (†). Therefore, the algorithm verifies (†). □

Algorithm 5 is extremely fast compared to other algorithms of this section.

Proposition 6. *For a word u picked up uniformly at random from the set Σ^n, Algorithm 5 works in $\Theta(\sqrt{n})$ expected time.*

Proof. By Lemma 2, the expected length of the word v found in line 6 is $|z| + \Omega(\sqrt{|z|})$ and thus, on expectation, the assignment in line 18 leads to skipping $\Omega(\sqrt{|z|})$ suffixes of u. Hence the expected total number of processed suffixes of u is $O(\sqrt{n})$. By the same argument, the inner cycle for a suffix z runs, on expectation, $O(\sqrt{|z|})$ iterations, so its expected time complexity is $O(\sqrt{|z|})$. Thus, processing the suffix of length ℓ, Algorithm 5 performs $O(1) + p_\ell \cdot O(\sqrt{\ell})$ operations, where p_ℓ is the probability to enter the inner cycle, i.e., the probability that two random ternary words of length ℓ are Abelian equivalent. One has

$$p_\ell \leq \max_{k_1,k_2,\ldots,k_\sigma} \binom{\ell}{k_1,k_2,\ldots,k_\sigma} \Big/ \sigma^\ell,$$

dividing the maximum number of A-equivalent words of length ℓ over Σ by the total number of such words. This maximum, is $\Theta(\sigma^\ell/\ell^{(\sigma-1)/2})$ by the Stirling formula. Thus $p_\ell = O(1/\ell^{(\sigma-1)/2})$. Then Algorithm 5 performs, on expectation, $O(1)$ operations per iteration of the outer cycle. The result now follows. □

4 Experimental Results

We ran a big series of experiments for α-A-free languages over the alphabets of size $2, 3, \ldots, 10$. Each of the experiments is a set of random walks in the prefix tree of a given language. Each walk follows the random depth-first search (Algorithm 1), with the number N of visited nodes being of order 10^5 to 10^7. The ultimate aim of every experiment was to make a well-grounded conjecture about the (in)finiteness of the studied language. Our initial expectation was that random walks will demonstrate two easily distinguishable types of behaviour:

- *infinite-like*: the level of the current node is (almost) proportional to the number of nodes visited, or
- *finite-like*: from some point, the level of the current node oscillates near the maximum reached earlier.

However, the situation is more tricky: very long oscillations of level were detected during random walks even in some languages which are *known* to be infinite; for example, in the binary 4-A-free language. To overcome such an unwanted behaviour, we endowed Algorithm 1 with a "forced backtrack" rule:

- let $\mathsf{ml} = k$ be the maximum level of a node reached so far; if $f(k)$ nodes were visited since the last update of ml or since the last forced backtrack, then make a forced backtrack: from the current node, move $g(k)$ edges up the tree and continue the search from the node reached.

Here $f(k)$ and $g(k)$ are some heuristically chosen monotone functions; we used $f(k) = \lceil k^{3/2} \rceil$ and $g(k) = \lceil k^{1/2} \rceil$. Forced backtracking deletes the last $g(k)$

letters of the current word in order to get out of a "trap": a very big finite subtree the search was supposed to traverse. The use of forced backtrack allowed us to classify the walks in almost all studied languages either as infinite-like or as finite-like. The results presented below are grouped by the alphabets.

4.1 Alphabets with 6, 7, 8, 9, and 10 Letters

In [21], it was proved (Theorem 3.1) that $\mathsf{ART}(k) \geq \frac{k-2}{k-3}$ for all $k \geq 5$ and conjectured that the equality holds in all cases. However, the random search reveals a different picture. For each of the languages $\mathsf{AF}(k, \frac{k-2}{k-3}^+)$, $k = 6, 7, 8, 9, 10$, we ran random search with forced backtrack, using Algorithm 3 to decide the membership in the language; the search terminated when N nodes were visited. We repeated the search 100 times with with $N = 10^6$ and another 100 times with $N = 2 \cdot 10^6$. The results, presented in columns 3–8 of Table 2, clearly demonstrate finite-like behaviour of random walks. Moreover, the results suggest that neither of these languages contains a word much longer than 100 symbols.

Theorem 1. *One has* $\mathsf{ART}(k) > \frac{k-2}{k-3}$ *for* $k = 6, 7, 8, 9, 10$.

A length-n word is called *n-permutation* if all its letters are pairwise distinct. Observing that a $\frac{k-2}{k-3}^+$-A-free word of length $k-1$ contains a $(k-2)$-permutation, one can easily prove Lemma 3 below. Reducing the search space with the help of Lemma 3, we were able to prove Theorem 1 by exhaustive search.

Lemma 3. *Let* $k \geq 6$, $\alpha = \frac{k-2}{k-3}^+$, *and let* L_1, L_2, *and* L_3 *be subsets of* $L = \mathsf{AF}(k, \alpha)$ *defined as follows:*

- $L_1 = \{w \in L \mid w$ *has the prefix* $01 \cdots (k-3)$ *and no* $(k-1)$*-permutations*$\}$;
- $L_2 = \{w \in L \mid w$ *has the prefix* $01 \cdots (k-2)$ *and no* k*-permutations*$\}$;
- $L_3 = \{w \in L \mid w$ *has the prefix* $01 \cdots (k-1)\}$.

Then L *is finite iff each of* L_1, L_2, *and* L_3 *is finite.*

Table 2. Maximum levels ml reached by random walks in some Abelian power-free languages. Columns 3–5 (resp. 6–8) show the maximum, average, and median values of ml among 100 random walks visiting $N = 10^6$ (resp., $N = 2 \cdot 10^6$) nodes each. Column 9 shows the length of a longest word in the language, found by exhaustive search.

Alphabet size	Avoided power	$N = 10^6$			$N = 2 \cdot 10^6$			Maximum length
		ml_{max}	ml_{av}	ml_{med}	ml_{max}	ml_{av}	ml_{med}	
6	$(4/3)^+$	112	98.9	98	114	101.1	101	116
7	$(5/4)^+$	116	100.3	100	124	103.9	102	125
8	$(6/5)^+$	103	94.8	95	102	96.2	96	105
9	$(7/6)^+$	108	95.6	96	107	98.8	99	117
10	$(8/7)^+$	121	107.7	108	128	111.6	111	148*

Remark 6. The number of nodes visited during the optimized exhaustive search proving Theorem 1 ranged from 0.43 billions for $k = 8$ to 615 billions for $k = 10$; the search required over 2500 h of single-core processing time by an ordinary laptop (Algorithm 3 was used to detect A-powers). For each $k = 6, 7, 8, 9$ we have also run a single search enumerating all lexmin words in the language $\mathsf{AF}(k, \frac{k-2}{k-3}^+)$. Thus we found the maximum length of a word in each language (the last column of Table 2) and the distribution of words by their length. For $k = 10$, such a single search would require too much resources; here the value in Table 2 is the length of the longest word found by the search based on Lemma 3.

As the next step after Theorem 1, we ran experiments for the languages $\mathsf{AF}(k, \frac{k-3}{k-4})$. The results for $k = 7, 8, 9, 10$ are presented in Table 3; random walks in these languages clearly demonstrate finite-type behaviour, while proving finiteness by exhaustive search looks impossible. On the contrary, the walks in the 6-ary language $\mathsf{AF}(6, \frac{3}{2})$ demonstrate an infinite-like behaviour: the average value of ml for our experiments with $N = 10^5$ is greater than $5 \cdot 10^4$. We note that the obtained words are too long for Algorithm 3, so we had to use slower Algorithm 2. Finally, we constructed random walks for the languages $\mathsf{AF}(k, \frac{k-3}{k-4}^+)$ ($k = 7, 8, 9, 10$). They also demonstrate infinite-like behaviour. The obtained experimental results allow us to state the part of Conjecture 2 for the alphabets with 6 and more letters.

Table 3. Maximum levels ml reached by random walks in some Abelian power-free languages. Columns 3–5 (resp. 6–8) show the maximum, average, and median values of ml among 100 random walks visiting $N = 10^6$ (resp., $N = 2 \cdot 10^6$) nodes each.

Alphabet size	Avoided power	$N = 10^6$			$N = 2 \cdot 10^6$		
		ml_{max}	ml_{av}	ml_{med}	ml_{max}	ml_{av}	ml_{med}
7	4/3	510	374.5	371	510	397.5	394
8	5/4	211	179.7	179	223	185.0	184
9	6/5	192	157.2	156	191	162.3	161
10	7/6	175	154.0	154	187	159.7	158

4.2 Alphabets with 2, 3, 4, and 5 Letters

Random walks in the prefix tree of the language $\mathsf{AF}(5, \frac{3}{2}^+)$ demonstrate the infinite-like behaviour; Fig. 3 shows an example of dependence of the level of the current node on the number of nodes visited. The obtained results give us sufficient evidence to support Conjecture 1 for $k = 5$.

Remark 7. As the language $\mathsf{AF}(5, \frac{3}{2}^+)$ is probably infinite, it is interesting to estimate its growth. Based on the technique described in [17], we estimate the number of words of length n in $\mathsf{AF}(5, \frac{3}{2}^+)$ as growing exponentially with n at the rate close to 1.5. The upper bound 2.335 [21] on this rate is thus very loose.

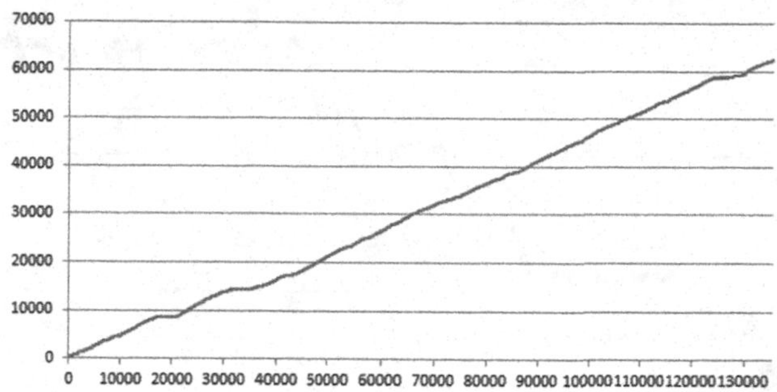

Fig. 3. An infinite-like random walk in the language $\mathsf{AF}(5, \frac{3}{2}^+)$: a point (n, m) of the graph means that the nth node visited by the walk has depth m.

Further, we studied the languages $\mathsf{AF}(4, \frac{9}{5}^+)$, $\mathsf{AF}(3, 2^+)$, and $\mathsf{AF}(2, \frac{11}{3}^+)$, indicated by Conjecture 1 as infinite; we replaced the last two languages with their reversals to benefit from the fast detection of A-powers by Algorithm 5 and its version for $\alpha > 3$. Random walks in each of three languages show the finite-like behaviour; see Table 4 and the example in Fig. 4 (multiple forced backtracks provide slightly better average results for longer searches). So the experimental results justify lower bounds from Conjecture 2 for $k = 2, 3, 4$. To get the upper bound for the ternary alphabet, we ran random walks for the language $\mathsf{AF}(3, \frac{5}{2}^+)$ with the results similar to those obtained for $\mathsf{AF}(5, \frac{3}{2}^+)$: all walks demonstrate the infinite-like behaviour; the level $\mathsf{ml} = 10^5$ is reached within minutes.

Overall, the conducted experiments justify the formulation of Conjecture 2.

Table 4. Maximum levels ml reached by random walks in some A-power-free languages. Columns 3–5 (resp. 6–8, 9–11) show the maximum, average, and median values of ml among 100 random walks visiting $N = 10^6$ (resp., $N = 2 \cdot 10^6$, $N = 10^7$) nodes each.

Alphabet size	Avoided power	$N = 10^6$			$N = 2 \cdot 10^6$			$N = 10^7$		
		ml_{max}	ml_{av}	ml_{med}	ml_{max}	ml_{av}	ml_{med}	ml_{max}	ml_{av}	ml_{med}
2	$(11/3)^+$	775	435.8	416	706	477.0	453	759	589.7	588
3	2^+	3344	1700.0	1671	5363	2228.8	2140	5449	3078.1	3148
4	$(9/5)^+$	1367	861.2	835	1734	986.8	956	2453	1414.7	1369

5 Future Work

Clearly, the main challenge in the topic is to find the exact values of the Abelian repetition threshold. Even finding one such value would be a great progress. Choosing the case to start with, we would suggest proving $\mathsf{ART}(5) = 3/2$ because in this case the lower bound is already checked by exhaustive search in [21]. For all other alphabets, the proof of lower bounds suggested in Conjecture 2 is already a challenging task which cannot be solved by brute force.

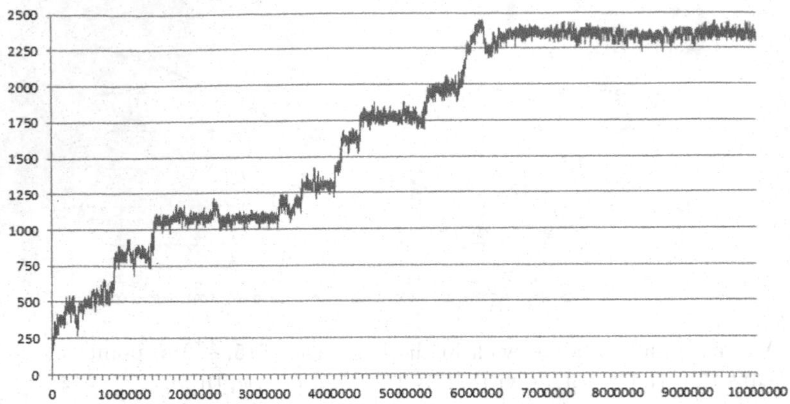

Fig. 4. A finite-like random walk in the language $\mathsf{AF}(4, \frac{9}{5}^+)$: a point (n, m) of the graph means that the nth node visited by the walk has depth m.

Another piece of work is to refine Conjecture 2 by suggesting the precise values of $\mathsf{ART}(2)$, $\mathsf{ART}(3)$, $\mathsf{ART}(4)$, and $\mathsf{ART}(6)$. For bigger k, random walks demonstrate an obvious "phase transition" at the point $\frac{k-3}{k-4}$: the behaviour of a walk switches from finite-like for $\mathsf{AF}(k, \frac{k-3}{k-4})$ to infinite-like for $\mathsf{AF}(k, \frac{k-3}{k-4}^+)$. However, the situation with small alphabets can be trickier. We tried 11/6 as the next natural candidate for $\mathsf{ART}(4)$. For the random walks in $\mathsf{AF}(4, \frac{11}{6}^+)$, with $N = 10^6$ and forced backtracks, the range of obtained maximum levels in our experiments varied from 3000 to 20000; such big lengths show that there is no hope to see a clear-cut phase transition in the experiments with random walks.

Third, we want to draw attention to the following fact. The quaternary 2-A-free word constructed by Keränen [14] contains arbitrarily long factors of the form xax', where a is a letter and $x \sim x'$; thus it is not α-A-free for any $\alpha < 2$. Similarly, the word constructed by Dekking [9] for the ternary (resp., binary) alphabet is not α-A-free for any $\alpha < 3$ (resp., $\alpha < 4$). Hence some new constructions are necessary to improve upper bounds for ART.

The algorithmic part of this work also rises some questions. As established by Radoszewski et al. [18], the commonly believed 3-SUM conjecture implies that it is impossible to decide in $O(n^{2-\varepsilon})$ time whether a word contains an A-square (and thus decide in $O(n^{1-\varepsilon})$ time whether a word contains an A-square as a suffix). So, what are the lower bounds for detecting fractional A-powers?

References

1. Carpi, A.: On Dejean's conjecture over large alphabets. Theoret. Comput. Sci. **385**, 137–151 (1999)
2. Cassaigne, J., Currie, J.D.: Words strongly avoiding fractional powers. Eur. J. Comb. **20**(8), 725–737 (1999)
3. Currie, J.D., Rampersad, N.: A proof of Dejean's conjecture. Math. Comp. **80**, 1063–1070 (2011)

4. Currie, J.D., Mol, L.: The undirected repetition threshold and undirected pattern avoidance. Theor. Comput. Sci. **866**, 56–69 (2021)
5. Currie, J.D., Mol, L., Rampersad, N.: Circular repetition thresholds on some small alphabets: last cases of Gorbunova's conjecture. Electron. J. Comb. **26**(2), P2.31 (2019)
6. Currie, J.D., Mol, L., Rampersad, N.: The number of threshold words on n letters grows exponentially for every $n \geq 27$. J. Integer Seq. **23**(3), 20.3.1 (2020)
7. Currie, J.D., Mol, L., Rampersad, N.: The repetition threshold for binary rich words. Discret. Math. Theor. Comput. Sci. **22**(1) (2020)
8. Dejean, F.: Sur un théorème de Thue. J. Combin. Theory. Ser. A **13**, 90–99 (1972)
9. Dekking, F.M.: Strongly non-repetitive sequences and progression-free sets. J. Combin. Theory. Ser. A **27**, 181–185 (1979)
10. Dolce, F., Dvořáková, L., Pelantová, E.: Computation of critical exponent in balanced sequences. In: Lecroq, T., Puzynina, S. (eds.) WORDS 2021. LNCS, vol. 12847, pp. 78–90. Springer, Cham (2021). https://doi.org/10.1007/978-3-030-85088-3_7
11. Erdős, P.: Some unsolved problems. Magyar Tud. Akad. Mat. Kutató Int. Közl. **6**, 221–264 (1961)
12. Evdokimov, A.A.: Strongly asymmetric sequences generated by a finite number of symbols. Soviet Math. Dokl. **9**, 536–539 (1968)
13. Gorbunova, I.A.: Repetition threshold for circular words. Electron. J. Comb. **19**(4), P11 (2012)
14. Keränen, V.: Abelian squares are avoidable on 4 letters. In: Kuich, W. (ed.) ICALP 1992. LNCS, vol. 623, pp. 41–52. Springer, Heidelberg (1992). https://doi.org/10.1007/3-540-55719-9_62
15. Moulin-Ollagnier, J.: Proof of Dejean's conjecture for alphabets with $5, 6, 7, 8, 9, 10$ and 11 letters. Theoret. Comput. Sci. **95**, 187–205 (1992)
16. Pansiot, J.J.: A propos d'une conjecture de F. Dejean sur les répétitions dans les mots. Discr. Appl. Math. **7**, 297–311 (1984)
17. Petrova, E.A., Shur, A.M.: Branching frequency and Markov entropy of repetition-free languages. In: Moreira, N., Reis, R. (eds.) DLT 2021. LNCS, vol. 12811, pp. 328–341. Springer, Cham (2021). https://doi.org/10.1007/978-3-030-81508-0_27
18. Radoszewski, J., Rytter, W., Straszynski, J., Walen, T., Zuba, W.: Hardness of detecting abelian and additive square factors in strings. CoRR abs/2107.09206 (2021)
19. Rampersad, N., Shallit, J.O., Vandomme, É.: Critical exponents of infinite balanced words. Theoret. Comput. Sci. **777**, 454–463 (2019)
20. Rao, M.: Last cases of Dejean's conjecture. Theoret. Comput. Sci. **412**, 3010–3018 (2011)
21. Samsonov, A.V., Shur, A.M.: On Abelian repetition threshold. RAIRO Theor. Inf. Appl. **46**, 147–163 (2012)
22. Shallit, J.O., Shur, A.M.: Subword complexity and power avoidance. Theoret. Comput. Sci. **792**, 96–116 (2019)
23. Thue, A.: Über unendliche Zeichenreihen. Norske vid. Selsk. Skr. Mat. Nat. Kl. **7**, 1–22 (1906)
24. Thue, A.: Über die gegenseitige Lage gleicher Teile gewisser Zeichenreihen. Norske vid. Selsk. Skr. Mat. Nat. Kl. **1**, 1–67 (1912)
25. Tunev, I.N., Shur, A.M.: On two stronger versions of Dejean's conjecture. In: Rovan, B., Sassone, V., Widmayer, P. (eds.) MFCS 2012. LNCS, vol. 7464, pp. 800–812. Springer, Heidelberg (2012). https://doi.org/10.1007/978-3-642-32589-2_69

Characterizing Level One in Group-Based Concatenation Hierarchies

Thomas Place[1,2] and Marc Zeitoun[1](✉)

[1] Univ. Bordeaux, CNRS, Bordeaux INP, LaBRI, UMR 5800, 33400 Talence, France
{Thomas.Place,Marc.Zeitoun}@labri.fr

[2] Institut Universitaire de France, Paris, France

Abstract. We investigate two operators on classes of regular languages: polynomial closure (*Pol*) and Boolean closure (*Bool*). We apply these operators to classes of *group languages* $\mathcal{G}$ and to their well-suited extensions $\mathcal{G}^+$, which is the least Boolean algebra containing $\mathcal{G}$ and $\{\varepsilon\}$. This yields the classes $Bool(Pol(\mathcal{G}))$ and $Bool(Pol(\mathcal{G}^+))$. These classes form the first level in important classifications of classes of regular languages, called *concatenation hierarchies*, which admit natural *logical characterizations.* We present *generic* algebraic characterizations of these classes. They imply that one may decide whether a regular language belongs to such a class, provided that a more general problem called separation is decidable for the input class $\mathcal{G}$. The proofs are constructive and rely exclusively on notions from language and automata theory.

Keywords: Regular languages · Group languages · Concatenation hierarchies · Membership

1 Introduction

An active line of research in automata theory is to investigate natural subclasses of regular languages. We are particularly interested in classes associated to fragments of standard pieces of syntax used to define the regular languages (*e.g.*, regular expressions or monadic second-order logic). Given a fragment, we consider the class of all languages that can be defined by an expression of this fragment. For each such class $\mathcal{C}$, a standard approach for its investigation is to look for a $\mathcal{C}$-*membership algorithm*: given a regular language L as input, decide whether $L \in \mathcal{C}$. Getting such an algorithm requires a solid understanding of $\mathcal{C}$. We are not only interested in a yes/no answer on the decidability of $\mathcal{C}$-membership but also in the techniques and proof arguments involved for obtaining this answer.

We look at classifications called *concatenation hierarchies.* A concatenation hierarchy is built from an input class of languages, called its *basis*, using two operators. The *polynomial closure* of a class $\mathcal{C}$, written $Pol(\mathcal{C})$, consists in all finite unions of languages $L_0a_1L_1 \cdots a_nL_n$ where $a_1, \dots, a_n$ are letters and $L_0, \dots, L_n$

Funded by the DeLTA project (ANR-16-CE40-0007).

A. S. Kulikov and S. Raskhodnikova (Eds.): CSR 2022, LNCS 13296, pp. 320–337, 2022.
https://doi.org/10.1007/978-3-031-09574-0_20

are languages in $\mathcal{C}$. The *Boolean closure* of $\mathcal{C}$, denoted by $Bool(\mathcal{C})$, is the least class containing $\mathcal{C}$ and closed under Boolean operations. We investigate level *one* of concatenation hierarchies: the classes $Bool(Pol(\mathcal{C}))$ (abbreviated $BPol(\mathcal{C})$). Moreover, we consider special bases $\mathcal{C}$. The *group languages* are those recognized by a finite group, or equivalently by a permutation automaton (*i.e.*, a complete, deterministic *and* co-deterministic automaton). We only consider bases that are either a class $\mathcal{G}$ containing only group languages, or its well-suited extension $\mathcal{G}^+$ (roughly, $\mathcal{G}^+$ is the least Boolean algebra containing $\mathcal{G}$ and the singleton $\{\varepsilon\}$). The motivation for using such bases stems from the logical characterizations of concatenation hierarchies [12,22]. A word can be viewed as a logical structure consisting of a sequence of *labeled positions*. Therefore, we may use first-order sentences to define languages. It turns out that $BPol(\mathcal{G})$ and $BPol(\mathcal{G}^+)$ correspond to the logical classes $\mathcal{B}\Sigma_1(<, \mathbb{P}_\mathcal{G})$ and $\mathcal{B}\Sigma_1(<, +1, \mathbb{P}_\mathcal{G})$ where $\mathcal{B}\Sigma_1$ is the fragment of first-order logic containing only the Boolean combinations of purely existential formulas. Here, the predicates "$<$" and "$+1$" are interpreted as the linear order and the successor relation. Moreover, $\mathbb{P}_\mathcal{G}$ is a set of predicates built from $\mathcal{G}$: for each language $L \in \mathcal{G}$, it contains a unary predicate that checks whether the prefix preceding a given position belongs to L.

In the paper, we present generic algebraic characterizations of $BPol(\mathcal{G})$ and $BPol(\mathcal{G}^+)$. They apply to all classes of group languages $\mathcal{G}$ satisfying mild hypotheses (namely, $\mathcal{G}$ must be closed under Boolean operations and quotients). Moreover, they imply that *membership* is decidable for $BPol(\mathcal{G})$ and $BPol(\mathcal{G}^+)$ provided that a more general problem, *separation*, is decidable for $\mathcal{G}$. Separation takes two input regular languages L_0, L_1 and asks whether there exists $K \in \mathcal{G}$ such that $L_0 \subseteq K$ and $L_1 \cap K = \emptyset$. From the decidability point of view, the results are not entirely new. In particular, for $BPol(\mathcal{G})$, it is even known [14] that *separation* is decidable for $BPol(\mathcal{G})$ when it is already decidable for $\mathcal{G}$ (on the other hand, this is open for $BPol(\mathcal{G}^+)$). Hence, our main contribution consists in the characterizations themselves and the techniques that we use to prove them. In particular, the proof arguments are constructive. For example, given a language L satisfying the characterization of $BPol(\mathcal{G})$, we prove directly that L belongs to $BPol(\mathcal{G})$ by explicitly building a description of L as a Boolean combination of products $L_0a_1L_1 \cdots a_nL_n$ where $L_0, \dots, L_n \in \mathcal{G}$.

With these characterizations, we generalize a number of known results for particular classes of group languages $\mathcal{G}$. Let us first consider the case when $\mathcal{G}$ is the trivial Boolean algebra, which we denote by ST: we have $\text{ST} = \{\emptyset, A^*\}$ and $\text{ST}^+ = \{\emptyset, \{\varepsilon\}, A^+, A^*\}$ (where A is the alphabet). In this case, we obtain two well-known classes: $BPol(\text{ST}) = \mathcal{B}\Sigma_1(<)$ defines the *piecewise testable languages* and $BPol(\text{ST}^+) = \mathcal{B}\Sigma_1(<, +1)$ the *languages of dot-depth one*. The famous algebraic characterizations of these classes by Simon [17] and Knast [6] are simple corollaries of our generic results. Another key example is the class MOD of *modulo languages*: membership of a word in such a language depends only on its length modulo some fixed integer. In this case, the logical counterparts of $BPol(\text{MOD})$ and $BPol(\text{MOD}^+)$ are the classes $\mathcal{B}\Sigma_1(<, MOD)$ and $\mathcal{B}\Sigma_1(<, +1, MOD)$ where "MOD" denotes the set of *modular predicates*. It is again possible to use our results to reprove the known characterizations of these classes by Chaubard, Pin and Straubing [4] and Maciel, Péladeau and Thérien [7]. Our result also applies to the important case when $\mathcal{G}$ is the class GR of *all* group languages [8]. In particular, there exists a specialized characterization of $BPol(\text{GR})$ by Henckell, Margolis, Pin and Rhodes [5], independent from GR-separation. While it is also possible to reprove this result as a corollary of our characterization, this requires a bit of technical work as well as knowledge of the GR-separation algorithm [2] which is a difficult result. Finally, another generic characterization of the classes $BPol(\mathcal{G})$ follows from an algebraic theorem of Steinberg [18] (though it only applies under more restrictive hypotheses on $\mathcal{G}$).

Our techniques differ from those used in the aforementioned specialized papers. Historically, classes of the form $BPol(\mathcal{G})$ or $BPol(\mathcal{G}^+)$ are often approached via alternate definitions based on an algebraic construction called "*wreath product*". Indeed, it turns out that all classes of this kind can be built from the piecewise testable languages (*i.e.*, the class $BPol(\text{ST})$) using this product [9,20]. The arguments developed in [4,5,7,8,18] build exclusively on this construction. The paper is completely independent from these techniques: we work *directly* with the language theoretic definition of our classes based on the operator $BPol$. This matches our original motivation: investigating classes of regular languages.

We introduce the needed terminology in Sect. 2, look at classes of the form $BPol(\mathcal{G})$ in Sect. 3, and devote Sect. 4 to classes of the form $BPol(\mathcal{G}^+)$. Due to space limitations, several proofs are postponed to the full version of the paper [16].

2 Preliminaries

We present the objects that we investigate and the terminology that we require to manipulate them. The proofs are available in the full version of the paper.

2.1 Words, Regular Languages and Classes

We fix a finite alphabet A for the whole paper. As usual, A^* denotes the set of all finite words over A, including the empty word ε. We let $A^+ = A^* \setminus \{\varepsilon\}$. For $u, v \in A^*$, we let uv be the word obtained by concatenating u and v. Additionally, given $w \in A^*$, we write $|w| \in \mathbb{N}$ for the length of w. A language is a subset of A^*. We denote the singleton language $\{u\}$ by u. We lift concatenation to languages: for $K, L \subseteq A^*$, we let $KL = \{uv \mid u \in K \text{ and } v \in L\}$. We shall consider *marked products*: given languages $L_0, \dots, L_n \subseteq A^*$, a marked product of $L_0, \dots, L_n$ is a product of the form $L_0 a_1 L_1 \cdots a_n L_n$ where $a_1, \dots, a_n \in A$ (note that "L_0" is a marked product: this is the case $n = 0$).

Regular Languages. All languages considered in the paper are *regular*. These are the languages that can be equivalently defined by a regular expression, an automaton or a morphism into a finite monoid. We work with the latter definition. A *monoid* is a set M equipped with a binary operation $s, t \mapsto st$ (called multiplication) which is associative and has a neutral element denoted by "1_M". Recall that an idempotent of a monoid M is an element $e \in M$ such that $ee = e$. For all $S \subseteq M$, we write $E(S)$ for the set of all idempotents in S. It is standard that when M is *finite*, there exists $\omega(M) \in \mathbb{N}$ (written ω when M is understood) such that s^ω is idempotent for every $s \in M$.

An *ordered monoid* is a pair $(M, \leq)$ where M is a monoid and $\leq$ is a partial order on M which is compatible with multiplication: for every $s, t, s', t' \in M$, if $s \leq t$ and $s' \leq t'$, then $ss' \leq tt'$. An upper set of M (for $\leq$) is a set $S \subseteq M$ which is upward closed for $\leq$: for every $s, t \in M$ such that $s \leq t$, we have $s \in S \Rightarrow t \in S$. For every $s \in M$, we write $\uparrow s$ for the least upper set of M containing s (*i.e.*, $\uparrow s$ consists of all $t \in M$ such that $s \leq t$). We may view arbitrary monoids as being ordered, as follows: we view any monoid M with no ordering specified as the ordered monoid $(M, =)$: we use equality as the ordering. In this special case, *all* subsets of M are upper sets.

Clearly, A^* is a monoid for concatenation as the multiplication (ε is neutral). Given an ordered monoid $(M, \leq)$, we may consider morphisms $\alpha : A^* \to (M, \leq)$. We say that a language $L \subseteq A^*$ is *recognized* by such a morphism α when there exists an *upper set* $F \subseteq M$ such that $L = \alpha^{-1}(F)$ (the definition depends on the ordering $\leq$, since F must be an upper set). Note that this also defines the languages recognized by a morphism $\eta : A^* \to N$ into an *unordered* monoid N since we view N as the ordered monoid $(N, =)$. It is well-known that a language is regular if and only if it can be recognized by a morphism into a *finite* monoid.

Remark 1. The only infinite monoid that we consider is A^*. From now, we implicitly assume that every other monoid $M, N, \ldots$ that we consider is finite.

Classes of Languages. A class of languages $\mathcal{C}$ is a set of languages. A *lattice* is a class closed under both union and intersection, and containing the languages $\emptyset$ and A^*. Moreover, a *Boolean algebra* is a lattice closed under complement. Finally, a class $\mathcal{C}$ is *quotient-closed* when for all $L \in \mathcal{C}$ and $u, v \in A^*$, the language $\{w \in A^* \mid uwv \in L\}$ belongs to $\mathcal{C}$ as well. We say that a class $\mathcal{C}$ is a *positive prevariety* (resp. *prevariety*) to indicate that it is a quotient-closed lattice (resp. Boolean algebra) containing *only regular languages*.

We rely on a decision problem called *membership* as a means to investigate classes of languages. Given a class $\mathcal{C}$, the $\mathcal{C}$-membership problem takes as input a regular language L and asks whether $L \in \mathcal{C}$. Intuitively, obtaining a procedure for $\mathcal{C}$-membership requires a solid understanding of $\mathcal{C}$. We also look at more involved problem called *separation*. Given a class $\mathcal{C}$, and two languages L_0 and L_1, we say that L_0 is $\mathcal{C}$-separable from L_1 if and only if there exists $K \in \mathcal{C}$ such that $L_0 \subseteq K$ and $L_1 \cap K = \emptyset$. The $\mathcal{C}$-separation problem takes two regular languages L_0 and L_1 as input and asks whether L_0 is $\mathcal{C}$-separable from L_1. Let us point out that we do *not* present separation algorithms in this paper. We shall need this problem as an intermediary in our investigation of membership.

Group Languages. A group is a monoid G such that every element $g \in G$ has an inverse $g^{-1} \in G$, *i.e.*, such that $gg^{-1} = g^{-1}g = 1_G$. We call "*group language*" a language recognized by a morphism into a *finite group*. We consider classes $\mathcal{G}$ that are group prevarieties (*i.e.*, containing group languages only).

We let GR be the class of *all* group languages. Another important example is the class AMT of *alphabet modulo testable languages*. For every $w \in A^*$ and every $a \in A$, we write $\#_a(w) \in \mathbb{N}$ for the number of occurrences of "a" in w. The class AMT consists of all finite Boolean combinations of languages $\{w \in A^* \mid \#_a(w) \equiv k \bmod m\}$ where $a \in A$ and $k, m \in \mathbb{N}$ such that $k < m$. One may verify that these are exactly the languages recognized by commutative groups. We also consider the class MOD, which consists of all finite Boolean combinations of languages $\{w \in A^* \mid |w| \equiv k \bmod m\}$ with $k, m \in \mathbb{N}$ such that $k < m$. Finally, we write ST for the trivial class $\text{ST} = \{\emptyset, A^*\}$. One may verify that GR, AMT, MOD and ST are all group prevarieties.

It follows from the definition that $\{\varepsilon\}$ and A^+ are *not* group languages. This motivates the next definition: for a class $\mathcal{C}$, the *well-suited extension of* $\mathcal{C}$, denoted by $\mathcal{C}^+$, consists of all languages of the form $L \cap A^+$ or $L \cup \{\varepsilon\}$ where $L \in \mathcal{C}$. The next lemma follows from the definition.

Lemma 2. *Let $\mathcal{C}$ be a prevariety. Then, $\mathcal{C}^+$ is a prevariety containing the languages $\{\varepsilon\}$ and A^+.*

2.2 Polynomial and Boolean Closure

In the paper, we look at classes built using two standard operators. Consider a class $\mathcal{C}$. The *Boolean closure* of $\mathcal{C}$, denoted by $Bool(\mathcal{C})$ is the least Boolean algebra that contains $\mathcal{C}$. Moreover, the *polynomial closure* of $\mathcal{C}$, denoted by $Pol(\mathcal{C})$, contains all finite unions of marked products $L_0 a_1 L_1 \cdots a_n L_n$ where $L_0, \dots, L_n \in \mathcal{C}$. Finally, we write $BPol(\mathcal{C})$ for $Bool(Pol(\mathcal{C}))$. It is known that when $\mathcal{C}$ is a prevariety, $Pol(\mathcal{C})$ is a positive prevariety and $BPol(\mathcal{C})$ is a prevariety. This is not immediate (proving that $Pol(\mathcal{C})$ is closed under intersection is difficult). This was first shown by Arfi [1], see also [10,12] for more recent proofs.

Theorem 3. *Let $\mathcal{C}$ be a prevariety. Then $Pol(\mathcal{C})$ is a positive prevariety and $BPol(\mathcal{C})$ is a prevariety.*

In the literature, these operators are used to define classifications called concatenation hierarchies. Given a prevariety $\mathcal{C}$, the concatenation hierarchy of basis $\mathcal{C}$ is built from $\mathcal{C}$ by iteratively applying *Pol* and *Bool* to $\mathcal{C}$. In the paper, we only look at the classes $Pol(\mathcal{C})$ and $BPol(\mathcal{C})$. These are the levels 1/2 and one in the concatenation hierarchy of basis $\mathcal{C}$. Moreover, we look at bases that are either a group prevariety $\mathcal{G}$ or its well-suited extension $\mathcal{G}^+$. Most of the prominent concatenation hierarchies in the literature use bases of this kind.

The hierarchy of basis $\text{ST} = \{\emptyset, A^*\}$ is called the Straubing-Thérien hierarchy [19,21]. In particular, $BPol(\text{ST})$ is the class of piecewise testable languages [17]. Another prominent example is the basis $\text{ST}^+ = \{\emptyset, \{\varepsilon\}, A^+, A^*\}$ which yields the *dot-depth hierarchy* [3]. Non-trivial group prevarieties also yield important hierarchies. For example, the group hierarchy, whose basis is GR was first investigated in [8]. The hierarchies of bases MOD and MOD^+ are also prominent (see for example [4,7]). These hierarchies are also interesting for their logical counterparts, which were first discovered by Thomas [22]. Let us briefly recall them (see [12,14] for more details).

Consider a word $w = a_1 \cdots a_{|w|} \in A^*$. We view w as a linearly ordered set of $|w|+2$ positions $\{0, 1, \dots, |w|, |w|+1\}$ such that each position $1 \leq i \leq |w|$ carries the label $a_i \in A$ (on the other hand, 0 and $|w|+1$ are artificial unlabeled leftmost and rightmost positions). We use first-order logic to describe properties of words: a sentence can quantify over the positions of a word and use a predetermined set of predicates to test properties of these positions. We also allow two constants "*min*" and "*max*", which we interpret as the artificial unlabeled positions 0 and $|w|+1$ in a given word w. Each first-order sentence φ defines the language of all words satisfying the property stated by φ. Let us present the predicates that we use. For each $a \in A$, we associate a unary predicate (also denoted by a), which selects the positions labeled by "a". We also consider two binary predicates: the (strict) linear order "$<$" and the successor relation "$+1$".

Example 4. The sentence "$\exists x \exists y\ (x < y) \wedge a(x) \wedge b(y)$" defines the language $A^*aA^*bA^*$. The sentence "$\exists x \exists y\ a(x) \wedge c(y) \wedge (y + 1 = max)$" defines A^*aA^*c.

We associate a (possibly infinite) set of predicates $\mathbb{P}_{\mathcal{G}}$ to every group prevariety $\mathcal{G}$. For every language $L \in \mathcal{G}$, $\mathbb{P}_{\mathcal{G}}$ contains a unary predicate P_L which is interpreted as follows. Let $w = a_1 \cdots a_{|w|} \in A^*$. The unary predicate P_L selects all positions $i \in \{0, \dots, |w| + 1\}$ such that $i \neq 0$ and $a_1 \cdots a_{i-1} \in L$. It is standard to write "$\mathcal{B}\Sigma_1$" for the fragment of first-order logic, containing exactly the Boolean combinations of existential first-order sentences. We let $\mathcal{B}\Sigma_1(<, \mathbb{P}_{\mathcal{G}})$ be the class of all languages defined by a sentence of $\mathcal{B}\Sigma_1$ using only the label predicates, the linear order "$<$" and those in $\mathbb{P}_{\mathcal{G}}$. Moreover, we let $\mathcal{B}\Sigma_1(<, +1, \mathbb{P}_{\mathcal{G}})$ be the class of all languages defined by a sentence of $\mathcal{B}\Sigma_1$, which additionally allows the successor predicate "$+1$". The following proposition follows from the generic logical characterization of concatenation hierarchies presented in [12] and the properties of group languages.

Proposition 5. *For every group prevariety $\mathcal{G}$, we have $BPol(\mathcal{G}) = \mathcal{B}\Sigma_1(<, \mathbb{P}_{\mathcal{G}})$ and $BPol(\mathcal{G}^+) = \mathcal{B}\Sigma_1(<, +1, \mathbb{P}_{\mathcal{G}})$.*

Remark 6. When $\mathcal{G}$ = ST, all predicates in $\mathbb{P}_{\text{ST}}$ are trivial. Hence, we get the classes $\mathcal{B}\Sigma_1(<)$ and $\mathcal{B}\Sigma_1(<, +1)$. When $\mathcal{G}$ = MOD, one may verify that we obtain the classes $\mathcal{B}\Sigma_1(<, MOD)$ and $\mathcal{B}\Sigma_1(<, +1, MOD)$ where "MOD" is the set of *modular predicates* (for all $r, q \in \mathbb{N}$ such that $r < q$, it contains a unary predicate $M_{r,q}$ selecting the positions i such that $i \equiv r \bmod q$). When $\mathcal{G}$ = AMT, one may verify that we obtain the classes $\mathcal{B}\Sigma_1(<, AMOD)$ and $\mathcal{B}\Sigma_1(<, +1, AMOD)$ where "$AMOD$" is the set of *alphabetic modular predicates* (for all $a \in A$ and $r, q \in \mathbb{N}$ such that $r < q$, it contains a unary predicate $M^a_{r,q}$ selecting the positions i such the that number of positions $j < i$ with label a is congruent to r modulo q).

2.3 $\mathcal{C}$-morphisms

We now introduce a key tool, which we shall use to formulate our results. Let $\mathcal{C}$ be a positive prevariety. A *$\mathcal{C}$-morphism* is a *surjective* morphism $\eta : A^* \to (N, \leq)$ into a finite ordered monoid such that every language recognized by η belongs to $\mathcal{C}$. Let us make a key remark: when $\mathcal{C}$ is a prevariety, it suffices to consider *unordered* monoids (we view them as monoids ordered by equality).

Lemma 7. *Let $\mathcal{C}$ be a prevariety and $\eta : A^* \to (N, \leq)$ a morphism. Then, η is a $\mathcal{C}$-morphism if and only if $\eta : A^* \to (N, =)$ is a $\mathcal{C}$-morphism.*

While simple, this notion is a key tool in the paper. First, it is involved in the membership problem. It is well-known that for every regular language L, there exists a canonical morphism $\alpha_L : A^* \to (M_L, \leq_L)$ into a finite ordered monoid recognizing L and called the *syntactic morphism* of L (we do not recall the definition as we shall not use it, see [11] for example). It can be computed from any representation of L and we have the following standard property.

Proposition 8. *Let $\mathcal{C}$ be a positive prevariety. A regular language L belongs to $\mathcal{C}$ if and only if its syntactic morphism $\alpha_L : A^* \to (M_L, \leq_L)$ is a $\mathcal{C}$-morphism.*

In view of Proposition 8, getting an algorithm for $\mathcal{C}$-membership boils down to finding a procedure to decide whether an input morphism $\alpha : A^* \to (M, \leq)$ is a $\mathcal{C}$-morphism. This is how we approach the question in the paper. We shall also use $\mathcal{C}$-morphisms as mathematical tools in proof arguments. In this context, we shall need the following simple corollary of Proposition 8.

Proposition 9. *Let $\mathcal{C}$ be a positive prevariety and consider finitely many languages $L_1, \dots, L_k \in \mathcal{C}$. There exists a $\mathcal{C}$-morphism $\eta : A^* \to (N, \leq)$ such that $L_1, \dots, L_k$ are recognized by η.*

Finally, we state the following simple lemma, which considers group languages.

Lemma 10. *Let $\mathcal{G}$ be a group prevariety and let $\eta : A^* \to G$ be a $\mathcal{G}$-morphism. Then, G is a group.*

2.4 $\mathcal{C}$-pairs

Given a positive prevariety $\mathcal{C}$ and a morphism $\alpha : A^* \to M$, we associate a relation on M. The definition is taken from [12], where it is used to characterize all classes of the form $Pol(\mathcal{C})$ for an arbitrary positive prevariety $\mathcal{C}$ (we recall this characterization below). We say that $(s, t) \in M^2$ is a *$\mathcal{C}$-pair* (for α) if and only if $\alpha^{-1}(s)$ is *not* $\mathcal{C}$-separable from $\alpha^{-1}(t)$. The $\mathcal{C}$-pair relation is not robust. One may verify that it is reflexive when α is surjective and symmetric when $\mathcal{C}$ is closed under complement. However, it is *not* transitive in general. We shall use the following lemma, which connects this notion to $\mathcal{C}$-morphisms.

Lemma 11. *Let $\mathcal{C}$ be a positive prevariety and let $\alpha : A^* \to M$ be a morphism into a finite monoid. The two following properties hold:*

- *for every $\mathcal{C}$-morphism $\eta : A^* \to (N, \leq)$ and every $\mathcal{C}$-pair $(s, t) \in M^2$ for α, there exist $u, v \in A^*$ such that $\eta(u) \leq \eta(v)$, $\alpha(u) = s$ and $\alpha(v) = t$.*
- *there exists a $\mathcal{C}$-morphism $\eta : A^* \to (N, \leq)$ such that for all $u, v \in A^*$, if $\eta(u) \leq \eta(v)$, then $(\alpha(u), \alpha(v))$ is a $\mathcal{C}$-pair for α.*

Application to Polynomial Closure. We now recall the characterization of $Pol(\mathcal{C})$ from [12].

Theorem 12. *Let $\mathcal{C}$ be a positive prevariety and $\alpha : A^* \to (M, \leq)$ a surjective morphism. Then, α is a $Pol(\mathcal{C})$-morphism if and only if the following condition holds:*

$$s^{\omega+1} \leq s^{\omega}ts^{\omega} \quad \text{for every } \mathcal{C}\text{-pair } (s,t) \in M^2. \tag{1}$$

By definition, one can compute all $\mathcal{C}$-pairs associated to a morphism provided that $\mathcal{C}$-separation is decidable. Hence, in view of Proposition 8, it follows from Theorem 12 that when $\mathcal{C}$ is a positive prevariety with decidable separation, membership is decidable for $Pol(\mathcal{C})$.

An interesting point is that Theorem 12 can be simplified in the special case when $\mathcal{C}$ is a group prevariety $\mathcal{G}$ or its well-suited extension $\mathcal{G}^+$. This will be useful later when dealing with $BPol(\mathcal{G})$ and $BPol(\mathcal{G}^+)$. We first present a specialized characterization of the $Pol(\mathcal{G})$-morphisms.

Theorem 13. *Let $\mathcal{G}$ be a group prevariety and $\alpha : A^* \to (M, \leq)$ a surjective morphism. Then, α is a $Pol(\mathcal{G})$-morphism if and only if the following condition holds:*

$$1_M \leq s \quad \text{for every } s \in M \text{ such that } (1_M, s) \text{ is a } \mathcal{G}\text{-pair.} \tag{2}$$

Finally, we present a similar statement for classes of the form $Pol(\mathcal{G}^+)$.

Theorem 14. *Let $\mathcal{G}$ be a group prevariety, $\alpha : A^* \to (M, \leq)$ a surjective morphism and $S = \alpha(A^+)$. Then, α is a $Pol(\mathcal{G}^+)$-morphism if and only if the following condition holds:*

$$e \leq ese \quad \text{for every } e \in E(S) \text{ and } s \in M \text{ such that } (1_M, s) \text{ is a } \mathcal{G}\text{-pair.} \tag{3}$$

3 Group Languages

In this section, we look at classes of the form $BPol(\mathcal{G})$ when $\mathcal{G}$ is a group prevariety. We present a generic algebraic characterization of such classes, which implies that $BPol(\mathcal{G})$-membership is decidable when this is already the case for $\mathcal{G}$-separation.

3.1 Preliminaries

We present two key results that we use to build languages of $BPol(\mathcal{G})$ in the proof. The first one is a concatenation principle for the classes $BPol(\mathcal{C})$ (where $\mathcal{C}$ is an arbitrary prevariety) which is proved in [15, Lemma 3.6]. It is based on the notion of "cover". Given a language L, a cover of L is a *finite* set $\mathbf{K}$ of languages satisfying $L \subseteq \bigcup_{K \in \mathbf{K}} K$. If $\mathcal{D}$ is a class, we say that $\mathbf{K}$ is a $\mathcal{D}$-cover of L, if $\mathbf{K}$ is a cover of L such that $K \in \mathcal{D}$ for every $K \in \mathbf{K}$.

Proposition 15. *Let $\mathcal{C}$ be a prevariety, and let $n \in \mathbb{N}$, $L_0, \dots, L_n \in Pol(\mathcal{C})$ and $a_1, \dots, a_n \in A$. For every $i \leq n$, let $\mathbf{H}_i$ be a $BPol(\mathcal{C})$-cover of L_i. There exists a $BPol(\mathcal{C})$-cover $\mathbf{K}$ of $L_0a_1L_1 \cdots a_nL_n$ such that for every $K \in \mathbf{K}$, there exists $H_i \in \mathbf{H}_i$ for each $i \leq n$ satisfying $K \subseteq H_0a_1H_1 \cdots a_nH_n$.*

Using Proposition 15 requires building a language $L_0a_1L_1 \cdots a_nL_n$ where $L_0, \dots, L_n \in Pol(\mathcal{C})$. We do this with an independent result which is tailored to the special case that we investigate in the section: $\mathcal{C}$ is a group prevariety $\mathcal{G}$. Let $L \subseteq A^*$ be a language. For every word $w \in A^*$, we associate a language $\uparrow_L w \subseteq A^*$. Let $a_1, \dots, a_n \in A$ be the letters such that $w = a_1 \cdots a_n$. We define $\uparrow_L w = La_1L \cdots a_nL \subseteq A^*$ (in particular, $\uparrow_L \varepsilon = L$). The next proposition is proved in the full version of the paper (the proof is based on Higman's lemma).

Proposition 16. *Let $H \subseteq A^*$ be an arbitrary language and let $L \subseteq A^*$ be a group language such that $\varepsilon \in L$. There exists a cover $\mathbf{K}$ of H such that every $K \in \mathbf{K}$ is of the form $K = \uparrow_L w$ for some word $w \in H$.*

3.2 Characterization of *BPol*($\mathcal{G}$)

We are ready to present the characterization. As announced, we actually characterize the $BPol(\mathcal{G})$-morphisms. Recall that since $BPol(\mathcal{G})$ is a prevariety, it suffices to consider unordered monoids by Lemma 7.

Theorem 17. *Let $\mathcal{G}$ be a group prevariety and $\alpha : A^* \to M$ a surjective morphism. Then, α is a $BPol(\mathcal{G})$-morphism if and only if the following property holds:*

$$(qr)^\omega(st)^{\omega+1} = (qr)^\omega qt(st)^\omega \quad \text{for every } q, r, s, t \in M \text{ such that } (q, s) \text{ is a } \mathcal{G}\text{-pair.} \tag{4}$$

Computing the $\mathcal{G}$-pairs associated to a morphism boils down to $\mathcal{G}$-separation. Hence, in view of Proposition 8, Theorem 17 implies that if *separation* is decidable for a group prevariety $\mathcal{G}$, then *membership* is decidable for $BPol(\mathcal{G})$.

Remark 18. The decidability result itself is not new. In fact, it is even known [14] that *separation* is decidable for $BPol(\mathcal{G})$ when this is already the case for $\mathcal{G}$. Our main contribution is the algebraic characterization and its proof, which relies on self-contained language theoretic arguments.

We may use Theorem 17 to reprove well-known results for specific classes $\mathcal{G}$. For example, since ST $= \{\emptyset, A^*\}$, every pair $(s,t) \in M^2$ is an ST-pair. Hence, using Theorem 17, one may verify that a surjective morphism $\alpha : A^* \to M$ is a $BPol$(ST)-morphism if and only if the equation $(st)^\omega s = (st)^\omega = t(st)^\omega$ holds for all $s, t \in M$. This is exactly the characterization of the class $BPol(\text{ST}) = \mathcal{B}\Sigma_1(<)$ of piecewise testable languages by Simon [17]. We also get a characterization of the class $BPol(\text{MOD}) = \mathcal{B}\Sigma_1(<, MOD)$. Though the statement does not really simplify in this case, it is easily shown to be equivalent to the one presented in [4]. Finally, there exists a simple characterization of $BPol$(GR) presented in [5]: a surjective morphism $\alpha : A^* \to M$ is a $BPol$(GR)-morphism if and only if $(ef)^\omega = (fe)^\omega$ for all idempotents $e, f \in E(M)$. This is also a corollary of Theorem 17. Yet, this requires a bit of technical work as well as a knowledge of the GR-separation algorithm [2] (needed to describe the GR-pairs).

Proof (of Theorem 17). We first assume that α is a $BPol(\mathcal{G})$-morphism and prove that it satisfies (4). There exists a finite set $\mathbf{H}$ of languages in $Pol(\mathcal{G})$ such that for every $s \in M$, the language $\alpha^{-1}(s)$ is a Boolean combination of languages in $\mathbf{H}$. Since $Pol(\mathcal{G})$ is a positive prevariety, Proposition 9 yields a $Pol(\mathcal{G})$-morphism $\eta : A^* \to (N, \leq)$ recognizing every $H \in \mathbf{H}$. Moreover, Lemma 11 yields a $\mathcal{G}$-morphism $\beta : A^* \to G$ such that for every $u, v \in A^*$, if $\beta(u) = \beta(v)$, then $(\eta(u), \eta(v)) \in N^2$ is a $\mathcal{G}$-pair for η. We know that G is a group by Lemma 10. We let $n = \omega(M) \times \omega(N) \times \omega(G)$.

We may now prove that (4) holds. Let $q, r, s, t \in M$ such that (q, s) is a $\mathcal{G}$-pair. We prove that $(qr)^\omega (st)^{\omega+1} = (qr)^\omega qt(st)^\omega$. Since $\beta : A^* \to G$ is a $\mathcal{G}$-morphism and (q, s) is a $\mathcal{G}$-pair, Lemma 11 yields two words $u, x \in A^*$ and $g \in G$ such that $\beta(u) = \beta(x) = g$, $\alpha(u) = q$ and $\alpha(x) = s$. Since α is surjective, we get $v, y \in A^*$ such that $\alpha(v) = r$ and $\alpha(y) = t$. Moreover, since G is a group, we have $\beta((uv)^n) = \beta((xy)^n) = 1_G$ by definition of n. Let $v' = v(uv)^{n-1}$ and $y' = y(xy)^{n-1}$. Since $\beta(u) = \beta(x) = g$, we also get $\beta(v') = \beta(y') = g^{-1}$, $\beta(uy') = 1_G$ and $\beta(v'x) = 1_G$. Hence, by definition of β, $(1_N, \eta(uy'))$ and $(1_N, \eta(v'x))$ are $\mathcal{G}$-pairs. Since η is a $Pol(\mathcal{G})$-morphism by definition, it follows from Theorem 13 that $1_N \leq \eta(uy')$ and $1_N \leq \eta(v'x)$. We may now multiply to obtain that $\eta((uv)^n(xy)^{n+1}) \leq \eta((uv)^n uy'(xy)^{n+1})$ and $\eta((uv)^n uy(xy)^n) \leq \eta((uv)^n uv'xy(xy)^n)$. By definition of n, y' and v', one may verify that this yields the inequalities $\eta((uv)^n(xy)^{n+1}) \leq \eta((uv)^n uy(xy)^n)$ and $\eta((uv)^n uy(xy)^n) \leq \eta((uv)^n(xy)^{n+1})$. Since η recognizes all $H \in \mathbf{H}$ by definition, it follows that $(uv)^n(xy)^{n+1} \in H \Leftrightarrow (uv)^n uy(xy)^n \in H$ for every $H \in \mathbf{H}$. Since all languages recognized by α are Boolean combination of languages in $\mathbf{H}$, we get $\alpha((uv)^n(xy)^{n+1}) = \alpha((uv)^n uy(xy)^n)$. By definition, this exactly says that $(qr)^\omega (st)^{\omega+1} = (qr)^\omega qt(st)^\omega$ as desired.

We turn to the converse implication. Assume that α satisfies (4). We prove that α is a $BPol(\mathcal{G})$-morphism. Lemma 11 yields a $\mathcal{G}$-morphism $\beta : A^* \to G$ such that for every $u, v \in A^*$, if $\beta(u) = \beta(v)$, then $(\alpha(u), \alpha(v))$ is a $\mathcal{G}$-pair. We write $L = \beta^{-1}(1_G) \in \mathcal{G}$. By hypothesis on $\mathcal{G}$, L is a group language. Moreover, we have $\varepsilon \in L$ by definition. Given a finite set of languages $\mathbf{K}$, and $s, t \in M$, we say that $\mathbf{K}$ is (s, t)-safe if for every $K \in \mathbf{K}$ and $w, w' \in K$, we have $s\alpha(w)t = s\alpha(w')t$. The argument is based on the following lemma.

Lemma 19. *Let $s, t \in M$. There exists a $BPol(\mathcal{G})$-cover of L which is (s, t)-safe.*

Before proving Lemma 19 we first use it to prove that every language recognized by α belongs to $BPol(\mathcal{G})$, thus concluding the argument. We apply Lemma 19 with $s = t = 1_M$. This yields a $BPol(\mathcal{G})$-cover $\mathbf{K}_L$ of L which is $(1_M, 1_M)$-safe. We use it to build a $BPol(\mathcal{G})$-cover $\mathbf{K}$ of A^* which is $(1_M, 1_M)$-safe. Since $L \in \mathcal{G}$ and $\varepsilon \in L$, Proposition 16 yields a cover $\mathbf{P}$ of A^* such that every $P \in \mathbf{P}$, there exist $n \in \mathbb{N}$ and $a_1, \dots, a_n \in A$ such that $P = La_1L \cdots a_nL$. We cover each $P \in \mathbf{P}$ independently. Consider a language $P \in \mathbf{P}$. By definition,

$P = La_1L \cdots a_nL$ for $a_1, \dots, a_n \in A$. Since $L \in \mathcal{G}$ and $\mathbf{K}_L$ is a $BPol(\mathcal{G})$-cover of L, Proposition 15 yields a $BPol(\mathcal{G})$-cover $\mathbf{K}_P$ of $P = La_1L \cdots a_nL$ such that for every $K \in \mathbf{K}_P$, there exist $K_0, \dots, K_n \in \mathbf{K}_L$ satisfying $K \subseteq K_0a_1K_1 \cdots a_nK_n$. Since $\mathbf{K}_L$ is $(1_M, 1_M)$-safe, it is immediate that $\mathbf{K}_P$ is $(1_M, 1_M)$-safe as well. Finally, since $\mathbf{P}$ is a cover of A^*, it is now immediate that $\mathbf{K} = \bigcup_{P \in \mathbf{P}} \mathbf{K}_P$ is a $(1_M, 1_M)$-safe $BPol(\mathcal{G})$-cover of A^*. Since $\mathbf{K}$ is $(1_M, 1_M)$-safe, we know that for every $K \in \mathbf{K}$, there exists $s \in M$ such that $K \subseteq \alpha^{-1}(s)$. Hence, since $\mathbf{K}$ is a cover of A^*, it is immediate that for every $F \subseteq M$, the language $\alpha^{-1}(F)$ is a union of languages in $\mathbf{K}$. By closure under union, it follows that $\alpha^{-1}(F) \in BPol(\mathcal{G})$. This exactly says that all languages recognized by α belong to $BPol(\mathcal{G})$.

It remains to prove Lemma 19. We define a preorder on M^2 that we shall use as an induction parameter. Consider $(s,t), (s',t') \in M^2$. We write $(s,t) \leqslant_L (s',t')$ if there exist $x, y \in A^*$ such that $xy \in L$, $s' = s\alpha(x)$ and $t' = \alpha(y)t$. It is immediate that $\leqslant_L$ is reflexive since we have $\varepsilon = \varepsilon\varepsilon \in L$. Let us verify that $\leqslant_L$ is transitive. Let $(s,t), (s',t'), (s'',t'') \in M^2$ such that $(s,t) \leqslant_L (s',t')$ and $(s',t') \leqslant_L (s'',t'')$. We show that $(s,t) \leqslant_L (s'',t'')$. By definition, we have $xy, x'y' \in L$ such that $s' = s\alpha(x)$, $t' = \alpha(y)t$, $s'' = s'\alpha(x')$ and $t'' = \alpha(y')t'$. Hence, $s'' = s\alpha(xx')$ and $t'' = \alpha(y'y)t$. Moreover, since $L = \beta^{-1}(1_G)$, we have $\beta(xx'y'y) = \beta(xy) = 1_G$, which yields $xx'y'y \in L$. We conclude that $(s,t) \leqslant_L (s'',t'')$, as desired.

We may now start the proof. Let $s, t \in M$. We construct a $BPol(\mathcal{G})$-cover $\mathbf{K}$ of L which is (s,t)-safe. We proceed by descending induction on the number of pairs $(s',t') \in M^2$ such that $(s,t) \leqslant_L (s',t')$. We handle the base case and the inductive step simultaneously. Consider a word $w \in L$. We say w *stabilizes* (s,t) if there exist $u, v \in A^*$ such that $uv \in \uparrow_L w$, $s\alpha(u) = s$ and $\alpha(v)t = t$. Observe that by definition, ε stabilizes (s,t) since we have $\varepsilon\varepsilon = \varepsilon \in L = \uparrow_L \varepsilon$. We let $H \subseteq L$ be the language of all words $w \in L$ that do *not* stabilize (s,t). Note that by definition $\varepsilon \notin H$. We first use induction to build a $BPol(\mathcal{G})$-cover $\mathbf{K}_H$ of H and then complete it to build $\mathbf{K}$. Let us point out that it may happen that H is empty. This is the base case, it suffices to define $\mathbf{K}_H = \emptyset$.

Let $P \subseteq M^2$ be the set of all pairs $(s',t') \in M^2$ such that $(s,t) \leqslant_L (s',t')$ and $(s',t') \not\leqslant_L (s,t)$. We define $\ell = |P|$ and write $P = \{(s'_1, t'_1), \dots, (s'_\ell, t'_\ell)\}$. For every $i \leq \ell$, we may apply induction in the proof of Lemma 19 to obtain a $BPol(\mathcal{G})$-cover $\mathbf{K}_i$ of L which is (s'_i, t'_i)-safe. We define $\mathbf{K}_L$ as the finite set of all languages $L \cap K_1 \cap \cdots \cap K_\ell$ where $K_i \in \mathbf{K}_i$ for every $i \leq \ell$. Since $L \in \mathcal{G}$, it is immediate that $\mathbf{K}_L$ is a $BPol(\mathcal{G})$-cover of L which is (s',t')-safe for every $(s',t') \in P$. We use it to construct $\mathbf{K}_H$.

Lemma 20. *There exists an (s,t)-safe $BPol(\mathcal{G})$-cover $\mathbf{K}_H$ of H.*

Proof. Since L is a group language such that $\varepsilon \in L$, Proposition 16 yields a cover $\mathbf{U}$ of H such that for every $U \in \mathbf{U}$, there exist $n \geq 1$ and $a_1, \dots, a_n \in A$ such that $a_1 \cdots a_n \in H$ and $U = La_1L \cdots a_nL$ (note that $n \geq 1$ as $\varepsilon \notin H$). For each $U \in \mathbf{U}$, we build an (s,t)-safe $BPol(\mathcal{G})$-cover $\mathbf{K}_U$ of U. Since $\mathbf{U}$ is a cover of H, it will then suffice to define $\mathbf{K}_H$ as the union of all covers $\mathbf{K}_U$. We fix $U \in \mathbf{U}$.

By definition, $U = La_1L \cdots a_nL$ where $a_1 \cdots a_n \in H$. Since $L \in \mathcal{G}$, $\varepsilon \in L$ and $\mathbf{K}_L$ is a $BPol(\mathcal{G})$-cover of L, Proposition 15 yields a $BPol(\mathcal{G})$-cover $\mathbf{K}_U$ of U such that for each $K \in \mathbf{K}_U$, we have $K \subseteq K_0 a_1 K_1 \cdots a_n K_n$ for $K_0, \dots, K_n \in \mathbf{K}_L$. It remains to show that $\mathbf{K}_U$ is (s,t)-safe. We fix $K \in \mathbf{K}_U$ as described above and $w, w' \in K$. We show that $s\alpha(w)t = s\alpha(w')t$. By definition, we have $w_i, w'_i \in K_i$ for all $i \leq n$ such that $w = w_0 a_1 w_1 \cdots a_n w_n$ and $w' = w'_0 a_1 w'_1 \cdots a_n w'_n$. We let $u_i = w_0 a_1 \cdots w_{i-1} a_i$ and $u'_i = w'_0 a_1 \cdots w'_{i-1} a_i$ for $0 \leq i \leq n$ ($u_0 = u'_0 = \varepsilon$). We also let $v_i = a_{i+1} w_{i+1} \cdots a_n w_n$ and $v'_i = a_{i+1} w'_{i+1} \cdots a_n w'_n$ ($v_n = v'_n = \varepsilon$). Note that $u_i w'_i v'_i = u_{i-1} w_{i-1} v'_{i-1}$ for $1 \leq i \leq n$. Hence, it suffices to prove that $s\alpha(u_i w_i v'_i)t = s\alpha(u_i w'_i v'_i)t$ for $0 \leq i \leq n$. By transitivity, it will then follow that $s\alpha(u_n w_n v'_n)t = s\alpha(u_0 w'_0 v'_0)t$, *i.e.*, $s\alpha(w)t = s\alpha(w')t$ as desired.

We fix $i \leq n$ and show that $s\alpha(u_i w_i v'_i)t = s\alpha(u_i w'_i v'_i)t$. By hypothesis, $w_i, w'_i \in K_i$. Since $K_i \in \mathbf{K}_L$ is (s',t')-safe for all $(s',t') \in P$, it suffices to prove that $(s\alpha(u_i), \alpha(v'_i)t) \in P$. There are two conditions to verify. First, we show that $(s,t) \leqslant_L (s\alpha(u_i), \alpha(v'_i)t)$. By definition of $\leqslant_L$, this boils down to proving that $u_i v'_i \in L$. By definition, $w_j, w'_j \in K_j$ for every $j \leq n$. Moreover, since $K_j \in \mathbf{K}_L$, it follows that $w_j, w'_j \in L$ for every $j \leq n$ by definition of $\mathbf{K}_L$. It follows that $\beta(w_j) = \beta(w'_j) = 1_G$ since $L = \beta^{-1}(1_G)$. Therefore, by definition of u_i and v'_i, we obtain $\beta(u_i) = \beta(a_1 \cdots a_i)$ and $\beta(v'_i) = \beta(a_{i+1} \cdots a_n)$. This yields $\beta(u_i v'_i) = \beta(a_1 \cdots a_n)$. Finally, since $a_1 \cdots a_n \in H \subseteq L$ and L is recognized by β, we get $u_i v'_i \in L$, as desired. It remains to prove that $(s\alpha(u_i), \alpha(v'_i)t) \not\leqslant_L (s,t)$. By contradiction, assume that $(s\alpha(u_i), \alpha(v'_i)t) \leqslant_L (s,t)$. This yields $x, y \in A^*$ such that $xy \in L$ and $s = s\alpha(u_i x)$ and $t = \alpha(y v'_i)t$. Since $xy \in L$ and $w_j, w'_j \in L$, it is immediate by definition of u_i and v'_i that $u_i x y v_i \in \uparrow_L (a_1 \cdots a_n)$. Hence, $a_1 \cdots a_n$ stabilizes (s,t). This is a contradiction since $a_1 \cdots a_n \in H$. □

We are ready to construct the desired (s,t)-safe $BPol(\mathcal{G})$-cover $\mathbf{K}$ of L. Let $\mathbf{K}_H$ be the $BPol(\mathcal{G})$-cover of H given by Lemma 20. We let $K_\perp = L \setminus (\bigcup_{K \in \mathbf{K}_H} K)$. Finally, we define $\mathbf{K} = \{K_\perp\} \cup \mathbf{K}_H$. It is immediate that $\mathbf{K}$ is a $BPol(\mathcal{G})$-cover of L since $BPol(\mathcal{G})$ is a Boolean algebra (recall that $L \in \mathcal{G}$). It remains to verify that $\mathbf{K}$ is (s,t)-safe. Since we already know that $\mathbf{K}_H$ is (s,t)-safe, it suffices to prove that for every $w, w' \in K_\perp$, we have $s\alpha(w)t = s\alpha(w')t$. We actually show that $s\alpha(w)t = st$ for every $w \in K_\perp$. Since this is immediate when $w = \varepsilon$, we assume that $w \in A^+$ and let $a_1, \dots, a_n \in A$ be the letters such that $w = a_1 \cdots a_n$.

By definition of $K_\perp$, we know that $w \notin K'$ for every $K' \in \mathbf{K}_H$. Since $\mathbf{K}_H$ is a cover of H, it follows that $w \notin H$, which means that w stabilizes (s,t) by definition of H. We get $u', v' \in A^*$ such that $u'v' \in \uparrow_L w$, $s\alpha(u') = s$ and $\alpha(v')t = t$. Since $u'v' \in \uparrow_L w$, there exist $0 \leq i \leq n$ and $x_0, \dots, x_i, y_i, \dots, y_n \in A^*$ which satisfy $x_0, \dots, x_{i-1}, x_i y_i, y_{i+1}, \dots, y_n \in L$, $u' = x_0 a_1 x_1 \cdots a_i x_i$ and $v' = y_i a_{i+1} x_{i+1} \cdots a_n x_n$. We write $u = a_1 \cdots a_i$ and $v = a_{i+1} \cdots a_n$. By definition $w = uv$. We show that $s = s\alpha(u x_i)$ and $t = \alpha(y_i v)t$. Let us first assume that this holds and explain why this implies $st = s\alpha(w)t$.

Since $uv = w$ and $w \in K_\perp \subseteq L = \beta^{-1}(1_G)$, we have $\beta(u)\beta(v) = 1_G$. Let $p = \omega(G)$. We have $1_G = \beta((y_i v)^p)$. Thus, since G is a group, it follows that $\beta(u) = \beta((y_i v)^{p-1} y_i)$. By definition of β, it follows that $(\alpha(u), \alpha((y_i v)^{p-1} y_i))$ is a $\mathcal{G}$-pair. Consequently, we obtain from (4) that,

$$(\alpha(ux_i))^\omega(\alpha((y_iv)^{p-1}y_iv))^{\omega+1} = (\alpha(ux_i))^\omega\alpha(uv)(\alpha((y_iv)^{p-1}y_iv))^\omega.$$

We may now multiply by s on the left and t on the right. Since $s = s\alpha(ux_i)$ and $t = \alpha(y_iv)t$, this yields $st = s\alpha(uv)t$. This concludes the proof since $uv = w$.

It remains to show that $s = s\alpha(ux_i)$ and $t = \alpha(y_iv)t$. We prove the former (the latter is symmetrical and left to the reader). For every j such that $0 \leq j \leq i$, we write $z_j = x_ja_{j+1}\cdots x_{i-1}a_ix_i$ (when $i = j$, we let $z_i = x_i$). We use induction on i to prove that $s = s\alpha(a_1\cdots a_jz_j)$ for $0 \leq j \leq i$. Clearly, the case $j = i$ yields $s = s\alpha(a_1\cdots a_ix_i)$ which exactly says that $s = s\alpha(ux_i)$. When $j = 0$, we have $z_0 = x_0a_1x_1\cdots a_ix_i = u'$ and $s\alpha(u') = s$ by hypothesis. Assume now that $1 \leq j \leq i$. Since $x_{j-1} \in L$ and $L = \beta^{-1}(1_G)$, we have $\beta(x_{j-1}) = \beta(\varepsilon) = 1_G$. Hence, $(\alpha(x_{j-1}), 1_M)$ is a $\mathcal{G}$-pair by definition of β. Applying (4) with the values $\alpha(x_{j-1})$, $\alpha(a_jz_ja_1\cdots a_{j-1})$, $1_M, 1_M$ yields that,

$$(\alpha(x_{j-1}a_jz_ja_1\cdots a_{j-1}))^\omega = (\alpha(x_{j-1}a_jz_ja_1\cdots a_{j-1}))^\omega\alpha(x_{j-1}). \tag{5}$$

By induction hypothesis, we know that $s = s\alpha(a_1\cdots a_{j-1}z_{j-1})$. Since it is immediate by definition that $a_1\cdots a_{j-1}z_{j-1} = a_1\cdots a_{j-1}x_{j-1}a_jz_j$, we get,

$$\begin{aligned}
s &= s\alpha(a_1\cdots a_{j-1}x_{j-1}a_jz_j)\\
&= s(\alpha(a_1\cdots a_{j-1}x_{j-1}a_jz_j))^{\omega+1}\\
&= s\alpha(a_1\cdots a_{j-1})(\alpha(x_{j-1}a_jz_ja_1\cdots a_{j-1}))^\omega\alpha(x_{j-1})\alpha(a_jz_j)\\
&= s\alpha(a_1\cdots a_{j-1})(\alpha(x_{j-1}a_jz_ja_1\cdots a_{j-1}))^\omega\alpha(a_jz_j) \qquad \text{by (5)}\\
&= s(\alpha(a_1\cdots a_{j-1}x_{j-1}a_jz_j))^\omega\alpha(a_1\cdots a_{j-1}a_jz_j)\\
&= s\alpha(a_1\cdots a_jz_j).
\end{aligned}$$

This concludes the proof. □

4 Well-Suited Extensions

We turn to the classes $BPol(\mathcal{G}^+)$ where $\mathcal{G}$ is an arbitrary group prevariety. Again, we present a generic algebraic characterization, which implies that $BPol(\mathcal{G}^+)$-membership is decidable when this is already the case for $\mathcal{G}$-separation.

4.1 Preliminaries

In this case as well, we start with preliminary results that we use to build languages of $BPol(\mathcal{G}^+)$. The first one is a simple corollary of Proposition 15 (the concatenation principle for $BPol(\mathcal{C})$) which is more convenient to manipulate when considering $BPol(\mathcal{G}^+)$ (see the full version of the paper).

Corollary 21. *Let $\mathcal{C}$ be a prevariety, $L \in Pol(\mathcal{C}^+)$, $\mathbf{H}$ a $BPol(\mathcal{C}^+)$-cover of L, $n \in \mathbb{N}$ and $n+1$ nonempty words $w_1, \dots, w_{n+1} \in A^+$. There exists a $BPol(\mathcal{C}^+)$-cover $\mathbf{K}$ of $w_1L\cdots w_nLw_{n+1}$ such that for every language $K \in \mathbf{K}$, we have $K \subseteq w_1H_1\cdots w_nH_nw_{n+1}$ for $H_1, \dots, H_n \in \mathbf{H}$.*

We complete Corollary 21 with a result that we use to build languages of the form $w_1 L \cdots w_n L w_{n+1}$ with $L \in Pol(\mathcal{C}^+)$. It is tailored to the case considered in the section: $\mathcal{C}$ is a group prevariety $\mathcal{G}$. Consider a morphism $\alpha : A^* \to M$ and a *nonempty* word $w \in A^+$. An *α-guarded decomposition of* w is a tuple $(w_1, \dots, w_{n+1})$ where $n \in \mathbb{N}$ and $w_1, \dots, w_{n+1} \in A^+$ are nonempty words such that $w = w_1 \cdots w_{n+1}$ and, if $n \geq 1$, then for $1 \leq i \leq n$, there exists an *idempotent* $e_i \in \alpha(A^+)$ such that $\alpha(w_i)e_i = \alpha(w_i)$ and $e_i\alpha(w_{i+1}) = \alpha(w_{i+1})$. The next result is a corollary of Proposition 16. It is proved in the full version of the paper.

Proposition 22. *Let $H \subseteq A^+$ be a language, $\alpha : A^* \to M$ be a morphism and $L \subseteq A^*$ be a group language such that $\varepsilon \in L$. There is a cover $\mathbf{K}$ of H such that for all $K \in \mathbf{K}$, there are $w \in H$ and an α-guarded decomposition $(w_1, \dots, w_{n+1})$ of w for some $n \in \mathbb{N}$ such that $K = w_1 L \cdots w_n L w_{n+1}$ (if $n = 0$, then $K = \{w_1\}$).*

4.2 Characterization

We may now present the characterization. As we explained, we actually characterize the $BPol(\mathcal{G}^+)$-morphisms. Recall that since $BPol(\mathcal{G}^+)$ is a prevariety, it suffices to consider unordered monoids by Lemma 7.

Theorem 23. *Let $\mathcal{G}$ be a group prevariety, $\alpha : A^* \to M$ a surjective morphism and $S = \alpha(A^+)$. Then, α is a $BPol(\mathcal{G}^+)$-morphism if and only if the following property holds:*

$$\begin{array}{c} (eqfre)^\omega (esfte)^{\omega+1} = (eqfre)^\omega qft(esfte)^\omega \\ \textit{for all } q,r,s,t \in M \textit{ and } e,f \in E(S) \textit{ such that } (q,s) \textit{ is a } \mathcal{G}\textit{-pair.} \end{array} \quad (6)$$

Again, by Proposition 8, Theorem 23 implies that if *separation* is decidable for a group prevariety $\mathcal{G}$, then *membership* is decidable for $BPol(\mathcal{G}^+)$.

Theorem 23 can also be used to reprove famous results for specific classes $\mathcal{G}$. As seen in Sect. 3, since $\text{ST} = \{\emptyset, A^*\}$, every pair $(s,t) \in M^2$ is an ST-pair. Thus, one may verify from Theorem 23 that a surjective morphism $\alpha : A^* \to M$ is a $BPol(\text{ST}^+)$-morphism if and only if $(eqfre)^\omega(esfte)^\omega = (eqfre)^\omega qft(esfte)^\omega$ for every $q,r,s,t \in S$ and $e,f \in E(S)$ (where $S = \alpha(A^+)$). This is exactly the well-known characterization of the languages of dot-depth one by Knast [6] (*i.e.*, the class $BPol(\text{ST}^+) = \mathcal{B}\Sigma_1(<,+1)$). Additionally, there exists a specialized characterization of $BPol(\text{MOD}^+) = \mathcal{B}\Sigma_1(<,+1,MOD)$ in the literature [7]. It can also be reproved as a corollary of Theorem 23. Yet, this requires some technical work involving the MOD-pairs.

Proof (of Theorem 23). Assuming that α satisfies (6), we prove that it is a $BPol(\mathcal{G}^+)$-morphism. The converse implication is proved in the full version of the paper (the argument is based on Theorem 23).

Lemma 11 yields a $\mathcal{G}$-morphism $\beta : A^* \to G$ such that for $u,v \in A^*$, if $\beta(u) = \beta(v)$, then $(\alpha(u), \alpha(v))$ is a $\mathcal{G}$-pair. Let $L = \beta^{-1}(1_G) \in \mathcal{G}$. By hypothesis on $\mathcal{G}$, L is a group language. Moreover, $\varepsilon \in L$ by definition. Given a finite set of languages $\mathbf{K}$, and $s,t \in M$, we say that $\mathbf{K}$ is *(s,t)-safe* if for every $K \in \mathbf{K}$ and $w,w' \in K$, we have $s\alpha(w)t = s\alpha(w')t$. The proof is based on the next lemma.

Lemma 24. *Let $s, t \in M$. There exists an (s,t)-safe $BPol(\mathcal{G}^+)$-cover of L.*

We first apply Lemma 24 to prove that α is a $BPol(\mathcal{G}^+)$-morphism. We use for $s = t = 1_M$. This yields a $BPol(\mathcal{G}^+)$-cover $\mathbf{K}_L$ of L which is $(1_M, 1_M)$-safe. One may now apply Proposition 15 and Proposition 16 to build a $BPol(\mathcal{G})$-cover $\mathbf{K}$ of A^* which is $(1_M, 1_M)$-safe from $\mathbf{K}_L$ (see the proof of Theorem 17 for details). Hence, for every $F \subseteq M$, the language $\alpha^{-1}(F)$ is a union of languages in $\mathbf{K}$. By closure under union, it follows that $\alpha^{-1}(F) \in BPol(\mathcal{G}^+)$. This exactly says that all languages recognized by α belong to $BPol(\mathcal{G}^+)$.

It remains to prove Lemma 24. We define a preorder on M^2 that we shall use as an induction parameter. Let $(s,t), (s',t') \in M^2$. We write $(s,t) \leqslant_L^+ (s',t')$ if either $(s,t) = (s',t')$ or there exist $x, y \in A^*$ and $e \in E(S)$ such that $xy \in L$, $\alpha(x)e = \alpha(x)$, $e\alpha(y) = \alpha(y)$, $s' = s\alpha(x)$ and $t' = \alpha(y)t$. One may verify that $\leqslant_L^+$ is a preorder. We may now start the proof. Let $s, t \in M$. We construct a $BPol(\mathcal{G}^+)$-cover $\mathbf{K}$ of L which is (s,t)-safe. We proceed by induction on the number of pairs $(s',t') \in M^2$ such that $(s,t) \leqslant_L^+ (s',t')$. The base case and the inductive step are handled simultaneously. First, we define a language $H \subseteq L$. Let $w \in L$. We say w *stabilizes* (s,t) if $w = \varepsilon$ or $w \in A^+$ and there exists $n \geq 1$, an α-guarded decomposition $(w_1, \dots, w_{n+1})$ of w, an index $1 \leq i \leq n$, $x_1, \dots, x_i, y_i, \dots, y_n \in A^*$ and $e \in E(S)$ which satisfy the following conditions:

- $x_1, \dots, x_{i-1}, x_iy_i, y_{i+1}, \dots, y_n \in L$, and,
- $s\alpha(w_1x_1 \cdots w_ix_i)e = s$, and,
- $e\alpha(y_iw_{i+1} \cdots y_nw_{n+1})t = t$.

We let $H \subseteq L$ be the language of all words $w \in L$ which do *not* stabilize (s,t). Observe that by definition, we have $\varepsilon \notin H$. We first use induction to build an (s,t)-safe $BPol(\mathcal{G}^+)$-cover of H. Then, we complete it to obtain the desired $BPol(\mathcal{G}^+)$-cover of L. It may happen that H is empty. In this case, we do not need induction: it suffices to use $\emptyset$ as this $BPol(\mathcal{G}^+)$-cover.

We let $P \subseteq M^2$ be the set of all $(s',t') \in M^2$ such that $(s,t) \leqslant_L^+ (s',t')$ and $(s',t') \not\leqslant_L^+ (s,t)$. We define $\ell = |P|$ and write $P = \{(s'_1, t'_1), \dots, (s'_\ell, t'_\ell)\}$. For every $i \leq \ell$, we may apply induction in the proof of Lemma 24 to obtain a $BPol(\mathcal{G}^+)$-cover $\mathbf{K}_i$ of L which is (s'_i, t'_i)-safe. We met $\mathbf{K}_L$ as the finite set of all languages $L \cap K_1 \cap \cdots \cap K_\ell$ where $K_i \in \mathbf{K}_i$ for every $i \leq \ell$. Since $L \in \mathcal{G}$, it is immediate that $\mathbf{K}_L$ is a $BPol(\mathcal{G}^+)$-cover of L which is (s',t')-safe for all $(s',t') \in P$. We use it to build $\mathbf{K}_H$.

Lemma 25. *There exists an (s,t)-safe $BPol(\mathcal{G}^+)$-cover $\mathbf{K}_H$ of H.*

Proof. Since L is a group language such that $\varepsilon \in L$ and $\varepsilon \notin H$, Proposition 22 yields a cover $\mathbf{U}$ of H such that each $U \in \mathbf{U}$ is of the form $U = w_1L \cdots w_nLw_{n+1}$ where $(w_1, \dots, w_{n+1})$ is an α-guarded decomposition of a word $w \in H$. For each $U \in \mathbf{U}$, we build an (s,t)-safe $BPol(\mathcal{G}^+)$-cover $\mathbf{K}_U$ of U. As $\mathbf{U}$ is a cover of H, it will then suffice to define $\mathbf{K}_H$ as the union of all covers $\mathbf{K}_U$. We fix $U \in \mathbf{U}$.

By definition of $\mathbf{U}$, $U = w_1L \cdots w_nLw_{n+1}$ where $(w_1, \dots, w_{n+1})$ is an α-guarded decomposition of a word $w \in H$. Since $L \in \mathcal{G}$, $\varepsilon \in L$ and $\mathbf{K}_L$ is a $BPol(\mathcal{G}^+)$-cover of L by hypothesis, Corollary 21 yields a $BPol(\mathcal{G}^+)$-cover $\mathbf{K}_U$ of U such that for each $K \in \mathbf{K}_U$, we have $K \subseteq w_1K_1 \cdots w_nK_iw_{n+1}$ for $K_1, \dots, K_n \in \mathbf{K}_L$. Let us prove that $\mathbf{K}_U$ is (s,t)-safe. We fix $K \in \mathbf{K}_U$ as described above. For $u, u' \in K$, we show that $s\alpha(u)t = s\alpha(u')t$. If $n = 0$, then $K \subseteq \{w_1\}$. Hence $u = u' = w_1$ and the result is immediate. Assume now that $n \geq 1$. We get $u_i, u'_i \in K_i$ for $1 \leq i \leq n$ such that $u = w_1u_1 \cdots w_nu_nw_{n+1}$ and $u' = w_1u'_1 \cdots w_nu'_nw_{n+1}$. For $1 \leq i \leq n$, we write $x_i = w_1u_1w_2 \cdots u_{i-1}w_i$ and $x'_i = w_1u'_1w_2 \cdots u'_{i-1}w_i$. Moreover, we let $y_i = w_{i+1}u_{i+1} \cdots w_nu_nw_{n+1}$ and $y'_i = w_{i+1}u'_{i+1} \cdots w_nu'_nw_{n+1}$. For $1 \leq i \leq n$, we have $x_iu'_iy'_i = x_{i-1}u_{i-1}y'_{i-1}$. Moreover, one may use the hypotheses that $w \in H$ and $(w_1, \dots, w_{n+1})$ is an α-guarded decomposition of w to verify that $(s\alpha(x_i), \alpha(y'_i)t) \in P$. Hence, since $K_i \in \mathbf{K}_L$ which is (s',t')-safe for every $(s',t') \in P$, we have $s\alpha(x_iu_iy'_i)t = s\alpha(x_iu'_iy'_i)t$ for $1 \leq i \leq n$. It is now immediate by transitivity that $s\alpha(x_nu_ny'_n)t = s\alpha(x_1u'_1y'_1)t$, *i.e.* $s\alpha(u)t = s\alpha(u')t$ as desired. □

We now define the desired (s,t)-safe $BPol(\mathcal{G}^+)$-cover $\mathbf{K}$ of L. Lemma 25 yields a $BPol(\mathcal{G}^+)$-cover $\mathbf{K}_H$ of H. We let $K_\bot = L \setminus (\bigcup_{K \in \mathbf{K}_H} K)$. Finally, we let $\mathbf{K} = \{K_\bot\} \cup \mathbf{K}_H$. Clearly, $\mathbf{K}$ is a $BPol(\mathcal{G}^+)$-cover of L since $BPol(\mathcal{G}^+)$ is a Boolean algebra (recall that $L \in \mathcal{G}$). It remains to verify that $\mathbf{K}$ is (s,t)-safe. Since we already know that $\mathbf{K}_H$ is (s,t)-safe, it suffices to prove that for every $w, w' \in K_\bot$, we have $s\alpha(w)t = s\alpha(w')t$. We actually show that $s\alpha(w)t = st$ for every $w \in K_\bot$. Since this is immediate when $w = \varepsilon$, we assume that $w \in A^+$.

By definition of $K_\bot$, we have $w \notin K'$ for all $K' \in \mathbf{K}_H$. Since $\mathbf{K}_H$ is a cover of H, this yields $w \notin H$, *i.e.* w stabilizes (s,t). Since $w \neq \varepsilon$, we get an α-guarded decomposition $(w_1, \dots, w_{n+1})$ of w, an index $i \leq n$, $x_1, \dots, x_i, y_i, \dots, y_1 \in A^*$ and $e \in E(S)$ such that $x_1, \dots, x_{i-1}, x_iy_i, y_{i-1}, \dots, y_n \in L$, $s\alpha(w_1x_1 \cdots w_ix_i)e = s$ and $e\alpha(y_iw_{i+1} \cdots y_nw_n)t = t$. Let $u = w_1 \cdots w_i$ and $v = w_{i+1} \cdots w_{n+1}$. We show that $s = s\alpha(ux_i)e$ and $t = e\alpha(y_iv)t$ (note that since e is an idempotent, this also implies $s = se$ and $t = et$) Let us first assume that this holds and explain why this implies $st = s\alpha(w)t$.

Since $(w_1, \dots, w_{n+1})$ is an α-guarded decomposition, there exist an idempotent $f \in E(S)$ such that $\alpha(w_i)f = \alpha(w_i)$ and $f\alpha(w_{i+1}) = \alpha(w_{i+1})$. By definition of u and v, we have $\alpha(u)f = \alpha(u)$ and $f\alpha(v) = \alpha(v)$. Clearly, we have $uv = w$. Thus, since $w \in L = \beta^{-1}(1_G)$, we have $\beta(u)\beta(v) = 1_G$. Let $p = \omega(G)$. We have $1_G = \beta((y_iv)^p)$. Thus, since G is a group, it follows that $\beta(u) = \beta((y_iv)^{p-1}y_i)$. By definition of β, it follows that $(\alpha(u), \alpha((y_nv)^{p-1}y_i))$ is a $\mathcal{G}$-pair. Let $q = \alpha(u)$, $r = \alpha(x_i)$, $q' = \alpha((y_nv)^{p-1}y_i)$ and $r' = \alpha(v)$. Since we just proved that (q,q') is a $\mathcal{G}$-pair, we obtain from (6) that,

$$(eqfre)^\omega(eq'fr'e)^{\omega+1} = (eqfre)^\omega qfr'(eq'fr'e)^\omega. \tag{7}$$

Since $\alpha(u)f = \alpha(u)$, we have $eqfre = e\alpha(ux_i)e$ and $qfr' = \alpha(uv) = \alpha(w)$. Moreover, since $f\alpha(v) = \alpha(v)$, we have $eq'fr'e = e\alpha((y_iv)^p)e$. Hence, since we have $s = s\alpha(ux_i)e = se$ and $t = e\alpha(y_iv)t = et$, it is immediate that $seqfre = s$ and $eq'fr'et = t$. We may now multiply by s on the left and t on the right in (7) to obtain $st = sqfr't = s\alpha(w)t$ as desired.

It remains to prove that $s = s\alpha(ux_i)e$ and $t = e\alpha(y_iv)t$. We concentrate on $s = s\alpha(ux_i)e$ (the other equality is symmetrical and left to the reader). For every j such that $1 \leq j \leq i$, we write $r_j = \alpha(w_jx_j \cdots w_ix_i)e$ and $u_j = w_1 \cdots w_{j-1}$ (we let $u_1 = \varepsilon$). We use induction on j to prove that $s = s\alpha(u_j)r_j$ for $1 \leq j \leq i$. This concludes the argument: when $j = i$, we get $s = s\alpha(w_1 \cdots w_{i-1}w_ix_i)e$. Since $u = w_1 \cdots w_i$, this exactly says that $s = s\alpha(ux_i)e$ as desired. The case $j = 1$ is immediate by definition: we have $s\alpha(w_1x_1 \cdots w_ix_i)e = s$. Thus, we now assume that $2 \leq j \leq i$. Since $(w_1, \dots, w_{n+1})$ is an α-guarded decomposition, there exist an idempotent $f \in E(S)$ such that $\alpha(w_{j-1})f = \alpha(w_{j-1})$ and $f\alpha(w_j) = \alpha(w_j)$. By definition of u_j and r_j, we have $\alpha(u_j)f = \alpha(u_j)$ and $fr_j = r_j$. Moreover, since $x_{j-1} \in L$ and $L = \beta^{-1}(1_G)$, we have $\beta(x_{j-1}) = \beta(\varepsilon) = 1_G$. By definition of β, it follows that $(\alpha(x_{j-1}), 1_M)$ is a $\mathcal{G}$-pair. Hence, we may apply (6) for $q = \alpha(x_{j-1})$, $r = r_j\alpha(u_j)$ and $s = t = 1_M$ to obtain,

$$(f\alpha(x_{j-1})fr_j\alpha(u_j)f)^\omega = (f\alpha(x_{j-1})fr_j\alpha(u_j)f)^\omega\alpha(x_{j-1})f. \tag{8}$$

Induction yields that $s = s\alpha(u_{j-1})r_{j-1}$. Moreover, it is immediate from the definitions that $\alpha(u_{j-1})r_{j-1} = \alpha(u_j)\alpha(x_{j-1})r_j = \alpha(u_j)f\alpha(x_{j-1})fr_j$ which yields,

$$\begin{aligned}
s &= s\alpha(u_j)f\alpha(x_{j-1})fr_j \\
&= s(\alpha(u_j)f\alpha(x_{j-1})fr_j)^{\omega+1} \\
&= s\alpha(u_j)(f\alpha(x_{j-1})fr_j\alpha(u_j)f)^\omega\alpha(x_{j-1})fr_j \\
&= s\alpha(u_j)(f\alpha(x_{j-1})fr_j\alpha(u_j)f)^\omega r_j && \text{by (8)} \\
&= s(\alpha(u_j)f\alpha(x_{j-1})fr_j)^\omega\alpha(u_j)fr_j \\
&= s\alpha(u_j)fr_j.
\end{aligned}$$

This exactly says that $q = s\alpha(u_j)r_j$ which completes the proof. □

5 Conclusion

We presented generic algebraic characterizations for classes of the form $BPol(\mathcal{G})$ and $BPol(\mathcal{G}^+)$ when $\mathcal{G}$ is a group prevariety. They imply that membership is decidable for these two classes as soon as separation is decidable for the input class $\mathcal{G}$. The most natural follow-up question is whether these characterizations can be generalized to encompass all classes $BPol(\mathcal{C})$ where $\mathcal{C}$ is an *arbitrary* prevariety and obtain a characterization similar to the one provided by Theorem 12 for $Pol(\mathcal{C})$. This is a difficult question. In particular, it seems unlikely that $BPol(\mathcal{C})$-membership boils down to $\mathcal{C}$-separation in the general case. Indeed, a specialized characterization for the class $BPol(BPol(\text{ST}))$ is known [13]. Yet, deciding it involves looking at a more general question than $BPol(\text{ST})$-separation.

References

1. Arfi, M.: Polynomial operations on rational languages. In: Brandenburg, F.J., Vidal-Naquet, G., Wirsing, M. (eds.) STACS 1987. LNCS, vol. 247, pp. 198–206. Springer, Heidelberg (1987). https://doi.org/10.1007/BFb0039607

2. Ash, C.J.: Inevitable graphs: a proof of the type II conjecture and some related decision procedures. Int. J. Algebra Comput. **1**(1), 127–146 (1991)
3. Brzozowski, J.A., Cohen, R.S.: Dot-depth of star-free events. J. Comput. Syst. Sci. **5**(1), 1–16 (1971)
4. Chaubard, L., Éric Pin, J., Straubing, H.: First order formulas with modular predicates. In: Proceedings of the 21th IEEE Symposium on Logic in Computer Science (LICS 2006), pp. 211–220 (2006)
5. Henckell, K., Margolis, S., Pin, J.E., Rhodes, J.: Ash's type II theorem, profinite topology and Malcev products. Int. J. Algebra Comput. **1**, 411–436 (1991)
6. Knast, R.: A semigroup characterization of dot-depth one languages. RAIRO - Theoret. Inform. App. **17**(4), 321–330 (1983)
7. Maciel, A., Péladeau, P., Thérien, D.: Programs over semigroups of dot-depth one. Theoret. Comput. Sci. **245**(1), 135–148 (2000)
8. Margolis, S.W., Pin, J.E.: Products of group languages. In: Budach, L. (ed.) FCT 1985. LNCS, vol. 199, pp. 285–299. Springer, Heidelberg (1985). https://doi.org/10.1007/BFb0028813
9. Pin, J.E.: Algebraic tools for the concatenation product. Theoret. Comput. Sci. **292**, 317–342 (2003)
10. Pin, J.É.: An explicit formula for the intersection of two polynomials of regular languages. In: Béal, M.-P., Carton, O. (eds.) DLT 2013. LNCS, vol. 7907, pp. 31–45. Springer, Heidelberg (2013). https://doi.org/10.1007/978-3-642-38771-5_5
11. Pin, J.E.: Mathematical foundations of automata theory (2020). www.irif.fr/jep/PDF/MPRI/MPRI.pdf. (in preparation)
12. Place, T., Zeitoun, M.: Generic results for concatenation hierarchies. Theory Comput. Syst. (ToCS) **63**(4), 849–901 (2019)
13. Place, T., Zeitoun, M.: Going higher in first-order quantifier alternation hierarchies on words. J. ACM **66**(2), 12:1–12:65 (2019)
14. Place, T., Zeitoun, M.: Separation and covering for group based concatenation hierarchies. In: Proceedings of the 34th Annual ACM/IEEE Symposium on Logic in Computer Science, pp. 1–13. LICS 2019 (2019)
15. Place, T., Zeitoun, M.: Separation for dot-depth two. Logical Methods Comput. Sci. 17(3), 1–4 (2021)
16. Place, T., Zeitoun, M.: Characterizing level one in group-based concatenation hierarchies. CoRR abs/2201.06826 (2022). https://arxiv.org/abs/2201.06826
17. Simon, I.: Piecewise testable events. In: Brakhage, H. (ed.) GI-Fachtagung 1975. LNCS, vol. 33, pp. 214–222. Springer, Heidelberg (1975). https://doi.org/10.1007/3-540-07407-4_23
18. Steinberg, B.: Inevitable graphs and profinite topologies: Some solutions to algorithmic problems in monoid and automata theory, stemming from group theory. Int. J. Algebra Comput. **11**(1), 25–72 (2001)
19. Straubing, H.: A generalization of the schützenberger product of finite monoids. Theoret. Comput. Sci. **13**(2), 137–150 (1981)
20. Straubing, H.: Finite semigroup varieties of the form V * D. J. Pure Appl. Algebra **36**, 53–94 (1985)
21. Thérien, D.: Classification of finite monoids: the language approach. Theoret. Comput. Sci. **14**(2), 195–208 (1981)
22. Thomas, W.: Classifying regular events in symbolic logic. J. Comput. Syst. Sci. **25**(3), 360–376 (1982)

How Much Randomness is Needed to Convert MA Protocols to AM Protocols?

Nikolay Vereshchagin[1,2,3](✉)

[1] Moscow State University, Moscow, Russian Federation
nikolay.vereshchagin@gmail.com
[2] HSE University, Moscow, Russian Federation
[3] Yandex, Moscow, Russian Federation

Abstract. The Merlin-Arthur class of languages MA is included into Arthur-Merlin class AM, and into PP. For a standard transformation of a given MA protocol with Arthur's message (= random string) of length a and Merlin's message of length m to a PP machine, the latter needs $O(ma)$ random bits. The same holds for simulating MA protocols by AM protocols: in the resulting AM protocol the length of Arthur's message (= random string) is $O(ma)$. And the same holds for simulating heuristic MA protocols by heuristic AM protocols as well. In the paper [A. Knop, Circuit Lower Bounds for Average-Case MA, CSR 2015] it was conjectured that, in the transformation of heuristic MA protocols to heuristic AM protocols, $O(ma)$ can be replaced by a polynomial of a only. A similar question can be asked for normal MA and AM protocols, and for the simulation of MA protocols by PP machines. In the present paper we show that, relative to an oracle, both latter questions answer in the negative and Knop's conjecture is false. Moreover, the same is true for simulation of MA protocols by AM protocols in which the error probability is not bounded away from 1/2, the so called PP·NP protocols. The latter protocols generalize both AM protocols and PP machines.

Keywords: Arthur-Merlin protocol · Merlin-Arthur protocol · Derandomization · Oracles

1 Introduction

Let MA$[m, a]$ denote the class of languages that have two-round Merlin-Arthur protocols in which Merlin starts the communication, the lengths of messages are m, a, respectively, and error probability is at most $1/3$. In a similar way the class AM$[m, a]$ is defined, but now Arthur is the one starting the communication.

The class AM includes MA [Bab85], more specifically, it holds that MA$[m, a] \subset$ AM$[m, O(ma)]$. This can be proved via amplification: we first

The results are supported by Russian Science Foundation (20-11-20203).

A. S. Kulikov and S. Raskhodnikova (Eds.): CSR 2022, LNCS 13296, pp. 338–349, 2022.
https://doi.org/10.1007/978-3-031-09574-0_21

decrease the error probability from 1/3 to 2^{-m-1}, at the expense of increasing a to $O(ma)$, as Arthur has to repeat his algorithm $O(m)$ times and then make a majority vote. Using derandomization via expanders [AFWZ95], we can replace $O(ma)$ by $a+O(m)$ and hence prove the inclusion $\mathrm{MA}[m,a] \subset \mathrm{AM}[m,a+O(m)]$. In this paper we try to understand whether it is possible get rid of $O(m)$ and replace in this inclusion $a+O(m)$ by a polynomial of a only.

Question 1. *Is there a polynomial p such that $MA[m,a] \subset AM[*,p(a)]$ for all polynomials m,a of the length of the input?*

Here $\mathrm{AM}[*,a]$ denotes the union of $\mathrm{AM}[m,a]$ over all polynomials m. This question is motivated by the following conjecture from Knop's paper [Kno15] about heuristic analogs of MA and AM.

Conjecture 1 ([Kno15]). *There is a polynomial p such that if there is a heuristic Merlin-Arthur protocol for a language L that on inputs of length n and confidence δ uses $q(n/\delta)$ random bits (q is a polynomial) then there is a heuristic Arthur-Merlin protocol for L using $p(q(n/\delta))$ random bits.*

Roughly speaking, a language L has a heuristic Merlin-Arthur protocol if there is an ordinary Merlin-Arthur protocol that errs only on a small fraction of inputs (called its confidence). The heuristic analog of AM is defined in a similar way.

This conjecture is interesting, since it provides a way to transform lower bounds for heuristic computations to lower bounds for normal computations. More specifically, the following holds: if Conjecture 1 is true then for all k some NP language has no Boolean circuits of size n^k ([Kno15]). Thus it would be very helpful to prove Conjecture 1.

A similar question arises for the inclusion MA $\subset$ PP [Ver92], where PP stands for the class of languages recognized by probabilistic polynomial time machines with error probability less than 1/2. It is important that the error probability is not bounded away from 1/2. This inclusion is also proved via amplification and its more detailed version reads $\mathrm{MA}[m,a] \subset \mathrm{PP}[O(ma)]$, where r in the notation $\mathrm{PP}[r]$ denotes the number of random bits available to PP machines.

Question 2. *Is there a polynomial p such that $MA[m,a] \subset PP[p(a)]$ for all polynomials m,a?*

If MA = P or MA = NP, then in both above simulations randomness is not needed at all, therefore both questions answer in positive. Hence to prove negative answers, we must show beforehand that MA $\neq$ P. The latter is equivalent to P $\neq$ NP since MA $\subset \Pi_2^p$ [BHZ87]. Thus we cannot hope to prove negative answers to both Questions 1 and 2 unless we show that P $\neq$ NP. On the other hand, positive answers seem implausible.

In such a situation, it is natural to ask whether one can answer Questions 1 and 2 using relativizable techniques. By the result of [BGS75] there is an oracle under which P $\neq$ NP. Under that oracle MA = P, since the Polynomial Hierarchy collapses. Hence under that oracle both questions answer in the positive and Knop's conjecture holds.

On the other hand, in the present paper we show that there are oracles under which both questions answer in the *negative* and Knop's conjecture does *not* hold. More specifically, we show that there is an oracle under which for every polynomial p the class MA$[m, a]$ is not included in both classes AM$[*, p(a)]$ and PP$[p(a)]$ where $a(n) = n$, $m(n) = p(n)$, and n stands for the length of the input. In particular, under that oracle MA $\neq$ NP thus the "full derandomization" of MA is impossible. Our result implies that we need a non-relativizable proof techniques to fully derandomize MA and even to show that MA$[m, a] \subset$ AM$[*, p(a)]$ for some fixed polynomial p. It remains an open question whether we can resolve both questions using algebrizable techniques in the sense of Aaronson and Wigderson [AW09].

Actually, we prove a stronger separation. Let PP·NP$[m, a]$ denote the class of languages recognized by Arthur-Merlin protocols with error probability less than 1/2 but not bounded away from 1/2. This class obviously includes both classes PP$[a]$ and AM$[m, a]$. In the present paper we prove that under an oracle, for all non-constant polynomials m, a there is a language L in MA$[m, a]$ such that for every PP·NP$[m', a']$ protocol for L it holds $a'(n) \geqslant m(n) + a(n) - O(\log n)$ for all n.

Using the same techniques, we then show that under an oracle Knop's conjecture is false, too. We also establish a similar theorem for MA protocols, where Merlin never fails. More specifically, let MAP$[m, a]$ denote the subclass of MA$[m, a]$ consisting of languages possessing a protocol for which the error probability is zero for all strings from the language. It is natural to ask whether MAP$[m, a] \subset$ AM$[*, \text{poly}(a)]$. From the Sipser–Gács–Lautemann theorem [Sip83, Lau83] about the inclusion BPP $\subset \Pi_2$ it follows that MAP = MA, more specifically,

$$\text{MA}[m, a] \subset \text{MAP}[O((m + a \log a)a \log a), O((a \log a)^2)].$$

Hence our theorem implies that under an oracle for all polynomials p there are polynomials m, a with MAP$[m, a] \not\subset$ AM$[*, p(a)]$. In the present paper, we establish a more tight bound: relative to an oracle, for every non-constant polynomials m, a there is a language L in MAP$[m, a]$ such that for any PP·NP$[*, a']$ protocol for L we have $a'(n) \geqslant \max\{m(n), a(n)\} - O(\log n)$ for almost all n. Compared with simulating MA protocols, $m(n) + a(n)$ is replaced by $\max\{m(n), a(n)\}$.

Summarizing, we show that we cannot prove Conjecture 1 or positive answers to Questions 1 and 2 using relativizable techniques.

2 Preliminaries

A language is a subset of the set $\{0, 1\}^*$ of all strings over the binary alphabet. The length of the string x is denoted by $|x|$. When we speak on probability, we always mean the uniform distribution.

A *polynomial* is a function $p : \mathbb{N} \to \mathbb{N}$ of the form $p(n) = b(n + 1)^c$ where b, c are positive integers. Thus any polynomial is a non-constant function with positive values. In the following definitions r, m, n, t denote some polynomials.

Definition 1. *A language L is in the class PP$[r]$ if there is a Turing machine V with input strings x, a, whose running time is bounded by some polynomial of $|x|$, such that*

$$x \in L \leftrightarrow Prob_{a\in\{0,1\}^{r(|x|)}}[V(x,a)=1] > 1/2$$

for all strings x.

Definition 2. *A language L is in the class MA$[m,a]$ if there is a Turing machine V with input strings x, y, z, whose running time is bounded by some polynomial of $|x|$, such that*

$$x \in L \rightarrow \exists y \in \{0,1\}^{m(|x|)} Prob_{z\in\{0,1\}^{a(|x|)}}[V(x,y,z)=1] > 2/3,$$
$$x \notin L \rightarrow \forall y \in \{0,1\}^{m(|x|)} Prob_{z\in\{0,1\}^{a(|x|)}}[V(x,y,z)=1] < 1/3.$$

for all strings x.

Definition 3. *A language L is in the class MAP$[m,a]$ if there is a Turing machine V with input strings x, y, z, whose running time is bounded by some polynomial of $|x|$, such that*

$$x \in L \rightarrow \exists y \in \{0,1\}^{m(|x|)} Prob_{z\in\{0,1\}^{a(|x|)}}[V(x,y,z)=1] = 1,$$
$$x \notin L \rightarrow \forall y \in \{0,1\}^{m(|x|)} Prob_{z\in\{0,1\}^{a(|x|)}}[V(x,y,z)=1] < 1/2.$$

for all strings x. Compared with the definition of MA, the number 2/3 is replaced by 1, and the number 1/3 by 1/2 (the latter replacement is not important).

Definition 4. *A language L is in the class AM$[m,a]$ if there is a Turing machine V with input strings x, y, z, whose running time is bounded by some polynomial of $|x|$, such that*

$$x \in L \rightarrow Prob_{z\in\{0,1\}^{a(|x|)}}[\exists y \in \{0,1\}^{m(|x|)} V(x,y,z)=1] > 2/3,$$
$$x \notin L \rightarrow Prob_{z\in\{0,1\}^{a(|x|)}}[\exists y \in \{0,1\}^{m(|x|)} V(x,y,z)=1] < 1/3.$$

for all strings x.

Definition 5. *A language L is in the class PP·NP$[m,a,t]$ if there is a Turing machine V with input strings x, y, z, whose running time is bounded by $t(|x|)$, such that*

$$x \in L \leftrightarrow Prob_{z\in\{0,1\}^{a(|x|)}}[\exists y \in \{0,1\}^{m(|x|)} V(x,y,z)=1] > 1/2. \tag{1}$$

for all strings x. Triples of the form (m,a,V) will be called PP·NP protocols. *We say that a PP·NP protocol* is correct on input x *if the equivalence* (1) *is true. Otherwise we say that the protocol* errs on x.

Definition 6. *(Heuristic classes) We say that a language L is in Heur-PP·NP$[m,a]$ if there is a Turing machine V with input strings x, y, z, δ, whose running time is bounded by a polynomial of $|x|/\delta$, such that for all n the equivalence*

$$x \in L \leftrightarrow Prob_{z\in\{0,1\}^{a(|x|/\delta)}}[\exists y \in \{0,1\}^{m(|x|/\delta)} V(x,y,z,\delta)=1] > 1/2. \tag{2}$$

holds for all but δ fraction of strings x of length n.

In a similar way the classes Heur-MA$[m,a]$ and Heur-AM$[m,a]$ are defined.

An oracle is a function $A : \{0,1\}^* \to \{0,1\}$. The classes MA, MAP, AM, PP·NP, *relativized by an oracle* A are defined as follows: now the machine V has an extra "oracle" tape. On that tape the machine can "query the oracle". That means that the machine can write any string u followed by a question mark on that tape. Immediately after that, the word u is replaced by $A(u)$ by "the oracle", which is counted as one step of computation. Complexity classes relativized by an oracle A are denoted by $\mathrm{MA}^A, \mathrm{MAP}^A, \mathrm{AM}^A, \mathrm{PP{\cdot}NP}^A$.

3 Constructing an Oracle Under Which Transformation of MA to PP·NP Protocols Requires Many Random Bits

The first result states that under some oracle some language in $\mathrm{MA}[m,a]$ has no $\mathrm{PP{\cdot}NP}[m',a',t']$ protocols unless $a'(n) \geqslant m(n) + a(n) - \log_2 t'(n) - O(1)$.

Theorem 1. *There is an oracle* $A : \{0,1\}^* \to \{0,1\}$ *with the following property. For all polynomials* $m(n), a(n)$ *there is a language in* $\mathrm{MA}^A[m,a]$ *that is outside any class* $\mathrm{PP{\cdot}NP}^A[m',a',t']$ *such that* $a'(n) < m(n) + a(n) - \log_2(3t'(n))$ *for infinitely many* n.

Proof. We first prove a weaker version of the theorem, assuming that the polynomials $m(n), a(n)$ are fixed.

The value of an oracle A on strings of length $m(n) + a(n)$ can be viewed as a Boolean matrix A_n with $2^{m(n)}$ rows and $2^{a(n)}$ columns. For the constructed oracle A for all n the matrix A_n will have one of the following forms:

- either some row in the matrix has more than two thirds of ones,
- or less than one third of entries in every row are ones.

Matrices of the first type are called *heavy*, and matrices of the second type are called *light*. We will call this property of A by $P_{m,a}$ (see Fig. 1).

$$\begin{pmatrix} 0&0&1&0&0&0&0\\ 0&0&0&0&0&0&0\\ 0&0&0&0&1&0&0\\ 0&0&0&0&0&0&0\\ 1&0&1&1&0&1&1\\ 0&0&0&0&0&0&0 \end{pmatrix} \qquad \begin{pmatrix} 0&1&1&0&0&0&0\\ 1&0&1&0&0&0&0\\ 0&0&0&0&0&0&1\\ 0&0&0&1&0&0&1\\ 0&0&0&0&0&0&0\\ 0&0&0&0&0&1&1 \end{pmatrix}$$

Fig. 1. The matrix on the left is heavy, and the matrix on the right is light.

The language $L = L(A)$ will consist of all strings 1^n such that the matrix A_n is heavy. The intuition is the following: the hidden heavy row is easy to guess in one step but hard to amplify and find.

The property $P_{m,a}$ of A guarantees that $L(A) \in \mathrm{MA}^A[m, a]$, since

$$1^n \in L(A) \to \exists y \in \{0,1\}^{m(n)} \mathrm{Prob}_{z \in \{0,1\}^{a(n)}}[A(yz) = 1] > 2/3,$$
$$1^n \notin L(A) \to \forall y \in \{0,1\}^{m(n)} \mathrm{Prob}_{z \in \{0,1\}^{a(n)}}[A(yz) = 1] < 1/3$$

(the respective machine V on input $(1^n, y, z)$ outputs $A(yz)$ by querying the oracle once).

Now we will define an oracle A so that $L(A)$ is outside $\mathrm{PP}\cdot\mathrm{NP}^A[m', a', t']$ provided $a'(n) < m(n) + a(n) - \log 3t'(n)$ for infinitely many n.

We first pick any PP·NP protocol (m', a', V) with $a'(n) < m(n) + a(n) - \log 3t_V(n)$ for infinitely many n. Here $t_V(n)$ stands for the polynomial that upper bounds the running time of V. W.l.o.g. we may assume that the running time of $\mathrm{PP}\cdot\mathrm{NP}^A$ protocols does not depend on the oracle.

Then we prove that there is an oracle A such that this protocol does not recognize $L(A)$. To this end we will need the following

Lemma 1. *Assume that a procedure P is given that on input (a Boolean matrix M of size $m \times a$, strings y, z) outputs a bit by querying at most $q < 2^a/3$ elements of the matrix M. Let a' be a natural number with*

$$2^{a'-1}q < (2^a/3 - q)2^m,$$

and m' any natural number. Then there is a heavy Boolean matrix M with

$$Prob_{z \in \{0,1\}^{a'}}[\exists y \in \{0,1\}^{m'}, P(M, y, z) = 1] \leqslant 1/2, \tag{3}$$

or a light Boolean matrix M with

$$Prob_{z \in \{0,1\}^{a'}}[\exists y \in \{0,1\}^{m'}, P(M, y, z) = 1] > 1/2. \tag{4}$$

Proof. For the sake of a contradiction assume that there is no such matrix. That is, for every heavy M we have (4), and for every light M we have (3).

Let first M be all-zero matrix. We will derive a contradiction by flipping certain M's entries in such a way that M is still light but there are $2^{a'-1} + 1$ pairs (y, z) with pairwise different first components and with $P(M, y, z) = 1$. We will find such pairs (y, z) one by one. For each new pair (y, z) we will *freeze* all elements of M queried in the computation of $P(M, y, z)$. This means that we will not change those elements on further steps and thus the equality $P(M, y, z) = 1$ will remain valid. On each step we will freeze at most q entries and the assumed inequality

$$2^{a'-1}q < (2^a/3 - q)2^m$$

will guarantee that on each step it is possible to find a row with few frozen entries. Flipping all non-frozen elements of that row we get a heavy matrix, which will allow to find a new pair (y, z).

More specifically, we make $2^{a'-1} + 1$ steps and on ith step we find one new pair (y_i, z_i). On the first step we flip all the elements of the first row of M. We obtain a heavy matrix. By assumption the inequality (4) holds. Hence there is

z_1 such that there is y_1 with $P(M, y_1, z_1) = 1$. Fix such y_1, z_1. Then freeze all elements of M queried in the computation of $P(M, y_1, z_1)$. Then we again flip all non-frozen elements of the first row and M becomes light. This follows from the assumed inequality $q < 2^a/3$, which implies that the number of ones in the first row is less than one third.

After ith step the matrix M is light and at most iq its entries are frozen. Besides that, there are distinct $z_1, \dots, z_i$ and (not necessarily distinct) $y_1, \dots, y_i$ with $P(M, y_1, z_1) = \dots = P(M, y_i, z_i) = 1$. On $(i+1)$st step we choose a row with minimal number of frozen elements. That number is less than $2^a/3 - q$, since at most $iq \leqslant 2^{a'-1}q < (2^a/3 - q)2^m$ entries of the matrix are frozen, that is, on average less than $2^a/3 - q$ per row. Then we make all non-frozen elements in that row equal to 1. The resulting matrix is heavy, as it has more than $2^a - (2^a/3 - q) > (2/3)2^a$ ones. By the assumption we have (4). Since $i \leqslant 2^{a'-1}$, there is z_{i+1} that is different from $z_1, \dots, z_i$ and there is y_{i+1} with $P(M, y_{i+1}, z_{i+1}) = 1$. Pick such y_{i+1} and z_{i+1} and freeze all elements queried in the computation of $P(M, y_{i+1}, z_{i+1})$. Then we make all non-frozen elements of that row equal to 0. The total number of frozen elements in that row is less than $(2^a/3 - q) + q = 2^a/3$, thus we again get a light matrix.

After $2^{a'-1} + 1$ steps we derive a contradiction: the matrix M is light and yet for more than half of $z \in \{0,1\}^{a'}$ there is $y \in \{0,1\}^{m'}$ with $P(M, y, z) = 1$.

Let us resume the proof of the theorem. Let us consider the procedure $P(M, y, z)$ that simulates the run of $V^A(1^n, y, z)$. If V queries oracle's value on a string of length $m(n) + a(n)$, then P queries the corresponding entry of the input matrix M. If V queries oracle's value on a string of length different from $m(n) + a(n)$, then P assumes that the oracle answer is 0. Note that for all sufficiently large n the running time $t_V(n)$ of V on 1^n, and hence the number of oracle queries, is less than $2^{a(n)}/6$. Indeed, $2^{a(n)}$ grows exponentially and $t_V(n)$ is a polynomial. For such n's, to meet the assumptions of the lemma, it suffices to satisfy the inequality $2^{a'(n)-1}t(n) < 2^{a(n)+m(n)}/6$, that is, $a'(n) < a(n) + m(n) - \log 3t(n)$. By the assumption there are infinitely many n satisfying this inequality. Thus there is n for which the conclusion of the lemma holds. We pick any such n and define the value of the oracle A on strings of length $m(n) + a(n)$ so that the matrix $M = A_n$ satisfy the conclusion of the lemma. For all other strings u we let $A(u) = 0$. By construction the chosen PP·NP protocol does not recognize $L(A)$.

Now we have to fool all PP·NP protocols (m', a', V), with $a'(n) < m(n) + a(n) - \log 3t_V(n)$ for infinitely many n. This can be done by a standard diagonalization. We enumerate all PP·NP protocols with oracle which satisfy the inequality $a'(n) < m(n) + a(n) - \log 3t_V(n)$ for infinitely many n. We first let $A(u) = 0$ for all u and then we perform infinitely many steps. On each step we freeze a finite number of oracle values. On ith step we fool ith PP·NP protocol (m', a', V). To this end, we choose n such that no value of A on strings of length $m(n) + a(n)$ has been frozen yet, $t_V(n) < 2^{a(n)}/6$ and $a'(n) < m(n) + a(n) - \log 3t'(n)$. Using the lemma, we change oracle values on strings of length $m(n) + a(n)$ so that the conclusion of the lemma holds. Then we freeze all oracle values queried by V in the runs on inputs y, z of lengths $m(n), a(n)$, respectively.

Finally, to construct an oracle A such that the statement of the theorem holds for all polynomials $m(n), a(n)$, we also enumerate all the pairs (m, a) of polynomials: $(m_1, a_1), (m_2, a_2), \dots$ and define

$$L_i(A) = \{1^n \mid A_{i,n} \text{ is heavy}\}.$$

Here $A_{i,n}$ is defined exactly as we defined A_n earlier for the pair (m_i, a_i) as (m, a).

Then we enumerate all pairs (a natural number i, a PP · NP protocol (m', a', V)) and for each such pair we make one step. On that step we fool the protocol (m', a', V) as a candidate protocol for $L_i(A)$. There is one obstacle however. In order to place the language $L_i(A)$ in $\text{MA}^A[m_i, a_i]$, we need the property P_{m_i,a_i} hold for all i. When we change $A_{i,n}$ to fool the protocol (m', a', V) as a candidate protocol for $L_i(A)$, we can violate the property P_{m_j,a_j} for n' with $m_i(n) + a_i(n) = m_j(n') + a_j(n')$.

To handle this problem, we will split the oracle A into countably many oracles, one oracle for each pair (m_i, a_i) of polynomials. For each i we consider the prefix encoding $\hat{i}$ of the number i. It is obtained by doubling each bit in the binary representation of i and then appending 01 (for instance, $\hat{5} = 11001101$). This encoding ensures that for $i \neq j$ strings of the form $\hat{i}u$ and $\hat{j}v$ cannot coincide.

Then we change the definition of the matrix $A_{i,n}$: now it is built from oracle's values on strings of the form $\hat{i}u$, where the length of u is $m_i(n)+a_i(n)$. Changing $A_{i,n}$ does not affect any of the matrices $A_{j,n'}$ for $j \neq i$. Therefore, when we change $A_{i,n}$ we cannot violate the property P_{m_j,a_j} for any $j \neq i$.

4 Refuting Knop's Conjecture Under an Oracle

Recall that Knop's conjecture claims the existence of a polynomial p such for all polynomials m, a, if $L \in \text{Heur-MA}[m, a]$ then $L \in \text{Heur-AM}[*, p(a)]$.

Notice that if $L \in \text{Heur-AM}[*, a(n)]$ then there is a normal $\text{AM}[*, a(2n)]$ protocol that is correct on at least half of inputs of each length and hence is correct on at least one input of each length n. We will build an oracle A under which Knop's conjecture is false in a strong way. Under that oracle, for all polynomials m, a there is a language in $\text{MA}[m, a]$ (and hence in $\text{Heur-MA}[m, a]$) such that every $\text{PP} \cdot \text{NP}[m', a', t']$ protocol with $a'(n) < m(n) + a(n) - n - \log_2(6t'(n))$ for infinitely many n errs on *all* inputs of length n for some n.

Let, for instance, $a(n) = n$ and $m(n) = p(n) + n$, where p is an arbitrary polynomial. We can see that all $\text{AM}^A[*, a'(n)]$ protocols for a language in $L \in \text{MA}^A[m(n), n]$ that are correct on at least one input of each length require

$$a'(n) \geqslant m(n)+a(n)-n-O(\log n) = (p(n)+n)+n-n-O(\log n) \gg p(n) = p(a(n))$$

random bits for almost all n.

Theorem 2. *There is an oracle $A : \{0,1\}^* \to \{0,1\}$ with the following property. For all polynomials $m(n), a(n)$ there is a language $L \in MA^A[m,a]$ such that any $PP{\cdot}NP^A[m',a',t']$ protocol for L with $a'(n) < m(n)+a(n)-n-\log_2(6t'(n))$ for infinitely many n errs on* all *inputs x of some length n.*

Proof (Sketch of proof). As before, we enumerate all pairs (a polynomial m, a polynomial a). Then we define

$$L_i(A) = \{x \mid \text{the matrix } A_{i,x} \text{ is heavy}\},$$

where $A_{i,x}$ is a Boolean matrix of size $m_i(n) \times a_i(n)$, $n = |x|$, defined by

$$A_{i,x}(u,v) = A(\hat{i}\hat{x}uv), \quad |u| = m_i(n), |v| = a_i(n).$$

Note that this time the matrix $A_{i,x}$ depends on the input x and not only on its length n. The oracle construction will ensure that for all i, x the matrix $A_{i,x}$ is either heavy, or light. Thus for all i the language $L_i(A)$ is in $\mathrm{MA}^A[m_i, a_i]$.

The construction of A will ensure that for all i and for all PP·NP protocols (m', a', V) with $a'(n) < m_i(n) + a_i(n) - n - \log 6t_V(n)$ for infinitely many n, there is n with the following property: for all x of length n,

either $A_{i,x}$ is heavy and

$$\mathrm{Prob}_{z\in\{0,1\}^{a_i(|x|)}}[\exists y \in \{0,1\}^{m_i(|x|)} V^A(x,y,z) = 1] \leqslant 1/2.$$

or $A_{i,x}$ is light and

$$\mathrm{Prob}_{z\in\{0,1\}^{a_i(|x|)}}[\exists y \in \{0,1\}^{m_i(|x|)} V^A(x,y,z) = 1] > 1/2.$$

This implies that the protocol (m', a', V), as a candidate protocol for $L_i(A)$, errs on *all* inputs x of a certain length n.

The construction of A proceeds in steps where on each step we fool some protocol (m', a', V) as a candidate protocol for some language $L_i(A)$. To this end we use the following

Lemma 2. *Assume that a procedure P is given that on input (a sequence of Boolean matrices $M = (M_1, \dots, M_{2^n})$ of size $m \times a$, strings y, z and $x \in \{1, \dots, 2^n\}$) outputs a bit by querying at most $q < 2^a/3$ elements of the given matrices in total. Let a' be a natural number with*

$$2^{a'} \cdot q \cdot 2^n < (2^a/3 - q)2^m,$$

and m' any natural number. Then there is a sequence of matrices $M_1, \dots, M_{2^n}$ such that for all *$x = 1, \dots, 2^n$ either M_x is heavy and*

$$Prob_{z\in\{0,1\}^{a'}}[\exists y \in \{0,1\}^{m'}, P(M,y,z,x) = 1] \leqslant 1/2, \tag{5}$$

or M_x is light and

$$Prob_{z\in\{0,1\}^{a'}}[\exists y \in \{0,1\}^{m'}, P(M,y,z,x) = 1] > 1/2. \tag{6}$$

Proof. The proof is similar to that of Lemma 1 and thus we explain only what is the difference. Now we make 2^n stages and on each stage we make $2^{a'-1}+1$ steps. On stage x we flip only entries of M_x to ensure the requirement for that x. However we need to freeze also entries of other matrices $M_{x'}$ in the case P queries their entries in the computation on the input (M, y_i, z_i, x). Thus the total number of frozen elements, in all the matrices, can now raise up to $(2^{a'-1}+1)\cdot q\cdot 2^n \leqslant 2^{a'}\cdot q\cdot 2^n$. Since we assume that this number is still less than $(2^a/3-q)2^m$, on each step each matrix has a row with less than $2^a/3-q$ frozen entries. This we can complete each step.

The rest of the proof is similar to that of Theorem 1. To fool a protocol (m', a', V) as a candidate protocol for the language $L_i(A)$, we apply Lemma 2 to the procedure P that simulates the run of $V^A(x, y, z)$. If V queries oracle's value on a string of the form $\hat{i}\hat{x}uv$ where $|u| = m_i(n)$ and $|v| = a_i(n)$, then P queries $M_x(u, v)$. To fool the protocol (m', a', V), we again choose n such that no value of A on strings of length $2\log i + 2 + 2n + 2 + m_i(n) + a_i(n)$ has been frozen yet, $t_V(n) < 2^{a_i(n)}/6$ and $a'(n) < m_i(n) + a_i(n) - n - \log 6t'(n)$. Using the lemma, we change oracle values so that the conclusion of the lemma holds. Then we freeze all oracle values queried by V in the runs on inputs x, y, z of lengths $n, m_i(n), a_i(n)$, respectively.

5 Constructing an Oracle Under Which Transformation of MAP to PP·NP Protocols Requires Many Random Bits

Our third result states that under some oracle some language in MAP$[m, a]$ has PP·NP$[m', a', t']$ protocols only if $a'(n) \geqslant \max\{m(n), a(n)\} - \log t'(n) - O(1)$.

Theorem 3. *There is an oracle* $A : \{0,1\}^* \to \{0,1\}$ *with the following property. For all polynomials* $m(n), a(n)$ *there is a language in MAP*$^A[m, a]$ *that is outside any class PP·NP*$^A[m', a', t']$ *such that* $a'(n) < \max\{m(n), a(n)\} - \log t'(n) - O(1)$ *for infinitely many* n.

Proof. The proof of this theorem is similar to that of Theorem 1. However this time heavy matrices are defined as those for which there is an all-one row, and light matrices as those in which there are less than one half ones (Fig. 2). Instead of Lemma 1 we use the following

Lemma 3. *Assume that a procedure* P *is given that on input (a Boolean matrix* M *of size* $m \times a$*, strings* y, z*) outputs a bit by querying at most* $q < 2^{a-1}$ *elements of the matrix* M*. Let* a' *be a natural number with* $2^{a'-1}q < 2^m$ *or* $(2^{a'-1}+1)q < 2^{a-1}$ *and* m' *any natural number. Then there is a heavy matrix* M *satisfying* (3)*, or a light matrix* M *satisfying* (4).

Proof. Assume first that $2^{a'-1}q < 2^m$. For the sake of contradiction assume that for every heavy matrix M it holds (4) and for every light matrix M it holds (3).

$$\begin{pmatrix} 0&0&1&0&0&0&0 \\ 0&0&0&0&0&0&0 \\ 0&0&0&0&1&0&0 \\ 0&0&0&0&0&0&0 \\ 1&1&1&1&1&1&1 \\ 0&0&0&1&0&0&0 \end{pmatrix} \qquad \begin{pmatrix} 0&1&1&0&1&0&0 \\ 1&0&1&0&0&1&0 \\ 0&0&0&0&0&1&1 \\ 1&0&0&1&0&0&1 \\ 0&1&0&0&0&0&0 \\ 0&1&0&0&0&1&1 \end{pmatrix}$$

Fig. 2. The matrix on the left is heavy, and the matrix on the right is light.

Let M be all-zero matrix. Flip all bits of the first row. We get a heavy matrix. By assumption we have (4). Choose any z_1 such that there is a $y_1 \in \{0,1\}^{m'}$ with $P(M, y_1, z_1) = 1$. Fix such y_1, z_1 and freeze all values of M queried in the run $P(M, y_1, z_1)$. Thus we guarantee that $P(M, y_1, z_1) = 1$. Then flip again all non-frozen elements of the first row. As $q < 2^{a-1}$, now the matrix M is light.

Then we make $2^{a'-1}$ similar steps. After ith step we have at most iq frozen elements of M, distinct $z_1, \ldots, z_i$ and (not necessarily distinct) $y_1, \ldots, y_i$ with $P(M, y_1, z_1) = 1, \ldots, P(M, y_i, z_i) = 1$. On $i + 1$st step we choose a row with no frozen entries (such a row does exist, since we assume that $iq \leqslant 2^{a'-1}q < 2^m$) and flip all elements of that row. We get a heavy matrix and hence it satisfies (4). Since $i \leqslant 2^{a'-1}$, there is z_{i+1} that is different from $z_1, \ldots, z_i$ and there is y_{i+1} with $P(M, y_{i+1}, z_{i+1}) = 1$. Freeze all entries of M queried in this computation. Then flip all non-frozen elements of the first row. As $q < 2^{a-1}$, now the matrix M is light.

After $2^{a'-1} + 1$ we get a contradiction as the matrix M is light and for more than half of $z \in \{0,1\}^{a'}$ there is $y \in \{0,1\}^{m'}$ with $P(M, y, z) = 1$.

Assume now that $(2^{a'-1}+1)q < 2^{a-1}$. In this case the arguments are simpler. Again, for the sake of contradiction assume that for every heavy matrix M it holds (4) and for every light matrix M it holds (3). Let M be all-one matrix and hence it is heavy. By assumption we have (4). Fix $2^{a'-1} + 1$ pairs (y, z) with $P(M, y, z) = 1$ and with pair-wise distinct first components. Freeze at most $(2^{a'-1} + 1)q$ entries of M guaranteeing $P(M, y, z) = 1$ for all those pairs. Flip all non-frozen elements of M. The inequality $(2^{a'-1} + 1)q < 2^{a-1}$ implies that less than half entries in each row are frozen. Hence we get a light matrix satisfying (4), a contradiction.

The remaining part of the proof is similar to that of the proof of Theorem 1.

6 Open Questions

1. Is it true that for some polynomial p for all polynomials m, a it holds $\mathrm{MA}[m, a] \subset \mathrm{AM}[*, p(a)]$?
2. Can we prove the inclusion $\mathrm{MA}[m, a] \subset \mathrm{AM}[*, p(a)]$ by algebrizing techniques (for some fixed polynomial p)?
3. Can we prove Conjecture 1 by algebrizing techniques?

Acknowledgements. The author is sincerely grateful to anonymous referees for helpful suggestions.

References

[AFWZ95] Alon, N., Feige, U., Wigderson, A., Zuckerman, D.: Derandomized graph products. Comput. Complex. **5**(1), 60–75 (1995)

[AW09] Aaronson, S., Wigderson, A.: Algebrization: a new barrier in complexity theory. ACM Trans. Comput. Theory **1**(1), 2:1–2:54 (2009)

[Bab85] Babai, L.: Trading group theory for randomness. In: 17th STOC, pp. 421–429 (1985)

[BGS75] Baker, T., Gill, J., Solovay, R.: Relativization of P=?NP question. SIAM J. Comput. **4**(4), 431–442 (1975)

[BHZ87] Boppana, R.B., Håstad, J., Zachos, S.: Does co-np have short interactive proofs? Inf. Process. Lett. **25**, 127–132 (1987)

[Kno15] Knop, A.: Circuit lower bounds for average-case MA. In: Beklemishev, L.D., Musatov, D.V. (eds.) CSR 2015. LNCS, vol. 9139, pp. 283–295. Springer, Cham (2015). https://doi.org/10.1007/978-3-319-20297-6_18

[Lau83] Lautemann, C.: BPP and the polynomial hierarchy. Inf. Proc. Lett. **17**(4), 215–217 (1983)

[Sip83] Sipser, M.: A complexity theoretic approach to randomness. In: Proceedings of the 15th ACM Symposium on the Theory of Computing, pp. 330–335. ACM, New York (1983)

[Ver92] Vereshchagin, N.: On the power of PP. In: Proceedings of 7th Annual IEEE Conference on Structure in Complexity Theory, Boston, MA, pp. 138–143 (1992)

Author Index

Printed in the United States
by Baker & Taylor Publisher Services